New Light on Dar

BEING THE NARRATIVE OF

The German Emin Pasha Expedition,

ITS JOURNEYINGS AND ADVENTURES AMONG THE NATIVE TRIBES OF EASTERN EQUATORIAL AFRICA, THE GALLAS, MASSAIS, WASUKUMA, ETC., ETC., ON THE LAKE BARINGO AND THE VICTORIA NYANZA.

RELATED BY

DR. CARL PETERS,

THE COMMANDER OF THE EXPEDITION.

TRANSLATED FROM THE GERMAN BY

H. W. DULCKEN, Ph.D.

WITH THIRTY-TWO PAGE ENGRAVINGS AND SIXTY-FIVE OTHER ILLUSTRATIONS FROM DESIGNS BY RUDOLF HELLGREWE, AND A LARGE EXPLANATORY COLOURED MAP, REPRESENTING THE PROGRESS OF THE EXPEDITION FROM DAY TO DAY.

WARD, LOCK, AND Co.,
LONDON, NEW YORK, AND MELBOURNE.
1891.
[*All Rights Reserved.*]

This scarce antiquarian book is included in our special *Legacy Reprint Series*. In the interest of creating a more extensive selection of rare historical book reprints, we have chosen to reproduce this title even though it may possibly have occasional imperfections such as missing and blurred pages, missing text, poor pictures, markings, dark backgrounds and other reproduction issues beyond our control. Because this work is culturally important, we have made it available as a part of our commitment to protecting, preserving and promoting the world's literature.

form in other books, and which are not at all necessary for the comprehension of the following narrative.

Now that I am giving to the public this history of the German Emin Pasha Expedition, I am obeying an impulse of my heart in once more expressing my thanks to those to whose co-operation it must be attributed that the undertaking ended in the manner described in the following pages, and that it did not collapse at the very beginning, or come to a tragic conclusion on the continent of Africa, as it often appeared about to do. In this place I publicly offer my thanks to the men who, in the German Emin Pasha Committee, backed and supported the undertaking at home, and to the high-hearted subscribers who, by their liberal and ready assistance, enabled our expedition to be realised. I also thank my comrades in the expedition yonder, among whom Herr von Tiedemann was my constant and faithful companion, while Herr Oskar Borchert proved, by his journey up the Tana, that he was imbued with the spirit which alone can achieve the right result in such affairs.

But after all, even with such support, I should not have been in a position to write a description of the German Emin Pasha Expedition had not a higher Hand manifestly led us, through all hindrances and dangers, back to our native land. In all humility we have to offer thanks to Providence that it has been vouchsafed to us to return home in safety from the elevated plateaus of Leikipia and from the incalculable entanglements in the countries on Lake Victoria.

CARL PETERS.

Essen, "Auf dem Hügel,"
    February 1st, 1891.

PREFACE TO THE ENGLISH EDITION.

THE book here offered to the English public, in a form which every effort has been made to render an attractive one, has already, in its original German garb, been received with emphatic appreciation and general approval by a large number of readers. Accordingly, the publishers consider themselves justified in looking confidently forward to an equal measure of success for this, the English edition of Dr. Peters's valuable and interesting work.

The question of the opening up of Dark Africa, with its vast prospects for trade, commerce, and agriculture, and still more important capabilities for the diffusion of Christianity and the spread of civilisation, is coming more and more to the front, and occupies a continually increasing amount of public attention. The natural desire for information on this great and important subject has been increased and stimulated by the works on the African continent, that have lately appeared from the pens of eminent travellers and explorers; the more so, perhaps, from the wide divergences in the views and the methods of action advocated by the various authors.

It has always been the custom in England, "according to the fair play of the world," to give an impartial hearing to the different statements put forward by those whose experience and labours entitle them to speak on an important subject. Englishmen like to know what each man has to say, rather than give their unhesitating adhesion to the perhaps dogmatic views of any one writer. "In a multitude of counsellors there is wisdom;"—and nowhere more than on the question of carrying forward the banner of culture and Christianity into regions now desert, but where, in future ages, civilisation's lofty scenes shall—

"Be acted over,
In states unborn, and accents yet unknown."

Among those writers who have earned an incontrovertible right to be listened to with respect, Dr. Carl Peters undoubtedly stands in the first rank. That he has, in the fullest sense of the term, thrown "New Light" upon Dark Africa, no unprejudiced and impartial reader of his work will for a moment be disposed to doubt. Fearlessly, and with a transparent honesty of intention which will especially commend itself to English sympathies, he claims for his country a share in the great work of the civilisation of Africa; criticises his competitors with outspoken frankness, without withholding from them his meed of admiration; protests boldly where he considers himself hardly dealt with; points out what he considers to have been errors in judgment and action, and gives his reasons in every case. He has the courage of his opinions, and his trumpet gives no uncertain sound; but while he frankly dispenses praise and blame, he tells his own story with an equally plain straightforwardness, and an absence alike of self-laudation and self-depreciation singularly graceful in a man who has passed through great perils, and achieved very remarkable results, with very moderate means.

Mr. Stanley, in a passage in his "Darkest Africa" (Vol. II., p. 406), says: "It is to be the destiny of the Germans to carry out this work" (the civilisation of Ugogo), "and," he adds, "I envy them." The leader of the enterprise here recorded undertook it in this spirit. No man more completely dedicated himself to a great task, or carried it out with more persistent devotion and daring; and in every page the reader will see vindicated the soundness of the judgment that placed Dr. Carl Peters in authority as the head of a most important national undertaking.

Various fallacies dissipated, a fund of useful information gained, and the ground prepared for future work and progress in Africa, may justly be chronicled as constituting the triumphant results of the German Emin Pasha Expedition.

H. W. D.

CONTENTS.

CHAPTER I.
IN GERMANY.

First Ideas of an Expedition.—Stanley's Departure for Africa.—Steps towards a German Expedition.—Managing Committee Appointed.—Amount of Money Required.—Dr. Peters Appointed Commander.—Arrangements with Lieutenant Wissmann.—State of Eastern Africa.—Encouragement from Prince Bismarck.—Proposed Tana Route.—Rumours concerning Emin Pasha.—Communication from Count Herbert von Bismarck.—The Expedition to Start under Dr. Peters.—Choosing Officers.—Doubts and Difficulties in Prospect . . . . 1—18

CHAPTER II.
IN ZANZIBAR AND THE BLOCKADED TERRITORY.

Insurrectionary Districts to be Avoided.—Supply of Soldiers and Porters.—Shipping Arms.—In Aden.—Commencement of Difficulties.—Prohibitions and Restrictions.—Landing at Merka Abandoned.—Vexatious Proceedings and Useless Efforts in Zanzibar.—Threats of the Sultan.—The *Neœra* Chartered.—Confiscation of Weapons.—Report to the Committee.—By Steamer to Bagamoyo.—Departure of Herr Bley.—Conference with Admiral Fremantle.—Authority from the Committee.—Departure for Dar-es-Salam.—The Voyage.—Alarm of Fire.—Scarcity of Water.—Danger of Shipwreck.—Arrival at Kwaihu Bay.—At Pasa.—Embarkation of Recruits.—Proceedings of Admiral Fremantle.—Navigation in Dhows.—Siyu Canal.—Passage to Shimbye.—Arrival in Witu . . . . 19—45

CHAPTER III.
IN THE SULTANATE OF WITU.

Success of the Commander's Plan.—Delay and Doings at Shimbye.—Report to Germany.—Visit to Wanga.—Exaggerated Reports.—A Hurried Departure.—H.B.M.S. *Boadicea* and the Blockade.—

Landing of the Expedition at Mgine.—Rendezvous at Hindi.—
The *Neœra* Brought to Book.—" Where is Dr. Peters ? "—Diplomatic Correspondence with Admiral Fremantle.—Letter Received
from Herr Borchert.—The *Neœra* Seized and Taken to Zanzibar.
—The Consequent " *Neœra* Lawsuit."—Difficulty of Procuring
Porters.—Division of the Expedition.—Porterage.—Disciplining
the Company. — Manners of the Natives. — Character of the
Somalis.—Troubles of the Rainy Season.—The Start from Hindi.
—Unruliness of the Porters.—Missing Loads and Deserting
Bearers.—New Recruits.—System of Rewards and Punishments,
Rules, etc.—Camp at Mansamarabu.—Our March to Witu.—The
Scenery, etc.—Swamp and Forest.—The Plain.—Sultan Fumo
Bukari.—Statistics of Witu.—Grand Reception.—Report to the
Committee.— Negotiations.— The Somalis.— Sheriff Hussein.—
Preparations for Departure.—Prosperous Condition of the Column.
—Departure for Engatana . . . . 46—76

CHAPTER IV.

UP THE TANA TO THE GALLAS.

The First Day's March.—Encampment in the Valley.—Buana Shamo
Promises a Guide.—Poetry of Camp Life.—Start for Ngao.—
Aspect of the Country.—Search for Water.—Camping in the
Wapokomo Quarters.—Arrival at the Tana.—German Missionary
Station at Ngao.—Scarcity of Food.—Discontent in the Column.
—Ants and Mosquitoes.—" Shauri " with the Porters.—Desertions. — The Missionary Würz.—Departure from Ngao.—The
Boats at Marfano.—Disappointment and Discouragement.—The
Monsoon.—Dr. Peters's Illness.—His Letter to his Friend Hofmann.—On the Banks of the Tana.—Supplies from Witu.—
Untrustworthy Somali Messengers.—Rumours of the English
Expedition.— Hussein's Diplomatic Proposal.— Smith's English
Expedition.—Camp at Engatana.—Hamiri's Failure.—Missionary
Heddenström.—Dangers at Mitole.—Parting from the Wapokomo.
—Scenery of the Tana.—The Steppe.—Animal Life.—Climate.
—A Cheerful March. — Complaints of the Elders. — Hamiri's
Eloquence.— Hiring Boatmen.—Foreign Hostility. — Departure
by Boats from Muina.—Good News.—Supplies.—Passage of the
Tana.—Arab Treachery.—Nderani.—Miaus.—Characteristics of
the Wapokomo.—Interview with the Sultan Suakini.—German
Flag at Malalulu.—Massa.—Wapokomo Festival.—The Galla
Regions.—Kidori.—Nature of the Mboni.—Hamiri and Pembo
moto.—Traces of the English Expedition.—Sources of the Tana.
—Scarcity.—Triumphal March to Oda-Boru-Ruva . . . 77-123

CHAPTER V.

WITH THE GALLAS IN ODA-BORU-RUVA.

Scouts Sent Across the River.—On the Tana.—Sultan of Gallas.—The Gallas.—The Wapokomo.—The Suaheli of the Tana.—Characteristics of the Gallas.—Negotiations with the Sultan.—Waiting for the Second Column.—Sultan Hugo's Concessions.—Mr. Pigott's Expedition.—Mr. Smith's Expedition.—Consultation with Sultan Hugo.—Explanation on Both Sides.—Treaty Between the Sultan and Dr. Peters.—Illness of Herr von Tiedemann.—Sojourn Among the Gallas.—Von der Heydt House.—Bad Conduct of the Gallas.—Alarming Reports.—Defeat of the Gallas.—Hostages.— Grain Stores Seized.—Hostile Somali.—Gall-Galla's Cunning.— Sultan Gallo.—His Deposition.—Sadeh made Sultan.—The Treaty.—Waiting for Rust's Column.—Difficulties.—Instructions to Lieutenant-Captain Rust.—Proposed Route of Dr. Peters.— Discretion Allowed.—Decision to Cross the Steppe . . . 124-151

CHAPTER VI.

ON THE UPPER TANA TO KIKUYU.

Exceptional Character of the Expedition.—Delays of the Gallas.— Grain Wanted.—Stragglers.—Galamba.—The Women and Children to be sent Back.—The Fugitives on the River.—Yembamba's Doleful Narrative.—Course of the Tana.—Its Islands.—Tana Settlements.—Glorious Hameje.—The Lion's Visit.—Cataracts of the Tana.—Hofmann Falls.—Branches.—Tiedemann's Hill.— Emperor William II. Mountains.—Boat Voyage.—Krapf's Conjectures Concerning the Tana.—Great Volcanic Elevated Plateau. —Jibije and Mountain Range.—The Wandorobbo Tribe.—Projected Route.—Embassy to the Wandorobbo.—Tokens of Approaching Strife.—Insolent Demands.—Negotiations.—A Bad Bargain.—Order of March.—Nogola's Misbehaviour and Punishment.—Attack with Poisoned Arrows.—Explorations on the Tana.—A Dangerous Position and Timely Rescue.—Somalis and "Strayed" Cattle.—The Tana: Question of Fords.—Barakka's Accident.—The Forest and its Animals.—The Kiloluma Fall.— Wakamba.—The Wadsagga and their Country.—Krupp's Mountain.—Marongo and his Demands.—War with the Wadsagga.— Their Punishment.—Tree Warriors.—Difficulties of the Mountain March.—Excited Somalis.—A Resolute Policy maintained.—Herr von Tiedemann's Position.—How to Cross the Tana.—The Raft and the Rope.—Building the Bridge.—Difficulties and Failure.—

The Augusta Victoria Fall.—Hunting Incidents, etc.—The Carl Alexander Cataract.—Schweinfurth Fall and Krapf Hill.—Steppe of Ukumba Kitui.—Passage of the Dika.—The Tana Conquered.—The Kenia Mountain. — The Friendly Wakikuyu. — Passage of the Marawa.—Solemn Entry into Konse . . 152—212

CHAPTER VII.

THROUGH THE MASSAIS, OVER THE LEIKIPIA PLATEAU TO THE BARINGO LAKE.

Stay at Kikuyu.—The Thievish Wakikuyu.—March through the Kikuyu Country.—Treacherous Customs of the Country.—Region of the Guaso Nyiro.—Mountain Region.—The Leikipia Plateau. —The Kenia Peak.—Guaso Nyiro River.—Question of Water Supply.—The Gretchen-Thal.—Plan of the Expedition.—The Massais and their Characteristics.—Nomadic Herdsmen.—Their Warlike Propensities.—The Elmorán, or Warrior Massais.—Their Equipment, Customs, etc.—The Gnare Gobit.—Meeting with Massai Warriors.—The Chief Kraal of Elbejet.—Rukua, our Interpreter.—Insolence of the Natives.—Hostile Demonstrations.—Attack on Elbejet.—Attack by the Elmorán.—Battle with the Massais.—Burning of Elbejet.—Orders for an Advance.—Rout of the Massais. — Precautions against Surprise. — Opportune Eclipse.—A Disturbed Christmas Eve.—The March Resumed.—Peace Proposals and Treaty.—The Döngo Gelesha Range.—Teleki Rock.—Hostile Massais.—Joyful Meeting with Herr von Tiedemann.—Difficult March.—The Guaso Narok.—Thomson's Route. —Desertion of Porters.—Water Found.—A New Year.—Talk with the Wandorobbo.—The Guaso Tien River.—Lake Baringo and its Surroundings.—Crossing the Guaso na Nyuki.—Arrival at Njemps . . . . 213—269

CHAPTER VIII.

FROM THE BARINGO TO THE VICTORIA NYANZA TERRITORY.

Ways and Means.—Herr von Tiedemann's Illness.—Massai Agriculture.—The Wakuafi, or Dealers.—Report to the Committee.—Communication with Oda-Boru-Ruva.—Treaty with the Wakuafi.—Mr. de Winton's and Other Expeditions.—Arrangements for our Advance towards the West.—The Kamasia Plateau.—Pemba Motu and the Wakamasia.—Land of Elgejo.—Demonstrations of the Natives.—Conversation with Arabs.—Report on Kawirondo.—Candle Manufacture.—Death of the Somali Achmed.

CONTENTS. xiii

—People of Elgejo.—Kirobani, the Guide.—A Carnivorous Camel.
—Elgejo Guides.—Fight with the Waelgejo.—Easy Victory.—
March to the Angata na Nyuki.—Grand Solitude of Nature.—
Violent Tropical Thunderstorms.—A Dream and an Imaginary
Conversation.—Wild Cattle.—Route to Kabaras.—News of White
Men.—A Letter to a Possible European.—The Kawirondo People.
—Mr. Thomson's Opinions.—A Land of Plenty.—Conversation
with the Sultan's Messengers.—The Sakwa's Possessions.—Town
of Sakwa.—Porters from English Expedition.—Arrival of Ali
Somal.—Accounts of Emin Pasha.—Bewildering News.—The
Sultan's Proposal.—Report on the Wasoga and Waganda.—
Sakwa's Politeness.—Triumph over the Mangati.—Treaty with
Sultan Sakwa.—Explanatory Letter.—Advance to Kwa Sundu.
270—311

CHAPTER IX.

ADVANCE UPON UNJORO AND DEVIATION TO UGANDA, TO ASSIST THE CHRISTIAN PARTY.

Visit from the Sultan and Chiefs.—Mr. Mackay's Despatch.—Muanga,
Son of Mtesa.—His Rebellion against Karema, King of Uganda.
—Mr. Stokes's Enterprise.—Expected British East African Expedition.—Proposal to Emin Pasha.—Political Missionary Interference.—Mr. Jackson's Proceedings.—Letter of Père Lourdel.—
Conversation with the Wasoga Men.—Kiswahili and Kisogo
Languages.—The Sultan's Information respecting Unjoro.—
Guides Required for Journey to Kwa Telessa.—Ali Somal's Dissuasions.—Hussein's Report.—Dr. Peters's Speech to the Somalis.
—Result of the Conference, or Shauri.—Crossing the River
Nsoia.—The Country of Kwa Tindi.—Messenger from Sultan
Tindi.—Attack on the Kraal by Robbers.—Particulars Concerning the Country.—March through the "Junker Range."—To
Kwa Tunga and Kwa Telessa.—White Men in Wanjoro.—Conjectures Concerning Emin.—Dr. Peters's Letter.—The Wissmann
Hills.—A Mysterious Visitor.—Marco and Talabanga.—Proposal
to Visit Unjoro.—Stanley's Camp.—Stanley's Refusal to go to
Uganda.—Letter to Monseigneur Livinhac.—Offer to Muanga.—
Life in Usoga.—Particulars.—The Napoleon Gulf.—The Banana.
—The Wasoga.—The Sultans and their Power.—The Wachore and
their Jovial Sultan.—His Visit.—Kamanyiro Kanta's Career.—
Return Visit to Wachore.—Report from H. M. Stanley.—Up to
Uganda!—Pleasant Journey towards Usoga.—Kamanyiro's One-
eyed Men.—Murder of Bishop Hannington.—Welcome from
Christian Waganda.—Passage Across the Nile.—Ripon Falls.—
First Encampment in Uganda.—A Dangerous Enterprise . 312—367

xiv   CONTENTS.

CHAPTER X.

IN UGANDA.

Fatal Accident to Rukua.—Letter from King Muanga.—Declaration of Kamanyiro Kanta.—March in Military State.—Dismissal of Kamanyiro.—Letter to Mr. Gordon the Missionary.—A Gloomy March Through a Desolate Region.—Message from King Muanga. Entry into Mengo, the Capital.—Audience of the King.—Muanga's Friendliness.—Père Lourdel's Ideas.—Dr. Peters's Advice.—Visit of the Katikiro.—At the French Mission.—Thoroughness of the Catholic Mission Stations. — Mechanical Ingenuity. — King Muanga's Palace.—Private Interview with the King.—Important Treaty Proposed and Signed.—Trade of Uganda.—Extensive Traffic with Usukuma.—Objections of Gordon and Walker.—Freedom of Residence for White Men.—Muanga's Plain Declaration.—Explanatory Letter to Mons. Lourdel.—Letter to Herr Arendt.—Letter to the Englishmen in Kawirondo.—Monseigneur Livinhac.—The Slave Trade.—Prospects of the Supremacy of Christianity.—Monseigneur Livinhac's Opinion.—The Waganda, their Great Abilities.—Their Customs.—Music, Architecture, etc. —Their Cruelty.—Advantages of Climate and Soil.—Origin of the Waganda.—The Beyma People.—Comparison of Languages.—Ancient Records.—The Mountains of the Moon.—Ancient Maps. Royal Tombs at Mengo.—Arab Account of Ancient Egypt.—Gumr and El Gumi.—Cave Dwellings.—Thomson's Account of them.—Historic Traditions and Unproved Theories.—The Katikiro, and Difficulties in Uganda.—Mr. Jackson's Letter.—Dispute between Muanga and the Katikiro.—Muanga's Message to Europe.—Collecting the Forces.—Defiance to Karema.—Mr. Walker's Visit.—Gabriel's Letter.—The Land of Bulingogwe.—Brilliant Expectations . . . . 368—438

CHAPTER XI.

ROUND VICTORIA NYANZA TO USUKUMA.

Mons. Lourdel in Bulingogwe.—Particulars of Mr. Stanley and Emin Pasha.—Sir William Mackinnon's Plan.—Arrival of Nugula.—Dilatory Boatmen.—Mons. Lourdel's Energetic Measure.—Its Fatal Consequences.—View on Lake Victoria.—The Sesse Islands. —Arrival at Mfoh.—Great Thunderstorm.—Letter from the Katikiro, and Reply.—Sesse Songs.—Starting Afresh for Sesse. —The French Mission.—Meeting with Herr von Tiedemann.—The

CONTENTS.

French Station Civilised Life.—Mr. Mackay and Monseigneur Livinhac.—Sunday at the French Station—Arrival of the Boats.—Resumption of the Journey.—French Missionary Boats.—Interchange of News.—Flat Shores of Lake Victoria.—Village of Boats.—Dumo.—Sango.—The River Kagera.—Conference with the Chiefs in Tabaliro.—Warning to the Wasiba.—Their Reply.—Letter from Père Lourdel.—Collection of Tribute.—Letter from Monseigneur Livinhac—Departure from Tabaliro.—Voyage Along the Coast to Busiba.—Island of Bukerebe.—The Sultan's Submission.—Easter Sunday.—Island of Bumbide.—Friendly Natives.—Towards Soswa—Volcanic Region of Lake Victoria.—Soswa Islands.—Arrival of Boats.—Encampment in Bandelundo and Kuru.—Catholic Mission of Nyagesi.—A Banquet.—News from Europe.—Condition of Massailand.—Prospects of Opening up Africa.—Means to be Adopted.—Principles of Christianity and Freedom.—Idea of a New Expedition.—Results Already Achieved.—A Prosperous Region.—Removal to Ukumbi.—Round through Usukuma.—Welcome by Monseigneur Hirth. . . . . 439—482

CHAPTER XII.

FROM LAKE VICTORIA TOWARDS HOME.

The Mission Station of Nyagesi.—Its Occupants.—Dry Season in Usukuma.—Good Qualities of the Wasukuma.—Flight of the Arabs.—Life of the Expedition in Ukumbi.—Luxuries of Civilisation.—Religious Services.—Musa Devoured by a Crocodile.—Lion Hunt.—" Walpurgis Night" Watch.—Illness of Dr. Peters and Herr von Tiedemann.—Departure from Ukumbi.—Probable Future Importance of the Wasukuma.—Encampment at Kabila.—The Difficult River.—Fording the Stream.—The Nera Country.—Tactics of the Wasekke.—The African Character.—Crossing the Wami.—Mr. Stokes's Business Activity.—Trade in Africa.—Caravan Routes.—Opening up a New Road.—Settlement of Busiba.—Keletesa's Cordiality.—March through Thicket and Scrub.—The River Sanguke.—Crossing the Wembaere.—Through the Wilderness.—People of Iramba.—Sultan Kilioma.—The Peaceable Iramba People.—Iramba Plateau.—An Unladylike Sultana.—Importance of Usure.—Illness, Rest, and Travelling.—District of Uweri-weri.—In Kabaragas.—District of Ugogo.—The Arab Mohammed Bin Omari.—Achievements of the Badutschi.—The Kilima Tindi Ridge.—The Wagogo People.—Makenge and Mr. Stanley.—Lesson to the Wagogo.—Demand for Tribute.—War with the Wagogo.—Burning of Wagogo Villages.—Arrival of the Wanjamwesi.—Wagogo Cattle Seized.—Makenge's Submission. — Wanjamwesi Caravan. — Mohammed Bin Omari's Caravan.—Circuit Round the Lindi Mountains.—A Caravan under the German Flag.—Tidings of Emin Pasha.—Kwam Yagallo.—The Marenga Mkali Country.—To Mpuapua.—Meeting with Emin Pasha.—Consultations with Emin.—Criticism of Stanley's Proceedings.—Emin's Position on the Upper Nile.—Discrepancy between Accounts.—Emin's Estimate of Stanley.—Character of Emin Pasha.—Parting from Emin.—Arrival at Usagara.—The Arabs of Mkondogna.—Stay at Loanga.—March to Bagamoyo.—News from Europe.—Crossing to Zanzibar.—To Italy and Germany.—A Few Words with Admiral Fremantle 483—560

APPENDIX.

SUPPLEMENT I.—The German Emin Pasha Committee . . . 561

SUPPLEMENT II.—Relations with Admiral Fremantle and the British Blockade 566

SUPPLEMENT III.—The *Neœra* Lawsuit 574

SUPPLEMENT IV.—The Fate of the Second Column 578

SUPPLEMENT V.—The Uganda Treaty 585

LIST OF FULL-PAGE ILLUSTRATIONS.

Portrait of Dr. Carl Peters		*Frontispiece*
Attempt to Land at Merka		*To face page* 25
Transfer of the *Neœra's* Freight to the Dhows		„ „ 40
Camp in Mansamarabu		„ „ 63
Reception of the Somali-Kawallala		„ „ 71
View on the Tana		„ „ 101
On the March		„ „ 121
Flotilla of the Expedition on the Tana		„ „ 133
Fight with the Gallas		„ „ 141
The Hofmann Falls		„ „ 159
View on the Emperor William II. Mountains		„ „ 161
Negotiation with the Wandorobbo		„ „ 168
In the Mumoni Mountains		„ „ 191
The Augusta Victoria Falls		„ „ 201
The Karl Alexander Falls		„ „ 205
The Kenia		„ „ 219
Elmorán Warriors advancing to the Attack		„ „ 227
Attack on Elbejet		„ „ 236
Attack on the Massais at Gnare Gobit		„ „ 238
Christmas Eve at Guaso Nyiro		„ „ 246
The Teleki Rocks		„ „ 252
By Lake Baringo		„ „ 267
Encounter with the Waelgejo		„ „ 289
In Camp before Kabaras		„ „ 296
Passage of the Nile		„ „ 366
Triumphal Entry into Uganda		„ „ 372
Reception by Muanga		„ „ 379
On Lake Victoria		„ „ 445
"How, Dr. Peters?—You are not dead?"		„ „ 456
Camp in Usukuma		„ „ 477
In Usukuma		„ „ 485
The Wagogo Attacked and Defeated		„ „ 525
The Meeting with Emin Pasha		„ „ 536

LIST OF ILLUSTRATIONS IN THE TEXT.

	PAGE
The German Emin Pasha Committee	9
Portraits of Rudolf von Bennigsen and Dr. George Irmer	11
Portrait of Lieutenant-Captain Rust	20
Portrait of Herr von Tiedemann	21
Portrait of Oskar Borchert	22

xviii   LIST OF ILLUSTRATIONS.

	PAGE
Portrait of Fritz Bley	25
The *Neœra* running out from Dar-es-Salam	34
"Is Kwaibu Peak in Sight?"	37
Landing in Shimbye	43
Loading the Camels	60
Instructing the Somalis	76
Rukua, First Servant to Dr. Peters	80
Hamiri's Illustration	103
Crossing the Tana at Mbuji	108
On the Tana	118
Tana Landscape, near Oda-Boru-Ruva	128
Von der Heydt House	138
The Von der Heydt Islands	157
The "Devil's Field"	164
Wadsagga	183, 184
Building the Bridge across the Tana	199
Hunting the Rhinoceros	204
Fording the Dika	208
Hut of the Wakikuyu	215
Annoyed by Bulls	232
Peace Proposals from the Massais	249
The Wakamasia demand Tribute	281
Wakawirondo	298, 299
Hussein, Leader of the Somalis	325
Shauri with the Somali Soldiers	327
Mount Schrœder and Arendt Bay	351
Dr. Peters Reads Stanley's Letter	361
A Missionary at the Plough	387
Monseigneur Livinhac	403
Musical Instruments of the Waganda	410
Household Utensils of the Waganda	413
Monseigneur Livinhac blessing his Pupils	453
Wasiba of the Island of Tabaliro	461
Voyage Along the Coast of Busiba	467
Usukuma Woman Preparing Corn	481
Wasukuma	485
Mission House in Ukumbi	487
The Chief Porter, Musa, Killed by a Crocodile	491
Animal Life in the Desert	499
An Usukuma Dandy	503
View of the Plain of Ugogo near Mtive	521
Destruction of the Wagogo Villages	528
Usagara Landscape	553

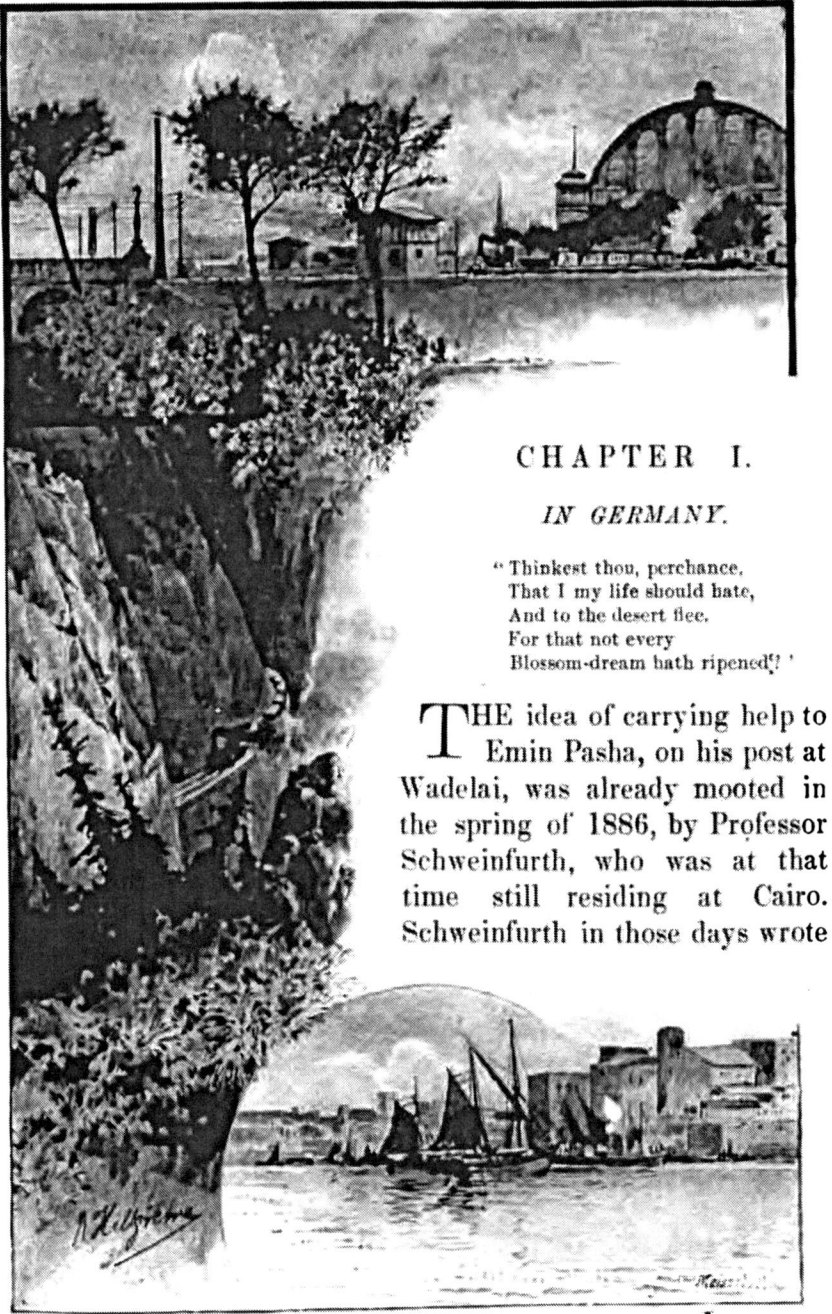

CHAPTER I.

IN GERMANY.

"Thinkest thou, perchance,
That I my life should hate,
And to the desert flee,
For that not every
Blossom-dream hath ripened?"

THE idea of carrying help to Emin Pasha, on his post at Wadelai, was already mooted in the spring of 1886, by Professor Schweinfurth, who was at that time still residing at Cairo. Schweinfurth in those days wrote me a series of letters, in which he made communications concerning Emin's situation, and drew attention to the great importance of his position on the Upper Nile. These letters, which I gave to the public, did not fail to produce an impression in the colonial circles of Germany; and already at that time a few efforts, though feeble ones, were initiated with the view of succouring our fellow-countryman. I, for my part, was so completely engrossed, in the year 1886, in business connected with the East African colonial acquisitions, and in founding the German East Africa Company, that, with the best will in the world, I was not in a position to give my attention to any less immediate tasks of the kind. It was the year in which Jühlke accomplished his Somali Expedition; the year in which the Universal German Congress held its sittings in Berlin, in which the financing of the East African undertaking was begun, and the so-called London agreement created the sphere of English interests in Eastern Africa.

First ideas of an expedition.

Soon afterwards, Stanley took up the idea of carrying help to Emin Pasha; and he quickly succeeded in financing the undertaking in England. Already at the beginning of 1887, he started from Europe for Eastern Africa, and in the spring of the same year he arrived at the Congo, with the band he had recruited in Zanzibar.

Stanley's departure for Africa.

I was in Zanzibar in that year, occupied in regulating the affairs of the coast, and in introducing a few fundamental measures of administration in our colony. I was successful, in July 1887, in inducing the Sultan of Zanzibar to conclude a preliminary treaty, which in principle established the transfer of the administration of the customs and the coast to the German East Africa Company. Nevertheless, the Stanley expedition to the territories of the Upper Nile naturally could not fail to draw the attention of the public circles more and more to itself, and especially the attention of all who were practically interested in the development of the regions around the lakes of Central Africa. In the first rank of these stood the German East Africa Company.

Public interest excited.

When I reached Europe again, in February 1888, after my recall from Zanzibar, the chairman of the German East Africa Company, Herr Carl von der Heydt, at Nervi, handed me a memorial, which set forth circumstantially the idea of a German Emin Pasha Expedition, and gave a prospect of a subscription of 300,000 marks (£15,000), provided I felt inclined to undertake the leadership. I acquiesced in the proposal in principle, but declared that my final decision must depend upon the manner in which the idea was received in Germany. German Emin Pasha Expedition projected.

Meanwhile the fate of our countryman in Wadelai had gradually awakened the purely human interest in large circles of the German people. This more general interest manifested itself in a motion by the Nuremberg division, of which my brother was at that time secretary. This was put before the directing body of the German Colonial Company in April 1888, and represented the succouring of our countryman in Wadelai as a duty that touched the honour of the German people. The directorate of the Colonial Company gave a favourable reception to this motion, and declared itself ready to support an undertaking conceived in the spirit of the proposal.

It was to get this carried into effect that I invited a number of friends of the colonial cause to meet, on June 27th in that year, for a private discussion in a hall of the House of Deputies. On that evening, gentlemen to the number of fourteen put in an appearance, and these determined, after an introductory deliberation, to constitute themselves a provisional committee for the relief of Emin Pasha. The provisional chairmanship of this committee was entrusted to me; it was further determined definitely to settle upon a form of appeal to be issued, and to work privately for an increase of the provisional committee, in order to carry it out. I here insert this appeal in the form in which it was drawn up on September 17th, 1888, as it accurately portrays the views in which the German Emin Pasha movement originated, and accordingly sets forth the ultimate basis of our undertaking :— First steps towards realising the idea.

"APPEAL!

"The insurrection of the Mahdi in the Soudan has destroyed the first holdings of European civilisation on the Upper Nile; the cultured world sees with terror how the horrors of an unbridled system of slave-dealing are spreading more and more.

Services of Emin Pasha. The report that our German fellow-countryman, Dr. Eduard Schnitzer, Emin Pasha, was able to maintain the Equatorial Provinces in the south of the Soudan, entrusted to him by the Egyptian Government, against the assault of the Mahdi, and is there defending with his troops a last bulwark of European culture, has awakened in Europe the hope that Emin Pasha's provinces will be able to furnish the point of departure for the civilising of Central Africa. With ample means Stanley went forth, commissioned by the English, to re-establish communications with Emin Pasha; unfortunately his expedition must be considered as a failure.

"Emin Pasha, however, is in urgent need of help; his letters announce that his ammunition and stores are becoming exhausted. Shall our heroic countryman, left without succour, be abandoned to destruction, and his province, won to civilisation by German energy, become the prey of barbarism? The attempts to reach Emin from the Congo have failed; but from Eastern Africa the best and safest way leads to the Upper Nile, and there is German territory that gives the safest points of departure and support for an Emin Pasha Expedition. The *Duty of the Germans towards him.* German nation is called upon to bring help to the German Dr. Schnitzer. But this help, if it is not to be too late, must be given without delay. Accordingly, the German Emin Pasha Committee turns to the nation for practical support. May each man contribute his share to the accomplishment of an undertaking, which not only aims to advance our transmarine position, and open new paths to German commerce, but is pre-eminently calculated to fulfil a duty of honour, incumbent upon the bold German pioneer. Considerable sums have already flowed in upon the undersigned Committee; but to proceed at once to the carrying out of the expedition, the promptest general and readiest liberal participation of extended circles is necessary. We beg that contributions may be made payable to our Treasurer, Carl von der Heydt, in Elberfeld, at the places appointed by him: The German East Africa Company, in Berlin, W., Krausenstrasse, 76; or the German East African Plantation Company, in Berlin, W., Kaiserin-Augusta-Strasse, 71; or to Herren von der Heydt-Kersten und Söhne, in Elberfeld."

(Here follow the signatures.)

In conclusion, it was determined, already at this first meeting, on the motion of Dr. Otto Arendt, to put forward my name as the leader of the expedition, with extensive powers. The following gentlemen, according to the report, took part in the sitting: Herren v. Steun, J. Wagner (classical-school teacher), Baron v. Langermann, Councillor v. Vedden, Governmental President v. Pilgrim, Schultz-Lupitz, Livonius, Lucas, Major-General v. Teichmann and Logischen, Dr. Schroeder, Dr. Timotheus Fabri, Dr. Arendt, and Ministerial Director Sachse. For the further prosecution of the affair, a managing committee of five members was chosen from among these gentlemen. It consisted of Herren Arendt, Livonius, Peters, Sachse, and Schroeder. *Managing committee appointed.*

This committee, which met on July 7th, determined, before any other steps, to send memorials to His Majesty the Emperor, and to the Imperial Chancellor Prince von Bismarck, soliciting their approval of the projected undertaking. In a sitting of July 18th we elected the following gentlemen as additional members of this committee: The Minister of State v. Hofmann, Professor Dr. Schweinfurth, Retired First Lieutenant Wissmann, and Assessor Lucas. From *Enlargement of the committee.* this day the attempts began to arrange a co-operation between Wissmann and myself in the leadership of the expedition. In Madeira, where he had been staying for three-quarters of a year, for the healing of a diseased lung, Wissmann had also conceived the idea of a German Emin Pasha Expedition, and we at once agreed, at any rate, to try whether it would not be possible to undertake the matter in common.

This attempt certainly did not offer any great prospect of a good result, because it placed in jeopardy the first condition of success in such an affair, namely, the unity of command. This was as fully recognised by Wissmann as by myself; accordingly, we very soon agreed upon the point that it would be necessary to bring about a division of the expedition itself, or, to put it more clearly, to set two expeditions on foot. Here, again, the difficulty arose, how to bring about unity of action in the locality itself, the Equatorial Province. To render this practicable, Wissmann made a written declaration, at Wiesbaden, that in carrying out the German Emin Pasha Expedition he would subordinate himself to me, in such measure as I should consider necessary.

Co-operation with Wissmann proposed.

In Wiesbaden the preparations could be made for the definitive constituting of the German Emin Pasha Committee and resolutions passed; and here, on the occasion of a public meeting of the committee of the German Colonial Company, this constitution was accordingly effected. The subscriptions had at that time already reached the amount of 224,413 marks (£11,220 13s.); and answers to the memorials sent by the provisional committee had been received from His Majesty the Emperor and Prince Bismarck, sympathetically welcoming the carrying out of a German Emin Pasha Expedition. The committee had, moreover, spread itself over the whole of Germany, and now counted more than a hundred members.

Approval of the Emperor and Prince Bismarck.

In the decisive sitting at Wiesbaden, on September 12th, 1888, the following gentlemen were present:—

Vice-Admiral Livonius, Berlin.
Chamberlain Count Behr-Bandelin, Gützkow.
Dr. Irmer, Hanover.
Professor Dr. Fabri, Godesberg.
Prince Hohenlohe-Langenburg.
Privy Councillor Simon, Berlin, deputy of the Landtag.
J. Ulrich, Pfungstadt, member of the Reichstag.
Rumpff Schloss Aprath, deputy of the Reichstag.
V. Palézieux, Weimar.
Dr. Schroeder, Poggelow.
K. v. d. Heydt, Elberfeld.
Dr. Otto Arendt, Berlin, deputy of the Landtag.
Privy-Commission Councillor Lucius, Erfurt, member of the Landtag.
Heszler, Erfurt.

Dr. Ritter, General Director, Waldenburg, in Silesia.
Dr. Fritz Becker, Worms.
Dr. Rud. Grosse, Strassburg, in Elsass.
Lieut. Maercker, Strassburg, in Elsass.
Wissmann, retired First Lieutenant.
Dr. M. Busse, Mining Councillor, Dortmund.
Dr. M. Lindeman, Bremen.
L. Friederichsen, Hamburg.
Max. Schubert, manufacturer, Chemnitz.
G. Wittenbrinck, teacher at the High School, Burgsteinfurt.
Dr. Wibel, M.D., Wiesbaden.
D. Kreszmann, retired Major, Karlsruhe, in Baden.
Grosz, advocate, Pforzheim.
Dr. Grimm, Ministerial President, retired, Karlsruhe, in Baden.
Gerhard Rohlfs, Weimar, Consul-General.
Chr. Frhr. v. Tucher, Government Councillor, Nürnberg.
Sachse, Director in the Imperial Post Office, Berlin.
Dr. R. Sernau, Berlin.
V. Hofmann, Minister of State, Berlin.
Dr. Carl Peters.
Heszler, Government Architect.
G. Truppel, Rudolstadt.
Heinrich Schaerer, Nürnberg.
Wilhelm, Prince of Wied, Neuwied.
V. Cuny, Privy Councillor of Justice, Berlin, deputy of the Reichstag and the Landtag.

The feeling in this meeting was entirely in accordance with the great thought for the realisation of which it had assembled. Almost unanimously, the conviction was held that the question of supporting our countryman in Wadelai involved a duty of honour for the German people, and that the circles who had inscribed the colonial-political idea on their banner were called upon, more than all the rest, to discharge this honourable duty. The colonial-political points of view have, in the whole movement, been regarded as of secondary importance. In accordance with this unity of view, the resolutions of the day were all carried unanimously. Among these the most important were the resolution to convert the provisional committee into an authoritative one, and the resolution, on the motion of Prince Hohenlohe, to instal myself, the Minister of State v. Hofmann, and Dr. Schroeder as presidents. Herr Carl v. d. Heydt was chosen as treasurer, and Dr. Arendt as secretary. The general committee requested the committee of management to carry on an extensive agitation in speech and writing, and on all sides the necessity of speedily putting our intentions into practice was emphatically insisted upon. The sum which we then considered necessary for carrying out the

Definite formation of the committee.

Emin Pasha Expedition we estimated at 400,000 marks (£20,000). The question was, accordingly, the collecting of 175,000 marks in Germany for the undertaking. But the assembly was under the impression that this would hardly occasion any serious difficulty, as in a very short time, in a narrower circle, the amount of full 225,000 marks (£11,250) had been reached. To give an impulse to such further subscriptions, the appeal, which had till then been pursued in a private manner, was now to be signed by the full committee and brought before the public.

<small>Amount of money needed.</small>

The sitting was closed in an enthusiastic spirit, with cheers for His Majesty the Emperor. But it was a very remarkable coincidence, that just at that moment I received the first detailed despatch on the spreading of the insurrectionary movement on the East Coast of Africa. The thought obtruded itself whether these occurrences in Pangani, Bagamoyo, and Dar-es-Salam might not perhaps necessitate, if not the entire cancelling of the plan for which we had assembled in Wiesbaden, at any rate considerable modifications in carrying it out. Meanwhile, however, already in the afternoon of September 12th the committee of management assembled for a private sitting, at which, in consequence of the answer given by Wissmann, the command of the entire undertaking was entrusted to me, with a co-operation that was to be as independent as possible on Wissmann's part.

<small>Troubles in the east of Africa.</small>

<small>Dr. Peters appointed commander.</small>

Concerning this determination there have been discussion and disputation in the press. We did not at that time make it public in its entirety, and, as is often the case, throughout the whole winter of 1888-89, public opinion, in its conjectures, moved along a false track. The question of the division of the command between Wissmann and myself occupied the committee of management once more on September 19th, 1888. On that day Herren Livonius, Sachse, and Schweinfurth were commissioned to conclude agreements with Wissmann and me, concerning the carrying out of the Emin Pasha Expedition, on the basis of

<small>Arrangements between Wissmann and Peters.</small>

the Wiesbaden resolutions. As a basis of our joint advance, it was determined—and in the main it was adhered to, so long as Wissmann remained in the combination—that he should start at once with a small column to march as far as the Albert Nyanza Lake. Meanwhile I was to organise the main column. At the Albert Nyanza we were to meet, and Wissmann, with his column, of which he was to retain the independent command, was then to take part in a plan of operations, to be *Instructions given to Wissmann.* delivered to him by me, and determined on by the committee. On September 23rd it was added that Wissmann was to start for Zanzibar on October 5th or 12th, and that the question of the route should be left to us two leaders, aided by the advice of competent persons. In the same manner, the selection of the guns was to be left to us two.

During this period the movement was going forward in Germany. On the foundation of the Wiesbaden resolutions the *Lively interest in Germany.* German Colonial Company joined it. In Hanover the North-West German Union for the assistance of Emin Pasha was founded, under the presidency of Rudolf von Bennigsen. An address which Herr Ministerial Director Sachse had delivered at Wiesbaden was circulated throughout the whole of Germany, and collections began to be made everywhere, in smaller circles, so that there was no longer any doubt that the required 400,000 marks would be raised.

But at the same time the insurrectionary movement on the East African coast went on side by side with it. The East *Progress of the East African disturbances.* Africa Company was compelled to evacuate, in quick succession, the coast places given over to it on August 15th, with the exception of Bagamoyo and Dar-es-Salam. In Kiloa Kirindshe the officials of the Company were murdered; and, looked at from Europe, it appeared as if the whole of Eastern Africa were bursting into flame. This certainly proved afterwards to be altogether an error; and the Emin Pasha Expedition especially was able, by its proceedings, to show that it was so. The agitation did not, in fact, extend to the real negro world of Eastern Africa, with the exception of the tribe of the Mafiti, who were personally stirred up by Bushiri. Even the Wapokomo, on the Tana, had no intelligence of this insurrectionary movement, much less the Gallas and the Massais.

Nevertheless, it is manifest that the leaders of the Emin Pasha movement found themselves compelled, at the end of September 1888, to consider the question whether the expedition could be carried out at that moment, when the state of things that had existed in the Wiesbaden days had been so entirely altered. This was the question that occupied the committee on the morning of September 30th. In this sitting,

RUDOLF V. BENNIGSEN,
President,

DR. GEORGE IRMER,
Vice-President,

Of the North-West German Union for the Succour of Emin Pasha.

besides members of the committee, Dr. Junker of Vienna also took part. I had to announce at the meeting the opinion adopted by the German East Africa Company, that the rising in Eastern Africa had become organised under a unity of leadership, and held possession of the caravan roads. At the conclusion of my report, I suggested the question whether an advance in union with England and the Congo State did not recommend itself, in view of this new condition of affairs. Wissmann declared on the same occasion, following up my announcement, that in his opinion the Emin Pasha Expedition, according to the original design, had now become impossible. Dr. Junker, too, sided with us,

<small>Question of co-operation with England.</small>

and recommended united action with England and Portugal for the subjection of the Arabs. My advice was that we should, in the first place, put ourselves in communication with the English Emin Pasha committee. In view of these proceedings, Herr Ministerial Director Sachse insisted on the necessity of going on with the collections under all circumstances, so that the favourable moment might be seized, when it should present itself, for putting the enterprise in execution. His Excellency von Hofmann and I supported this method of procedure, and drew up the following motion, which was unanimously adopted :—

"Considering that according to the declared opinion of competent persons whose counsel has been sought on the subject,* the accomplishing of the Emin Pasha Expedition, according to the plan hitherto proposed, has become impossible at the present moment, in consequence of the disturbances that have broken out in Eastern Africa, the committee resolves to postpone the expedition until such time as it shall appear possible in the view of the Imperial Government, but meanwhile to proceed with the collections for the undertaking in the way already adopted."

<small>Resolution for postponement.</small>

The contents of this resolution were published by us at the time, and the news was welcomed with great jubilation by our opponents in the press. It was considered the undertaking had failed.

In consequence of this sitting, a report was made to the Imperial Chancellor, Prince Bismarck, who in his reply, dated Friedrichsruh, October 16th, expressed a wish that the managing section of the German Emin Pasha committee should enter into relations with the German East Africa Company, and endeavour to agree upon a plan for a common advance and mutual support. Thereupon the managing committee resolved, on October 21st, 1888, to inform the Imperial Chancellor that it would obey the suggestion offered in his letter, and place itself in communication with the German

<small>Encouragement from Prince Bismarck.</small>

---

* Schweinfurth also took part in this sitting.

East Africa Company. Negotiations were accordingly opened with the aforesaid Company, and led to an agreement which was reported to the Foreign Department; but a new position taken up by the Government, with respect to East African affairs in general, caused the business to deviate into an entirely different direction.

Meanwhile, in view of the state of things prevailing in the German East African protected territory, the question arose in the managing committee, whether it might not be possible, for the carrying out of the expedition, entirely to avoid this insurrectionary region. Wissmann especially, and various others, drew attention to the Tana route as a possible way of reaching the Equatorial Province. This route, if it were practicable, certainly offered the advantage that the undertaking would be commenced forthwith. There could not, indeed, be a question of a definite Tana route, for the caravan traffic of Eastern Africa had never yet taken that direction; and in such cases the existence of certain physical obstacles may always be counted on, that hinder traffic along so great a river as the Tana. It was hardly to be supposed that commercial intercourse would not have taken its way along the Tana if that route had really been suited to the peculiar conditions of East African commercial life. There was moreover the fact that the greater part of the subscriptions had emanated from the circles of the German East Africa Company, which supported the Emin Pasha Expedition, in the hope that this undertaking would develop itself chiefly in the German East African protected territory. These questions became the subject of discussion in the German Colonial Company on November 22nd. Wissmann on that occasion recommended the Tana route, about which I expressed doubt. These debates on pure matters of detail, which moreover were concluded by a complete understanding, already on November 25th, furnished the hostile press with matter for outbursts of joy, on the dissension in the German Emin Pasha committee—" Wissmann *contra* Peters!"

Proposed route by the Tana to the Equatorial Province.

Opinions of Wissmann and Peters.

On November 25th, the German Emin Pasha committee

resolved unanimously to take in hand, without delay, the starting of the Emin Pasha Expedition; and Wissmann, to whom, according to the decision of September, the free choice of his route was left, was to betake himself, as quickly as possible, to Africa, where he could study the circumstances on the spot, and select his route according to the information obtained. It was noted as desirable that, if it could be done without undue loss of time, the route should be through the German East African territory. It was further arranged that I also should prepare the part of the expedition entrusted to me as quickly as possible, and begin carrying it out. On the strength of this resolution, we both at once set about purchasing the equipments necessary for the expedition.

Resolution to proceed with the expedition.

Affairs were in this state, when Prince Bismarck resolved to take Government action in East Africa, placing First Lieutenant Wissmann in command. Wissmann accordingly retired from the German Emin Pasha Expedition; and now the plan of a dual expedition was naturally abandoned. Although a valuable power was thus withdrawn from the enterprise, on the other side all the means were now placed in one hand, and, above all, the unity of command was assured; and whatever aspect affairs in German East Africa might assume, the first condition for the success of the undertaking was thus fulfilled.

Prince Bismarck's change of front.

It is well known that during all this time various rumours concerning Emin Pasha were spread abroad from England throughout all Europe. At one time Emin Pasha and Stanley were both said to have been killed by the Mahdi; at another the former was reported to be alone in captivity at Khartoum; again, both were said to be retreating from the province of Wadelai. These rumours, which were at first believed here in Germany, were, however, so contradictory, that we at last came to the conclusion, which was not confuted by the subsequent actual departure of Emin Pasha with Stanley, that they were inventions put about with a purpose, and calculated to prevent the carrying out of the German Emin Pasha Expedition. For of the

Conflicting rumours concerning Emin Pasha.

departure of Emin and Stanley nothing at all was known in England at that time, and there was consequently no objective foundation for the appearance of these reports. Accordingly we were resolved not to be deceived by them.

Our position was different with regard to the plans of the German Imperial Government in Eastern Africa. It was, of course, altogether alien from our intention to undertake anything whose accomplishment might be obstructive or even inconvenient to the Imperial procedure. We had, indeed, planned the German Emin Pasha Expedition solely with the object of thereby doing service to our German East African colonial undertakings. How could it have entered into the thoughts of the German Emin Pasha committee, consisting as it did entirely of national men, to advance otherwise than in full agreement with a Government which at that very time was about to act in accordance with the wishes of the colonial-political elements of Germany in Eastern Africa? If even one or another had cherished the wish to carry out, under all circumstances, that German Emin Pasha enterprise, on which so much strength and time had been expended, a resolution in this sense was entirely precluded, in a large majority of the committee, in the event of an intimation from the Imperial Government, to the effect that in the present state of affairs in Eastern Africa it no longer thought this expedition desirable.

Embarrassing position with regard to the Government.

Thus in January 1889 we were especially desirous to ascertain definitely the actual attitude of the Foreign Office. On January 3rd, the managing committee determined, on the motion of Herr Ministerial-Director Sachse, " to abandon the hitherto contemplated division of the command of the expedition; to entrust to Herr Dr. Peters the leadership of the entire expedition, according to the stipulations agreed upon with Captain Wissmann in the compact of December 20th, 1888, those regulations being omitted, which were made in contemplation of a second expedition." This resolution was at once made known to the Foreign Office, and was not followed by any withdrawal

Resolution for unity of command.

of the former expressions of sympathy with the carrying out of the expedition. I was privately informed, through Wissmann, that a written answer would not be given to our last communication; but that the Secretary of State Count Herbert von Bismarck gave me to understand that the Imperial Government was now, as formerly, favourably disposed towards the project, and only requested that I should maintain an understanding with it concerning the steps I intended to take. In this case the German Government would be glad to support the expedition, so far as was compatible with its action on the Eastern coast of Africa. This declaration, which Herr Dr. Arendt and I were able officially to announce at the sitting of the general committee on January 31st, 1889, appeared to the committee sufficient ground for resolving on the immediate carrying out of the German Emin Pasha Expedition.

[margin: Communication from Count Herbert Bismarck.]

At this sitting the following gentlemen were present:—

Parliamentary deputy Lückhoff.
Dr. Wagner, teacher at the Latin School.
Major von Steun.
Assessor Lucas, Director of the German East Africa Company.
Parliamentary deputy Government President von Pilgrim.
Ministerial Director Sachse.
Vice-Admiral Livonius.
Imperial deputy Count von Mirbach-Sorquitten.
Parliamentary deputy Count Hue de Grais.
Count von Hake.
His Excellency von Drigalski Pasha.
Imperial deputy Count Arnim-Muskau.
Parliamentary deputy Professor Dr. Friedberg.
Parliamentary deputy Robbe.
Parliamentary deputy Syndic Tramm.
Parliamentary deputy Muhl.
Parliamentary deputy Privy Councillor Simon.
Imperial deputy Woermann, of Hamburg.
Imperial deputy Rudolf von Bennigsen.
Imperial deputy J. Ulrich.
Parliamentary deputy Gerlich.
Minister of State von Hofmann.
Parliamentary deputy Dr. Otto Arendt.
Parliamentary deputy Government President von Tiedemann.
Imperial and Parliamentary deputy von Kardorff.
Dr. Irmer, of Hanover.
Dr. Carl Peters.

These gentlemen unanimously resolved to commence the

expedition immediately, and to commission me to proceed to Africa at the first opportunity, to undertake the command there in person. In my proceedings in East Africa I was to keep myself in accord with the impending Government action. <small>The expedition to start under Dr. Peters.</small>

By this resolution the German Emin Pasha movement had provided the basis on which we were to work in Eastern Africa. It was a very serious moment for me, when I expressed my thanks to the committee for the confidence displayed towards me, by placing me at the head of such an enterprise in such a difficult time. I resigned the chairmanship of the committee. which the Minister of State von Hofmann undertook; for now, as its commissioner, I was to labour for the object in view. The preparations in Germany were fully completed in the course of the month of January; the officers for the expedition were engaged, and Herr Fritz Bley in Zanzibar was already authorised to proceed with the hiring of porters. <small>Preparations; officers chosen.</small> The very next day, February 1st, on the strength of the resolutions of the preceding evening, I directed Lieutenant-Captain Rust and Herr Fricke to start on the evening of that day for Aden, there to recruit one hundred Somali soldiers for the expedition. Those indeed, who opposed German colonial enterprise on principle, now as ever, took up a position of protest against the expedition; and especially in various circles of the nation, the confidence in my ability to carry such a task into execution, was very far from strong. But after the resolutions of January 31st, opinions and dispositions of mind at home were of little importance, as the basis for the work was here fully assured; the position of affairs at Zanzibar and on the coast would now determine the future fortunes of the expedition, and the manner in which we should set about our task on our arrival. <small>Doubts and forebodings.</small> Opinions and humours at home had no more importance in that moment than the blowing of the autumn wind round the battlements of a strong castle. But already more real obstacles were looming on the horizon, obstacles which we could only make head against in Africa itself; and it

18   *NEW LIGHT ON DARK AFRICA.*

was these obstacles that diverted the course of the German Emin Pasha Expedition into far different ways than we could have anticipated for it on January 31st, 1889. When on February 25th of that year I set out from Berlin for Eastern Africa, I perfectly understood what kind of difficulties and dangers I was going to encounter; and my parting with my friends at the Anhalt railway station was characterised rather by seriousness and emotion than by joyful hope.

Difficulties to be encountered.

CHAPTER II.

IN ZANZIBAR AND THE BLOCKADED TERRITORY.

Aequam memento rebus in arduis
Servare mentem !
(HORACE.)

ON February 20th I had despatched Lieutenant von Tiedemann to Aden, to assist Lieutenant-Captain Rust in transporting to Lamu the hundred Somali soldiers enlisted by the latter. After mature deliberation I had determined to organise my expedition far away from the turmoil of the East African disorders, in Witu. In Germany I had not altogether made up my mind to take the Tana route, being fully aware of the technical difficulties it presented ; but I foreboded that I might be compelled to it. At all events, the tranquil condition of the sultanate of Witu offered a far more convenient basis for the building up and combination of an expedition than the unquiet state of affairs in Zanzibar and on the East African coast, where the Imperial action might at

The insurrectionary districts to be avoided.

any moment be compelled to thrust aside the interests of the German Emin Pasha Expedition. If, on my arrival, I should find it practicable to carry out my great wish of leading the expedition through the disturbed territory, I could, even then, have my whole troop carried across from Witu to Dar-es-Salam or Bagamoyo.

Accordingly, I communicated by telegraph with Lieutenant-Captain Rust in Aden, and sent him corresponding instructions

LIEUTENANT-CAPTAIN RUST.

through Herr von Tiedemann, in the first place to lead the hundred Somalis across to Witu, and to proceed to drill them as the nucleus of the troop I should organise. I had received from Herr Fritz Bley from Zanzibar the preliminary intelligence that he expected to be able to supply nearly two hundred porters. I now commissioned Herr von Tiedemann to push forward the engaging of porters as energetically as possible in Witu and the surrounding region, in conjunction with Lieutenant-Captain Rust. By the kind

Supply of soldiers and porters.

intervention of the Witu Company, I procured an introduction for these two gentlemen to its representative, Herr Toeppen, in Lamu; and thus I might hope, if I could not do it in the protected territory, to raise a troop here, which would render practicable an energetic advance into the interior of Africa.

HERR VON TIEDEMANN.

For the transport of my weapons to Eastern Africa, the Imperial Commissary Wissmann granted me permission to ship them on board of one of his steamers, the *Martha*. I could therefore expect to avoid the disagreeables and difficulties that might otherwise arise from the blockade of the coast that had been recently ordered. I took it for granted that, also in English quarters, there would

Arms shipped on the "Martha."

be consideration for an expedition organised by a nation with which the English were then, as it seemed, working together in a friendly manner in Africa; the more so, as we were determined to advance there in strict accordance with the action the German Empire had taken.

After taking these measures, I proceeded with Herr Oskar Borchert to Egypt, in the hope of there gaining some definite

OSKAR BORCHERT.

information as to the position of Emin Pasha. Not succeeding in this, I went on to Aden, to work personally at the recruiting of an effective Somali or two, but especially to procure camels for the use of the expedition. I reached Aden in the third week in March; and here, to my great satisfaction, I found Count Teleki and Herr von Höhnel, who had just returned from their expedition in Massailand, and gave me very valuable information on the position of affairs by Lake Baringo, through which territory my course would surely lead me, and concerning the regions northward of the lake, especially Engabot and Turkanj. I also had the pleasure, at Aden, of seeing and speaking to our friend Professor Dr. Schweinfurth, who was just returning from his Arabian journey. On the evening of March 24th, Wissmann likewise arrived at Aden from Cairo; and after I had arranged my affairs, we started, on March 25th, 1889, with Wissmann and a few of his gentlemen, Dr. Bumüller and Herr Janke, for Zanzibar, where we arrived on March 31st, towards two o'clock in the afternoon.

Already during this passage Wissmann had shown me a telegram from his representative in Zanzibar, announcing that Rust had landed my Somalis in Bagamoyo. I could not make up my mind to accept the contents of this telegram as correct, as this proceeding was directly contrary to the instructions I had given to Rust. But, on March 31st, immediately on my landing in Zanzibar from the *Mendoza*, I received the necessary explanation through Herr Fritz Bley, and this explanation, at the same time, threw a hard light upon the prospect of the things that awaited me in Zanzibar. I found that, although Lieutenant-Captain Rust had at Aden asked for tickets to Lamu for himself and the Somalis, and had duly obtained them from the British India Steam Navigation Company at that place, the agents of the company had nevertheless forbidden the disembarkation of the people at Lamu. The steamer of the British India line had been obliged to turn round in front of the harbour of Lamu, and had gone with my people to Zanzibar. There, probably at the instigation of the English representatives, the Sultan of Zanzibar had likewise opposed the disembarkation of the Somalis, and thus it had become necessary to carry them across to Bagamoyo. I also heard, at the same time, that the Sultan of Zanzibar was determined to forbid me the passage through Lamu, and to prevent my taking it; and by this, as it seemed, the Tana route was lost to me. As, moreover, the whole blockaded territory, German as well as English, was closed against me, there seemed to be no access to the interior for the German Emin Pasha Expedition from Delagoa Bay to the Juba Islands, and I could not help seeing that the position for me in Zanzibar was much more difficult than my worst forebodings in Germany had allowed me to expect.

On the following day I resolved personally to inspect the position at Lamu, and perhaps also beyond it, on the Somali coast, which in case of need might be brought into the question; and on April 2nd, on board a Sultan steamer which happened to be navigating in those waters, and had meanwhile been chartered by the British East African Company, I went away in company with Lieutenant-Captain Rust and Herr Friedrich Schroeder towards the north. I had previously instructed Herr Fritz Bley to take action in my name against the British East India Steam Navigation Company for breach of their contract to land my Somalis at Lamu, laying the damages at £15,000, or 300,000 marks.

Difficulties with the steamers.

When I arrived in my Sultan steamer, the *Kiloa*, at Mombas, I was informed by Mr. Buchanan, the representative of the British East Africa Company, that although I had taken passage for Lamu, the steamer must not touch at the harbour there, unless I gave my word of honour that, in the event of the ship's running in there, which would only be for a few hours, I would not go on shore at Lamu. Willingly or not, I found myself obliged to give this pledge, because I still had the hope of having a short talk on board with my representative at Lamu, Herr von Tiedemann, who had gone to that place a few days before in the *Barawa*, and of thus giving him new instructions. It happened as I expected; and besides Herr von Tiedemann, I saw at Lamu, though only hurriedly, Herr Kurt Toeppen and Herr Gustav Denhardt. With Herr Toeppen I arranged that he should endeavour, for an adequate indemnification, privately to procure for me, through an Arab, porters for the German Emin Pasha Expedition. I wished to have these porters sent to Lamu. I requested Herr von Tiedemann to give me information concerning the bays and landing-places northward of Lamu.

Vexatious restrictions.

Engagement of porters.

ATTEMPT TO LAND AT MERKA.

After this had been done, our vessel steamed out again, and we ran to the Somali coast to Barawa, Merka, and Mogdishu. Before each of these places we lay at anchor for some days; but the Arab administration there was so weak and cowardly, and perhaps, also, so malicious towards the Europeans resident in Zanzibar, that until then it had been quite an unusual thing for the captains of the ships that ran in, or for their super-

FRITZ BLEY.

cargoes, to go on shore. The dealers used to come on board the ships and do their business. After submitting to this treatment at Lamu, I determined on my own responsibility to make an attempt at landing at Merka. With Lieutenant-Captain Rust I passed in a canoe through the somewhat formidable breakers. But when we came to land, there arose such a tumult on the beach,—to which was added an official order from the Arab governor commanding us to turn back,—that we, who were only armed with revolvers, were

Attempt to land at Merka abandoned.

obliged, whether we liked it or no, to abandon our design of getting a nearer view of the circumstances of the place, so far as they concerned our expedition.

Thereupon I betook myself back to Zanzibar; and here fresh events had occurred, that rendered the successful accomplishment of our undertaking more and more improbable. Contrary to the express instructions I had given in Europe, my hunting weapons had been shipped from Antwerp by the North German Lloyd to Aden, and transhipped from thence to the British India line. By this line they had arrived in Zanzibar while I was on the Somali coast, and, in pursuance of a literal interpretation of the blockade regulations, had been at once seized by the English Admiral Fremantle. As the weapons had been marked by the firm which consigned them to me, not as "ammunition," but as "merchandise," the British India Company also assumed an attitude as if it were pursuing an action against me for £15,000, or 300,000 marks, damages.

Vexations at Zanzibar.

Now I knew that my real weapons of war and the Remingtons which I was to take to Emin Pasha were likewise lying at Aden. There was a pressing danger that these also would be carried on board the British India line and seized at Zanzibar. I immediately put myself in active telegraphic communication with the German Consulate at Aden, to procure the transhipment of these weapons of war to one of Wissmann's steamers, preferably to the *Martha*, which was expected from Hamburg. The captain of the *Martha*, Freiherr von Gravenreuth, declared, however, to the Consulate at Aden, that the ship was full, and could not take my chests of arms. Then by means of the telegraph, in which Wissmann supported me, I endeavoured to get my weapons on board the *Harmonie*, which was expected later. But, to my painful surprise, I received, in answer to my last telegram, an intimation from the German Consul at Aden that the arms had been shipped on board the British India line. I now tried at the German General Consulate in Zanzibar to prevent the seizure of this part also of my equipment, by showing my telegraphic correspondence with Aden, and thus

Telegraphic negotiations with Aden.

Useless efforts for help at Zanzibar.

proving how it was against my express instructions that the consignment of arms had been put on board the English Zanzibar line. But I found it impossible to get any kind of support here; and thus this part likewise of my store of weapons fell into English hands so soon as it got to Zanzibar, and was first deposited on board an English ship of war, and afterwards sent back to Aden by order of the British Admiral.

On my return to Zanzibar, a second great disappointment awaited me. Zanzibar had always been the traditional furnishing-place, with regard to porters, for all expeditions proceeding from Middle Eastern Africa into the interior. Here the Pagasis are engaged, and until lately there was not an expedition that could do without calling at Zanzibar. Accordingly I lost no time in making the usual application to the German Consulate, with the request that the permission might be obtained for me to hire porters there from the Sultan of Zanzibar—a mere formality, the permission being granted to every expedition as a matter of course. Considering my old relations with the Arabs, it could not be difficult for me to procure porters in Zanzibar, and in fact several hundreds of persons had already offered themselves to me in that capacity. When I returned to Zanzibar on April 17th, I heard, to my astonishment, that no answer had been received to my application to the Consulate; and at the same time I was informed that the Sultan had caused it to be made known that every black man who took part in the expedition should have his head struck off at whatever time he might return to Zanzibar, and that I must not reckon on engaging porters.

Application for leave to hire porters disregarded.

The Sultan's threat.

To meet these difficulties, Herr Fritz Bley, who was at that time my representative at Zanzibar, had, very judiciously, on his own responsibility, cast about for a steamer for us; and he had succeeded, by the intervention of the Indian Sewa Hadji, in securing one for me, namely the *Neæra*, from the Bombay Steam Navigation Company. I had originally wished to work with sailing boats, but, in view of these quite unexpected and entirely unusual hindrances, it was exceedingly likely that the possession of a steamer would be necessary, if I was to take up the contest at all. So with a heavy heart I resolved to disburse the large sum required for the chartering of the *Neæra*; and this resolution naturally involved a very important change in my plan of organising the expedition. As I was compelled to spend nearly 75,000 marks (£3,750) only to secure the landing on the coast, —a thing for which, as a rule, every other expedition received facilities on all sides,—I could no longer hope to carry out an expedition estimated to consist of a hundred soldiers and six hundred porters.

The "Neæra" chartered at heavy cost.

Accordingly, already in April I made up my mind to dismiss at least two-thirds of the Somali force; and I now began to contemplate an expedition of a hundred and fifty to two hundred porters.

But fate seemed bent on forbidding the execution even of this design. The following weeks were characterised by efforts on my part, if not to recover all my arms, at least to release my hunting weapons from the English blockade; and on the other hand, by diplomatic intervention of the Empire, to procure access to Lamu. With this object in view I telegraphed on April 29th to the Emin Pasha committee in Berlin, requesting that an application might be made to the Foreign Office, to procure for me, from the English, permission to proceed to Witu. After waiting for some days without receiving news, I renewed the application on May 6th; and on the 10th I begged for mediation that my confiscated arms might be given up. On May 13th I received the reply, "Foreign Office refuses all mediation and support." Thus I was cut off from all further hope in this direction. I was now thrown back entirely on my own resources, and had to put the question seriously to myself, whether I really believed I could carry out the expedition under these circumstances, or not. My weapons were confiscated, with the exception of the muzzle-loaders and breech-loaders, which Wissmann had formerly bought for his section of the expedition, and had handed over to me in Berlin. These were

Endeavour to interest the Foreign Office.

Difficulties; confiscation of weapons.

lying at the depôts of the Imperial Commissariat at Bagamoyo and Dar-es-Salam. But it was still a question whether the delivery of these weapons would not also be refused from Berlin. Such was the condition of the affair in the middle of May. I expressed my opinion of the general position, in a report from Zanzibar to the German Emin Pasha committee, dated May 17th, from which I give the following extract:—

"If the Imperial Government did not wish that the German Emin Pasha Expedition should be undertaken, it should have forbidden the project, which it was the more bound to do, as it had from the commencement approved of the movement, and indeed had set it going. Moreover, we have at once informed the Imperial Chancellor of each of our resolutions. But to have allowed the development of the project to the present point, and now to permit its being hindered under every imaginable pretext, amid the derision of all the nations represented here, and even with the co-operation of the German authorities, is certainly a very peculiar method of advancing German interests and German honour on the shores of the Indian Ocean, and a curious application of the 'Civis Romanus sum' of which Prince Bismarck formerly spoke in the Imperial Diet." In conclusion, I explained my position, in view of our difficulties, in the same report, in the following manner:—

Extract of report to Emin Pasha committee.

"But in face of the difficulties in every direction, in face of the intrigues with which we have to fight daily, all of us here, I am proud to say, are only the more firmly resolved to carry on the undertaking to the utmost verge of possibility. The blockade extends from 2° 10' to 10° 28' south latitude, and there are still points of access enough, which the European powers, Germany and England, have no legitimate pretext for closing against the German Emin Pasha Expedition. If our weapons are permanently confiscated, we shall procure compensation. We shall certainly be powerless against violence by sea. But once in the interior we shall, for the time, be masters of the situation."

Determination to proceed.

The report concludes with the expressed conviction: "If

the political circles in Germany and we here work on together, resolutely and unbewildered, in this persuasion, we shall accomplish our purpose, as there is a providential Power that rules over human affairs. In this firm conviction I remain, with perfect esteem, etc."

Thus the resolution was firmly upheld, under no circumstances to abandon the expedition until mechanical obstacles rendered a further advance entirely impossible.

Meanwhile, in the beginning of May, the *Neœra* had arrived at Zanzibar. The steamer proved to be a very sturdy little craft, that could make her eleven miles an hour, and I considered her of the first importance for the prosecution of our enterprise. By means of the *Neœra*, if it came to the worst, I had the power of bringing weapons from some other part of the Indian Ocean, and, before all other things, it became possible for me to collect porters on the coast, and eventually to evade the blockade. In the first instance, I put the little craft in the service of the Imperial commissariat, as the Wissmann steamers had not yet arrived, and it was especially important, before all things, to get my muzzle-loaders and my ammunition away from Bagamoyo and Dar-es-Salam. I also depended especially, for the enlisting of porters, on Bagamoyo, where Lieutenant-Captain Rust, who commanded our Somalis there, had already established relations for this purpose with the French mission.

On May 17th I crossed over for the first time to Bagamoyo, in the *Neœra*; and during this passage, as happened to me repeatedly during the expedition, I suddenly felt penetrated with a profound certainty that the undertaking was destined to be put into practice in spite of all difficulties, and, so far as we were concerned, to be accomplished. During the following days I took some hundreds of Wissmann's troops, with Wissmann himself, across to Dar-es-Salam, and obtained from him permission to take away a hundred muzzle-loaders and fifty breech-loaders from his depôts, where they lay.

When I returned to Bagamoyo, a few days afterwards, I

received the very agreeable information that Brother Oskar, of the French mission, had about sixty Central-African porters ready for me. Besides the breech-loaders and the hundred muzzle-loaders, the manager of the depôt in Dar-es-Salam had delivered to Herr Oskar Borchert seventeen repeating weapons, for which Wissmann at Bagamoyo very kindly gave me three thousand ball cartridges. I deposited all these stores of weapons in the houses inhabited by the Somalis at Bagamoyo, and on Sunday, May 26th, betook myself back to Zanzibar to transport my tents and other equipments from thence to Bagamoyo. I took seventy-three Somalis across with me to Zanzibar, and dismissed them there.

Resources of the expedition.

Here, in the meanwhile, Herr Fritz Bley and Herr Borchert had practically concluded the re-packing of the loads, diminishing their numbers. From Herr Bley, however, I was obliged on the following morning to part, as the state of his health urgently necessitated his return to Europe, and it was obvious that for undertakings such as we had in view only sound and vigorous constitutions were available.

Departure of Herr Bley.

I remained in Zanzibar until Saturday, June 1st; and this week was important in two directions for the carrying out of the Emin Pasha Expedition. On the one hand, we commenced negotiations during this week with Herr Gasch, who stood in communication with the southern places, and received advice from him, concerning the further procuring of porters, perhaps in Tungi Bay, or Mozambique, or Delagoa Bay. Through these conferences there arose in Zanzibar the settled conviction that I should, in the first place, go with the *Neæra* to Mozambique, to get porters from thence; and this conviction was remarkably useful to us during the next week in the accomplishment of my real plan. For, though I had not myself made any communications in reference to it, this opinion was held, in a certain degree, by the commanding admirals in Zanzibar. On the other hand, during the concluding week in May, I entered into personal communication with Admiral Fremantle, with the view of effecting, at

Plan of proceeding determined on

least, the delivering up of my hunting weapons; and in this I succeeded.

I myself went on board the British flagship, and had a lengthy conference with Admiral Fremantle, which threw a clear light on the situation of affairs. A few days previously, the Deputy Commander in Zanzibar had announced to me, in the absence of Fremantle, that I had no right to put with the *Neœra*, although she did not in general fall under the blockade regulations, into any place that was under blockade, especially Mompas, whither I had wished to go to have a conference with Fremantle. I asked Fremantle what were the reasons and motives of this peculiar order, and he declared to me, in the plainest possible manner, that I was inconvenient to the English in Eastern Africa, and might therefore not reckon upon enjoying, with their sanction, the same right that any one else would have. Twice he openly gave me to understand that, with respect to me, it was a state of war— "C'est la guerre!" If this did not suit me, I should send a despatch to my Government in Berlin; a despatch from Berlin to London, and from London to him, would completely alter the state of things. This he explained to me repeatedly. He deplored all this condition of things, but must obey his instructions. Nevertheless, at the conclusion he promised me not to come in my way outside the line of blockade, and to put no difficulties in the way of the *Neœra*, in case I wished to send her to Lamu, provided that neither I nor contraband of war was on board.

margin: Conference with Admiral Fremantle.

margin: The Admiral's declaration.

"C'est la guerre!" With these words Fremantle had also indicated to me my position in the affair. If I found no legal protection it behoved me, in carrying out the commission entrusted to me, to try how much I could accomplish without it. I considered it more consonant with our national honour and our national interests to perish, on the sea or on the land, with my whole expedition, than to retreat before this paltry mass of obstacles and intrigues. To do this with a good conscience, it was certainly necessary that I should have another expression of authority from the body

margin: Reference to the committee at home.

whose commission I held, the German Emin Pasha committee. It happened fortunately that, on my arrival at Zanzibar, I had found a telegram waiting for me, asking for information concerning the state of the expedition and our condition as regarded weapons. I telegraphed back that the arms had been replaced, and that I hoped to be able to start in four weeks. Then, on May 30th, I received the welcome reply: "All right! Authority forward! Hofmann." I had now what I wanted, and to advance. was resolved to delay no longer, but to extricate myself at once from this state of thraldom in the blockaded territory with the means that were still at my disposal, however limited they might be, and to seek in a freer field the scene of further development of events. I was now determined to lead my expedition northward round the line of the blockade, and to seek more suitable points of support for the advance, in Witu and on the Tana.

On June 1st, in company with Herr Oskar Borchert, and with Herr Friedenthal, who had been engaged expressly for packing the cases, I crossed over to Bagamoyo, having Departure my hunting weapons and the other paraphernalia of from Bagamoyo for the expedition on board. The whole of the following Dar-es-day, and on June 3rd, I was shipping my arms and Salam. ammunition in Bagamoyo, and on the 4th I caused Lieutenant-Captain Rust to take into actual service the porters enlisted through Brother Oskar. On June 5th I embarked all my forces, and on the morning of the 7th we steamed out of the harbour of Bagamoyo, bending our course towards Dar-es-Salam. In Bagamoyo it was thought that I should lie for a week at Dar-es-Salam, to procure additional porters, and then betake myself to the south. I should indeed have been very glad to get more porters at Dar-es-Salam, as I had procured only fifty-three men in all at Bagamoyo. I feared, however, that by longer tarrying in Dar-es-Salam I should risk everything without a proper equivalent, and consequently contented myself with hiring some fifteen more men there on June 8th; and already, on the morning of the 9th, a Sunday, I proceeded onward from Dar-es-Salam.

Herren Teramin, Maercker, Küsel, and Rabe had helped me with all their might, in the kindest manner. I took leave of them at eight o'clock in the morning, on the quay at Dar-es-Salam, and shaped my course at first towards the south, to get safely clear of the entire blockade territory. The guns of the station saluted the departing *Neæra*, and we took leave of our countrymen on the coast with a return salvo from our repeating rifles.

It was a glorious moment when the outlines of the islands

THE "NEŒRA" RUNNING OUT FROM DAR-ES-SALAM.

of Dar-es-Salam faded away behind us. A stiff breeze came up from the north-west, and the sea was strongly agitated.

Hopes for the future. The future, indeed, lay before us shrouded in uncertainty, even in darkness; but the sentiment that moved us three—Lieutenant-Captain Rust, Oskar Borchert, and myself—at that instant, was certainly one of relief, of release from a heavy pressure, the feeling of liberty, of movement. If we made our way into the free ocean, we could shape our plans as we chose, and had not to apprehend being crushed unceremoniously by measures of brute force. It was only on the preceding evening that I had disclosed my definite plans to the captain of the *Neæra* and to Lieutenant-Captain Rust. I was going to hold a northward course outside of the islands of Zanzibar and Pemba, and endeavour to gain Kwaihu Bay, that lies north of the blockade territory. Technically, this undertaking was no easy one, for Kwaihu Bay is blocked from the outside by reefs, and generally cannot be entered without a pilot's help. We had naturally not been able to procure a pilot in Zanzibar, for this would have frustrated the whole plan. *Plan of proceeding.*

But it was necessary that I should run this risk, if I did not wish to give up the expedition as such. So we took the responsibility on ourselves. After we had run for ten miles to the south-east, the course was altered towards the east, in which direction, by six o'clock in the evening, we had steamed about fifty miles. Then we shifted our course to north-north-east, and in the night ran past Zanzibar and Pemba, steering directly for Lamu. Till four in the afternoon we steamed on through a very rough sea, till about the latitude of Lamu, and from thence we held on to the north-west, shaping our course for Kwaihu. Zanzibar and the whole blockade were far out of sight astern. *A devious course.*

On the evening of the 10th our expedition was near coming to a sudden end. I was sitting after supper on the quarter-deck, over a cigar, with Lieutenant-Captain Rust and Oskar Borchert, when suddenly a bright glare of fire shone from the saloon, where all our powder and ammunition were stored. The heavy rolling and pitching of the vessel had overthrown the petroleum lamp, which exploded about three feet from the first powder barrel. We rushed down at once with the captain and engineer, caught up a number of woollen blankets, which we threw upon the fire, making a kind of package of the whole, and threw the flaming mass overboard. Except a few burns on Rust's hand, there were no casualties to record. I took this as a fortunate omen, and a complete confidence in the further fortunes of the expedition filled my heart. *Alarm of fire.*

On the morning of the 11th we awoke with the impression that we were in the latitude of Kwaihu Bay. We skirted an island which, according to the marine charts, corresponded to Kwaihu Bay. There was a heavy sea, the wind whistled from the south-west, heavy rollers broke continually over our little boat, which threatened every moment to capsize. The chests were thrown violently to and fro, and my people groaned with sea-sickness and alarm. Till nearly eleven o'clock we were sounding and tacking. Then I had the gig lowered, to attempt a landing through the roaring breakers. But the boat was nearly overturned, and we had to get it back on board quickly, or we should have lost it. An imperfect observation of the sun's altitude at noon indicated that we were about 1° south latitude, consequently thirteen miles north of the Hohenzollern harbour, or about sixty miles from Kwaihu Bay, and in sight of one of the Dundas Islands. So strongly had the coast current carried us towards the north.

A stormy passage.

We steamed at full speed towards the south-west until seven in the evening, making only seven (German) miles against the monsoon; and we had, beyond this, to reckon for about three miles of leeway towards the north; so that our actual progress on our course comprised only four (German) miles. By seven in the evening we had made about forty miles. From that time we went at half-speed, to avoid getting into the English blockade, until four in the morning, when we put on full speed again. After long soundings, etc., and observation of the sun's altitude at noon, we simply found ourselves in about the same position as yesterday. So greatly had we still under-estimated the set of the stream towards the north.

Harassing navigation.

Now matters became really serious, for a want of water began to make itself felt. At Zanzibar I had ordered the captain to take about a week's supply of water on board, and he had done so; but he had only reckoned for his own ship's company, and had not allowed for the people I was to bring. In Dar-es-Salam I had endeavoured to supply this want. It had, however, been impossible to get large

Scarcity of water on board.

DOUBTS AND DIFFICULTIES. 37

quantities of water on board; and thus, in the expectation of being in Kwaihu Bay in three days at the latest, I had steamed away with an insufficient store of water—undoubtedly a great mistake in administration. The captain began to lose courage. Then I made arrangements for catching the rain water, and

"Is KWAIHU PEAK IN SIGHT?"

away we went again, under press of steam, to the south-west, against a heavy sea and roaring wind, like yesterday. Sleep was not to be thought of, as we were all berthed on the afterdeck; it was the more impossible, as heavy downpours of rain wetted everything through. We steamed at full speed till four in the morning; then steered west by north towards the land and sighted—one of the Dundas islands. The captain was much depressed, and demanded to go back to Zanzibar. Accordingly I issued a written instruction to him to cruise before Kwaihu Bay, until he should receive a different order from me. I threatened, if he did not obey my directions, to hold his company answerable for the loss of £20,000. That sufficed for the day. By dint of more extensive measures I further succeeded, on this Thursday morning, in collecting and storing in the tanks about 1,500 buckets of rain water.

Difficulties with the captain.

At half-past twelve we had a gleam of sunshine, and the captain took the sun's altitude for 2° south latitude, so that we must be near our goal. At half-past one I drew Herr Borchert's attention to the fact that I thought I descried Kwaihu Peak, the landmark of Kwaihu Island. Immediately afterwards a very heavy squall arose, with black rain clouds, so that everything vanished, and we had hurriedly to steer away from the land, lest we should be thrown upon the reefs. At four o'clock the captain came on the after-deck, and asked me to step on the bridge and see if the island opposite was not Lamu. I thought it was, and Lieutenant-Captain Rust was even more decidedly of the same opinion. We slowed down; then, as we imagined, passed Manda Island northward, till we thought we saw the entrance to Manda Bay. Now we seemed to know where we were. We were obliged to hold off from the shore because the sun sank. Through the night we cruised in sight of the island. The next morning we were to go along Patta and to Kwaihu Bay. In such a mood as used to be mine in my boyish days in anticipation of Christmas Eve, I lay through the night sleepless on my swaying chair. Next morning at dawn we went on. Yonder was Manda, yonder Patta—now Sewy Point and Sewy Spit and Kwaihu Bay with Botteler's Ledge must come. Sure enough there it was. But the bay was obstructed by a barrier of reefs and by violent breakers. And what was yonder island in the middle, that was not marked on the marine chart; and why did the soundings not correspond? At twelve o'clock the solar observations showed us that we were in 1° 34′ S. latitude,

Danger of shipwreck.

Doubts as to our position.

consequently twenty-nine to thirty German miles northward of Kwaihu Bay. The coast formations along the Benadirland are so uniform, that such mistakes as happened to us must not be too much wondered at. I believe we may have had Fairhead before us on this mournfully fine Friday.

Off we went again, under full steam, towards the south! In the evening we were opposite the fancied Lamu, where we had cruised the night before. Next morning onward to the south-west! And there it rose before us. The peculiar, unmistakable Kwaihu Peak was there at length, and finally Kwaihu Bay itself! It is impossible to picture the feeling of deep satisfaction I experienced. It must be remembered how much was at stake on this occasion. With what derision we should have been received, and how kindly the English blockade would have welcomed us if, as might easily have happened, we had stumbled into it! A slight accident to our engines or our screw might have overthrown everything. However, these were *curæ passatæ,* and between ten and eleven o'clock on Sunday, June 15th, we passed through the breakers of Kwaihu Bay. At eleven the *Neæra* anchored. Behind us lay the breakers of Siyu Spit, and before us, though certainly at a distance of five miles, the continent of Africa. What very seldom happens to me now, after these four days of exhaustion and sleeplessness I felt somewhat excited.

Arrival at Kwaihu Bay.

But there was no time for recreation. We had no boats, and a fresh breeze was blowing into the bay, and more than a hundred persons and about twenty thousand pounds of cargo had to be landed. Consequently, at half-past eleven I stepped into the gig with Lieutenant-Captain Rust, to proceed to Siyu and secure people for unloading and carrying. As a precaution I took with me the jolly-boat with six of my soldiers; and it was only towards three o'clock that we reached the village of Siyu, on the north side of Patta. We quickly succeeded in establishing friendly relations. But I learned that dhows were only to be had in Pasa from Buana Mse, with the concurrence of the Arab governor. Quickly resolved, I sailed on westward, with Rust, in the jolly-boat to Pasa. Herr

To Siyu for recruits.

Friedenthal, who had meanwhile arrived with the other jolly-boat, was directed by me to follow me slowly in this second boat, with ten soldiers, and to lay to in front of Pasa.

Pasa is a town of between four and five thousand inhabitants, with a fort and an Arab garrison. Hundreds of people surrounded us when we were ceremoniously ushered into the Governor's presence. At Pasa the sympathies were decidedly English, as Mr. Mackenzie had shortly before been strewing gold around. The inhabitants took us for Englishmen, as the *Neæra* sailed under the English flag. I saw no reason to undeceive them in this matter; and half-an-hour later I sailed back with two great dhows to the *Neæra*, which we reached towards seven o'clock. Buana Mse had also secured for me a hundred and fifty porters, whom, however, he did not afterwards produce.

Our fortunes at Pasa.

That same night, with the sea running high, we succeeded in getting all the contraband of war, powder, ammunition, etc., into one of the dhows, with twelve soldiers to guard it. The second dhow we loaded next morning at daybreak; and as at this moment a third dhow ran up to the steamer, I was now able to embark all my people at once. On Sunday morning towards eight o'clock we made all clear for leaving the *Neæra*. Indeed, as is usually the case, it appeared at the last moment that all the things had not been got out of the boat; but as the ebb was setting in fast, and I would no longer run the risk of exposing the whole business to the chance of a *coup de main* of the English, I made up my mind to leave Herr Friedenthal behind, and to let the remainder of the things follow us on that day or the succeeding one. I should probably have done this far more zealously if I had been aware of what was taking place meanwhile, just south of Kwaihu Bay.

Embarkation of the recruits.

Fremantle, whose attention must have been attracted by my departure and my sudden disappearance from the Zanzibar waters, had meanwhile put himself in motion, with his flagship and three other men-of-war, in the certain hope, as it appears to me, that I should endeavour to run into Manda Bay, and

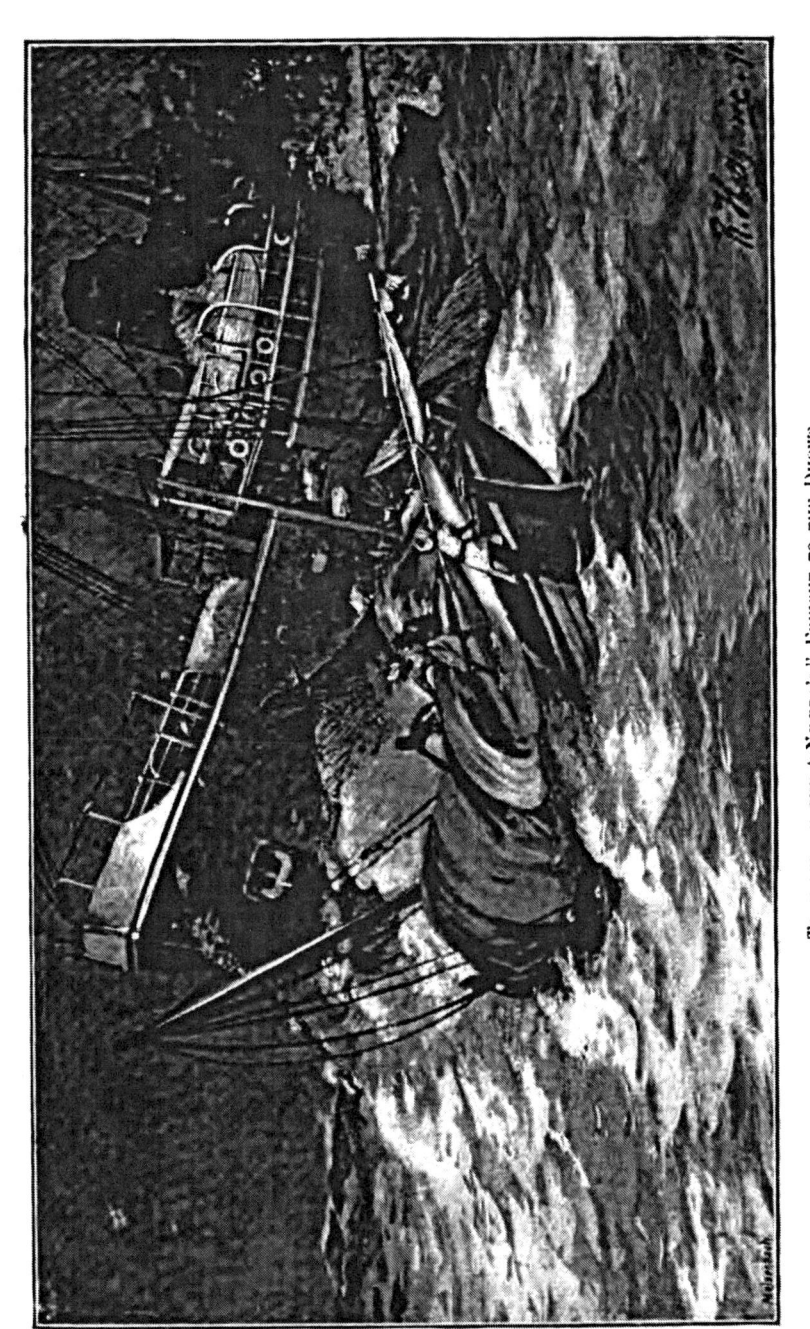

Transfer of the "Neera's" Freight to the Dhows.

PROCEEDINGS WITH THE DHOWS. 41

that he should succeed in laying hold of me there. His flagship lay about two German miles from me. He had neglected to occupy Kwaihu Bay, because he looked upon the entrance to it as closed up; which I consider an unpardonable error on his part. That he did not, as was afterwards affirmed in English quarters, consider Kwaihu Bay as lying outside the region of his blockade and that I had a right to land there, is shown by the fact that a few days later he forbade the *Neæra* to land her effects in Lamu or in the adjoining bays and harbours,—a prohibition that undoubtedly included Kwaihu Bay. Thus Fremantle was quietly lying in Manda Bay, when at about ten o'clock I with my three sturdy dhows parted company with the *Neæra*. In the first of these I had embarked with Lieutenant-Captain Rust, in the second was Herr Borchert, the third I had carelessly left without any white man on board, as it was to be commanded by Herr Friedenthal, whom at the last moment I had ordered back to the *Neæra*. It was with a feeling of exaltation that I saw the white line of breakers gradually disappear behind us. Such may have been the emotions of the much-enduring Ulysses, when Circe's island disappeared beneath the ocean.

At eleven o'clock a heavy shower of rain drew up, veiling before as in twilight the islands of Kwaihu and Fazy, and also the continent. Thus we could not accurately control our course, and were anything but pleasantly surprised when, towards twelve o'clock, the dhow suddenly struck heavily, and at the same time the sail came down, without any command from us. The "captain" of the dhow informed us that the Arab governor had given orders we were to come once more to Pasa before we betook ourselves to the continent. As I afterwards ascertained, the gentlemen had held councils during the night, and after learning who we were had resolved to keep us at Pasa until the British Admiral Fremantle sent to decide what should be done with us. To acquiesce in this was certainly not now my intention. I could not think of making the success of the whole undertaking dependent on the humours of Arabs who were in the pay of the English. I gave orders to hoist the sail again. After a short resistance my people succeeded in carrying out the order, at which the Patta people half voluntarily and perhaps half under compulsion sprang overboard, and we were now completely masters of the boats. I requested Lieutenant-Captain Rust to take the helm in my boat; the two other pursuing dhows that now arrived, and manœuvred like the first, had also to turn round, when Herr Borchert at my call interposed energetically; and after I had succeeded in putting some determined Somali soldiers into the third, by means of swimming, we drew off hastily from the land, when we saw masses of people coming along with loud cries, and now with full sails we steered for the continent of Africa.

Energetic measures.

The rain, which had ceased for a time, now began to fall again more heavily, and a grey mist hid the Siyu Canal, into which we now ran. At half-past one o'clock we anchored before a place that was designated to me as Kiwani. I wondered at seeing no houses, but caused myself to be carried by three men a long distance through the sea, to look about me. There was the usual mangrove thicket. A grey swell struck incessantly into the knotted tree roots on which we stood. Lieutenant-Captain Rust, who had landed with six Somali soldiers, agreed with me either that this was not Kiwani or that Kiwani was not the place for us. Therefore back into the boats! I now took my place in the third boat, ordering Lieutenant-Captain Rust into the first one, so that each boat was furnished with a commander.

Kiwani does not suit us.

Before us lay the Siyu Canal, which runs into Manda Bay. On the left, in graceful lines, extends the island of Patta, which I knew very well from having visited it a year and a half before. In the north the continent of Africa winds boldly along, curving into a series of bays. A soft rain was rippling down, and wrapped all things in a mysterious grey tint. This invited us to the execution of a plan which had appeared tempting to me already at Zanzibar, but which I had not ventured seriously to contemplate.

The Siyu Canal: a new plan.

QUESTION OF LANDING THE GOODS. 43

Whoever looks at the map will see that the Siyu Canal, nearly opposite the town of Patta, makes a wide curve to the north. We should have had to avoid the northern bend of this

LANDING IN SHIMBYE.

canal if we had landed opposite Kwaihu. With a full complement of porters this would have taken us three days to do, but with our limited supply would require at least six or seven. But this northern bay is already bounded on the west by the sultanate of Witu. If we could enter it, unperceived, from the Manda Bay, the problem of evading the blockade would be successfully solved this very day. I made up my mind to make use of the opportunity afforded me, by the secure possession of three dhows, to carry this plan into execution. Forward, therefore, with a good wind, to the west! The two front dhows lowered their sails to obey this new order of proceeding; and then we rushed along, at about the same latitude. Opposite Siyu we inclined to the north, and at four in the afternoon, drenched to the skin, we cast anchor at Mbaja. I had the little dhow unloaded at once, as I wished to send it back immediately to the ship with Herr Borchert; meanwhile we established ourselves comfortably at Mbaja.

I had intended to cross that very night to Shimbye in the sultanate of Witu; but the complete state of exhaustion of captains and crews alike compelled me somewhat to delay these proceedings. We supped on a little cold meat, put a sufficient number of soldiers into the dhows, and at half-past seven o'clock all went to sleep; but our rest was uncomfortably disturbed by the continual leaking of the rain through the roof of the negro hut.

At four o'clock in the morning Herr Borchert, with four soldiers to guard the possession of the dhow, returned to Kwaihu Bay. At half-past five Lieutenant-Captain Rust and I had all the things stowed in the third dhow, and all the people placed in the two others, which floated deep in the water and were crowded; and at sunrise we again put to sea. Æolus was gracious to us; the sun shone pleasantly, and already at half-past seven we were able to cast anchor at Shimbye. The place itself lies some twelve minutes from the anchoring-ground. I went at once into the village; found that it was admirably suited to our purpose; secured the hire of a few houses from the elder; and went back to the strand to superintend the landing of our effects. This business was continued till about twelve o'clock, and furnished a very lively and, for us, an exceedingly satisfactory spectacle. When everything had been landed, I went back into the village to take in hand the stowing of the baggage, while Lieutenant-Captain Rust remained on the shore. The porters ran to and fro; and by two o'clock in the afternoon of June 17th everything was snugly housed at Shimbye, in the sultanate of Witu, under the flag of Fumo Bakari that waved above us.

Safe arrival in the sultanate of Witu.

CHAPTER III.

IN THE SULTANATE OF WITU.

"But wildly did they fare,—
I fear 'twill rend;—
God makes not the account
At each week's end." GOETHE.

THE impediment of brute force offered by the blockade had thus been overcome; and the task of conquering this difficulty had not been a very difficult one. A little cool calculation and, above all, complete discretion had been sufficient to stultify the prophecies of friends and foes in Zanzibar. There the German Emin Pasha Expedition had already been looked upon as a lamentable failure, and there had been rejoicing over the fact. But the English had been too confident of success, which in general appears to me to be a national fault with them, and one that may some day cost

Success of the commander's plan.

them dear; and so the *Neœra*, in spite of four English ships of war, had happily run into the northernmost bay of the system of the Lamu harbours. The consciousness of having prevented this ignominious stifling of the expedition at Zanzibar was naturally calculated to call forth in us a certain feeling of triumph. But, on the other hand, the position in which we were now placed was scarcely of a kind to keep alive in me feelings of satisfaction. *Conflicting feelings.*

I had landed, all in all, at Shimbye, some sixty porters and twenty-seven soldiers. With these, on June 17th, I had in the first place to confront the task of getting more than two hundred and fifty loads of ammunition and other stores to Witu, in the face of the British fleet. That in the event of further violence on the part of the English I was entirely destitute of rights, I understood perfectly well. Moreover, so long as I remained on the coast I was not safe for a moment in my own camp from the danger of a visit of English marines. Though I had been obliged to make use of stratagem against the English ships of war, I was certainly resolved to employ the means far more sympathetic to me, the *vis vim vi expellit*, in opposing any such violence by land. But the position of the German Emin Pasha Expedition was hardly improved by this resolution. *Danger of hostile interference.*

At Shimbye I was obliged to wait for a few days to give the whole column a little rest. The people were greatly exhausted by the hardships of the sea passage. It was also requisite thoroughly to clean the arms, which had suffered greatly from the sea water, to mount the gun, and to take the tent-loads to pieces. In addition I had to wait for news from Herr Borchert, and the dhow, with the remainder of our things from the *Neœra*. With regard to these things I had directed that everything which falls under the designation of "merchandise" should, according to the permission given me by Fremantle, go to Lamu, from whence I could have it delivered to me on the continent by means of nine camels I had formerly bought at Aden, and that were now stationed at Lamu; that, on the contrary, everything *Doings at Shimbye.*

which fell under the designation of "contraband of war" and, consequently, under the regulations of the blockade, should be brought to me by dhow to Shimbye, which lies to the north of the blockade line. On June 18th, Herr Friedenthal arrived at Shimbye with this portion of the things. Herr Borchert sent me word that he had considered it better for his part to go to Lamu with the goods intended for barter than personally to superintend the loading of the camels. Already before the arrival of Herr Friedenthal from Shimbye, on June 18th, I had put myself in communication with Herr von Tiedemann and Herren Toeppen and Gustav Denhardt in Lamu. On that day I wrote a report to Germany, which, with regard to Jackson's expedition, concluded with these words: "We will just see if the English, with all the start they made, have overtaken us." My whole attention during the next few days was directed to procuring additional porterage power. For this purpose I betook myself on June 19th to Wanga, with a few people. Close by the shore there I found a house which had quite a European character. I entered, and found in it Herr Schönert, an official of Herr Denhardt. He received me kindly, and at once pointed out to me, in the bay before his windows, a ship well known to me, the *Boadicea* of Admiral Fremantle, which had arrived shortly before. At one o'clock in the day Herr Schönert accompanied me back to Shimbye, and here I had the agreeable surprise of seeing Herr von Tiedemann, who, on receiving the news of our landing, had at once betaken himself with Toeppen, Denhardt, and Gerstaecker on board a dhow, to seek us in the environs of Kwaihu Bay. It was somewhat late before they discovered us at Shimbye. Already before my letters arrived at Lamu rumour had carried thither the announcement of our landing. But with what exaggeration! A thousand Germans were reported to have landed in Kwaihu Bay, and there was great excitement among the white and black population. To my sorrow I soon convinced myself that my hope of procuring porters through Herr Toeppen had little chance of being realised. But I arranged with him that he should undertake the fitting out of my expedition, with suitable articles of barter, for the Tana route. I had caused ninety-six loads of articles of barter to be brought together from Zanzibar in view of a Tanga-Massai route. I was at that time still possessed with the traditional views of African travel, that it was necessary to provide, with the most anxious care, a selection of articles of barter for each separate route, suited to the tastes of the inhabitants of the districts through which a man would pass, if he wanted to travel at all in Africa.

Articles of barter, etc.

Accordingly I arranged with Herr Toeppen that he should take over the articles of barter I had brought with me, and conveyed to Lamu. The part that could be used he was to include in the collection to be made by him; the rest he was to sell on the best terms he could get; and then, from his own camp, and from other wares that were to be procured at Zanzibar, he should put together the articles I should require on my route.

New arrangements.

On this afternoon I also learned for the first time that four English men-of-war were cruising in these waters without any ostensible reason. But to me the reason was ostensible enough; and in consequence of this news I determined to start with my expedition at once towards the south-west, to get away in the first instance from the vicinity of the sea. Therefore on the same evening, at half-past five, I sent my ammunition by the land road to Wanga, and in the night, between eleven and twelve, I despatched a dhow laden with provisions under Herr Friedenthal to Mgine. June 20th and 21st afforded us the diverting sight of our dhows, with the stores for the expedition, moving, in view of Admiral Fremantle and the *Boadicea*, from Shimbye towards Mgine, at which place they all arrived in good condition. The gentlemen perhaps took us for quite ordinary slave dhows, which were not worth chasing,—especially as by so doing the interests of their new friends of Patta or Manda might be compromised. Certainly, the *Boadicea* was lying here pursuant to the orders of the blockade, quite irrespective of

A hurried departure.

The "Boadicea."

us, to watch the dhow traffic with respect to contraband of war, ammunition, and slaves ; and the excuse that they could not be aware that dhows were transported by sea to Mgine would accordingly not have been valid. It was indeed a system of surveillance calculated to inspire respect !

On the morning of June 20th I myself went, in company with Herren Toeppen, Denhardt, and von Tiedemann, with a number of loads to Wanga. On this day the *Boadicea* fired many salutes, and had run up the Wali flag; a proof that Walis were on board, my friend Buana Mse being probably among them. In every case the fact of our landing must now be undoubtedly known to the English. In spite of this, judging from the proofs I had already had of their vigilance, I resolved, as I wished to get matters concluded quickly at Shimbye, to work that day with dhows also on the sea. We got together three such dhows, two of which I sent to Shimbye with new instructions for Lieutenant-Captain Rust, keeping one for myself.

<small>Necessity for quick action.</small>

Besides this, behind the bushes which hid them from the view of the English man-of-war, my people were all day long carrying loads of ammunition for me from Shimbye to Wanga. Rust put the remainder of the things in the two dhows sent to him ; and on June 21st, by ten o'clock at night, the whole expedition had been transported to Mgine, from whence the much frequented land road leads to Witu. Already on this day, at nine in the morning, Herr Friedenthal arrived with his dhow, then Herr Gerstaecker on one of the two Shimbye dhows. The ammunition I did not send from Wanga quite to Mgine, but landed it opposite Wanga on the further side of a creek, under the supervision of Herren Toeppen and Tiedemann, to have it carried from thence by the land road to Mgine. This overland transport I superintended myself, with Herr Denhardt. I arrived with about fifty loads at Mgine, at half-past six o'clock, and at once sent the people back to bring up the remainder, which Herr Tiedemann was guarding, the same night. At ten o'clock, as we all sat in very cheerful mood at supper in Mgine, to my great satisfaction

<small>The landing at Mgine.</small>

ASSEMBLING OF THE EXPEDITION.

the last dhow arrived, under Lieutenant-Captain Rust; and at daybreak next morning I had everything deposited in safety on shore, and immediately sent sixty loads of ammunition further inland to Hindi, which was about nine miles distant.

I had selected Hindi as the spot where I would gather together all the means and powers I possessed, and organise my expedition. The place was situated some miles from the sea, immediately behind Lamu, in the midst of a richly cultivated region, and appeared therefore to fulfil all the conditions for my work of organisation. *The rendezvous at Hindi.* I betook myself thither on the 23rd in company with Herren Denhardt and von Tiedemann, while Lieutenant-Captain Rust once more remained behind to superintend the reserves. Through the whole of the 23rd, 24th, and 25th we worked to get all the loads housed at Lamu; in which business my camels, drawn from Lamu on the morning of June 24th, proved themselves very useful.

On June 25th, 1889, the whole expedition was assembled at Hindi. I had the tents set up in the middle of the place, my guns loaded, and the houses around occupied. On the road towards Lamu, from which direction further forcible proceedings on the part of the English were perhaps to be expected, I had a guard maintained, day and night, to get timely notice of any such movement. The gentlemen, however, did not favour us with a visit. These last measures of mine might appear exaggerated, if it were not taken into consideration what feelings must have been awakened in us by the events that had taken place, in the interval, at Lamu.

At that place Herr Borchert had arrived on June 20th with the *Neœra*, which had meanwhile suffered damage by sea. On the way it had almost appeared as if the *Neœra* must go to pieces. They had been obliged to cast out the sheet anchor; and the captain advised Borchert to be prepared for the worst. *The "Neœra" brought to book.* Nevertheless on June 20th, on the day when from Herr Borchert's window I was, with peculiar interest, watching through a telescope the proceedings on board the English flagship *Boadicea*, the *Neœra* reached the harbour of Lamu. As she ran in she was met by a pinnace from the English ship of war *Mariner*, whose officer called up from the boat, " Where is Dr. Peters ? " The question was asked in a tone as if the officer were enquiring, not whether I was at Zanzibar or in the interior, but in the cabin or on the quarter-deck. The more startling, accordingly, was Herr Borchert's answer, " Dr. Peters? Dr. Peters is gone into the interior, to Emin Pasha." Next morning Fremantle himself appeared, and summoned the captain of the *Neœra*. To our general regret we heard at Hindi that Admiral Fremantle had been very angry indeed in the presence of the captain. We were told he gave manifest signs of considerable disturbance of spirit. For five days, he exclaimed, he had been cruising in these miserable waters with three men-of-war, the *Boadicea*, the *Mariner*, and the *Cossack*, for the sole purpose of intercepting us—for five days, five days! And now, after all !—Poor Admiral Fremantle! We all pitied him sincerely. But from his anger—which appeared to me personally somewhat inexplicable, inasmuch as he had given permission for the *Neœra* to land at Lamu provided neither I nor ammunition were on board—there were evolved in him manly resolutions, which promised him satisfaction.

The two following letters should be read by those who would form an opinion of what occurred at Lamu subsequently to June 20th. They were written in English, and I herewith give them :—

" BAGAMOYO, *June 9th*, 1889.

" YOUR EXCELLENCY,—I have the honour kindly to inform Your Excellency that I shall most likely have to send the *Neœra* to Lamu.

" According to the promise kindly given by Your Excellency to me, that you will raise no objections to my doing so in case there are neither arms and war ammunitions nor my own person on board, I kindly beg from Your Excellency to instruct the commander of H.M.S. at Lamu of my intention.

" I probably shall send to Lamu either Herr Borchert or

Herr Friedenthal or both, and this will be about from June 25th to 30th. With the expression of my sincere respect,
"I remain Your Excellency's most obedient Servant,
"(Signed) CARL PETERS."

"BOADICEA" AT ZANZIBAR, *June* 11*th*, 1889.

"SIR,—I have the honour to acknowledge the receipt of your letter of the 9th instant, informing me of your intention to send the *Neœra* to Lamu, but that in accordance with what I mentioned in our recent interview you would not go yourself, and no arms or ammunition would be on board the ship.

"Under the above circumstances I shall not object to the *Neœra* going to Lamu, and I will give instructions to our blockading ship accordingly; but her proceedings there will be watched, and I shall direct that she is ordered to quit the port if anything whatever is being done or suspected which would at all be liable to create disturbance or injure the British Imperial East Africa Company.

"It would tend to remove suspicion if you were to make a candid statement of the object for which the *Neœra* is required to go to Lamu.

"I have the honour to be, Sir, your obedient Servant,
"FREMANTLE, *Vice-Admiral.*

"To DR. CARL PETERS, BAGAMOYO."

This letter of Admiral Fremantle I did not receive until afterwards at Witu, and was consequently unable to send an earlier reply. To further elucidate the position I also append the following letter:—

"LAMU, *June* 21*st*, 1889.

"To OSKAR BORCHERT, ESQ.,
"Member of the German Emin Pasha Expedition, Lamu.

"SIR,—I have the honour to inform you that I have received order from Arbuthnot, Commander of H.M.S. *Mariner*, to prevent the ss. *Neœra* from landing the cargo consigned to the German Emin Pasha Expedition in Lamu.

"I further have to state that I have examined every

package, and hereby certify that I have found neither arms nor ammunition nor powder amongst them.

"I have the honour to be, Sir,

"(Signed) D. R. ROBERTS, *Seaman H.M.S. 'Mariner.'*"

When, on June 23rd, I arrived at Hindi, Herr Oskar Borchert had come over in person from Lamu, to report to me on the contents of this letter. The matter no longer formally concerned me, as already in Kwaihu Bay I had transferred to Herr Borchert the right of directing the movements of the *Neæra*, and had left the articles of barter which were on board the steamer, as already stated, at the disposal of Herr Cust Toeppen, at Shimbye. Nevertheless I was naturally materially affected by these occurrences, inasmuch as I was anxious, from financial considerations, to get a fresh charter for the *Neæra* as soon as possible, and, on the other hand, Herr Toeppen was going to furnish my new equipment for the expedition partly from the articles of barter I had surrendered to him. Consequently I gave Herr Borchert new instructions for his conduct in the affair, and hoped, looking at the concluding sentence of Roberts's letter, that it would be quickly settled. Accordingly, who shall describe my astonishment when on June 24th Herr Borchert sent me a copy of the following letter :—

"H.M.S. 'MARINER,' AT LAMU,
June 22nd, 1889.

"To OSKAR BORCHERT, ESQ.,

" Member of the German Emin Pasha Expedition.

"SIR,—Acting under orders from the naval Commander-in-Chief in these waters, and in consideration of the existing blockade of this part of the coast of Africa, I have to inform you that the stores at present on board your ship for Dr. Carl Peters cannot be landed at this place, or at any other part within or adjacent to that part of the coast which is at present under blockade. Those stores now in a lighter alongside your ship must be taken on board again, and you are to quit the port as soon as this is accomplished. I shall send an officer and an armed party on board to support you in carrying out this order.

The officer will accompany you to Zanzibar, in order to see that the stores are not landed at any other port on this part of the coast. His passage to that place will be taken and paid for.

"(Signed) CHARLES R. ARBUTHNOT,
"*Commander.*"

This order was apparently the means adopted by Admiral Fremantle of airing his displeasure at the landing in Kwaihu Bay. I may emphasise only one point—that in the matter of the confiscated goods there was no question of the equipment for my expedition, but simply of merchandise, from which Herr Toeppen was going to select articles of barter for its use, and which I might in any case hope, at least in part, to find procurable in the stores at Lamu itself. Thus the proceeding of Admiral Fremantle was evidently not so much intended for a blow at the German Emin Pasha Expedition as for a means of expressing his anger at what he had not been able to prevent. Enough to say, twenty-five English marines were sent on board the *Neœra*, the steamer's engine was demolished, and the vessel itself towed to Zanzibar. As afterwards became manifest, the course of the expedition was considerably altered in consequence of this measure. After a few weeks it was found that the articles of barter required for the Massai country were not to be had at Lamu, and in the course of the following months it became manifest that I should never be put in possession of the new articles procured from Zanzibar, which Lieutenant-Captain Rust was to bring after me. The English succeeded in bringing it about that the German Emin Pasha Expedition acquired a character that differed in every way from that of usual African travels. But they were not able to thwart the undertaking, or even essentially to weaken its action; and in looking back upon these events during the course of the expedition, the biblical text frequently came into my mind: " Ye thought evil against me, but God meant it unto good."

Practically these proceedings of Fremantle's had the effect of entirely removing from the sphere of my action, for the whole further course of the expedition, Herr Oskar Borchert, whom I had intended to take part in it in closest contiguity to myself.

Borchert and the "Neœra."

He was obliged to go to Zanzibar, because I was determined to defend myself with the utmost seriousness against this clumsy infringement of rights on the part of the English. There he prosecuted with effect the so-called *Nœra* lawsuit, which, so far as I have ascertained, awakened general interest throughout the whole of Europe, and of which I give a few particulars in the Appendix. Not until the conclusion of the suit was Herr Borchert able to lead the second column of the expedition up the Tana.

<small>The "Nœra" lawsuit.</small>

To this first blow which fell upon me at Hindi was soon added a second, in the painful consciousness that it would not be possible for me to increase my force of porters in the Witu territory, in such a manner as to let me hope that I should be able to carry up the Tana, in one column, even the loads that I had remaining. The Suaheli of Witu and Lamu has not the enterprising spirit possessed by the Wangwana on the German East African coast. There is no idea of any intercourse, by means of caravans, with the interior, and thus it was only one by one that candidates appeared to take part in my expedition; and those who came were not just the best of their tribes. All kinds of disreputable rabble appeared, with the intention of getting porter's pay for one or two months in advance, and then running away. I could, moreover, scarcely meet such fraudulent proceedings effectually in those regions, because the only possible measure against them, namely, that of putting suspected characters in chains, and punishing such deserters as were captured with the most rigorous severity, could not, from political considerations, be here put into practice. The highest number of porters I ever nominally had under my authority amounted to about ninety; but in reality we probably never possessed more than seventy porters. I was, therefore, the more anxious to strengthen my camel column, and to supplement the deficient carrying power by the purchase of asses. I succeeded in bringing my column of camels up to seventeen head, and in purchasing nine donkeys. Thus it was clear that I might not hope to convey all my loads at one time up the Tana. I was obliged to divide the expedition

<small>Difficulty of procuring porters.</small>

into two columns, the second of which I placed under the command of Lieutenant-Captain D. Rust. He was to organise a boat expedition on the Tana, and to join me again in Oda-Boru-Ruva, with the loads left behind, and especially the articles of barter expected from Zanzibar. As it was not possible to strengthen myself with new porters among the Suahelis, I now put my hope in the Wapakomo or Gallas on the Upper Tana, where this attempt might perhaps succeed, and where, in any case, I should be in a position, in case the articles of barter from Zanzibar reached me, to equip a caravan of asses, and with these to get to the Equatorial Province. These were the hopes that animated me in Hindi and Witu, and in accordance with which I made my resolutions. How small a portion of them was destined to be fulfilled in the end! *Division of the expedition.*

On the other hand, a thing completely accomplished in Hindi was the ordering of the burdens. The portion of the water that had been spoilt was rejected; the rest was accurately booked, and divided between the two columns. From Lamu Herr Toeppen sent in all about thirty loads of powder, biscuit, lucifer matches, and woven stuffs, all very useful things, only that none of them were of any value for the route I had selected through the Massai lands, as here nothing will pass current but iron, and copper wire, and beads. On the whole I estimated the loads my column was to carry up at about a hundred and fifty, and left behind with Lieutenant-Captain Rust the same number, to be brought up after me. Herr von Tiedemann was to go up in my company. *Porterage arrangements.*

Besides these obvious labours, I especially occupied myself at Hindi in disciplining and organising my originally very disorderly column. As I was compelled to begin the march into the interior without any real articles of barter, I could not pay my way, as Thomson and other people were accustomed to do, by giving tribute to the native chiefs; therefore the discipline of my people, and the control I could exercise over them, became of the very greatest consequence for the success of the undertaking. If I could not carry out the German Emin Pasha Expedition in the usual *Disciplining the company.*

peaceable fashion, as I had originally hoped to do, I must face the fact that I might ultimately be compelled to organise our column as a warlike band. Now it is a well-known physical law, that the effect of a power may be increased quite equally in one of two ways—either by the augmentation of the mass, or by the increase of velocity. To increase the mass of my troops, looked upon as a warlike force, was not in my hand; the possibility of increasing their quickness or availableness depended solely upon the carrying out of an unwavering discipline. To attain this, I had to turn my attention principally to the Somalis of the column, by means of whom, if I got them well in hand, I could carry out a thorough physical authority over the porterage element, which was made up chiefly of Central Africans. Such African masses of men can only be kept in control by a determination uncompromisingly to carry out one's own will in the teeth of all opposition. I, too, have found this the only thing that makes an impression upon one's own people. The so-called *Bwana Wasari* (good masters) will not, under critical circumstances, possess the authority which is necessary to carry an expedition safely through the vicissitudes and dangers of the elements and of warfare. The impression I should recommend leaders of expeditions to aim at producing must be the verdict of the people: "*Kali sana laikini hodari sana*" (Very strict but very thorough). By this feeling in separate things there is woven in time around the leader and his followers an almost demoniacal bond, which is sufficiently strong to withstand the crises and catastrophes in a life of African travel. The Somalis possess great sensibility, and if they are properly managed, and their prejudices are respected, they are easy to lead. Of course, with them also, one must not think to manage matters entirely on the lines of the " point of honour." In the course of the expedition I had even for my Somalis to introduce corporal punishment, and to inflict it rigorously.

The development of all this, which naturally could only evolve itself during the course of the expedition, was already begun during the week we spent at Hindi. It was a wonderful time of cares, labours, plans, and hopes. The tardy rainy season poured whole waterspouts down upon us every day; and it was seldom that the sun shone upon us, as we laboured at the burdens. In these days I had caused a saddle-horse to be bought for me in Lamu, and repeatedly rode out on excursions in the environs of Hindi. I rode for hours along the way to Lamu, until I saw before me the peculiar dune of that place. I knew that if I went into Lamu I should run the risk of personal arrest. I had the feeling that banished men may experience, of being cut off from Europe and my home. For me there was only one thing:

> " To westward, oh, to westward yet,
> My gallant bark, speed on ;—
> Dying, my heart's last wish shall greet
> The land I would have won." *

There was no thought of turning back. Whether the goal of our desires could be reached appeared at Hindi more than improbable. But then there was only one fate for us all—destruction! Thus a peculiarly mournful and emotional tone characterised these our first days on the continent of Africa. There was only one consolation, that of bowing the soul entirely under the mysterious dispensations of Providence.

On Wednesday, July 3rd, I at length set out from Hindi, having the day before received my articles of barter from Lamu. I wished first to lead my column as far as Witu, and there to wait for the second column under Rust, and the first march was to be only seven miles, as far as the place called Kibokoni. First, I had the camels loaded; then the asses received their burdens. How clumsily the whole work was still managed is shown by the fact that it was ten o'clock before we had completed this business. At a later period of the expedition, the loading of the camels and asses was always finished by six o'clock in the morning. Everything has to be learnt, especially the leading of an African expedition. That I had still something to learn in this respect was

* From " Columbus," a poem by Luisa Brachmann.—TR.

manifested by myself, in the fact that after the beasts of burden had been loaded, I marched off with them instead of waiting, as I ought to have done, to be the very last to quit the camp, especially on that day; and that I left to Lieutenant-Captain Rust and Herren von Tiedemann and Friedenthal the task of loading and superintending the porters. But I altered this as early as the following day.

As my horse had been somewhat chafed by the saddle, I

LOADING THE CAMELS.

marched on foot out of camp, at a quarter past ten, on July 3rd, and I may declare that I sallied forth in the best of spirits. The landscape before me was richly planted with wheat and mtama. The sun lit up field and woodland, and now I was at last, as it appeared, beginning in earnest the great journey towards the west. It appeared that I was about to frustrate definitely the calculations that had sought to nullify my expedition at Zanzibar; and this filled me, during the whole march, with a sort of joyous satisfaction.

High hopes.

This feeling, however, was much diminished when I came

DIFFICULTIES WITH THE PORTERS.

to think over the result of this first day's march. Some of the asses broke down under badly-packed loads; but the greatest failure was in the discipline of the porters. I had arrived at Kibokoni at half-past twelve o'clock with the camels and a small proportion of the porters, had immediately caused my tent to be set up, ordered fires for cooking, and then waited for Herr von Tiedemann and the rest of the caravan. Not a man appeared. As corn for cattle and men was not to be had at Kibokoni, I had sent at once to Hidio, distant about two miles, to purchase grain. Towards half-past two Herr Friedrich, the owner of the plantation there, appeared at my tent, with the intelligence that he could supply us with the corn. I at once sent two camels to fetch it. Six o'clock came, and then at length Herr von Tiedemann arrived, and reported that a portion of the carriers had disappeared, or, in fact, had run away, manifestly because they objected to carrying loads. Thus twenty loads had remained behind at Hindi; the other portion was on the way under Friedenthal. I at once ordered two camels back to Hindi, and determined to investigate the affair thoroughly next day. Herr von Tiedemann had to return to Hindi next morning, and at noon brought the last loads, with the news that there were no more porters at Hindi. They must, therefore, have arrived at Kibokoni. *[margin: Unruliness of the porters.]*

I now counted our loads over, with the list in my hand, and ascertained afterwards that the porters were all actually present. I then arranged the loads in three heaps, for camels, donkeys, and porters respectively, and thought myself sure of my affair when, at two o'clock, I gave the signal for marching onward to Mansamarabu. But again thirty porters' loads were left behind. The experiences of the previous day had determined me for the present to take my position at the rear of the column, and I accordingly sent Friedenthal forward with the first loads and a few soldiers. The way from Kibokoni to Mansamarabu leads through a creek which is not passable for beasts of burden. The way for these leads round the creek, and takes two hours, while on the direct road only an hour to an hour and a half is required. After starting the *[margin: Missing loads.]*

porters I intended to march with the beasts of burden round the creek. At three o'clock I had the camels put in motion, and the neighbourhood was scoured for my porters. As a few *Deserting porters.* continued to come in, I suspected the missing ones to be still at Kibokoni, and accordingly left Tiedemann behind with orders to bring the rest of the column by the direct road to Mansamarabu, while I myself started with the asses at four o'clock. Two miles short of the place some laden asses broke down, and I had to return to Kibokoni. All this was very discouraging. At five o'clock I was back in the abandoned camp. I immediately sent letters to the Rust column at Hindi, and to Friedenthal at Mansamarabu, with orders to verify the number of porters, and to send all that were present to me. I then had my tent set up again, and passed a few very uncomfortable hours, waiting with Herr von Tiedemann for news. At eleven o'clock eighteen porters came from Mansamarabu, whom I sent back loaded the same night, under Herr von Tiedemann.

Friday, July 5th, broke dark and heavy with rain. Early in the morning came thirty to forty porters, who carried the rest of the things quickly away. Thus I was able to send off the donkeys that morning with quarter-loads, and at half-past *New recruits.* seven I mounted my horse and rode rapidly along the longer road round the creek to Mansamarabu. There I arrived at ten o'clock, completely wet through; found the gentlemen and all the loads waiting; and immediately held a general muster of the people.

The result showed that all the porters were present. It was therefore manifest that on the previous day, also, a number of men must have slunk away without loads. I made the porters a speech, in which I told them that I knew the good people, and also the bad ones; that I was a good master to the good ones, *Rewards and punish-ments.* but stern to the bad ones. I gave double pocho to the men who had carried loads the previous night, and succeeded in identifying a porter who, on July 3rd, had thrown down his load in a maize field and run back to Hindi. I had him laid in chains and flogged before all the people. In

CAMP IN MANSAMARABU.

the same way a few other persons were punished, concerning whom I could prove that they had carried no loads on the previous day. I now announced to the porters a scale of punishments, to be inflicted for running away, and for the throwing down of loads. This communication, which was made intelligible on the spot by a few examples, produced a decided impression. I concluded this memorable display by the distribution of a slaughtered ox and the meting out of a measure of maize to each man.

At five o'clock in the evening I assembled the people again. Not a man was missing. I made another short speech, in which I communicated the following command: "Each morning at half-past five o'clock, at the sound of the trumpet, every man has to appear. Then to each will be given his load, once for all. At a quarter before six the caravan is to take the road in due order of march. On arriving in camp every load is to be given up, when it is to be verified by the list if a man or a load is missing. Each load is numbered, and each porter has his load, which is noted in the list for the day." *Rules for mustering, etc.*

I have chronicled these arrangements in detail because, after their introduction on July 5th, essential order reigned in the caravan. The success of the expedition depended in a great measure upon the maintenance of this order. Some amount of time was still requisite before my expedition had so accustomed itself to this order as to march, to a certain extent, by itself.

Our camp at Mansamarabu presented an exceedingly picturesque appearance. Our three tents had been set up in a glorious park, under splendid mango trees and baobabs. Before my tent, which stood in the centre, the German flag waved on the right, and, so long as we were in the sultanate of Witu, the flag of Sultan Tumo Bakari on the left—white and red, with a white pentagram in a red field. *Camp at Mansamarabu.* Under the German flag the artillery was placed, guarded night and day by a sentinel. Behind the tents, on the greensward, camels, donkeys, and my Arabian horse grazed. Before them the loads were piled up, likewise guarded by regular posts of Somali soldiers. Behind these are the houses in which the porters are lodged, in many cases with their trim young wives,—strong, robust figures, contrasting advantageously with the Suahelis of Witu. The rain of the morning had passed over, and we were sincerely sorry that there was no painter present to perpetuate the sunny scene by a sketch.

During that day Herr Friedrich from Hidio was with us again, and very obligingly related for our benefit his experiences of the country and people. On the following morning I was *Order of march.* obliged to leave Herr von Tiedemann behind, as it appeared that we had taken eight loads too many of guns with ammunition from Rust's camp at Hindi, and had no porters to carry them. But I had the great satisfaction of seeing that the last porter marched with his load at six o'clock; that at seven the artillery followed, dragged by two Gallas; and that in the course of certainly two hours more donkeys and camels went away loaded. I brought up the rear on horseback, with my two dogs. Our way led through a flat country, to which its flora imparted a very peculiar character. I soon rode past the beasts of burden, which I knew to be under the direction of trustworthy Somalis, and was alone in the wilderness. Recollections and pictures of my childhood's days arose before me involuntarily in this charming, blooming landscape, which is overgrown with a shrub that reminded me forcibly of our heath-plant, and on which bees and butterflies were hovering. Not a sound breaks the solemn silence. Above me the blue vault of heaven is spread out, under which an eagle soars at intervals in sweeping circles. Thus I ride onward through the *Scenery and surroundings.* Saturday afternoon. My dogs soon get tired of hunting through the open field and searching for game in vain, so they trot along behind my horse, and give the soul leisure for quiet contemplation. At about two o'clock I ride past Pemba, where the ground assumes a heavy character, and maize and wheat-fields appear, ranged side by side. Here I dismount for a moment, let my horse and my dogs have some water, and inquire about the state of provisions at Funga Sombo ("Tie thy bundle"), the goal of our march for to-day. The required information is cheerfully given, and I ride further, following the track of the artillery. At a quarter to three o'clock the road leads past Massivatato ("the three lakes"), and a quarter of an hour later I am hailed with joyous shouts by my porters, who have already found quarters, and of their own accord come to meet me with fruits. As they had done their duty to-day, I caused another ox to be slaughtered, and the meat to be distributed among them.

The evening was passed in preparations for the following day's heavy march of seven or eight hours, the first real achievement for the heavily-laden caravan. I secured a few more porters to assist, and commanded the march for Sunday, July 7th, to begin at five in the morning. *On the march to Witu.* At that hour the call of the trumpet resounded through the village, and immediately after the porters gathered together beside their loads, which they now already knew. At a quarter to six the last porter was with Herr Friedenthal on the road to Witu! At half-past six the camels and donkeys marched away with the last packages. I was just going to mount my horse, when it was announced to me that there were people from Conumbi, who wanted to sell me a camel. It took half-an-hour to conclude the bargain. I wrote a longer letter to Herr von Tiedemann, to whom I sent the purchased camel, so that it was half-past seven o'clock before I myself followed my caravan. But in an hour's time I overtook the donkeys, and soon afterwards the camels, which I could for the time leave behind me, as they were under secure guard. I rode forward, and once more the solemn gloom of the wilderness surrounded me. This time it was a wilderness indeed. The Sultan of Witu had well understood how to secure his seat thoroughly from attack. In Funga Sombo, in 1855, stood the Arab advanced posts. From that place to Witu the way leads for hours through swamp and forest. *Swamp and forest.* The solitude is the more impressive, as it is not broken even by the cry of a wild animal. I had been told at Funga Sombo that the region abounded with lions and panthers, and that only a few days before a man had been devoured in broad daylight by a lion; so that I had already made up my mind to some interesting occurrences. But not a solitary animal appeared. There was, however, the less time for dreaming to-day, as I had soon overtaken my porters, and had to give a few directions to Herr Friedenthal. So I fell back again, to personally conduct the camels and donkeys through the swamp. To make this practicable, I had to get a way made through the forest, which took two hours to do. A camel fell down in the swamp, and had to be unloaded, and then loaded afresh. Thus it was three o'clock in the afternoon before we reached the real plain of Witu. Our approach to that place was made manifest to us, in the first instance, by thirty soldiers of the Sultan, who came to bid us welcome in their master's name.

The plain of Witu.

About a mile from Witu I was greeted by Sheriff Abdallah, a very cultured Suaheli, accompanied by Herr Doerfer, an official of Herr Denhardt, who also bade me welcome. I sent the caravan forward under our flag, and in charge of Herr Friedenthal, and determined for my part to wait for the camels, which had again remained behind. But as soon as they appeared in sight on the horizon I entered the smiling valley of Witu, in company with Herr Doerfer. Here I found good heavy corn ground, and the land was laid out in maize and wheat fields.

Witu itself lies on a slight ridge of hills, and is thoroughly surrounded by a fastness of forest. The entrance to the place is by two gates strongly fortified, with sentries keeping guard night and day. Witu has perhaps three thousand inhabitants; but, by the number of civilised Suahelis, the idea is kept alive that the stranger is here in one of the centres of East African life. The court does not afford the brilliant aspect of that of Zanzibar, but makes a more satisfactory impression through the general and patriarchal unanimity of its constituents, and was to my mind more interesting, through the elements of population that were new to me. Here types of Gallas and Somali crowd among the Suaheli, and beside these appear the strange head-dresses of the Waboni, and the muscular forms of the Wapokomo.

Importance of Witu.

Amidst an enormous thronging of the crowd, I rode into

Witu. I noticed our flag hoisted in front of a house, and learnt that the Sultan had put at the disposal of our people four houses, and an ox for their entertainment. I requested Herr Doerfer to oblige me by going at once to Fumo Bukari, to report my arrival, to thank him, and announce my intention of paying him a visit on the morrow. Fumo Bukari conveyed to me the expression of his satisfaction at my arrival, and his desire that I should always make him acquainted with my wishes, for that I was a welcome guest, and he would be glad to receive me to-morrow morning at nine o'clock. When I had seen my people settled, I went with Herr Doerfer to his country house, which was about twelve minutes distant, to seek a place wherein to quarter the camels and my horse. Meanwhile I had the tents set up in the largest open square. After Herr Doerfer and I had taken a bath, we returned to my tent, where we supped together in exceedingly good spirits.

Sultan Fumo Bukari.

The sultanate of Witu, which I have traversed chiefly in a direction from north to south, appears in its whole extent as a very flat country, well cultivated here and there. In its northern part it is manifestly less fertile than in the southern portion, and probably no part of it has the luxuriance that is found in southern districts, as, for instance, in Usambara. The population, too, is generally poor. Only in a few places did I find possessors of large herds, whose property could be estimated at a hundred thousand rupees. The native inhabitants generally present a feeble aspect, which may be chiefly ascribed to insufficient nourishment. Especially noticeable to persons coming from Zanzibar is the reversal of the usual credit system, which is carried out to the smallest detail. When I want to buy cocoa-nuts or any other trifling article, I must first lay down the money on the table, and then my purchase is handed over to me. If I order any work to be done for me by an artisan, he demands payment in advance. On the other hand, he himself takes each and every article from the European, on credit. All this makes a very poor impression. On the whole, I feel convinced that the productive

Statistics of the Witu sultanate.

power of the country might be very much increased if the conditions of labour were more favourable. There can be no question that the ground, at certain points, can produce anything. The natural flatness of the country, with arms of the sea intersecting it deeply everywhere, also presents favourable conditions for transport. If greater powers of capital were brought to bear here, a very rapid development of culture might be expected. The hopes, however, with which I once regarded the back regions of Witu have proved to be entirely erroneous. Witu is nothing more than an oasis in the great East African steppe, thrusting a line of cultivation, along the Tana, into the steppe itself.

On Monday, July 8th, I for the first time met the ruler of this territory. The Sultan Fumo Bukari had fixed the hour of nine in the morning for my reception. I resolved on this occasion, so far as I possibly could, to show him the honour due to a prince acknowledged by Germany. Consequently I caused my soldiers to march out, with the German banner and the Sultan's flag at their head. They were made to present arms when we entered the Sultan's house and when we quitted it. The highest officials of the court, Sheriff Abdallah, and the first officer of the Sultan's troop, Omar Hamadi, came to fetch me; the latter wore the uniform of a Prussian officer of artillery. I had put two of my servants into rich red Cavasse uniforms embroidered with silver; they had to follow me, bearing the presents for Fumo Bukari—a handsomely gilded Arab sword, with a real Jehalla blade, and two unused Dreysesch repeating guns of the newest construction, with three hundred cartridges. I was accompanied by Herr Doerfer and Herr Friedenthal. The Sultan, on his part, had about forty soldiers on guard to receive us, and welcomed us surrounded by his whole court. His stone house, indeed, made a very plain effect; but the assembly did not materially differ from the surroundings of the Sultan of Zanzibar on similar occasions.

A grand reception and council.

Fumo Bukari came as far as the door to meet me, and conducted me to an armchair on the left of his raised seat;

a chair similar to mine on his right being occupied by the heir to the throne, a brother of the Sultan. Fumo Bukari is a man of about forty, with a gentle, benevolent expression of countenance. His conversation was in the Kiswahali language, and its subject was naturally the purpose of my expedition, which the Sultan promised to further, so far as he could. At my request he at once granted me a written order to his elders to forward Rust's column directly to Witu. He also declared himself willing to furnish Tana boats for me; and in general he repeated his message of the day before, that I was to let him know each of my wishes, for that he was too good a German not to be ready to meet them in every particular.

Fumo Bukari's declaration of friendship.

The audience lasted an hour, and during the rest of the day the great men of the place hastened, one after another, to pay their visits. Some of them were truly cultivated and dignified men. The same evening I ordered my camels back to Hindi, with the Sultan's letter, to bring up Rust's column to Witu.

On the following day I had the satisfaction of seeing Herr Tiedemann arrive at Witu with the baggage that had been left behind; so that my own column was now reunited. I now took the greatest pains to strengthen myself as much as possible; but it soon became apparent that porters were not to be had at Witu in anything like sufficient numbers, and that as a point of support to an expedition, the country was not in any direction sufficient. I especially noticed how small was the knowledge of the territory of the Tana, and of the whole back districts of Witu generally. The land resembles an island which has no communication at the back. The intelligence, also, that I had obtained from a few Gallas and Wapokomo in Witu, afterwards proved utterly inaccurate, and indeed mendacious. So much was perfectly clear at Witu, that I must seek other points of support for carrying out my expedition, perhaps on the Upper Tana or further in the interior, if I would hope to reach my goal, the Equatorial Province. All this was not encouraging; I often had the feeling as if everything I arranged turned out against

Preparations and precautions for the march.

me, and every day the doubt pressed heavily upon me, whether it would not, after all, be better to give the affair up. Actuated by these feelings I wrote on July 20th to the committee:—

<small>Report to the German committee.</small> "I have the honour on this occasion to repeat the declaration I made from Alexandria, that I will carry on the undertaking to the very utmost bounds of possibility. In the summer of 1888 I maturely considered the question whether I should undertake the task. Now that heaven and earth seem to rise up against me, the committee may be assured that I know my duty."

In the same report I added:—

"This one remark I still wish to make: If our expedition succeeds, I certainly believe that the almost overwhelming opposition will, in fact, contribute to make it useful to Germany. For England the whole course of events till now, the motives of action being known, is plainly a humiliation. I do not believe that this will be, or can be appreciated in Germany,—the whole inimical press-manufacture from above and below will take care of that; but in spite of this it is fortunate for us that the German Emin Pasha undertaking has, after all, not succumbed to the English counteracting efforts. And this much I will answer for, that we shall not experience the fate of the English expeditions into the interior. We may perish, but in somewhat different fashion from Messrs. Jackson, Last, and Martin."

<small>Stay at Witu.</small> I had to remain waiting at Witu throughout almost the whole month of July; partly because I still hoped to procure porters from Lamu, and furthermore because I heard that, in this month, there was no possibility of supporting even a small expedition on the Tana. It was requisite to buy corn from the Arabs on the coast, and to transport it for me to Engatana, to convey it up the stream in boats, alongside of the caravan, if I wished to undertake an advance in that direction. All this required time.

The constituents of my expedition, as I at last made it up by the exertion of all my forces, were as follows:

1. Sixteen camels. 2. Eight donkeys. 3. One riding horse. 4. Two dogs. 5. Eighty-five porters (on paper: the worshipful

RECEPTION OF THE SOMALI-KAWALLALA.

porters from Witu, as a rule, took to their heels very soon after receiving their payment in advance, which I was not able fully to ascertain until the day before my departure). 6. Thirteen women—porters' wives, who only carried the private baggage of their lords. 7. Twenty-five Somalis (twenty-one soldiers and four camel drivers*); of these I took twelve soldiers and four camel drivers for my column, the others remained for Lieutenant-Captain Rust. 8. Eight private servants (including cook's boys, cook, etc.). 9. I had engaged Hamiri, a Lamu man, as a guide.

Strength of the expedition.

With this force I had to move one hundred and fifty to one hundred and sixty loads. At Witu this did not appear a very difficult task; but it soon became manifest how uncertain transport by camels was. Already in Engatana I lost, on the whole, six camels; and on the Lower Tana the porters also were quickly reduced by desertion to their original number of sixty. While I lay encamped at Witu, Herr Clemens Denhardt arrived there, with Herr von Karnap, Herr Gustav Denhardt, and Herr Gerstaecker, whereby our social life became a very lively and stirring one, especially as Lieutenant-Captain Rust also made his appearance during the second week of my stay. These gentlemen were with us almost every day, and in the evening the soldiers of the Sultan, and also my Mangemas and Wangamwesi, used to entertain us with war dances. I look back upon these weeks at Witu with a kind of mournful pleasure. It was, in a certain way, the last glimmer of European life that played around us. Often during the expedition we looked longingly back on the comfort and sociability which here for the last time brightened our days.

Pleasant intercourse.

---

* One of my camel-Somalis had committed suicide at Witu. One evening he had stolen a sheep from me. Accordingly, the next morning I called the Somalis together, and explained to them that I would have nothing to do with thieves; I should load the thief with chains, and in that condition send him back to Aden to be punished. The Somalis declared themselves ready to execute the order. When they approached the criminal he shot himself through the head with the rifle, which he fired off with his toe.

A very interesting and useful incident for me, during my residence at Witu, was the appearance of an embassy of the Kawallala Somalis, which came to negotiate with the Sultan concerning the opening of a free road of commerce towards Wanga. These Kawallala Somalis dwell between Djuba and Tana, and have of late also spread southward across the Tana in their warlike expeditions. They press more and more upon the Gallas, who are compelled to retire step by step before them. It is like a powerful flood, which will probably only be arrested by the strong dam of the Massai kingdom. On the Lower Tana all tremble before these tribes, and only the Witu sultanate itself forms the strong rampart before which they stop. In view of the breech-loaders of the Witu soldiers, these worthies, as we have said, condescend to negotiation; whereas, in general, they simply take whatever they have a mind to. On July 10th twenty-three warriors, under Sheriff Hussein, arrived at Witu. On that day there was no milk to be had in Witu, because all the Gallas, notwithstanding that they were under the protection of the Sultan, had fled in panic terror into the woods, with their herds, before the Somalis.

With us the Somalis endeavoured at once to enter into friendly relations. At the news of their approach, my Mangemas, my Central African porters, had rushed to their weapons without orders, and my soldiers had loaded the cannon to receive these wild visitors. Thus our camp made a very warlike appearance when the Kawallala went past; and this did not fail to produce its effect. On July 11th Sheriff Hussein also appeared with all his people, to pay his respects and conclude a treaty of amity with me. He said his tribe had heard of my landing at Kwaihu, and the Sultan, Ali Nurr, had especially ordered him to convey to me the friendship of this tribe. I assured him of the high value I had always set on the friendship of the Somalis, and added that it had been my intention to march through their country, but that the way was shorter to my goal through Witu; that he was perhaps aware that the Somalis were not popular in Europe, but I hoped he had heard that I had always been their friend, and had consequently already several times sent expeditions to them. Sheriff Hussein replied, that this was known to him and to all the Somalis, and therefore now also they would help me. My enemies, he said, were theirs, and whoever was my friend should be reckoned by the Somalis as their friend likewise. I rejoined, that I hoped I should not stand in need of help; let him look at my arms and my artillery. It was strong enough to overcome every attack by force; but what I wanted was stores— oxen and camels. I knew that his tribe ruled over the countries to the west, between Djuba and Tana. I was about to travel in that direction, and requested him to provide me with cattle and camels for purchase, and with good guides to the Kenia. Sheriff Hussein promised he would take counsel with his people concerning these matters. *Conversation with Sheriff Hussein.*

In the days next following we had various consultations, and the result was that the Sheriff declared himself ready to sell me five camels immediately, and to have more driven together for my inspection. He declared himself especially anxious, as he dwelt in the neighbourhood of Oda-Boru-Ruva, that I should remain neutral in a campaign against the English that he was planning. The English, he declared, had shot one of his people, and it was consequently a matter of honour that he should make war upon them. That, therefore, was the reason why the Kawallala afterwards scattered Mr. Smith's expedition. *Hussein's stipulations for neutrality.*

I have never had to fight with the Somalis, and this I attribute to the treaty of peace which was set up in writing between me and Sheriff Hussein, and was concluded on the last day of my stay at Witu; wherein the Somalis expressly acknowledged that they would recognise me not only as their friend, but, if I demanded it, as their leader also. Several times, when the affairs of our expedition on the Lower Tana were in a desperate state, I entertained the idea of betaking myself to these Somali tribes, in case things should come to the worst, and to try if it were not possible to excite them to a march against the Massais, and lead them to Wadelai. The further course of events happily obviated the necessity of adopting this measure.

Sheriff Hussein is a tall and dignified figure of a man, with an entirely European cast of countenance, sparkling eyes, and prominent nose. His face is surrounded with a full, close-cut beard. Like him, the other envoys of the Kawallala tribe were of slender and elastic build, recognisable from afar by their haughty gait and cavalierlike bearing; born warriors and commanders! They wore their hair long, parted in the middle, and falling in ringlets upon their shoulders, so that they had almost the appearance of wearing full-bottomed wigs. They created an impression by their behaviour, similar to that made by the proud Elmoran of the Massais. The presence of a certain courteousness in their manner makes their inborn pride appear the more plainly. On the day of my departure from Witu they performed a war-dance to my honour, in which was expressed, in a very characteristic way, the ultimate destruction of certain presumptuous foes.

After various postponements I had at last fixed upon July 26th as the day of my departure. To secure a firm point of support in Witu, and especially with a view to Rust's column, I had invested Herr Clemens Denhardt with the management of our expedition there, and had also opened a credit for him with Hansings at Zanzibar. I hoped that, before all things, Denhardt would get the loads of the Rust column sent for me to Ngao on the Tana, and from thence by boat up to Oda-Boru-Ruva, where I purposed to wait for the said column. With respect to my own column, I had requested Herr Clemens Denhardt to send me a hundred loads of corn, and the necessary transport boats, to Engatana, to enable me to lead my men along the course of the Tana.

On July 25th it was reported to me that the loads were lying ready for me at Engatana; and now there was no longer any reason further to delay my departure from Witu. On that day I parted from Herr Friedenthal, who wished to go back to

READY FOR THE MARCH.

Zanzibar, and definitely appointed Herr von Tiedemann to my column. With him alone I intended, in the first instance, to march up to the Gallas on the Upper Tana, a territory which, according to Ravenstein's maps, which we had before us, would lie close to the eastern declivities of the Kenia. This afterwards proved to be a very gross blunder. On July 25th my column was quite ready for the march; all loads were packed, and according to the estimated amount of my carrying powers, I had even reserve porters at my disposal. My Somalis were under good discipline, and nine of them were armed with repeating rifles, for which I carried with me two thousand rounds of ball cartridge. For my little bushpiece I had one hundred rounds of grapeshot and the same number of bombshells. I myself carried a capital express rifle by H. Lenne, in Berlin, with Mauser cartridges, besides a double shot gun, a Lancaster repeater, and a six-barrelled revolver. Herr von Tiedemann was armed in the same way. The rest of my Somalis and my private servants and a few reliable porters I armed with breech-loaders, for which I had unfortunately allowed myself to be persuaded in Europe to take cartridges with paper cases. Besides this, every porter carried a serviceable muzzle-loader, and for these I had five loads of cartridges, and in case of need five hundred pounds of powder, which I had certainly, in the first instance, brought with me for Emin Pasha. Thus, small as our number was, we were well enough equipped; and if I could only manage fully and properly to discipline this column, and if the necessary resolution and prudence in the leading of it, on which everything principally depended, were not wanting, I might venture to push forward into the land of the Somalis and Gallas, and whatever might lie behind them.

To do this I was now resolved; and on the afternoon of July 25th I took my leave of Fumo Bukara, to whom I declared: "Nitapeleka bandera ako katika barani"—"I shall carry your flag into the wilderness." In the evening all the Europeans in Witu were assembled at my quarters to celebrate our leave-taking once more. The Somalis had organised a great dance on the space in front of my tent in honour of this parting, the melodies of which have also accompanied me throughout the expedition. Early on the morning of July 26th the trumpet sounded through the streets of Witu, summoning my people to the march, and shortly after six o'clock Herr von Tiedemann led forth the porters into the steppe which divides the sultanate of Witu from the Tana, marching towards Engatana. I had still business in the house of Herr Clemens Denhardt, where I gave my final directions to Lieutenant-Captain Rust, settled accounts with the Somalis, and ordered ten camels to be packed. At eight o'clock I gave instructions for the camels to start, and rode forward myself at a sharp trot, after Herr von Tiedemann, towards the camping-ground that had been agreed upon. The die was now cast. When once I had left the gates of Witu behind, there was no way back for me but by the circuitous route across the Tana, Baringo, Nile, and, God willing, through the Equatorial Province.

Departure for Engatana.

INSTRUCTING THE SOMALIS.

CHAPTER IV.

UP THE TANA TO THE GALLAS.

"... And, be thou counsell'd,
Love not the sun too dearly, nor the
stars."—(GOETHE.)

WHEN I broke up my camp on July 26th I had the intention of marching from Witu straight upon Engatana. The Suaheli there had given me accurate information with regard to the road, and had declared to me that I could quite well reach Engatana in what would certainly be a somewhat severe day's march. As, however, this had been represented to me in other quarters as doubtful, and a first day's march always brings with it a number of unexpected hindrances and difficulties, I had determined once more to set up my camp, for July 26th, in the neighbourhood of Witu, at a distance of from five to seven miles, in a

The first day's march.

plantation belonging to the Sultan Fumo Bukari, and I had issued instructions to Herr von Tiedemann accordingly.

After the camels had been loaded, I hastened on, alternately at a trot and a gallop, behind the porters, to make the necessary arrangements myself for the pitching of the first camp. I arrived at the Sultan's country seat, but no expedition was to be seen there. I was informed that the column had betaken itself into the forest, in a north-westerly direction. Towards twelve o'clock I came up with it, and Herr von Tiedemann reported to me that, in consequence of the peculiar features of the ground, as the Suaheli had predicted, a further advance in the direction we had taken seemed to him impracticable for the camels, and he therefore proposed to me that we should halt for to-day at the place we had reached, there being water in the neighbourhood. It was a charming valley in which we found ourselves: on the left a declivity, along which a watercourse took its way; on the right a gradually rising ground, covered with maize and mtana. Though with some reluctance, I made up my mind to act upon Herr von Tiedemann's proposal, and gave orders to pile the loads and set up the tents.

Encampment in the valley.

These operations, during the first days of our march, were always carried out with a certain slowness, as the people had not been sufficiently schooled in the art of setting up the tents. On this occasion the circumstance was added, that some very high grass had to be cleared away before a place could be gained for the tent; and so we sat on our boxes, in the burning sun, in a somewhat depressed frame of mind. The discouraging thing was the fact that if the Suaheli of Witu were not able to give us accurate particulars even concerning the way to Engatana, it could hardly be expected that what I had heard from them with respect to the Tana regions would have any practical significance; and that therefore the march into these regions to a certain extent meant a leap in the dark, which for an expedition like ours is generally extremely dangerous. For in such expeditions, in the end, everything depends on the disposition of the porters,

Doubts and difficulties.

on which the leader has altogether to rely. But the porter, on his part, is exceedingly sensitive until he has become bound to the leader personally, and unfavourable impressions during the first days may easily once and for all decide the fate of an expedition. I was always conscious of the fact that there were in no direction any reserves for me, and that I must therefore only reckon upon the materials I had immediately in my hand; and that was little enough in comparison with the extent of the journey before us. However, immediate exertion was effectual then, as always, in banishing such moods of discouragement.

I at once sent back to Witu to procure that very day a guide to Ngao, as the road to Engatana was impracticable. This certainly involved a circuit that would cost us two or three days; but, in proportion to the periods of time we had now to take into consideration, that was practically of no importance. Meanwhile the encampment had been completed, my Central African porters had built up their huts of wood and leaves in a remarkably short time, and when I had had an ox slaughtered, the whole assembly was soon busy cooking, and in remarkably good spirits. I myself was gratified, in the afternoon, by the appearance of a Witu Suaheli of rank, the Wali of this district, Buana Shamo by name, who announced to me that the guide would be with me that very evening. He himself remained, with his wife, as my guest in the camp, until my departure. *Buana Shamo promises a guide.*

Towards evening there arrived also in the camp from Witu Herren Denhardt, Doerfer, and Friedenthal; and it was, in truth, for all of us, an equally picturesque and pleasing sight to view the men of the column encamped in the wilderness round their many fires, with the various groups feasting, singing, and narrating adventures. It was, for the first time, a real inland African expedition, now that we were clear of the civilised districts of the Witu sultanate. It was the poetry of camp life that we had now before us. Unfortunately, the pleasant impression of this fresh picture was in some measure disturbed by the announcement of the Somalis, that one of the sixteen camels I had with me had strayed from *The poetry of camp life.*

the pasture-ground in the forest, and was not to be found. As I did not like to abandon this camel to its fate, I determined to postpone the march from this place for a day, and on the next morning to try every means to find the animal in the forest, which did not appear a very difficult matter. It was only necessary to follow up its traces; and if we did not get hold of it, we should at least satisfy ourselves as

A prosaic loss.

RUKUA, FIRST SERVANT TO DR. PETERS.

to its fate,—if, for instance, it should have fallen a prey to some wild beast during the night. And, in truth, that very evening the Wali sent intelligence to his slaves, who appeared in the camp next morning, as early as ten o'clock, with the missing camel, that had been somewhat severely hurt with the thorns, and had lost its saddle into the bargain.

This July 27th, a Saturday, was probably in every respect a joyful day for Herr von Tiedemann, as it was for me. Herr

Friedenthal came back once more to pack up a few loads, whereby the number was brought to a hundred and fifty-three. In the morning we fired the trial shots from our little cannon, and in the afternoon, in the forest, from our rifles and other guns. It was the powerful poetry of the wilderness that was irresistibly borne in upon us, and that still imparts a hallowed character to that day in the memory of us all. It was not until eleven at night that the kiongosi, or guide, ordered from Witu, arrived in camp; and already, at three in the morning, I had the alarm beaten and the trumpet sounded. I had been told that the distance to Ngao would be a journey of twelve hours. *A joyful day.*

Accordingly, I was desirous of starting at four o'clock in the morning, to reach our destination by four in the afternoon. But the night was so dark, that the porters with Tiedemann did not move from their position till half-past five; and the camels and donkeys, with which I was to follow, were not loaded and ready until past seven. So sluggish were even now the movements of our expedition.

I rode off with my camels in a westerly direction, hoping that I should not meet the column of porters till my arrival at Ngao. But, to my disagreeable surprise, I came upon it already at ten o'clock. The guide sent me by the Sultan of Witu did not even know the frequently traversed road to Ngao. Consequently, my column had gone astray, and was now encamped. I at once caused them to make a fresh start, while I myself stayed behind to wait for the camels. But once more, no later than twelve o'clock, I came again upon Tiedemann's column, encamped beside some water; and its elders, the Mangema Nogola and the Dar-es-Salam man Musa, begged permission to rest for to-day. This I refused, and we journeyed onward, further and further towards the west, through the burning heat of that Sunday afternoon. *An inefficient guide.*

The landscape, in its flatness, has a Dutch appearance. The eye ranges far away across the steppe, which is only here and there scantily clothed with bushes, and the hot air lies brooding over the moorland waste, deceiving *Aspect of the country.*

the eye with atmospheric mirages and fata morgana. Water was nowhere to be seen; here and there the dry bed of a river, or a ditch. The affair began to become wearisome. Towards three o'clock I rode forward, past the caravan, to look round in advance for the road, always keeping the imbecile guide before me. Thirst began to make itself felt, and I lounged lazily in the saddle, while my fancies began to present to me pleasant pictures from home. At about four o'clock we came into a wooded district, where the few people whom I had with me—Hamiri was among them—at last discovered a swampy pool, to which they rushed with great rejoicing. Behind it was a clear space of three thousand yards in breadth, beyond which the forest began again. In this second forest I discovered a camping place, on which Wapokomo had probably rested.

In the belief that I was close to Ngao, I again declined the proposal of Hamiri to stay there for the night, cut through the wood, and came anew into a bushy region, characterised by the presence of great hills of the termite ant, which from a distance looked almost like Wapokomo houses and villages. As my horse was exhausted, I marched on foot with Hamiri and my servant Rukua till towards half-past five, without seeing anything of Ngao. Then I was incautious enough to throw myself down under an acacia to rest, and to remain half an hour stretched on the ground, waiting for my people. Not a man came. Desolate, oppressive silence over the whole plain! Where was my caravan?

The sun was going down. I went back, and near a thicket I found nine of my camels, with some Somalis; I was obliged to have a way cut for them in a quarter of an hour. I ordered the Somalis to march on, and not to halt till they came to the river; and they obeyed my command. I myself went further back, and found one set of my porters at the Wapokomo camping-place I had before discovered, and another at the swampy pool we had found that afternoon in the wood. Whether I liked it or no, I had to make up my mind to set up the camping-place here for sixty porters and five camels. Five porters and one camel had remained behind in the steppe. I myself encamped in the Wapokomo camp, where I had the tents pitched, with my private servants and a few porters. Towards nine in the morning a heavy thunderstorm came on, with a deluge of rain, which thoroughly wetted my column; and in the night we had, for the first time, the pleasure of hearing lions roaring close to our tents.

On Monday morning at six o'clock I first sent forward all the camels that had remained behind (the sixth had made its appearance at an early hour), and then I despatched Nogola, one of the best of the Mangema men, and two of the best Somalis to look for the five straggling people. At half-past seven o'clock the caravan of porters was in complete order, and marched forth with beat of drum, with the black, white, and red flag carried in the front. I followed as usual on horseback; but Ngao was still not to be descried. When we had quitted the wooded tract we came once more into the burnt-up steppe which had made such a melancholy impression on us the evening before. No water, no grass; only a darker strip in the distance. Was it, perhaps, the course of the Tana? *Marching with all the honours.*

At ten o'clock I ordered the procession to incline to the south; for in this way we must strike the river somewhere. At eleven, there it lay before us! Very invigorating to us was the sight of this water, rolling its yellow flood towards the Indian Ocean. The Tana is here about as broad as the Weser below Münden. We reached it about six miles above Ngao. I now rode forward, still following the river, in a south-east direction. Amid the beating of drums and the joyous shouts of the porters, who reckoned upon a good meal after the fatiguing march, I halted at twelve o'clock before the house of the German missionaries in Ngao, and was welcomed by Herren Würz, Weber, Heyer, and Böcking. At two o'clock Herr von Tiedemann arrived with the last of the porters, and at six o'clock Nogola appeared with two of the Pagases and Somalis we had lost the day before. The impression made by the steppe between *Arrival at the Tana. German missionary station, Ngao.*

Witu and Ngao had been too much for the nerves of the other three. They had let the Emin Pasha Expedition be the Emin Pasha Expedition, and shown it a clean pair of heels. Most likely they had gone back to Witu.

I immediately sent off two men with a donkey to bring in their loads, and at the same time despatched a letter to Witu, to have them arrested there if possible. All this was in the highest degree annoying.

But altogether alarming was the news I at once received at Ngao, that no food was to be had there for the porters, for that *Disagreeable tidings.* the Wapokomo themselves were suffering from hunger, were even dying of hunger. This was certainly a very agreeable piece of intelligence! It absolutely seemed as if our expedition were destined to end in a truly miserable manner; and that, too, when it had just begun. I heard, however, that soldiers of the Sultan of Witu had gone in boats to Engatana the day before, to carry corn for me there from Kau.

Acting on this intelligence, I at once, that very Monday afternoon, sent Hamiri with two Somalis by boat up to Engatana to bring down immediately to Ngao eight loads of the grain stored up there, for I feared that otherwise my whole column would run away altogether on the very first day. Without these eight loads I could not even hope to reach Engatana, as probably no food would be obtainable on the road between Ngao and that place. At the same time I wrote back to Witu to Herr Denhardt, commissioning him immediately to purchase there ten oxen for slaughtering, and to send them to Engatana.

I hoped by these measures to counteract the first heavy disappointment. I called my people together, explained the state of affairs to them, told them that there was corn enough for them at Engatana, and that on the Upper Tana the new crop *Explanations not successful.* was already ripening. But the negro does not love the music of the future; he is a realistic politician of the first water. And the next morning I was confronted by the very reassuring fact that seven of the Dar-es-Salam men had considered it preferable to seek their fortune elsewhere.

A NIGHT AMONG THE MOSQUITOES.

Perhaps the unpleasurable experiences of the night had contributed to this result. We had suffered comparatively little from mosquitoes during the expedition; but on no night were we molested by such swarms of these little pests as attacked us at Ngao. The mission had built its house close by the Tana, amid a wild, luxuriant grass steppe. Here milliards of mosquitoes swarmed; and so soon as the sun went down they threw themselves ravenously upon the welcome guests, who seemed to offer them a fresher nourishment than they were accustomed to. It was of no use that we surrounded our tents and ourselves with a smoke that brought tears into our eyes; it was of no use that we put on drawers and wrapped up our hands in cloths. The sharp sting of the mosquitoes, who threw themselves upon us in black serried ranks, pierced through trousers and drawers; nor was the mosquito-net any protection against our unwelcome visitors. Thus the nights passed away, bringing us disturbed sleep, and, unrefreshed, we rose to encounter the labours of the day that brought one disappointment after another.

Ants and mosquitoes.

I endeavoured at Ngao to procure at any rate fish for my people, but was told that no fish could be got from the Tana at this season of the year. There was only the mambo to be had—a kind of eel—and these, unfortunately, but in very sparing quantity. I immediately sent soldiers in pursuit of my runaway porters, and especially hunted for them among a tribe of Gallas who had established themselves in the neighbourhood, whose chief came to bring me a tribute of five sheep, three of which I handed over at once to my porters. I held a council with these Gallas in the midst of the whole congregation of my men. In order to terrify these from further desertion, I charged the Gallas, in the event of my runaway porters refusing to return, simply to cut them down. I also held a *shauri* (conference) with my porters, in which I explained to them that I would not have people in the column who were not willing to go with me, and called upon them to give me notice at once if they wanted

The Gallas as police.

"Shauri" with the porters.

permission to go home. No one presented himself; but as I very well discerned, the temper of the men was very unsatisfactory and doubtful. If a leader cannot feed his men well, especially at the beginning of an expedition, they go away; and for this they can hardly be blamed.

Thus Monday went by, and no news from Engatana, towards which place I was looking hopefully for corn. My soldiers came back; not a trace of the fugitives had they discovered. I was obliged to confine myself to sending the names of the runaways also to Lieutenant-Captain Rust at Witu, in the hope he would succeed in bringing at least one or two to punishment there. The men engaged at Witu left me in pairs; during these days, among others the private servant of Herr von Tiedemann, whom we used to call Fremantle, betook himself home to his Penates. But this worthy could not make up his mind to depart without a remembrance of his master, and accordingly took with him some good shirts and coats, and, unfortunately, also a money pouch containing 700 marks (£35). The affair was the more deplorable as there was nowhere a gleam of hope of better things. How could I expect it would be better at other points of the Tana than in Ngao, which was comparatively nearer to civilisation? Or how could I assume that the main body of my porters would be intrinsically more faithful than those who had already deserted me? But if my porters went off, the whole undertaking would prove a fiasco of the most ridiculous kind; and the landing and the difficulties we had already overcome would assume an altogether comic character. To make things worse, Herr von Tiedemann, who had gone across the river on Monday, in the heat of the sun, to the English mission, to see after our runaway porters, had got an affection of the head from the sun, and was suffering from the most violent cerebral pains.

Further desertions of the Witu men.

Importance of the porters.

During those days I had much intercourse with the missionary Würz; but our conversation on the Gospel according to St. John and the Lutheran dogma hardly sufficed to free my mind from the gloomy cares that oppressed it,

Missionary Würz.

and made our thoughts revert continually to the miserable circumstances of the moment.

On July 30th, towards evening, the eight loads ordered arrived at last from Engatana. It was a positive heartfelt comfort to me to be able to serve out rice and maize in abundance to my people. This was certainly more calculated than my address to raise the sinking courage of the men. On August 1st I marched away from Ngao, still in a very depressed frame of mind, to betake myself at least as far as Engatana, where I hoped to find waiting for me some ninety loads of grain, and the necessary boats for transporting it onward. We wanted to sleep this night at Marfano; and I was accompanied by Herr Weber, from the mission at Ngao, who wished to look at Engatana, with a view to a possible missionary settlement there.

<small>March from Ngao.</small>

This marching day very considerably strengthened the impressions of discouragement which the Tana route had awakened in me when I first entered upon it. There was no real road, for the Wapokomo carry on their trade by boats. So we had to march continually through bush and steppe, always in danger of losing our way, which indeed happened to us several times. Then at last we got into a broad and deep morass, in which the porters disappeared to their hips, and the camels got embedded in such a way that they had to be unloaded and hoisted up with levers, a work in which the whole force of porters, already sufficiently wearied by a ten or twelve hours' march, were obliged to help. Moreover, at Marfano there was nothing to eat; and in the night another porter ran away, and I could never learn what became of him. That was the Tana route, to which we now stood committed.

<small>Marching in a morass.</small>

On this day I determined at any rate to make use of the advantages of this route, by partly unloading my heavily burdened column, and having a portion of the things transported up the river in boats. Already at the beginning of July seventy or eighty Arabs had gone up the river, whether on English instigation I do not know, but at all events to English satisfaction, to stir up the inhabitants of the

<small>Inimical feelings aroused.</small>

Tana banks against my expedition, and especially to stop its progress, and neither to sell me provisions nor give me the use of boats. But the gentlemen who proceeded in this manner against me had not reckoned upon one thing, namely, that these continual hindrances and oppressions would necessarily compel me, on my side, to meet extremities with extremities, and where I found people refusing to let me purchase what they possessed, to fall back upon the right of self-preservation and the right of arms, which is everywhere acknowledged in Africa, and simply to take what I required. I had a formal right to do this, inasmuch as I appeared here, to a certain extent, as an authorised agent of the Sultan of Witu, whose flag I carried, and whose influence I had undertaken to spread towards the west. The Sultan's Walis have everywhere the right to requisition boats and men for the objects of their lord; and I appeared in these lands, in some measure, invested with this power by a document from Fumo Bukari. Therefore I took possession of two boats at Marfano, and requested the proprietors to forward a part of my loads to Engatana under the guard of some Somalis; and the goods arrived there at the specified time. Thus relieved to some extent, I set forth from Marfano on the morning of August 2nd, and arrived at about eleven in the morning with my whole column safe and sound at Engatana.

Necessity of self-help.

The boats at Marfano.

Here I encountered the great disappointment with regard to my measures from Witu, and this disappointment was nearly overturning everything. At Witu I had made a contract with the Banyans of Kau for the delivery of six *miaus* or Tana canoes, with one hundred loads of grain, at Engatana; the six miaus were to be at my disposal for use up the river. As in the meanwhile Herr Clemens Denhardt had undertaken to represent me at Witu, I made him acquainted with this arrangement. Herr Denhardt offered to manage the affair in a safer way for me, through the Wali of the Tanga territory, Buana Shaibo in Kau. Two days before my departure from Witu, I sent Tiedemann to Denhardt with the inquiry whether I might depend upon finding the grain and the

Failure of the grain and miau contract.

miaus at Engatana. When Herr von Tiedemann brought me an answer in the affirmative, I broke off my own negotiations with the Banyan, and marched to Engatana. But on August 2nd I found at Engatana, instead of the expected hundred loads, only fifty-four, and *not a single miau*. Buana Shaibu had believed he had herewith sufficiently fulfilled his engagement!

For the time, this decided the fate of my column. Without miaus I had no means of shipping the grain up the stream, and had consequently to remain in Engatana. Herewith began the darkest weeks of the German Emin Pasha Expedition. Our position appeared to me almost hopeless. In spite of the greatest economy, I was obliged to expend from two to three loads of grain each day to satisfy the hunger of my people. The grain decreased more and more from day to day, and the time could be accurately calculated when it would come to an end. Whatever was to be got at Engatana, in the way of unripe bananas and other articles of food, was soon completely consumed. *Serious delay and discouragement.*

It happened, in addition, that the rainy season this year was unusually prolonged. Night after night cataracts poured down from the skies, and soon sickness began to rage among my camels, which in a short time were reduced to the number of ten. My people also fell ill, and the desertion of men, one by one, continued, until I made up my mind, once for all, to chain up every doubtful character among them, under the guard of a Somali, day and night. But worse than all this was the circumstance that I myself began to lose my elasticity of mind. *Rainy season and sickness.*

Opposite Engatana is situated a wide region of swamp, the so-called Shechababu lake. This lake afforded for our support an inexhaustible shooting-ground for ducks, fowl, and geese. At this time we lived almost entirely on birds.

But the south-west monsoon, which continually blew with unusual violence across our camping-ground, incessantly drove the marsh vapour over upon us; and as we were in the habit of carelessly sitting, often for hours, after supper, in the open air in the front of my tent, I was seized in *The monsoon; illness of Dr. Peters.*

the course of this detention at Engatana with a rheumatic fever, which shook me violently for two days, and then left behind it a painful lameness in my left knee, and also in my right arm. Against this rheumatic suffering I used strong doses of Salicin, but I did not succeed in completely overcoming it; and, on the other hand, the use of quinine and salicyl had the disagreeable effect of greatly depressing my spirits, and especially my power of will. How could I thus hope to command an Emin Pasha Expedition under ordinary conditions? how much less to face the quite unusual difficulties of my exceptional position? But how could I have reconciled myself even to continue to live, if the Emin Pasha Expedition broke down in this manner? Thus I sat for weeks in Engatana, brooding over my fate and the future, while the south-west wind whistled round my tent, and the sky, from its murky clouds, poured down torrents of rain on our expedition.*

Weeks of dreary waiting.

* I cannot more forcibly express the feelings that pervaded me at the beginning of our detention at Engatana, than by reproducing a letter which I addressed on August 3rd to Government Architect Hofmann. This letter is not without interest for me, because it especially indicates the hopes to which I still clung at that time. The literal text is as follows:—

"I must confess that this Emin Pasha Expedition makes unusual demands upon my patience and strength of purpose. The famous Tana route is, just as I said in the autumn, in reality quite unavailable for expeditions. At that time the whole river plain is in a state of famine. This it was that ultimately caused the failure of the English (Pigott's) expedition, and I must exert all my powers to escape such a fate. I have my provisions carried with me in boats, which naturally gives occasion for delays. So I only get forward slowly. In three or four weeks the crops will be ripe, and the misery past. We are looking forward to an abundant harvest. Now, the people here are living literally on grass and the bark of trees. There is *nothing at all* to be had except water, of which there is enough in the river. You would not believe the difficulties that arise in provisioning, especially in furnishing supplies for my camels, donkeys, and my riding horse. To this must be added the quite unusual days' marches we have to make. Repeatedly we have had to march from quite early in the morning until from four to six in the afternoon, before we get to a halting-place. The Tana valley, in its formation, is quite like that of the Nile on a small scale. The river has carried a fertile but narrow alluvial surface into a quite desolate steppe. Along this region I journey; that is to say, I encamp in it. I do not follow the windings of the river, but travel diagonally across the steppe towards my camping-ground.

On the 24th, my condition of mind had become considerably more passionate, by the state of tension throughout these weeks. On that day I wrote a letter to Dr. Denicke, from which I extract a few passages:—

"Meanwhile, every attempt to cause me to waver in my fixed determination to carry out my task, whether through hunger, negro mobs, rain, wind, or sickness, appears to me downright ridiculous. I do not for a moment think of retreating. . . . I am cut off from my rear. Germany will, as usual, since I have the distinction to work for German interests, be 'indignant' at me. I have 'contrived' to make myself

Here I must again wait for a few days," (such was my expectation even on August 3rd) "for grain from Kipiri and Kau, and for my boats.

"So soon as I am at Korkoro, which will be God knows when, but *without question* will be effected, I shall profit by the immediate neighbourhood of the Kawallalah Somalis" (which was also destined to be a sweet delusion), "and shall also immediately put myself in communication with the Massais. The former made a compact with me the last day I was in Witu; they came after me. I was to remain neutral in case the Wagalla" (and Englishmen with them) "attacked them; in return they will bring cattle and camels to me to Korkoro, and also to Oda-Boru-Ruva" (which they never thought of doing); "and I am always to be their Sultan so long as I remain in Africa. So runs the concluding part of the treaty set up by Sheriff Hussein. The Massais must furnish me with donkeys. Then I think I shall be able to get easily to the great caravan road of Baringo, where further means of help are to be found. I must operate in this way because I am cut off from Zanzibar, and from the rear.

"I have already several times experienced in my life how apparently invincible obstacles yield to a persistent will; and I also believe that Providence actually wills this undertaking, however all appearances seem to declare against it. For it is only now that I see, with complete clearness, what this undertaking is capable of becoming for this part of Africa. Steamers must run up the Tana; then the Baringo trade will certainly be drawn this way" (which was an error). "The Wapokomo must be protected against the Somalis and Massais, so that they gain courage to follow cattle-breeding and agriculture on a large scale. Stations must make the north-west trade route safe, far into the south. Perhaps the task of breaking the ground here is reserved for me. In that case I should understand the contrarieties that beset me, and that have compelled me to have recourse again to camels, and always force me back upon the river. I have been obliged to emancipate myself from all the received traditions of Central African expeditions. But thus this undertaking may in reality form an epoch in the history of Central 'unpopular' in wide circles there. It is a worse thing that Zanzibar and the coast are cut off from me, with regard to porters and provisions. This certainly throws me back on my own resources. . . . Once more. The billows that roar against me may perhaps bewilder my temper here and there, but never my resolves. Whatever my feelings may be, facts will always find me meet them like a man. . . . My dear Denicke, I hope —and God will not be so cruel as to will it otherwise—that I shall do you no dishonour; and if, to avoid this, I should perish here with all I am and possess, it will be in the strife, and whatever may happen, I shall fall as a man! . . . People like myself will, probably, not usually get beyond a certain limit,

Africa. Firm as a rock in this conviction, I work from morning till evening, and in this confidence I am determined to oppose my whole being to all difficulties and troubles, in full trust that if I aid myself, God will also aid me in the end.

"From Ngao I have taken with me Herr Weber, one of the Neukirchen missionaries, that he may take a survey of this land in connection with his duties. He will probably go a few days' journey further up with me." (This was not done, in consequence of our lengthened detention.)

"You and all friends in Germany only require to have patience with us. Though we drag ourselves forward but slowly, you may be sure that we still get on as quickly as ever it can be done; our base as far as Witu remains permanently secured, and at all events I shall avoid a catastrophe. This is my first duty. The German Emin Pasha undertaking must in every case be carried out, and have a practical result. By this undeviating resolve I will stand or fall, if my force of will be not broken by sickness. But this I do not apprehend.

"I have especial pleasure in putting myself in communication with you to-day. Close in front of my tent flows the Tana, very like the Weser at Hameln. The opposite shore is luxuriantly covered with bananas and maize. Weber and Tiedemann have gone out hunting, and it is a calm, fine morning, one in which the soul can thoroughly go into and strengthen itself. Behind me lies all the jarring of Europe, like the blustering sea, of which not a whisper, much less an angry sound, penetrates to us here. Let wind and waves rage behind us; before me lies the future, and 'Forward!' is my watchword.

"When I look up from this letter my glance always falls upon the mirror of the Tana, whose waters glide by me, dumb and mysterious. Whence does it come? Perhaps it may be vouchsafed to me to behold its source. That is in the hands of the Eternal Powers, that regulate the fate of individuals and of the whole. Farewell."

even of life. And they fail, indeed, in this manner: on the one hand, they want to display qualities which, in fact, *must* go beyond the rule and measure of prescribed bounds if they are to fulfil their task; on the other hand, their qualities are to remain within the limits of private action. The reconciliation of a contrast and contradiction is here demanded."

The Tana here rolls through a pleasant scene, onward towards its mouth. Close by the margin of the shore was a Wapokomo hut, with a barasa or verandah. Here Herr von Tiedemann and I were accustomed to take our early breakfast, and I used then for hours to gaze down the river, hoping that round one of its windings help might appear from the coast. In the evenings we would again sit before our tent, having left the cares of the day behind us. Opposite us, on the further shore, stood a knotted tree, which from the varied effects of light assumed fantastic forms and outlines. Sometimes it looked like an old man with a ragged beard, stretching out his hands threateningly towards us; sometimes it appeared in the mist like the Erl-king, with hand thrust forth, pointing to the west. To my somewhat melancholy fancy it always had a threatening appearance. But it was not on ghosts and apparitions that my fate depended. If there was any help for us, it must after all be in ourselves.

I shall pass briefly over the many efforts I made in this direction. I at once sent Hamiri down river to Ngao to bring up fresh supplies of grain. He actually succeeded in procuring thirty-four loads, and getting them to Engatana. From Witu, through the exertions of Herr Denhardt, I received nine oxen, and if anything could keep my people in good heart it was the appearance of the nine oxen in question. I used to tell Herr von Tiedemann that so long as a single one of these oxen walked in front of the expedition the people would follow him, as iron is drawn by the magnet. What modest views we still had at that time with regard to cattle—and how entirely different had our ideas become, a few months later, when we marched along, with herds of hundreds and even thousands of oxen, the prize of war!—Our expedition, still so hungry at that time, was destined to become one of the best fed that ever marched onward in Africa. I further succeeded in procuring two large miaus from the Arabs.

On August 8th I sent a few people up the river to look about, as far as Kosi Nderani, for miaus, and to bring down any they could get. However, as it usually happens, the Somalis came back without fulfilling their commission; they declared there were no miaus; they had not been able to get any. Thereupon I sent Herr von Tiedemann up the river; and next morning already he sent me down a miau, and after several days, to my great satisfaction, came back himself with a second one. This last miau had certainly cost a few lives, as the Wapokomo of Nderani, who were being goaded on by the Arabs, had refused to let us have one. Not only had they insulted Herr von Tiedemann at a council, but, when he, notwithstanding, went away with the miau, they had even shot at him, so that he was obliged to return their fire in self-defence, on which occasion four of the Wapokomo fell.

Untrust-worthy Somali messengers.

The captured miau.

So, after all, I had for the present a little flotilla of four miaus lying at Engatana, guarded day and night by Somali sentries. On account of the total want of provisions with which we were threatened, I reduced the posho or allowance for the porters to a load and a half per day. The people resisted this in their peculiar manner, by declaring they would not accept a load and a half. But when I told them, in reply, that this would suit me all the better, for that then I should save all my grain, they came to me in the evening, and begged me to give them the load and a half, and they would be content; which I, on my part, did not do, for I put them off to the following day. Hereby I put an end, once and for all, to this kind of resistance, in my own column, for the whole remaining period of the expedition. The people got more and more accustomed to leave it to me to decide for them what was to be done in the expedition. Such "shauris" as, according to the books of travel, were usual in other expeditions, especially in those of Stanley, I never

Short allowance.

Strict discipline.

tolerated in the German Emin Pasha Expedition. Nevertheless, as a precaution, when I adopted the before-mentioned measure on August 6th, I had all the people put in chains who had been engaged at Lamu and Witu.

The longer I remained at Engatana the more did suspicious Arab characters show themselves, day by day, around my camp. Already at the beginning of August reports came daily of the approach of an English expedition to Engatana. Naturally I listened to all these communications with the greatest interest. The English expedition was said to be commanded by Mr. Smith, as proved to be the case, and had specially put itself in communication with the Kau Arabs. As it was now reported to me that the Arabs from Kau were trying to stir up my people to desert, and as men belonging to the approaching English expedition had already been seen in my quarters, I determined to put a stop to this, by one day chaining up some yellow gentlemen from Kau, and keeping them with me, to a certain extent, as hostages. The envoys from the English expedition, who had manifestly endeavoured to persuade my people to desert, I caused to be flogged, and sent them back.

Rumours of the English expedition.

By this means I established something like peace towards the end of my stay; but the general condition of the expedition was only negatively improved thereby, inasmuch as there was one danger less, to threaten us. From Witu, to which place I continually looked for help, none appeared; on the contrary, the expedition was looked upon there as having already failed; and an endeavour was made to persuade me that this could not have been otherwise, that it had been predicted. Among the peculiar plans that were discussed among us day by day, to help us out of the blind alley in which we were, I cannot forbear giving an account of a proposition made to me, in all seriousness, one morning by Hussein Fara.

A time of suspense.

I was accustomed at that time to get some hours' instruction every morning from Hussein in the language of his people, that I might give my commands to the Somalis, who did not understand the Kiswahili tongue. Then Hussein one morning came out deliberately with the observation that my porters were very powerful and well-built people. When I assented to this proposition, he went on to remark that Sheriff Hussein in Witu had already said the same thing. I observed to Hussein that every one could see this for himself, and that I did not wonder at it. Yes, he said, Sheriff Hussein was desirous to buy himself a lot of slaves. Now, our porters were in the habit of running away, and so he had agreed with Sheriff Hussein, that when we came into the district where the latter was with his herds, I should give over my porters as slaves to him, and he would give me five camels in exchange for every porter. He advised me to conclude this business. In the first place, a camel carried much more than a porter, and then I could afterwards sell the camels on the coast when the expedition was over, and I should make a good profit by the transaction. Hussein made me this proposition on August 22nd, and frequently reverted to it later on in the expedition. He could not understand why I should not make up my mind to so manifestly profitable a transaction, and he had noticed with astonishment that the whites did not enter into such little undertakings on the coast. During the course of this conversation Hussein also expressed his opinion, that when I had once seen how lucrative such an affair could become, I should perhaps make up my mind to do business more frequently in this manner in Africa. But, tempting as the matter appeared in his eyes, I could not bring myself to close with his proposal.

Meanwhile the English expedition, under Mr. Smith, actually marched past Engatana, on the opposite side of the Tana river. But if Mr. Smith had been commissioned to close the path against me there, I must confess that, from his first appearance on the scene, he did not follow his instructions very conscientiously. For, instead of keeping close to my camp, and if possible drawing over my porters to his side, he seemed to find it more convenient to march round it in a wide circuit, so that altogether I did not get sight of him and his column. This relation between us was practically maintained during the whole time we were both marching along the Tana. When, later on, I followed his traces, Mr. Smith, whom I repeatedly expected to meet, had always started again a few days earlier; so that of him personally I saw nothing at all, and of his people only so many as fled to me after the Smith expedition, one hundred and sixty strong, had been scattered by the Somalis. One day, moreover, two boats passed our camp, carrying grain up the Tana for the Englishmen.

During the whole time I had the camp closely guarded by day and night, because reports were continually reaching our ears of Arab machinations to attack and plunder us; and it was necessary for me, at all hazards, to resist any raids that might be attempted on my cattle or my boats. I need hardly say that I was not much afraid of this Arab coast rabble. <small>Danger of Arab raids.</small> I had too much confidence in the discipline we had introduced in my troop for that, and in my artillery and our repeating rifles. Seen from the river, our camp at Engatana had a sufficiently picturesque look. In the foreground was my fine large tent, with the German and the Witu flags. In front the artillery was placed. On the right <small>The camp at Engatana.</small> was the smaller tent, of Herr Tiedemann, and behind my tent, and to the left of it, the Somalis, and further off the porters. The whole presented a handsome and warlike appearance.

On August 23rd I had ordered Hamiri to a rich Suaheli in the sultanate of Witu, to try and procure me grain from that place. I had given him eight camels, to bring home the grain into camp. But already on the morning of the 24th Hamiri came back. The camels had not been able to <small>Hamiri's failure.</small> pass through the primeval forest, and so he had been compelled to return. Now I only wished to wait for the definite decision from Witu, from whence I still reckoned on assistance, before making my final resolve. The grain on the Upper Tana was already ripening. Like the first swallow in spring, an Arab had a few days before passed Engatana in a boat with twenty loads of rice, which he said he had "bought" on the Upper Tana. The maize cobs, too, were already gleaming golden, and came out deliberately with the observation that my porters were very powerful and well-built people. When I assented to this proposition, he went on to remark that Sheriff Hussein in Witu had already said the same thing. I observed to Hussein that every one could see this for himself, and that I did not wonder at it. Yes, he said, Sheriff Hussein was desirous to buy himself a lot of slaves. Now, our porters were in the habit of running away, and so he had agreed with Sheriff Hussein, that when we came into the district where the latter was with his herds, I should give over my porters as slaves to him, and he would give me five camels in exchange for every porter. He advised me to conclude this business. In the first place, a camel carried much more than a porter, and then I could afterwards sell the camels on the coast when the expedition was over, and I should make a good profit by the transaction. Hussein made me this proposition on August 22nd, and frequently reverted to it later on in the expedition. He could not understand why I should not make up my mind to so manifestly profitable a transaction, and he had noticed with astonishment that the whites did not enter into such little undertakings on the coast. During the course of this conversation Hussein also expressed his opinion, that when I had once seen how lucrative such an affair could become, I should perhaps make up my mind to do business more frequently in this manner in Africa. But, tempting as the matter appeared in his eyes, I could not bring myself to close with his proposal.

Meanwhile the English expedition, under Mr. Smith, actually marched past Engatana, on the opposite side of the Tana river. But if Mr. Smith had been commissioned to close the path against me there, I must confess that, from his first appearance on the scene, he did not follow his instructions very conscientiously. For, instead of keeping close to my camp, and if possible drawing over my porters to his side, he seemed to find it more convenient to march round it in a wide circuit, so that altogether I did not get sight of him and his column. This relation between us was practically maintained during the whole time we were both marching along the Tana. When, later on, I followed his traces, Mr. Smith, whom I repeatedly expected to meet, had always started again a few days earlier; so that of him personally I saw nothing at all, and of his people only so many as fled to me after the Smith expedition, one hundred and sixty strong, had been scattered by the Somalis. One day, moreover, two boats passed our camp, carrying grain up the Tana for the Englishmen.

During the whole time I had the camp closely guarded by day and night, because reports were continually reaching our ears of Arab machinations to attack and plunder us; and it was necessary for me, at all hazards, to resist any raids that might be attempted on my cattle or my boats. I need hardly say that I was not much afraid of this Arab coast rabble. I had too much confidence in the discipline we had introduced in my troop for that, and in my artillery and our repeating rifles. Seen from the river, our camp at Engatana had a sufficiently picturesque look. In the foreground was my fine large tent, with the German and the Witu flags. In front the artillery was placed. On the right was the smaller tent, of Herr Tiedemann, and behind my tent, and to the left of it, the Somalis, and further off the porters. The whole presented a handsome and warlike appearance.

Danger of Arab raids.

The camp at Engatana.

On August 23rd I had ordered Hamiri to a rich Suaheli in the sultanate of Witu, to try and procure me grain from that place. I had given him eight camels, to bring home the grain into camp. But already on the morning of the 24th Hamiri came back. The camels had not been able to pass through the primeval forest, and so he had been compelled to return. Now I only wished to wait for the definite decision from Witu, from whence I still reckoned on assistance, before making my final resolve. The grain on the Upper Tana was already ripening. Like the first swallow in spring, an Arab had a few days before passed Engatana in a boat with twenty loads of rice, which he said he had "bought" on the Upper Tana. The maize cobs, too, were already gleaming golden, and

Hamiri's failure.

7

could furnish good food. It was towards the close of August, when the chief harvest time of these lands is approaching. On the 25th, in the morning, came the report that there was nothing more to be expected for us from Witu. Five minutes afterwards I gave the order to make the four boats clear, and to load them. The time of gloomy brooding was now to be over. If the fate of the expedition was to be accomplished it seemed to me more desirable to follow the old Virgilian motto, "*Tu ne cede malis, sed contra audentior ito,*" than to receive our kismet with the resignation of the Mahometan.

No hope from Witu.

Sixty-seven loads were deposited in the boats. Wapokomo of Engatana were requested to embark in them as boatmen. In every boat a soldier was posted, with a loaded repeating gun, and the command of the whole fleet was entrusted to the brave Hamiri. Towards three o'clock in the afternoon the boats went off, each displaying a little black, white, and red flag, that fluttered gaily in the breeze. An hour later the camels followed with forty loads. Then I sat down with Herr von Tiedemann to breakfast, when suddenly it was reported to me from the Somali post that a white man, an Englishman, wished to speak to me. This last designation was incorrect; for the white man who now stepped into the tent was the Swedish missionary, Heddenström, from Kulesa, above Engatana, whom we had already, on the previous evening, seen passing our camp in a boat, and who came to make us a certainly not very edifying communication.

Onward by boat.

Missionary Heddenström.

The next station between Engatana and Nderani was a village called Mitole, near which there is a tolerably large forest. Missionary Heddenström now informed us, he had certain intelligence that there were concealed in this forest three hundred men belonging to Futilla, a formidable Somali in the sultanate of Witu, under a Kau Arab named Bwana Omari, and that their object was to attack our camp, or lie in wait for us in case we marched through the forest.

At this news I was not, indeed, anxious about our expedition as such, but I feared that the Arabs might attempt to

get possession of my boats in case they put to shore at Mitole;
—I consequently gave immediate orders that Herr von Tiedemann should betake himself at once to Mitole with six Askaris, the camel men, and the artillery, to clear the wood and protect the boats. Herr von Tiedemann accordingly set out at once, but saw nothing of the reported three hundred Arabs. I may mention at once that two days later, in a wood between Muina and Mbuji, I came upon a few hundred figures, who might have furnished the foundation for Heddenström's report. I immediately had my ordnance brought up, and went forward, armed only with my revolver and accompanied by five men, towards the hill where the fellows stood; and we had not even to fire a shot, so quickly did the whole assembly vanish, like chaff before the wind.

Dangers at Mitole.

After Herr von Tiedemann had marched away with the Somalis on Sunday afternoon from Mitole, I called my porters together, and gave orders that they should make everything ready for setting out on the following morning. I told them I had intelligence that the harvest was ripe on the Upper Tana; that I had had enough of the hungry time for my people, and would now lead them into districts where there would be plenty to eat, if they were prepared to do their duty. These words did not fail to produce a good effect. "*Maneno masuri kapissa*" ("Exceedingly good words!"), replied Nogola in the name of all the porters, and the feeling with regard to the departure from Engatana was manifestly one of pleasurable excitement.

Encouraging address to the people.

It is a remarkable peculiarity of human nature that we perhaps feel a greater attachment to places in which we have had to suffer, than towards those where we have passed happy days. That was my experience on Sunday, August 25th, after Herr von Tiedemann had marched away. My feeling with regard to quitting Engatana was one of deep sadness. I once more visited all the spots where I had brooded over the hard strokes of fortune that had alighted on our expedition, and could hardly refrain from tears. I learned to my joy on the same evening that Heddenström's

Remembrances of suffering.

report had been unfounded. Next morning, in a pouring rain, I sent away the caravan of porters likewise to Mitole.

The Wapokomo of Engatana hypocritically assumed the appearance of a kind of sorrow at their parting with me, but put on a very joyous air when, at the last moment, I made them a present of a few empty boxes and chests. We parted ostensibly as good friends; but this did not prevent their sending an embassy to the Sultan of Witu, with the declaration that my expedition had ruined them, and a petition to be allowed to found a new village. Ingratitude is the world's reward also in Africa. It was a great satisfaction to me that, when we began our march, not one of the porters was missing. The experiences I had had, nevertheless, caused me to secure with cords all I still had of the people from the Lamu district, and to lead them up to Oda-Boru-Ruwa under especial guard.

Parting from the Wapokomo.

When all were on the road, in a continuous pouring rain, I left Engatana with Hussein Fara, my servant Rukua, and Tell, the last remaining one of my dogs. The ground was so clayey and slippery that we only advanced slowly, and did not reach Mitole until towards twelve o'clock, though it is only seven and a half miles distant from Engatana. I was very glad to be able to substantiate, on this journey, that the remains of my rheumatism had disappeared.

The way by the Tana is always outside the belt of river scrub that runs uninterruptedly along by the stream in its lower and middle course. Especially in the middle course this underwood is comparatively broad, so that in the morning we had to work our way tolerably far from the camp out of the thicket, and in the afternoon were obliged to work back to it. This wood is only broken, in the immediate vicinity of the villages, by plantations. Here are growing bananas, mtama, maize, batatas, and various kinds of bean fruits.

Scenery of the Tana.

Seen from the river, the banks of the Tana throughout present a very charming landscape appearance, whether they are bordered by plantations or by bush forest. Outside this belt

VIEW ON THE TANA.

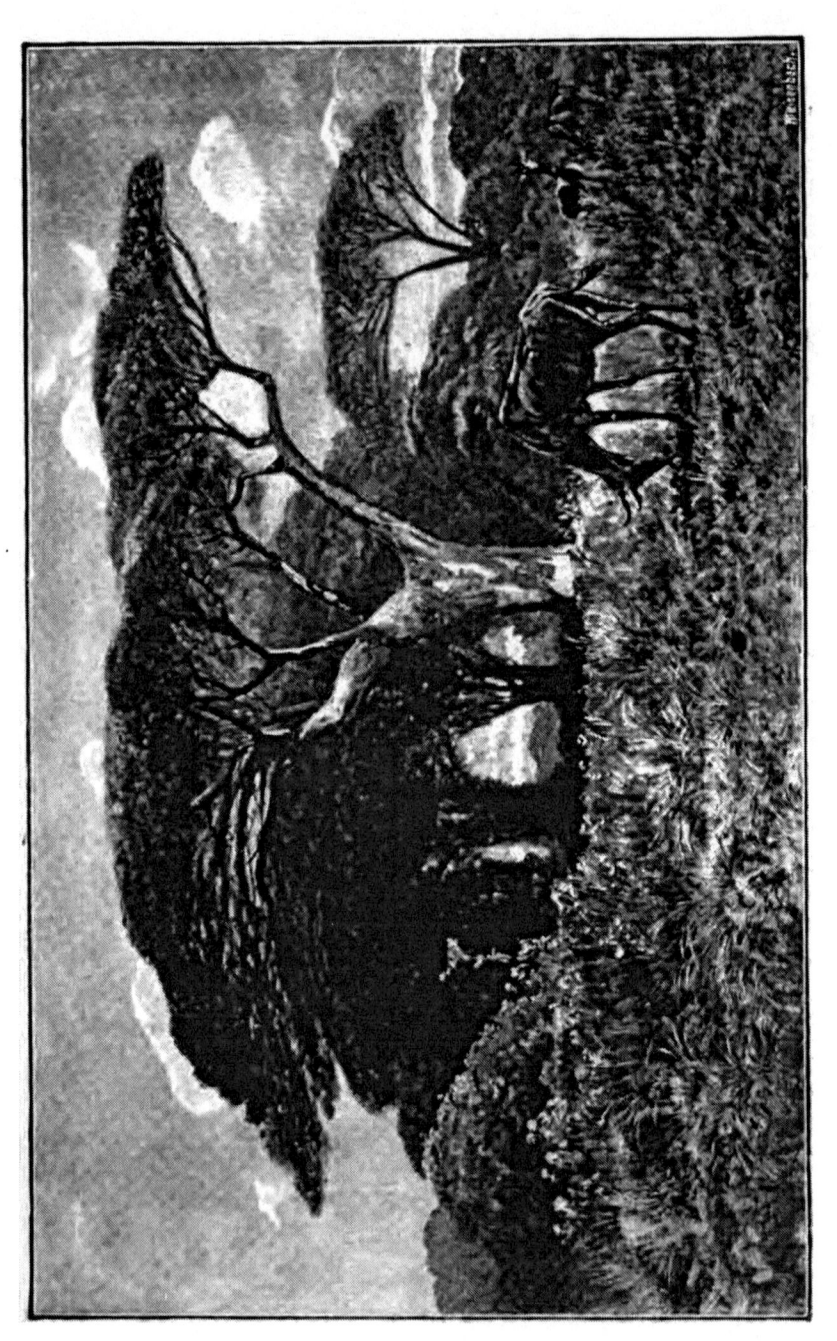

one comes upon the dry steppe, a region exceedingly convenient for the march, covered with mimosas of various kinds, whose thorns, however, often unmercifully tear the clothes and skin of the horseman. Frequently the march is for hours through tracts of cactus, whose hard prickles become dangerous to the feet of porters and beasts of burden. This steppe, through which the Tana rolls its flood along, forms a part of the great North-East African border plains, the abode of Somalis and Gallas. Unfruitful as it is, from its aridity, for plantations of any kind, it yet offers a very picturesque and lovely scene to the eye of the traveller, especially after the rainy season, and also affords a lively and exciting picture from its wealth in game and animals. There is the antelope in large flocks; there may be seen each morning the heavy traces of the elephant and the rhinoceros; there great companies of baboons and other apes pursue their gambols, and bucks of all kinds afford welcome occupation for the rifle. In the air, pea-hens and other fowl fly abroad, the wild duck and the wild goose sweep by, and here are seen the great pelican, vulture, and eagle. *[Region of the steppe. Animal life of the steppe.]*

Nothing more delightful can be imagined than a march through this Tana steppe at an early morning hour. When the column was on the road, in good order, and I left the camp in the rear of all, either riding my horse, or striding with Hussein and my servants through the dewy steppe, the eye roved delighted over the plain covered with its strange formations of bush. Seldom in Europe can such a delicious elastic clearness of the air be enjoyed as is found in the morning hours in Africa, almost under the Equator. On the left, after we had crossed to the right bank of the Tana, the river winds along, a dark-green, snaky line; before us, on the horizon, is seen the column of porters, like a little straight thread; and behind it the camels, with their strange swinging movement. In all the leaves and blades of grass millions of dewdrops are gleaming like diamonds, in the bright but not oppressive tropical sun. The heart beats higher with joyous excitement, and all the privations of the life, com- *[Exhilarating climate. A cheerful march.]*

pared with that of Europe, are forgotten in this pure feeling, in viewing this manifestation of the greatness of God, which offers itself to our contemplation more immediately here than where man has mingled his creations with it. These were wonderful hours, which were further brightened by the consciousness that we were moving towards the appointed goal; that we were on our way to Emin Pasha in the Equatorial Province. Over this first part of the expedition lies in our remembrance a bright, sunny glow; perhaps because the impressions of Zanzibar and the coast were yet recent in us, and formed a dark background.

On these marches it was my custom to leave the camp last of all, and then, when we approached the goal of our day's march, to overtake the others; so that I generally arrived first at the new camping-ground. It was Herr von Tiedemann's duty to march immediately behind, and with the porters. This arrangement was modified several times during the course of the expedition. When we had passed beyond the districts where we could procure guides, and it became necessary to settle our own route with maps and the compass, I made it a rule to march at the head of the expedition. But here we were still in the territory of the Wapokomo tribe, where in every village a few ells of stuff would purchase the services of a guide to the next. To-day we are encamped at Mitole, a little cheerful place, surrounded by plantations of maize and bananas.

Order of the procession.

Already, as I drew near the village, the elders of the place came out to meet me, to complain that my porters had plundered their maize fields. Sorry as I was for the Wapokomo, this was, in one respect, an agreeable piece of news for me, as it proved that the maize harvest was really ripe, and that I should accordingly, in all likelihood, find subsistence for my people, during the continuance of the expedition along the Tana. I have already mentioned that I had with me a writing from the Sultan of Witu, addressed to the village elders of the Wapokomo.

Complaints of the elders of Mitole.

The reading aloud of this despatch was always the proud achievement of fat Hamiri, who, according to the varying wants of the expedition, read all kinds of things out of it, with a fluency that perfectly amazed us. If it was grain we wanted, he would announce to the elders in a loud voice, how it was the particular desire of the Sultan of Witu, that all the Wapokomo should hasten to bring corn and maize. If we required boats, it was boats that formed the subject of the Sultan's letter. Astonished, like the fowls at the preaching of Reynard the fox, the Wapokomo would stand

Hamiri's imaginative eloquence.

"THAT'S THE HEIGHT OF THE ENGLISHMAN!"

in a half circle, listening; and they were filled with the most profound respect when, at the end of this oration, Hamiri exhibited to each in turn the seal of Fumo Bukari, with which the letter was stamped. Then, in conclusion, he would proceed to explain to the people the difference between the Englishmen and me. The Englishmen, of whom every one in the district knew that they wanted to prevent the expedition, he declared to be "kidogo kapissa" (exceeding small), and he would hold his outspread hand about six inches over the ground; I, on the contrary, was "mkubua sana;" and he would hold his hand high—as high as he could, and, as his own height did not seem to him sufficient for the occasion, he would jump two or three feet from the ground. The worthy chiefs of the Wapokomo were then accustomed to quit the conference with a secret shudder, and at its conclusion they would bring together as much as they could collect of the articles demanded by Hamiri; the only deplorable circumstance was that the said Hamiri was much given to the practice of demanding, say, one half of the supplies thus afforded, for his own worthy person. Whatever could be obtained disappeared in his insatiable maw; a fact that did not greatly conduce to his popularity in the caravan.

If at Mitole we succeeded in some measure in supplying the wants of the caravan, affairs unfortunately wore a very different aspect on the next day at Muina, a village lying about ten miles further up the stream. The journey thither was already very exhausting and toilsome. The place lies very much hidden in the river forest, and I was obliged to send forward Wapokomo to cut a way for porters and camels through the tangled underwood. Thus we did not arrive at the place until between three and four o'clock. Here the Wapokomo, if indeed they still possessed anything in the way of supplies, had carefully carried it away, and I saw myself compelled to have one of the six oxen I had with me slaughtered, that my people might have something to eat. I immediately entered into negotiations with the chiefs of this place for the supply of boatmen as far as Oda-Boru-Ruwa, and these negotiations were terminated in a peaceful manner. The twelve Muina men whom I had with me took the boats up safely to the Gallas territory. I put them all under Hamiri's special superintendence, and thus I had personally very little to do with the management of the boats.

A difficult and hungry march.

Hiring boatmen.

But in Muina my expedition had to experience a porter's tragedy, which, if it had no other result, at any rate decreased my confidence very considerably. After I had made all preparations for next morning's march, I went to bed at nine o'clock; but I was aroused even before eleven o'clock by my servant

DETAINED AT MUINA.

Rukua, who came to tell me "Pagasi wiote wamekimbia" ("All the porters have run away"). This certainly proved to be an exaggeration, for Nogola came directly afterwards, and reported that eight porters had just absconded, taking their wives with them; but these were not coast people, but Mangemas. In the fact that the Central African men were beginning to desert lay the alarming element of the affair, quite apart from the inconvenience of the reducing of the expedition by the loss of eight bearers. I immediately had the Somalis mustered, and at once despatched six of them in a boat down the Tana to Mitole, with orders to capture the porters, who would make their way to the place by land, or to shoot them down. The Somalis, under the command of Nurr, posted themselves in ambush in the forest near Mitole. As they could not get the porters, who were seen approaching at dawn of day, to stand, they shot two of them, whose corpses were thrown into the river.

Exciting news concerning the porters.

Meantime I lay dozing, with very unquiet dreams, in my tent. I fancied myself back at Neuhaus, on the Elbe, my native place, but still occupied in getting back the absconding porters. The dream ended each time with the sudden discovery that all my porters had run away. Next morning, however, I so far restrained myself as to compliment Nogola, to whose tribe the runaways belonged, in the presence of all the people, on his vigilance. I thus effaced the evil impression which the absconding of eight men might have made, by putting the others in good humour. I was now obliged to stay at Muina until my Somalis returned from Mitole; but towards noon, having succeeded in obtaining some maize from the neighbourhood, I sent Herr von Tiedemann with the porters up the river to Mbuji. Meanwhile I remained encamped at Muina, with very gloomy prospects for the future. I derived a certain amount of comfort from the perusal of a chapter in Schopenhauer's "Parerga" and "Paralipomena," on the apparent design in the fate of the individual, wherein Arthur Schopenhauer demonstrates the necessity of everything that has happened. But after all, in situations of

Making the best of it.

Despondency and philosophy.

packages of ammunition was transported to the opposite side. The Wapokomo of Kosi Nderani, who had assembled on the opposite bank at our arrival, disappeared like chaff before the wind, so soon as we began to operate with our boats.

The passage of the Tana. We worked the whole afternoon; camels, oxen, and donkeys were fastened behind the boats, and thus taken over to the opposite side. In the evening at six o'clock the passage of the Tana had been accomplished. I had

CROSSING THE TANA AT MBUJI.

the camp pitched, and the porters were watched all the night through by five sentries with loaded guns.

When the Nderani people saw that we had succeeded in establishing ourselves upon their bank, and heard that I intended to march next morning upon Kosi itself, the Sultan *Visit of the Sultan.* appeared in the evening with some of the chief men of the place, threw himself on the ground before me, and begged for peace. I enjoined him to furnish a guide on the morrow, to have a way cut through the forest, and to supply two miaus. When, on his part, though in a frightened tone, the man demanded presents as restitution for the men shot by Herr von Tiedemann, I answered him roughly, and this item disappeared from the order of the day. Meanwhile our relation to each other remained but a "sour-sweet" one.

During the night I three times visited my sentries, who were guarding the porters. While my attention was entirely concentrated on this point, a Kau Arab, named Ahmed, who was in my service, managed to play me a shabby trick. He unmoored a miau containing nine loads, broke up the loads with an axe, and sank them down the stream, afterwards overturning the miau. On the following morning I managed, indeed, to recover the miau itself and two loads of preserves, but we had lost two chests of bombshells and grenades, the whole of our library, two loads made up of tea, cocoa, coffee, sugar, and salt, a chest containing tow, revolvers, parts of guns, etc., the only load of beads I possessed, and a load of cognac. Nevertheless I caused the column to march away next morning for Nderani, carrying with me all the boat-loads, which from that time I always had regularly landed. In Nderani I established myself in a strong camp, which I caused to be completely surrounded by sentries; and on August 31st I went with two boats, four soldiers, and two porters back to Mbuji, where I succeeded in finding out the place where Ahmed had sunk the loads. *A piece of Arab treachery. Fortified camp at Nderani.*

The first thing we fished up was Thomson's "Through Massailand," which afterwards did me good service. We worked the whole day long, and presently got up a number of bombshells and grenades. To continue this work I myself remained at Kosi Nderani on September 1st, on which day I sent away Herr von Tiedemann with porters and camels to Makere. Kosi Nderani is a charming and exceedingly fruitful peninsula, running out into the Tana, where the French missions of St. Mary and the Sacred Heart established a station only half a year later; which, however, had to be abandoned, as the place was too much subject to inundations of the Tana. The Wapokomo here have a wealthy and *Description of Nderani.*

prosperous appearance, for we are now reaching the most productive districts of the Lower Tana.

On September 1st I succeeded in recovering about half the lost goods from Mbuji, and in procuring two more miaus at Kosi. I had now seven miaus in all, of which I sent one down to Ngao to Lieutenant-Captain Rust, under guard of a Somali soldier, with the order to send me part of the articles of barter as soon as he should have got together a small array of boats. On the morning of September 2nd, with a few of my people, I followed Herr von Tiedemann to Makere, after taking a friendly leave of the Sultan and his followers. I was struck by the enormous number of game animals on this tract. Great herds of antelopes awoke the instinct of the chase, and I practised, for the first time, the art of pursuing the herds of antelopes on horseback, and shooting one of them down from the saddle,—certainly with a negative result. This is the manner in which the Somalis are accustomed to hunt; they kill the lion from their horses with lances. In Makere I found my people safe and sound, and at once entered into friendly relations with the Wapokomo. But when I enjoined them to bring in provisions and to provide guides for the following morning, to lead me to Keredja, the whole population vanished at once; and to prevent my people from suffering again from hunger I was obliged to supply myself on my own account, from the ripening maize fields. When my men made use of the permission accorded them, the Wapokomo sought to drive them away by force, on which occasion, to my regret, two of them were wounded by my people. The foolish suspicion of the Wapokomo was continually, during the further course of the expedition, giving rise to similar incidents. They could not imagine that any one who had so much power in his hands as we possessed could make up his mind loyally to fulfil the obligation incurred, and, like the real "Friend Lampes"* that they are, they preferred to abandon house and home, and, if necessary, wife and

* Lampe is the hare in the burlesque epic of "Reynard the Fox." He is depicted as exhibiting the proverbial timidity of his race.—TR.

child also, rather than maintain relations with us. To get them to come back to Makere I at last threatened that if this were not done I would burn down their village; but even this threat, which, by the way, I did not carry into execution, did not induce them to return; and thus it happened that on the following morning I had, for the first time, to start without a guide on my way to Keredja.

Characteristics of the Wapokomo.

This day again it rained very heavily, and my column had to suffer considerably, especially the camels, which I could not put under shelter at night, and which succumbed, one after another, to the hardships of this Central African climate. Here, at Keredja, however, I had at least friendly intercourse with the natives, who brought me food, and sold me a large miau, which would carry fifty loads. When I had completed this purchase, I sent away two of the miaus I had brought with me to Lieutenant-Captain Rust at Ngao. On September 4th I arrived at Kina Kombe, the chief place of the whole territory of the Lower Tana. The place is so hidden in the primeval forest that in the afternoon we had, in the first instance, marched past it, and only arrived, by a very circuitous route, towards five o'clock. Here is a comparatively intelligent Sultan, the only Wapokomo on all the Tana who makes anything like a dignified impression upon one. Kina Kombe is a great village, surrounded by a strong fortification; besides the Wapokomo who live here, it is inhabited also by Gallas and Waboni. The Sultan led me into a house belonging to Herr Schlumke, who from here had carried on ivory-hunting. In this house I stayed the night. The Sultan declared his willingness to sell me food, and asked me to forbid my Somalis to go into the place, as the Somalis on the one side and the Gallas and Wapokomo on the other were deadly enemies. Food was also brought in abundance, and I determined to stay here through September 5th to feed my people up a little.

Arrival at Kina Kombe.

Interview with the Sultan.

On the morning of September 6th we resumed our route, to reach a camping-place, not far from the English station of

Subakini, by five in the afternoon, after a very heavy march. According to the accounts I had received at Kina Kombe, I had to expect that I should at length meet the English expedition of Mr. Smith, whose intention it was, I had been told, to cross my further advance up the Tana. Consequently, I did not march that evening as far as Subakini, for I wished to bring a fresh and a quiet mind to the contemplation of this English problem next morning. As the affair greatly interested me, I marched the next day, with ten soldiers and my loaded ordnance in advance, towards the English station. I presumed that I should find Mr. Smith just at breakfast, and already rejoiced when I thought of our salutation. Just before the place, I drew my column of camels around me, made a circuit round the English station, and appeared suddenly on the western side, in sight of it. A lively rattle of musketry resounded in the station when they saw me. I galloped up, and as my Wapokomo ran away the moment they heard the firing, in order to give them courage I jumped my horse over the not very high enclosure of the station. This was certainly not a very prudent proceeding, supposing, as I at first thought, the firing had a hostile intention. But hardly had I jumped down from my horse, revolver in hand, in the midst of the Arab garrison, than they all bowed before me, and kissed my hands. They said the firing had been intended as a salute; and I heard immediately that Mr. Smith had already marched away a few days ago, and was accordingly still in advance of me. I also received positive intelligence here that the Pigott expedition had gone to wreck on the Upper Tana. The very intelligent chief of the station, a half-breed Arab from Zanzibar, behaved very amiably to us, pointed out a very beautiful camping-place under a mighty fig-tree in a field of maize, brought me rice for my private use, and also poultry, and procured me miaus from the inhabitants of the place, so that I was able to dispatch two more boats the next day to Lieutenant-Captain Rust at Ngao. Unfortunately on this day my own six miaus did not arrive, and therefore I resolved to wait for them, with some few of my people, on

September 8th at Subakini, sending Herr von Tiedemann forward once more with the porters. He was to march upon Sissini, where I would overtake him on September 9th. He was to accomplish the long march to Sissini in two days, so that no loss of time might arise from my waiting at Subakini. Here, from Subakini, I wrote a detailed report to the German Emin Pasha committee, sent the two miaus, as I have stated, to Lieutenant-Captain Rust, and at about two o'clock I was rejoiced to see my own flotilla of miaus, under Hamiri, sailing up with colours flying. I sent this flotilla onward towards Sissini the same day. Thus things developed themselves at Subakini in a very satisfactory way. How the report could have originated, that was afterwards despatched in telegrams to Germany, that I had established myself here for a lengthened stay, and was waiting at Subakini for goods from the coast, has never been clear to me. Perhaps it arose from the fact that I had my letter from here forwarded through the agency of the English mission at Goldbaute. *Arrival of Hamiri with the miaus.*

Already on September 9th I marched to Sissini, where I rejoined my main column. Here also I succeeded in procuring plentiful supplies of food for my people. I still continued to have their firearms taken away from all the porters every evening, and posted two sentries to prevent any possible further desertions; but gradually I began to show more confidence with respect to the people, as the relations between us had desirably altered to my advantage. On September 10th I arrived at Malalulu, where we were altogether out of the territories of the Sultan of Witu. Here I resolved to hoist the German flag for the first time on the north side of the Tana, to make it clear to the English that the sphere of their interests extended only to the southern side of that river. On a lofty mast our flag was run up, and waved in these regions, for the first time, in the evening breeze, saluted with volleys of musketry and some cannon shots. I had brought over from the Sultan of Malalulu, on the opposite bank, a sheep, to celebrate the day, and on my *Sissini. The German flag hoisted at Malalulu.*

part bestowed on the Wapokomo, as a return gift, a camel which had fallen that day.

From here we went forward in long marches towards Massa, which we reached on September 12th. The grain was now completely ripe, and the whole Wapokomo community in a very jovial humour in consequence. In the next villages to which we came it was rather difficult to meet with sober people with whom we could negotiate, as the yellow grain is consumed chiefly in the form of brown pombes or beer. The consequence to us was, however, that we also had enough to live upon, and the expedition accordingly consolidated itself more and more. Massa is the name of a whole region, whose settlements lie on both sides of the river. The chief place is on the northern bank of the Tana, and the Sultan of it asked me to hoist the German flag there, and concluded a treaty of protection with me. To make the relations between us more intimate, I remained in this district on September 13th, because for me and for Rust's column it was of especial importance to completely assure ourselves of this last great place, before entering upon the Tana steppe proper.

Arrival at Massa.

The Massa region.

Some distance above Massa the lower course of the Tana, where that river has formed a fruitful alluvial tract in the dry steppe, comes to an end, and we get to the middle part of the river's course, in which the character of the steppe is completely maintained. The middle course is marked by the absence of alluvium and by the close approach to the stream of high steppe-shores. We hoisted the German flag on September 18th at Massa in the middle of the village square. It was, as before, saluted with firing of cannon, and in the evening a great popular festival was held in the place, duly to celebrate the joyful occasion. Hamiri was the manager of this popular entertainment, which consisted in a general dance of the Wapokomo; that is to say, of the male part of the population. To the beat of drum and the rhythmical hand-clapping of all the ladies in the place the old Sultan and the different Wapokomo danced

Lowest middle course of the Tana.

Cheerful dance of the Wapokomo.

along, in all kinds of more or less graceful or ungraceful evolutions, in front the old Sultan, who, during the afternoon, had enjoyed himself over the cognac in my tent, and in his own quarters had already done adequate justice to the pombe. After supper we crossed over to the right side of the river, to get a nearer view of this spectacle; and when I considered the cowardice of these robust fellows, which had exhibited itself all along the Tana in a perfectly comic fashion, I was obliged involuntarily to think of friend Lampe, with his family, how he enjoys life guilelessly and merrily, but yet is always on the alert to escape by flight from real or fancied danger. Till late into the night the sounds of the "ngoma," or drum, sounded across into our camp, till at last I made them call out to the people beyond the river, that now there had been enough of it, and I requested they would go to sleep.

Nocturnal festival.

From Massa we marched on September 13th to Bura, which also lies on the left bank of the Tana. Here we arrived as early as eleven o'clock in the morning. I sent to ask the Sultan, on the opposite side, to come across, which he immediately did; and, early as the hour was, the old gentleman was considerably heated; in fact, he and his whole following were completely drunk at eleven in the morning. They laughed incessantly, and made the most absurd remarks. Consequently, I sent the Sultan back again, and pointed out to him that he should despatch to me some one who was not drunk. So, after an hour, his brother appeared, and made excuses for the lofty potentate, who had been enjoying his early pombe, and lamented that the Sultan was in general too much addicted to that liquor. Unfortunately, I had to point out to the brother that he was in no better condition than the Sultan; but as he replied by naïvely declaring that he was the least intoxicated man in the whole village, I retained him in my company, with an intimation that he would have to remain in my camp until the Wapokomo had brought food across for my column. There were, it appears, some difficulties connected with this; accordingly, in the afternoon I despatched some soldiers to Bura, which, however,

An excited assembly.

The Sultan as a hostage.

only resulted in setting the whole populous element scampering. Only the servants of the Sultan's brother, wishing to rescue their master out of my hands, towards evening sent a few boat-loads of maize, for which I paid. As my repeated requests were ineffectual in drawing from their forest retreats the Wapokomo, who must by that time have got over their fit of intoxication, I found myself compelled to borrow a fine large miau without their express permission; but, as a pledge, I left behind me at Bura one of the small miaus I had brought with me.

The question of provisioning began to be a serious one for me, as I knew that I was close to the entrance to the steppe, and that I must get together a supply for a few days for my people, to enable me to get to Oda-Boru-Ruva. On the following day, at Ischarra, I accordingly saw myself necessitated, inasmuch as I was sufficiently acquainted with the cowardly tactics of the Wapokomo, to take into custody all the three chiefs of the place immediately on my arrival, to detain them until sufficient corn should be brought in for my column. Here I heard for the first time that hordes of Somalis were roving in the surrounding country. The Wapokomo told me that a few days previously some Somalis had visited them, and plundered them completely out.

Strong measures for procuring provisions.

At Ischarra we first came into the regions of the Galla language. Until we arrived there, the men of higher rank among the Wapokomo had always talked a little broken Kiswahili; the language of the Gallas now took its place. From olden times the Gallas ruled here, who have now been thrust back upon Oda-Boru-Ruva. I managed, with the utmost exertion, to procure sustenance for us at least for one day, and also to obtain a little meat for the morrow. In view of the danger from the Somalis, I arranged a strict sentry service for the night, with great fires before the camp, which were kept up all night long; however, no Somali made his appearance among us. On September 15th we reached Kidori, the last settlement of the Wapokomo on the lower course of the Tana. I consider this place as forming

The Galla regions.

Kidori, on the Tana.

ON TO THE UNINHABITED STEPPE. 117

the point of separation between the lower and middle course of the river. The inhabitants complained that they had been eaten out of house and home by the English expedition of Mr. Smith, and gave me more accurate details on the wrecking of the English expedition by Somalis, which had occurred at a point somewhat above this place. Already at Massa I had received into my column a few porters who had fled there before the catastrophe happened, and had learned the fact that Mr. Smith had been surprised and beaten by a horde of Somalis. Here I heard that in broad day, at three in the afternoon, thirty Somalis had managed actually to defeat the English expedition of one hundred and sixty men armed with guns, and to hurl it back upon Kidori. This seemed to me not so much to evidence the efficiency of the Somalis as the miserable spirit in the English expedition. For me, it had the effect of making me much more cautious in arranging the details of management of my expedition. *Reported defeat of Smith's expedition.*

At Kidori I only succeeded in provisioning my people to a very small extent; I had therefore to trust to my fortune, and strike into the steppe without a supply of corn. Thereby the position of the expedition became a very difficult one. In this steppe, which we entered on September 16th, we certainly found here and there settlements of hunting Mboni; but of these people themselves we nowhere caught sight. There was something quite unearthly about the fashion in which they were acquainted with every one of our movements, to the smallest detail, without our even once getting to see them. The Mboni is swift-footed as the antelope he pursues, and keen-sighted as the falcon he brings down from the air with his bow and arrow. I had taken two guides with me from Kidori, who were originally to have led me only as far as Oda. So soon as I ascertained that I could not procure other guides onward from this place, I saw myself compelled to put them in chains, and carry them with me through the steppe. Though they were not acquainted with the route by land across the steppe, they had several times gone up the river, and knew its bendings. By hard severity *Scarcity of grain.* *Nature of the Mboni.*

I effected thus much in a few days, that they at least only made such assertions as they were sure of being able to verify.

As regards the road itself, I was entirely unable to make enquiry in any other direction.

At Oda an incident happened that is characteristic of the spirit existing in my expedition, and may therefore be related by me. Hamiri had, as was quite right, the command of the boats; but through his whimsical egotism, that made him arrogate everything to himself, a bitter hatred had been gradually aroused in the whole column against him.

Hamiri and Pembomoto's quarrel. A Mangema bearer, Pembomoto, had gone to the place where the boats lay, to wash himself. Hamiri wanted to turn him away, and without further preface the two were engaged in a violent fight, in which their chief weapons, horribly enough, were their teeth. Pembomoto bit Hamiri in the breast, and Hamiri tore Pembomoto's eyebrows from his forehead. Thereupon the Mangemas came to me, and demanded that Hamiri should be punished. When I caused Hamiri, and Pembomoto also, to be put in chains, they suddenly rose up, and

ON THE TANA.

threatened that if I would not punish Hamiri, they themselves would attack him and cut him down. The spokesman of the Mangemas was Nogola, a demagogic champion of the first order, who terrorised his people, and at that time still kept the whole column in fear of him. At that moment the question was whether Nogola or I was to be master of the expedition; and I met his impudent words by ordering all the people to fall in, stationing the Somalis with loaded repeating rifles around the porters, having the latter deprived of their guns, and Nogola put in chains. This settled the affair. From that day Nogola's credit declined rapidly, and the recurrence of a riot such as that of September 16th was out of the question. Here Hussein once more rejoiced me by a very neat proposition, and one that is characteristic of the Somalis. *Hussein's idea of justice.* "Master," said he, "dost thou wish Nogola dead? Then, do not have him shot before the porters, or they will all run away. Simply tell him he is to march with the camels to-morrow, and then we will shoot him down from behind." As a distinguishing mark of this proposal, I must add that Hussein and Nogola were very good friends, and continued so during the whole further course of the expedition. Hussein could never rightly understand why, on my part, I declined this exceedingly practical offer of his.

On Tuesday, September 17th, the real difficulties of the march through the steppe began. In the afternoon, at half-past one, after an eight hours' march, all steaming and glowing with heat, we reached, instead of the camping-place traced out for us, a primitive forest, without finding water. *A weary march.* I now perseveringly looked for the traces of the English caravan, which, after being surprised by the Somalis, had advanced again on this side of the river; and I knew for a certainty that if we did not find the English spoor on this Tuesday, we should undoubtedly be compelled, wanting food as we did, to turn back. Therefore I left to Herr von Tiedemann the command of the expedition, which presently found water, and I betook myself, with Rukua and Nogola, to the search for the English road. At about two o'clock we succeeded in finding traces of footsteps. So soon as I had found this, I sent Rukua back into the camp to inform Herr von Tiedemann that I should follow the English traces till I came to their camping-place by the water, and I desired that something to eat and a blanket might be sent to me.

Traces of the English expedition.

It is quite unnecessary to give here the description of a march through the steppe, with the sun in the zenith and the torments of thirst. This has been very often done, and the reader would after all not get a clear conception from a description. After close and repeated observation of my own sensations, I have come to the conclusion that the tortures of thirst bear the closest resemblance to the torments of suffocation. Perhaps the proportion between them may be thus stated: the torment of suffocation is in the same measure more intense, as the time required for dying by thirst is longer than that for death by suffocation. It is, in truth, a fearful torment. On September 17th I had to experience it in all its anguish. We continued marching till sunset, and it was only just before the coming on of darkness that I succeeded in breaking through the thicket towards the river, and reaching the bank. To give my servants who might follow me an indication of the way, I ordered Nogola to set trees on fire; and soon the sea of flame, visible for miles, towered above the steppe, mirrored in the flood of the Tana; and with its roaring and hissing voice singing a mighty slumber song to me, as, weary to death, with my boots under my head for a pillow, and my loaded double-barrelled rifle resting on my arm, I stretched myself to rest. Towards nine o'clock I heard shots fired at a distance. I answered them, and half an hour later I was surrounded by a few of my servants, who brought me some food. Herr von Tiedemann had even packed up one of the last half bottles of sekt. With what comfort I set about the business of eating and drinking, only those will understand to whom such situations are known. The feeling of comfort, through contrast of the present circumstances with the past endurance, is converted into sauciness and joviality. Next

More marching through the steppe.

Fire signal at the river.

ON THE MARCH.

morning at five o'clock I sent Nogola back to the expedition to serve as guide. I myself once more followed the English traces. At ten o'clock I came to the camping-place of that expedition by the river, and here I awaited the arrival of my column that was marching from the south-east. This day we continued our march till three in the afternoon.

On the track of the English.

Such a journey through the steppe is always hot, and as a rule also dusty, but it has great attractions for the leader of an expedition. Beasts of burden and men pass along with equal pace and uninterruptedly, inasmuch as the latter also do not see much temptation in the shadowless plain to fall out of the ranks and rest. When, therefore, the caravan is once set in motion, at least towards the afternoon, it lies entirely in the will and pleasure of the leader in what direction it shall bend its course, or where it shall halt. The preparations for the march used now to begin regularly at five in the morning, and at about a quarter to six the porters, under Tiedemann, would start, while it was generally six before the camels and donkeys could follow. I left the camping-ground when the last beast and the last man had gone. Then I would remain behind till the word was passed and the steppe reached; thereupon, as a rule, I rode past the loaded animals, to get the porters in sight. Generally I would turn back once more, to let the camels defile past me. Towards midday I was accustomed to leave these behind me, and gradually to advance to the head of the column. Such had been the rule of march under ordinary circumstances.

Severity of the steppe journeys.

The routine of marching.

Matters assumed another form now on our march through the steppe, where I had to make out the way and take the head of the column. This steppe would, but for the Tana, be altogether untraversable for an expedition with porters; it is only the Tana, which is here entirely without tributaries, that furnishes the life-giving element of water. That it was able to roll such ample masses of water through the sandy plain to the Indian Ocean, made me already at that time form an estimate of the great volume of the sources from which it

Sources of the Tana.

gushes forth. The Tana receives its waters from the same plateaus from which the Nile issues forth to flow northwards. In fact, in its whole conformation it may be called a Nile on a small scale. Like the larger river, it has carried its own arable land into the desert, and, as with the Nile, the middle course of the Tana has the real steppe character which I have described.

Through this steppe we travelled in a march of five days. It was a march for life or death. After I had slaughtered the last ox, on September 18th, we were for three days without food of any kind, and were exposed, besides, to the danger of perishing of thirst. On the 17th we reached the region of Korro-korro, which we passed in one day, as we were in continual danger of losing the English spoor, finding no way to the river, and succumbing to thirst. I now made my people march from five in the morning until sunset.

Terrible suffering from want.

So we went on uninterruptedly on September 18th, 19th, and 20th. The worst day was September 21st, when I marched at the head of the expedition from early in the morning until half-past six in the evening, when at last, in the darkness, I made my way to the Tana, and not only found water, but also the prospect of obtaining provisions next day. On September 21st, a Saturday, I found the first settlement of the Gallas in Odagalla. Herr von Tiedemann, with the majority of the porters, did not reach the camp at all on this occasion. He was compelled to pass the night in the steppe, amid frightful torments of thirst, although on that night, between Saturday and Sunday, I had the whole forest by the river set on fire, so that the flames blazed up to the firmament, as a signal from us to the Gallas that the expedition of the Germans had arrived. It was not until towards noon on the Sunday that Herr von Tiedemann arrived; all the rest of the day, stragglers were coming in. In the morning I had already succeeded in procuring some maize from the island opposite us, and here, to my regret, I had again been obliged to put in practice the expedient of chaining the Sultan when he paid his visit, because otherwise my column would have

Arrival at the Galla settlement.

ODA-BORU-RUVA IN SIGHT. 123

run a great risk of actually perishing through hunger. In the afternoon I was also fortunate enough to get a purchase of hens from a neighbouring village, so that Herr von Tiedemann and I were able once more to refresh ourselves with flesh meat. I remained at Odagalla throughout Monday the 23rd, because one of my people had not made his way in from the steppe,—a certain Amdurabi, who carried the load containing my private blankets. He appeared at last on September 26th, emaciated and three parts dead, at my camp at Oda-Boru-Ruva. On Tuesday, September 24th, while it was yet early, I broke up my camp at Odagalla; and now, with waving flag and beat of drum, we went forward to the great Galla sultanate of Oda-Boru-Ruva, seven English miles distant. Towards eleven o'clock we found the path through the primeval forest to the river, and half an hour later we saw for the first time before us, on the other side of the Tana, the rich plantations and the villages of the Gallas of Oda-Boru-Ruva.

Beginning of better things.

Triumphal march to Oda-Boru-Ruva.

CHAPTER V.

WITH THE GALLAS IN ODA-BORU-RUVA.

"Within thy bosom are thy fateful stars."
SCHILLER.

TOWARDS noon I encamped with my caravan in the primeval forest of the Tana, opposite the settlements of the Gallas, which were seen gleaming from the opposite side. We had the pleasure— the first occasion for a long time —of once more seeing maize plantations. But the thing to be done was to establish communications with the opposite shore of the river, which was a matter of difficulty, as my boats had not yet arrived. I therefore sent some Somalis across the river, which is tolerably broad at this point, and they succeeded in getting possession of a boat, which they brought over to

Scouts sent across the river.

us. They reported that the whole district was deserted. I sent the boat back once more, and made them bring two more Galla boats across. I now crossed with a few soldiers and my servants to the left bank of the Tana, leaving the actual column behind under the guard of Herr von Tiedemann. As I could not at all tell how the Gallas would behave at our arrival, I at once ordered one of the boats to the maize-fields, to have it filled with grain, and then taken to the camping-place we had yet to find out. Meanwhile we rowed past a broad fork of the river, followed the southern arm, and at last landed, after an hour and a half, at a little village on the right hand, where I saw a few people. This was a slave settlement of the Gallas, and consisted chiefly of Suahelis of the sultanate of Witu, who had been kidnapped by the Gallas and dragged to this place. It happened by chance that Bin Omar, whom I had with me, had formerly been a very good friend of one of these slaves, named Mandutto, and at once resumed his old relations with him. Under a mighty tree a bench had been fixed, and here I sat down, at once sending back my boats to bring more men across; and I sent, moreover, an invitation to the Sultan of the Gallas, asking him to give himself the trouble to come to me, that we might consult about our quarters. They brought me fruit and maize cobs to eat, and apparently the Suaheli were much rejoiced at the arrival of our expedition.

On the Tana river.

An old acquaintance recognised.

An hour had passed before Sultan Hugo appeared with his suite. He was a little man, with a very cunning look, dressed in a kind of brown toga gown, and decked out with a copper chain round his neck, and thick bracelets of the same material. In his hand he carried a lance, according to the custom of the Gallas.

The Sultan of Gallas.

These Gallas are, as a rule, of an imposing appearance. Tall and of slender build, they exhibit the same type I had formerly admired in the Somalis. The shape of the face is entirely different from that of the negro, and in its narrow, delicately-cut features reminds one entirely of the Caucasian. Their dark eyes have a melancholy look in them, but begin to sparkle when their hearts are stirred by passion. The Gallas belong to the handsomest peoples of the earth, and have something very noble in their carriage. In their language they have a close affinity to the Somalis, with whom, nevertheless, they live in deadly enmity. Wherever a Somali and a Galla may meet, they stand towards each other in a state of warfare. The Somalis themselves say that the two had formerly been one nation, but parted, because the Gallas remained faithful to the old national belief, while the Somalis adopted the teaching of Mahomet. The Gallas of Oda-Boru-Ruva, especially, belong manifestly to the race of the Borani Gallas that still ruled in the north, but were in the course of centuries carried down by the Somali flood into the country of the Bararetta Gallas, from whence, according to their own assertion, they were again chased towards the north by the Wakamba. They had now been settled for a long time on the great island of the Tana, which they called Oda-Boru-Ruva,—Oda signifying fork of the river; Boru, to-morrow morning; and Ruva, rain;—and from hence they held under their dominion the Wapokomo, who are seated along the Tana to the neighbourhood of Hameje. These Wapokomo have, indeed, still their own Sultan, who has his place in the councils of the Gallas, but are obliged to do menial service for the ruling Gallas caste, especially in the matter of boat navigation. Besides this, as I have already mentioned, the Gallas keep slaves, who have to do their work in the fields, and other labour of the kind. These slaves are settled in special villages, and also hold possession of some arable land for themselves and their families; but they are never in a position to accumulate property, because what they have is regularly taken from them by their masters, the Gallas. To all appearance the two races lived in a good understanding with each other, the intelligent Mandutto being the representative of Suaheli interests with the Gallas; but a bitter hatred had arisen in secret between the governing race and the governed, and this was destined to have a very remarkable influence on the fortunes of our expedition. The Suaheli of the Lower Tana considered themselves as really the superior race, and gnashed their teeth at the haughtiness with which the proud Gallas treated them. They were especially enraged at the fact that the young Galla warriors seized their wives and daughters at their pleasure. Among the sufferers from this state of things was Mandutto, with whom I soon entered into closer relations, and who afterwards became a valuable member of my expedition.

Taking all things together, the Gallas of Oda-Boru-Ruva are in a very constrained position, threatened on all sides. In the north they have to defend themselves against the Somalis; in the west they fight against the Wandorobo, and from the south-west the Wakamba make raids upon their herds. According to my estimate, the Sultan Hugo had, in the year 1889, still about one thousand two hundred warriors at his disposal. *Dangerous position of the Gallas.* "Look at my warriors," he once said to me, when I made it a reproach that the once powerful race had retreated to this island of the Tana; "only look at my warriors! Once they numbered many thousands; they have now shrunk to hundreds. In every direction we have to fight, and I can see the day coming when the foot of a Galla shall no longer speed through the steppes on the Tana." Thus these Gallas resemble the tribes of North American Indians—stubborn in resistance, but destined to perish; and there is a mournful strain in their fate. From the outset I had a strong sympathetic feeling for this warlike and heavily-oppressed race—these proud men with the melancholy eyes, and the reserved, pensive-looking girls, whose outward appearance forcibly recalled the type of the gipsy women. This interest was not extinguished in me when, later on, I was obliged, through the development of events and the hard necessity of self-preservation, to use *Their personal appearance.* forcible measures against the Gallas; and it had a great share in deciding the position I took up with regard to the tribe, after the combat I had to wage with them in the night of October 6th.

The settlements and villages of the Gallas spread themselves out in a pleasing manner over Oda-Boru-Ruva. The

128   *NEW LIGHT ON DARK AFRICA.*

foot wanders there as through a garden, maize field after maize field appears, interspersed with banana plantations and batata fields. The houses are certainly small and round, after the manner of haycocks, but they are clean and neat. Oda-Boru-Ruva had its origin in the alluvium of the Tana, and is an oasis in the midst of the steppe, which separates it towards the east from the cultivated strips of land of the Lower Tana, and towards the south, west, and north,

Beauty of their country.

TANA LANDSCAPE, NEAR ODA-BORU-RUVA.

from Wapokomo, Massais, and Somalis. Here every kind of cultivation would be possible; for instance, the native tobacco is quite suited to European taste, and was smoked by us for a long time. As the river affords the means of a cheap communication with the coast, so also the fruitfulness of the soil and the enchanting loveliness of the landscape directly invite the foundation of a station, the more so as the Gallas themselves declare that from this part a trade in ivory is already carried on with the elephant countries in the west, and that it seems capable of ready development.

In bold sweeping curves the Tana rolls along by Oda-Boru-Ruva, and the eye roves delighted over the river, whose shores are covered either with plantations or with stately woods, and which, besides Oda-Boru-Ruva, forms a number of larger and smaller islands at this part. A breath of sweet poetry rests upon the landscape, and invites the spirit to dreamy and abstracted contemplation. *Course of the Tana.*

When, on September 24th, I entered into my first negotiations with Sultan Hugo, I could not suppose that this sunny and poetic region would very soon be the scene of the first serious battle, for the German Emin Pasha Expedition. Sultan Hugo at the very beginning gave permission for my expedition to take up its quarters opposite the island of Oda-Boru-Ruva, on a place that should be assigned to us. He also said that he would take counsel with the elders of the tribe, to open a regular market for the provisioning of my people. Among the Gallas, the Sultan cannot by himself decide any important question; he is rather a chosen magistrate than a hereditary ruler. Although it would appear that, in general, the lineal succession is maintained, the Gallas are not bound to observe it, and the Sultan is even liable to be deposed if he administers his office badly. The decision is always with the council of elders, which also pronounces sentence in cases of heavy crimes committed against members of the community. It was to a council of this sort that Sultan Hugo at once betook himself, in the interior of the island, promising to send me boats, to bring me to the landing-place that should be assigned to me. For further explanation he left with me Gall-Galla, a Galla who had been stolen in his childhood from the Arabs, and had long lived as a slave in the sultanate of Witu. He had gone through an adventurous career, and had lived for years among the Kavallala Somalis; in consequence, besides knowing the Galla language, he was master of the Arabic, Kiswahili, and Kisomali, which was of great value for us. At my wish, he at once sent messengers to my column in the forest, to bring them to the landing-place appointed for them. *Negotiations with the Sultan.*

During this time I was waiting for the boats the Sultan had promised; and with the two boats at my disposal, I caused about twelve men to be carried across the river to me. The boats promised by Hugo not arriving, I declared, towards three o'clock, that I would march down the river bank towards the island till I came to the point opposite the landing-place, and then the Gallas should set me across. The Gallas refused to do this, and I had to threaten them with war, to avoid damaging our position at the outset, and to carry my point. For three-quarters of an hour we marched under Gall-Galla's guidance up the island, and past the settlements of the Gallas. We were not conducted into any of these. At the entrances there were always standing fierce troops of Galla warriors, who gazed with hostile, threatening looks upon the strangers. At length, after passing several Wapokomo villages, we reached a clear space by the Tana river, from which, to my great joy, I could already see my people and camels on the opposite shore. Under a giant tree, with which I was destined to become much better acquainted in the course of the next few weeks, I awaited the boat, which soon carried me across to my column on the opposite side. The boat laden with maize, which I had ordered in the morning, had already arrived, and I was accordingly able to distribute food to my people at once. But a really joyous state of mind was not to be attained.

Difficulties and delays.

Our camping-place was a burnt-out steppe, from which the wind continually whirled up black masses of ashes. The view upon the Tana was certainly a charming one, and the landscape in the background presented a striking and yet pleasant woodland scene; but I found immediately on my arrival that the locking of our ordnance would not act, and this present case at once suggested serious anticipations as to what might be further in store for the expedition. Here I had to wait for the second column under Lieutenant-Captain Rust. Suppose a misfortune happened to it, and it did not join me? Was not perhaps Oda-Boru-Ruva the ultimate point of our German Emin Pasha Expedition altogether? Yes, for the moment itself I was in grave embarrassment. My boats,

Waiting for the second column.

with the few articles of barter which I possessed, had not arrived. Would they be sufficient to secure for us so much as a lengthened, peaceful stay at Oda-Boru-Ruva?—Such were my cogitations as, sitting on a chest, I ordered the camp to be pitched.

Towards half-past five o'clock Sultan Hugo suddenly made his appearance, with some hundreds of his warriors, on the opposite bank, and summoned me to come to a conference under the above-mentioned great tree. I made a few soldiers step into the boat, and rowed across to Hugo. But these little Tana canoes are so rickety, and my people were so unskilled in managing them, that before we could reach the opposite shore our boat was upset, and I had to proceed, swimming, to the conference with the Gallas; a somewhat comic episode, which was frequently repeated during the next weeks, and lost us a load of goods and several guns. When I emerged from the water among the Gallas, dripping with wet, Sultan Hugo announced to me that the Gallas were ready to open a market for us for our necessaries, and that he personally intended to give me some fowls. But when I asked him to send me one at once, as I had not yet eaten anything that day, he considered it would be time enough to-morrow morning; and I could not induce him to change his opinion. Thus it happened that on this evening we had to satisfy our hunger on boiled maize and butter, and that the newly-awakened feeling arose in my mind, that perhaps the peace policy I had taken up was not, after all, the right one in the face of this arrogant tribe, but that we should perhaps for the first time have to resort to an appeal to arms, to demonstrate whether it was necessary to starve, when the land produced such a store of food for man and beast. I determined, under all the circumstances, to assume for my part a higher tone towards these proud sons of the steppe; and next morning, when the Sultan appeared again for a conference beneath the tree, I sent Herr von Tiedemann to represent me.

Sultan Hugo's concessions.

Herr von Tiedemann was to offer the Sultan a few presents, tokens of friendship from me; but only on condition that the

Sultan, on his side, offered me proportionate gifts. This was done. I received a few boat-loads of grain, and bananas, and several fowls, so that on this day, for the first time, we could at least begin again to take our regular meals. To-day also, to my great satisfaction, my boats with the articles of barter came in; and, for the time, we should have obtained a regular supply of provisions, by purchase from the Gallas, if they had at once fulfilled their promise of opening a market for us. To induce them to fulfil the obligation they had undertaken, and, above all, to secure ourselves from the danger that continually threatened us, of perishing from hunger, I caused another foray for grain to be undertaken, on the following night, by three boats, under Herr von Tiedemann. It was completely successful, and caused the Gallas to proceed with the opening of the market without further delay.

Change of policy.

Its success.

Here in Oda-Boru-Ruva, half a year before, the Englishman, Mr. Pigott, had stayed with his expedition, concerning whose fortunes I had heard particulars already on the day of my arrival. According to the account given by the Gallas, Mr. Pigott had attempted to push forward in the north of the Tana. But when he had seen the settlements of the Galla tribes to the north he had become apprehensive, and had turned back. According to other accounts, which seemed to me more credible, Mr. Pigott was reported to have come upon desert steppes in the north, and had turned back for that reason. Then he had attempted an advance southward from the Tana, but had found no food there, and consequently had been compelled to march back to Mombassa. Mr. Pigott was said to have founded two stations among the Gallas, and to have left a garrison behind in one of them; but this garrison had betaken itself down the river ten days ago. Mr. Smith and his expedition had arrived about a week before, after the English garrison had already gone. He had lived there for a few days; but when the news came to Oda-Boru-Ruva of our approach, Mr. Smith had one morning quite suddenly gone, and he, also, had marched back through Ukumba to Mombassa. The Gallas added that there was no connection for an expedition

Mr. Pigott and his expedition.

Mr. Smith's expedition.

FLOTILLA OF THE EXPEDITION ON THE TANA.

COUNTERACTING MEASURES. 133

towards the west, because no people lived there, and nothing but the broad steppe was before us. If one marched further towards the west, one would get into the mountains, which we could already see when the sun was going down, rising here and there on the horizon.

According to the London agreement, the Tana was to be the boundary of the territory of English interests; therefore the English had no kind of right to establish stations northward of the Tana. Mr. Pigott had, notwithstanding, done this, wherein I was neither able nor desirous to alter anything. But in order to get the spirit of the London agreement acted upon here, I began on my side systematically to work at bringing the Gallas under German sovereignty, and to induce the Sultan and the elders of the tribes, as an outward sign of this, to solemnly hoist our flag in the north of the Tana. These matters occupied me very seriously during the next days, and led to a very favourable result for us. *The London agreement.*

It was on September 28th, at two in the afternoon, that I met the Sultan Hugo and the great men of the Gallas, under the before-mentioned tree on the further side of the Tana, at a great consultation, to bring the question to a definite conclusion. I sent several boat-loads of soldiers in advance, then I myself followed, and gradually had my whole force, with the exception of the camp sentries, ferried to the island. I had our two carriers' chairs taken across for Herr von Tiedemann and myself, and on these we at once took our places. Besides Sultan Hugo, three sultans of the Wapokomo had made their appearance, to take part in the deliberations. From the Sultan Hugo, with whom I had discussed the affair beforehand, I had heard that there was among the Gallas a strong opposition to my proposals, and I therefore made up my mind for an interesting assembly. Beside and behind Hugo reclined the warriors of the Gallas, with whom my Somalis exchanged looks of defiance. The hatred between the two races was so strong, that several times I had the greatest trouble to prevent a sudden outbreak and bloodshed. Every moment the Gallas were starting up, brandishing *Great consultation with Sultan Hugo.* *Threatenings of strife.*

their spears, to rush upon the Somalis, or my Somalis were bringing their musket stocks to their shoulders to shoot down the Gallas. To prevent this, Sultan Hugo recommended me to send back my soldiers to the opposite shore; but in view of the many hundreds of Galla warriors assembled there, I could not make up my mind to this. While we were negotiating, there was a continual streaming to and fro of the people, so that the whole produced a very lively effect.

I opened the proceedings with a short address, in which I asked the Gallas if they wished to have peace or war with me. Thereupon Sultan Hugo and the elders of the Wapokomo expressed their opinion at great length something to the following effect: "We know that thou art a great man, and hast much power, and that thou mayst have still more. We have also heard that more Germans are following thee, and will soon arrive here. Thou art as God, compared with us, and we wish for peace with thee. There have been Englishmen here, too. But we know that the Englishmen are quite little, and thou art very great. Thou art as God. Give us peace, great Lord; we will do everything that thou desirest." To this I replied as follows, after the general sentiment of the peace party among the Gallas had been thus declared: "I have been sent hither by the great nation of the Germans ('Wadutschi'). We dwell in the middle of Europe, and are the strongest of all the nations of the earth. You know the English and you know us; you can judge for yourselves which of us is the greater. But we make war upon those who attack us first; we overthrow them and kill them; while we give peace to all those who wish to live peaceably together with the Germans. We protect the weak; we cast down the strong, if they rise up against us. I am now only passing through the country of the Gallas, and am going to march far to the west, through the Massais, to a great German who lives alone in the middle of Africa; and in this, if you wish to be our friends, you must help me. Westward of this is a great mountain, which is white; to that I wish to go first, and what I

Fair words and peaceful professions.

Explanation of our intentions and demands.

want of you is, that you give me guides thither. That is the mountain Kenia, in the land of the Massais; thither I want guides from you. I know that on the way thither there is no food for us, therefore I want food from you, and boats to carry it up the river. If you will help me in these two things, I am ready here to hoist our flag, which the Somalis know very well, and which will prevent them from attacking you. Here is a writing of the Somalis, that I will leave here with you. It is from the Sheriff Hussein. In case the Somalis should come, show it to them, and they will be your friends."

Long discussions now arose, after the Gallas had declared themselves willing to grant my requests generally. Twelve boatmen were provided for me at once, whose names I entered, and who only asked permission to go to their homes and take leave of their families, before removing into my camp. Three guides were also brought before me, who were to show me the way over Hamege, and from thence to the Kenia. It was five o'clock when these matters were settled, and I laid before them the treaty, which, in pursuance of the unanimous decision of the popular assembly, Sultan Hugo signed next morning in the name of the Gallas. The treaty is worded thus:—

"The following treaty is this day concluded between Dr. Carl Peters and the Galla Sultan Hugo:

"Dr. Peters acknowledges as Sultan's territory the land on the Tana, from Massa to the Kenia.

"Sultan Hugo places himself, with all his territory, under the protection of Dr. Peters. Dr. Carl Peters will endeavour to obtain for the Galla sultanate the friendship of His Majesty the German Emperor.

"Nevertheless this treaty is not dependent upon the granting of the protection of the German Empire or upon its ratification by any European power.

"Sultan Hugo cedes to Dr. Carl Peters the right of working the country above and below the ground in every direction.

"This right especially includes the exclusive commercial monopoly, the right of establishing plantations, and the exclusive mining monopoly.

"If gold is found, Sultan Hugo is to have a quarter of the net profit from the production of it.

"Dr. Carl Peters is to be supreme lord in the country of the Gallas, to command the armed forces, and judge the people.

"This is done for the blessing and welfare of the Galla land.

"After several long conferences, and after its contents have been deliberated, and unanimously resolved upon, in a great public popular meeting by the Gallas in general, this treaty is formally concluded this day by Sultan Hugo and Dr. Peters.

"Dr. Peters.
"Hugo's mark.

"*Witnesses* { Von Tiedemann.
Mark of Hugo Valogalgal, brother and Prime Minister of the Sultan.
The Interpreter's mark."

This treaty was accepted amid lively acclamations, and was signed by us the next morning. Meanwhile my people provided a tall stem of a tree, and dug a hole, to raise the German flag with all due ceremony. I considered it more correct to have the actual business of hoisting done by the Gallas themselves. So the Sultan and his great men had to accommodate themselves to fastening up the flagstaff and running up the flag. When the sun disappeared in the west behind the mysterious chains of mountains, which, according to the opinion we held at that time, bounded the Massai territories, the black, white, and red flag waved for the first time in the evening breeze over the Upper Tana, saluted with three volleys by the whole of my people, while the slim forms of the Galla warriors danced around it. That this whole procedure made a deep impression upon the people is proved, among other circumstances, by the fact that at the end of December, two months after my departure, Herr Oskar Borchert found the flag still there, and regarded by the Gallas with a kind of superstitious awe.

Raising of the German flag.

During the following days, I had the opportunity of making nearer acquaintance with the lovely island of Oda-Boru-Ruva and with the peculiar manner of the Gallas. Unfortunately, on September 29th, Herr von Tiedemann fell so sick, whether of an affection of the spleen or the liver we did not know, that I was most seriously alarmed for his life, and made him the proposition that he should go back to the coast in our great boat. Thus for the weeks that were next to come I was to depend entirely on myself; and the powerful magic of solitude is thrown over the recollections of these sunny days of Oda-Boru-Ruva. Sunny days they certainly were. Between two and three o'clock the thermometer, in the deepest shade, regularly attained a height of 45° (centigrade thermometer). The heat was now and again simply almost intolerable, but the ground was dry, and there were no real cases of fever in the expedition. Of an afternoon, when the sun was sinking, I was in the habit of having my horse saddled, and making excursions into the wide and wonderful steppe. I would gallop for two or three miles towards the west, to a hill, from which the eye could range far to the dark mountains behind which our destiny would have to be fulfilled. When evening drew on, and the moon shone down upon the dreamy landscape, I was accustomed to sit in front of my tent, and listen to the rushing of the Tana, bringing down mysterious tidings of the countries beyond the mountains. A deep peace and sweet repose lay spread over this region in such tropical nights. When Orion flames exactly over us, or the Southern Cross stands in the heavens, and the whole firmament glitters with the sparkling of the stars, the heart trembles with awe at the Eternal, and the Godhead is vividly brought before the soul. In face of the wonderful vicissitudes of this expedition, the heart, from a natural necessity, reverted more and more to this last source of comfort; and herein was the sublimity of these lonely hours.

That we might not altogether waste our time in idleness, I began already on September 29th the task of founding a German settlement on the island of Oda-Boru-Ruva. In the course of the next fortnight a neat little house arose on the opposite shore, thatched with straw and built of wood; it contained three rooms. A strong fence ran round the little building on three sides, and on the fourth, the river front, I had a landing-place made for the boats. This settlement, to which I had a shed for goods added, I called "Von der Heydt House." I had caused it to be erected especially with reference to the second column, whose arrival I expected, and in the hope of establishing a route for traffic from here to the Baringo, where I purposed founding a second station. My idea was to be able, from hence, to direct

New settlement. The Von der Heydt House.

VON DER HEYDT HOUSE.

the ivory traffic of the Massai territories to Germany, and to establish a rivalry with the English Mombassa route.

The English station, which still stood on the opposite side of the river, was in those days burnt by the Gallas, and I was powerless to prevent it. If the hopes I entertained while founding the Von der Heydt House have not been realised, at least the little settlement afforded me, during those October days of 1889, the full and pure enjoyment of labour as such. When the house was completed we made a little tablet, on which we inscribed in Roman characters the name, "Von der Heydt Haus, 1, 10, 1889," and we fastened the tablet to a pole on the left of the house. Herr

Completion of the house.

Borchert found both house and tablet in perfect preservation in December.

But fate refused to fix the pure impressions of peaceful industry upon our residence at Oda-Boru-Ruva. My relations with the Gallas, which were at first hearty enough, gradually began to cloud over. The burning of the English station (an act committed without my order) annoyed me, and I was put still more out of humour by the fact that when, on October 5th, I sent to the second English station for the articles of barter there, which I wanted to have deposited in security at my own place, these articles had vanished, and were already in the hands of the Gallas. Accordingly, on October 6th, I despatched a categorical request to Sultan Hugo for the restoration of these English articles of barter. He came to me personally, in a very friendly manner, and remained all the afternoon in my camp, explaining to me that he had not had the custody of the English wares, for that the Englishmen had confided the care of them to another Galla; and that altogether he did not believe there had been English goods left at the station at all. I was not in a position to test the truth of these assertions, but declared myself satisfied with Hugo's explanation. Meanwhile, however, another affair had been maturing, which led to strife and combat. The Suaheli slaves Mandutto and Yembamba had put themselves into communication with Hamiri, in the first instance, and through him with me, with the enquiry if, in case of their coming into my camp with their fellow-tribesmen, I should be willing to take them under my protection against the Gallas. After some negotiation, I declared that I would protect all those Galla slaves who could prove that they had neither been bought by the Gallas, nor had become prize of war, but had simply been stolen. Thereupon thirteen men had had themselves inscribed on my lists, being able to furnish the required proof. I informed the Sultan Hugo of this on October 6th, and he replied that I was lord of the Gallas, and could do as I thought right, but that his tribe would look upon such a proceeding on my part as a violent measure. Sultan Hugo had a very beautiful wife, of gipsy-like appearance, but no children. He hoped that I could give him a charm to remove this trouble, and this formed one of the subjects of our conversation. I promised to give him a final answer the next morning.

A fine moonlight night was ushered in by the evening of October 6th. I had been still sitting in front of my tent towards nine o'clock, and then I went to bed. Towards ten o'clock I was aroused by the sentry before my tent, who reported that Yembamba and Mandutto had appeared on the other side of Alarming reports. the Tana, with the news that the Gallas were holding a great stormy council, and had just determined to put the Suaheli slaves in chains, and to attack my camp that same night. I have from the beginning, throughout the whole expedition, where I considered a conflict as unavoidable, adopted the tactics of being the attacking party, so as to secure to myself the advantages of the initiative. I was much too weak in numbers to afford to practise concession in dealing with the warlike propensities of the proud tribes of Northern East Africa; and I am convinced that we should have all been lost men, if I had attempted such a yielding policy as would have strengthened the lust for combat in our opponents and weakened the courage of my own men. If the Gallas really attacked my camp on October 6th, in the night time, it was Difficult position. very probable that they would be beaten back. On the other hand, the task of resisting them would probably cost a great many more cartridges than an attack on my part; and, what was more important than all, the *morale* of my troops must suffer considerably, if they found that my position was not even strong enough to deter black men from attacking our camp. Therefore I made up my mind at once to bring the whole thing to an issue that very night.

I got up, ordered a short trumpet signal to be given, took ten soldiers and twenty-five porters with me, and without acquainting the sick Herr von Tiedemann, whom I supposed to be asleep, with my intention, I crossed to the opposite side of the Tana. For half an hour we marched towards the south-

Fight with the Gallas.

south-east upon the Sultan's kraal, in which the council was being held. When I look back upon the events of this night, I can see that the attitude I took up showed a great want of experience in these matters. Later, I should not have thought of doing what I did on October 6th, which was to advance with eight men of my main column, and with these first eight, among whom was not one of my Somali soldiers, to step, without ceremony, into an assembly of Gallas, who were excited by the liberal use of beer. But I did not yet believe in an impending battle; I thought that I should succeed in overawing the people by my appearance, and in adjusting the points in dispute between us by a consultation. So I entered the Galla kraal, from which hoarse cries had reached me from afar, and called twice aloud to the assembly, "Amani, amani!"("Peace, peace!") But I had considerably over-estimated the effect of my appearance. The answer to my coming was, that a Galla warrior hurled his lance at my head, grazing my ear, while a second made a thrust at my chest, which attack I only escaped by Hamiri's dragging me on one side, whereby I fell on the ground, and struck my head against the barrel of his gun. I pulled out my revolver to shoot the Galla down, but unhappily my revolver cartridges missed fire, and I had to seize my rifle to defend myself. For a moment the position was critical; but after we had fired on the whole about six volleys, by which the Sultan and seven of his chief men were laid low, the matter was decided within three minutes, and the whole tribe was scattered abroad. The Gallas were so completely frightened, that some of them fled as far as the coast, and there spread the report that I had fallen; by which means Europe for several months stood under the impression that our expedition had been wrecked by the Tana, and that I myself was dead.

Decisive measures against the Gallas.

Defiance of Galla warriors.

Sudden discomfiture of the Gallas.

When the fight was over I felt, indeed, the proud intoxication of the victor, but also a great disturbance of the nerves at the thought of the first shedding of human blood. But there was no time for such reflections; circumstances urged us to action. I at once perceived that it would be of the greatest importance for the safety of my expedition, if I could secure myself by a pledge against further enterprises of the Gallas. Accordingly I had all the women who were hidden in the kraal, twenty-three in number, brought out of their houses, to carry them with me into my camp. I also found some men, whom I likewise carried off as prisoners of war. I could not help perceiving, also, that it would probably be no longer possible to obtain grain from the Gallas by purchase, and so, the same night, I took possession of all the stores I could find, and on the following days I increased these by further boat-loads that I caused to be brought across to me. On the whole I succeeded in heaping up about eighty boat-loads of corn in my camp. Proud as Thusnelda,* the wife of Sultan Hugo marched back, with her companions in misfortune, into my camp, when towards one o'clock we left the island. From the Sultan's kraal I had marched at once into the slaves' village, and had here set free about thirty slaves, men, women, and children, and immediately taken them into my camp with all their property.

When I awoke on the morning of October 7th I stood face to face with quite a new condition of affairs. Now I was the true lord in these regions; "there was nothing that did not belong to me." But my situation, nevertheless, looked at in its true light, was a worse one than that of the day before; for how, without the Gallas, was I to find my way up the Tana river? How could I hope to regain communications with my second column if I lived in enmity with this race, who could always interrupt the communications between Massai and Oda-Boru-Ruva? How, in conclusion, could my plans, which I attached to the founding of the Van der Heydt House, be fulfilled, if the Gallas quitted the neighbourhood and it became converted into a desert, like that which bordered Oda-Boru-Ruva to the east and west?

---

* Thusnelda, in the history of the ancient Germans, was a heroic German woman, the wife of Hermann, or Arminius, the conqueror of the Roman general Varus, at the battle of the Teutoburg Forest, A.D. 9.—TR.

NEGOTIATIONS REOPENED WITH THE GALLAS.

Added to this, I had just received the news, on October 7th, that the Somalis had encamped by the river, between me and the coast, and, in a body five thousand strong, were cutting off the communication down stream. A few days before I had sent off a report to Germany and to Lieutenant-Captain Rust. On October 7th my messenger Abocca returned with the announcement that he had found it impossible to make his way through the Somalis. *The hostile Somalis.*

These considerations determined me to make the attempt to resume peaceful relations with the Gallas; accordingly, already on October 7th I dismissed the men I had captured, with a message that the Gallas might return, for I was willing to deliver up their wives to them. At the same time, I began that day to fortify my camp, by having strong palisades and an almost impenetrable thorn fence raised around it. Three gates gave access to the camp—one above and one below, close by the river, and the third at the back. A double post of sentries was established at these gates night and day, and the sentries were visited every night by me or by my worthy Hussein Fara. I may mention that it was my principle, in the further prosecution of the expedition, to consider the deep responsibility of guarding against chance surprises by hostile tribes. I knew that I owed it to my people to take care that a surprise, either by night, or on the march, or under any circumstances, should be a thing that could not happen to the German Emin Pasha Expedition, and that, whatever our fate might be, it was for me to secure to the expedition the possibility of fighting against destruction to the last. Therefore I determined to be bold in my general decisions, but in details to cultivate the greatest and most painful caution. Thus there was now introduced in the German Emin Pasha Expedition a guard system that has not, I think, been surpassed, up to the present time, in the history of African explorations. In the Massai lands, afterwards, eight posts were established, almost regularly every night, and the sentries were visited every hour. Before the posts I caused great fires to be lighted, that we might overlook *Fortifying the camp.* *Boldness and caution alike necessary.* *Outposts and watch-fires.*

The negotiations were this day conducted in the Von der Heydt House, and were accompanied by all the ceremonial of the Galla state. They were confirmed by the present of a sheep which Sadeh had brought with him. This sheep afterwards had a somewhat curious destination, half of it being made into invalid soup for one of the camels, a medicine which had been hit upon by those wise gentlemen, my Somalis. "Give him some soup, sir," said Hussein.

The treaty ratified.

During those days I wrote down a series of observations and notes concerning the Gallas, which I intended to send to Germany. I left this budget behind me at Oda-Boru-Ruva; but unfortunately it has not been delivered up to Herr Oskar Borchert. Probably the Gallas were afraid, and that with reason, that in my reports I had given information of my fight with them; and thus they preferred to suppress the whole packet. Thus it happened that in Germany they were for months without any news of me, as later reports, which I sent off for Germany from Hargazo and Murdoi, also did not get further than Oda-Boru-Ruva.

Missing reports.

I likewise resumed my excursions in the neighbourhood, during which I saw a mountain ridge gleaming to the north of Oda-Boru-Ruva; probably it represented the watershed between Juba and Tana. I have called these mountains Galla Mountains. But I especially devoted much pains to procuring information concerning the upper course of the Tana, as well from geographical interest as with reference to the further march of my expedition. The moment when we should resume our march was necessarily approaching. Week after week went by, and in vain did I look longingly down the river, waiting for my second column under Lieutenant-Captain Rust, or at least for a sign of life from that direction. The full moon came and waned, and no news reached me. The Somalis advanced to Oda Galla, about six miles off. Where was Lieutenant-Captain Rust, and what had become of my second column? Already on October 8th I had made the sacrifice of sending Hamiri with Muhamed, a Somali, down the river to re-establish the communications

Discovery of mountain ranges.

Waiting for Rust's column.

with Rust. Two weeks went by, and of them, too, there was no intelligence!

I was now obliged to look a very serious decision in the face. I did not possess any articles of barter for the Massai lands, with the exception of a load of iron wire and half a load of beads. Should I, setting at nought all African traditions, risk the march among the dangerous tribes of the west, or should I, under all the circumstances, wait at Oda-Boru-Ruva, at least until I heard news as to the fate of my second column? But this waiting consumed the collected supplies to no purpose, and depressed the spirits of my troop. Beyond this, every month of delay might jeopardise the fate of the undertaking in the Equatorial Province itself. I could not expect an answer to this question from without. The stars to which I gazed up enquiringly remained voiceless, and no token was vouchsafed to me by Providence; unless, indeed, I chose to interpret as such a jesting oracle I one evening set up on my own account. My expedition was still in possession of a herophon, into which I placed plates for playing different pieces of music. One evening I determined to seek for an omen in reference to the further fortunes of the expedition by means of this instrument. In the darkness I put in the first plate that came to hand, with the idea of taking the character of the piece that turned up, as a sign from Heaven. I could not help smiling when, all at once, the well-known march from Carmen rang out. I shall, however, be believed when I say that my decision was not actively influenced by this circumstance. But I certainly was now to march away.

Perplexities and dangers.

An appeal to fate.

The considerations that led me to this step, I have noted in the instructions which I left behind me at Oda-Boru-Ruva for Lieutenant-Captain Rust. This memorandum of instructions was as follows:—

"ODA-BORU-RUVA. FROM THE VON DER HEYDT HOUSE,
"*October* 20*th*, 1889.

"To LIEUTENANT-CAPTAIN RUST.

"For four weeks I have waited here in vain for you, or for any sign of life from you. This long delay of any kind of

intelligence, in spite of my repeated attempts, I can account for to myself in four ways:

"1. My letters may have been lost.

"2. Some deplorable physical accident may have happened to you personally.

"3. Your column may have been temporarily wrecked, by the running away of your boatmen.

Instructions for Lieutenant-Captain Rust.

"4. You may have been prevented from carrying out the commission entrusted to you by those machinations from behind from which we have already suffered so much.

"However this may be, in the absence of all intelligence, although as lately as the 8th instant I sent off Hamiri to you, my honour and my duty now compel me, with the small forces I have at my disposal, to undertake to push forward at once to Emin Pasha. If I did otherwise, I should expose the expedition to the danger of total wreck, being utterly unable to ascertain what has taken place in my rear. You will yourself be able to judge with what grave consideration I expose myself to this new *salto mortale*, thus marching away, without any articles of barter, for Massailand and the territories situated behind it. Nevertheless I have made up my mind to grasp at the last chance of success, which now lies entirely in prompt action, in view of the tolerably certain prospect of failure if I remain here longer; and I start from here to-morrow, with about ninety loads.

"My plan is, supposing I find a guide at Ukamba, to march past the Kenia direct to Kawirondo, by the Victoria Nyanza to Massala. If I do not find a guide, I must go to the Kitui of Count Teleki, to get from thence to the Baringo, and so onward to Massala. As I take guides from here, you will learn whither I have marched; which you can, moreover, at all times ascertain on any march you may undertake. From Massala I will travel along the northern shore of the Nyanza, to where the Nile flows out of the lake, and there set myself right as to whether the route is to be taken through Uganda, or if Uganda is to be skirted to the east. My next

Proposed route of Dr. Peters.

chief point would be Mruli, in Unjoro, from which it requires only a week to get to Emin Pasha. I reckon to Massala, not taking interruptions into account, five weeks, and from thence to Mruli two to three weeks. From the Kenia I shall perhaps go by the so-called Thomson route, which, according to his book, leads to Massala over Njemps in four to five weeks. I hope, however, to find Teleki's guides at Kitui.

"I now leave behind me the following instructions for you:—

"Make use of the relations I have established here with the Gallas. The first sultan whom I met here, Hugo, I considered, in consequence of his treachery, which threatened our camp, as an enemy, or at any rate as a lukewarm friend, and he fell, with seven Gallas, in a nocturnal fight against us. His first successor, Gollo, who behaved with considerable insolence towards us, and was called to order by me with some asperity at a public assembly of the people, and threatened with war, was deposed by his subjects. He must be kept in view as the so-called leader of a possible war party. The present sultan, Sadeh, was appointed with my sanction. He has made a treaty with me, in which he acknowledges me as lord of the Gallas, cedes territory to me, etc.; in return for which I secure to him life and property, so far as I come into question. He promises in the treaty especially to support our expedition. He has promised me by word of mouth, in the presence of witnesses, to provide porters for you to the Kenia. If he does not fulfil this, it is said that donkeys are to be had, three days' journey from here. The Wagalla are to help you to organise an expedition with donkeys to the Nyanza. *Policy to be adopted towards the Gallas.*

"This I commission you to do, if you are ready by December 15th, and can follow me. But if I should march over Kitui and the Baringo, I further commission you to establish stations in each of these places, and eventually to complete those I have founded. As guards, dependable people belonging to the place itself are always in the first place to be kept in view. At Massala you would hear further from me. *Measures to be taken by Rust.*

"If you consider the organising of a donkey expedition by December 15th of this year as impracticable, I request you to disband your column as quickly as possible, to provide the station here with articles of barter, and to leave Hamiri behind with a few Askaris. The rest of your column I request you to dispose of in Lamu or Zanzibar to the best possible advantage, for the benefit of the German Emin Pasha committee. I should relieve you of your responsibilities with regard to my expedition, without, however, shutting you out from our undertaking. Until the result is decided, I entrust you with the representation of our interests first at Lamu, then in Zanzibar, until you hear further concerning the fortunes of my column. Kindly suggest to the committee, if necessary, to summon you to Germany to make your report. In such case, I request you to order home Herr Borchert to Germany, regard being had to my obligations made under contract, and the commercial accounts being settled; for I have heard that his health has suffered. I request you to send a copy of these instructions, as soon as possible, by the quickest way to Europe, and likewise beg you to send the accompanying packet down river as soon as you can.

Discretion allowed to the Lieut.-Captain.

The report to Europe.

"With the best wishes for your prosperity, and for the completion of your commission,

"I remain, with friendly sentiments,

"Yours faithfully, and with esteem,

"CARL PETERS.

"P.S.—Let an attempt be made, moreover, to purchase ivory; and please take under your protection the station garden and the plantations that are to be laid out. Signed (C. P.)"

The decisive cast had now been made. On October 18th I had the articles of barter packed and marked anew; and on the 19th my whole column was employed in pounding maize, for I had ordered that each man should take with him a supply of meal for twenty-five days. The steppe which lay before us had, until now, completely resisted every attempt to penetrate through it. Two English expeditions before mine had been wrecked. In the maize flour I hoped to find the magic key that should open to me the portals of the desert. On the 18th there appeared, provided for me by the Gallas, eight guides, whom, for the sake of security, I immediately caused to be chained. On the afternoon of October 20th I once more visited the beautiful island of Oda-Boru-Ruva, which was still deserted by the Gallas, and sat for the last time, for a quarter of an hour, in my Von der Heydt House, the erection of which had afforded me so much pleasure. My frame of mind was grave, yet mingled with joyful emotion. The sinking sun that day again showed me the mysterious ridges of mountains in the west, which hid from me the world of the Massais. My resolution was taken; all preparations were made. We will try if we can succeed where the two English expeditions failed. Let us penetrate into the girdle of wilderness that guards the lands of the West, and let us see if the magic key we hold is able to unlock for us the gates of the territory of the Nile.

The decision to cross the steppe.

Hopes and anticipations.

CHAPTER VI.

ON THE UPPER TANA TO KIKUYU.

"To be, or not to be: that is the question."
SHAKESPEARE.

THE determination to advance, without the requisite articles of barter, from Oda-Boru-Ruva into the Massai lands, once for all decided the character the

DEPARTURE FROM ODA-BORU-RUVA.

German Emin Pasha Expedition was for the future to bear. It was plain that if I was not in a position to go forward in the Massai land, paying the usual tribute, I must expect to experience warlike opposition in that territory. I did not go away from Oda-Boru-Ruva with the intention of leading the expedition onward, in this sense. As a last resource, I thought at that time I could have still made use of the powder which I carried with me for Emin Pasha, as an article of barter in these lands. I also cherished the hope of meeting with Arab dealers at the Baringo or the Victoria Nyanza, from whom I could perhaps purchase articles of barter, paying by a cheque on Zanzibar. Nevertheless, when on the morning of October 21st I quitted the Oda-Boru-Ruva that had become so dear to me, it was with a feeling that our expedition was now gliding away from the tracks of the calculable into the region of the adventurous. The one thing that comforted me, under this impression, was the certain conviction, that the only way to carry out the task proposed was the one upon which I was that morning entering.

Exceptional character of the expedition.

The future incalculable.

The night before, I had sent an order to the Gallas to provide four great boats for me, to convey corn up the river. As these boats had not yet appeared at six o'clock next morning, I was compelled to send my column forward towards Galamba, and to wait with a few Somali soldiers. I had received about twenty slave-women, with their children, into my camp, and at the last moment I resolved to send these also by boat up the Tana. Towards seven o'clock the Gallas arrived with the four boats I had ordered, and I could then follow my column on horseback to Galamba. How right it was to have sent grain up in boats, was not fully shown till a week afterwards, when I found that my people had already, in the first days, either eaten up or thrown away the grain served out to them, that was to have lasted them for twenty-five days. By means of these four boat-loads of maize I had it once more put into my power, at Hargazo, to provision my column for several days. And this was partly

Delays of the Gallas.

Necessity of providing grain.

the reason why we did not experience the fate of the English expeditions, in the steppes into which we had now advanced.

The impressions of the first day's march from Oda-Boru-Ruva up the Tana were for me very depressing. Though I had put most of the slave-women, with their children, into the boats, a few had preferred to march with their husbands. As I rode onward, in the rear of my expedition, I found these new elements lying, some here, others there, by the wayside, and was repeatedly compelled to adopt measures of punishment, to maintain the old order of march. At this first march, I at once recognised the fact that it would not be possible to carry on the German Emin Pasha Expedition further, with the wives and children of the newly-enlisted Gallas, and consequently I made my decision on the evening of that day, at Galamba. This place lies opposite the point in the river where the island of Oda-Boru-Ruva terminates. Wapokomo and Gallas live here together, and by the latter we were welcomed in a friendly manner, immediately upon my arrival.

Inveterate stragglers.

Galamba.

From Galamba onward I began, so to speak, to hunt for the " Kiloluma," which was marked on the maps of that day as a tributary of the Tana. For this purpose I made a boat excursion up the Tana this afternoon, whereby I ascertained that here at least no Kiloluma existed ; and, by enquiries I made, I conceived a suspicion that no tributary of the kind flows into the Tana. When I returned to my camp from this excursion, in the evening, I found all my people employed pulling fish out of the river. Behind Oda-Boru-Ruva the Tana begins to be very full of fish ; a circumstance by which my column learned to profit more and more.

Supply of fish in the Tana.

This day was not fated, however, to close amid such cheerful impressions. At seven o'clock I caused the slaves of the Gallas who accompanied me to assemble for a consultation, and represented to them that it would be quite impossible to carry their wives and children with me into the interior of Africa. They had all seen to-day, I said, how wearisome such a march was, and yet to-day we had only had half or a quarter of a day's

SLAVE WOMEN AND CHILDREN SENT BACK. 155

marching. We were as yet still in countries where we could journey onward in peace. But it would be certain destruction to women and children, when once we should have got into the territory of the Massais. I was very sorry for it, but I must put it to them, whether they would betake themselves, with their families, back to the Gallas, who were friendly to us now; or, as an alternative, I should be willing to send the latter under an escort, this very evening, in some of my boats down the Tana to Ngao. At that place there was a station of Germans, to whom I would write that they were to give the needy people a kind welcome; and this they would certainly do, as they had come to help the black people. The slaves declared that they were prepared to die, all of them, with wives and children, sooner than let their families fall once more into the hands of the Gallas. They could see plainly that they would probably lose many of their people in the interior, if they went with me; therefore they accepted, with great joy, my proposal to send the women and children to Ngao, until the expedition was finished. Yembamba and another old slave should accompany them, and the others would go forward with me, to return to their wives and children within a year. I immediately had two large boats unloaded, and placed at the disposal of the Gallas. *Decision concerning the women and children.* *Good sense of the men.*

It was urgently necessary that they should pass by Oda-Boru-Ruva that very night, because it was to be feared that by daylight the Gallas would pursue the boats, and get them into their possession. Accordingly, I urged an immediate departure. During the next half-hour a very touching and heart-rending scene was enacted. Men were taking farewell of their little ones, who cried and wept aloud. Women packed their things into the boats, and my Somalis cursed at the whole affair, which gave them so much work in the hours of night. The boats rode deep in the water, when, towards nine o'clock, all was ready for departure. I urged the necessity of rowing quickly down the river; and if my exhortation had been attended to by Yembamba, there is no doubt that, in the deep darkness that reigned around, they would *Parting scenes.* *The fugitives on the river.*

have got past Oda-Boru-Ruva unperceived. I felt quite easy in my mind as to the fate of the column, when towards eleven o'clock the Galla Sultan Sadeh, and his brother Parisa, appeared in a most innocent manner in my camp, to pass the night with us. I naturally assumed that they had not seen the fugitives making their way down the river, or else that their fear of us was still sufficiently strong to protect the latter in their retreat.

Concerning the fate of the party I was first enlightened three days afterwards, when Yembamba rejoined us, bleeding and half-starved. The boats had, it appeared, run on a sand-bank in the dark night, and could not be floated off until towards the morning. They had then been chased by the Gallas, and after Yembamba had killed three of the pursuers, all the fugitives had fallen once more into the hands of their mortal enemies. Yembamba had escaped to the right bank by swimming; and from thence, pursued by the Gallas, he had made his way back to my column.

Yembamba's doleful re-appearance and narrative.

It was one of the cruel necessities to which I was exposed during this expedition, that it was not permitted me to turn back once more, to release those women and children from the hands of the Gallas. With a heavy heart I was compelled to pursue my march towards the west, where greater questions were awaiting settlement.

From Galamba upwards, the Tana presents an uninterrupted succession of island formations. About forty-six miles above Oda-Boru-Ruva its upper course changes to its middle course. Flowing onward through a rocky bed thus far, it enters the sandy steppe at Hargazo, and in the varying height of the water new channels of streams continually are produced, and corresponding formations of islands. At intervals are expanses in the form of lakes, so that the river reminds one vividly of the Havel between Potsdam and Spandau. All these islands, whose uniform character was first noticed by us, I afterwards entered in the map under the common appellation of the Von der Heydt Islands. The shores are here clothed with a

Course of the Tana.

thick fringe of forest, which, seen from the river, appears in parts like a hanging wood. The islands rise, dark green in colour, from the bright surface of the water, so that boat excursions here on the Tana, of which I undertook several, offer unusual charms of landscape. On the left bank are still found some Wapokomo settlements, which extend as far as Hameje. The right side of the river, along which we marched, is already a completely desert steppe, unpeopled by the wars of centuries between Gallas and Wakamba, *The islands in the river.*

THE VON DER HEYDT ISLANDS.

who extend their predatory raids as far as this region, and whose camping-places we had an opportunity of observing, already in the first days of our march, behind Galamba.

The river deviates here more and more from its northwestern course to a western direction, but from Hargazo begins to turn back towards the south-west. The names entered upon the map, such as Gakashamorra, Iposa, Galangogessa, Hameje, and so on, do not signify towns, but only places by the river. I conjecture that they were once Galla settlements. The forest on the margin is here unusually broad, and the openings to the river can hardly be descried, *Settlements on the Tana.*

so that my messengers whom I had sent up the stream a fe[w] weeks before from Oda-Boru-Ruva had almost perished fro[m] exhaustion. We had, however, three efficient Gallas as guide[s] under the leadership of Parisa, the brother of Sultan Sade[l.] Thus, by a five days' march through the steppe, we arrived safe[l] at glorious Hameje, where, with its luxuriant island and lake-like expansions, surrounded by magnificen[t] hanging woods, alive with all kinds of game animal[s] and fowl, the stream assumes an altogether imposing appea[r]-ance. Hameje represents a ford to the water, and forms on[e] of the broad dry arms of the stream, where tracks of wil[d] animals lead to the water. As had been often the case befor[e] in the night we heard the roaring of lions immediately i[n] front of our tents, and Herr von Tiedemann was even oblige[d] to vacate his tent in rather quick time, because one of thes[e] amiable guests, moved probably by a kind of curiosity, fe[lt] himself impelled to bring his head a little too near the ten[t.] Tiedemann struck at him several times with th[e] revolver, whereupon both parties took a most summar[y] leave of each other—one betaking himself into the forest, th[e] other to the camp-fires of the Somalis. The next mornin[g] when we started I enjoyed the still more original spectacle of [a] lion stretched out, in broad daylight, close by our line of march[.] I was unfortunately on horseback, and had given my rifle to [my] servant to carry, so that our meeting was to a certain exten[t] only a platonic one; though the lion did not seem at all in [a] hurry to get up, but measured me for a tolerably long tim[e] with his eyes, before he slowly betook himself into the forest.

On the afternoon of October 25th I made a boating excur-sion of several hours up the Tana, still searching fo[r] the Kiloluma; the non-existence of which river, as fa[r] as Hameje, I had already proved by the boats I sent up. Thi[s] day I navigated along the northern bank of the Tana, till clos[e] to Hargazo, without seeing any stream running into it from th[e] north. Next morning I caused my boats to follow me t[o] Hargazo, and the boatmen corroborated the fact that there wa[s] no river-mouth on the north as far as that place.

The Hofmann Falls.

A bright halo encircles that day at Hameje in the memory of us all. Here for the first time the mountain chains in the west came clearly into view. My people revelled in the enjoyment of the supplies that were brought to us here in the boats, and tumbled about merrily in the broad shallow river, after the six days' marching through the scorched steppe. We all imagined we had the Kenia before us, and fancied ourselves a month and a half nearer to the goal of our journey than we were in reality. In the most cheerful of spirits we marched next morning upon Hargazo.

Reminiscences of Hameje.

The surface of the country here for the first time begins to lose the character of a steppe, and to assume a more undulating form. The character of the bush flora becomes more luxuriant. In cool valleys a fresher wealth of grass and a richer store of flowers appear. Many-coloured butterflies hover above the glittering array of blossoms, and the granitic ground gives indication that we are very near the mountains. At Hargazo, where we arrived at eleven in the morning, the Tana again spreads out in a lake-like form; and here it seemed to be at last, the fork of the river that we had been seeking so long. The Tana here falls from its upper into its middle course, in a series of rapids and a cataract of about 20 to 22 feet in height. To this fall I at once betook myself, by boat, with my servant Rukua and a few Wapokomo. "Kiloluma!" cried the Wapokomo when they saw it. To the left of the fall a broad arm bends away in a south-west direction. Towards the north-west the Kiloluma falls down. There it was at last, as it seemed! Full of joyful emotion, I had myself rowed close under the fall, whose refreshing spray I enjoyed to the utmost. I climbed up the rock on the left, from which it poured down, and thus ascertained its height with tolerable accuracy. In honour of the President of the German Emin Pasha committee, Minister of State von Hofmann, I named it "Hofmann Falls," and then I immediately returned down river to the camp, to impart my discovery to Herr von Tiedemann, and to

Richness of the country.

Cataracts of the Tana.

Hofmann Falls.

note it down at once. On that morning I did not yet know that "Kiloluma" is merely the Ukamba word for a rushing stream or waterfall, and that the whole Upper Tana is known by this name among the Wakamba.

That the fork of the river I had seen in the morning had nothing to do with a second river coming from the north, but was simply a dividing of the Tana itself into two arms, I was able to verify as early as the afternoon of October 26th.

Branches of the Tana. On that afternoon I determined to follow up my discovery of the morning, and therefore directed Herr von Tiedemann to proceed with two boats up the left arm of the river, while I myself, with a company of people, followed the course of the stream on the same side by land. Something more than a mile above the place where the river separates into branches below the fall, I came upon the boats, which had stuck fast in the rapids of the southern arm. To my astonishment I could perceive, from the high river bank, that these *The rapids.* rapids in the southern arm rush down somewhat above a branching of the stream towards the north, so that we had manifestly an island formation before us. Could the upper arm of the river perhaps be identical with the current that I had seen from below in the morning, and which throws itself into the Hofmann Falls? This trace must be followed up.

Accordingly, I had a boat brought over to me,—which was done with great difficulty,—embarked upon it with Herr von Tiedemann, a Somali, and two Wapokomo, and then had it taken into the northern arm of the river. Along this we drove down for some distance, and then went on shore to the north, to get a general survey of the surrounding country. On the *Tiedemann's Hill.* proposal of Herr von Tiedemann we ascended a hill to the north of the Tana, which I have called, after him, Tiedemann Hill. From this point we had the view we wanted. There, to the west, in front of the setting sun, rose an important chain of mountains, losing itself in unlimited distance towards the north. Those were the mountains which we had already seen, under peculiarly favourable conditions of light, from Oda-Boru-Ruva,—the chain which here met our view,

VIEW ON THE EMPEROR WILLIAM II. MOUNTAINS.

and which, following the old maps, we had always considered as connected at least with the Kenia mountain system. Especially magnificent rose, to the north-west of where we stood, a mountain peak, whose summit had something of the form of a round half-overturned garden table. Behind the first chain, peak after peak reared its head. We stood, strongly interested, opposite an entire region of mountains, which the eye of no white man had yet beheld. In the glowing evening sky the outlines of the mountains stood forth with especially picturesque distinctness. It was the first time the German Emin Pasha Expedition stood in view of a magnificent formation of land; and mindful of the powerful bond which, here in the far-distant land, united us two Germans the more closely with our German home, I christened these mountains the "Emperor William II. Mountains," and called the most prominent peak, towering before us, the "Hohenzollern Peak."

Mountain chains of the Tana.

The "Embond peror William II. Mountains."

The sun sank in the west, and, willingly or unwillingly, we were obliged to tear ourselves from the sight before us, for fear of losing our way to the boat and the camp, in the rapidly-approaching darkness. With some difficulty we succeeded in getting back to the boat; and now, in the grey twilight, we drove down the current of the northern Tana into the rapids, that rolled more and more wildly. The little boat flew hissing through the foam of the rushing river. The people had to be continually baling out the water that poured in over the gunwales to keep the boat from sinking. At times there was a danger of its being shattered on a pointed rock; sometimes of its capsizing in a hissing whirlpool. It was a nerve-bracing passage, lasting about half an hour, when suddenly we heard the roaring of the cataract in front of us. At first our boatmen had launched with reluctance and fear into the foaming rapids; but gradually they had gained courage, probably imagining that we possessed a charm against capsizing, and now they were for boldly rowing down the Hofmann Fall itself, which is from 20 to 24 feet high. With the greatest difficulty we managed to bring the

An adventurous boat voyage.

Danger to the boat.

have got past Oda-Boru-Ruva unperceived. I felt quite easy in my mind as to the fate of the column, when towards eleven o'clock the Galla Sultan Sadeh, and his brother Parisa, appeared in a most innocent manner in my camp, to pass the night with us. I naturally assumed that they had not seen the fugitives making their way down the river, or else that their fear of us was still sufficiently strong to protect the latter in their retreat.

Concerning the fate of the party I was first enlightened three days afterwards, when Yembamba rejoined us, bleeding and half-starved. The boats had, it appeared, run on a sand-bank in the dark night, and could not be floated off until towards the morning. They had then been chased by the Gallas, and after Yembamba had killed three of the pursuers, all the fugitives had fallen once more into the hands of their mortal enemies. Yembamba had escaped to the right bank by swimming; and from thence, pursued by the Gallas, he had made his way back to my column.

Yembamba's doleful re-appearance and narrative.

It was one of the cruel necessities to which I was exposed during this expedition, that it was not permitted me to turn back once more, to release those women and children from the hands of the Gallas. With a heavy heart I was compelled to pursue my march towards the west, where greater questions were awaiting settlement.

From Galamba upwards, the Tana presents an uninterrupted succession of island formations. About forty-six miles above Oda-Boru-Ruva its upper course changes to its middle course. Flowing onward through a rocky bed thus far, it enters the sandy steppe at Hargazo, and in the varying height of the water new channels of streams continually are produced, and corresponding formations of islands. At intervals are expanses in the form of lakes, so that the river reminds one vividly of the Havel between Potsdam and Spandau. All these islands, whose uniform character was first noticed by us, I afterwards entered in the map under the common appellation of the Von der Heydt Islands. The shores are here clothed with a

Course of the Tana.

THE COURSE OF THE TANA. 157

thick fringe of forest, which, seen from the river, appears in parts like a hanging wood. The islands rise, dark green in colour, from the bright surface of the water, so that boat excursions here on the Tana, of which I undertook several, offer unusual charms of landscape. On the left bank are still found some Wapokomo settlements, which extend as far as Hameje. The right side of the river, along which we marched, is already a completely desert steppe, unpeopled by the wars of centuries between Gallas and Wakamba, <small>The islands in the river.</small>

THE VON DER HEYDT ISLANDS.

who extend their predatory raids as far as this region, and whose camping-places we had an opportunity of observing, already in the first days of our march, behind Galamba.

The river deviates here more and more from its north-western course to a western direction, but from Hargazo begins to turn back towards the south-west. The names entered upon the map, such as Gakashamorra, Iposa, Galangogessa, Hameje, and so on, do not signify towns, but only places by the river. I conjecture that they were once Galla settlements. The forest on the margin is here unusually broad, and the openings to the river can hardly be descried, <small>Settlements on the Tana.</small>

so that my messengers whom I had sent up the stream a few weeks before from Oda-Boru-Ruva had almost perished from exhaustion. We had, however, three efficient Gallas as guides, under the leadership of Parisa, the brother of Sultan Sadeh. Thus, by a five days' march through the steppe, we arrived safely at glorious Hameje, where, with its luxuriant islands and lake-like expansions, surrounded by magnificent hanging woods, alive with all kinds of game animals and fowl, the stream assumes an altogether imposing appearance. Hameje represents a ford to the water, and forms one of the broad dry arms of the stream, where tracks of wild animals lead to the water. As had been often the case before, in the night we heard the roaring of lions immediately in front of our tents, and Herr von Tiedemann was even obliged to vacate his tent in rather quick time, because one of these amiable guests, moved probably by a kind of curiosity, felt himself impelled to bring his head a little too near the tent. Tiedemann struck at him several times with the revolver, whereupon both parties took a most summary leave of each other—one betaking himself into the forest, the other to the camp-fires of the Somalis. The next morning when we started I enjoyed the still more original spectacle of a lion stretched out, in broad daylight, close by our line of march. I was unfortunately on horseback, and had given my rifle to a servant to carry, so that our meeting was to a certain extent only a platonic one; though the lion did not seem at all in a hurry to get up, but measured me for a tolerably long time with his eyes, before he slowly betook himself into the forest.

On the afternoon of October 25th I made a boating excursion of several hours up the Tana, still searching for the Kiloluma; the non-existence of which river, as far as Hameje, I had already proved by the boats I sent up. This day I navigated along the northern bank of the Tana, till close to Hargazo, without seeing any stream running into it from the north. Next morning I caused my boats to follow me to Hargazo, and the boatmen corroborated the fact that there was no river-mouth on the north as far as that place.

THE HOFMANN FALLS.

A bright halo encircles that day at Hameje in the memory of us all. Here for the first time the mountain chains in the west came clearly into view. My people revelled in the enjoyment of the supplies that were brought to us here in the boats, and tumbled about merrily in the broad shallow river, after the six days' marching through the scorched steppe. We all imagined we had the Kenia before us, and fancied ourselves a month and a half nearer to the goal of our journey than we were in reality. In the most cheerful of spirits we marched next morning upon Hargazo. *Reminiscences of Hameje.*

The surface of the country here for the first time begins to lose the character of a steppe, and to assume a more undulating form. The character of the bush flora becomes more luxuriant. In cool valleys a fresher wealth of grass and a richer store of flowers appear. Many-coloured butterflies hover above the glittering array of blossoms, and the granitic ground gives indication that we are very near the mountains. *Richness of the country.* At Hargazo, where we arrived at eleven in the morning, the Tana again spreads out in a lake-like form; and here it seemed to be at last, the fork of the river that we had been seeking so long. The Tana here falls from its upper into its middle course, in a series of rapids and a cataract of about 20 to 22 feet in height. To this fall I at once betook myself, by boat, with my servant Rukua and a few Wapokomo. "Kiloluma!" cried the Wapokomo when they saw it. To the left of the fall a broad arm bends away in a south-west direction. *Cataracts of the Tana.* Towards the north-west the Kiloluma falls down. There it was at last, as it seemed! Full of joyful emotion, I had myself rowed close under the fall, whose refreshing spray I enjoyed to the utmost. I climbed up the rock on the left, from which it poured down, and thus ascertained its height with tolerable accuracy. In honour of the President of the German Emin Pasha committee, Minister of State von Hofmann, I named it "Hofmann Falls," and then I immediately returned down river to the camp, to impart my discovery to Herr von Tiedemann, and to *Hofmann Falls.*

note it down at once. On that morning I did not yet know that "Kiloluma" is merely the Ukamba word for a rushing stream or waterfall, and that the whole Upper Tana is known by this name among the Wakamba.

That the fork of the river I had seen in the morning had nothing to do with a second river coming from the north, but was simply a dividing of the Tana itself into two arms, I was able to verify as early as the afternoon of October 26th. On that afternoon I determined to follow up my discovery of the morning, and therefore directed Herr von Tiedemann to proceed with two boats up the left arm of the river, while I myself, with a company of people, followed the course of the stream on the same side by land. Something more than a mile above the place where the river separates into branches below the fall, I came upon the boats, which had stuck fast in the rapids of the southern arm. To my astonishment I could perceive, from the high river bank, that these rapids in the southern arm rush down somewhat above a branching of the stream towards the north, so that we had manifestly an island formation before us. Could the upper arm of the river perhaps be identical with the current that I had seen from below in the morning, and which throws itself into the Hofmann Falls? This trace must be followed up.

Branches of the Tana.

The rapids.

Accordingly, I had a boat brought over to me,—which was done with great difficulty,—embarked upon it with Herr von Tiedemann, a Somali, and two Wapokomo, and then had it taken into the northern arm of the river. Along this we drove down for some distance, and then went on shore to the north, to get a general survey of the surrounding country. On the proposal of Herr von Tiedemann we ascended a hill to the north of the Tana, which I have called, after him, Tiedemann Hill. From this point we had the view we wanted. There, to the west, in front of the setting sun, rose an important chain of mountains, losing itself in unlimited distance towards the north. Those were the mountains which we had already seen, under peculiarly favourable conditions of light, from Oda-Boru-Ruva,—the chain which here met our view,

Tiedemann's Hill.

VIEW ON THE EMPEROR WILLIAM II. MOUNTAINS.

and which, following the old maps, we had always considered as connected at least with the Kenia mountain system. Especially magnificent rose, to the north-west of where we stood, a mountain peak, whose summit had something of the form of a round half-overturned garden table. Behind the first chain, peak after peak reared its head. We stood, strongly interested, opposite an entire region of mountains, which the eye of no white man had yet beheld. In the glowing evening sky the outlines of the mountains stood forth with especially picturesque distinctness. It was the first time the German Emin Pasha Expedition stood in view of a magnificent formation of land; and mindful of the powerful bond which, here in the far-distant land, united us two Germans the more closely with our German home, I christened these mountains the "Emperor William II. Mountains," and called the most prominent peak, towering before us, the "Hohenzollern Peak."

Mountain chains of the Tana.

The "Emperor William II. Mountains."

The sun sank in the west, and, willingly or unwillingly, we were obliged to tear ourselves from the sight before us, for fear of losing our way to the boat and the camp, in the rapidly-approaching darkness. With some difficulty we succeeded in getting back to the boat; and now, in the grey twilight, we drove down the current of the northern Tana into the rapids, that rolled more and more wildly. The little boat flew hissing through the foam of the rushing river. The people had to be continually baling out the water that poured in over the gunwales to keep the boat from sinking. At times there was a danger of its being shattered on a pointed rock; sometimes of its capsizing in a hissing whirlpool. It was a nerve-bracing passage, lasting about half an hour, when suddenly we heard the roaring of the cataract in front of us. At first our boatmen had launched with reluctance and fear into the foaming rapids; but gradually they had gained courage, probably imagining that we possessed a charm against capsizing, and now they were for boldly rowing down the Hofmann Fall itself, which is from 20 to 24 feet high. With the greatest difficulty we managed to bring the

An adventurous boat voyage.

Danger to the boat.

11

boat up, at the last moment, on the right bank, where it was drawn ashore, and carried down to a point below the falls. We were, in truth, below the Hofmann Fall that I had discovered that morning; and thus the fact was confirmed, that in this "Kiloluma" there was no question of a tributary from the north, but simply of a fork of the river; and that consequently the land in the south is merely an island, which I have named Hofmann Island. I was able still further to establish this *Geographical results.* when, on our passage back to the camp, we again passed the forked point to the south-west that I had seen in the morning. Thus on October 26th, 1889, a very noticeable negative result was gained for the geography of the Upper Tana; and in consequence we returned in a very jubilant frame of mind into the camp, where on the same evening I wrote a report of the morning's and afternoon's observations for transmission to the German Emin Pasha committee at home.

My Galla guides were desirous of returning to their country that very evening, according to the terms of their agreement, *The Galla guides.* made in Oda-Boru-Ruva. I ordered two of them, however, to accompany me further up the river, until I should succeed in procuring fresh guides. I sent one of the Gallas, with a few Wapokomo, during the night, to their people, to satisfy the latter concerning the fate of their fellow-countrymen who were with us. Thus with fresh courage, on October 27th, we resumed our wandering towards the unknown west.

As I was entirely uninstructed in the geography of these countries, I determined to make an attempt to get my boats *Krapf's conjectures concerning the Tana.* farther up the Tana. Krapf had, in his time, expressed his opinion, from Ukamba Kitui, that the Tana might be navigable down to its mouth. I resolved, in summary fashion, to established the correctness or error of Krapf's conjecture. The very first day brought the proof that his hypothesis was utterly untenable; which is not at all surprising, when the fact is taken into account that the level of the land at Hargazo is about 1,000 feet above that of the sea, and that after the first day's march of about nine miles we had already reached a level of 1,500 feet. In consequence

NATURE OF THE UPPER TANA COUNTRY.

of this scale of ascent from Hargazo, which is uninterruptedly maintained up to the source of the Tana, the stream from this point presents a series of cataracts and rapids, which in several instances exhibit themselves on a magnificent scale. The descent from this part is through a series of terraces, and these terraces slope generally in an abrupt form towards the east. To the traveller coming from the east, a terrace ridge of this kind appears, from the distance, as a sharply-defined mountain ridge. After ascending it, he finds himself in a flat steppe, like that of the lower and middle Tana, and sees towering on the horizon a new mountain range, which afterwards, in its turn, proves to be the ridge of a terrace. *Nature of its course.*

Thus it goes on uninterruptedly as far as Kikuyu and the Leikipeia plateau, where we have before us, at an elevation of 7,000 feet, the culmination of this grand elevated plateau formation, which on the other side slightly declines again towards the Victoria Nyanza. This general swelling upward of the great mass of land surface evidently shows a peculiar formation, the centre of which is the volcanic hearth of the Baringo territory, and on which the conical peaks of the Kenia, the Subugula Poron, the Tchibcharagnani, and the Elgon, all similar in character, are superimposed. These four, in tolerably regular declivities, surround Lake Baringo, which is manifestly nothing more than an extinct crater. The great mass of this elevated plateau is divided in the midst by a tremendous rift, in which, among others, are situated Lake Nairwasha and Lake Baringo, besides a series of smaller lakes. I shall have to return to this peculiar formation. It will suffice here to remark that the ascent continues uninterruptedly from Hargazo, and that, accordingly, from this place the Tana takes the form of a Kiloluma, or noisy river, and therefore there can be no question about its being unnavigable. *The great elevated plateau. Volcanic nature of the region.*

Our camping-ground on October 27th was at a place called by the Gallas Jibije. Here the line of hills of the Emperor William's chain crosses the Tana, and they appear as very extraordinary rocky formations. One of these peaks, 2,000 feet high, I ascended in the afternoon with Herr von Tiedemann; and we had once more the full view over the Emperor William II. Mountains; and in the north-east we again saw the line of the Galla mountains displayed.

Jibije and the mountain range.

My people had not been able to bring the boats up to Jibije; and if, on that evening, I attributed the non-arrival of those vessels to want of energy in my followers, I was able on

THE "DEVIL'S FIELD."

the following day to convince myself, by the witness of my own eyes, of the complete impossibility of navigating the Tana. For on this day the stream poured itself along over rough grey boulders, which reminded me vividly of some parts below the Brocken, and which I was inclined to insert in my map as "Devil's Field." The river here merges into a series of raging torrents. All is lost in a grey foam, and there is nothing like a regular stream. But directly we have ascended the terrace, we have suddenly before us once

The Tana not navigable.

more the quiet Tana river, standing out darkly in the shadow of the forest trees. From this point the Tana receives a number of small tributary streams coming from the north, from the mountains. Along the stream, growing higher with each day's journey, rises a chain of mountains, forming, perhaps, the southern slope of the Emperor William Mountains, and which I have named Bennigsen Chain.

To the south of the Tana we here arrive in a land which till then was not marked on the maps,—Murdoi. About fourteen miles beyond Hargazo this little country begins; I have not been able to determine its extension towards the south. Here the Massai tribe of the Wandorobbo ranges with its herds through the steppe, which, so far as I know, here alone rejoices in independence of the real Massais. Between Wakamba and Gallas they roam over the country with their great herds of oxen, sheep, goats, and asses, exhausting one pasturage after another. Like the Somalis below Oda-Boru-Ruva, they likewise were compelled in the year 1889, through the drought in the back districts, to keep, with their herds, near the Tana;—a piece of great good fortune for the German Emin Pasha Expedition. For some distance beyond Hargazo we had still come upon traces of Pigott's expedition. But suddenly these traces of encampment had ceased, and we had been able to ascertain that the expedition had turned off towards the south. It had been compelled to this by want of provisions. This fate we should scarcely have experienced, as we still had some stores in hand, and I should in no case have marched upon Mombas, but under all circumstances should have tried to work my way through to Ukamba Momoni, from thence to Ukamba Kitui, and so to the Baringo. Still the situation already began to be very embarrassing, as my people now only carried with them a portion of the provisions that had been given them. Consequently I felt a most lively interest in the footsteps which we discerned for the first time on October 28th.

The Wan-dorobbo tribe.

Traces of Pigott's expedition.

Projected route.

On the following day, when, to ascertain the way, I was marching with the Gallas and a few Somalis in front of the expedition, we suddenly saw female footsteps of the preceding day, which led to a river ford. I now at once resolved to make an end of the uncertainty I felt, through the lack of all information concerning the countries in front of us. If women had come to the river the day before, their tribe must be in the immediate neighbourhood, for it would hardly have allowed its most valuable possession, which was represented by the women, to wander to any distance. Accordingly, it might be assumed that the tribe, of whatever race it might form a part, to which these female footsteps belonged, must dwell in the immediate neighbourhood of the river ford. This could also be conjectured from the many foot tracks of sheep and oxen which covered the whole ford. Now these tribes used to drive their herds to the water at noon. It was now eleven o'clock. I determined, consequently, to let Herr von Tiedemann and the column pass by, and to commission them to choose a suitable camping-place, but myself to remain in ambush, with a few soldiers and able-bodied Mangemas, around the ford, to establish relations in this manner with the natives. My people hid themselves in the thicket, and I seated myself, well hidden, on a block of stone in the river ford itself. We had hardly been there half an hour, after the departure and marching past of the expedition, when suddenly the lively chattering of girls was heard from the south. There were eleven girls, more or less young, coming towards the Tana with water-pitchers. Suddenly they were challenged, and great was their astonishment when they saw me, an apparition such as they had never seen, rising out of the bed of the river. With the help of the Gallas I succeeded in ascertaining that they belonged to the Wandorobbo tribe. Strangely enough, they looked upon me with far more astonishment and curiosity than fear, and made no sort of resistance when I made them understand that they must follow me into my camp. That is the right of war in these lands; and the women know that, in surprises of this kind, they run no peril of their lives.

I informed them that I should let them go immediately, if their tribe, which for some days had kept timidly aloof from

A BRUSH WITH WAKAMBA WARRIORS. 167

us, would consent to communicate with me, for the sale of food and the supplying of guides. After about an hour's march I came upon our camp, and at once sent away two of the girls with presents, to carry my proposals of peace to the Wandorobbo. *Embassy to the Wandorobbo.*

While they were away, fate decreed that the want of guides, at least, should be supplied in a different manner. Suddenly three new figures appeared in my camp—three young men of lofty stature, completely naked, with only a piece of stuff wound round the neck and hanging on the back, and each man with a sort of travelling bag bound round his forehead with a string. I requested them to draw near, which they readily did. But so soon as they saw my Gallas, they jumped up suddenly with long leaps, and wanted to take to flight. I caused my Somalis to prevent them from doing this, and had the three secured, for safety. They were Wakamba warriors, from the Mumoni mountains, and had gone out on a foraging expedition after female slaves. They knew the lands before us very accurately, and I informed them, in all friendship, that they were to have the kindness to show us the way to Ukamba, where I would dismiss them with presents. They had wanted to go slave-catching, and were not at all agreeably surprised at having fallen into the toils themselves. I was still pacifying them on this subject, when suddenly war cries and the rattle of musketry were heard from the direction where a portion of my Somalis had encamped with the camels. The Wandorobbo, instead of entering into friendly negotiations with me, had preferred at once to attack my camp; but they were at once driven back with volleys from our repeating rifles, and chased beyond view of our camps. Only one of them was left dead on the field in this attempt. *Wakamba warriors.* *Ominous sounds of strife.*

I now sent away to the tribe two more of the women we had brought home, with the intimation, that if they continued such foolish proceedings, I should make war with them on my part, and they would very soon have to repent their rashness. If, however, they would live in friendship *Dr. Peters' speech to the Wandorobbo.*

with me, I would at once send back the rest of their girls to them. But I must insist, as I had guides from elsewhere, that they should at least bring me a few sheep and goats for sale. My column had been so excited by the occurrences of the morning, that repeatedly, both by day and night, the men allowed themselves to be startled by false alarms, and rushed to entirely unrealised encounters with imaginary enemies. At one time came the report that one of my porters had been killed at the river by the Massais; at another, one of the men was firing blindly into the thicket, because an enemy had been descried there. All this made a very disagreeable impression, and, in consequence, I again had a fence erected around the camp.

Adverse reports.

Towards three o'clock in the afternoon appeared the ambassadors of the Wandorobbo, two wonderful apparitions, to us who came from the east. They were entirely nude, with their whole bodies besmeared with red clay, their hair artfully arranged in ringlets round the head, the quiver full of poisoned arrows, and the bow over their shoulders, and the lance and Massai shield in their hands. The feeling involuntarily arose, that we had now penetrated among entirely new tribes, and into completely strange regions. While among the Gallas there had always been a certain maintaining of relations with the coast such relations were here entirely absent, and there was not the slightest sign that these people had ever seen Suaheli or Arabs, much less white men. The Wandorobbo ambassadors brought out their demands in a loud, imperious tone, so that I had to admonish them several times to moderate their voices, as this shouting was not the way to my heart. They demanded that their girls should be given up; I, on the other hand, declared, I must first have my sheep; and when they protested that they had not the power to give me them, I ordered them, if that were so, to come again the following morning, and to bring the sultan of the tribe with them. Not until then would I negotiate with them for the delivering up of the women. I made use of the evening hours further to fortify

The Wandorobbo ambassadors.

Insolence of their manner and demands.

Fortifying the camp.

NEGOTIATION WITH THE WANDOROBBO.

the camp, and in the night I had good watch kept. But with the exception of a few false alarm shots, we remained undisturbed.

I now wrote a last report for Europe, in which I related the occurrences until the evening of this day, and especially my discoveries on the Tana. I purposed next morning to send the Gallas and the Wapokomo I had brought from Oda-Boru-Ruva back to their homes, and to get my packet to Europe in this way, through the intervention of the second column, which might be coming up, or perhaps by the post messenger whom I expected with news from the coast. *Report for Europe.*

They departed on the morning of October 30th, already before sunrise, as the Gallas feared to be seen and killed by the Wandorobbo or the Wakambas. As I was afterwards informed by Herr Borchert, Parisa arrived home safely at Oda-Boru-Ruva with his people, but did not deliver any of the reports for Europe that had been sent by him. *Parisa's neglect.* Early in the morning I was gratified by the agreeable intelligence that there was no meat for our breakfast, and that our private servants had had nothing to eat since yesterday. A very charming piece of news, if we consider the complete isolation of such a position. It is certainly much more easy to criticise, after the fact, the manner in which any one has extricated himself from such a desperate situation, than to manage extrication at the place itself. *Prospect of famine.*

I threw my gun over my shoulder and, that I might at least do something for us, went forth from the camp, with my servant Rukua, into the steppe to shoot. Two thin pigeons were the entire result of my foray, from which I returned half dead with hunger two hours afterwards. *A useless chase.*

The pigeons were as quickly forgotten as eaten. The Wandorobbo question began, indeed, to become a burning one. Then, towards eleven o'clock, the Wandorobbo elders at length appeared before the camp, with the five sheep I had demanded. After we had demonstrated and sworn, by spitting at each other several times, that our intentions towards each other were good, we entered upon the negotiation for exchanging the women

the camp, and in the night I had good watch kept. But with the exception of a few false alarm shots, we remained undisturbed.

I now wrote a last report for Europe, in which I related the occurrences until the evening of this day, and especially my discoveries on the Tana. I purposed next morning to send the Gallas and the Wapokomo I had brought from Oda-Boru-Ruva back to their homes, and to get my packet to Europe in this way, through the intervention of the second column, which might be coming up, or perhaps by the post messenger whom I expected with news from the coast. *Report for Europe.*

They departed on the morning of October 30th, already before sunrise, as the Gallas feared to be seen and killed by the Wandorobbo or the Wakambas. As I was afterwards informed by Herr Borchert, Parisa arrived home safely at Oda-Boru-Ruva with his people, but did not deliver any of the reports for Europe that had been sent by him. *Parisa's neglect.* Early in the morning I was gratified by the agreeable intelligence that there was no meat for our breakfast, and that our private servants had had nothing to eat since yesterday. A very charming piece of news, if we consider the complete isolation of such a position. *Prospect of famine.* It is certainly much more easy to criticise, after the fact, the manner in which any one has extricated himself from such a desperate situation, than to manage extrication at the place itself.

I threw my gun over my shoulder and, that I might at least do something for us, went forth from the camp, with my servant Rukua, into the steppe to shoot. Two thin pigeons were the entire result of my foray, from which I returned half dead with hunger two hours afterwards. *A useless chase.* The pigeons were as quickly forgotten as eaten. The Wandorobbo question began, indeed, to become a burning one. Then, towards eleven o'clock, the Wandorobbo elders at length appeared before the camp, with the five sheep I had demanded. After we had demonstrated and sworn, by spitting at each other several times, that our intentions towards each other were good, we entered upon the negotiation for exchanging the women for the sheep. The Wandorobbo must have thought us very bad men of business to give them back their women for the five sheep. In these countries the price of a woman generally rises to fifty sheep; and according to African ideas of polity, our right of possession was indefeasible after the occurrences of the day before. Two sheep were quickly slaughtered; one of them was given to the people, and one was consigned to the cauldrons for us and the Somalis, and within an hour it had been consumed.

Wandorobbo negotiations: a bad bargain.

I now caused a start to be made, to get, as soon as possible, to Ukamba Mumoni, which, according to the statements of the Wakamba, lay only two or three days' journey before us. The way lay through rugged bush and over some stony and ever-rising ground. On the way I succeeded in killing a guinea-fowl, which I gave Nogola to carry. The march was exceedingly fatiguing; the camels, especially, could only advance with difficulty, and every now and then they had to be unloaded to climb up the heights. At four o'clock, as I was marching at the head of the column, I discovered a ford in the river, and determined to encamp there. I sent Nogola to the chief column, to Herr von Tiedemann, to show him the place, to which I myself proceeded with a few Somalis to commence the work of clearing away, before pitching the camp. Five o'clock came, the sun began to sink, and not a human being appeared. I sent two Somalis back, and towards half-past five had the pleasure of seeing at least my camels clambering down the steep declivity leading to the ford. But where were the porters, and where was Herr von Tiedemann? Towards six o'clock we succeeded in ascertaining that the column had marched round the ford, and must be already at a considerable distance to the west of us. The chief loads belonging to my tent were with it—my camp bed and my blankets. Whether I liked it or not, I had to make up my mind to do without those articles for that night. But the principal task was to put myself into communication with the chief column that same evening. I therefore sent some reliable people behind the main body of the column, and,

The order of march.

Anxiety for the column.

A disagreeable night.

THE FALL OF NOGOLA. 171

according to my custom, set fire to the bush forest on a hill to the westward of us. At ten o'clock I had the satisfaction of hearing a few dropping shots in the distance, and soon afterwards several of the porters appeared with my private luggage, which Herr von Tiedemann had sent to me for the night. Now at least each of us knew where the other was encamped, so that there was no difficulty about our meeting the next morning, as I had directed Herr von Tiedemann to defer his departure until I joined him.

Thus, as early as five o'clock next morning, we broke up towards the south-west, and at about half-past seven I met Herr von Tiedemann, who with his column was waiting for me, in readiness to march. Nogola, who was to blame for the mishap, had meanwhile been enjoying himself over my guinea-fowl. Perhaps he had only led the column round the ford at which I was encamped, to accomplish this in all quietness of mind. But the matter had a bad ending for him. I administered an emetic to make him give up the stolen goods as far as practicable, and, in addition, caused him to receive twenty-five lashes, which were duly counted out to him in the presence of all, as a warning and a lesson to the whole community. The impudent fellow was, in addition, put in chains for the rest of the day. From that time his position in the caravan sank rapidly; and he did not recover it to the day of his death, which happened on the 22nd of the following December. *Nogola's misbehaviour and punishment.*

On October 31st I pitched my camp in a glorious wood by the Tana river. On that day I had repeatedly met Wandorobbos on the road, and I invited them to visit me, and to bring me sheep for sale. In spite of all that had happened, the whole set of them were, and remained, brazen and impudent. When, on the march, I took hold of one of these people with my crooked stick by one of the earholes that hung down to his shoulders, because he would not come on, he tried, in return, to seize me by the ears too. But as we sat at table the chief of the Wandorobbo appeared in my camp. This was reported to me in my tent. I rose from the dinner table, and went out to *Wandorobbo insolence.*

him to ask him where the sheep were, that I had ordered. He replied that the sheep would come on the morrow or the day after. Now this, it will be allowed, is very cold comfort when one has a hungry column to provide for, and has oneself hardly meat enough left for one day. Consequently, I explained to the Sultan that this delay was not according to my wish, as I proposed to march forward the next day, and that he must remain in the camp until his tribe furnished the sheep. Hereupon on a sudden he raised his loud war-howl, like the cry of the jackal; and in a moment the poisoned arrows of the Wandorobbo came flying into our camp from every direction. One of them struck into my trousers, and was within an ace of killing me. I at once had the Sultan knocked down, and fettered; then took him by the ears, and shoved him in front of me, as a kind of shield, towards the shooting Wandorobbos. I forbade my people to fire on these people, as I wished to have peace with them.

[sidenote: Visit from the Wandorobbo chief.]

[sidenote: Attack with poisoned arrows.]

As they did not like, of course, to shoot at their Sultan, they were obliged also to pause; and by signs, with the help of a few broken words of their language, I contrived to announce to the Sultan, and through him to his people, that if by the evening they brought me five sheep and four donkeys, I would deliver up their Sultan to them, and give them stuffs for clothes. This treaty was sealed before the people by my spitting several times at the Sultan, while he spat at me; and the Wandorobbos withdrew to bring the ransom for their chief, who remained with me. Quite friendly relations were established in the course of the afternoon between myself and him; and when, in the evening, no donkeys, indeed, but eight sheep made their appearance, I presented the chief and several of his principal men with red clothing material, and dismissed them, unharmed, to their people.

[sidenote: A peace patched up.]

Next morning I expected to see the Wandorobbo once more, according to agreement made on the previous evening, to buy more meat from them. Not to let the time until their arrival pass by unused, I went with Hussein Fara and Rukua along the upward course of the Tana, to find

[sidenote: Explorations along the Tana.]

FALLING INTO A TRAP. 173

out if there were a way for the camels, in the immediate neighbourhood of the river, by which I might escape the tiring devious road through the steppe, as I should have to come back to the river in the evening. After a reconnaissance of two or three hours, we ascertained, to our discomfiture, that there existed no such way along the river, as the rocks here began to offer a steep descent towards the rushing Tana. I returned to the camp, and was just passing through the dry bed of an affluent from the south, which poured its waters into the Tana during the rainy season—we were in the middle of this watercourse—when suddenly nearly a hundred figures of Wandorobbo sprang up before me out of the thicket, with their arrows ready to shoot. I was going to withdraw from these disagreeable neighbours into the bush on the other side of the river bed, when Wandorobbo rose up there also, and suddenly the side of the river towards the Tana was likewise lined with them. I had managed to fall into a trap, and these gentlemen might now have taken their revenge for yesterday. I did not, however, let them perceive my embarrassment, but laughed in friendly fashion, and beckoned with my hand to ask them to wait a moment, while with a face of apparent amusement I approached a tree on the upper side of the dry river course. So soon as I had reached this, I pulled out my rifle, which was in its case, and made ready to fire, at the same time continually waving tufts of grass in the air as a sign of peace, this being apparently everywhere the accepted international African form. I now made the Wandorobbo understand that my servant Rukua should hasten into my camp to bring presents for them; and that in return I expected a present of sheep from them.

Threatened attack by the Wandorobbo.

A temporising policy.

Rukua accordingly hurried into camp with the order to bring the presents, and twelve of my soldiers besides. As the poison of the Wandorobbo arrows, which they prepare from the bark of a tree, is immediately fatal, my position during the ensuing three-quarters of an hour was not the pleasantest. The Wandorobbo continually tried, though perhaps not with hostile intentions, to get nearer to me; and I as continually motioned them to stay where they were until the presents arrived. At length my soldiers appeared, and the position of affairs was altered. I placed my soldiers in a half-circle behind me, with their repeaters prepared; then I put down my own rifle, and made the Sultan of the Wandorobbo, my friend of yesterday, understand that he also should lay aside his bow and arrows, and give me a personal meeting in the middle of the dry river bed. After we had spat three times at each other, there was no further danger of an attack at this place; and we now arranged that the Wandorobbo should bring ten sheep to a cleared space by the river above my camp; in return for which, I undertook for them that they should be allowed, without molestation from us, to drive their flocks to water at the ford, which I could command from my camp. I also promised them some fine clothing stuffs as presents. We shook hands upon it; on which occasion neither I nor the Sultan omitted, as a sign of the honesty of our arrangements, each to spit into his own hand, which is, indeed, the recognised form of greeting among friends in all the Massai tribes. We spat once more in each other's face, and thereupon parted good friends, each going his own way.

On arriving at the camp, I at once ordered the camels, with Herr von Tiedemann, round the bush forest into the steppe. I would only wait, with a part of my people, for the ten sheep promised by the Wandorobbo, and then quickly follow the camels, which marched but slowly. Accordingly, I betook myself, with ten or twelve men, to the clearing by the river, where the Wandorobbo also appeared immediately afterwards. But they had not yet brought the sheep. First, we must eat liver together, they said, as a sign that our nations, the Germans at home and the Wandorobbo in Murdoi, were at peace, and then they would give me the ten sheep. The sun began to burn hot; and, as the Wandorobbo commenced taking all kinds of liberties,— demanding that I should show them my breast, and pull off my boots, with various other jests of the kind,—I became considerably angry, because I had no inclination to creep through among these tribes, in the clowning manner of Thomson. Accordingly, I forbade their bold proceedings in a sufficiently rough tone, and sent them away with the injunction to bring the sheep at once, or I should no longer recognise our compact of the morning.

My humour became none the more rosy when I suddenly saw the camels come marching back from the side of the river. Herr von Tiedemann had not found any road. It was plain, accordingly, that I must remain to-day in the same place; and I only transferred my camp from the forest into the clearing where I was, that I might be nearer to watch the development of events that would no doubt take place at the ford. The tents were pitched, and I sat down with Herr von Tiedemann to our scanty meal, when suddenly the Somalis came rushing, with very disturbed looks, into the tent, and told us the Wandorobbo were driving an immense number of cattle to the river. The Somalis always looked disturbed, when they saw cattle in other men's hands; but here especially, because the Godsend was so well within their reach, and they were in a hungry condition. In mere absence of mind five of them had brought twenty kids into my camp, which, as they averred, they had "found" by the river. Inasmuch as such a manner of keeping treaties does not generally square with our German ideas, I stood up from table, and myself brought the twenty kids to the Wandorobbo up the river, where these people were certainly driving herd after herd to the water, and away again. As a proof of my friendly intentions, I had only brought two men with me, and for myself I had my six-shooting revolver in my pocket. Now I had the clothes stuffs brought, to redeem my promise with regard to the presents; but I demanded, once more, that the Wandorobbo should deliver to me the promised ten sheep. With discontented faces they at last brought up five at their Sultan's orders. One of these was at once slaughtered, the liver was taken out, and without much ceremony laid in the fire, whereupon each of us received a piece of it to

An enforced encampment.

Excited Somalis; prospects of plunder.

"Reciprocity" to be on one side.

Renewed peace.

eat. And herewith the treaty of peace was sealed between the German nation, as such, and the Wandorobbo.

I now once more demanded my ten sheep, and became somewhat suspicious when I noticed that the warriors, or Elmoran, of the Wandorobbo began to snigger, and that some figures posted themselves near me, on the left, in the bush. The Wandorobbo refused my pieces of stuff, and I said I would send to my camp, and have a load of iron wire brought, which Measures of precaution against treachery. they would perhaps prefer. I sent Hussein Fara into the camp with a note to Herr von Tiedemann, in which I requested him to come, with thirty men, to our place of council, and ordered the Somalis immediately to start for the dry ford, which they were to occupy some distance up, and, at a trumpet signal from me, to drive as many head of cattle as they could get together into our camp; and directly they had secured a herd they were to fire a shot, that I might know what was going on.

Herd after herd belonging to the Wandorobbo went away from the river; when the last had quitted the water-side, the people suddenly let three of the five sheep there go, so that only one very skinny specimen remained for me. All at once an Tokens of hostility. arrow flew past my ear. I coolly rose, and called out to them, "Take care of yourselves, you dogs!" and quietly had my things packed up, and ordered them to be carried back into the camp. Hussein Fara soon reappeared with the intelligence that my orders were being executed, and Herr von Tiedemann presently came marching along with thirty men. Now I suddenly caused the trumpet to be blown, and quietly fell back upon my camp. When my people came hurrying up, the Wandorobbo disappeared with one accord into the Herr von Tiedemann's position. bush. I requested Herr von Tiedemann to follow them through the clearing and the dry river bed, which he was to occupy with his thirty men. Then, on my side, I went back quietly into the camp, when suddenly the shot I was so anxiously awaiting rang out from the bush. I immediately ordered the people who had remained in camp to get up a fence for the cattle that Heaven was going to send us, then sat down in my tent to a cup of tea and cognac, and took up "Mommsen." I had been sitting there for about twenty minutes, when there came a trampling like an approaching cavalry attack, sheep and goats jumping along merrily in a crowd, and a donkey also had "strayed" over to us—so the Somalis reported, who came running behind them in a state of enthusiastic excitement. The sheep were now driven to the water, and surrounded by my people, till the fence was finished. After about ten minutes came also Herr von Tiedemann, who was to have taken the Wandorobbo, if necessary, between two fires; he had not got sight of one Wandorobbo. He was naturally highly delighted when he saw the sheep. {*The Somalis and the "strayed" cattle.*}

Now we settled down to a mighty slaughtering and feasting. To every five men a sheep was given, and to every two men a kid. Joy, jovial dancing, and merry songs were the order of the day. We had two hundred and fifty sheep in our possession, and with this there was an end, once and for all, of famine in the German Emin Pasha Expedition. The pleasurable part for me, in the occurrences of this day, was that, in the first place, no human blood had been spilt, and, secondly, that I felt myself, morally, entirely in the right in the measures I had put in action. {*A valuable prize.*}

In the night I had the camp well watched, and now and then I ordered rockets to be thrown up over the bushes. But these measures of precaution proved to be superfluous. The Wandorobbo, who, as I heard from Wakamba, were under belief that the fiend himself had personally, and with a great following, appeared in their land and among them,—to which conclusion they were brought especially by the contemplation of my broad-brimmed flapped hat, and also probably of the black shining spectacles in which I was accustomed to appear at the conferences—vanished in the darkness of night, going down stream with their herds. I never set eyes upon them afterwards.

Next morning I wished to cross the Tana at this place, as Herr von Tiedemann shared the opinion with the Somalis, that outside the bush forest there was no road up the stream, on the right bank of the Tana. For that reason I caused my people to go through the river, which was very broad here, in the early morning, to ascertain if it was fordable for us at this spot. Strangely enough, from the earliest morning this November 2nd, a continuous rising of the Tana occurred, so that already in the afternoon the whole sandy cleared space by the brink, where the negotiations of the former day had taken place, was under water, and in the night the water penetrated into our camp. My people lost all relish for working in the Tana, on the sudden approach of a row of suspicious dark objects, which were soon identified as so many crocodiles. I was able, indeed, to scare these creatures away from the surface with bullets from my rifle, but hardly altogether to banish them from the vicinity.

The Tana: the question of fords.

So from nine o'clock I devoted myself, with entire zeal, to constructing a raft, for which I made my people bring fifty trunks of trees, as uniform in size as possible. Towards twelve o'clock the raft was finished; but when I made the attempt, even quite alone, to trust myself to the currents with it, the heavy wood sank beneath the surface. The trial resulted in complete failure. Now there was nothing for it, but to devote the remainder of the day to finding a way for my caravan on our side of the Tana. I sent the best of my people out on this business, and they succeeded in establishing the possibility of a march for the next day. On the morning of November 3rd we therefore started with beat of drum, always up hill, up hill, through bush and forest. But still we made progress, and, what was most fortunate, our flock of sheep and goats got forward with us cheerily enough.

Attempt to cross with a raft.

All these herds are accustomed to nomadic wanderings, and must therefore not be judged entirely by a European standard. From this time, during the whole further course of the expedition, I carried herds along with me. Thus the sordid care for the body's food and nourishment was removed. We could look forward with pleasure to the march, the arrival in camp, and dinner, instead of contemplating with

Marching with the herds.

a kind of horror this arrival, and the ugly scenes that would be associated with it. Herewith the advance assumed a much more pleasant character. The heavy wrong the Englishmen had done us in Lamu, by the confiscation of our articles of barter, had in some degree been remedied by Providence, and I began to get rid, more and more, of the doubt as to the definite accomplishment of my task.

On this day I encamped by a beautiful cataract of the Tana, just beneath the fall, near a ford of the river, so that, if we wished, we could enjoy the refreshing rain of spray in front of our tent. On the other side of the Tana the Bennigsen chain day by day exhibited more imposing forms. Lovely bush forest surrounded my camping-place, in which a cheerful busy life appeared, for the people were now in good humour, in consequence of winning the herds. On this day I again wrote reports for Germany, in which I described our adventures with the Wandorobbo. *Cheerful aspect of the country.*

I was busy with this task, when all at once the Mangema Barakka, surrounded by his followers, came rushing into my tent with loud howls. My people were accustomed regularly to fill up the afternoon hours with fishing. Barakka also had drawn forth with the hook from the cooling flood a great, a very great, inhabitant of the Tana. But the fish, taking the joke in evil part, had bitten Barakka soundly in the finger. When a black man sees blood he thinks it his duty to howl, and the people were very much astonished at my not taking the affair tragically; and it was certainly not tragic, for a little chloride of iron sufficed to stop the bleeding. *Barakka's formidable accident.*

In the night a heavy storm drew up, the rolling thunder mingling harmoniously with the sound of the waterfall—the first practical token that the short rainy season was at hand. The landscape became more and more magnificent, the onward sweep of the Tana more turbulent, ever more majestic the forms of the mountains and the primeval forest that surrounded us. The Tana here rushes downward through short stretches in mighty cataracts to the depths. Terrace after terrace were we obliged to climb. *Stormy indications of the rainy season.*

Next day we made a long march, and had throughout the afternoon to endure a pelting fall of rain, which set in regularly, and was repeated almost daily for the next month and a half. On this day, we first came again upon traces of men. My people thought they descried in the distance "shambas" (plantations), and the pleasant expectation was strengthened in the afternoon by the appearance of two Wakamba, who said that on the morrow we should reach inhabited districts.

Indications of inhabited districts.

According to my custom, I kept these visitors in the camp through the night. But as I did not like, on the following morning, to lead them back to their countrymen bound with cords, they got away, with one of the Wakamba I had brought with me from Murdoi, as soon as I set my column in motion. On November 7th I felt slightly indisposed, which occasioned me to take strong doses of ipecacuanha, and in a few hours I had quite recovered. On this day also the Somali, Daud Wais, fell sick with dysentery, from which he suffered till the end of the expedition. The land we approached on the following morning was, to my astonishment, not Ukamba, as I was obliged to assume from the maps, but the land of Dsagga, which stretches out, in lovely ranges of noble outline, over the Tana. The land is richly cultivated, and makes a most picturesque appearance, with its little villages, built in the Swiss style, and surrounded with strong circumvallations. It is situated in front of the Bennigsen Mountains, and to a certain extent corresponds with Kikuyu, which lies in front of the plateau, only that in Kikuyu the mountain chains are higher, and the air is in consequence still more pure.

Securing the Wakamba.

The land of Dsagga.

The Wadsagga, again, are Bantu, and closely related to the Wakamba and the Wakikuyu, as also to the people of Mbe, with whom they possess a common language. According to enquiries made by Krapf, the Wakamba are said formerly to have had their dwellings on the Kilima-Ndsharo, and to have been driven thence towards the north by the Massais. Perhaps this has to do with the similarity of sound

The Wadsagga tribe.

in the names Dsagga and Dshagga at the Kilima-Ndsharo. The foremost tribes, in this emigration, made their way across the Tana forward into a region which by those who dwelt behind it was called Mbere, Mbele, or Mbe (front). This is the land that stretches from Dsagga along the left bank of the Tana, and belongs to tribes of quite the same race as Ukamba.

The Wadsagga, like the Wakamba, have something of high blood in their demeanour. They love to deck themselves in chivalrous style, to ornament themselves with feathers, and to wear on their feet bits of iron which clink like spurs at every step. Their women are voluptuous, cheerful looking creatures, plentifully adorned with beads and rings. They were fond of promenading saucily with their adorers in front of our encampment, to have their beauty admired.

High breeding and haughtiness of the Wadsagga.

Into this country also, no knowledge of white men had yet penetrated. I believe they did not know even Arabs or Wangwana. They took our guns for cudgels, and when they looked at our feet, clad in high boots, they began to laugh aloud; for they thought we had thrust our feet into donkeys' legs that we might march the better, or that we ourselves had donkeys feet. On the declivities of the charmingly-situated land long ranges of plantations appear, between which great herds and flocks, oxen, sheep, and goats are pasturing in peaceful sunny groups. The whole scene, with the Tana traversing it, makes an idyllic impression; and when, on November 8th, we encountered these people for the first time, we thought we had come upon a " peaceful shepherd tribe."

A primitive community.

This impression was very quickly altered when I entered into commercial relations with them anent the purchase of grain. I asked them to furnish me with a great bulk of grain at once, and in return I was ready to make a proportionate present. But as all monarchical unity was wanting here, it was not possible to enforce this demand. Each individual brought a little pot or a little bundle of mtama, for which he asked his own utterly exorbitant price. As I was, above everything, in urgent want of strong food for my riding horse and the camels, I at last made short work of it, by taking possession of the grain that had been brought, and paying an entirely adequate price for it in cloth. At this there arose a great outcry, so that, to avoid a breach of the peace, I had the whole company turned out of the camp. For all that, our relations continued to be of the most friendly kind. The Wadsagga, of their own accord, provided a guide, who was to lead us as far as Mbe, so that I could now dismiss, with rich gifts, Mkamba, who was still with me; and on the morning of November 9th we went forth, amid friendly greetings from all sides, through the beautiful land;—now past villages from which men and women rushed forth to gaze at us; then on well-kept woodland paths, uphill and downhill, until towards noon we came into a second district of the Dsagga land. Before we crossed the frontier, hundreds of the Wadsagga, who had now grown quite confidential, took leave of us, and we marched into the second district, under the impression that we should be able to traverse the whole country as friends, and thus might reach Mbe in the most agreeable manner. Beyond Mbe, we were told, there was a ford of the river, which I designed to cross.

Egotistical ideas of trade.

WADSAGGA.

March through the country.

THREATENING OF A STORM. 185

When I entered the second district of Dsagga, by way of a high hill that sloped gradually down, I saw on the other side of the shore a great mountain, which remained in sight as a landmark for us for days afterwards. The Bennigsen chain, which had run, as far as this mountain, in a south-south-west direction, here deviated a little towards the west, and ran south-west, so that the mountain we had seen stands at the angle of the range. I decided to name it the Krupp Mountain, and encamped opposite it, at one in the afternoon, by a ford of the Tana. Presently numerous Wadsagga came in; their insolence of manner, in communicating with us, at once impressed me disagreeably. I asked them to bring food for us to purchase, within an hour; but immediately learned, to my complete astonishment, that one of my porters, Ajabajir, who was somewhat unwell, and consequently had been marching in the rear of the column, had disappeared, having probably been captured by the Wadsagga. To get at the truth of this I immediately sent back some soldiers, who presently returned bringing me a confirmation of the news.

The Krupp Mountain.

Insolence of the Wadsagga.

We were just sitting at breakfast, when it was suddenly announced that the gentlemen Wadsagga had set about driving off my five donkeys. They had indeed been put to flight by prompt action on the part of the Somalis; but the intention of paying no respect to our rights of property was apparent enough. In this condition of affairs I determined to take vigorous measures, and replied by giving my men the order to drive as many head of cattle from the surrounding pastures into my camp, as they could get possession of without a breach of the peace. The command was promptly obeyed, and by half-past four we had six hundred sheep and about sixty oxen in the enclosure. The herdsmen had been driven away by a few shots fired in the air.

Aggression and reprisals.

Towards sunset one of the patriarchal elders of the district came to the camp, begging from afar for peace. As it seemed hardly possible to keep the somewhat unruly oxen with us through the night, I sent the greater number of them back to the elder, with the remark, "He should have

A peace-seeking elder.

peace." If he wanted to treat, he must come to me next morning. In the morning, accordingly, the old and really venerable-looking man made his appearance, with a few younger warriors. I took him to task, and asked how the Wadsagga had dared to carry off one of my people and to try to drive away my donkeys. I told him, before I would negotiate further with him he must deliver up my man, and that I further wished the Wadsagga to bring corn for my beasts of burden. I had already, yesterday, ordered them to do this, but not a grain had been voluntarily brought in. The elder thereupon departed, but returned about one o'clock in the day, when I was just returning from an excursion in the neighbourhood; he brought with him nothing but my porter's gun. Accompanying him was a personage, who, for weeks afterwards, was one of the principal figures in my expedition. This was Marongo, a tall lanky Mkamba, who had come from Ukamba to Dsagga to buy beer, with a little bundle of things, which was still lying in the hands of the Wadsagga, and a mouth that stretched almost from ear to ear. His face was characterised by a half crafty, half good-natured expression about the eyes, and his arms swung to and fro by his sides, extending down almost to his knees. The man spoke a little Kiswahali, and consequently at once excited in me a desire to secure him for my expedition, so that the wearisome exchange of broken words and pantomimic systems of conversation might cease.

I gave the elder one of my jackets with red and white squares, which I put on him myself. To my inquiry concerning Ajabajir, he replied, he thought he could inform me that the man was no longer with him; he had fled to the Wakamba, but here was his rifle. I informed the elder that I did not believe his assertion, and once more complained that no grain had yet come. I said I had wished for peace with the Wadsagga, but they seemed to prefer war. If that were so, they could also have war. Then we sat down to table, while the Sultan, with Marongo and the Wadsagga, remained sitting outside the tent. Then I went and sat down with them again, whereupon the peripettia of the whole incident came quickly. Suddenly Morango began to talk, in the elder's name, of sheep that I was to deliver up. "What sheep?" I asked. "Well, the sheep that had been driven into my camp yesterday evening." Thereupon I replied, that he had seized Ajabajir yesterday, adding, "And to-day, when I want to have him back, you say that he has run away to the Wakamba. Now I will tell you, that is exactly the state of things with your sheep. I am afraid that your sheep will also run away to Wakamba with me. If you bring Ajabajir back, there can be a council held to decide what is to be done with the sheep that are in my hands. If you don't do this, the matter will remain as it is. We can even then part in peace if you wish it. If you do not wish it, you may do what you can." All at once the Wadsagga sprang up, seized their spears, and hurried out of the camp. *A plain statement of facts.*

As Marongo was also about to follow them, I asked him, through my Somalis, to stay, as I should want him for the further negotiations. After some resistance, he yielded to necessity with a good grace, only asking that his bundle should be obtained for him from the Wadsagga. I now dismissed the Wadsagga guides, as Marongo knew the way to Mbe, and at once sent off five men to the Wadsagga to have his bundle brought into my camp. I had no foreboding of evil; and as the sun was shining hotly down, I seated myself in my tent to pass my Sunday afternoon in quiet. All at once my people rushed into the tent, and announced to me that the Wadsagga were attacking our herds, and already advancing upon the camp from the other sides. At the same moment I also heard firing from the direction of the herds, and saw my embassy of five men running in headlong flight from the opposite side, towards the camp. With a force of more than a thousand men, the Wadsagga attacked our camp on every side. I entrusted Herr von Tiedemann with the command on the upper side of the river, and threw myself, with a few people, upon the enemies who came crowding up from the lower side. *Marongo submits to his fate.*

Attack by the Wadsagga.

Suddenly the Wadsagga came to understand what sort of cudgels our guns were. A row of them came tumbling head over heels down the hill; the others stopped bewildered; but as man after man was picked off, they turned suddenly back, and took to flight wildly. On the other side, also, Herr von Tiedemann succeeded in making an end of the affair, and in half an hour all was decided. Behind a hill in the south-west, the Wadsagga collected like ants whose nest has been destroyed. The sun was already low in the west, and I considered it more prudent to conclude the whole affair by daylight, than to run the risk of being roused up once more at night by an attack.

Therefore I took some twenty of my people, leaving the command of the camp to Herr von Tiedemann, and determined to attack the hill on which the Wadsagga then were. Below the camp, a deep rain gully or stream ran into the Tana. Along this we noiselessly crept, as it went in the direction of the hill aforesaid. But we must have been observed; for as we crept up the hill, at the back, it was suddenly deserted. I now turned towards the neighbouring villages of the Wadsagga, to give them a serious lesson before the night came on. At our approach the villages, too, were speedily deserted. I *Reprisals on the foe.* ordered everything that could be of value to us to be quickly taken out, and had six of these villages set on fire, one after another. It appeared to me necessary to make the people understand *c'est la guerre*, because the safety of our further march depended, in the last instance, entirely upon this. When the sun went down, the glare of the flames spread over the wide hilly region, plainly discernible from the camp, where our column was naturally watching these occurrences with the keenest interest.

Heavily laden, I returned with my band to the camp, from which the other people came forth singing and dancing to meet me. I was able that night to feed my beasts of burden, *The "Kupanda-Sharo" feeling.* and also to distribute some grain to the column. Now the state of mind arose more and more in my camp which I was accustomed to call the "Kupanda-Sharo" feeling. Kupanda-Sharo, that is to say, climber of mountains, was the name which I had borne from the beginning of my expedition, and which is now becoming more and more known among the native tribes. My people had composed special songs upon this name, and these they were accustomed to sing upon such occasions as the present, especially the Wanjamwesi girls. I remember how, on that very evening, one of these girls, as she husked the corn, sang a song of which the burden always was: "Others have nothing to eat; Kupanda-Sharo gives us to eat."

From this time I could count more and more on the completely reliable spirit in the expedition, at least among the great majority. This evening I prepared a spectacle for the people, by having the last load of petroleum poured over a dried mimosa bush, and setting it on fire. *A grand bonfire.*
On the morning of this day one of the porters' wives had given birth to a child, and therefore I had consented to encamp for a day opposite Krupp Mountain. But next morning before sunrise we were on our onward path towards the south-west for Ukamba, which I hoped to reach the same day. Of the Wadsagga at first nothing was to be seen. But soon, first singly, then in hundreds, they popped up on the hills to right and left of us, following our track like jackals, to see if they could not find an opportunity to attack us. During the whole marching day there was skirmishing, and the rattle of the guns never ceased. Unfortunately the Wadsagga succeeded in capturing the above-mentioned porter's wife, who could not keep up with us, and carried her off with her child. A bloody retribution was exacted; but a loss of this kind, to a hostile tribe, is always very painful to the feelings of a leader. Whatever villages of the *Retribution on the Wadsagga.* Wadsagga could be reached during the march were set on fire. At twelve o'clock, the procession was moving through a narrow pass. I thought the Wadsagga had at length gone back, and therefore galloped my horse from the rear to the head of the column, to find out a suitable place for our camp. But just in front of this defile the Wadsagga were lying in ambush, and were within a hair's breadth of succeeding in

driving off our herd of cattle. The attempt only failed through the cleverness of the Somalis in driving the beasts. The herd was made to rush at a wild gallop through the narrow pass, which Herr von Tiedemann meanwhile covered with a few Somalis.

I found a very suitable camping-place in a deserted plantation, into which I threw myself with my caravan. As the Wadsagga immediately occupied all the heights round about, I caused a circuit of one of these heights to be undertaken by the Somalis, under the leadership of Hussein. So soon as the volleys from our repeating rifles flew among the Wadsagga from the rear, causing some of them who were perched in the trees to descend involuntarily to the earth with unwonted celerity, they abandoned the field in the most violent haste, and were seen no more. Only on the hill towards the west, a company of Wadsagga remained standing for the rest of the day. After dinner I myself went towards this post; but the people there sent to ask me why we were always shooting at them, inasmuch as they had no war against us. "Why are you perched up there?" I called up to them. "Because," they cried, "we are at war with the Wakamba, who are on the other side of the hill, and we are defending ourselves against them." "Oh, indeed," I called up, "then I wish you a pleasant afternoon!"

An enemy in the trees.

With the Wadsagga on the other side of the river peace was also concluded at midday. They declared, likewise, that they had nothing at all to do with the Wadsagga tribe with whom we were at war. They would be our friends, and would show us the way to Ukamba next morning. It was a marvellously beautiful afternoon that we passed in this plantation. Just like the mountains of the Danube between Passau and Vienna, the western continuation of the Bennigsen chain here stretches along the stream.

Peace and fair promises.

On the opposite side, up the stream, mountains extended to the Tana, filling me with a certain disquietude, because they threatened to put new difficulties in the way of our advance. Nevertheless, I still hoped that I should succeed in finding

IN THE MUMONI MOUNTAINS.

a way between these mountains and the river; and, for the rest, I depended upon the knowledge which Marongo declared he possessed of the roads in this region. These were the Mumoni Mountains, and we marched into them on November 12th. At first there certainly was a way between them and the river; but presently the rocks approached so closely and so steeply to the Tana, that I was compelled, whether I liked it or no, to leave the river, and betake myself to the valleys that slanted into the mountains. As I liked to sleep by the river, on account of the water, I turned back towards it after a march of about three hours; and now began about as difficult and uncomfortable a climbing match as can well be imagined. The mountains then assumed a very steep and precipitous character. They were covered, throughout, with thicket, like a primeval forest, and thorny bushes, which made marching very difficult and painful. It must be remembered that we had here to march not only with porters, but with a column of camels that still numbered seven, and with many hundred sheep. Sometimes we had to climb up a steep declivity, sometimes to scramble down an abrupt descent, and continually we were cutting our way with the axe.

March through the mountain regions.

Considerably tired, I fixed my camp, at about three o'clock, in a less precipitous place, and gradually gathered the whole column about me. My people were in anything but a cheerful humour, and their spirits did not greatly rise, even when I gave them, in addition to their regular daily fare, a number of sheep as an extra present. I saw well enough that an advance in this direction was impossible. Throughout the whole afternoon I accordingly caused various little excursions to be organised, to try in what direction a better way could be found for us; and I learned, before evening, from the Somali Musa and my servant Rukua, that by going away in the first instance entirely from the river, in a south-east direction, we should get to an open country.

Further advance impracticable.

The Tana here turns more and more completely towards the south, so that to all the difficulties of our advance was added the uncomfortable feeling, that at the end of each marching day of this kind we should be farther from, instead of nearer to, our real goal, the Equatorial Province. Next morning we marched away in a south-easterly direction, therefore exactly opposite to that in which Emin Pasha was to be sought. However, by this means we got out of the primeval forest, and into an open region, though it was pouring with rain. Then I gradually inclined towards the south, and then towards the south-west, always keeping the margin of the wood at my right hand.

Change of direction.

Towards ten o'clock we descried some people at a distance, and Marongo informed me that these were Wakamba Mumoni. Marongo, who now was literally of vital importance to us, was usually led in advance of the column, with a cord round his neck, under the guard of a Somali. He now begged to be allowed to conceal the cord from his countrymen. Accordingly, a handsome cravat was made for him out of a great piece of red stuff, which was only fastened at the back, in the most discreet manner possible, to the cord covered by the material. When this toilet had been completed, Marongo beckoned his countrymen to approach, and informed them of my wish to be shown a way through the mountains. We enforced the request by a present of stuff, and the Wakamba at once put themselves in motion in advance of us.

Marongo securely guarded.

They were desirous of showing me a place by the river, where the native caravans were accustomed to cross the water to get to Mbe. I had already given them their advance pay, but at every hundred paces the fellows would sit down and demand a fresh payment before they went further. I had made up my mind to practise patience in this country to the utmost possible extent, to get through peacefully; but practically I could not help seeing how impossible it is to get on with natures like these negroes without recourse to corporal punishment. But for this resource, a man is entirely powerless against such breaches of contract and hindrances of every kind; and for these people themselves it is much better, if they are made clearly to understand that lying, thieving, and cheating are not exactly the things that

Severity necessary with negroes.

ought to be in this world, but that human society rests upon a certain reciprocity of responsibility and service. Beyond all question, that is the manner in which the way will be best and most safely prepared for the opening up of Africa. To make oneself the object of insolence of the natives is the very way to confirm the blacks in the lowest qualities of their characters, and especially to degrade our race in their eyes. The practice of undertaking such responsibilities, and then leaving them unfulfilled, under all manner of pretexts, is always founded upon a certain under-estimation of the other party. It is quite a mistaken motto of travellers, that in Africa one must learn patience, and that no one who has not patience should travel there. It certainly is far more consonant with our interests and with civilisation if we take it as our motto, on the other hand, that we will impart some of our characteristics to the natives of Africa, instead of simply truckling to their faults. The great principle that makes itself felt through the universe, even in inorganic nature, is the principle of unlimited justice. But this principle is quite as much disregarded when the black man is allowed to overreach the white man, as in the opposite case. During the whole time of my leading the expedition I was always conscious of acting upon this principle. *Justice to be shown and enforced.*

In the middle of the day, between one and two o'clock, we at length came upon a high hill, with a very steep declivity towards the Tana, down which the column was led with much trouble, to the ford designated by the Wakamba. Here we found cooking stones and other signs of the camping of caravans and expeditions. At this place the Wakamba entered into commercial relations with the people of Mbe. But at that time the Tana was so high that the carrying across of the porters with their loads was not to be thought of, much less, even, the transport of the cattle. On that day four attempts were made to find a suitable place, but they all failed. The Wakamba told us that expeditions often had to wait here for many months till the river had subsided. That is just the way of the black men. Instead of *Abortive attempts to cross the Tana.*

13

buckling all together to the work of making an ordinary boat, they will wait for half a year until the river has gone down. I was now compelled, willingly or unwillingly, to continue my march on the right bank.

In laboriousness and in lack of result our next march was quite equal to that of the previous day. It was always up hill and down hill, through primeval underwood, where only the axe could make something like a path. It was, in truth, very depressing, especially when the ultimate object of the journey was considered. Whither would the Tana, thus running continually southward, ultimately lead us? There was something ridiculous in the idea of journeying in a direction just opposite to the goal of the journey, merely because it was impossible to cross a particular river. It recalled to the mind certain campaigns of the Turks south of the Danube. I began to consider, more and more seriously, whether it would be well to devote a few days to throwing a bridge across the river.

Doubts as to the route.

On November 14th I encamped on a small clearing in the forest, and here we were very agreeably surprised, in the evening, by the visit of about a hundred Wakamba to our camp. If any one could do it, they were the people to help us out of the disagreeable position in which the expedition then was. Moreover, they declared their readiness to do this, and asserted that we should soon come to the end of the mountains. On the advice of these Wakamba, I marched entirely away from the river, first to the east, then to the south-east, afterwards to the south, and gradually towards the south-west and west. On that day we absolutely made a circular movement, and though marching over more than seven miles of surface, we were only some 1,100 yards from our old camping-place when we halted in the afternoon. I was once more led by the Wakamba to a place where the Tana was wide, and where, according to their assertion, the people of Mbe crossed the river in the dry season. Here I determined to make an attempt to get across, or, as we were pleased to call it, I resolved " to force the Tana."

Advice of the Wakamba.

A DIFFICULT TASK.

Hemmed in between the river and the mountain range, with its thick growing wood, I had a lengthened encampment made here. With the help of Marongo and of the Wakamba who accompanied me, I put myself at once in communication with Mbe people on the other side of the river. I offered them rich presents, cattle and stuffs, if they would transport me and my whole expedition across the Tana. The conversation is here carried on by the natives on the opposite banks in a very remarkable manner. They speak with voices hardly raised, and yet each side can perfectly hear what the other says. Every sentence is answered by the cry of "eh!" in token that it has been understood. We found just the same practice afterwards in Kikuyu, Kamasia, and Elgejo. *Communication with the Mbe people.*

As the Tana was altogether too high to be crossed by wading, I resolved, in order, in the first place, to establish a communication with the opposite shore, to get a rope on to an island lying opposite, which was only separated from the further bank by a narrow arm of the river, which did not seem likely to present many difficulties. The Mbe people professed themselves ready to help us, and already in the afternoon they contrived, by wading up to their shoulders in the water, to reach the island from the opposite side. There was a second declivity about fifty yards above the island on our side of the river. From this point I made attempts the whole afternoon to reach, from our own bank, the island lying below. In the course of these attempts Hussein at one time was caught in the rapids, and shot, swift as an arrow, down the Tana and past the rapids, so that I feared for his life; but by exerting his utmost strength he contrived to regain the right hand shore. At last the Somali, Omar Idlé, managed to reach the island, so that he could hail the Mbe people from thence. But this brought us little practical advantage. On this first day I had also acquired a complete knowledge of the characteristics of the water at this place, and I decided, on the following morning, to proceed with the building of a great raft, which I intended to have strongly secured with ropes, and then to draw to and fro between our side and the little island lying lower down near *The problem of crossing the river.* *Omar Idlé's exploit.*

the opposite bank, and thus to get the column across in sections.

My people worked with perfect zeal, as I had promised rewards; and a raft about six times as large as the one we had made at Murdoi was constructed in the course of the day. At the same time I made the attempt to draw a rope across to the island, by which the people might swing themselves over, and their packages also. With their utmost strength the best swimmers of the expedition, among whom was Herr von Tiedemann, toiled to reach the island with the rope. Either each fastened it round his breast, which was important as preventing them from being carried down into the whirlpool, or two persons took hold of it, to reach the island with it by swimming. But directly they were a certain distance from the island, the strong current swept man and rope on one side, or drew them under the surface.

The raft and the rope.

Meanwhile the Tana was continually sinking. I had made a measuring rod, which I fastened in the river, and by which I could accurately gauge the height of the water. As the river had fallen about one foot in the night between November 16th and 17th, I continued the attempts with the rope. At the same time I caused the Mbe people on the opposite side to be asked to show us a place where the Tana was narrow, and where we might hope to throw a bridge across the river. They said that there was such a place a little way higher up. I sent a few people there; and when they came back and reported that a bridge seemed possible in that place, at noon I gave up the attempt to reach the island by the rope, inspected the place proposed for the bridge, and decided, as the scheme of the raft must always be exceedingly dangerous, on account of the rushing current and the heavy woods, to proceed with the construction of the bridge instead.

The river falling.

The usual method of building bridges of this kind in Africa is by pushing forward heavy piles on both sides into the river, as far as the current will allow. The piles are then fastened together by cross beams, and over these long slender trees are stretched across, the thrust being always from below upward.

When beams can no longer be used, the work is continued with hurdle work, tier upon tier being pushed forward as far as the supporting power of the wood will bear. If this hurdle work, which is pushed forward from both sides at the same time, does not suffice, the last space is spanned by tough ropes made of the bark of trees. In this manner a bridge is produced, unsteady, indeed, but strong in itself, if the supports are able to stand against the current. *How to build a bridge.*

My people, assisted by the Mbe men, worked with the greatest energy and with truly heroic exertion at this bridge, from November 18th to the 22nd. On the 21st the wattles had been pushed so far forward on each side that only a space of about fifteen feet remained to be joined by ropes. In the afternoon three such ropes were drawn from one side to the other. The whole hung down, indeed, somewhat close to the surface of the water, but I determined that when the ropes had been bound together by a cross-plaiting, I would have a fencing made on either side to keep my people from being drawn into the current. Of course I could not have the smaller animals driven across such a bridge, but each one had to be carried across separately. But as a row of porters could be posted for this duty, to pass the sheep and goats from hand to hand, and as this had only to be done across the middle space of the bridge, it only involved the expenditure of a few hours' time. *Energetic operations.*

On the 21st, at night, I went to bed in the firm hope that on the morrow the bridge could be completed, and the passage effected. We had had the great good fortune, that since the beginning of the building of the bridge the rain had suddenly ceased; a fact the Wakamba attributed to my magic power. But in the evening, on the 21st, I saw with disquietude that the whole western horizon was covered with thick clouds. Still, next morning, the bridge was completely above the water, though the Tana had risen somewhat in the night. Evidently there had been rain higher up. At seven o'clock I went to where the bridge was building, and found my workmen zealously employed in filling up the last gaps. Six *Completion of the bridge.*

ropes had been drawn across; and through these, cross-piece after cross-piece of wood was twisted, and firmly attached to the ropes. Over the cross-pieces other pieces were to be bound lengthwise, and the whole was to be finally secured by a strong paling at the sides. The cross-pieces were laid down, and at nine o'clock I returned to the camp, and gave orders to prepare everything for crossing at eleven.

I retired into my tent for an hour to do some writing, when all at once my attention was drawn to a wonderful rustling and splashing in front of it. Looking out, I found that the Tana had suddenly risen to the entrance of my tent. I hastened *Rising of the waters.* towards my bridge. The whole bottom of the valley, which until then had been partly dry, was under water. People from the bridge itself came hurrying towards me. The bridge had been torn away and carried down the stream, the spiteful river having thus destroyed in a moment the arduous work of six days. In half an hour the Tana had risen about four feet.

By the carrying away of the bridge, my people, who had been at work on the other side of the river, were suddenly cut off from us; and as they had no weapons they were actually in *Our workmen cut off.* danger of their lives. By the most strenuous exertions our brave Somali, Mahomed Ismail, at length succeeded, after several useless attempts, in getting a rope across, and fastening it on the other side, so that I could draw the people over to me.

To keep up the spirits of the caravan, I now, in spite of our failure, distributed rewards to the most diligent of our people for the work they had done in the bridge-building, and commented on the whole affair rather from the humorous point of view. I also at once despatched a column up the *Change of plan of advance.* river, to settle on a path for the march of the following morning. But I felt very heavy at heart as I returned to my camp, for again we were to encounter all the misery of a march through the forest in a direction that was turned away from the goal of our journey; and I did not even know whither this march would ultimately lead us, as the position of the source of the Tana was as yet unknown to me.

PERSEVERANCE UNDER DIFFICULTIES. 199

In the afternoon the river suddenly began to fall again, and once more the delusive hope played around me, as I had once set my heart upon it, that I should cross the Tana after all, and get rid of it. The following morning I started for a reconnaissance down the river, and discovered a place where, from our side, great blocks of rock projected for about a third into the narrower river, while on the opposite side, as I was assured by the Mbe people, who were proceeding parallel with me on the other shore, a flat sandbank thrust

<small>Another chance.</small>

BUILDING THE BRIDGE ACROSS THE TANA.

itself into the waters. In the midst, the water was naturally all the deeper, and roared along with enormous power; but this space only comprised about thirty feet, and it might be assumed that it could be bridged over with hurdle work and ropes.

I will pass in silence over the labours of the next days. On the evening of November 25th I once more believed that we should be able to cross the river on the morrow. Herr von Tiedemann was unwell on that day, and I sat alone in front of my tent. On this evening I enjoyed the strange spectacle of beholding, not indeed the setting of the moon, but rather the rotation of the earth, in a manner I had never before experienced. The moon stood like an immovable point, exactly on the horizon, in an atmosphere that, above the Tana, had been completely cleared by thunderstorms. When I fixed my eyes steadily upon it I saw, not by any means the moon moving away, but the earth turning upward, like a huge balloon, from west to east, whereby the moon disappeared from my view.

A strange optical delusion.

Towards nine o'clock heavy masses of cloud drew up from the west, and soon the crashing of thunder and the glare of the lightning became incessant, while plashing rain poured down on us like a deluge. My people were some of them crying out in the midst of the flood, and I experienced a downright feeling of shame to think I should be lying dry in my tent, while outside all were roused up in wild confusion, and had to suffer.

With dismal forebodings I went next morning to the place where the bridge stood. The river had risen again five feet during the previous night, and I could see already, from a distance, that the bridge was entirely below the surface of the water; it was only on the opposite side that some of the beams stood forth. Like Frederick the Great at the battle of Kollin, I was ready, as I could not induce any of my people to go across to the other side, to throw myself alone on the rope into the raging current. But so soon as I reached the furthest point of the rock, and heard the roaring, howling, and hissing of the floods, I understood that any attempt of the kind would be constructive suicide; and I at once gave the order for breaking up the camp and resuming the march down the margin of the river.

Failure of the bridge.

In half an hour the expedition was on the march, with beat of drum, and the black, white, and red flag displayed in the van. I was the last in the camp, and stood there with very peculiar feelings. "Idly gazing and astounded, seeth he his works destroyed."* I ordered them to saddle my horse. But my horse, dead beat from the rain deluge of the

A day of misfortunes.

---

* From Schiller's "Lay of the Bell"—describing the impotence of man against the forces of nature.—TR.

AUGUSTA VICTORIA FALLS.

last days, stood with trembling knees, and when we tried with cuts of the whip to get it to move, it suddenly sank to the ground with half-extinguished eyes. So I had to part from the faithful beast, and pursue my way with the wanderer's staff in my hand.

The march soon led through a high leafy wood, always up hill, till towards eleven o'clock we were about five hundred feet above the level of the river, and now looked straight down upon the current. What a magnificent view was displayed before us! Below our feet the river poured down a glorious cataract, and we heard the roaring of this fall in all its majesty. Looking towards the north-east, the eye wandered for a long distance over the rapids below the fall, and like a silver thread the Tana wound its way through the rocks, that reared their heads in bold outline, and the green woodlands. I was obliged to acknowledge that if the Tana with its powerful current was inconvenient enough from a practical point of view, it produced an elevating and, indeed, an altogether overpowering impression, contemplated thus objectively. And up here, under the deep blue vault of heaven, face to face with the development of power in the depths, rested the peace of God. The sun beamed all the clearer after the storm of the preceding night; it played with the tops and crowns of the trees, and painted varied shadows on the ground, which was gay with fresh grass and flowers of every kind. In the branches could be heard the cries of the feathered world, and over the blossoms in the woodland shade hovered many-coloured glittering butterflies, and the fresh forest air poured with an invigorating flow into the lungs. Over the sordid cares of the moment the soul soared away amid these impressions, and new hope came into the heart.

A grand forest scene.

I determined to chronicle on the map of the Tana the union of powerful grandeur and moving loveliness presented by the landscape at this part, and called the cataract with its rapids, after the name of Her Majesty the German Empress, the "Victoria Augusta Fall."

The " Victoria Augusta Fall."

Towards one o'clock I found Herr von Tiedemann, with the

column, waiting in the wood, expecting me. Our march was finished. I went with Hussein and Rukua and the elder of the porters, Musu, to look for a camping-place. Towards three o'clock we had found one, and I sent Rukua back to lead the column to it. The porters came, but the camels delayed to make their appearance, and when at last they arrived, at about seven o'clock, I was informed that besides my horse the list of victims for the day included a camel, a donkey, and a porter named Omari Washikura. At all events there was a completeness about the losses of this day.

<small>Various losses.</small>

On the morrow we marched about seven thousand paces further, in a tremendous rain. I pitched my camp in a clear space by the river, where the current in the middle was so strong that it caused waves like billows of the sea to roll to the banks. As on this day the Tana repeatedly rose and fell again, a man might easily imagine himself by the shore of the ocean.

The following day deserved to be marked with red letters. At first we still moved on among mountains. All at once the declivities became gentler, and then they suddenly ceased altogether. We were on level ground. The mountain chain was passed, and once more we had the steppe before us. We were now about 2,500 feet above the level of the sea. I cannot describe what a feeling of satisfaction it was to have these Mumoni Mountains behind us, with their difficulties and discomforts, that for a time had almost threatened to spoil our expedition.

<small>A "red-letter day."</small>

Once more I pitched my camp by a dry affluent of the Tana. A glorious afternoon, full of sunshine, dried the exhausted column, and soon brought back the old confident tone of mind among the people. As Omari Washikura, to whom I had, on the day before, immediately sent his brother, Ben Omari, proved to be utterly incapable of following us, his brother came back to me to-day, asking permission to remain with him, and as soon as the sick man was convalescent to return with him to the coast. I gave him the required permission, and fitted him out richly with five sheep, cartridges, and pieces of stuff. I also gave him letters for the

<small>"Sick-leave" granted.</small>

coast; but unhappily the two brothers never reached Lamu. Probably they were slain by the Wakamba, or captured as slaves.

In the night between November 28th and 29th, to the terror of my people, three lions appeared in our camp; but they soon rushed away. For the next few days we were once more surrounded by the complete solitude of African bush steppes. We came into regions where the wealth of animal life was greater than anything we had yet met with. On the march, on the 29th, we heard for a long time the roaring of lions close by the column, and we repeatedly came upon rhinoceroses, which in their stupidity rushed full upon us, till the bullets from my double-barrelled rifle, catching them in the region of the eyes, forced them to turn round. On the left a mountain region now appeared, which was called by Marongo the Tia mountain land. He informed me that it was a day and a half's journey from thence to the place Kitui. *Lions in the bush.*

Thus we came once more into regions where a white man had been before us, if only for a short time—the old faithful Krapf. I now began to hope that we should soon come upon the fords of the river indicated by him. *Krapf's country.*

The vegetation assumed ever a fresher and more attractive character. Magnificent fan palms formed a lovely screen to the Tana, and great colonies of cacti shot up amid the various kinds of acacia in the steppe. On November 30th I succeeded in killing two hippopotami in a little affluent of the Tana,—a welcome addition to the store of meat for my Waniamwesi. *Hippopotamus shooting.*

On December 1st we came to a place in the river where it divides into seven forks. "Here," thought I, "is where we must cross," and I at once began to ascertain the depth of the separate arms of the river. Meanwhile my column had come up, and we halted on the right hand shore, while my people waded across one arm after another. As we were thus taking our ease, an enormous rhinoceros suddenly rose up, in one of the little islands situated in the river, and was about to cross the arm of the river *Hunting a rhinoceros.*

that separated us from the island, exactly in the face
our column. My people jumped up in alarm, but a shot
the head from my rifle induced the colossus to retreat, a[nd]
attempt the passage of the river somewhat lower down. B[ut]
this brought the animal directly into the line of fire, and n[ot]
only Herr von Tiedemann, but several of the Somalis also sh[ot]

HUNTING THE RHINO-
CEROS.

at it, so that the rhin[o]
ceros fell on the ground n[ot]
far from the place where [we]
had intended crossing. This was a slight encouragement, b[ut]
not enough to sweeten the failure of the passage.

Six of the arms were fordable; but the seventh represent[ed]
the real course of the Tana, and hard as my people tried [to]
find a place where they could wade across, the thing th[is]
time again proved to be impossible. I remained at this fo[rd]

THE CARL ALEXANDER FALLS.

of the river all the day, and next day marched further up the stream amid a succession of showers of rain. En- counters with rhinoceroses now formed part of the incidents of each marching day. On December 2nd I moreover lost my last faithful dog Tell, who suddenly ceased to follow me, and, when I coaxed him, all at once fell down trembling, with glazed eyes; so that I had to leave Rukua behind, with a request to Herr von Tiedemann to shoot the poor creature. On such expeditions as these it is, in fact, unadvisable to take dogs, or anything to which our heart grows attached, for it is necessary to part from one after another, and each parting has its separate heartache.

The difficult Tana again.

Death of faithful Tell.

According to Marongo's assertion, we were to arrive in Kikuyu to-day, but this prophecy turned out to be a great mistake. We did, indeed, come once more to a wooded mounted region, in front of which the Tana spreads out into a broad, lakelike form. This I caused to be sounded at various places with regard to its depth, and thus gained something like a measurement of its surface, which I should estimate at an average of 3,300 square yards.

A little above this lake-like broadening of the river the mass of water flings itself down in a cataract, which, though it rushes over several terraces, must, according to the aneroid barometer, have a total height of more than three hundred feet, and may accordingly be safely reckoned among the greatest waterfalls of the earth. As it began to rain towards noon, I pitched my camp on the slope of a hill, about 90 feet below the summit of this cataract, and here the rock literally trembled beneath us. The uproar was so loud that we could hardly keep up a conversation. If this waterfall were situated in any other part of the world it would certainly every year be a goal for the journey of the cultured world. I named it, after His Royal Highness the Grand Duke of Saxony, the " Karl Alexander Fall."

A grand cataract, the "Karl Alexander."

From the heights I could see, in the north, a quite peculiarly formed mountain region, which I was a few days later to identify as Kikuyu Muea. Mbe was, accordingly, now behind us, and the hope that we should be quit of the wearisome Tana became stronger.

From the mountains that had so much frightened us on December 2nd we emerged on the following day. The Tana likewise began to depart from its southern direction, and to incline first towards the west, and soon afterwards even a little towards west-north-west. This likewise was a hopeful sign.

On this day, December 3rd, I shot a magnificent waterbuck and an antelope; and now it was that I suddenly astonished Herr von Tiedemann with an art which he did not at all suspect me of possessing. I began to occupy myself with the kitchen, and prepared pieces of the back of the waterbuck with a sauce that almost excited Herr von Tiedemann to admiration. He thought he had never tasted anything like it at Hiller's or Uhl's. As we always had a supply of milk and cream, and the proportion of meat in the strong broth was of no great consequence, and we had also salt and pepper still in store, the preparation of a strong sauce did not present very formidable difficulties. From that time we occupied ourselves more and more with the labours of the kitchen, and practically degraded to the character of a scullion the brave cook, Bamberger, who seemed to be of opinion that, for possible scientific investigations in Europe, he ought to accumulate every kind of East African remnant in our cooking pots. Bamberger was one of the originals of the expedition, and entirely disproved the dogma of the educational importance of the whip of hippopotamus hide. In the best natured manner he opposed all measures of mine that were directed towards cleanliness, or even the punctual accomplishment of work. When the hippopotamus hide whip was flourished over his back, he prayed to Allah, which he never did at other times. When the unpleasant performance was closed, he would betake himself with a cheerful smile once more to his cooking pots, which might have done well for the retorts in the witch's kitchen at a performance of Faust. In the further course of the expedition I appointed him as drummer; and as he showed himself completely competent for this office, and also fought most manfully in our combats, a reciprocal feeling of esteem was developed between him and us, towards the end of our intercourse.

On December 3rd, about ten miles above the Karl Alexander Fall, I discovered another waterfall, which poured down its waters like a note of interrogation. It turned towards the north, then towards the east, shot down in that direction, and immediately below the fall the river turned to the south, and then, by the west, took its way back directly to the north. This fall I entered on my map, after the name of our most prominent scientific African investigator, as the "Schweinfurth Fall." At noon on this day I pitched my camp below a conical rock, which is situated about at the place where Krapf must have reached the river. The spot cannot be determined with complete accuracy, as the statements of Krapf are too undecided. In honour of the old German missionary and honest investigator I called this hill "Krapf Hill." *The "Schweinfurth Fall" and "Krapf Hill."*

The forest that skirts the Tana now, to my great joy, receded more and more, and on the following day ended entirely. Instead of it, there extended before us the wide, red grass-covered steppe, over which the eye could range for many miles, where on the horizon great herds of antelopes or bucks stood forth, and among them zebras and giraffes; where the rhinoceros thundered along, and where at night the lion lifted up his voice. This is the actual elevated steppe of Ukamba Kitui, which we now entered, and the sight of which made our hearts beat higher, in view of the fact that from here we should come direct into the region of Kikuyu. *Steppe of Ukamba Kitui.*

In this steppe the Tana began to receive affluents from the south side likewise; a proof that we were approaching the western chains of mountains. On December 6th we crossed several of these southern tributaries, that cut their way deeply in the red clay soil, but generally contained only a little water. I had learned from the people of Mbe that the Wakamba of Kitui, when they went to Kikuyu and the Baringo, *Tributaries of the Tana.*

crossed the Tana at a place where it becomes two rivers (mito mibili). The name of Dika was given as that of the second river, which was described as coming from the south. For some days we had been looking for this division of the river. On December 6th I made a long excursion up the Tana for this purpose with Hussein Fara. The river had here taken a course exactly towards the west-north-west, and my servant Rukua had declared, already on the preceding day, that he had seen the Kenia, which is not improbable, as he had very sharp eyes. Hussein and I discovered the long-sought fork, on the

FORDING THE DIKA.

6th, in the far distance. Greatly elated by this fact, we returned to our camp that afternoon.

On December 7th, after a two hours' march, this division of the river was reached towards the south-west, among the mountains towards the Naiwasha lake, and the passage over the Dika, in which the people had to wade up to the chest in water, with all the cattle and the burdens, was happily accomplished in about the same space of time. I made the people stand in a row across the Thika river, which is about 90 feet wide, and thus one sheep after another was passed from hand to hand to the opposite bank. From this spot the Tana turns more and more towards the north.

Passage of the Dika.

We are now at an elevation of about 4,800 feet, and the nights begin to be refreshingly cool. The thermometer at night falls to 15° C. (58 Fahrenheit), and the evenings are agreeable and refreshing. The firmament in the hours of night appears more immeasurably lofty than anywhere else on account of the more rarefied atmosphere. The grasses and herbs be- *The steppe:* come sweeter and fresher, and entirely new kinds of *its plants* trees appear. The number of game animals is enormous. *mals, etc.* Zebras, antelopes, rhinoceroses, wild hogs, and waterbucks are often seen feeding peacefully together. Every day's march yields prizes to the gun. The enclosure of the Tana again increases, but it has lost the hard character that marks the lower steppe, and offers an easy access to the waters. On our left the mountain chain begins; its outlying ridges extend to the river. It can be none other than the Kenangop range that borders the Naiwasha lake on the north-east. Already on December 6th we *Traces of* had suddenly, to our great joy, come upon traces of *travellers.* mankind, in the shape of a place with cooking stones and tent pegs that had been left behind. These traces soon ceased again, but we could perceive that they led across the river. I was informed in Kikuyu that they were those of an Arab caravan, which had marched from Mombassa to Lorian.

All this led us to suppose that the time of our laborious march on the Tana was drawing to its conclusion, and that we must be near Kikuyu. After the passage of the Tana, *The Tana* as I was accustomed to express it, the "poison fang" of *difficulty* the river had been extracted. Its volume of water had *overcome.* decreased by one half, and it flowed quietly and modestly onwards. On December 8th we suddenly came upon some men. They were upon the opposite side of the Tana, but with Marongo as an interpreter, we were able to make ourselves understood by them. They were people from Kikuyu, who had driven their herds down stream, and they told us that we should reach their country on the morrow.

On this day we descried for the first time, though it was to some extent veiled, the mighty cone of the Kenia, just in front of us, on the horizon in the north. When towards evening the clouds parted, its snowclad summit was also to be seen. That was an impressive sight; and our hearts beat higher when we thought amid how much toil, care, and exertion we had been led thus far. On October 25th we had thought we beheld the Kenia before us; and now December 8th had come before our passionate longing had been realised. What a wealth of impressions and experiences filled the space between those two dates! Unhappily, on that evening, one of my porters from Dar-es-Salam, Amdallah, was left behind. He had for some time suffered from consumption, and I had long since relieved him of his burden. The lions, which roared on that night louder than usual behind us, unfortunately left no doubt as to the poor fellow's fate.

The Kenia Mountain.

Poor Amdallah.

On December 9th, the Tana again turned a little more towards the north. We crossed a second western tributary, and now quitted the Tana altogether, which from this place turns, in curves visible at a long distance, towards the Kenia, from which it flows. About noon on this day, we came to a little water pond in the neighbourhood of the Marawa, after we had journeyed all the morning over long-drawn ridges of hills with gradual declivities. The Kenia was continually half to our right, and on the left were the mountains of the Naiwasha Lake, called by Thomson the Aberdare Range.

The Aberdare Range.

We were now in Kikuyu, a high plateau region between Kenia and the western mountain ranges, in which the Tana really collects its volume of waters. In the afternoon the proud, noble Kenia Mountain stood for the first time before us, in its whole unsullied purity, in the sunlight, with its snow-fields sparkling in the brightness. Towards four o'clock on this day my Somalis and Rukua, whom I had sent out to settle on the road for next day's march, suddenly brought five Wakikuyu into our camp. These were the first strange faces we had encountered for more than a fortnight; and for the first time again, since that period, vegetable food for us and our people! They told us, that they would lead us next morning to their villages, and declared themselves willing to pass the night in camp. They also immediately inquired

Wakikuyu men in the camp.

AMONG THE WAKIKUYU. 211

whether I had come to buy slaves of them, announcing themselves as having some of both sexes for disposal.

Violent showers poured down upon us at night, as they had previously done by day. Next morning early we were already on the march, in a north-westerly direction. The Wakikuyu showed me the place, in the distance, where Count Teleki had lived. At eleven o'clock, when we mounted a far-extending acclivity, we came upon the first settlements of men. The people hurried to meet us, bringing flour, sugar, and mtama for sale, of which my people bought as much as they were at all able to carry. Then, accompanied by a crowd that could be counted by thousands, we ascended another range of heights, and so through thick grass, waving like a sea, down to the margin of a little river, the Marawa, which we had here to cross. The Wakikuyu knew the white race, and indeed in a manner advantageous to us, for Count Teleki and Herr von Höhnel had lived here. These two had taught the people of Kikuyu a certain amount of good manners; and it amused me to see how, in consequence, the natural insolence of these natives was continually mingled with outbreaks of fear. *Friendly intercourse with the natives.*

Of this I had immediate experience when, by the river Marawa, people came towards me, with the demand that I should pay tribute before I crossed. I gave them to understand that such was not the custom with us; but I was obliged to order them in peremptory tones to stand away from the ford, before they suddenly declared themselves entirely willing to let us pass the Marawa without tribute. Here, in the afternoon hours of December 10th, a very original passage of a river was effected, my people and the Kikuyu working harmoniously together. The water reached about to our necks, and it may be imagined what difficulties were experienced in getting the cattle and the loads of powder through the rushing current. I had at once caused a rope to be stretched across the river, by which the men could hold fast. The work went on diligently, the camels and donkeys were pulled across by the rope, and at about four o'clock the last had been carried over. *Passage of the Marawa.*

Here it was that the brave Marongo manifested all the noble qualities of his character. His time of suffering was now over, and I intended to send him, rewarded with presents, back to his home. For the first time he walked with us to-day as a "gentleman," unguarded. His heart, filled with gratitude, swelled high when I presented him, in addition, with an old gun and some ammunition. He brandished the gun like a lance, high above his head, pointing it at the Kikuyu people, and marching upon them with enormous strides whenever, during the passage, they came too near the baggage. He maintained strict order, and was thoroughly impressed with his own personal importance. "The Wakikuya take me for a European," he said, glancing with a grin at his European costume.

Marongo a gentleman at large.

A little above the ford by which the caravan had passed over was a swaying bridge, high over the river; and by this I myself, with Herr von Tiedemann and a few soldiers, crossed to the opposite side. Our tents had already been pitched there. A crowd, some thousands strong, surrounded our camp, curiously and importunately. Partly from a freak of ostentation, I resolved to have a solemn entry. Two Somalis were sent on in advance, incessantly blowing the trumpet, and behind them came a drummer beating a march. Then followed Rukua with the black, white, and red flag; behind him came I, and behind me Herr von Tiedemann. Two Somali soldiers closed the procession. In this way we proceeded along the distance, some hundred paces, to our camping-place. The first thing I did was to have the crowding Kikuyu people, who had come dangerously near our flock of sheep, driven back twenty or thirty steps in every direction by the Somali soldiers, and to inform the elders that any raids upon our herds or upon the goods of the expedition would be answered by shots from my guns. Then I entered my tent. We were now in Konse, about five miles from Kitura, the Kitui of Count Teleki. The way to Baringo appeared to lie open before us, and we thought we had left behind us the technically difficult portion of the German Emin Pasha Expedition.

Solemn entry into Konse.

CHAPTER VII.

THROUGH THE MASSAIS, OVER THE LEIKIPIA PLATEAU TO THE BARINGO LAKE.

"Who helped me 'gainst the Titans' insolence,
Who rescued me from death, from slavery?"
GOETHE.

IN Kikuyu seven days of rejoicing refreshed the expedition, which was greatly exhausted by marches on the Upper Tana. **Stay at Kikuyu.** Kikuyu is a land that can feed its people, a region literally flowing with milk and honey. It is a mountainous country, with gently-sloping lines, inclining towards the Kenia on the south, richly watered, and with a fresh and verdant appearance everywhere.

There are two divisions of this country: Kikuyu Mbi on the right side of the Tana (Kikuyu 2), where we now were, and Kikuyu Mnea on the left bank of the river (Kikuyu 1). Thomson has much to say of the untameable cruelty of the inhabitants—exaggerated like all the pictures of the dangers among the inhabitants of this steppe offered by Thomson to the wondering European. Count Teleki and Herr von Höhnel had thoroughly impressed the thievish Wakikuyu with the superiority of European weapons; accordingly, as I have already stated, we were brought face to face with a whimsical mixture of impudent, thievish propensities and sentiments of timid submission. The native chiefs hastened to make their peace with us, which was ratified by the slaughter of a goat or a sheep. The younger inhabitants, however, could not restrain a propensity to thieving, confirmed by transmission through many generations, even after, with the concurrence of the elders, I had ordained that every attempt at robbery should be visited with capital punishment, and a number of them had suffered the penalty for indulging their thievish proclivities. If the flocks were driven through the land, luxuriant with grass, a black arm, its possessor entirely hidden in the bush, would be suddenly thrust forth from one side, and seizing a sheep by the hind leg, would endeavour to vanish with the prize as quickly as it had appeared. Then the Somalis would fire into the bushes, out of which a yell of pain would burst forth, proclaiming that just punishment had overtaken the evildoer.

Thus for seven days did we travel through this beauteous Kikuyu, whose flora already exhibits the forms of the temperate zone. Here we met with a kind of tree that reminded us vividly of our European oaks. Here I saw the fresh green clover of the North German borders, on which donkeys, goats, and sheep browsed with much enjoyment. Clear rivulets gushed onward through all the hollows, with an average temperature of only 14-15° C. (55-58° Fahr.). The nights were already bitterly cold; the thermometer fell by ten o'clock to 8-9° C. (44-47° Fahr.). In the morning the hoarfrost lay spread over the fresh landscape. On December 16th the registering "lowest temperature" thermometer for the first time exhibited the register at the freezing-point.

The ways here generally lead along by the far-extending hills. When we had reached the heights, we every morning enjoyed the view of the grave and majestic lines of the Kenia,

HUT OF THE WAKIKUYU.

which appeared more and more prominently in the north. The Wakikuyu snatched greedily at the coloured and white pieces of stuff which we still had with us, and brought in return into our camp quantities of poultry, milk, and honey, besides abundance of grain of all kinds, so that black and white revelled alike in the treasures of this beautiful land.

Trade with the natives.

Kikuyu is, beyond all question, the pearl of the English

possessions, with the exception of Uganda. It is unfortunate that this cool and fruitful land lies so far distant from the coast; otherwise it would most certainly be suited for colonisation by European agriculturists.

On December 17th we were approaching the western rampart of Kikuyu. On this morning I had endeavoured to engage fifteen fresh Kikuyu porters, as far as to the Baringo. The impudent fellows, not taking warning by the experiences of the preceding days, had believed they could completely overreach us by demanding payment in advance, in stuffs, for their services to the Baringo, and then absconding with their booty. But I was prepared for an attempt that was so exactly in their way. The fugitives were at once laid low by a few bullets from our guns, and we succeeded in getting hold of and securing eleven of these Kikuyu people, who were now compelled to make up their minds to undertake with us the march into the Massai lands they detested. This happened in the midst of a crowd of people that might be counted not by thousands only, but certainly by tens of thousands; for the whole of Kikuyu is extraordinarily populous. But the multitude was so intimidated that the people dared not attack us, though there were only about fifty of us in all.

The cheating Kikuyu porters.

We were led by the High Priest Kikuyus, who, with all manner of mysterious ceremonies, blessed the bridges we had to cross, and sprinkled the roads. We were also requested every moment, when we came to a parting of the roads, to spit. The Wakikuyu declared it was to avert the evil omen; but I suspected it was to deliver us over to evil spirits. We passed by a number of pleasant-looking kraals and fish-ponds, with the glittering Kenia beside us, towards the right hand. Gradually the cultivated land was left behind. A dense primeval forest separates Kikuyu from the land of the Massais. Climbing plants twist themselves among the primeval thickets, and malignant stinging nettles make any deviation from the beaten track practically impossible. Over the only path that leads out of Kikuyu they have made strong fences, between which deep *chevaux-de-frise*, concealed

Magic ceremonial.

Defences made by the natives.

from the traveller, have been sunk, their beds studded with sharp pegs, to receive the unsuspecting stranger falling into them. I had one of these trap pits opened, and found that it was at least eighteen feet deep. Whoever falls among these sharp pegs is lost beyond all question. To the left, through the wood, I was obliged to have a way cut, to avoid such dangers for my column. We came immediately to a great clearing, where for the first time for a week we again saw great herds of game animals. Here we halted, and took leave of the chiefs of the Wakikuyu who had accompanied us. I only took three guides forward with me; they were to lead us out of the primeval forest to the elevated plateaus of Leikipia, as far as the boundaries of the Massailands. In the west, to the left of us,—for we were now marching continuously to the north-west,—rose sharply and clearly defined the mountains of the Naiwasha Lake, called by the Massais Subugu la Poron. To the right, permanently in our view, rose the Kenia, an invaluable landmark for the further progress of the expedition, as I knew that it is situated exactly on the equator, and that the Baringo Lake, which I was trying to reach, is about ¾° north. I had, with the exception of the question of water, no difficulty as to keeping the line of march for the following weeks. {margin: Guide to the Massai-lands.}

On the margin of the primeval forest, in a second clearing of the wood, I had my camp pitched, towards noon, near a pool from which the column could draw water. All the waters of Kikuyu pour themselves into the Tana. We now stood on a watershed, for we came this day to the river region of the Guaso Nyiro, which, emerging from the mountains of the Naiwasha Lake, makes its way towards the north, past the Kenia and the Endika Mountains, where it turns towards the east. We stood here, on December 17th, at a parting from whence a portion of the waters flows towards the north, while close by, the Tana, having its source in the Kenia, pours its flood towards the south. In Kikuyu the Tana bears the name of Sagana, which is identical with Kilima, meaning simply "mountain." {margin: Region of the Guaso Nyiro.}

To-day the Wakikuyu guides left us. They could be of no further use to us, as they did not know the Leikipia Plateau, through which the Massais range.

The thermometer this night sank to 28° (Fahr.). It was true Christmas weather, suitable for the approaching feast. *Coldness of the nights.* The lightly-clad people cried out with cold and pain; and I myself used, from this time, to wake regularly every morning between three and four o'clock, shaking with cold, though I was ensconced in four blankets, wore woollen drawers and shirts, and spread my winter wrapper over me. In the morning, when we marched through the frost-whitened grass, the cold seemed to cut into our feet, though we wore woollen stockings and boots up to the knee.

When the sun got higher, we had the most lovely weather of a German August and September. The air above was so thin that the eye seemed to rove through immeasurable distance. A hill, a tree, even a single leaf on the tree, stands out in the crystal air as though it might be grasped. The game animals, feeding in the sunlight in crowded groups, seem so entirely within range, that involuntarily the traveller raises his gun again and again for a shot at them. But, behold! the ball strikes midway between the hunter and his intended prey. But *A mountain region.* throughout the whole bright morning, on the right, rises the Kenia, with what appears to us its seven-peaked, icy crown towering into the blue sky, lifting itself proudly and royally above the eminences around. Spotless and pure it stands, not like a thing created, but like an embodiment of the Eternal Himself; and involuntarily the heart is lifted up above the petty cares and thoughts of every-day life. When, at noon, the sun rises to the zenith, the temperature likewise rises to 30°. But now the Kenia begins to veil his icy head in the clouds, and early in the afternoon a hailstorm, or a driving rain-shower, descends upon our camp, by which the temperature is at once cooled down again to 17-13° C. (62-55° Fahr.), so that from five o'clock we have congenial and cool November weather.

Thus the march through the Leikipia Plateau goes on, so

THE KENIA.

long as we are under the north-east monsoon that sweeps down from the Kenia. This whole country has something spectral and unearthly about it. We are here, perhaps, on the oldest piece of earth, which has certainly been turned towards the sun for millions of years. Leikipia stood above the surface of the sea at a period since which South America has twice been buried deep in the waves, and thus it still confronts the gazing wanderer. It is an ancient, wrinkled woman, weary of life, and withered; ready, on her part, once more to dive down, rather to-day than to-morrow, into the reposeful abyss of death. To the right and to the left it has set up its sons— similar to itself, and ancient likewise—Subugu la Poron and the Kenia. But the Kenia is the firstborn. He wears the kingly crown that sparkles like diamonds, and with him is the habitation of the dark forms of the primeval forest that here perform their mysteries. According to the belief of the Massais, the Godhead itself dwells on the Kenia, and, unapproachable, this seat of the Divine is cut off from the contact of the finite. To ascend the towering height of 23,000 feet will be a problem which only the boldest and most stout-hearted of our Alpine climbers might hope to accomplish. Proudly he draws around him the threefold girdle of bristling, impenetrable virgin forest, of boulders of the wilderness, and, lastly, of iron-bound glacier ice. If the Hellenes had seen the Kenia they would have dethroned Olympus, and have transferred hither the abodes of the Eternal Ones. Had Shakespeare wandered upon the plateau he would have made it the scene of the witches' incantations in Macbeth; for here, and not in the Scottish Highlands, is the grandest background for the creations of Ossian.

This plateau we reached on December 18th, penetrated with the awe of the eternal in the presence of these mysterious and minatory scenes of nature. On the 19th we had still to traverse a lengthened woodland district, to cross several rushing brooks, which brawled along over volcanic débris towards the north. On this day we set up our camp at the Guaso Nyiro, which, cutting its course deeply through volcanic stone, rolls to the north, to the left of the Kenia. On the afternoon of this day I ascended a hill, which commanded the surrounding country. There all at once the sight stretched immeasurably into the endless distance of the north. The land undulates gently, and there is nothing to limit the observer's gaze. The fancy is awakened, and the sight seems to stretch to Abyssinia, to Egypt; a delusion, certainly, occasioned by the transparency and elasticity of the atmosphere.

I determined, in the first place, to traverse this steppe in a northern direction till the Kenia turned off to the south-east, and then to turn westward, to hit one of the southern affluents to Lake Baringo.

<small>Line of march.</small>

The land seemed deserted. On the summits of the hills appeared the peculiar circumvallations of the Massai kraals. No human beings were to be seen. All this increased the gloomy character of the landscape in the highest degree. The danger in this marching through pathless regions, without guides acquainted with the locality, is principally connected with the question of water. The finding of water is entirely a matter of chance. How could I know, when I broke up my camp in the morning, where I should find water, or if I should find it at all? With this object in view, I used always, with a few of my people, to precede the column by at least an hour's march, always keeping a look-out for the course of a brook, or a pond of standing water.

<small>Important question of water supply.</small>

On December 20th, I certainly succeeded in solving my problem in an especially favourable way. That day we encamped due east of the Kenia by an affluent of the Guaso Nyiro, the most charming camping-place we had found on the whole expedition. The shore is here fringed with a growth of fine grass, which in the autumn is bright with all kinds of colours. This carpet is studded with picturesque groups of trees, among which the acacias, with their sharp outlines, are especially prominent. On account of its loneliness I named this valley—which I can recommend to future travellers as a camping-place—the "Gretchen-Thal." This name suddenly occurred to my mind when, on returning from a prospecting excursion towards the north, I looked down

<small>Camping in the Gretchen-Thal.</small>

on the pleasant picture of my encamped column, engaged in cooking, and on the grazing herd, the camels and donkeys, and the cheerful people. On the afternoon of December 20th, just as I was working at a report for Germany, in which I declared that Leikipia appeared deserted, and that it seemed as though the Massais had fled before us, the Kenia suddenly, and for the last time, poured down on my tent such a hail-storm as threatened almost to crush it to pieces, as though to express utter scorn of my delusion. The Kenia, whose sons the Massais call themselves, knew his children better! He was perfectly aware that they retreat before no man, and least of all before a little expedition like ours; and of this we were to receive proof next day. *A tropical storm.*

Before continuing my narrative, I will here insert a short account of the general plan of the German Emin Pasha Expedition under my leadership. Previously to my expedition, the Massai route had in general been considered as practically almost impassable. Entirely exaggerated opinions were held as to the dangers of this road. In view of these difficulties, Stanley had made up his mind to make the long circuit round the Cape and up the Congo, although, compared with ourselves, he had unlimited means at his disposal, and had the support of all official circles working in Africa. An assertion of Stanley's has been communicated to me, in which he gave it as his opinion, that to get through the Massais in warlike fashion, a man must have a force of at least one thousand Europeans at his back. A large part of the German Emin Pasha committee continued to hold similar opinions. Wissmann, as well as Reichardt, declared the Massai route to be impracticable; and Wissmann especially, when he laid before the committee his plan for the march up the Tana, had included in it, as a matter of course, the avoiding of the Massailand and Uganda. *Plan of the German Emin Pasha Expedition. Reichardt's opinion.*

This view, moreover, could not appear altogether unwarranted, after perusing the reports of the two travellers who up to that time had traversed Massailand, namely, that of Dr. Fischer, and that of Thomson especially. Thomson commanded an expedition in Massailand, compared with which our resources must appear altogether ludicrous; and yet he had in that country submitted to a treatment which, judged by a European standard, not only falls below the notion of "gentlemanlike," but must be plainly designated as unworthy. Proofs of this are plentifully found in his book of travels. Thomson thought he could produce an impression on the Massais by all kinds of tricks, as, for instance, by playing the part of a great magician, taking out his set of false teeth and putting it back again, preparing effervescing lemonade with Eno's Fruit Salt, and declaring the devil was in the mixture. I have tried to produce an impression on the Massais by means of forest fires, by fiery rockets, and even by a total eclipse of the sun that happened to occur on December 23rd; but I have found, after all, that the one thing which would make an impression on these wild sons of the steppe was a bullet from the repeater or the double-barrelled rifle, and then only when employed in emphatic relation to their own bodies.

The results of the Thomsonian manipulation were what might have been expected. I will cite a few passages from his book of travels which prove this very clearly. I do this, on the one hand, to prove what ideas the Massais in these regions must have had of the white race, and, on the other, because for my part, on my first meeting with the Massais, I myself was influenced by the impressions produced by Thomson's descriptions. I was firmly resolved, let come what would, not to put up with such behaviour towards myself.

Among other things, the Massais had forbidden Thomson to shoot on their territory. Thomson himself tells us that though there were oxen, showing the neighbourhood of Massais, about a mile off, he resolved, in consideration of their starving condition, to risk a shot. The beast falls, and Thomson's servant rushes up to it, and at once tears off a piece to eat raw. Thomson tells us, in continuation (3rd edition, p. 368), "My exclamations of disgust were stopped by hearing warning voices, and, turning about, I saw my men pointing in the direction of the Massai kraals. 'We are in for it now!' I mentally ejaculated, as I saw great numbers of warriors with their gleaming spears coming towards us at full trot. I retreated at once towards my men, Brahmin bringing a huge chunk of zebra with him. The warriors were soon down upon us, and in response to their cries we stopped, and closed up. The Elmoràn, in the most savage manner, demanded an explanation. As they stuck their great spears in the ground, they asked us if we wanted to fight. If so, they were ready! We at once put on our most 'umble,' Uriah Heep manner, and looked profoundly contrite. We were deeply grieved, we said, for thus infringing their customs, but we had done it for the purpose of getting a particular part of the creature's entrails, which was necessary for the making up of our medicine. They had to be further softened by a *largesse* from our sadly-diminished stores, and then they consented to let us go on."

On page 379 Thomson further says, concerning the Massais of the region into which we were now going: "Certainly they were rude to a degree I had not yet seen. They scrupled not to stop us, by holding their spears at my breast, and demanding beads. . . . The Massais were in very great numbers, and continued nasty to a degree that was maddening. They played with us as a cat does with a mouse, and the ending would, without doubt, have been the same, but for a certain hazy respect and fear they had of me, as a phenomenon the power of which it was not safe to rouse." (So Mr. Thomson imagined!) "I had to sit continually on exhibition, ready to take their filthy paws, pull out my teeth for their admiration, and spit upon them, to show that I did not mean them any harm."

On page 381 he says: "I was plundered of almost everything. The warriors were quarrelsome, and the slightest accident at any moment might be the signal for a massacre. The Massais in front ordered us not to come near them till they had discussed all the *pros* and *cons* of my case. . . . At last, after four days' detention, we were rejoiced to hear that we might proceed."

Thomson also relates how one day a Massai took hold of him by the nose to see if it were as loose as his teeth; that another day the Massai warriors cut down his guards, and that he was then compelled, in addition, to pay tribute to the Massais because blood had been shed on Massai soil.

<small>Massai arrogance.</small>

Such had been the previous record, in the relations between the white race and the arrogant Massai nation, which I was to encounter on the following day.

For a long time it was believed that the Massais belonged to the great Hamitic race in the north-east of Africa, and were related to Somalis and Gallas. According to newer investigations, they are said to belong to a Great Central African race, from the regions of the Upper Nile and Mambukuland. This point I must leave undecided. Like Attila's Huns and other nomadic peoples, they have developed, in the highest degree, a propensity for plunder and a thirst for blood. The continual flesh diet on which they live has physiologically increased their natural savageness, and the brutalising of the feelings that must ensue with people who are in the habit of slaughtering and devouring, in a cold-blooded manner, the domestic animal they themselves have reared, appears here in a very decided manner. A people of herdsmen, where the shepherd is not at the same time the butcher of the cattle, will be able to develop the gentler feelings of the heart, as we have often found them described in the Arcadian songs. But where, through centuries of generations, the herdsman has been also the slaughterer of his cattle, as is the case with the Mongols on the elevated plains of Central Asia, and with the Massais on the elevated plains of Central Africa, there, by inheritance, an almost absolute state of brutalisation must ensue. This law has always explained why the herdsmen of the nomadic races have constantly furnished the most savage phenomena in the world's history, as we have seen them embodied in Europe, in personages like Jhengis Khan and Attila.

<small>Character of the Massais.</small>

<small>Social status of the nomadic herdsman.</small>

In addition to this psychological law comes the fact, that such races are prevented, by the peculiarity of their employment, from establishing themselves anywhere permanently. The possession of great herds necessitates a continual change of domicile. While the agriculturist is obliged to remain on his soil, to which his heart becomes attached, the nomad is indifferent to the charms of owning a home. Where there is pasture for his cattle, where there is water for them to drink, thither he goes with his herds; and the practice he thus gets, from his youth up, makes him capable of undertaking warlike expeditions across great tracts. Thus the Massai has become the terror of the whole of East Africa. Living in the elevated plains eastward of the lakes, where winter and summer, following each other not within the round of twelve months, but within the space of twenty-four hours, dwell together all the year round, where night has taken winter for itself, while tropical heat rules by day, he is hardened to all discomforts of climate. With hasty foot he traverses the steppes to the rich lands of the Bantu in the south, and even to the places on the coast. Faithful to the natural character of his kind, he has built up for himself a religious belief, according to which only the Massais are sons of the Deity, and as such have a natural right, confirmed by God, to all the cattle of the earth. Any man, not being a Massai, found in possession of cattle is guilty of death, and the Massai remorselessly murders not only the able-bodied men, but the infant at the mother's breast, girls, and old women. Slaves from other tribes he altogether despises.

Warlike propensities of the nomad.

Religious and moral status.

But if all the conditions are present that tend to bring to full development the wild and brutal qualities of the man, on the other hand, among the Massais there may be recognised the ennobling influence which is produced in every people by the inherited consciousness of rule. Accustomed to see all around them tremble at the name of Massai, the warriors of the race have acquired a natural pride, which cannot be designated otherwise than as aristocratic. From the first the Massais assumed towards me the deportment of young haughty noblemen. They recognise only one kind of work, namely, war and the protection of the herds. All industrial occupations, such as trading with passing caravans, the

Haughty and overbearing deportment.

manufacture of weapons and implements, and the driving of the herds, are undertaken by the Wandorobbo, a kind of Massai, who live here intermingled with the warrior tribes.

The haughty and warlike spirit innate in the Massais is considerably strengthened by the peculiar matrimonial institutions, and by the constitutions of the race. Their form of government is the very ancient patriarchal one which we meet with in the Old Testament. The elders of the families manage the great affairs of the tribe in their councils, and represent the tribe abroad. The family and the tribe, into which it has developed, is self-contained with regard to those without; consequently here, as everywhere under the same conditions, the vendetta has developed itself in its purest form. If a member of one tribe is murdered by a member of another, retribution is exacted from the second tribe as such, whether the vengeance strikes the murderer or another.

Form of government.

But the point that seems, above all others, peculiar to the Massai community is the strict social separation of the married from the unmarried element. The unmarried Massai, called Elmorán, is simply a warrior. He may live only on milk or flesh, at any rate only on animal food, and, more than this, he may only take *one of these* at a time. If he wishes to go from the milk to the meat diet, or the reverse, he must begin by taking an emetic, so that the two kinds may never meet in his stomach. This also is an arrangement that has been hallowed by religious consecration. He is likewise fond of sucking the blood from a live ox, a hole being cut in the neck or the nape of the beast, out of which the Massai warrior drinks the blood in full flow, afterwards stuffing up the hole with grass. Vegetable diet is only permitted to the married Massais and the women. The warrior considers it effeminate. But amid the great plateaus, far from the borders of any tribes who practise agriculture, this must be only a very rare interruption of the daily milk diet. The milk is generally eaten sour, in the form of curds, when it certainly affords a very wholesome and palatable food.

The Elmorán among the Massais.

Milk diet.

On entering a Massai kraal, this precious beverage is seen

ELMORAN WARRIORS ADVANCING TO THE ATTACK.

in a number of gourds, standing against the walls in the houses, that are built of clay and cow-dung. The milk is in various stages of sourness, up to ten days old.

The Elmorán, the unmarried Massai warriors, live in villages of their own; with them are united, by free-love bonds, the girls of the tribe, each of whom has a right to choose a lover according to her fancy. This is a new incentive to the warlike rough spirit of the Elmorán; for a girl will choose the man who rushes into the battle with the greatest fierceness and temerity, who kills the greatest number of enemies, and brings home the largest booty in cattle. Thus even the soft impulse of love impels the Massai warrior to his marauding foray, and when he creeps along to the villages of the Wasagura, or penetrates into the streets of Mombassa, he has perhaps in his heart the image of some fair one of the elevated plains under the Kenia, to whom he wishes to do honour. *Separate Elmorán villages.*

While the Massai warriors stride along absolutely naked, in the right hand the broad handsome lance, on the left arm the broad shield adorned with heraldic devices, which covers almost the whole body, and perhaps a short fur, embroidered with beads, thrown over the shoulder, and falling to the hips, the girls are clad very decently in furs, reaching up to the neck, as I have found customary among all the proud and warlike tribes of north-eastern Africa. On the other hand, the more slothful and effeminate tribes of the Bantu in the north-east of the Victoria Nyanza, and the people in Kawirondo, let their girls go nude. Somalis, Gallas, and Massais prefer keeping the charms of their fair ones for themselves. *Equipment of the Massais.*

Widely different from this more poetical relation between the sexes in the kraals of the Elmorán is the actual marriage state among the Massais. It is a mere matter of purchase, which is managed by the father for the son, who is not always much gratified to change the freer life of the Elmorán kraal, by a removal into the kraal of the old married people. In contrast with the impulses of jealousy *Marriage among the Massais.*

which characterise the relations of the Elmorán kraal, the Massai in the married state is said to be exceedingly indifferent with respect to his wife's faithfulness. To have as many children as possible, especially sons, in whatever way it may be, is the chief object of the mature man, who altogether, as far as the idea of possession was concerned, in his practical stolidity, reminded me greatly of our peasants in the Lower German marches

On December 21st, I was destined to make the acquaintance of these remarkable tribes. On that day I had kept the course of my expedition towards the north-north-west, in order to approach, in some measure, the mountains that run from the Naiwasha Lake northwards; at the angle I hoped to come upon *A hunting country.* the Guaso Narok. As I was pursuing my way, in advance of the column, with Hussein and two of my servants, I came upon great herds of zebras, and with my gun I brought down two. I left a servant behind with the slain beasts, with orders for my column, when it came to the place, that the zebras should be cut up, and their flesh carried into the camp. I went on with Hussein only, to continue the search for water, beside which to encamp. On the way Hussein informed me that the Somalis did not care for zebras, and consequently I promised him to shoot an antelope for the Somalis and myself. Towards eleven o'clock we came to a running stream, which we afterwards ascertained to be the Gnare Gobit. After some difficulty we succeeded in finding a place for crossing; whereupon I sent Rukua back to bring up the column. I *Crossing the Gnare Gobit.* myself fastened a piece of paper to a tree for Herr von Tiedemann, with a request to pitch the camp at this spot, and then I continued my way in a northern direction, to shoot the promised antelope for Hussein. The Gnare Gobit is skirted throughout its whole course by a strip of high forest, which, however, does not extend beyond the margin of land fertilised by the river. In this strip of forest, by the ford of the river, the camp was to be set up; and through it we now strode on to look for antelopes. It may be about three hundred feet broad on the left side. We had

MAKING ACQUAINTANCE WITH THE MASSAIS. 229

not yet passed through it, when on a clearing on the left I suddenly saw great numbers of oxen. On an acclivity beyond the forest I also saw great herds. *Massai herds.*

I called Hussein's attention to this phenomenon, and he immediately informed me, in his broken English, that he saw "too much men." These could be none but Massais. I whistled through my teeth, and thought we had better leave the antelope hunting alone for that time. It would be more prudent, after all, to go back to our camping-place, and wait there for the advancing column. We had scarcely got once more to the tree with the paper on it for Tiedemann, when all at once, cheerfully singing, "O ho! O ho!" from our side of the river, and up stream and down stream on the opposite bank, in groups of three and four, Massai warriors came pouring in upon us. As we had established no kind of relations with these Massai tribes, I ordered Hussein to guard the rear, and presented my gun at the group that was approaching. *First meeting with Massai warriors.* I had laid my revolver on the ground beside me, to have it ready at hand. The Massais, so soon as they saw my proceedings, laid down their shields and spears, and thus unarmed came in a friendly way towards me. I also laid down my rifle, and the Massai warriors greeted me with an amiable "Wadsak," after first, in token of their friendly sentiments, spitting at me and likewise at Hussein Fara. To my questions they answered, that I was in the territory of Elbejeto. In an instant we were surrounded by twelve or fourteen young slender Massai warriors, who immediately began to sing a monotonous song, and to dance round us in a row.

Gradually, to my great satisfaction, my column came up; first a few Somalis, who in general are not at all behind the Massais in haughtiness, and were accordingly at once acknowledged by them as equals, whereas no Massai condescended to greet one of my porters. The Massais endeavoured to frighten my people, by exhibiting to them the effect their lance thrusts could produce, and also that of their poisoned arrows. I was very glad to see that my Somalis simply laughed at it, while they retorted by trying, by pantomimic representa- *A game of brag.*

tion, to give the Massais a notion of what our repeating guns could do.

Suddenly some new Massai warriors came, with the request that I should look out another place for my camp, as this was the ford at which they were accustomed to water their horned cattle. I informed the Massais that I did not feel inclined to do this. "You can, however, drive your cattle to the ford, although we are encamped here." After a long hesitation they gave way; and so, on that morning, everything went on in a friendly manner enough.

Symptoms of trouble to come.

I resumed my interrupted sporting excursion beyond the forest, ordering four men of my following to go with me. On stepping forth from the wooded enclosure, the traveller sees before him a low hill, entirely covered with pasture grass, which runs parallel with the Gnare Gobit, and gradually shelves away towards the south-west and north-east. On this hill in the south-west lies the chief kraal of Elbejet, and in the northern slope the Elmorán kraal that belongs to it. Further kraals are also situated on the right bank of the Gnare Gobit, and towards the north all the heights are occupied by such villages.

The chief kraal of Elbejet.

Some of these kraals consist only of huts of clay, standing contiguous to one another in a circle, and open on the inner side; but others are surrounded outside the exterior walls of these clay huts with a fence a yard thick and three or four high, made of thorns and underwood, with gates leading through it to the interior; and, according to African circumstances, the place becomes absolutely impregnable if well defended. The Massais, who on their foraging expeditions always sleep out in the open, trusting only to their own vigilance, have, in their own country, perhaps the best fences that are to be found in all Africa; and herein, again, is manifested the practical warlike spirit of this nation.

Fortified kraals.

On the declivities of the hill, by the Gnare Gobit, thousands of oxen and sheep were grazing, guarded by Elmorán warriors, or by Wandorobbo. The Elmorán are armed only with lance and shield; the Wandorobbo and the older Massais with bows and arrows.

Our appearance before the gates of Elbejet naturally produced a considerable sensation. From all directions warriors came hurrying up to welcome us, and the Massai girls also pressed forward, manifesting curiosity; and they, too, welcomed us with a grasp of the hand. Unfortunately I shot twice at a vulture with my rifle, and missed each time; whereupon there arose contemptuous laughter, especially among the old Massai women. The conceit of the Massai women, with regard to their sons, beats anything one can ever meet with in the way of unreasoning or monkeylike affection; and they are fond of showing this feeling as ostentatiously as possible, by contemptuous behaviour towards other men. *Reception at Elbejet.*

When I returned into camp, towards two o'clock, I met some bulls of the Massais that had turned wild; and from the right hand a few elders of the Massais came hastening towards us. As one of the bulls was preparing for a hostile attack upon us, I stretched him on the ground with a shot from my rifle; an incident which evidently impressed the Massais in a very disagreeable manner. I then requested the elders to follow me into my camp, to hold a conference with me. When we approached my quarters, I noticed large numbers of the Massai warriors drawn up beneath a tree, and about to regale us with a war song. I knew that the sequel of this would be their demanding tribute from me, which I was resolved not to pay. Besides, I had very vividly before my eyes the ill-treatment that Thomson had suffered at this very place, and wished to clear up certain matters between myself and the Massais without delay. Accordingly I shot at a vulture on the tree under which the Massai warriors were seated; and when a fat elder came to me in front of my tent, where I was sitting in an arm-chair, to forbid my shooting, I twice fired off my rifle over his head. Then I at once gave orders to my Somalis to turn all the Massais out of the camp; but I myself followed them, and summoned them to a conference outside its precincts. *Putting on a bold front.*

As I could only speak a little of the Massai language in a broken fashion, the negotiations had to be conducted through one of the Kikuyu prisoners as interpreter, for Rukua, my servant, could in some degree make himself understood by that people.

Rukua as interpreter.

ANNOYED BY BULLS.

I proposed to the elders of the Massais that they should furnish me with guides as far as the Baringo Lake, and sell me a few donkeys. In return, I would give them the only load of iron wire I possessed, and also a few beads, of which ornaments I had a small bag with me. We would mutually secure each other in our possessions, and part as friends.

"You must know," I said, "that among white men also there are differences. Five years ago, a white man came to you, whose race differs from our race as much as, for instance, the Wakikuyu differ from yours. The white man who was here was an Englishman (Inglese), and you treated him badly enough. But I belong to the race of the Germans (Badutschi), and we would rather die than submit to such treatment. If, therefore, you will not agree to all friendly proposals, you have only to tell me so, and you can also have war with us." The Massais thereupon caused it to be made known to me that, in the first instance, I must pay tribute for their young warriors, before they would consent to treat further with me. When I simply refused to do this, they rose up suddenly, without a word of leave-taking, and the Kikuyu man told me that now we should have war. *Systematic speech to the Massais. The Massais decide for war.*

I went into the camp to breakfast, and resolved to bring the matter to an issue that very afternoon. I gave over the command of the camp to Herr von Tiedemann, and betook myself with thirty men to the chief kraal of Elbejet, to make sure of the intentions of the Massais. I posted my people in a half-circle behind me, and stepped into the foreground with Rukua and a Kikuyu interpreter, beckoning the elders of the Massais to come to me. I now waived my demand that they should sell us donkeys, and asked only for a guide to the Baringo, offering to pay for the accommodation. The exasperation on the part of the Massais, who had restrained themselves in the morning, was so great, that several of the Elmorán came rushing onward with levelled lances to transfix me. But I was glad to find that my people replied to this demonstration with shouts of laughter. In fact, two or three volleys would have been sufficient to lay low all the Massais who were present. *Preparations and proposals.*

While I thus negotiated with the Massais, an old Massai woman came and stood next to us, breaking out into a scornful laugh at every word I spoke. I had her put aside by two of my Somalis, and came to an agreement with the elders of the Massai that both sides should keep the *An agreement arrived at.*

peace, that they should next morning furnish me with a guide to Baringo, for which service I was to pay, and that they were to respect my property and I theirs.

My Kikuyu man had contributed greatly to the procuring of this agreement. When he had tried to intimidate the Massais by saying, "You cannot make war against the white man, he comes from God. See! he leads eleven of us Wakikuyu bound with cords,"—the Massais answered curtly and proudly, "But we are not Wakikuyu, we are Massais."

After the treaty which I had concluded with them had been sealed by the spitting ceremony, I went back to my camp, with the feeling that, diplomatically, I had after all been beaten by this arrogant Massai elder. My attempt to make head against their last plans had failed when opposed to the cold arrogance of this man, whose equal in imperturbability could hardly be found, and who, quite at the close of the conference, when he had concluded the treaty with me, expressed his contempt for my porters, who were sitting inside the enclosure, by stepping up close in front of them, pointing at them with a derisive gesture, and breaking out into a short scornful laugh.

Insolent behaviour of the natives.

He may probably have scattered Zanzibar caravans often enough. Firearms do not in themselves intimidate the Massais at all. Even in the year 1887 they cut down, to the last man, an Arab caravan numbering two thousand guns, laid all the corpses in ranks and rows side by side, and in scorn put each man's gun across his shoulder. Generally, in fact, the caravans fire their guns once, and then immediately take to flight; whereupon they are regularly massacred to the last man by the swift-footed Massais. The Massai knows how to protect himself from the first shot by throwing himself on the ground, or sheltering himself behind a tree; and long before the muzzle-loader has been made ready for a second discharge, he has come bounding up, to finish the matter with a thrust of his lance.

Behaviour of Zanzibar caravans.

In the evening I had four sentries posted round the camp, and towards nine o'clock I betook myself to the margin of the wood, to send up blue and red rockets, as a token to the Massais that we were on the alert. I heard the turmoil and roaring of the Massais in both kraals when I turned back to my camp. *Precautions in camp.*

In the night, I was awakened several times by shots from my sentries. When I enquired the reason, I was told that Massais were prowling about the camp, and had just been attempting to steal a load of cartridges from it. Already in this night the thought came into my mind whether it would not be best to attack Elbejet without hesitation. As yet our people had beaten all who had stood against them; but terror of the Massais was still alive in the majority of the porters, and I knew very well that it was just the first result that would here be decisive. I let the idea go, however, in the hope that the Massais would next morning fulfil the obligation they had taken upon themselves, of providing a guide for the journey, and that I should be able to leave the whole disagreeable state of things behind me by a rapid march. *A critical position.*

When I rose next morning it was reported to me, in the first place, that the promised guide had not come; secondly, that, in spite of all our vigilance, two loads of stuff had been stolen out of the midst of the camp during the previous night; and, thirdly, that we had been pelted with arrows. Quite a number of these arrows were exhibited to me as a proof. *Hostile demonstrations.*

My resolution was now taken. If the Massais had so little respect for our agreement of the previous day, it was clear that if, after the kind behaviour I had exhibited on Saturday, I left this breach of the treaty unpunished, they would proceed to far greater acts of aggression. It was one of the most critical decisions of the expedition, and I asked Herr von Tiedemann for his opinion. As he agreed with me, I gave him the order to hold thirty-five men ready for action. Silently we strode onward through the forest, when suddenly all the Somalis fell on their knees at once, and began to implore the protection of Allah from what we were now to encounter. On reaching the border of the wood we formed a *Preparations to fight the Massais.*

long line. I took the right wing, and gave the left to Herr von Tiedemann, while Hussein Fara led the centre. The black, white, and red flag was carried by Rukua, who hurried on a few steps in advance of the line. Thus we marched rapidly to the north, directly upon the kraal. Between the kraal and ourselves were a great number of cattle, and the man who kept them called out to us in the most insolent tone to go round his herd, or we should drive the beasts away. That we few men should intend to attack Elbejet, the worthy fellow in his conceit never supposed, until a bullet passed through his ribs, and permanently silenced his insolent tongue.

On account of the cold in the morning the Massai are fond of sleeping late, and consequently we completely surprised Elbejet. Our firing woke up the sleepers. On a sudden, the men came rushing out of the gate against us, while women and cattle ran down the declivity on the other side in precipitate flight. I was opposed especially by the elder with whom I had negotiated on the previous day, and by his following. They tried to defend the entrance into the kraal. Three of the elder's arrows flew past me; and, for my part, I also missed my mark twice. My third bullet crashed through his temples. And now the Massais poured down the opposite declivity in headlong flight. We succeeded in this first fight in killing seven of them in all, and, so far, we had not yet suffered a single casualty.

Attack on Elbejet.

I was now master of Elbejet, the dominant position of this whole region, and had also a herd of cattle numbering more than two thousand in my possession. I now determined to send back a part of my company to the camping-place by the river, and at once to bring up all my column to this capital position. This resolve, though undoubtedly judicious in itself, could not be carried into execution, because suddenly the rattling of musketry sounded from the camp, and I saw that great bands of Massais were rushing towards it from all sides. If the camp should be taken by the Massais, and our ammunition thus fall into their hands, we were all of us lost. Therefore, back to the camp

Design to hold Elbejet.

Back to the camp.

ATTACK ON ELBEJET.

A DANGEROUS MARCH. 237

at full speed to guard it. For my part, I had shot away all my cartridges, and was obliged to hasten to my loads of ammunition. The trumpet gave the signal for a retreat, which was accordingly commenced by us in perfect order. For all that, in the course of it, three of my people were laid low by the Massais, Nogola, the Mangema elder, being one of them.

On arriving in the camp I at once had ammunition served out—to the Somalis as many cartridges as each of them was able to carry; for myself seventy-five cartridges, fifty of which I entrusted to Rukua. In an instant the tents were down, and the order was given to march out of the wood towards the right. I went on in advance with Musa Somal, Alo Agal, and my two servants, Rukua and Buana Mku, to decide upon the road for the column. The great herds, the camels, the donkeys, and women, were placed in the centre, and Herr von Tiedemann, with another detachment of Somalis, brought up the rear. *The order of march.*

We had been marching only three minutes through the forest, some thirty yards in advance of the column, when Alo Agal suddenly reported, "Mimanka brenjehei!" (Many men!) And there they were coming on, the proud Elmorán of the Massais, like a great pack of wolves, in hundreds, passing tree by tree to get at us. Alo had scarcely made his report to me, when he fell dead at my side, pierced by an arrow. Rukua and Buana Mku, as soon as they saw what was coming upon us, were seized with a panic, and fled precipitately towards the column. I knew perfectly well that if I did the same the Massais would come thronging after us with their battle-cry, and we should be defeated and overthrown in an instant. Consequently I made up my mind to take up the gauntlet there and then; and it was fully clear to me that now every bullet must find its billet, if this day was not to bring the end of things for me, and perhaps for the German Emin Pasha Expedition also. *Attack by the Elmorán.*

Then a very singular combat occurred here in the river forest of the Gnare Gobit. From tree to tree the Massais advanced, but always with caution, to cover themselves from the bullets. I may say truly, that for the next few minutes I gave up my life and all of us for lost; nevertheless, on noticing the perfect skill of their method of attack, I could not suppress a kind of admiration of my opponents, whom, at the same time, I mortally hated. Several times I succeeded in knocking over two of the foremost Massais with a double shot; whereat the others were startled, and left me time to load again. But it was especially Musa's repeating gun that had quite a remarkable effect upon them. With the muzzle-loaders they had already made acquaintance, but the system of the repeaters must have appeared to them supernatural, and therefore uncanny. Meanwhile I was calling for Hussein; and after five minutes of the most painful anxiety I was joyfully surprised at seeing my people at last hastening up from behind to the rescue. A Massai, who was just preparing to thrust at me, was first laid low by a bullet in the face from our kitchen-boy Fargalla; and now, with a hurrah, I advanced upon the Massais. At first they stood firm, but gradually they gave ground; and after half an hour of fighting we reached the margin of the wood, from which the Massais, with their faces still turned towards us, slowly retreated towards Elbejet, drawing off on each side.

By this time the rear column, with Herr von Tiedemann, had also been attacked, and the rattle of musketry at times increased to an extent that was somewhat alarming for me. Herr von Tiedemann got into imminent danger of his life, by the sudden failure of the mechanism of his repeating rifle, while the Massais were likewise pressing in upon him. But the intervention of the porters—the preliminary fight having allowed the time necessary for bringing them into line—very soon decided the affair on this side also; and now I pressed forward more and more upon Elbejet, driving away the Massais right and left, until I had two-thirds of the hill in my power.

The command, "Misigo miote embele!" ("All loads to the front!"), which I called into the wood, was a welcome signal to Herr von Tiedemann that the affair in the front had been decided in our favour; and presently there appeared,

ATTACK ON THE MASSAIS AT AGARE GOBIT.

on the margin of the forest, first my camels, then the goatherds, and, lastly, all the porters with their loads. These loads I caused to be laid down, two-thirds of the way up the hill, and drew up the people for the second attack on Elbejet itself.

At first we moved cautiously towards one of the gates, in front of which we took up our position; and then we moved round the kraal to the other gates. As we slowly approached the entrance to the kraal we became aware, to our satisfaction, that Elbejet was abandoned. At the second attack we had also discovered our two loads, that had been stolen the previous night. Now I gave orders to have Elbejet plundered, and set on fire at eight corners.

Second attack on Elbejet.

There were howls and roars of rage when the Massais, who were concealed by thousands in the thicket round the hill, beheld what we intended to do, and saw that what they had been accustomed to inflict upon others was now for once happening to themselves, in their own country.

What time the Advent bells were calling to church in Germany, the flames were crackling over the great kraal on all sides, and mounting towards the heavens. We felt a short glow of triumph; which was, however, very soon removed by the thought of what had now to be done.

Burning of the kraal.

At the side where I had fought, we found forty-three Massai corpses, all killed by bullets in front. But the loss of the Massais must certainly have amounted to three times that number, as the fighting had been just as hot in the rear as in front, and the enemy had in most cases been able to carry off their fallen fellow-tribesmen. As those who had fallen on our side, seven in number, had been mutilated in a shameful manner, we made reprisals, for our people cut the heads off the Massai corpses, and hurled them high through the air, and down among their fellow-countrymen by the hill below.

But we had lost seven men in the fight; a loss which was sufficiently grave, considering our scanty numbers. But much more serious was the fact of which I became aware while the flames of Elbejet were soaring up, namely, that the Somalis had shot off nine hundred cartridges from their repeating guns, and that consequently I had only six hundred cartridges left. The porters, too, had fired away quite inordinate quantities of ammunition. In fact, I could have exclaimed with Pyrrhus, "One more such victory, and I am lost!" For I was not even in a position to go through with a second fight like the one I had just waged. The Massais had only to keep on attacking us, and they would with mathematical certainty hunt us to death.

Serious expenditure of ammunition.

Added to this, I was entirely without guides for the road, and in a hostile country where we could not expect to receive any information as to the whereabouts of water.

It was eleven in the forenoon. My column was to the last degree exhausted. Some of the people had also been wounded with arrows. I had a great mind to encamp up on the hill for the rest of the day. On the other side of it the Elmorán kraal was still standing, into which I could throw my column. But in that case I should probably have had to fight my way anew to water, and, beyond this, I should be exposed to the far greater danger of the Massais drawing reinforcements from the neighbouring district of Lashau, so that on the next morning we should have a much more perilous battle to fight out than we had fought to-day. In such a position as mine, thoughts of retreat will flash for a moment through a man's brain. How if I marched back to Kikuyu, and from thence undertook an advance in some fresh direction? The sweet peace of the evenings lately passed came with seductive power before my soul.

Difficulty of proceeding.

I rejected both the ideas that occurred to me, and at half-past eleven gave orders for marching onward in a course towards the north-east. There I might hope to find a water-course, either the Gnare Gobit or the Guaso Nyiro. But the chief thing was, that I should thus get out of the centre of the infuriated Gallas, and might hope, by making a circuit, to avoid their whole territory.

Orders for an advance.

Forward, therefore! The great herds in the centre, all loads packed, I set the column in motion along the hill. On the opposite side I first had the Elmorán kraal set on fire, and then marched in slow time down by the north-east slope of the hill. Not a single nail of all our property was left as a prize to the Massais; not one head of all the cattle we had taken was left behind. The Massais, who did not at first understand our movements, presently set out on the march behind us, at a convenient distance. But the bullets that we sent towards them from time to time, from my double barrel and from Tiedemann's repeater, kept them far from the column. *The Elmorán kraal fired.*

Towards three in the afternoon I succeeded in finding an approach to the river, by which I could water my thirsty caravan, men and animals. Northward of this place I saw a hill above the river that commanded the surrounding region, and here I would pitch my camp. I made towards it with my advanced guard, and found that it was occupied by many hundred Massais. My nerves were so relaxed, and the occurrences of the previous night and of the present morning had made us so indifferent to danger, that, without waiting for the main column, I marched forward towards the hill with the few men I had with me, and fired into the Somalis. And the defeat of that morning had made such an impression upon these people, that they rushed from the place in wild flight, and crossed over to the right bank of the Guaso Nyiro. *The Massais routed from their position.*

Above, I found an enclosure for cattle. I at once had twelve sentries posted round about the hill to watch the Massais, who occupied the heights around, had the tents pitched, and established my column comfortably. Each man received permission to kill as many beasts as he liked, and then a terrible slaughter began among the oxen and sheep. The digestive powers of a negro are of a magnitude of which we in Europe can hardly form a conception. If he has one sheep he eats it up; if several are given to him he makes them disappear in the same manner. *A feast for the black men.*

Towards evening I betook myself, with some of my soldiers, to a ford below the hill by the river, and had great quantities of water carried up for the column for cooking purposes. Not a Massai was to be seen.

Our frame of mind was a very grave, but by no means an unhappy one. Herr von Tiedemann wrote a conclusion to his journal on that day, because he thought we should not outlive the night. I also was of opinion that the Massais would attempt an attack in force during the night, and consequently kept the half of the column commanded by Herr von Tiedemann under arms until midnight, and the other half, which I commanded, watched from midnight until morning. I had outposts pushed far forward, which were visited continually, and watchfires were lighted as far down the slopes of the hill as possible.

Precautions against surprise.

The night was pitch dark. Showers of rain fell at intervals. I also caused rockets to be thrown up, to show the Massais that we were on guard. The noise of these rockets unfortunately scared away a part of our herd, on which we never set eyes again.

An anxious night.

In all these troubles the only comfort was resignation to the unalterable decrees of Providence, and the conviction, that whatever might happen I had no need to give the hated foe the satisfaction of having themselves given me my death. In such a case I considered I should be fully justified in reserving my last revolver bullet for myself.

Before daybreak I marched away in a northerly direction. Whatever we could not carry off with us of the Massai furniture we had captured I had broken to pieces, so that it should not fall again into the hands of the enemy. The whole morning we skirted the margin of the river in a north-west direction. Not a Massai showed himself. The boundless steppe seemed dead, as it had appeared two days before.

March along the river.

After a march of seven hours, necessarily slow, as the herds of cattle had to be kept to right and left of the column, we came to a bend in the river, where it turns suddenly towards the west. Here I found a ford, on which I made the whole column cross to the right shore, and then again set up my camp in a Massai kraal on the hill, on the opposite bank.

Could it be that the Massais were giving up the notion of taking revenge for their defeat of the previous day? We tried to persuade ourselves to nourish this hope; and for a little distraction from our cares Herr von Tiedemann and I, after breakfasting, sat down in my tent to a game of écarté.

Doubtful tactics of the Massais.

Towards five o'clock my servant came into the tent to report, "Massai wanakuga!" ("The Massais are coming!") We went out to the entrance of the tent, and, sure enough, there they were, advancing across the chains of hills that lay by the shore; marching on silently, in columns, ever from east to west. A troop came close up to the other margin of the river, and established itself under a tree on the shore, exactly opposite our camp. I called for my rifle, and shot across, hitting one fellow in the leg, whereupon the whole column incontinently decamped.

An attempted lodgment frustrated.

I had now made up my mind for the last and decisive combat. If the Massais attacked again, after their defeat of the previous day, I could only assume that all this was done in the full determination to destroy our column at any cost. That was only to be effected by simply rushing upon us regardless of the number slain on their side, and thrusting us to death with their lances.

Then, suddenly, a thing happened such as I had until then been accustomed to read of only in romantic pictures of travel. At about five minutes past twelve the sun all at once began to be darkened. At first we did not ourselves know the meaning of this, but very soon saw that a total eclipse of the sun was commencing its course. More and more deeply did the gloom spread over the wide desert landscape, out of which the Kenia and the Subugu la Poron yet reared their heads threateningly aloft. As though the earth would throw itself once more into that chaos and old night whence it issued forth, so lay the lofty plateau of Leikipia before our gazing eyes. The shudder of the infinite crept even into our hearts, lifting them above the present, and the cares that were before us. My own people were seized with terror at

An opportune eclipse of the sun.

this sign from the Godhead which was being displayed in the heavens. So much does each individual feel as if he were in the centre of the created world, that he associates even the great phenomena of nature with his petty destiny.

The Massais, whom I had allowed, two days before, to entertain the belief that I was commissioned by their Engai, believed, as I heard a few days later, that in this appearance in the sky they beheld a great stroke of magic of my effecting. Or perhaps they thought that there was in the eclipse of the sun a warning from their god to themselves. Certain it is, that when the sun illumined the landscape once more, we saw them marching away westward, in separate bodies, silently, as they had come; and there was no attack made upon us that evening. Only a single outpost was established on the hill beyond the river. The Massais set fire to one of their own kraals, probably to warm themselves, and as I assumed, to keep us awake. In the evening my servants waited at supper, each with his rifle on his shoulder, as we sat at table, and I was again compelled to keep half the column under arms through the night. Real sleep was, of course, not to be thought of.

Effect of the phenomenon on the Massais.

On the alert.

Next morning I searched the valleys by the river for hostile spies, and I succeeded in starting a few on the opposite bank. I shot at these fellows, but without hitting one of them.

At six o'clock I started on the march, with the conviction that the Massais were certainly on the right road to annihilate us. They had only to keep us constantly awake, so as to shatter our nervous power, and to attack us from time to time, that we might shoot away our cartridges, and there could be no question but that we should fall victims to them at last.

Fabian tactics possible.

It was December 24th, a day on which we are accustomed in Germany to light up the Christmas tree. On this day we marched until one o'clock in the afternoon, always in a north-west direction. On the march a number of sheep and goats dropped down, and I had them killed, for I would not let them fall alive into the hands of the

March of December 24th.

Massais. My attention was kept on the alert the whole of this morning by Massais, who continually marched in a parallel line with our expedition on the opposite bank of the river. I shot across several times, but uselessly, for the distance was too great.

At one o'clock I had the camp pitched once more upon a hill that commanded a view of all the surrounding country, on the right bank of the Guaso Nyiro. I distributed a load of powder among the bearers, and kept them casting bullets the whole afternoon. I also completed the supplies of repeating gun cartridges carried by the Somalis, so that each man had again sixty cartridges in his bag. Then I gave each of my bearers a piece of red cloth, as a head covering, from the flag stuffs we had brought with us, to make their outward appearance more warlike, and to imbue them additionally with the feeling of the soldier. *Preparing ammunition.*

Thus the state of feeling in the camp was one of considerable liveliness, and the cheerfulness was increased when, shortly before three o'clock, I succeeded in bringing down, with a good shot at eight hundred yards, the leader of the seven Massais, who had also halted on the further shore opposite to us.

The Guaso Nyiro flows round the hill on which we lay, in almost an exact half-circle. That evening I established eight outposts round the camp, and again had fires kindled in advance of these.

At six o'clock we were at supper, and something like a Christmas feeling came into our hearts. I asked Herr von Tiedemann to keep watch for a few hours, and to wake me a little before midnight. I wanted to celebrate Christmas Eve by stretching myself on my camp bed as early as half-past seven, though fully dressed, and endeavouring to get a few hours' sleep. *A disturbed Christmas Eve.*

At ten o'clock I was awakened by a shot, which was followed by a whole volley. Directly afterwards I heard from the south-south-east the hyena-like battle-howl of the Massais.

The Massais had advanced from the north, along the course of the river, and thought to surprise our camp from the south.

They had come upon Daud Wais, who kept watch here, and he had at once knocked one of them over, by which means the Somalis had been alarmed. I came out of my tent, and, to encourage my men, called out to the Massais, "Karibu, Elmorán, mutakufa wiote!" ("Come on, Elmorán, you shall all die!")

An impending attack.

I at once had everything in the way of camp-fires extinguished, gave over to Herr von Tiedemann the command on the river side where we were not attacked, and myself turned to the further side, where the Massais were howling. I had everything we possessed in the way of chests and loads pushed forward, and ordered my people to lie down behind this rampart, to shelter themselves from the hail of arrows from without. Till this was done they were to keep up a partial fire of volleys upon the Massais, to frighten them from attempting to storm our camp. Then I had rockets brought, and one rocket after another flew hissing up into the black sky of night, giving just enough light to enable our best shots to pick out their mark among the threatening figures. A fantastic picture, which could not fail of its effect upon sensitive nerves. My people set up a rhythmical song, always ending with the burden, "Kupàndu, Kupàndu Scharro!"

Plan of operations.

This night was indeed a whimsical illustration of the biblical text, "Glory to God in the highest, and on earth peace, goodwill toward men!" The crackling of the rockets, the roaring of my own people, and the banging of the shots, together made a din that truly appeared more consonant with the Walpurgis night of the First of May than with the solemn seriousness of the celebration of the birthday of Christ.

Till one o'clock did the din continue. Then we heard the roaring of the retreating Massais gradually dying away in the south. On our side only one man had been wounded, a porter of the name of Boma; he had been shot through the arm by the Somalis, in the line of whose fire he had foolishly placed himself. The Massais had had greater losses, as was proved next morning by numerous pools of blood and various shields that had been left behind.

Results of the fight.

CHRISTMAS EVE AT GUASO AVIRO.

Thus the surprise had failed; but our situation next morning was more gloomy than on the previous day. The Massais had it in their power to attack when they would. If they were beaten, the situation remained for them unaltered. But if we were only once beaten we were all of us lost. Added to this was the fact that for four nights I had been without real sleep.

Continued danger.

Towards sunrise I started once more with my exhausted column. I marched onward, for an hour, along the right bank of the Guaso Nyiro, which I then crossed by a ford. I wished on that day to try and make an advance in a more westerly direction across the steppe, as I could not know at all whither the Guaso Nyiro would lead me.

We were now away from the districts that are touched by the winds which sweep down from the Kenia. We came into completely dried-up plateaus, which had been burnt by the Massais only a short time before. The plains which southward of the Leikipia appear slightly undulating, here exhibit themselves in a more massive and compact form. They are real border plateaus, of which the one that is placed higher always leans steeply towards the lower one, forming to a certain extent a fringe. In the north, peculiarly-formed groups of stone are found on these plains, and give the landscape a strange and remarkable appearance.

Features of the country.

The wind, whistling in a ghostly manner from the north over the dreary steppe, whirled up columns of ashes, that went sweeping across the plain, visible from afar like forms from the shades below. The north wind droned or rather sighed through the half-burnt flute trees, in melancholy fashion, a spectral tune to the procession of these phantoms of ashes.

A feeling of infinite desolation and solitariness fell upon our hearts, when, on the left bank of the Guaso Nyiro, we had climbed to these plateaus. The black expanse seemed to stretch out to infinity. Nowhere a river course or a water pool to be seen. Here and there on the horizon forms of Massais emerged, to disappear again so soon as I fired my far-carrying double-barrelled rifle at them.

248   NEW LIGHT ON DARK AFRICA.

So we went onward continually in a north-west direction, till the sun shone perpendicularly down. Then suddenly fresh green shone before us, and there was a decided declination in the plateau. Could it be that we had a stream of water before us? Alas, no! An anxious and accurate investigation brought the certainty that the declivity was dry, and there seemed to be no water far and wide.

Anxiety concerning water.

Nature confronts us here in all her bitter cruelty; and thus brought face to face with iron necessity, to hold discourse only with inexorable fate, the soul is ready to sink into despair. If there is no water here, we all run the risk of dying of thirst on our further advance. Therefore, "Back to the river!" was the command. And from our north-west course we deviated towards the east.

We marched on for two hours more. Then all at once we saw the Guaso Nyiro again before us. At least for this afternoon we have water!

Suddenly Rukua reports, "Massai Tele!" ("Many Massais!") True enough, all the hills are covered with figures! Then there must be more fighting.

I say, "Then we will beat the Massais here!" But Rukua drew my attention to an enclosure by the river, into which we could drive our herds, and where we should have better prospects for the fight.

Reappearance of the Massais.

Forward then! In with the herds into the enclosure, which is at once shut. "Bunduke teare?" ("The guns ready?") I cry to my people. "Teare," is the reply of all.

So we wait for the decisive combat, perhaps with a secret wish that it may put a period to our troubles.

But not a Massai appears. Suddenly an old Massai woman approaches, waving the bunch of grass.

"What is that?" I say.

"The Massais want peace," the Wakikuyu tell me in reply.

Perhaps I never approached a lady with greater eagerness than I now displayed, with an expenditure of all my gallantry, towards this repulsive-looking old Massai woman. I also caught up a bunch of grass, and took care that there should be a flower among it. I came forward as grace-

Pacific overtures.

THE MASSAIS INVITE A PARLEY. 249

fully as possible towards the lady, and seized her by the hand, to induce her to seat herself beside me.

PEACE PROPOSALS FROM THE MASSAIS.

The confabulation was soon in progress. I heard that the Massais wished to have peace with me, provided I would refrain from burning any more of their villages, shooting at them, or carrying off their herds.

I replied to the Massai woman that I was quite ready to promise this, if the Massais would furnish me with guides to the Baringo. "But," said I, "whither does this river run beside which we are now?"

Dialogue with a Massai ambassadress.

She indicated that the Guaso Nyiro, in the first instance, flowed on to the north, but that northward of the Endika Mountains it turned towards the east.

"How far is the Guaso Narok from here?"

"About a day and a half, if you follow the Guaso Nyiro; one day, if you march across to the Guaso Narok."

"And where does the Guaso Narok come from?"

She pointed in the direction towards the Baringo.

"How far is the Baringo lake from here?"

"Five days, if you march well."

"Do Massais live there, too?"

"The Massais live everywhere," she answered.

"Surely it is not the custom with you for women to decide concerning peace and war? If the Massais wish to have peace with me, let them send to me men of their tribe, to whom I can give presents, and with whom we will conclude the treaty of peace in due form."

She promised that towards evening eleven men of the Massais should come to me into the camp; and so went away, with a ring on her finger that I had put there, and with the flowers in her hand, to carry the message of peace to her tribe.

At the dinner which now followed, I took the opportunity of delivering a short address to Herr von Tiedemann on Arthur Schopenhauer's negativity of the perception of pleasure. After all, it seemed that the Christmas message was to find its fulfilment with us. A costlier Christmas present even Europe could not have offered us.

Arthur Schopenhauer's philosophy.

Unfortunately, on this day, for the first time, the early symptoms appeared in Herr von Tiedemann of a serious disease, dysentery, by which he was attacked two days later.

I have forgotten to mention that since our departure from

Kikuyu we had no longer vegetable food, but had to confine ourselves entirely to a flesh diet. To this were added the cold nights and the exciting incidents; the result being that several cases of illness occurred among my people.

At six o'clock in the evening eleven Massais appeared, but did not venture to come into our camp. I did not feel inclined to expose myself unarmed to their lances, as I knew well enough the malignity of these fellows. So I took a few people with me armed with rifles, which were laid down in a demonstrative manner, while I requested the Massais to do the same on their side, and to meet me at a spot half way between the two piles of weapons. This was done, and conditions of peace were at once settled by both sides on the basis of the agreement of the afternoon, and ratified by the men mutually spitting at each other three times. I then gave a finger ring and a few beads to each of the Massais, and in token that our tribe and theirs would live in friendship and peace together I killed one of the sheep I had myself taken from the Massais, and gave it to them. They asked permission to sleep that night in the camp; but this I cautiously declined, telling them it would be better if they slept some distance away. If they came to the camp at night, my sentries had orders to fire at them. I was the more cautious, just because we had made peace, and instead of the usual eight outposts I doubled them that night. I also remained, the greater part of the night, sitting on my chair, in front of my tent, in the open air; on such occasions I was accustomed to make astronomical observations with Hussein Fara.

A treaty of peace.

Massais excluded from the camp.

Next morning the Massais duly made their appearance, ostensibly to fulfil the part they had undertaken of the contract, by leading us to the Baringo. The negotiations with them continued to be conducted by a very worthy young Kikuyu man, who looked so strikingly like old Voltaire, that I had bestowed upon him that name, which at once became popular with my expedition and among the Massais.

Our Kikuyu "Voltaire."

The Kikuyu people began to feel very comfortable with the column. First of all, it had been a matter of great rejoicing to them to see their deadly enemies, the haughty Massais, so thoroughly beaten. Then they feasted to their hearts' content on the number of sheep and goats I caused to be given to them.

The Kikuyu mode of killing cattle. They do not slaughter these creatures, but strangle them, so that all the blood remains in the flesh. Slaughtered meat is just as detestable to them as strangled beasts would be to us. The sight of one of them holding a sheep or a goat by the throat, and choking it to death, always struck me as something completely disgusting.

Quitting the river, we now again ascended the elevated plateau to the left, on which we moved forward, still keeping a north-west direction. Soon, there came in sight to the west-west-north-west the long ranges which, the Massais informed us, were called the Subugu la Baringo (Subugu signifying a fringe of mountains). That, therefore, must be the Döngo *The Döngo Gelesha Range.* Gelesha. On the plateau we found great herds of Massai cattle, and for the sake of peace and quietness I willingly consented to halt until the Massais had driven these away from our, to them, unwelcome vicinity. When this had been done, young Massai warriors hastened up to us to greet us with the usual salutations of "Sotua" (friend). All this had a very pleasant appearance.

Towards noon we descended from the plateau, to the right, to a dry river-bed, and came upon an entirely black volcanic region. The name Guaso Narok signifies in the Massai language Black River, because it flows over black stones; for me, therefore, this dark ground was a satisfactory sign that we were *The "Teleki Rock."* really approaching the river. A dark, high-towering volcanic group of rocks, that we left on our right between the affluence of the Guaso Narok and the Guaso Nyiro, I called the "Teleki Rock," after my forerunner on the Guaso Nyiro territory.

The heat upon the black stones began to be disagreeable. We now came upon a broad sheep track. The Massais informed me that I had only to follow this track, and I should reach the Guaso Narok in an hour. In the meantime, they said, they would go to their houses to get provisions. So I went on with

THE TELEKI ROCKS.

Hussein and Rukua, in front of the column, in search of the Guaso Narok.

The behaviour of the native population entirely changed in these mid-day hours, inasmuch as all we saw hurried away from us in an altogether inexplicable flight. All this was very suspicious. *Alteration in native behaviour.*

Towards two o'clock I found eight donkeys and a loaded ox. They had been abandoned by their masters, and were carrying household implements and milk. Following up the ox spoor, I came into a narrow valley. By this time it was three o'clock, and the affair began to be very serious. I *The narrow valley.* resolved to halt and await my column, but meanwhile to send out Hussein and another Somali, who had come up, to ascertain if the course of the Guaso Narok was to be found in a long valley that opened before us. The messengers had not yet returned, when suddenly the rattling of musketry sounded behind me.

All at once the surrounding heights were covered with Massai warriors. Now all was explained. I had the loads at once deposited together, and commanded fifteen porters, who had arrived in the meantime, to go back with me. But my people had become so tired and stiff through the burning march that I could not get six men together. So I hurried back myself, accompanied only by one Somali, to see what had happened. *Hostile appearance of the Massais.*

Directly afterwards, I met Herr von Tiedemann with the camel-driver. He reported that our Massais of the evening before had, on a sudden, treacherously stabbed our sick porter Saburi. They had, indeed, been at once scared away by himself and the Somalis, but Saburi had expired in terrible agony. So the racket was all to begin afresh! Exhausted as I had before felt, I was filled with such rage at the thought of the dastardly assassination, and, at the same time, with such contempt for these Massais, that the idea of fighting them was altogether agreeable to me.

" Forward! Drive the donkeys to the porters! " I cried to the Somalis, when I saw the eight Massai donkeys still standing there, that I had till now refrained from taking. "Let us kill the cowardly rascals like dogs!" The Somalis were not exactly edified by this prospect, nor could they understand my indignation at the tactics of the Massais, which seemed to them entirely justifiable, as the blood spilling of December 22nd had not yet been expiated. However, I succeeded in seizing five of the donkeys; a very welcome booty for the overladen column.

The Somalis discouraged.

When I got back to the resting-place Hussein reported to me that the long valley before us was dry. On the right hand, joining it at right angles, there was certainly a river course, but it contained not a drop of water.

Here lay the real danger! Judging by all that had happened, I was obliged to consider that I had been completely overreached by the Massais. The thermometer stood at about 50° C. (122° F.). We were steaming with the glowing heat. Our dry tongues clave to the roofs of our mouths. And here we lay, surrounded by hostile warriors, who only awaited the moment when we appeared entirely exhausted to make an attack upon us. In such moments Nature assumes something of an unpitying, even of a cruel character, as I once experienced in the English Channel, where I was hurled down by the raging billows, apparently to inevitable destruction. There is no deliverance from without; a man feels unsparingly thrown back upon himself. But it is just in such positions that the despairing heart is suddenly penetrated with the thorough conviction of a protecting Providence. Even separate resolves then appear like inspirations from above.

A distressful predicament.

Thus it was with me at that moment. All at once the thought thrilled through me, that if I hurried forward over a declivity in the west of the neighbouring valley I should find water. Therefore forward! "Blow the trumpet! Beat the drum! The flag in advance, and away with the Massais!" An impression, as of the supernatural, must have been made upon these Massais, who were watching us on all sides, when they saw us make this sudden movement, exactly in the direction in which water really lay. There was no real

A sudden inspiration.

resistance on their part, when we suddenly turned off at a right angle from our road. Whatever men showed themselves on the rocks were at once shot down, and thus we started off on a march for life or death towards the west.

Behind us the Massais followed like hyenas; but they cautiously kept out of gunshot. Now and then I heard the sound of the guns echoing from the hills in front of me or behind me, just as the double crack of my rifle was heard by the rear. But what did we all care, at that moment, for the Massais? Within us there was a cry for water, water! Yonder a river course becomes visible. "Webigi!" cried the Somalis. "Madgi!" cried the porters. We came up to it, and—the watercourse was empty! It was evidently the same that Hussein had already seen lower down. *A bitter disappointment.*

The sun is sinking low! It is four in the afternoon! What is to be done?

"We will cross over the next row of heights, to see if we can perhaps find water on the other side!" I called out to Hussein and Musa, who, with me, formed the advanced guard. Onward, therefore! When I had climbed half-way up the hill, Tiedemann came hurrying up, calling to me from below, "Come back, Doctor; the Massais are attacking us from the rear!" "Then do you beat back the Massais; I shall search for water."

Aloft on the height stood a broad Massai kraal, near which a man was sitting. Like wolves we sprang upon him; the Somalis seized him, and I held the muzzle of my six-chambered revolver to his temples. "Show me the Guaso Narok, or depart into the world below." "Guaso Narok," he answered, trembling with fear; "Guaso Narok häna" ("Guaso Narok there"), pointing with his hand to the valley below. It was an Andorobbo who gave us this joyful news. I believe that no angel's voice could at that moment have inspired me to offer more sincere thanks to the Highest. "Who saved me from death, from slavery! Hast Thou not Thyself accomplished everything, holy, glowing heart?" Ah! how humbly, on this evening of December 26th, *An opportune capture.* *Thankful feelings.*

did I put away from me any such expression of Titanic daring! How devoutly did I bend before that mysterious Power that shapes the fate of men, and had once more saved us from perishing miserably!

Gradually the porters came dropping in, and I at once sent twenty-five of them, with a suitable military escort, down to the river with the Andorobbo to bring water. Then Herr von Tiedemann came in. I had sat down in my arm-chair at the entrance to the kraal, had already quenched my thirst from the Andorobbo's jug, and was smoking a pipe. "Well, Herr von Tiedemann, a little tired?" "Water; have we any water?" "Water," I rejoined, with feigned indifference, "why should we not have water? Down yonder is the Guaso Narok. Meanwhile do you take this," and I handed him the jug by my side, "or would you like a mouthful of brandy with it?" Herr von Tiedemann seized my hand with both his own. "THANK GOD! Then we shall perhaps get to Lake Baringo after all."

Joyful meeting with Tiedemann.

I threw my column of porters and the herd of cattle into the Massai kraal, which I made defensible by burning a few of the outlying buildings. Our tents, and that of the Somalis, I caused to be erected outside. I again established eight outposts, as the camp-fires of the Massais glared threateningly down from all the hills around. At nine o'clock we were sitting comfortably in the moonlight over a mutton cutlet, with cognac and water, and I had once more an opportunity of explaining to Herr von Tiedemann Schopenhauer's theory of the negativity of pleasurable sensations.

A comfortable supper.

This night I had, for the first time since many days, a lengthened sleep, and I made my servant Rukua lie down before the door of the tent; and the Somalis had assured me that, for their part, they would keep the sentries sufficiently awake. I had also arranged that the column should not take the road next morning until half-past six; and so I woke up, on December 27th, refreshed, and like a new man.

Unhappily, such was not the case with Herr von Tiedemann. On the preceding night he had not been able to sleep, and on that morning dysentery definitely declared itself.

Herr von Tiedemann's illness.

Towards seven o'clock, with my herd and my whole column, I crossed the Guaso Narok, which rushed below clear and fresh over the rocks.

On the opposite side of the river a few Wandorobbo came towards me, and informed me that the donkeys which I had taken away on the previous day belonged to them. As they were not, however, able to bring any proof of this statement, I rejected it as "unfounded." On their part they declined my proposition that they should approach a little nearer, to discourse with me concerning the way to the Baringo.

Amid enormous difficulties, partly through hard and thorny thickets, we got to the summit towards nine o'clock. Before us lay a black, charred steppe, over which the north wind swept, while a deserted Massai kraal appeared here and there. When we looked down the slope we had climbed the eye could follow, to an apparently immeasurable distance, the course of the Guaso Narok, bending off towards the south-west, and behind it, in the far distance, the slopes of the Elbejet district.

Difficult march across the steppe.

We now advanced in a west-north-west direction. Of Massais not a trace was to be seen. All kraals were empty. Until one o'clock I marched, according to the compass, exactly keeping the direction I had taken. Soon it was reported to me that the herd could no longer follow, and that a part of it had already given in on the way. This compelled me to halt to draw the column together again. I gave the people half an hour's rest, and intended then to go on until the evening. But Herr von Tiedemann reported to me that he was ill, and would not be able to make a forced march of this kind. Of course, this decided the matter.

A compulsory halt.

I had had the plateau inspected, far in advance, by Rukua. When he came back at two o'clock, with the announcement that water was nowhere to be found, I gave up the advance I had

17

planned, and turned in a southerly direction towards the Guaso Narok.

At four o'clock, hastening on far in advance of my column, I came upon a deserted Massai kraal, in which I hoisted our flag, and took possession of it for our use. It was soon cleaned up by my people, and by a little help put in a condition of defence. So soon as Herr von Tiedemann was established there, I went off with a few of my people in a southern direction in search of water.

Hoisting the German flag.

At about five o'clock we found a pool of water among some boulders of stone, and the whole column was able to cook something for supper.

That night I found it only necessary to establish three posts around the kraal, and for the second time I had a healthy sleep, as we were in perfect safety within our enclosure, supposing an efficient watch to be kept.

For December 28th I resolved to give the exceedingly exhausted column, and especially Herr von Tiedemann, a day's rest. I confined myself to removing the camp some distance nearer to the water we had discovered the evening before, and again threw the column into a strong Massai kraal, which, by burning the outworks and strengthening the enclosure, I converted into a perfectly impregnable fortress.

Fortifying the camp.

It was grey, dreary weather, and of the Massais there was not a trace to be seen by day or night. But the disquieting circumstance was, that regularly by night their camp-fires gleamed upon the neighbouring hills; a sign that now, as ever, they were prowling like hyenas round our column by night, and that the greatest caution must be our permanent rule.

As Herr von Tiedemann was now confined to his bed, I was more than before compelled to depend upon myself; and in these weeks I found comfort in reading Carlyle's "Frederick II.," whose shining example now wrought its effect in troublous times, even in the distant Leikipia plateaus.

On December 29th we again pressed forward, through a tolerably dense woodland thicket, to the Guaso Narok, whose course I now followed, throughout a somewhat severe day's march, ever towards the south-west. The Kenia still reared its height behind us in the south-east. The mountain, which had been my delight a few weeks ago, had now a very depressing effect upon us all. We did not want to see it any more, because we had suffered so much on its declivities. But immovably it looked down upon us. What cared he, the mighty Kenia, apparently created for eternity— what cared he for the petty movements of human suffering? *March by the Guaso Narok.*

Wherever we now came the Massais had fled before our expedition. The kraals on the opposite side of the Guaso Narok were likewise all of them deserted, though they exhibited traces of quite recent occupation; for instance, smoking fires. This was a very satisfactory indication. On the other hand, our caravan was again attacked on December 29th by a stupid rhinoceros, until a ball from my rifle caused it to deviate from its course towards us, and after running furiously round in a circle, to take to flight towards the north. Unfortunately, a number of our people let themselves be carried away by excitement, and sent a quantity of powder and ball rattling uselessly behind it. *The Massais scared.*

At one o'clock I again established my column in a Massai kraal, which lay exactly to the north of the Subugu la Poron, a mountain that had here just the appearance of the Kenia. To my joy, the Kenia on this day began to glimmer blue, while on the western side the boundary mountains of the Leikipia plateau stood out more sharply. If the eternal flesh diet, without any vegetable additions, had not begun to become disagreeable to us, our position might by degrees have taken the character of comfort, for we had gradually become accustomed to the system of keeping watch. *Improved prospects.*

On the following day a march of seven hours brought us to a large handsome Massai village, about at the place where the Guaso Narok begins decidedly to bend its course to the south, around the northern spurs of the Aberdare Chain. On this day we had marched past a series of great papyrus marshes, which are nothing more than stagnant portions of the Guaso Narok on the plain, that here presents an entirely *Papyrus swamps.*

horizontal level. These seem to be the same marshes which Thomson saw on their southern side.

In the afternoon I sent out eleven of my best people, to ascertain if the Guaso Narok here really bends towards the south. If this were the case we had reached the point from which, in his time, Thomson had turned off in a north-west direction to Lake Baringo, and on the next morning we should have to undertake the same *salto mortale*. It would truly be a *salto mortale* for us, inasmuch as Thomson marched in the rainy season, whereas we were now in the dry time of the year, and ran the risk of finding no water. Accordingly, before we started I had all our cattle watered, and after about an hour's marching we entered the dense thorny thicket, of which, in his book of travels, Thomson has given a doleful description. But the affair did not appear to us so bad as Thomson makes it out.

Thomson's route unadvisable in the dry season.

A few Somalis marching in front, with sharp swords and axes, opened a path for us in a north-west direction, from which, however, I deviated at noon towards the west, hoping, in this way, more quickly to reach the Guaso Tien, which flows into the Baringo Lake, and was to be my basis for the further advance.

While we were thus working our way through the thicket, all at once the Kikuyu people threw down their loads, and disappeared towards the right. I thought at first they had seen some Massais, and sprang towards the left side; but as no one appeared in that direction, it dawned all at once upon me that this was not so much a case of panic, as one of simple desertion on the part of these gentlemen, for which I could not altogether blame them. Only two of the Kikuyu people had been kept hold of by the Somalis, and had to go with us as far as the Baringo. But I was obliged now to burden the camels with the loads that had been thrown down, whereby our march was still further retarded.

Desertion of the Kikuyu porters.

All the woodland brooks we found here were dry; and our state of mind was the more despondent, as we had no points of intelligence, by which we could judge when we should succeed in working our way out of the thicket, or if we should do so at all.

At noon I allowed the column a short rest. The Somalis, and Hussein especially, prayed aloud to Allah for help, which I always encouraged them in such circumstances to do, to keep up their moral tone. The porters showed, as they did generally in these days, a touching confidence in me personally. They said, "We shall find water, for the chief has said it, that we should find water to-day."

<small>Confidence in the "chief."</small>

Throughout the whole afternoon we worked on. At length, from four o'clock, the thicket began to grow a little lighter. We came to a broad rhinoceros spoor, and at five o'clock into an open, but, unfortunately, an entirely dry valley, evidently the one designated by Thomson the Marmose valley. Here I pitched our camp.

Herr von Tiedemann told me, directly we were in camp, that he had decidedly identified his symptoms with those of dysentery. I had had a tub of water brought for the two of us, and now had some cocoa boiled for Herr von Tiedemann. But my heart was very heavy. How could I help him? Dysentery requires peculiar treatment. Thomson had been brought down, almost to death, by this disease during his return march out of Africa, and we had scarcely half of our march into Africa behind us.

<small>Grave condition of Von Tiedemann.</small>

But it was more important, for the moment, to find water for the caravan. For this purpose I sent two columns in a south and south-west direction respectively, while I myself, with Hussein Fara, went off in a north-west direction on the same quest. Towards six o'clock we came back with our errand unaccomplished, and I ate a scanty supper alone in front of my tent, after posting the sentries round about the camp. Rukua had also returned, with his troop, from the south unsuccessful.

<small>Seeking for water.</small>

It was New Year's Eve, and my friends in my own country were probably sitting within the circle of their dear ones, assembled round the punch bowl. The temperature was still cool during the nights, and above me the stars of the equatorial world were flaming like thousands of mysterious signs of interrogation. In the thicket around were heard the sounds of the wilderness—the jackal howled, and in the distance sounded the roar of a lion.

I was making mournful reflections on this conclusion of the year 1889, when towards midnight joyous cries suddenly resounded from the southern side of the camp, and directly afterwards the Galla man, Mandutto, was led up to me in triumph by some porters. He had just returned from his foraging expedition to the south-west, and on his shoulders he carried two jugs of water. "Mandutto has found water," was the joyful tidings, which ran at once from mouth to mouth through the whole camp, and suddenly transformed the general temper from melancholy brooding into a lively state of joy.

Water found by Mandutto.

With a heart full of thankfulness, I now laid myself down to rest. In a somewhat marvellous way this danger also had been averted; and full of cheerful confidence I slept into the year 1890.

The water discovered by Mandutto was brought from a rain pool on the slope of the western margin of the Leikipia plateau. The pool was hidden in the reedy grass, and had thus been prevented, so far, from drying up in the sun. To this pond, which was situate about four miles from our camp in a south-west direction, I transferred my camp on the morning of January 1st, and there I again held a day of rest, before accomplishing the march to the Guaso Tien on the following morning. The wind whistled raw and cold from the north, true January weather; but we had water! We could drink cocoa and cook soup; and so I spent a fine holiday, thinking of what lay behind us. On that day I began to work out my Massai report for Europe, and I also wrote letters to my beloved ones at home.

Beginning a new year.

We were now at an elevation of more than eight thousand feet, and would certainly next morning come to the slope of the Leikipia plateau towards the west.

As I sat in my tent that afternoon a report was suddenly

brought to me that there were people in the vicinity who apparently wished to enter into communication with us. I had them invited by signs to approach, and found that they were young Wandorobbo.

Talk with the Wandorobbo.

"Do you know the way to the Guaso Tien?" I asked them, when they had seated themselves in my camp.

"The Guaso Tien is very near," said they.

"It leads to the Baringo, does it not?"

"The Baringo is out yonder." They pointed to the northwest.

"Then that mountain yonder which we see is probably the Döngo Gelesha?"

They answered by lively signs in the affirmative, evidently astonished that I knew the name.

"Now I will tell you something, my good Wandorobbo. You are to show me the way to the Guaso Tien and to Njemps. In return, I will give you some head of cattle, and handsome clothes, when we arrive in Njemps."

They looked at one another, and did not seem inclined to agree to the proposals. Accordingly I continued,—

"Where I come from, it is the custom to show the way to strangers who come into the country when they ask it. Whoever does not do that of his own free will is compelled to do it. You do not seem inclined to follow our custom. Therefore I must ask you to sleep the night with my Somalis, so that you do not steal secretly away in darkness and mist. For the rest, you will receive good treatment."

A startling announcement.

When, in spite of my friendly words, the two men suddenly attempted to escape, they were seized by the Somalis, and secured. The next day we marched in a very friendly manner with them to Njemps, from whence they were allowed to return to their tribe with rich presents. Thus the chief care of the past week was overcome, and to-day, for the first time, I looked forward with complete confidence to the cheerful prosecution of our expedition.

Start for Njemps.

Next morning we crossed the western margin of Leikipia, guided by the two Wandorobbo, first passing through burnt-up and tangled bushes, then suddenly towards the west, on a broad way appearing almost like an avenue, down the declivity.

Suddenly my whole column broke out into a loud cry of rapture. A green valley opened before us, into which the Leikipia plateau fell perpendicularly down. Along this valley meandered a river. "Guaso Tien," was the answer of the Wandorobbo guides to my question. Thus we had reached the river domain of the Baringo. We had left behind us the rough and inhospitable plateau of Leikipia, and probably with it, for ever, the anxiety of fighting the Massais.

[margin: The Guaso Tien river.]

Through grass that grew to a man's height we marched on for a quarter of an hour to the Guaso Tien. The river was for the most part dry, and only in the places where a tangle of high reeds kept off the rays of the sun was a little water, from which the caravan refreshed itself. I resolved, accordingly, to march farther down the river, where, according to the assertion of the Wandorobbo, better water was to be had.

It was nearly three o'clock when we came to a mighty gorge, where the Guaso Tien begins to cast itself, with a steep fall, into the depths. Over rough boulders and great blocks of stone, where we had often a difficulty in picking our way, we clambered down. But at last the path became very narrow, and disappeared altogether when we came to a massive rock, that entirely filled up the bed of the river, presenting a perpendicular descent of at least sixty-five feet. Here was an insuperable obstacle to further climbing, and I therefore made up my mind to pitch my camp for the night by a little bend higher up the river, where there was a little water under the rock.

[margin: A difficult path.]

The shores rise steep on either side, so that every word, even if spoken softly, makes a loud echo in the gorge. Here I needed only to establish two outposts, one above and one below, to be safe from any hostile surprise; and when in the evening the camp-fires of the expedition blazed up by the rocks and in the river gorge, we had the most magnificent scenery of a wolf's glen* before us that can be imagined.

* The "Wolfsschlucht," or wolf's glen, it will be remembered, is the scene of the incantation of Caspar in Weber's *Freischütz*.—Tr.

On the day before, while attempting to descend with the camels, my Somalis had discovered a path to the right of the Guaso Tien, by which I travelled next morning. It led us first, at an elevation of 8,100 feet, to the furthest margin of Lake Baringo, from which the Döngo Gelesha appeared only like a hill of slight elevation. I had from here a complete view round this very remarkable margin land, and think I may assert that we have here to do with an enormous crater ring, the diameter of which, as it reaches to the ascent of Elgejo, I was afterwards able to determine at fifteen German miles (seventy English). Within a great ring a number of little crater rings appear to be set up, the deepest of which is Lake Baringo itself. Thus we here stand opposite a crater formation, to which not one that I know in the world can be likened, and which I could compare only with one of the annular systems in the moon. The descent from this margin to the deep land is almost perpendicular, and as a landscape is truly magnificent.

A new path found.

Volcanic region.

On a path winding down in a zigzag shape we now descended, to strike the Guaso Tien again at a point where it turns from its southern course, almost at a right angle, towards the west. From here we had to follow the course of the river itself. The rocks to the right and left, which completely close it in, rise to the height of about eight hundred feet. In some places they are close together, at others they are farther apart. It seems as though the rock had here been split asunder by some convulsion of the earth, developing a large cleft, into which the Guaso Tien precipitates itself. A remarkable thing in the course of this river was, moreover, that wherever it was in deep shadow it had a certain depth of water, but in those places where the sun shone down perpendicularly upon it only a dry river-bed appeared. It was difficult to see where the water at once came from again.

Course of the Guaso Tien.

In one place the rocks were so close together that a donkey could hardly force its way through the passage, and the camels actually stuck fast. Consequently I had the camp pitched for the second time below this spot, in a wider part of the gorge itself, and remained encamped here a whole day, to pull out the camels, which was done after much exertion.

So it was not until January 5th that we quitted the gorge of the Guaso Tien, a river which reaches to the south-west angle of Lake Baringo, to turn our steps, in a westward course on the edge of the declivity, directly across the plain of Njemps. The Döngo Gelesha now lay to the north-east, and soon appeared, looked at from below, in all its imposing slope, before us. On this day I had the camp pitched below the Döngo Gelesha, by a little affluent of the Guaso Tien. While this was being done one of the porters let a burning brand fall into the tinderlike grass. It caught fire at once; and with express-train speed the conflagration spread, happily in a direction away from the camp, over the slopes and the grassy steppe. This occurrence fortunately occasioned me to seek a camping-place that had already been burnt bare, and consequently presented no danger of fire. I say "fortunately," for in the evening the wind veered round, and now all at once the fire, which at noon had rushed forth across the steppe, came back upon us by a circuitous route, and, indeed, with a speed which, if we had been among the masses of grass, would have rendered flight almost impracticable. With difficulty we succeeded in getting the donkeys and the ammunition into the centre of the little bare camping-place I had selected. Herr von Tiedemann, who had set up his tent on the edge of the grassy steppe—indeed, in the steppe itself—was obliged to rush out, unclothed, in headlong flight, to escape the danger of being burnt alive in it. As is always the case where there are high and low grounds in close proximity, perfectly malicious gusts of wind prevailed here on this day, so that all night long we were in danger of seeing our tents suddenly blown down.

An accidental fire.

A dangerous position.

We were glad enough next morning to leave this inhospitable place, in the hope that before night we should see Lake Baringo itself. Even with such longing may Moses have gone forth, when it was declared to him that he should now behold the promised land.

By Lake Baringo.

Thomson had drawn seductive pictures of Lake Baringo. We hoped to find food there in abundance, and to regain the feeling of security for life and limb. Patiently, therefore, we accepted the fact that we had to march for hours through the parched prairie, and then to ascend towards the last circumference around Lake Baringo. Towards eleven o'clock this was reached; and there, in truth, lay the lake before us! A green grassy steppe extended far and wide, shading off, here and there, into brownish and reddish tints. Opposite, just below us, a steep group of rocks rose up, which, according to the maps, could be nothing else but Kamasia. This was, moreover, corroborated by the Wandorobbo, who were astonished, as before, that I could tell them of such names. But to the right the lovely basin of Lake Baringo bends like the bay of Sorrento, or that of Naples, and towards the north scattered islands rise above its surface. Thus the Baringo looks up with its deep blue eye at the gleaming heaven. One hardly knows if that blue surface that appears below, or the canopy that stretches its expanse above, is the real sky. Like a scene from fairy-land the picture lay spread out that we there viewed below us. *Lake Baringo and its surroundings.*

So it is really to be vouchsafed to us that we shall quit, as living men, the inhospitable steppes of the Massais? Yes, it has been vouchsafed to us! We have only to descend, to grasp the reality.

For about an hour we revelled in the contemplation of the picture glorified by every poetic charm. Whether the enthusiasm of my corn-lacking porters was not chiefly called forth by the anticipation of what they should find to fill their cooking-pots withal, I will leave an open question. *Improved prospects.* At all events, the feeling of satisfaction was universal, and on the strength of this general feeling the very troublesome descent was made more rapidly and easily than would probably have been the case under other circumstances. We had to clamber down an almost perpendicular space of about twelve hundred feet; certainly not a pleasurable task for the camels, or for the porters, with their loads that weighed sixty pounds. On reaching the utmost verge of the crater circumference, I halted to collect the whole column. Unhappily I had lost one of my camels that morning, so that I had only three left.

But what did that signify, weighed against the fact that we had now, of a certainty, reached the Baringo territory? Towards two o'clock we marched away with beat of drum, through the grassy steppe, towards the west. For the first time after a long interval, acacias and mimosas again appeared on our horizon. They grew on the borders of the Guaso na Nyuki, towards which we were pressing. At about five o'clock we crossed it, and, as I had formerly done in the quiet days by the Tana, I set up my camp under the widespreading shade of the mimosa trees; and it was with a sensation of heartfelt joy that I sat down to my evening meal in front of my tent, at seven o'clock, with the moon shining silently and peacefully down.

Crossing the Guaso na Nyuki.

Of the natives we did not, on this evening, get a glimpse. The two Massai settlements, Njemps Ndogo and Njemps Nkubua (Little Njemps and Great Njemps), are situated on the Guaso Tigerish, which rolls towards the Baringo, two or three miles westward of the Guaso na Nyuki. To-night I again lay down to rest, with satisfaction like that I had felt on Christmas Eve.

Next morning early we were up and away, with the drum beating, towards the south-west. Soon we came upon a broad road, and presently I heard human voices calling to us on my left. It was almost like a home feeling to hear the old " Iambo " of the coast repeated here in the heart of Africa. At once we felt that we were once again in peaceful communication with the outer world. A few hundred paces more, and the thick thorny ringwalls of Njemps rose before us. The elders of the tribe came out, and replied to my " Iambo " with a friendly " Iambo sana." Hands were duly spat in and shaken.

Arrival at Njemps.

Presently a troop of the natives placed themselves at the head of the column, and led us round Njemps in a circuit towards the west. We crossed the Guaso Tigerish, and found ourselves under the shade of the cool mimosa trees, by the northern wall of the place, on the old camping-ground of the travelling caravans, where Mr. Thomson, Dr. Fischer, and Count Teleki had all dwelt in their time. Quickly the loads were deposited and the tents set up, and soon we experienced the pleasant feeling of reposing comfortably among a friendly tribe.

Camping among friends.

The toils and dangers we had endured among the Massais of the Leikipia plateau began, like the stormclouds when a tempest has spent its rage, to sink gradually away on the horizon of our memory.

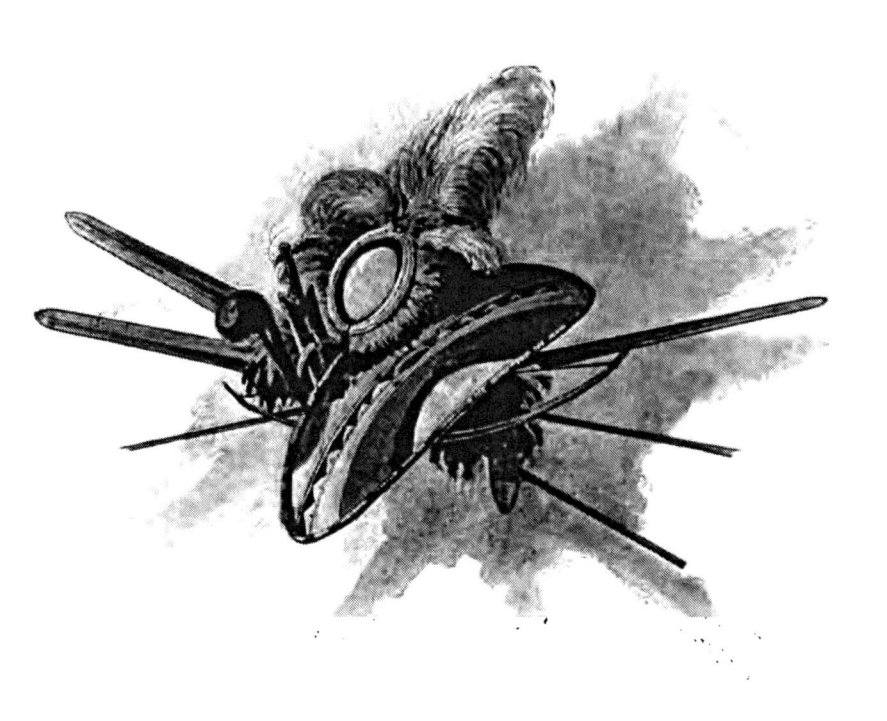

CHAPTER VIII.

FROM THE BARINGO TO THE VICTORIA NYANZA TERRITORY.

"In the realm of dreams and magic
Have we, as it seemeth, entered."
                                    GOETHE.

NJEMPS lies about five miles south of Lake Baringo. I am sorry to say I cannot join in the Thomsonian hymn of praise concerning this place and its inhabitants. He was enchanted with the security of the life he enjoyed here, and that may have biassed his spirit. We had won our own safety, until now, by fighting, and we had not paid tribute anywhere, so that these two considerations did not weigh heavily in the scale of our well-being.

<small>Question of ways and means.</small>

But as regarded the important question of our bodily food and necessities, thanks to the circumstance that we could pay for food with food, we were able to procure from the Massais grain, honey, and fish. They were themselves suffering hunger, and would hardly have declared themselves ready to part with eatables for clothes-stuffs, and still less for ornaments. But I paid in goats and sheep, and thus succeeded in purchasing for myself and my people a corresponding supply of "veri-veri," a kind of small red millet, and also in getting some honey and a daily supply of fish. Of the corn we prepared a kind of meal, which, boiled in salt water, made a very tasty addition to our milk. *Purchasing supplies.*

Among the sheep we brought with us, the Massais here and there recognised animals that had been stolen from them by their cousins of Leikipia, with whom they lived in deadly feud. Of course I could not consent to give these back without an equivalent; had I done so, I should soon have got rid of my whole flock. All things considered, we lived in good friendship with each other, being united by our common enmity towards a third nation.

I had very soon recovered from the fatigues of the march over Leikipia, but, unfortunately, Herr von Tiedemann was not able to regain his health in the four days we spent by Lake Baringo. *Herr von Tiedemann's illness.*

The depressed region between the Döngo Gelesha in the east, and the Kamasia plateau, that falls off steeply at about the same elevation, in the west, was 3,400 feet above the sea level, and for the first time, after a long interval, we had now warmer nights, while the days still remained tolerably cool.

The whole of this depression is filled with a kind of reddish clay, in which the sun burns great cracks and clefts. The drawback in this region is the remarkable dryness, which often destroys the harvest and occasions famine. The Massais, who, in contrast to their brethren on the elevated plateaus, practise agriculture, have indeed arranged a very ingenious method of irrigation; but this irrigation depends upon the state of the Guaso Tigerish, which also almost dries up at this season of the year. *Massai agriculture.*

I visited Lake Baringo on Sunday, January 12th. By the

way we saw great numbers of game animals of all kinds. But of the lake itself not much was to be seen, for it is surrounded on its southern shore with a broad margin of reeds, which must be pressed through before the expanse of water is descried.

<small>Shores of Lake Baringo.</small>

Lovely as this lake appears seen from the heights, there is little charm of landscape on its shores themselves. The inhabitants of these regions, called by the Wangannœsi "Wakuafi," that is to say, dealers,—a name which, by the way, is not known among the Massais themselves,—have been much reduced in number and humbled by wars, and are consequently more modest than their insolent cousins on the plateaus. They belong to a great tribe which, as it appears, was entirely defeated and scattered in all directions by the other Massais, at the beginning of this century, being partly driven still further north to the lakes discovered by Count Teleki, partly to Usaguha, partly to Kawirondo, and close to the shores of Lake Victoria. The people are intelligent, and certainly capable of culture. They are favourable to strangers, because they expect through them to get protection from the Massai tribes, who fall upon them again from time to time. The trading strangers, whether they be Arabs or Europeans, have likewise an interest in permanently maintaining here this colony of peaceable and friendly Massais.

<small>The Wakuafi or dealers.</small>

I expressed myself on this point in a report which I prepared at Baringo, on January 10th, for the German Emin Pasha committee, and which was not published for a long time:—

"A Baringo nation would be of the very greatest importance for the general opening up of Central Africa, and for the great plateaus, over which our way led. Here, in what resembles a peaceful oasis, the expeditions which, approaching from the east, are making their way to the north and west, can rest and gain strength for the further difficulties that lie before them. It is also known that Njemps and the Baringo form one of the great centres of the ivory trade of Eastern and Central Africa. I consider it equally important in the interests of civilisation and of a general European trade to

<small>Report to the committee.</small>

defend, and permanently to secure, the colony of intelligent and submissive Wakuafi dwelling here from the destruction with which they are continually threatened at the hands of the Massai and Wosuk. In a word, I consider the establishment of a strong European station by the Baringo to be called for in the interest of the whole further development of civilisation in Eastern and Central Africa. Five white men and twenty-five well-armed Askari, with a piece of ordnance, would, according to my estimate, be quite sufficient to secure this charming valley in a military point of view; and I also believe that such an establishment would very soon pay for itself as a commercial factory. Which nation it is that establishes such a station here is of no consequence, from the point of view of civilisation. I should unquestionably do it myself, if I did not require all my powers for the further prosecution of the task before me; for the greater part of my resources have been taken from me, by brute force, in Zanzibar and on the coast. Meanwhile, in order at least to effect something, I have concluded a treaty with the Wakuafi, which assures to them the friendship of the Germans, and places their land at my disposal with regard to further steps to be taken in the matter. At the same time I hoisted the German flag at Njemps on January 9th. I think I am warranted in assuming that, at the present moment, the black, white, and red flag is the one most dreaded by the Massais; and until the matter is decided in Europe, I hold it to be the most practical thing that this flag should wave here. Accordingly, I proclaim Njemps to be a European and especially a German possession. I consider myself entitled to do this, because the Baringo, with Njemps northward of the Equator, is, according to an objective explanation, manifestly not included in the London agreement.

"From hence, as I assume, a lasting communication with Oda-Boru-Ruva could be best established and maintained to the north of the Kenia; and if Emin Pasha is still in Wadelai, and is willing to co-operate in this plan, a European chain of stations might be established, extending into the heart of Africa, which would have its support in the navigableness of the Tana, and might become exceedingly important, alike as regards commerce and civilisation, for Eastern and Central Africa."

As the conclusion of this chain of reasoning I had already, on January 8th, concluded the following treaty with the elders:

"NJEMPS, on the Baringo,
"*January 8th*, 1890.

"The elders of the Wakuafi at Njemps and on the Baringo come and solicit the friendship of Dr. Carl Peters.

"They have heard that he has beaten the Massais, who are their enemies.

<small>Treaty with the Wakuafi.</small> "They declare that they acknowledge Dr. Peters as their lord, and beg him to make application to His Majesty the German Emperor for the incorporation of the Baringo country in the German protected territory.

"Dr. Peters, after a negotiation of several hours with an assembly of the Wakuafi, declares himself ready to grant them his friendship, and to protect them against the Massais so long as he tarries on the Baringo. He declares himself ready to hoist the German flag, thereby to show to the Massais, in the time to come, that he looks upon the Baringo territory as his, and that it stands under his protection.

"The regulating of the further relations of Njemps and the Baringo territory Dr. Peters reserves to himself.

"The cession of Njemps and the Baringo territory to Dr. Carl Peters, and the acceptance of it on the part of Dr. Peters for himself and his friends, is solemnly ratified by the signatures of both the contracting parties, and with the forms usual among <small>Ratification of the treaty.</small> the Wakuafi; as also the taking possession, by hoisting the German flag within the enclosure, of Njemps Mkubua; and Dr. Peters declares himself still prepared, in case it should yet be possible, to enter into negotiations with

Emin Pasha, with a view to transfer his territory of power to these regions. "CARL PETERS.

"Elders of the Wakuafi of Njemps and Baringo:

SIGNATORY MARK OF LAONAMA.	SIGNATORY MARK OF LONGOLETEA.
SIGNATORY MARK OF SOMBEJA.	SIGNATORY MARK OF LENDEKA.
SIGNATORY MARK OF BARZALAT.	SIGNATORY MARK OF NENDALOM.

Witnesses { HUSSEIN FARA, MUSA DAR-ES-SALAAM, "VON TIEDEMANN. | BWANA MKU, RUKUA, }

"This testifies that the foregoing act has been accomplished in the form of a treaty, on the present day, between Herr Dr. Peters and the Wakuafi of Njemps and the Baringo.

"NJEMPS, *January 8th,* 1890."

On January 9th the German flag was accordingly hoisted within the enclosure of Njemps, and it was visible far over the region around.

I had really expected to find an English expedition here, inasmuch as Mr. de Winton, so early as in the winter of 1888, had dissuaded us Germans from sending me out, on the ground that I should meet an English expedition that would then be already returning from Emin Pasha. *Mr. de Winton's expedition.* On this point also I expressed my opinion in the above-quoted report, and I will reproduce my expressions here, literally, as they clearly indicate what was my disposition in those days.

"I had expected a white man here, perhaps Mr. Martin, but there was no Mr. Martin anywhere to be seen. I had supposed that here at last the prophecies of Mr. de Winton would be fulfilled, and that the returning English expedition of rescue would appear on the scene. I had, indeed, repeatedly come upon traces of English expeditions engaged in effecting a retreat. Already at Aden, when I was still on my way to Zanzibar, I had encountered Mr. Swaine, who had been mentioned as the leader of the English East African Expedition. In Mombas, in April, I saw Mr. Last, who was coming back from Ukamba 'to fit himself out afresh.' When I was in Witu, at the beginning of July, I heard that somebody belonging to Mr. Jackson's expedition 'had come back in haste from the interior, and was fitting himself out anew in Malindi.' Afterwards I had been privileged with my own eyes to behold the return of Messrs. Pigott and Smith on the Middle Tana.

"There was, in truth, a sufficiency of returning English East African expeditions; but while Mr. de Winton and his friends counselled that I should on no account be invested with the com-

Previous Emin Pasha Expeditions. mand of the German Emin Pasha Expedition, they had nevertheless said that *one* Emin Pasha Expedition was already encamped by the Baringo, and that I should meet it here, if, on my side, I marched to Emin Pasha. Here, on the Baringo, no one has seen anything of that expedition.

"Even if I were to assume that the English leaders of it had moved onward—invisible, by some kind of spiritualist manipulation—I am too well acquainted with the masticatory

Question of their route. processes of Zanzibar porters to be able to believe, that four hundred of them could be pushed past the Baringo, without leaving tangible traces. I am accordingly inclined to think that no English Emin Pasha Expedition has ever been here. But then, how came Mr. de Winton and his friends to tell this to the world? And what reason has the world to attach more credit to other tales these gentlemen may put forth than to this one?"

It was afterwards told me, in Kawirondo, by Ali Somal, who was with the Jackson expedition, that Mr. Pigott had originally been intended for the Baringo. Whether this is true or not, I am unable to say. At any rate, we had at this point again got the better of English competition, and, very naturally, we were not exactly sorry in consequence.

For our further advance towards the west, I had the burdens solidly packed together, so that, as a rule, from that time for-

Adjusting the burdens. ward, only the porters were told off for the carrying of them, and the beasts of burden, especially the three camels, were only to be used in case of necessity. "Sir, let them go like gentlemen!" said Hussein Fara.

Besides this, I attended to the provisioning of the column, as I knew very well that the uninhabited Angata na Nyuki was now to be passed by us. As I have already noticed, the question of commissariat in African expeditions really constitutes the chief task of the leader, who must do justice to it, if he would show himself at all equal to his position. And here I may quite candidly declare, that the management of an expedition makes no figure, in my eyes, unless it is quite perfect from this most important point of view. Stanley has much to tell of the sufferings his expedition had to endure from hunger on their march up the Aruwimi. In reading that narrative I could not avoid thinking, "Yes, but does Stanley not feel at all that in these pictures he exposes an inexcusable fault of his own?" In the description there is not a syllable to indicate this. Now, I will grant that one cannot always be held responsible for a misfortune of this kind, although in general I feel convinced it is exactly in this particular that the commander of an expedition should make enquiries concerning his route, before he leads hundreds of men into such regions; or, if such a prosecution of enquiries is not possible, he should guard against the starving of his people by driving herds with him, or by previously establishing victualling stations proportionate to his needs. But that Stanley, even in his third journey through the forest, when he was thoroughly acquainted with all the circumstances, has again to tell of a "starvation camp," does not, I confess, maintain at its height the admiration I was formerly inclined to bestow on him, especially as a leader of an expedition. For my part, I should consider very seriously, before entrusting a great expedition to a man, who looks upon such a neglect of the principal duty of an expeditionary chief, as quite in the proper order of things, and even seems to be of opinion that he will awaken the sympathies of Europe, by giving a picture of the sufferings that resulted from such carelessness.

Provisioning the column.

Importance of the commissariat.

On the Baringo I gave each of my people a twelve days' ration of flour, and as I had still about four hundred head of cattle at my disposal, I considered, on January 13th, that I might, with a good conscience, begin the advance westward towards Kawirondo.

State of our supplies.

That day we encamped about seven miles westward of

Njemps, at a lovely bend of the Guaso Tigerish, where, in his time, Count Teleki had pitched his camp for weeks.

Climbing to the Kamasia Plateau. Next morning we had to climb the wall of the Kamasia Plateau, which inclines steeply down into the plain. We began our march before sunrise, and now we went climbing upward continually, while the sun shone down more and more hotly upon us.

The Kamasia Plateau is, in every respect, the opposite to the Döngo Gelesha and the Leikipia Plateau. Like the latter, it forms a series of levels, or terraces. It was as though we had to climb up a succession of crater walls, lying in annular form one within another.

I had induced my friend Laonania to show us the way as far as the first watering-place in Kamasia. We marched until *A confined camping-ground.* past noon, as water was nowhere to be found. At length we halted at a spring that trickled very sparingly in the dried-up bed of the Guaso Kamnje, where we were obliged to pitch the camp, in a very crowded manner, by the slope of a mountain; before us was the steep slope of the last portion of the eastern acclivity of Kamasia.

The people of this land are Massais, like the rest, and have much of the insolence of the inhabitants of Leikipia. Though they knew that we had beaten these latter, they came noisily crowding about us, and behaved turbulently enough, so that I turned them out of the camp. However, they brought capital honey to sell to us, and their boldness did not go so far as to bring on a fight.

On January 15th our way led, in zigzag windings, to the crest of the Kamasia, a complete climbing expedition, which, to my surprise, was accomplished even by the camels, who certainly marched along without burdens as " gentlemen," only having to carry Somali Achmed, who had fallen ill of pleurisy.

The eastern part of Kamasia. While the eastern slope of Kamasia is very dry, a series of brooks are to be found on the western side, and consequently fresh plantations also.

At Njemps, at the request of my porter Pemba I had left his sick wife behind, in the care of the Massais there; and the day before, my porter Chamsin, who carried some iron utensils and limped, had not arrived in camp. On the morning of January 15th, Pemba Motu was suddenly seized with a longing for his wife's company, and just before the expedition started on the march he absconded, leaving his load behind him.

This day I again set up my camp on a very confined space at the corner of a mountain slope, just above a little spring. Until then, the people of Kamasia had abstained from hostile demonstrations against us. At midday, the report was made that they had attempted to steal sheep from our flock, but had been quickly put to flight by the Somalis firing at them. Towards three o'clock, Pemba Motu suddenly made his appearance in headlong flight, completely naked, and without his weapons. He reported that the Wakamasia had felled Chamsin to the ground, and taken away his load; that they had also attempted to capture him, Pemba Motu, and that it was only by leaving all his things behind him that he had managed to escape, and to rejoin the expedition. *Pemba Motu and the Wakamasia.*

Though there was here a manifest *casus belli*, I could not make up my mind once more to make the difficult march back, across the crest of the Kamasia, but contented myself with issuing an order to my people to meet every hostile act perpetrated by the Wakamasia, from this time forward, with reprisals. *Question of reprisals.*

So we travelled onward on the morning of January 16th, continually traversing hilly and, in some parts, steep ground, towards the west. The Wakamasia repeatedly endeavoured to break into our herd of cattle, but were driven back by the Somalis, several of them being struck down.

It was nearly twelve o'clock when we reached the western declivity of the Kamasia Plateau; and, to our no small consternation, we perceived before us, separated from us by a broad valley, another steep, rocky wall, apparently extending down perpendicularly into the deeper ground, which seemed to stretch out in limitless length northward and southward. I was told that this was the land Elgejo, where the people were very bad; much worse than in Kamasia, the *The land of Elgejo.*

Njemps, at a lovely bend of the Guaso Tigerish, where, in his time, Count Teleki had pitched his camp for weeks.

Climbing to the Kamasia Plateau. Next morning we had to climb the wall of the Kamasia Plateau, which inclines steeply down into the plain. We began our march before sunrise, and now we went climbing upward continually, while the sun shone down more and more hotly upon us.

The Kamasia Plateau is, in every respect, the opposite to the Döngo Gelesha and the Leikipia Plateau. Like the latter, it forms a series of levels, or terraces. It was as though we had to climb up a succession of crater walls, lying in annular form one within another.

I had induced my friend Laonania to show us the way as far as the first watering-place in Kamasia. We marched until past noon, as water was nowhere to be found. At *A confined camping-ground.* length we halted at a spring that trickled very sparingly in the dried-up bed of the Guaso Kamnje, where we were obliged to pitch the camp, in a very crowded manner, by the slope of a mountain; before us was the steep slope of the last portion of the eastern acclivity of Kamasia.

The people of this land are Massais, like the rest, and have much of the insolence of the inhabitants of Leikipia. Though they knew that we had beaten these latter, they came noisily crowding about us, and behaved turbulently enough, so that I turned them out of the camp. However, they brought capital honey to sell to us, and their boldness did not go so far as to bring on a fight.

On January 15th our way led, in zigzag windings, to the crest of the Kamasia, a complete climbing expedition, which, to my surprise, was accomplished even by the camels, who certainly marched along without burdens as "gentlemen," only having to carry Somali Achmed, who had fallen ill of pleurisy.

The eastern part of Kamasia. While the eastern slope of Kamasia is very dry, a series of brooks are to be found on the western side, and consequently fresh plantations also.

At Njemps, at the request of my porter Pemba I had left his sick wife behind, in the care of the Massais there; and the day before, my porter Chamsin, who carried some iron utensils and limped, had not arrived in camp. On the morning of January 15th, Pemba Motu was suddenly seized with a longing for his wife's company, and just before the expedition started on the march he absconded, leaving his load behind him.

This day I again set up my camp on a very confined space at the corner of a mountain slope, just above a little spring. Until then, the people of Kamasia had abstained from hostile demonstrations against us. At midday, the report was made that they had attempted to steal sheep from our flock, but had been quickly put to flight by the Somalis firing at them. Towards three o'clock, Pemba Motu suddenly made his appearance in headlong flight, completely naked, and without his weapons. He reported that the Wakamasia had felled Chamsin to the ground, and taken away his load; that they had also attempted to capture him, Pemba Motu, and that it was only by leaving all his things behind him that he had managed to escape, and to rejoin the expedition.

Pemba Motu and the Wakamasia.

Though there was here a manifest *casus belli*, I could not make up my mind once more to make the difficult march back, across the crest of the Kamasia, but contented myself with issuing an order to my people to meet every hostile act perpetrated by the Wakamasia, from this time forward, with reprisals.

Question of reprisals.

So we travelled onward on the morning of January 16th, continually traversing hilly and, in some parts, steep ground, towards the west. The Wakamasia repeatedly endeavoured to break into our herd of cattle, but were driven back by the Somalis, several of them being struck down.

It was nearly twelve o'clock when we reached the western declivity of the Kamasia Plateau; and, to our no small consternation, we perceived before us, separated from us by a broad valley, another steep, rocky wall, apparently extending down perpendicularly into the deeper ground, which seemed to stretch out in limitless length northward and southward. I was told that this was the land Elgejo, where the people were very bad; much worse than in Kamasia, the

The land of Elgejo.

Wakamasia declared. I was now in the south-west district above Kapte, the region which surrounds the western declivity of Kamasia.

After slaughtering a "goat of peace" with the people on the higher ground, I began the descent, which was more readily accomplished than we could have anticipated from the higher position. Suddenly I saw that a green barrier had been placed across the way, and behind it fifty or sixty natives were lying in wait, lances in hand, and with bows and arrows ready to shoot. The people were simple enough to demand tribute from me, but immediately gave up this friendly intention when I pointed my gun at them, and threatened them with war. They had been spoilt by Thomson, who, with regard to this system of tribute, tells us in his work "Through Massailand," that he and his men had several times to halt, until they received permission to go on. The way was closed by putting green twigs over the footpath, and their stepping across that sacred symbol, before permission had been given, was enough to throw the people into paroxysms of uncontrollable excitement.

Demonstrations of the natives.

When the Wakamasia afterwards tried to take forcible possession of the tribute they demanded, by seizing some of my cattle (remembering also the assassination of Chamsin of which they had been guilty), three of them were shot down in the act of robbery, and by this means peace was restored in the land. They now came to explain to us that they were willing to be our friends, without receiving tribute.

This day I encamped somewhat to the south of Kapte, on the western slope of the mountain range. The Kamasia people, who now were quite amiable in their behaviour, brought us eatables of every description for sale, and we looked forward to a quiet afternoon, when our attention was suddenly attracted to a rattling of musketry at some distance below the terrace on which our camp had been pitched.

The friendly Wakamasia.

What could it be? Surely, a coast caravan, if not Europeans. An English expedition? Perhaps Stanley, or even Emin Pasha himself?

The Wakamasia who stood around soon relieved me from my state of doubt, by informing me that this was a caravan of Juma Kimameta, well known to me from Thomson's and also from Teleki's descriptions of travel.

Presently the foremost of the new-comers appeared on the

THE WAKAMASIA DEMAND TRIBUTE.

slope of the hill. In quick succession they fired their guns in the air, and I replied by a shot from my tent. I sent my leader of the porters, Musa, and my servant Buana Mku, to meet the new arrivals, and welcome them.

Arrival of Arabs.

Soon afterwards six picturesquely-attired Arabs, the leaders of the approaching expedition, made their appearance in my tent.

I felt as the mariner may feel, who, sailing on an entirely desert ocean, perhaps in the Polar Sea, suddenly sights another ship. The Arabs appeared to us almost like fellow-countrymen, for they spoke Kiswahili, with which we were well acquainted, and they came from Pangani, which I knew so well from former years. Here in the Massai tribes the opposition of interests to those of the Arab race disappears. We have all a common interest, namely, to assert ourselves against the wild natives, who, on their part, make hardly any difference between Europeans and Arabs.

The new-comers told me that they had come down from Turkang, and had tarried for some time in Engabot.

I asked them, naturally, if they had any news of Emin Pasha.

"Emin Pasha—who is he?"

Conversation with the Arabs. "A white man, who lives on the other side of Turkang, by the Nile. Have the people of Turkang never spoken to you of such a man?"

"No, never."

"Have they not told you that on the western boundary of their territory the 'Turki' are seated?"

"No, nor that either."

"What news do you bring us down from the north?"

"Turkang is a dry land. The inhabitants are peaceable, but last year the Massais came up, and they have driven away the camels of the natives."

"You were also in Engabot—had you food there?"

"The people of Engabot were formerly good, but now they have become bad."

"Have you any kind of news from Kawirondo?"

"They say that there is a white man in Kawirondo, in Kabaras, who came round the lake. So the people in Elmuttiey told us yesterday."

"A white man? what kind of white man? Does he come from the coast, or from the interior?"

"He does not come from the coast. He is said to have many women and soldiers with him. But who are you, and where do you come from?"

"I am a German, and my name is Kupanda Sharo—in Europe, Dr. Peters. We have travelled up the Tana, through the Gallas, and across the Leikipia Plateau through the Massais. We have beaten the Massais, and burnt Elbejet. You see yonder the remains of the herds which we have driven away from them." *Dr. Peters's account of himself.*

"Beaten the Massais? That is very fine! (Ngema sana!) The white men beat everyone now. Buana Mkubua (Count Teleki) beat the Wasuk in the north last year."

"We are obliged to fight everywhere, as we will pay no tribute, and the people attack us. Here in Kamasia, too, we had a skirmish this very day."

"Very good. But where do you want to go?"

"I will go to the white men on the Nile, and in the first place to Uganda. Have you news from Uganda?"

"Not from Uganda, but you will get every information in Kawirondo. There the people are very good. You may go out walking there without a gun—with a stick. There is much to eat there, too, and you will get all the information you can possibly want. Wangwana are living there, too, from whom you may buy stuffs." *Report on Kawirondo.*

This was an interesting communication, but our imagination was particularly excited by the news about the white men. The information brought by the Arabs sounded mysterious, and we conjectured that it must have a connection of some kind with the aim of our expedition. I made the Arabs a present of some oxen, and asked them if they would carry a writing with them for me to the coast. They said they would; and, amid a general salutation from my people, they went back to their column, promising to return in the evening. *Arrangement for guides.*

Great was the rejoicing among my people at the news we had heard. The generally expressed opinion declared that if a white man, with great herds of cattle, was in Kawirondo, he must be a German, for other people did not drive herds of cattle—so thought my porters and soldiers.

After breakfast I wrote a short report to the German Emin

Pasha committee on the progress of the expedition up to that time. This report arrived safely in Zanzibar at the beginning of April, and was the first actual evidence that our expedition had not been destroyed. This agreeable work occupied me until six o'clock in the evening.

After dinner the Arabs, among whom especially the very intelligent Buana Mku, from Pangani, led the conversation, came to us once again. I treated them to cocoa and sugar, and while the rain was falling without, we chatted away several agreeable hours in my tent, the Arabs questioning me closely, to get information concerning Leikipia, which they seemed inclined to prefer to the Naiwasha route. Our conversation was carried on in the dark.

Another visit from the Arabs.

I have forgotten to mention until now, that from Massa onward we had been entirely without lights. There can hardly be a notion, in Europe, of the quantity of privation involved in this slight circumstance. It makes one entirely dependent on the sun and moon; and when the moonlight failed us, we were compelled to sup before six o'clock, and to go to bed directly afterwards. It was not till we came to Uganda that the idea occurred to me of manufacturing the means of illumination, from our store of fat and twisted cotton stuff.

Candle manufacture.

I may mention, in this place, that the English in Lamu had taken from me six hundred cigars, so that for this narcotic enjoyment we had to depend entirely on our pipes and native tobacco. On the Baringo the last bottle of cognac was also expended; and now we were restricted, for beverages, to coffee, tea, and cocoa, which, I may observe by the way, we found eminently conducive to our health.

At parting I presented Buana Mku with a keg of powder and a new robe, and, bearing our despatch, the Arabs withdrew for the night. Next morning there was another leave-taking, and with mutual pious wishes we parted from each other—we to proceed to Uganda, they to make their way back through the Massais of the Kilima Ndsharo.

Parting with Buana Mku.

This meeting with the Arab expedition was like the first

faint dawning of day for us, with respect to our expedition's aim. In the white man, who was said to dwell in Kawirondo, we had a subject that occupied our thoughts during the march, and often enlivened our conversation afterwards. Each of us was now greatly thrown back upon himself, as Herr von Tiedemann's illness continued, and he generally went to bed so soon as the day's march was over.

From Kapte we journeyed to Elmuttiey in a march of eight hours. Elmuttiey lies in the great depression which extends between Kamasia and Elgejo in a north-west direction, and is traversed by the Weiwei river.

On this day died the Somali Achmed, who was buried in the evening, by the light of flaming fires, by his fellow tribesmen. A very fantastic spectacle was that of his burial. They uttered their Mohamedan prayers in a kind of wild convulsion. Each man solemnly laid it on the dead man's conscience, to mention his name in the presence of Allah. Strangers who witnessed this singular scene must have taken it for a grisly incantation, with magic formulas and exorcism of evil spirits.

Death of the Somali Achmed.

In these depressions, between two towering walls of rock, a very singular appearance is presented at night by the fires maintained in the villages built on the hills. This spectacle had already attracted us at Lake Baringo, and here it appeared still more peculiar.

I had heard that there was plenty of food at Elgejo; but the people here kept aloof from us in a singular manner. Inclined from the beginning to insolence, just like the Wakamasia, they still did not feel quite safe in approaching us, having heard of the fate of their tribal relatives of Kamasia, and especially of what had befallen the Massais. They are clothed like the Wakamasia, whom they also resemble in appearance, wearing a short cloak hung over the shoulders, that leaves the body itself completely nude. They carry a slender spear, about seven feet long, besides a bow and arrows. The language here, as in all the lands of this region, is that of the Massais.

The people of Elgejo.

On the recommendation of Buana Mku, I had, immediately

on my arrival here, enquired for a guide, Kirobani, who, it was said, knew the way to Kawirondo, and, for an adequate reward in cattle, would perhaps be inclined to show us the road. Kirobani declared himself willing, after we had settled to pay him five sheep and a reasonable quantity of stuff, for his services.

<small>Kirobani, the guide.</small>

As the supply of provisions the column possessed did not seem sufficient for the march across the steppe that lay before us, I determined to remain here for the following day, to increase our stock. In the morning I at once sent my people into the villages, on the slope of the mountains, to purchase, but they came back in the afternoon with their commission unfulfilled. The natives would not sell anything; and all my own efforts in this direction, continued until the evening, were of no avail.

To my chagrin there also arrived at my camp, on this day, a deserter from the Arab ranks, whom unfortunately I could not send back, as the distance between the two expeditions was already too great, and whom I was, therefore, compelled to receive into my column. The man's name was Buana Maramba, and he was a native of Mombassa.

<small>Arrival of a deserter.</small>

When I resumed the march with my column on January 18th, Kirobani, in spite of his emphatic promise, had not made his appearance. I therefore sent out men to seek him, and in the meantime set forward with my column towards the wall of rock which we had to climb.

Kirobani, who had already received part of his payment, was discovered by my people, hiding in a mtama field. I went up to him and said, "Forward now, old boy! Show us the way to Kawirondo." A short dogged "Ä-ä-ä!" was the reply to my encouraging address. I said, "Forward!" Again the snarling, "Ä-ä-ä!" Thereupon I took him by the shoulder, and gave him a slight shake. Then he snarled, just like a cat setting up its back against a dog. My patience was exhausted. A well-aimed blow in the face, and a cord fastened round his neck by the Somalis, made it manifest to Kirobani that I was not inclined to have my contracts broken in that unceremonious way. He immediately assumed a very polite and

<small>Misconduct of Kirobani.</small>

modest demeanour, and strode onward, up the mountain, in the most cheerful manner, followed by my column. This morning I was compelled to have the last but one of my camels killed, as it was entirely unable to march up the rocky path.

A little before twelve o'clock, I encamped on a promontory, half way up the ascent, where a little brook went rippling by.

I caused Kirobani, who was now our very good friend, to be chained up; and in this situation he received the visits of his family. I had him well fed, and he said I might quite safely set him at liberty, for he was glad to go with us to Kawirondo. But I was not sufficiently convinced of this gladness of heart in him, and consequently persevered in the measures I had taken.

To strengthen our last remaining camel, the Somalis cooked a whole sheep for it. To our great astonishment the beast ate up the flesh, quite ravenously, to the last morsel. *The carnivorous camel.*

On this day also, all our efforts to procure food for the caravan failed. The natives would not sell anything, while on the other hand their behaviour was not such as to justify a declaration of war.

In the evening a violent shower of rain poured down upon us, which we welcomed gladly, because it strengthened the hope that we should succeed in finding water on the Angata na Nyuki (red plain). But the night was dark as pitch, so that one could not see one's hand before one's eyes, and the outposts had taken refuge from the sheets of rain under the tent-roof of the Somalis. Here was an opportunity for Kirobani, of which he did not fail to take advantage. Next morning he had vanished, with the chain round his foot. He had only been able to take the shortest of steps, like Gretchen on the Blocksberg, when Faust beheld her in the distance; but, for all that, he was nowhere to be found. Accordingly, I had to face the disagreeable necessity of marching forward upon Kawirondo without a guide, after all. *Escape of Kirobani.*

All night through, there had been a wild yowling and roaring noise in the villages above us. The inhabitants had been holding high revel throughout the dark hours, and looked dissipated enough when we continued our march up the rocky incline next morning.

The ascent became steeper and steeper. After passing the villages, we presently came to a strip of forest. Here we succeeded in striking a bargain with three men from Elgejo, who agreed, in consideration of a stipulated number of arm-lengths of stuff, to lead us up to the plateau, and then to return. When the belt of forest had been passed, we came to another shoulder of the mountain, where I halted, to wait for my herd and the donkeys. Here it was reported to me that two donkeys had fallen down, and could go no further, and that a part of the herd had also dropped behind.

Three Elgejo guides.

From all sides Waelgejo came running up in many hundreds, even in thousands, and their demeanour towards us was manifestly more equivocal than on the two preceding days. At length the herd emerged from the wooded thicket, and now we went on, upward along the dizzy path on the margin of the rock.

At its highest point the Elgejo Plateau is crowned by a lava cap, which descends perpendicularly, and would be quite inaccessible, but that it is traversed by a cleft, in which one can climb upward, as on a staircase. But to do this, it is of course necessary to know where this cleft is situated.

The great Elgejo Plateau.

Where the lava cap surmounts the rock is another shoulder, on which there is room for the encampment of a caravan. This point was occupied by a crowd of Waelgejo, and when I appeared upon it, with the advanced guard, my three guides suddenly stepped aside, and refused to show me the entrance to the rocky staircase. All my persuasions were answered with a stubborn, "Ä-ä-ä!" and when I at last laid my hand upon one of the men, to compel him to do his duty, for which he had been paid in advance, a wild war-cry suddenly arose among the Waelgejo. They brandished their spears, advanced upon me in a demonstrative manner, and from rock to rock the war-howl echoed across the land.

Quarrel with the Elgejo.

All at once musket shots rattled from below. The

ENCOUNTER WITH THE WARLORJO.

Waelgejo had thrown themselves across the path of the Somalis and my herd to steal the cattle. This was enough! As the Waelgejo now also began to shoot at us from above with arrows, we fired among them, whereby three of them were killed; whereupon the rest quickly disappeared behind boulders of rock to the right. We succeeded in getting hold of at least one of the guides, whom we secured with cords, to compel him in this manner to show us the last ascent. *A combat*

From behind their rocky screens, the Waelgejo continued their war-howl and their shooting with arrows, which, however, was entirely without result. I contented myself with firing off my double-barrelled rifle, for which I had still five hundred cartridges, in their direction every now and then, to keep the horde at a distance. The Somalis below had also very soon put their opponents to the rout; and, after waiting an hour, I had the satisfaction of seeing not only my herd, but also the remaining camel and the donkeys make their appearance at our halting-place. *The easy victory.*

We now went onwards towards the last rocky ascent. The guide had to show us the approach, willingly or unwillingly, and we began to climb upward step by step. Unfortunately, however, in spite of my warning, he suddenly sprang aside from the rocky path right into the depth, clinging to the bushes, in an attempt at flight. One of my people shot down at him, and so, to my regret, this Elgejo man fell also; for which I was the more sorry, as we knew the way now, and the skirmish with his fellow-tribesmen might be considered as ended. *The incorrigible guide.*

At length we had gained the summit, and before us, on the heights of Elgejo, at an elevation of 2700 feet, lay a thick forest of juniper trees, into which a path led. Here I halted, to wait for the whole column. Gradually the porters came panting along, and I had to send them back immediately to bring up the burdens of the animals. It was reported to me that the camel had unfortunately stuck in the narrow path, and could neither be moved forward nor back. I *Death of the last camel.*

was obliged to give the order to have its throat cut, to prevent it from falling into the hands of the Waelgejo, and to make room for the column. After two hours of strenuous labour all of us were at the top.

Under us, at a dizzy depth, lay the settlements of the Waelgejo, from whom we were now delivered; before us the wood, which must lead us to the Angata na Nyuki. Forward, therefore, on the path, at whose entrance we were encamped, and which, in the meantime, I had already had inspected by <small>A difficult</small> Rukua and a Somali. The road was rendered much <small>path.</small> more difficult by a kind of sharp stinging nettle, which hung across it on both sides. But half an hour brought us to the opposite end, and now there lay before us the Angata na Nyuki, which separates Elgejo from Kawirondo. The afternoon was grey and cold, as in the Highlands of Scotland. Now and then a slight shower of rain descended upon us, and a cold autumnal wind whistled from the north across the steppe that lay spread before us.

This day I encamped a couple of miles further on, at the edge of a thick wood. We found no water to-day, but I descried a black swampy ground, out of which my people pressed a liquid, that though sufficiently sandy, yet made it possible for us at least to boil soup and meat in the evening, and to drink a cup of tea.

Next morning we proceeded in a due westerly direction up to the completely bare Angata na Nyuki (red plain). To the right, just in the north, we sighted the Ischibscharagnani, and <small>March to</small> half to the right, in the north-west, the Elgon, the two <small>the Angata</small> corresponding mountains to the Kenia and Subugu la <small>na Nyuki.</small> Poron on the other side of the Baringo Falls. This Angata na Nyuki, in its whole character and structure, exactly corresponds to the Leikipia Plateau, which it even somewhat exceeds in elevation. The equivalent to Kikuyu, which stretches beyond the Leikipia in the south, is furnished on this side by the land of Wandi in the south. The whole enormous ridge gradually declines towards the west, towards the Victoria Nyanza, to about 4,000 feet, and to any one who traverses it with an observant eye the unity of its geological character becomes indisputably apparent. The action of the expansive central forces, which have thrown it upward in immeasurably distant times, must be acknowledged in the Baringo territory.

But whereas the Leikipia Plateau had been peopled by human beings, here in the Angata na Nyuki we came into an entirely uninhabited region. Not so very long ago there lived here tribes related to the Wakamasia and Waelgejo. These have been exterminated, to the last man, by the southern Massai tribes, and at this day the empty steppe is traversed only by the flying feet of great herds of antelopes and zebras, and by the rhinoceros and buffalo. Each rising and each declivity appears in clear outlines through the transparent air. Before us, on the horizon, rise the Surrongai Hills, which we shall have to traverse to reach Kawirondo. *A deserted country.*

A dreamy feeling steals over the heart in this magnificent solitude ; a solitude only broken once in a couple of years by a caravan wending towards the west. Yonder is the Elgon, apparently so tangibly near that it seems as if we might get to it in a few hours. Does it not seem to look scornfully and contemptuously down upon us puny mortals, and to ask what we are seeking here, where Eternity itself has set up its habitation, and gazes down upon us ? *Grand solitude of nature.*

In Elgon, according to Thomson, there are to be found singular cave structures, which led him to conjecture that ages ago a civilised people had laboured here. What a historical past has once run its course on this marvellous scene ! Are they the voices of old hero-races that speak to us in the strange accents of the north wind sweeping across the plain ?

We have now emerged from the dry zone. The clouds are fantastically piled up on the horizon, and press forward with the storm over the Angata na Nyuki. Daily the dark heaven pours down its waters in heavy showers of rain upon the thirsty earth, which is already becoming overspread with a new freshly green surface of grass. Like the rolling of drums, the heavy raindrops fall pelting down upon the tents, and the organ pipe of the wind sounds among the reeds *Violent tropical thunderstorms.*

on the river's brink. In Nature more violent combats are exhibited. The firmament rolls its stormy clouds together, to call forth the dark forces in the womb of the earth. Threateningly the cloud army is marshalled onward, and flash upon flash of lightning darts across the dark plain, now blinding white, now glittering blue, and, like the discharge of cannon, roll peal upon peal the short, echoless thunder-claps; and we have now, every evening, the opportunity of observing the spectacle of the sheet lightning flashing before us in the south-west, from the region of the Victoria Nyanza.

The temperature is cool and agreeable. The nights are not so cold as on the Leikipia Plateau, and, on the other hand, the days are less hot. We have almost the temperature of northern Europe during the latter half of September. The water question has also assumed a satisfactory appearance.

Already on the first day we came to a southern tributary of the Nsoia, and the farther we marched towards the west the

Success and good spirits.

more quickly did brook succeed to brook, so that we had often to cross about a dozen of them on one morning. The cares of the weeks we have left behind us are flown, and the soul can look into itself with tranquillity.

Yonder before us, in the north-west, to the left of Elgon, opens the gate which might lead us to the lands of Emin Pasha. How if we were to press forward directly towards it? The temptation is sufficiently strong, but we are still entirely without intelligence of what may have happened, in the interval, in the Equatorial Province; and, on the other hand, Kawirondo beckons us, and the mysterious form of the white man, of whom we have been told in Kamasia. Forward, therefore, in a direct line, towards the Surrongai Mountains!

I was startled out of such lucubrations as these, on the Angata na Nyuki, by a dream that had about it almost the character of clairvoyance. As a general thing, I dream little or not at all; but already, on the Upper Tana, I had had three times one and the same dream, which was bound to influence my frame of mind, if not my decision. Three times, on the Upper Tana, when the continuous barrier of the river began to tire us all out, I had dreamt that I had given up the expedition at this stage, that I had marched back to Mombas, and was now in Germany. On each of the three occasions, the first joy at meeting my friends again in my native country had been succeeded by an exceedingly painful feeling, because the expedition had been interrupted here in the midst; and immediately a lively wish had arisen, to take it up again where it had been abandoned. Each time I had awoke with the anxious feeling,—How shall I again get through the blockade into the interior, and to the place from which I returned home? On the Angata na Nyuki I lay sleeping one night, and dreamt I was in the place where, in fact, I had encamped that day, but that the appearance of Africa had changed. I was not in my tent, but in a stone house, which had been built by Germans, and where, besides the Government architect, Hoernecke, there dwelt some other engineers and several ladies. I entered the house, mentioned my name, and told how we had come here after heavy combats against the Massais, and that I proposed to march to Emin Pasha. I was received very amiably by all, but to my last observation they replied unanimously, "To Emin Pasha! But he is in Berlin. How is it you are seeking for Emin Pasha here in Central Africa?"—I said, "Emin Pasha is in Berlin? But what are you doing here?"—"Do you not know that either? We are here to build a railway to Uganda."—"And what is Emin Pasha doing in Berlin?"—"He has left the Equatorial Province long ago." —"I do not believe that. At any rate, I must ascertain that at the place itself."

A curious dream.

Imaginary conversation.

During this last part of our conversation we continually heard a discontented growling, as of something supernatural. It was as though a ghostly thing were rushing onward, nearer and nearer.

In the perturbation it occasioned I awoke, and found myself in the midst of one of the tropical rain-showers of which I have spoken.

Thus ended this dream, which made a certain lasting impression on my fancy. This is not the place to touch upon the secret of dream-life; but perhaps it may occur now and then that the enigmatical power which surrounds and enfolds life can, in certain situations, exert an influence in this manner on the resolutions of individuals.

As a landmark for my march, I had, from the very first day, chosen a lofty eminence in the Surrongai Hills, which, in contrast to the other heights, looked quite white, and manifestly formed the eastern projection of these mountains. The white colour arose, as I afterwards ascertained, from the fact that the grass on the other hills had been burnt up, and only remained on this one.

A useful landmark.

On January 22nd we crossed the Guaso Marim, and on the following day we entered the Surrongai Hills themselves. The Angata na Nyuki becomes more and more luxuriant the further we advance to the west. Towards the west, also, are glorious stretches of wood, and by the courses of the springs we again, after a long time, came upon the fan palm. The number of game animals increases more and more. Herds of buffalo, to be counted by thousands,—or, I may say, tens of thousands of head,—graze by the margin of the forest, rushing off in a thundering gallop when the rifle bullet crashes in among them. On January 24th I shot five buffaloes, which all fell, though I could only secure one gigantic specimen, as a pursuit, even of a quarter of an hour, would have been too great an interruption to the business of the expedition. To give my people time to cut up the great beast, I set up my camp at noon near the western slope of the Surrongai Hills, once more halting this side of Kawirondo.

Enormous herds of wild cattle.

It was a dull, rainy day, but we were all in a state of joyous excitement; for now we knew for certain that next morning we should reach the fruitful land of Kawirondo, where we hoped to receive news concerning the object of our expedition.

Just before two o'clock, four Wandorobbo suddenly appeared at my camp. I invited them to stay the night with us, and on the next day to show us a convenient way down into Kawirondo, which was situated at a considerably lower level. On this day, January 25th, it was proved that the course I had pursued, without alteration from Elgejo, had been entirely the right one. In an almost direct line we struck Kabaras, having deviated from the chief town only half a mile, towards the north.

Fortunate route to Kabaras.

A march of three-quarters of an hour brought us to-day, first to the edge of the Surrongai Mountains, and then we all at once beheld before us the villages and plantations of Kawirondo, from among which cheerful, fair-promising clouds of smoke rose towards the sky.

The Wandorobbo accurately pointed out the chief place of Kabaras, and then begged permission to return, as they were at war with the Kawirondo people. I granted their request.

We had now before us the difficult task of finding a way down to the lower ground. The Angata na Nyuki here forms an almost perpendicular wall of 1,400 feet, and, at first sight, it seemed impossible to commence the descent. Twice we were obliged to turn back, because again and again there were places where the descent was literally perpendicular, and which were impassable. At last I discovered a more gradual slope; and here, going on in advance with the Somali Omar Idlé, I found a way for my caravan, first over loose rocks, and then through grass as tall as a man.

A difficult scramble.

Within two hours, all had arrived below, and I now resumed my march exactly in a western direction, according to a landmark I had fixed upon above. I marched till nearly three in the afternoon, and halted when I found myself by the side of a stream, opposite the first plantations of the Wakawirondo. According to my custom, I wished to meet the inhabitants of the country for the first time, not with a weary and hungry caravan, but on the next morning, with one refreshed by rest.

I had marched in advance, with Rukua, Hussein, and two other Somalis, and I now sent two Somalis back to bring up my people. It was more than an hour before they succeeded in bringing in the herd, and it was almost six o'clock when Rukua, whom I sent off later, managed to find the porters and Herr von Tiedemann, who had lost their way, and branched off in a wrong direction to the south. There was just enough time t set up the tents before it grew dark, and then the usual storm rain came splashing down upon us. But the kitchen was unde

Cooking under difficulties. a tent-roof, and so we could enjoy a strengthenin soup and some roast mutton,—each of us separately however, as Herr von Tiedemann was still ill; an afterwards over a pipe, while the rain, now more gentle an melodious, continued to fall, we gave ourselves up to pleasan contemplation of the improved prospects of our expedition.

A short march of hardly half an hour brought us, nex morning, to the first villages of the people of Kabaras. I fire off two shots as a greeting, and then, with the flag borne i advance, we marched with beat of drum upon the capital Kabaras, a place encircled by a wall of clay, at the norther entrance of which sat the elders, ready to give us a friendl welcome. "Jambo Sána!" was the cry. We turned off to th left outside the town, and under some mighty cotton trees, little below the southern enclosure of Kabaras, we pitched ou camp.

My first enquiry was naturally after the white man i *News of white men.* Kawirondo. "Are there any white men in Ka wirondo?"

"Yes," was the simultaneous reply of all.

"How many?"

"Some say two, and others four."

"Have the white men many soldiers?"

"Yes, a very great number, and every morning they blov the trumpet, just as you do."

"Do you know the names of the white men? Is one o them called Emin Pasha? And are Turkis among them?"

"Emin Pasha? We don't know him."

"Where do the white men come from? Do they come fron the coast, or have they come from the interior?"

"They have come from the south, round the Nyanza."

"Then perhaps their leader is called Stanley?"

"Yes, yes, quite right, Stamuley."

These questions I addressed repeatedly to several of th

IN CAMP BEFORE KABARAS.

Wakawirondo, and always got the same answer, "Yes, certainly, Stamuley. They have also cattle with them—a great herd, and their head man is called Stamuley!"

That was certainly a very notable piece of news for us. Could Stanley, of whose movements I knew nothing further than that he had marched back, the first time, from Mwutan Nzige to the Congo, perhaps have marched to the Victoria Nyanza by the Udidji Tabora road, and from thence to Kawirondo, to get in touch with Emin Pasha from that place; or was Emin Pasha with him, though perchance the natives did not know the Pasha's name?

I immediately sat down, and wrote the following letter:—

"KABARAS, *January 26th*, 1890.

"SIR,—On my arrival here this morning I got news, that Europeans are in Kwa Sundu. As I shall arrive at Kwa Sundu on Wednesday or Thursday next, I shall be charmed to meet any gentleman who may be at that place, and shall be obliged for a line to tell me whom I may have the pleasure to see. *Letter to a possible European.*

"I have the honour, Sir, to be, yours truly,

"DR. CARL PETERS.

"To any European gentleman who may be in Kwa Sundu or in Kawirondo."

This letter I immediately sent off by the two Somalis, Sameter and Jama Ismael, with a Kawirondo man for a guide, to Kwa Sundu, with orders to send me the answer to Kwa Sakwa, to which place I intended to march next day.

Meanwhile I observed, with real interest, the remarkable figures of the Kawirondo people, who crowded into my camp. In great gourd bottles they brought grain of all kinds, and honey, besides eggs, fowls, and milk. The men are clothed with an apron, but the ladies of the land are as unclad as possible; a remarkable contrast to the Massailands, where exactly the reverse was the case. Only the married women wore an apron of very limited size, and had also rings *The Kawirondo people.*

298   *NEW LIGHT ON DARK AFRICA.*

on their arms and legs and in their ears, and chains about their necks. The unmarried girls went about exactly as Heaven had made them.

Mingled with the Bantu population are here to be found,

WAKAWIRONDO.

everywhere, fragments of the once mighty Baringo-Massai tribe, called Wakuafi, who were driven out from the Angata na Nyuki by the Southern Massais. Here they generally do landsknecht-service for the native sultans, and, in fact, supply the principal warrior contingent for the whole of Kawirondo.

MANNERS OF THE WAKAWIRONDO.

Thomson has much to tell of the danger of his position in Kawirondo. He was very apprehensive of being killed. I must confess that we experienced no anxieties of the kind, among these simple and sociable people. In fact, it was true what the Arabs in Kapte had said, one could go out walking here without arms, and only with a walking-stick. Among the Massais themselves, Thomson had exhibited

Mr. Thomson's opinion.

WAKAWIRONDO.

a good nature of which I have already spoken. That this good nature did not altogether emanate from the Christian feeling of love for one's neighbour, in pursuance of the command to offer the right cheek when the left is smitten, Thomson manifests by the description of his behaviour towards the Massais in Kawirondo, in his work entitled "Among the Massai." He tells how the Wakawirondo attempted the same insolent braggadocio and arrogance, but how he soon made them understand that what he had put up with from the Massais in their own country, he would not endure from them; and further acknowledges that, from a certain desire of vengeance, long suppressed, it gave him no small satisfaction to encounter those rascals wrathfully, when any one of them tried his patience; and that his people were equally charmed to have it out with them, and to threaten, with tremendous objurgations, to inflict unspeakable torments upon them.

I have also always found the Massais in Kawirondo quite well behaved with respect to us, and was not obliged, on a single occasion, to repel insolence on their part.

The luxurious plenty in food, in this country, had a perfectly inspiring effect on us and my people. The fowls were fat and tender, and three of them were scarcely sufficient to satisfy the appetite of one of us at breakfast, so strong was the craving of our bodies, after the toils of the last months, *A land of plenty.* to patch themselves up anew. The honey was perfectly white, like sugar, and deliciously fragrant of flowers. We had also milk and eggs, which latter were eaten in the poached, and especially in the omelet form. Beans and corn, and grain fruits of all kinds, eaten with milk, as porridge, or with strong gravy as a concomitant of meat, formed an agreeable change from our ordinary meat diet; and glorious bananas, eaten raw, or baked in fat and sugar, made a capital dessert. The whole world appeared in new colours; and then, the mysterious white men were in the immediate vicinity.

On January 27th we celebrated the Emperor's birthday by a special dinner, and with beat of drum we went, on the 28th, with our guide in advance, on well-made paths, towards the south. The landscape put on a more and more cultivated appearance, with villages close to each other, and well-fed herds of oxen to be seen in the meadows. When we marched past, a settlement of people would come and offer corn, milk, and honey *Fear of the Massais.* for sale. Here the reputation of the conquerors of the Massais produced its full effect. I dare to assert that on the strength of this fact we were more popular in Kawirondo than in any other part of our march, for here the Massais are sufficiently known in all their brutal cruelty and dangerous wildness.

Between two villages, on a lovely declivity in a richly-cultivated plain, I pitched my camp on this day, and unfurled the great flag of the expedition at the margin of the slope, so that it was visible over the whole landscape.

Scarcely had I had the tents set up, when suddenly shots were fired in the low ground beneath us, and directly afterwards five men, clad in white shirts, came hurrying up at full speed, with friendly greetings. *Messengers from the Sultan.*

"There come the messengers from the white men!" said the Wakawirondo, and forthwith the newcomers were led by my Somalis in front of my chair.

"Who are you?" I enquired.

"We are Wangwana from the coast, and these are the sons and the people of the Sultan Sakwa, of Kawirondo. The Sultan sends us to bid you welcome to his country."

"What white men are there in Kawirondo, and what do you know about them?"

"They are Englishmen—Mr. Jackson, Mr. Martin, and two more."

"How long have they been here?"

"For many months; but a short time ago they went to Elgumi, and farther up, to shoot elephants."

"What are they doing here?"

"They have made a station in Kwa Sundu, and are buying ivory. Messengers have come to them, too, from Uganda, but in Uganda there is war, and no one can go there. The Arabs have driven away Muanga, and killed all the Christians. The Englishmen do not like to go into this country."

"Are they friends with your Sultan?"

"Sakwa, our Sultan, is great and rich. He does not love the people who come here to buy ivory and shoot game. Sakwa loves the thorough people who understand war. We know that you, Sir, have beaten the Massais, and therefore Sakwa will be your friend. He sends us to announce this to you, and invites you to march to-morrow *An important conversation.*

to his residence at Kwa Sakwa, to make a station there; Sakwa will not have the English, he loves the Germans. But whither are you journeying?"

"I am journeying into the land of the Turki, to Emin Pasha. Have you any tidings of him?"

"The Turki are said to be yonder" (pointing to the north), "but they are very far away. We have no tidings of them. Emin Pasha we do not know."

"Do you know the way to Unjoro?"

"Unjoro is very far off; we do not know the way there. Six years ago a white man came here; he wanted to go to Uganda, but the Waganda killed all his people. The Waganda are very bad, and none of us go out in that direction."

"Send messengers back to your Sultan, and tell him I shall come to him to-morrow; that I want to go to Uganda, and come as a friend. Everything else I will talk over with him personally to-morrow."

So now we had the explanation concerning our white men in Kawirondo; and, in truth, it was the *nascitur ridiculus mus*. We had come across the Jackson Emin Pasha Expedition, and probably the people of Kabaras had heard the name of "Stanley," with whom this expedition was to co-operate, mentioned in it.

The following days would bring us further explanations, and therefore for to-day we entirely refrained from conjecture.

Next morning we proceeded in a south-west direction over some high ranges. Everywhere we saw enormous herds of cattle. "All those belong to the Sakwa," said the guides. The Massais who tended the cattle hurried up to greet us respectfully, and after we had crossed an affluent of the Nsoia, all at once the great red walls and the lofty gates of Kwa Sakwa rose before us, not like a village, but like a town.

The Sakwa's possessions.

A dense crowd came streaming out of the gate towards us, and I was immediately informed that the Sultan himself, with his brothers, was coming to meet us, to give us suitable greeting. But as I did not sufficiently know the intentions of these

ARRIVAL AT KWA SAKWA.

people, I gave orders to have the firearms ready for action, for whatever might happen.

Thus in close order we marched towards the north-east gate of the town. About three hundred yards to the right, by the wayside, was a gigantic tree, and under this tree Sakwa sat with his people. A great bronze chain hung round his neck, and his arms were profusely ornamented with artistic copper rings. He carried a lance in his right hand, and a shirt of a cotton fabric covered his body. When I marched towards him, he rose from his seat, with all his following, and strode towards me with his hand extended. Hand in hand we then moved with ceremonious gravity towards the entrance gate of Kwa Sakwa. A wide ditch surrounds the walls of the place, over which a dam leads to the gate. On entering the en-closure, the stranger first comes upon a great open space, surrounded by the houses of the war garrison of the place. From thence he comes to a second great space, which is surrounded, in a wide circle, by the many houses of the sultan. All these houses are full of hundreds of women, in whose midst he himself dwells. The king pointed out to me that this place belonged to me. I might either dwell in his houses, or have my tents set up. At the same time he pointed to two fat oxen, that were to be my food for to-day, and every morning, so long as I stayed there, two other oxen would be ready for us. Then brown beer was brought for us in great jugs, and to this were added honey, eggs, poultry, and milk, as well as golden yellow bananas. Soon houses had been prepared for my people; the tents were set up, and at the hour of noon the black, white, and red flag waved for the first time in the midst of Kwa Sakwa.

The town of Sakwa.

Scarcely had I established myself comfortably in my tent, and bathed and shaved, as I was accustomed to do every day so soon as the march was ended, when a sudden firing of guns from the southern gate announced a new visit. Porters belonging to the English expedition came to welcome us, and from them I received more definite information concerning its objects, and especially about Ali Somal,

Porters from the English expedition.

who was, they told me, chief of the station, in the absence of the four white men. They said that the expedition had a strength of five hundred porters, and was armed with Remingtons, and well supplied with ammunition. They had more than fifty loads of cartridges still in stock.

In the afternoon Ali Somal came over himself from Kwa Sundu to greet us—a young Somali, of intelligent appearance, and almost gentlemanlike bearing, in a completely European garb, who very courteously bad us welcome, and immediately *Arrival of Ali Somal.* came out with an invitation that we should shift our quarters, as soon as possible, to his place in the English station. He said, "Mr. Jackson would be much offended with me if I allowed you to live here with the Sakwa. He will regret very much that he is absent just now; but at all events you must wait until he returns."

"But where has Mr. Jackson gone? Has he perhaps marched through Elgumi to Emin Pasha?"

"By no means. If he had gone to Emin Pasha he would certainly have taken me with him. No, he is hunting. He has been hunting for some time—several weeks—yonder on the Elgon, and has killed several elephants, and has probably now marched further to the northward for the same purpose."

"But if he only wants to hunt, why does he take four hundred and fifty men, and all the white men, to the northward with him? Has he only come into this region to hunt?"

"Not so. We were commissioned to put ourselves in communication with Stanley from this place, to support his expedition in the Nile countries. But Stanley has marched back, by the western side of Lake Victoria, to the coast, and so we could not help him."

"Stanley has marched off, by the western side of Lake Victoria? But then he has gone back for the second time to Emin Pasha; and has Emin Pasha perhaps even gone away with him?"

"No, Emin Pasha has remained behind in his country.

With Stanley another white man went southward. Emin Pasha has been at war with the Wangoro, who have beaten his people, and driven him up towards the north. He is quite alone now in the Equatorial Province, and to reach him from here is impossible."

Accounts of Emin Pasha.

" How do you know that ? "

" Mr. Jackson would have been uncommonly glad to march to Emin Pasha, or at all events to Uganda ; but he might not do this, as all the tribes to the west of us are hostile, and we should simply have gone to our death if we had marched thither. The Wangoro will have nothing to do with the whites, and the Arabs rule in Uganda. The Waganda kill every white man who comes into the country, and an expedition that advances into these regions is lost from the beginning."

" Have you had news from Uganda ? "

" Yes, repeatedly. The people of the last Waganda deputation are at present still in my camp, and you can question them yourself. The Christians of Uganda have already sent to us several times, asking us to bring help to them, and then they would accept the English flag ; but Mr. Jackson has always declined this, saying he was too weak for it. Wait for Mr. Jackson ; he will relate all this to you more clearly himself. In fourteen days he must be back."

" I cannot wait here for fourteen days, for in a few days I shall march away from here to the west."

" You intend to march from here to the west ? "

" Most certainly. If Emin Pasha is alone in his province now, he has the more need of help."

" But to go to the west is quite impossible. You will be leading yourself and all your people to death. Emin Pasha has been beaten, and is no longer what he was."

" If Emin Pasha has been beaten, he needs help all the more. Moreover, how do you know for certain that an advance to the west is impracticable ? "

" We have good intelligence from every quarter. I can show you the letters from Uganda itself, if you care to see them. You will then see it all yourself, and give up the plan of leading all your people to destruction. I have an especial interest in this, as there are twelve brothers of my own in your expedition, whose lives I would wish to save. Read the letters from Uganda yourself to-morrow, and you will say I am right."

"Very good. Now go to the Somalis, who will give you news from your country. So long as you remain with me in Kwa Sakwa you are my guest."

What tidings were these that I received here? The great English Emin Pasha Expedition had been lying for months past on the borders of the Nile countries, without venturing an advance in this direction. Emin Pasha beaten by the Wangoro, and remaining behind, solitary at his post, while his white companion (evidently Casati) had gone away with Stanley to the coast! Uganda in the hands of the Arabs, and Kaba-Rega, whom, from Emin's description, I knew to be his faithful friend, now the enemy of the Europeans and of Emin himself! It will be understood that I was excited to the utmost degree by these tidings, whose authenticity we had no reason to doubt. But out of the chaos of my feelings the solitary figure of Emin Pasha rose again and again, amid a world of hostile powers, forsaken by all, assailed by the Mahdi in the north and the Wangoro in the south, with nothing left before his eyes but ruin, and, as it appeared to us, resolved to encounter it. How could we for a moment waver in our determination, now more than ever, to hasten to him, either to give him help, or, if it must be, to fall with him?

Bewildering news concerning Emin.

But let us first wait to see what the next day will bring in the way of further explanations. It brought, in the first place, a peculiar request on the part of the Sultan Sakwa. Early in the morning he appeared in front of my tent, to make me the following proposal:—

"Two hours to the north of this place," said he, "dwells the robber tribe of the Mangati, in a land which we call Ngoro. These people are continually making inroads into my territory, threatening my herds, and burning down my villages. They have laid waste the whole west, from the Nsoia River. I have begged the English repeatedly to beat back these Mangati, and offered, if they would do this, to accept their flag for Kawirondo. But the English are people of fear; they have shut themselves up in their stations, and are afraid of the strife with the Mangati. Now you Germans are come, you who have beaten the Massais themselves, I will give you all my Askaris. You shall then beat the Mangati, and I will accept your flag, and give you half of the cattle that shall be taken from the Mangati." *Proposal of the Sultan.*

"But what have I to do with the Mangati? I have no thought of fighting with the Mangati. We have been obliged to fight with the Massais because they attacked us first. We Germans, in fact, only fight when we are attacked, or when people are attacked who are under our protection."

"Well, we will come under your protection. You shall be our lord if you beat the Mangati for us."

"Even if I wished to do you that favour, I could not at the present moment. I must march to the west, to a great white man who lives there. If I shoot away my cartridges here, how am I to get to my friend on the Nile?"

"You cannot get to the Nile, anyway. There dwell the Waganda, who are very bad, and kill every one who comes to them. A little while ago a white man was among us here, who also wanted to march into those lands. The Waganda killed him and all his people."

"But are the Wasoga as bad, too? If I march on this side of the Nile, through Usoga, and afterwards on this side of the river past Unjoro, I have no occasion to fear the Waganda."

"The Wasoga and the Waganda are just the same," said he. "The Wasoga are slaves of the Mfalme (king) of Uganda, and must do everything he tells them."

"But by the time the news of our marching through arrives at Uganda we shall have long passed Usoga; and if the Wasoga hinder us in doing so, we will beat them just as we have beaten the Massais."

"In Usoga there are many Waganda, and they have there very many guns. All the tribes behind you you could beat, but if you attempt to make war on the Waganda and the Wasoga, you will perish. Beat the Mangati for us, and accept our hospitality. Meanwhile, we will send tidings to the white man. If he is as great as you say, he will send you soldiers, so that you may come safely to him. We know very well that yonder, towards the sinking sun, the Turki dwell, and that they have many guns. If their sultan is a white man, wait here for news from him, and then you will get to him safely."

<small>Report on the Wasoga and Waganda.</small>

"I have now understood all your words. Go now, and leave me alone, that I may refer it to my God. This afternoon I will give you my answer."

The alluring part of Sakwa's offer was that by accepting it I should be sure of being strongly backed from Kawirondo. If we beat the Mangati, our credit towards the west would also be considerably increased; and this, again, might possibly be decisive in the matter of our march to Usoga. On the other hand, it was not in accordance with my principles to attack, under the German flag, a tribe that had not first committed acts of hostility towards us. Accordingly, I resolved that while I would give support to the Sultan in putting down the plundering tribe in the south, I would not allow the German flag, or any one of us white men, to have a part in the affair.

<small>Partial acceptance of alliance.</small>

I granted him, for the next morning, thirty-five men, under the leadership of Hussein, with the stipulation that, on his side, he should also put under Hussein's command all his Askaris, his Massais, and his Bantu, and should give them an opportunity of pushing forward to the Mangati that very night, that they might attack their foes, and beat them next morning before sunrise.

Sakwa acquiesced in everything; but, as the negroes do, he only half fulfilled his promises. Instead of Hussein's being conducted to meet the enemy between four and five o'clock, as I had demanded, it was between seven and eight before they reached Ngoro, which was not four, but between six and eight miles distant.

<small>Sakwa's politeness.</small>

The Mangati had taken the alarm, had driven their herds to the rear, and were awaiting my people in order of battle. A very obstinate and even murderous combat ensued, in which Hussein committed a fault, by not following the tactics we had always put in practice, of advancing with a "Hurrah!" after a few volleys, but still cautiously, and keeping distance, and thus routing the foe. *The best tactics in fighting.*

The whole morning we heard the lively rattle of the percussion guns, and the sharper ring of the long barrels; and we also saw the flames rising from some villages in the south.

Towards three o'clock in the afternoon the soldiers of Sakwa were the first to come marching back in great bodies, each some hundreds strong, singing a harsh war-song, with a rhythmic measure, something like the following, "Hu, hu, hu, hu, hu! hu, hu, hu, hu, hu!" and then my people came marching home, intoning their own war-song. The Mangati had indeed been thoroughly beaten, had lost two villages and fifty-six men; but Hussein had not succeeded in getting possession of herds of cattle, and the expedition's store of cartridges, already greatly lessened before this combat, had by it been reduced to the utmost. I had now only forty to fifty cartridges per man for the repeating rifles, and, into the bargain, we had several men wounded. On the other hand, all Kawirondo was certainly full of admiration of our little troop, and this was speedily communicated towards the west as far as Uganda. That same evening, Sakwa brought oxen to be slaughtered for my people, and on the following afternoon hoisted the great black, white, and red flag, on a hill in his capital, on a flagstaff fifty feet high. His wives performed dances in honour of us. *Triumphal return of the army.*

But, after all, what did this signify, compared to the fact that we had so few cartridges left, and with this reduced strength were now to march away into the dangerous territory of the Nile?

The treaty which I concluded with Sakwa on February 1st was in the following words:—

"Sultan Sakwa, of Kawirondo, begs Dr. Carl Peters for his flag. He acknowledges Dr. Peters unreservedly as his lord.

"Dr. Carl Peters promises to protect Sultan Sakwa according to his power, and to help him in the conquest of the whole of Kawirondo, so far as is consonant with Dr. Peters's other plans.

The treaty with Sultan Sakwa.

"Sultan Sakwa solemnly hoists the German flag to-day in his capital. Both parties complete this treaty by the signatures of witnesses.

"Dr. Carl Peters.
"Mark of the Sultan of Witu.

Witnesses
{
"Son of the Sultan Lutonia, Wasua.
"Brother of the Sultan, Kueju.
"Son of the Sultan, Sanialute.
"Hussein Fara, leader of the Somali; and
"Musa, headman of the porters."
}

On the basis of this treaty, I left with the Sultan the following letter for the English:—

"Sultan Sakwa has asked me for my flag, and I have granted his request, that I may have a support behind me for my further advance to Emin Pasha. Sultan Sakwa has accorded to me that he will look on his place as my property, for the purposes of my expedition, and for any other plans I may have in this part of Africa. I accordingly declare the land of Kawirondo to be my possession, until I may dispose of it otherwise with the concurrence of Sultan Sakwa. Accordingly I shall deal with any infringement of the rights of Sultan Sakwa as with an infringement of my own rights.

Letter explaining the treaty.

(*Signed*) "Dr. Carl Peters."

Next morning, in spite of the importunate entreaties of Sakwa that I would stay longer, I marched away, with beat of drum, through a well-cultivated country, towards the south, to set up my camp on that day in the English station of Kwa Sundu. Here I should receive definite information concerning the state of things in the west, and could make up my mind accordingly, whether I might risk the march through Uganda, or whether I had the choice of passing round that country and pushing forward direct upon Unjoro.

Advance to Kwa Sundu.

CHAPTER IX.

ADVANCE UPON UNJORO AND DEVIATION TO UGANDA, TO ASSIST THE CHRISTIAN PARTY.

"For, with the gods, there shall no man presume
Himself to measure."
GOETHE.

WE were very soon comfortably established in the English station. The young sultan received us with a present of honour of three oxen for slaughtering, though he certainly added to the gift the cool request: We had beaten the Mangati in the vicinity of Kwa Sakwa, and therefore he begged that to-morrow we would beat the Mangati in the vicinity of Kwa Sundu. There came, besides, the chiefs of the Massais in Kawirondo, with presents of honour, and the request to be allowed to enter into the position of a treaty, and into friendly relations with me. They declared they were all of them ready to acknowledge me as their lord and chief. I put them all off till my return from the Equatorial

Visit from the Sultan and chiefs.

Province. So soon, I said, as I had reached my German brother there, I would come back with an increased force, and then we would hold introductory councils on their relation to my tribe.

From the written communications laid before me by Ali Somal I first obtained the following authentic intelligence out of a despatch from Mr. Mackay, dated Usumbiro, August 25th, 1889, to Emin Pasha, which was evidently lying here, in the English station, to be forwarded, and I herewith give an extract of the substance of its contents:— *Mr. Mackay's despatch.*

"Muanga, the son and successor of Mtesas, King of Uganda, developed more and more, in the year 1887, into a malignant tyrant, until in September or October 1888, after he had attempted to murder his guards, most of whom were either Christians or Mahometans, these guards suddenly mutinied, and drove him from the throne. The dethroned king escaped in a canoe to the south side of Lake Victoria. *Muanga, son of Mtesas.*

"A brother of Muanga's, named Kiwewa, was invested with his power, and, in the first instance, proclaimed freedom for all beliefs; but soon afterwards he turned against the Christians, and, after a slaughter among them, drove them all away. They took refuge in Buragalla (Usagara), which is also called Ancore, whose king, Antari, received them as colonists. (See on this subject Stanley's 'In Darkest Africa,' vol. ii., ch. 32, pp. 333-37). Only a few escaped in canoes to the south side of the lake, and were received, some by the Romish priests in Ukumbi, and some by the Englishmen in Usumbiro. Mr. Gordon and Mr. Walker, as well as the Romish missionaries in Uganda, were kept prisoners for a week, and both the mission stations were plundered and destroyed, and thereupon all missionaries were allowed to leave Uganda in the Christian boat. Naturally, the Arabs were the chief instigators and the principal agents in the overthrowing of the Christian missions; but they themselves did not long enjoy the favour of Kiwewa. He found them too zealous in their desire to circum- *The rule of Kiwewa.*

cise him, and one day he caused all their chief men, declared Mahometans, to be arrested in Burgah, and with his own hand killed three of their leaders. In some way or another the others, however, got back their freedom immediately afterwards, and now Kiwewa had to fly for his life.

"Then another brother, named Karema (or Kalema), was chosen king, and his troops succeeded in annihilating the army assembled by Kiwewa. The latter fell into the hands of Karema, and was chained up, and killed. Muanga at first took refuge with the Arabs of Nuya, but afterwards left them, disgusted at the bad treatment he had received, and betook himself to the French in Ukumbi, where he resided until April 1888. Meanwhile Mr. Stokes, formerly a member of the English expedition, now a trader, arrived from the coast with a boat of his own. Muanga pressed him to take him back to Uganda, and to make an attempt to regain his lost throne. The boat was landed in the neighbourhood of the mouth of the Kagera, where Muanga raised the standard of rebellion, and soon gained a great following, especially among the brotherhood of the banished Christians in Busagala or Ankora. Karema sent a strong army to meet Muanga, and destroyed his warlike force.

Karema chosen king.

Rebellion raised by Muanga.

"Muanga himself escaped to the Sesse Islands, where he was acknowledged by the islanders. He once more found himself at the head of a not inconsiderable force, with all the canoes of the land. With these he advanced to Murchison Bay, and disembarked on a little island opposite Munyonyo, formerly the residence of a king. It was called Bulingogwe.

Muanga at the Sesse Islands.

"Karema sent out an army to prevent Muanga from landing, under the leadership of an Arab named Hamis Belul; but this force soon retired. Muanga's troops landed, and burnt Munyonyo. A battle also took place in Kyagore, in which Karema's army was beaten."

So far the information extends in Mr. Mackay's writing. He goes on to say that Mr. Stokes soon afterwards returned to

Ukumbi, and now, namely, in August 1889, had the intention to return with a new supply of weapons and ammunition to Muanga's assistance. Muanga had sent an invitation to the French and the English to come and establish themselves in the Sesse Islands. A few Frenchmen had already started, and Mr. Gordon and Mr. Walker were going off in canoes to Sesse next day.

Mr. Stokes's enterprise.

Mr. Mackay adds his own reflections: "Of course the missionaries cannot assist Muanga in the fight, but their presence is able to give prestige to his name, while it may also give courage to their respective communities, who at this time contribute almost the sole force of Muanga. Protestants and Catholics together, they number about fifteen hundred men, but according to their own estimate, two thousand. They have, I believe, one thousand guns in all, but very little powder. Besides these, Muanga has several thousands of heathen adherents, armed with spear and shield, while Karema has more than two thousand guns, and all the Arabs and their slaves at his back. But Karema is, I believe" (which was a mistake of Mackay's), "not inclined to Islam, and only uses that party as his chief means of defence. A short time ago he murdered all the princes and princesses on whom he could lay his hands, for fear one or other of them should come forward as a rival for the throne.

Opinion of Mr. Mackay.

"This has not increased his popularity, and I hear that several of his leading adherents are rebellious; but they are afraid to attach themselves to Muanga, as he is bitter against all who have made profession of Mahometanism. My counsel to Muanga is, for the present, to remain quietly in possession of the Sesse Islands, and with the help of the numerous canoes he possesses (while Karema has none) to blockade the coast of Uganda, (Buganda in the Kiganda language), and to hinder the Arabs from obtaining reinforcements. In this way he will gradually gain many adherents. In fact, most of his former chiefs, offended by Karema, have already attached themselves to him, though certainly with only a few followers.

Position of Muanga.

"When Mr. Stokes left Uganda the news had reached there of the arrival of a few white men in the vicinity of Wachores land. This, we believed, must be the advanced guard of the British East African Expedition, on its way to Wadelai with provisions and ammunition for you (Emin), for whose assistance Muanga has sent, to put himself in alliance with them; but we have no further news of them." (This information evidently had reference to the English expedition in Kawirondo, in whose own camp we were tarrying just then.)

<small>Expected British East African Expedition.</small>

Mr. Mackay now continues with a somewhat cool proposal to Emin Pasha, to whom it appeared no less quaint when I afterwards communicated it to him at Mpuapua, than it did to me when I first read it.

"Now is the time to strike a strong blow for the right to win Uganda. For if they (Jackson and his companions) assist Muanga in pulling down Karema and his Arabs, and bring Muanga himself back to the throne, the land will afterwards be virtually in their hands, and they will possess the key to all the western environs of Lake Victoria. But, I fear, the British East Africa Company has for soldiers Zanzibar porters, on whom little reliance can be placed."

<small>Chances of an attempt on Uganda.</small>

Now comes the point.

"You (Emin Pasha) have the army, and only by the assistance of one or two regiments of your troops, under suitable leaders, does it become possible to overthrow Karema's fanatical army, and to restore the ex-king Muanga to power, not, as before, as an independent sovereign, but as an agent of the British East Africa Company." (Certainly exceedingly attractive for Emin Pasha. Fancy a German missionary making such a proposal to an Englishman of birth, to win a kingdom for a German Colonial Company!) "His deposition and banishment appear to have taught him a lesson, and I at least have some hope that if he once again gets into power, he will rule more wisely than he has done. Nevertheless, according to my

<small>Proposal to Emin Pasha.</small>

conviction, it is especially desirable that it should not be left to him to rely upon his own sources of help, but that he should become dependent upon outsiders for his kingdom; that is to say, upon yourself and the British East Africa Company. In this way his future good behaviour will be secured.

"I have asked Messrs. Walker and Gordon to write to you on your arrival in Sesse, and accurately to explain the situation of affairs as they found it. I HAVE BEEN REQUESTED, THROUGH THE CONSUL-GENERAL IN ZANZIBAR, AS WELL AS THROUGH THE AGENTS OF THE COMPANY (MESSRS. SMITH, MACKENZIE AND CO., AND BY MR. MACKINNON HIMSELF), TO PROMOTE THE INTERESTS OF THE COMPANY SO FAR AS I CAN." (Surely this means to work as its political agent!) "I do not see how I can do this better, from my standpoint, than by making you and the gentlemen at the head of the expedition acquainted with the exact position of things at this time in Uganda, in the belief that there is at present a rare opportunity, which might never recur in our lifetime, not only to secure the market in Uganda, but also to acquire the control over the whole country. The fact that my 'brethren,' as well as the French missionaries, are prepared to attach themselves to Muanga will, I am sure, be to you an efficient guarantee that this side must be preferred. Karema is fanatical, and so long as he is in power he will ever be the enemy of all those who, like ourselves and the British East Africa Company, have at heart the welfare of the maritime territory."

Decided political missionary interference.

This letter will, in the first place, form a not uninteresting commentary on Stanley's assertion ("In Darkest Africa," vol. ii., p. 350): "The Christian converts gave them (the missionaries) an excellent character, and repeated much of the good advice Mr. Mackay had bestowed on them; which were undoubted proofs that though the yoke of Muanga was exceedingly heavy to them, the missionaries had in this abstained from meddling in the politics of the country."

Stanley's opinion of the missionaries.

I have given it here in its entirety, because it really gives a very clear picture of the position of affairs in Uganda, and especially of the English designs upon these lands.

From other documents, of which I got a view in Kwa Sundu, I further learned that, with the assistance of Stokes, Muanga had, in fact, beaten Karema's followers on October 4th, 1889, and regained possession of the throne, and that he had de-*Victory of Muanga.* spatched two embassies to the English expedition in Kawirondo, with the request to Mr. Jackson to bring him assistance, professing himself ready, if this were done, not only to bestow on the British East Africa Company the monopoly of trade in Uganda and all his lands, but also to place himself under a British protectorate.

This correspondence was signed by Muanga himself, by the English missionaries, and also by Père Lourdel. From the series of letters I was able to ascertain that Mr. Jackson had first delayed this affair, and then in writing declined it altogether. This answer I did not see until later in Uganda, and *Mr. Jackson's proceedings.* there I found that, with his five hundred Remingtons, he had not considered himself strong enough to march upon Uganda, where, according to all that he knew, the parties were pretty equally balanced, but preferred to go out hunting to the north, where he was at that time. From the last letter signed by Père Lourdel, dated on December 1st, from the Island of Bulingogwe, it appears that at the end of November the army of Muanga must again have been beaten (which had really happened on November 22nd), that the Christians had once more taken refuge on the islands of Lake Victoria, and from thence had despatched a more urgent prayer than ever to the English expedition for assistance. The document bearing upon this I herewith reproduce:—

"BULINGUGE, 1, XII., 89.

"BIEN CHER MONSIEUR,—Nous avons appris avec peine que vous ne pourriez pas venir, au moins pour le moment, porter secours à Muanga et aux chrétiens du Buganda comme nous l'espérions.

"Le roi Muanga m'avait chargé de vous écrire en son nom

la lettre Kiswahili que je vous ai envoyée, lorsqu'il n'avait pas encore appris la nouvelle de la défaite de son armée. Ayant été forcé de se réfugier dans l'île de Bulinguge il demande plus que jamais votre secours avec instance. En récompense outre le monopole du commerce dans le Buganda, il vous offre comme cadeau cent brasilas d'ivoire, (=3,500 Pfd.), qu'il vous donnera, lorsqu'il sera remis sur le trône. Il se charge aussi de la nourriture de vos hommes et accepte votre drapeau. Pour nous missionaires catholiques, nous serons très-heureux et très-reconnaissants de profiter de la protection, que vous pourrez, je l'espère, accorder aux missionaires et chrétiens de ce pays, si vous parvenez à chasser les musulmans. Veuillez avoir la bonté de présenter mes salutations empressées à vos intrépides compagnons de route. Je prie Dieu de continuer à bénir et favoriser votre entreprise.

"Daignez agréer, bien cher Monsieur, l'expression de mes sentiments de profond respect et de ma parfaite considération, avec lesquels j'ai l'honneur d'être, votre très humble serviteur,

"SIMEON LOURDEL,
"*Premier Catholique dans le Buganda.*"

(TRANSLATION.)

"VERY DEAR SIR,—We have heard with pain that you could not come, at least not at present, to bring assistance to Muanga and to the Christians of Buganda, as we hoped you would.

"King Muanga had charged me to write to you, in his name, the Kiswahili letter I have sent to you, WHEN HE HAD NOT YET RECEIVED THE NEWS OF THE DEFEAT OF HIS ARMY. Having been forced to take refuge in the island of Bulinguge, he more than ever urgently asks your assistance. In return, besides the monopoly of commerce in Buganda, he offers you, as a present, a hundred pasilas of ivory (equal to 3,500 lbs.), which he will give you when he is restored to the throne. He also takes upon himself the provisioning of your men, and accepts your flag. For our part, we Catholic missionaries shall be very glad and very grateful to take advantage of the protection which you will be able, I hope, to grant to the missionaries and Christians of this country, if you succeed in driving out the Mussulmans. Have the kindness to present my special greetings to the intrepid companions of your journey. I pray God to continue to bless and favour your enterprise.

"Deign to accept, very dear Sir, the expression of my sentiments of profound respect and perfect consideration, with which I have the honour to be, your very humble servant,

"SIMÉON LOURDEL,
"*First Catholic in Buganda.*"

So far, including the knowledge that the English, upon such information, were gone, not into this disagreeable Uganda, but elephant hunting to the north, did my own information in Kawirondo extend.

I have here related these facts, accepting the danger of incurring suspicion of having violated the secrecy of letters in Kawirondo; but I hope such a reproach will be considered unjustified. In the first place, it is not a question of opening letters, on my part, but of documents which were laid before me by the acting official chief of the English station, with the **Reasons for quoting the documents.** observation that he knew that "my brethren," his masters, would be glad to communicate all these facts, and further information also, to me, if they were on the spot, and with the express permission to take copies of them. Secondly, my position must be taken into account— the responsibility I bore with regard to the expedition and my people, which made it my simple duty to gain all the knowledge I could in any way acquire with regard to the lands that lay before us.

After I had thus, in general, found where I was, I had the Wasoga, who had carried the last Uganda post into the English camp, brought before me, to question them at large.

"You are Wasoga. Who has sent you hither?"

"We are compelled by the Waganda to show them the way to the English camp in Kawirondo."

"What news have you from Uganda? Who is the master there?"

"In Uganda there is war. A little while ago Muanga had beaten the Arabs; but at last Karema was king again, and Muanga and his people had fled to the islands."

Conversation with the Wasoga men.

"What kind of country is Usoga? Do you belong to Uganda, or have you chiefs of your own?"

"We have chiefs of our own, but they are all subject to the Kabaka of Uganda."

"Are strangers allowed to travel through Usoga without permission from the Kabaka of Uganda?"

"If a stranger comes to Usoga our sultans have to report to the Mfalme * of Uganda."

"Is there food in Usoga?"

"Food, as the sand by the sea," and they went through the movement of heaping up sand in both hands.

"What kind of food?"

"Bananas, grain, and flesh of all kinds."

"Do the Wasoga love the whites, or do they make war upon them?"

"The Wasoga love the whites, but they must do what the Waganda tell them."

"Are there Waganda in Usoga?"

"Yes; they come every year to get tribute from thence, and now many of them are there who have fled from the war in Uganda."

"Do the Wasoga belong to Muanga's party, or do they hold with Karema?"

"Muanga is the Mfalme of Uganda, and Karema is only a wicked man, who makes war upon him."

"Now I want to know, what is the Kisogo for a quantity of words from the Kiswahili language."

---

* Kabaka or Mfalme is the title of the King of Uganda. I conjecture that Kabaka is a Bantu word, while Mfalme is perhaps of Semitic origin. The title Kabaka is evidently the same as the Kaba in the title of King Kaba Rega of Unjoro.

I noted down a number of words, which show that the language of the Wasoga is mainly of pure Bantu origin :—

	English.	Kiswahili.	Kisogo.
Kiswahili and Kisogo languages.	the way	ndjia	njola
	goes	anakwenda	elegenda
	where?	wapi?	ekuba?
	to the Turks	qua Turki	kubo Turki
	want corn	nataka veri veri	dsagga limere.
	water	madji	madsi
	fowl	kuku	koko
	eggs	majai	magi
	milk	masnia	amata
	forward	twende	tugende
	I want	nataka	ndgale
	a guide	kiongosi kwa	munlu (man Twhahili) wakuntare
	to Unjoro	Unjoro	Unjoro
	slowly	pole pole	genan pole
	give	nipe	npa.

I then sent for the Sultan and his suite, and asked him,—

"Do you know a country called Unjoro?"

He pointed in a north-westerly direction.

"Are the Wangoro your friends or your enemies?"

"The Wangoro are our friends; the Waganda our enemies."

"If you want to march to Unjoro, must you pass through Usogo or Uganda?"

"No; if we want to go to Unjoro we have to go by way of Kwa Telessa. From thence we go to Akore or Akola, and thence direct to Unjoro. It takes four days to reach Akore, and another four days to get from there to the Nile, at Unjoro, and one day to cross the Nile; so that we have a nine days' march to Unjoro from this place."

"Have you much intercourse with the Wangoro?"

"Yes; the Wangoro come to Kwa Telessa, and bring us powder and ammunition. We take cattle and corn to them, and receive powder in exchange."

"Is Kwa Telessa a large place?"

"Kwa Telessa is a large town, and there you hear news rom all the countries of the west."

"Can you give me guides to Telessa?"

"Certainly; I am your friend, and you may command here. If you want guides to Telessa I will give you them."

"How many days' march is it from here to Kwa Telessa?"

"We sleep the first day in Kwa Tindi, the second in Kwa Surga, and the third day we reach Kwa Telessa." *Information about Kwa Telessa.*

"What sort of people live in these countries?"

"The Walukuma live there."

"Are you friendly with them, or do you live at war with them?"

"The Walukuma are our friends; but close to them live the Walunda. They are very bad people, and with them we are at war."

"Then when I march to Kwa Telessa, and from there to Unjoro, I have no need to go by way either of Usoga or Uganda?"

"No. You leave those countries to your left, and you go straight to Unjoro."

"Then get me some guides to Kwa Telessa. To-morrow I shall remain here, and the next day I shall march from here to Unjoro. When I come back I will beat your Mangati* for you."

The next day the negotiations were continued, and the final result of them all was that I engaged three guides (Gasia, Amoquaja, and Waschitoba) to lead us to Kwa Telessa.

February 3rd was one of the most unsatisfactory days of the whole expedition. I had certainly the pleasure of seeing Herr von Tiedemann completely restored to health; but an incident occurred on this day which threatened to upset all my plans for the future, and forced upon me, to my dismay, the conviction that I was by no means so absolutely sure of my own followers as I had supposed already. In the morning Ali Somal came to me, with Hussein, endeavouring to persuade me not to undertake the march towards the west. "The Doctor is

* I afterwards came to be of opinion that a confusion between Wangoro and Wachoro was involved in this information of the Sultan's.

very fiery, is the universal opinion," they told me; "he is not afraid, but he will lead us all to destruction." "Pray wait here," added Ali Somal, "till Mr. Jackson and his three gentlemen come back with our people. Then you can all take counsel together, and I know that Mr. Jackson will be very glad to carry out a plan in concert with you."

"But Mr. Jackson has already been lying here for more than four months, and you told me yesterday that so soon as he returned from the north he would march back to the coast. How can you say that he will be glad to carry out a plan in concert with me?"

Mr. Jackson's proceedings.

"Mr. Jackson would have been only too glad to go to Uganda himself, but he was afraid to do so because of the uncertainty in the whole state of affairs. If he sees that you are determined to advance, he will probably attach himself to you."

"Well, then it would, after all, be better for me to go on first and see if the roads are safe. Then I will write to Mr. Jackson, and I shall be glad if he will follow me."

"I cannot decide as to that," said Ali Somal; "but I should like to save the lives of my brethren, the Somali, who all say you are too fiery, and would rather wait here than go on with you at once."

"Is that true?" I asked of Hussein.

"Yes, sir. I will gladly go with you, to die with you; but the others think you ought rather to wait here. They are tired of carrying on war every day."

"Well, then, go and tell your people that I have heard your words. I thought I had men and soldiers with me, but I see now that such does not seem to be the case. Tell the Somalis, that to each one among them who may prefer to stay here with the English I will give permission to do so, and that I do not mean, either, to deduct anything from the pay which they have earned until now. But tell them also that I shall know, by the decision which each man comes to, whether we Germans have been deceived in the Somalis or not. And ask them what report of your brethren I am accordingly to give some day in Aden."

"Very good, sir."

Hussein went away, and returned in an hour with the answer that the Somalis thought that, from my having asked them whether they wished to stay behind, they might assume that I had no further need of them. Accordingly, they asked permission that all of them might remain here.

"Hussein, do you want to stay here, too?"

HUSSEIN, LEADER OF THE SOMALIS.

"No, sir. I should like to go with you, but I should like the other Somalis to come too."

"Well, then, call your people together for a conference with me."

Thereupon the Somalis appeared before my tent, and I spoke to them to the following effect:—

"You know that I had you all engaged in Aden, to go with me in search of a great German who rules in the land of the Turki. We marched together up the Tana, where the English Expedition was forced to turn back, and we reached Baringo

Meanwhile the bearers had got wind of what was going on among the Somalis; and thereupon they too held a meeting, and sent a deputation to the Somalis with the message, "If you do not wish to go any farther with Kupanda Sharo we shall not go either. Let us know what you have decided to do."

To this the Somalis replied, "We are Somalis, and you bearers are different people. We obey the commands of our chief, and if you are not willing to do so we shall fight against you at his command, and shoot down every man who runs away." This answer was confirmed to me afterwards by Musa, the headman of the bearers from Dar-es-Salam, who had headed the deputation.

The Somalis reply.

The plan which I had laid before the Somalis was the result of information of different kinds which I had received in Kwa Sundu, and was based upon the repeated assurances of Ali Somal, that Emin Pasha had remained alone in his province. In this case it was of course impossible to neglect any chance or refuse any effort to reach him, and I was firmly resolved once more to stake all for this purpose. Any other decision would have seemed to me as futile as if I had received the commission to explore the interior of Vesuvius, and after collecting everything necessary for the purpose, had proceeded to the edge of the crater, and then faced about, and returned home with my report, "It cannot be done!"

Dr. Peter's decision.

After the communication from Uganda I was obliged to desist from passing through that country, because by so doing I should have needlessly increased the risk twofold; and if I were successful in crossing Uganda alive, the dangers in Unjoro would not be diminished in the least.

On the other hand, I was able to hope that, if I had the good fortune of falling in with Emin Pasha I might, together with him, take into consideration what was possible to be done for the Christians in Uganda. It was evident that we should have to make the question of Uganda our first subject of deliberation, because it comprised within itself the quickest possibility of procuring ammunition for the Pasha. The plan of my farther advance, which I decided to put into execution on the following morning, was framed to suit these considerations. There was no object now in our remaining any longer in Kawirondo. Our doing so would simply waste the stores of the expedition for no purpose, and weaken the spirit of my people. And, in the last place, I should have rendered myself completely independent of the English.

Reasons for the decision.

Nevertheless, since it was impossible to foresee the result of the advance, Herr von Tiedemann and I resolved to leave behind our letters and reports at the English station, to be forwarded to the coast for Europe; a fatal resolution, which had for its result the loss of the whole packet. Exactly the same fate befell me with respect to all the letters sent to me at Zanzibar by the English mail. "Horse and horseman saw we never more!" As it seemed to me desirable, if it was in any way possible, to secure the stores of ammunition collected by the English for Emin Pasha, I left a letter for Mr. Jackson at his station, in which I informed him of my march in the direction of Uganda, and offered him my friendly cooperation. I promised to keep him constantly *au courant* of the characteristics of the route, and hoped that he would then decide, in the interests of civilisation and humanity, to follow me with his expedition into the Equatorial Province, in order to work in union with me for the relief of Emin Pasha.

At sunrise on February 4th I marched out of the English station at Kwa Sundu with beat of drum. I had previously tried to make it clear to the Sultan and his relations, that they would do better not to bring into play the intrigues and faithlessness of the black races, of which all travellers complain. As I was preparing to depart the guides declared, all at once, that they did not wish to go with me to-day; and when I urged them to fulfil the engagement into which they had entered with me, I was again treated to the dogged "Ä-ä-ä-ä!" which I have already described.

Faithless guides.

A few well-directed blows distributed among the whole population and the English intimated delicately to the Sultan and his family that this behaviour was not to be tolerated by us. But it was not until I had threatened to burn the place over

their heads that they resolved to undertake the guiding of our party, for which I had already paid them on the previous day.

On this morning I was in an especially irritable frame of mind, because I had been told that one of my Somalis, named Ismael Ali, had deserted. This could only have been possible if either the English garrison or the native population had connived at it. But we had something better to do than to stay here looking after a deserter, and so at about six o'clock we started off in the direction of the north-west. At seven o'clock we crossed, with some trouble, the stony river Nsoia, which flows into the Victoria Nyanza below Kwa Sundu, after draining the Angata na Nyuki.

On the march again.

The Wakawirondo, under the protection of our dreaded expedition, pressed forward with their herds to the river, to seek the pasture-ground on the opposite bank, which they had formerly avoided out of fear of the western tribes.

The Nsoia is very swift in this place, and the crossing was attended with great difficulty. Again and again some of my cattle were carried down stream, and had to be recaptured with much trouble. By nine o'clock all were on the right bank, and now our way lay onward into the distant unknown West.

The scenery through which we marched presented, indeed, a dreary spectacle. Everywhere ruined plantations and burned or half-burned villages. The Mangati had been "at work" here, and if up to this morning I had been rather angry with myself for having allowed myself to be drawn in to take part in the fight against them, I now rejoiced at having for once given these robbers and bandits a well-merited lesson.

So we went on for six hours through long stretches of hill districts. The mountains which shut in Kawirondo in the east and Samia in the north, lay extended before us in a south-westerly direction.

Through the hills.

At about three o'clock in the afternoon we reached their north-eastern spurs, and here I set up the camp by the little river Manieni, which flows into the Victoria Nyanza about three miles to the west of Nsoia.

The landscape here puts on a somewhat fresher character.

We found ourselves again in inhabited districts and among kraals, which were surrounded by fields of grain.

This was the country of Kwa Tindi, that is to say, of the Sultan Tindi, who rules over the western part of Kawirondo. No white man had ever been here before us, but the natives had heard of us, and the women, including the naked daughters of Kawirondo and the Massai women, who are clothed up to the neck, soon crowded round my expedition, offering for sale fire-wood and provisions of all kinds. Moreover, the Sultan Tindi had no sooner heard of our arrival, than he sent messengers to me from his capital, which lay about a mile away to the westward, with the reproachful question, "Why do you set up your camp so far from my capital? Why do you not come to me, who would so gladly be your friend?"

I answered the messenger,—

"Tell your sultan that my people are too tired to be able to march as far as Kwa Tindi to-night. For all that, the sultan may be assured that I have come into his country with intentions wholly pacific. To-morrow I intend to pass through his land toward the west. Ask your lord whether I can do so in peace, or whether he prefers to measure his strength with us in war." *Message to the Sultan.*

"Tindi desires your friendship, but we hasten to carry your words to him."

In an hour and a half, towards evening, they came back.

"The sultan bids us say, Why does the great white man, who has beaten the Massais, our enemies, and the Mangati, who plunder our villages, speak to me of war? I and my land belong to him, and I only wish that he would come to-morrow and set up his tent in my capital. We will give him all he desires, and show him every honour which is his due."

I replied to the messenger,—

"Tell your sultan that I have heard his words of peace, and received them as such. To-morrow I shall march by his capital, because I am going on farther to Unjoro, but when I come back, then I will stay with him, and we will exchange gifts of friendship."

On the evening of this day I was again to have an opportunity of learning from ocular demonstration more about the "settled" condition of this district. I had just lain down in bed, when all at once a diabolical row broke out in the kraal that lies ten minutes' walk to the east of our camp, and by which we had marched in the afternoon. Horns, drums, pipes, shrieking, and wild howling clashed together in a chaos of sound. From time to time there came a pause; but then the tumult broke out with renewed violence. I called my sentry into the tent, and asked what was the matter. He brought the guides from Kawirondo to me, and from these I learned that robber bands from Elgumi had just attacked the kraal, and that its defenders were now fighting.

<small>Attack on the kraal.</small>

"That is what Tindi's Massais say," they told me; "they are just gone by to beat back the Waelgumi."

I sent for Hussein, and bade him give out about a hundred cartridges for my people immediately. The danger to our camp was twofold. It was possible that the Wakawirondo, in case they were defeated, would flee to us, and that so we should be involved in the struggle; or, on the other hand, that the Waelgumi, even if this did not occur, might attack us in the mere wantonness of their victory. It is significant of the indifference with which we were all of us accustomed by this time to regard such possibilities, that we all stayed quietly in bed. Not until the noise broke out on the other side of the kraal and in the immediate vicinity of our camp did I get up, put my guns in order, light my pipe, and sit down in my armchair in front of my tent. I sent to beg Lieutenant von Tiedemann to join me, and we had, from ten o'clock to one in the morning, the curious experience of being able to observe, at least as far as the sound is concerned, a battle between natives close at hand.

The moon shone bright above the scene, the crickets chirped, frogs croaked in the brook below, and man alone demonstrated his likeness to his Maker by the tumult and cries of pain which continually clashed upon our ears, amid the sweet peacefulness of nature.

<small>The combative natives.</small>

Towards one o'clock the Massais, who were in the pay of

Tindi, advanced to their attack, and gradually the din of battle died away in the north, where, however, the natives were still awake, and received their retreating friends with cries and yells.

The whole affair passed away like a vision, and once more the earth lay at our feet in softest repose and deepest peace under the floods of moonlight. My people had paid so little attention to the whole transaction, that they peacefully snored all round us during all the noise of the warfare.

At dawn on the following day I gave orders for the trumpet to call the march out, and we started at once in the direction of the north-west. A little after six o'clock we crossed the Sio, and towards seven we reached Kwa Tindi. The town is picturesquely situated on a height, between basalt rocks. It is surrounded by a strong wall of red stone and a deep dike; the gates boldly and picturesquely arched, and connected by dams with the outer world. *Particulars concerning the country.* As soon as we approached any village the drummer had orders always to beat a tattoo, and in this manner we passed by Kwa Tindi. The population streamed out of the gate in crowds to stare at us, and I thought I saw among the throng the Sultan himself, with his retinue, recognisable by his ornaments. However, I did not choose to make any demonstration of greeting. At a short distance I passed by the town, and soon the whole scene lay behind us like a Fata Morgana. We now crossed two more streams, tributaries of the Sio, one of which is named Nogombe. When we had passed the latter the guides suddenly turned away from the north-western to a westerly direction. When I protested against their doing so they answered,—

"To the north of us live the Walundu, with whom we are at war. We cannot go thither. But be of good courage, we will lead you to Kwa Telessa to-morrow by this road."

I asked, "What land lies yonder to the left of us?"

They said, "That is the land of Samia, and behind it lies Usoga. We will not bring you there, but to Kwa Telessa, from where you can go on to Unjoro."

"What is the name of those mountains yonder to the left, behind which Samia lies?"

"That is the Fukulu."

"And the mountains here to the right of us, that reach across from Elgon?"

"That is the Eshekulu."

(*Kulu* is certainly the same root as the Kiswahili *kili*, meaning mountain.)

Between these two chains of hills, which we had seen already from Kwa Sundu, and which from that place looked like one uninterrupted uniform mountain range to the west of Kawirondo, we now passed on. There is a gap of from fourteen to eighteen miles wide between the two, forming a well-cultivated plateau, still at an elevation of nearly four thousand feet. As the first white man who ever marched through this gap and explored the formation of these mountains, I named the mass of mountains in the south, after our countryman whom we were endeavouring to reach, the "Emin Pasha Mountains;" while I christened the chain to the north, after his friend and companion, the "Junker Range." The two ranges have nothing in common in their formation. The Emin Pasha Mountains extend in an east and west direction, turning only their counterslope towards Kawirondo, and belong altogether to the volcanic girdle of the Victoria Nyanza Lake; while the Junker Range is nothing more than the south-westerly spur of the Elgon. Of course they both belong to the magnificent volcanic system to which the whole plateau, over which we marched, owes its origin. When, on the morning of February 5th, I fixed upon these designations, I felt that we were now indeed entering the regions in which the activity of these two men was displayed.

Kawirondo now lay behind us, and the landscape gradually assumed a new character. The doom-palm appeared again, and the character of the inhabitants themselves gradually appeared under a new aspect. We marched on over valley and mountain, through stream and swamp, till two o'clock in the afternoon.

We then reached the great place called Kwa Tunga, also surrounded by proud walls and with high gates, over which appeared gables and roofs, which reminded me, in some degree, of India. "Habesch!" cried my Somalis, when they came in sight of the place; and when I asked them what they meant by that, they said, "Just like those of Kwa Tunga are the villages of Abyssinia built."

[sidenote: March to Kwa Tunga.]

Kwa Tunga lies exactly to the north of the Emin Pasha Mountains, and marks almost the centre of the chain. I set up my camp by the southern ramparts of the town, opposite the mountain range which I had before my eyes all the afternoon.

Below the hill on which the place and my camp were situated flows a little brook. The air was as clear and pure as on an August day in Germany. Our relations with the natives were of a friendly character, and in a hopeful and joyous mood we spent the afternoon and evening.

[sidenote: Friendliness of the people.]

Although we had food in plenty, one of my bearers deserted on the following morning, with his wife. Uganda, in fact, still rose before my people as a menacing phantom of terror.

On this day we marched on again, in a west-north-westerly direction, towards Kwa Telessa. The aspect of the country became more and more cultivated and fertile along the green slopes. Village after village appeared, with large herds of oxen and flocks of sheep pasturing. The natives were very demonstrative in their friendliness. Our guides had only to tell them that we were the people who had beaten the Massais and the Mangati, to call forth stormy salvos of applause from them.

[sidenote: March to Kwa Telessa.]

The method of salutation here is by snapping with the thumb and forefinger, which, when it is done by large numbers of men together, has a very pleasing and attractive sound.

Whenever we passed by a kraal, the women and girls came out to bring us water and steaming batatas. The way these Walukuma fortify their villages is peculiar. The clay wall, such as is seen even at Kwa Tunga, now disappears, and in its place great enclosures of cactus are made, which surround the whole place to a height of from eight to twelve yards; a defence equally tasteful and efficacious. At one o'clock we reached Kwa Telessa.

This place is surrounded by a thick growing hedge, and lies

completely hidden in a grove of bananas, within which the huts are picturesquely grouped. More and more we began to realise that we were in Central Africa. Kwa Telessa was the first place to which the description of the Seribas of Central Africa, written by Emin Pasha and Schweinfurth, applied. At the same time we made our first acquaintance with the dress materials of Uganda, namely, the brown bark of the wild fig-tree, woven into a kind of cloth. The dialect itself was different; and already among the sounds which we had heard at Kawirondo were blended the more indistinct accents of Uganda.

Description of the town.

We pitched our tents under a mighty cotton-tree, inside the hedge rampart of the place, while the men were quartered in the neighbouring huts in the shade of the banana trees. Readily and amicably the natives came forward. When, after my arrival, I was taking a short rest, reclining in my arm-chair, my attention was suddenly aroused by a tittering at the door at the back of my tent. I turned round, and saw, standing there, three really charming young girls, in dresses of red stuff, and adorned with beads, who, as soon as I turned my head towards them, greeted me almost roguishly with the usual snap of the fingers. The girls, in their demeanour, reminded me in some degree of European young ladies.

Ladies of the country.

There was food to be had here in abundance, and presently the Sultan Telessa came from a neighbouring plantation to greet me—an old man, looking much like a German of Lower Saxony, with square-cut broad features, which, however, bore the stamp of very considerable strength of will.

Visit of Telessa.

Telessa and his suite crowded in front of my tent, while he examined me with unfeigned astonishment, but with a certain reserve that spoke of tact.

"Peace be with you," was my greeting to him. "I rejoice to be in Telessa's country. I have heard of you already in Kawirondo, and have come here to make your acquaintance and receive from you information about the lands to the west."

"Let the Msurgu (white man) ask what he desires to know."

"I wish to know whether you have any acquaintance with the country to the west. Do you know Unjoro and its king Kaba Rega?"

"The Wanjoro I know, but Kaba Rega I do not know."

"Do you know the great river in the west, the Nile, which the people here call Kyira?"

"I know the Kyira well. The children of my people often travel thither."

Questions concerning the Nile.

"And how many days' journey is it from here to Kyira?"

"Five days. In how many days have you come here from Kwa Sundu?"

"In three days."

"Then you have still five days' journey to reach the Nile."

"And how far is it to the Wanjoro?"

"To the Wanjoro you will come in four days from here."

"Have you any news of white men who live in Wanjoro?"

"Oh, yes, I have news of that kind. Two great white men live there, who possess many soldiers and great houses. One of my people has been for a long time in the service of the white men."

White men in Wanjoro.

"Are the soldiers of these white men Turki, or what kind of men are they?"

"I think they are Turki. But my man will be able to tell you all this better than I."

"Is this man to be found here in Kwa Telessa?"

"He lives not far from here."

"Then send to him, and bid him come, and let him know that I have rich presents for him. This evening, when the sun sinks in the west, come back with him, and then we will hold a further Shauri concerning the business."

The enquiry adjourned.

I was determined to tarry the next day in Telessa, to collect all the information which was to be had in the place. Although I was not inclined to put faith in the signs which seemed to open out before me, yet it was evident that before I went further I must, with especial vigilance, study my position again and again with regard to the circumstances of the case, that I might not lead my column blindly to destruction.

In the evening Telessa returned, and we began by exchanging the usual gifts in sign of friendship. He brought cattle, eggs, and milk, honey, and bananas, while I presented him with bright coloured stuffs, a little powder, and some beads.

<small>Second interview with Telessa.</small>

"Well, have you brought the man with you who was in the service of the white men at Unjoro?"

"I have sent to him, but he will not be able to be here till to-morrow morning."

"So you know for certain that there are white men living in Unjoro?"

"I am as sure of it, as I am of the fact that we are here together."

"And do you also know the place where they live?"

"Yes, I know it well. They have a large house, and many, many people."

"Then I daresay you will be willing to forward a letter from me to these white men, if I pay your messengers, and give you some more presents for yourself?"

<small>Concerning the white men.</small>

"I will very gladly do that, and you can wait here for the answer, to see whether I speak the truth, or am lying."

"And in how many days do you think the messengers can be back here?"

"In three days they can be here again from the white man."

"Well, then, I will tell you what. Give me messengers who can carry my letters in advance, and give me guides who will conduct me, by the same road, after them. Then the messengers, in returning, will meet me on the way, so that I can receive their news from them on my journey. If the white man is so near, I shall soon be back here with you, and then we will exchange more presents with each other. You shall have my flag, and we will make a lasting friendship."

<small>Proposal of Dr. Peters.</small>

"I will gladly take your flag, for I know that you have beaten the Massais. Two years ago the Massais came as far as here, and drove away my cattle."

"Good; then, to-morrow, do what I have commissioned you to do."

A lively snapping of fingers, from the assembled people, showed with what satisfaction the conclusion of our agreement was received by the multitude.

On the following morning, at seven o'clock, there was another great assembly of the people. The mysterious servant of the white men of Unjoro was certainly not yet there; but Telessa had brought two messengers who, he said, knew the way thoroughly, and would carry my letters forward. I drew up two documents, therefore, in presence of the large circle of people, and these were despatched in the course of the same morning. I was not at all inclined to apply to Emin Pasha the news which Telessa brought; nevertheless there might be some trace given in this direction. *Telessa's two messengers.*

When Emin Pasha received news of Dr. Fischer's advance, as he himself relates, he pushed forward his troops to Mruli. Might he not now, after Stanley's departure, have heard rumours of the approach of East African Relief Expeditions, and might he not be working to establish communication with them in that direction by means of advanced posts? *Conjectures about Emin.*

Accordingly, since I could not take for granted that Emin Pasha himself was to be found here in the east, but at most could only conjecture that Casati, or some Egyptian officers, might be there, I wrote the following letter in English and in French:—

"*February 7th*, 1890.

"To any gentleman, or any official of His Excellency Dr. Emin Pasha, who is stationed in Unjoro.

"On my arrival yesterday in Kwa Telessa, on my way to His Excellency Dr. Emin Pasha, I received the news that a

European was in East Unjoro. If such is the case I shall be much obliged for some brief particulars. I shall despatch this letter to-day, and follow on the same road with my small expedition to-morrow. An answer will find me on the route by which this letter has come.

Experimental letter of Dr. Peters.

"This answer will greatly oblige,

"Dr. Carl Peters."

When this letter had been sent off, I dismissed my guides from Kwa Sundu, by whom I sent the news of the incidents of our advance, to the gentlemen of the English expedition, and to whom also I gave a letter for Messrs. Hansing & Co., in Zanzibar.

In the course of the day, my people were again disquieted by news of dangers of war in the west. The Walandu, it was said, were making the passage towards the north-west impossible.

Disquieting rumours.

My people seemed to have changed altogether. They were thoroughly infected by the apprehensions that reigned in the ranks of the English expedition. It was as though the bandages had been suddenly torn away from their eyes, and they now saw on the edge of what a precipice they were walking in my company.

They forgot that the path, up to this time, had not been exactly a safe one. To guard against further desertions, I called them together in the evening, took their guns from them, and once again put the suspicious characters among them in chains.

Tendency to desertion.

In spite of this I was informed, on the following morning, that one of them had run back to Kawirondo.

On the following morning I had, first of all, the usual explanation with Telessa, who had no intention of fulfilling his promise of furnishing me with guides, but who was induced to perform his duty by the usual arguments. Then we began our march westward, along a chain of heights which rose before us, lying in a north to south direction, exactly under the thirty-fourth degree of east longitude as

March towards the west.

far as one degree north of the lake. I ordered the guides to lead us to the northern end of this chain of mountains; but they explained that it could not be done, for fighting was going on there; we should all be killed if we marched that way. It was a fact that, during our march, we had repeatedly heard the noise of fighting to the north of us; and in consideration for the demoralised state of my people, I consented to cross the hills in front of us, a little below the northern end. These hills, which formed the boundary of Usoga proper in the east, I have named "Wissmann Hills." Where they are approached from the east they present a precipitous and steep aspect, but on nearing them it is found that the ascent is a very easy one. In reality it is accomplished almost imperceptibly, through groves of bananas and other plantations.

The "Wissmann Hills."

The next day was an unpleasant one for me, for my people repeatedly pressed me to stay in Kwa Telessa until the answer came to the letters I had sent forward the day before to Emin Pasha, before travelling further into a region of uncertainty. I concluded the matter by decidedly forbidding any interference with my leadership of the expedition; and so we went on, past crowds of people, who also warned us against going further towards the Wissmann Hills. When we had nearly reached the foot of these hills, Herr von Tiedemann suddenly gave the trumpet signal to halt. I was eager to know what could have happened, when all at once I saw a handsomely-dressed young man, with a small suite, likewise of stately appearance, hastening to me along the column. The young man was dressed in a dark Arab kaftan, embroidered with gold, and wore a red turban. When he came up to me he fell on the ground before me and kissed my feet. We were unable to make out in the least who he was, or what he wanted; but he immediately placed himself at the head of my train, drew out a flute, and led the way, playing at the same time, sometimes in pathetic, sometimes in strange, quaint, short melodies, which his followers accompanied with rhythmical, peculiar kind of singing. In this way we went on through very bare country, along winding paths, in a south-easterly direction. There was

A mysterious visitor.

something mysterious in the whole occurrence. The young stranger seemed to me like the prince in a fairy tale, who had come to lead us to his castle, and my fancy was excited to penetrate the secret of his appearance. The idea began suddenly to awake in me that this might have some connection with the object of my expedition, and that some decided explanations lay before me in this direction.

When we reached the crest of the Wissmann Hills the whole character of the landscape changed on a sudden, as in a fairy tale. Emerging from the steppe, which for three hours had surrounded us, we at once passed into a fruitful, cultivated district. *A region of plenty.* The way led through bananas, and yet again through bananas; and this day we noticed, for the first time, the grey parrot. My people feasted to their hearts' content on the rich treasures; and again, as in a fairy tale, we suddenly found everything at our disposal. The people came pouring out of the houses, offering us fat quails in little baskets, and fatted fowls, grain, and fruits. Banana wine was brought out in great bowls for the drinking of healths, and on all sides were heard the lively notes of the flute, or the beating of the fiery drum. Every one bowed low before my mysterious guide, and I could at once perceive that he was a man in authority in these parts.

At the western foot of the Wissmann Hills I pitched my camp and made my toilette, during which my young unknown friend favoured me with another concert on the flute, when suddenly two shots resounded from the south, and two new figures appeared on the scene. These were the Waganda Marco and his companion Talabanga; and now the veil of mystery, which had given a character of excitement to our encampment, was suddenly to be dropped. *Marco and Talabanga.* Marco was a man with small features, indicative of unusual intelligence. Like his companion Talabanga, he was a Roman Catholic Christian, and both of them spoke Suahili. They had no sooner taken their seats on the ground before Herr von Tiedemann and myself, than I demanded their names and station. When they had answered me on this point, I asked,—

"In what country are we here?"

"We are here in the territory of Muanga, the Mfalme of Uganda, in Usoga. He yonder" (pointing to my friend of the morning) "is Mlamba, son of the Sultan Wachore, whose country, Akola, lies to the north of us, and can be reached in one day."

"What are you doing here in Usoga?"

"Muanga, King of Uganda, has sent us to the English in Kwa Sundu, in Kawirondo, to entreat them to give help to the Christians; but the English are afraid, they have not come. Now we have received intelligence that Badutchi are approaching who have beaten the Massais, and that is why we have waited for you here. The letters which you sent yesterday from Kwa Telessa arrived here in the night. I have sent them on to Muanga." *The envoys' account of themselves.*

"Where is Muanga now?"

"Muanga is on Balingogwe, an island on the Lake Victoria Nyanza. With him there are five white men. Write to him that you have arrived in Usoga, his country, as is the custom with the Waganda. Muanga will be glad if you will come to him."

"I shall be glad to visit Muanga, and glad to help my Christian brethren in Uganda. But to be able to do this, I must first of all bring up more assistance, and that is why I am now marching direct to Unjoro to the chief of the Turki, who is a German, and a brother of mine. I will take counsel with him, and he shall give me more men, with whom I will then come to the aid of the Christians in Uganda." *Dr. Peters's proposal to visit Unjoro.*

"You want to go to Unjoro? But do you not know that Kaba Rega is the enemy of the Europeans, and that he will make war against you?"

"Yes, but with the help of Emin Pasha I think I shall be in a position to get the better of Kaba Rega."

"Emin Pasha? Who is Emin Pasha? There are no more white men left in Unjoro. They are all gone away with Stanley."

"You are mistaken," I said; "not all the white men of Unjoro are gone away with Stanley. The chief of them, Emin Pasha, has stayed behind. Do you not know Emin Pasha?"

<small>Question of Emin's whereabouts.</small>

"I speak the truth. All the white men are gone away, and there is not a white man left in Unjoro (Wiote wametoka na hapana wasungu Katika Unjolo). Send letters, and enquire of the white men who are with Muanga. If I am telling you a lie, take my life."

"But how do you know this?"

"How should I not know it? Have I not myself been with Stanley in Busagalla (Ankore), to beg him to give help to the Christians of Uganda?

"In his camp I have seen not only his officers, but also Amdallah and Amdallah's daughter, Emin's white man, and besides these many, many Turkis. Some time ago Amdallah sent to Uganda to buy stuffs from us; but the people were set upon and plundered by the Wanjoro, and he never received the stuffs. That is why he and all his people, whom I saw with Stanley, were clothed in skins. I have seen them all; there is no white man left in Unjoro."

<small>Stanley's camp.</small>

"You exhorted Stanley to bring help to Muanga? Was not Stanley willing to do this, then?"

"No; he said he must go to the coast. The English are afraid, and that is why they do not come to Uganda. But, for your part, do you write to Muanga before you go farther towards Unjoro. Write to your white brothers who are with the king, and they will confirm to you what I have said. We will march together to Wachore's capital, and you can wait there till the answer comes. If there is a white man left in Unjoro, you can go there. If, however, all the white men are gone from Unjoro, then come and help the Christians in Uganda, and then, if you will, we can all go together against the Wanjoro afterwards."

<small>Proposal to write to Muanga.</small>

"When can I have the answer from Muanga?"

"In six or seven days."

"Good; then I will send letters to Bulingogwe. Now go; I

will take into consideration what you have said besides, and give you my answer this afternoon."

As to this communication of Marco's, I have to remark, that Stanley's account of the request of the Waganda to send them help, appears calculated to weaken the importance of the whole affair. At all events, what he says about it in his book (vol. ii., pp. 333-37) does not agree with what I heard confirmed from another quarter in Uganda. Stanley says nothing at all about King Muanga's having put himself in communication with him; and yet already, on February 13th, Père Denoit wrote to me as follows from Bulingogwe:—

"Quant à Emin Pascha, il doit être arrivé en ce moment à Zanzibar, ou même en Europe. Il était au sud du Nyanza vers la fin d'Août. Il y était arrivé en compagnie de Stanley par la route de Ounyoro, Ousagara, Oucaragwe, etc, sans toucher à l'Ouganda, quoique les Chrétiens de ce pays l'appelassent à leur sécours." *Père Denoit's letter.*

Thus Père Denoit says here, then, that the Christians of Uganda had appealed to Stanley for help; while Stanley himself represents the case as if only the Christians of Ankore had been to him. As Muanga himself told me afterwards, he had sent Marco first to Stanley, with a formal petition for assistance, exactly as he sent him afterwards to the English in Kawirondo. Subsequently, Emin Pasha gave me some exceedingly interesting details about the story of the refusal of this petition on the part of Stanley. From what I was told, Emin Pasha pressed Stanley to grant the Waganda what they wished, but Stanley immediately became downright angry about it. "We are much too weak," he declared repeatedly. "You do not know Uganda, if you think that with our force" (which, by the way, amounted to 1,000 men) "we could go to Uganda." Thereupon Emin Pasha offered to undertake the help of the Waganda Christians by himself with his own people. Stanley flared up at this, declaring the Pasha had no longer a right to any such independent action; he would have him put under supervision if he tried to carry out any such plan. He, Stanley, was responsible for the safe return of the Pasha and his people to the coast, and without the command of the Queen of England he did not choose to mix himself up with the affairs of Uganda.

This information, which Stanley does not give in his account, certainly throws a substantially new light on the whole of the proceedings. It shows that Stanley did not feel himself strong enough to go to Uganda, and he accordingly omitted this remarkable opportunity of drawing this country into the interests of his own nation. It is the same blunder which Stanley, in my opinion, repeatedly committed, and which gives the whole undertaking such a contradictory, and, to outsiders, such an almost incomprehensible character, to which I shall on occasion again refer.

<small>New light on important events.</small>

Meanwhile I wrote letters to King Muanga in Kiswahili, to Monseigneur Léon Livinhac in French, and to Messrs. Gordon and Walter in English. As the contents of the three letters were identical, I extract the following from the translation of the letter to Livinhac:—

"MONSEIGNEUR,—I have the honour to inform you that with a small expedition I have arrived in the land of the Sultan Wachore. When I crossed over the boundary of this land your servant Marco came to me, and told me that the Europeans whom I supposed to be in Unjoro were in Uganda, and that he had sent my letters for them to you. Besides this, he gave me important information concerning the departure of Emin Pasha with Stanley for Europe. If this news is true, my expedition for Emin Pasha is obviously at an end.

<small>Letter to Monseigneur Léon Livinhac.</small>

"Marco tells me that King Muanga would be much gratified if we would come into his land. Monseigneur would oblige me very much by a brief account of the occurrences in the Equatorial Provinces, and of the reported departure of Emin Pasha. If this news is confirmed, and King Muanga invites me, I am prepared to march to Uganda.

"In case the news of the departure of Emin Pasha is not confirmed, and you, meanwhile, send me word that the route through Unjoro is not practicable, I shall still be prepared to take my route through Uganda."

In my letters to Muanga and the Englishmen I added to this, that I was ready to place my small force at the service of civilisation and Christianity, in case the king requested me to do so. *Offer to Muanga and the English.*

In the afternoon I sent for Marco again, delivered to him these letters, which were forwarded on the morrow to Uganda, and imparted to him my decision in the following manner:—

"I have given you these letters, which you are to send to Uganda. Meanwhile I shall continue my march towards Unjoro, as far as the north-west boundary of Wachore's land; so that in case I receive no satisfactory answer to my enquiry in Uganda I may be able to resume my advance, either on this side of the Nile, or through Unjoro direct. If it turns out that you have spoken the truth, and if, as I do not yet believe, Emin Pasha has gone away from the territory of the Turki, I shall be ready to go to Uganda to make war against Karema and the Arabs, and to bring back the Christians, my brethren, to Uganda. Therefore, send messengers now to Wachore, and inform him that I shall come into his land to-morrow, and into his capital on the next day, and that I have already put myself in friendly communication with Muanga." *Decision communicated to Marko.*

A loud joyful clapping of hands was the answer to this announcement, and my commands were immediately put into execution. The more I thought over the information which Marco had brought, the more I was gradually inclined to disbelieve its accuracy. I conjectured rather than Amdallah might be one of the Egyptian officers of Emin Pasha, who had, perhaps, been put in command of a troop of Egyptian soldiers under Stanley. I thought this all the more when, in answer to my question, "Who is the chief of the whole expedition, Stamuley or Amdallah?" Marco replied, "Stamuley." This appeared to me scarcely compatible with what I then imagined to be Emin's position. *Approval by the audience.*

A cheerful activity was now displayed in my camp. The supply of meat and drink was abundant, and the whole evening the Wasoga ran about through the camp with great torches, to light up the drinking, dancing, and playing. *A festive evening.*

On the next day we marched onward in a northerly direction, keeping the Wissmann Hills always to the right hand. We met large troops of fantastic-looking Wasoga warriors, who carried tasteful shields of twisted wood, ornamented at the sides with monkeys' and other skins. They were travelling eastward to the war against the Walandu.

The march resumed.

On this day another porter ran away from me. I did not have him pursued, since the fate of the expedition now depended on quite other conditions. We went forward through bananas and richly-cultivated land, until, at eleven o'clock, we again pitched our camp in a splendid banana plantation.

Our life in Usoga was particularly pleasant. We had guides for the march, so that I myself was able to walk along in quiet contemplation. When we arrived at any place the natives at once had to turn out of their houses, in which my people were installed, and plenty of food was at once brought, without any one thinking of demanding that we should pay for it.

Pleasant life in Usoga.

A farther march brought us southward to the capital of Wachore, and now, according to the statement of the natives, we had only three marches, or about six expedition marches, to bring us to the Lake Kioga, in the Nile. From that place I could have easily established a communication with Emin Pasha, supposing that he was in his old stations. I had immediate communication by the river with his stations Kodyi and Fauvera. Amid extraordinary difficulties and dangers we had arrived as far as the borders of the Equatorial Province from the east. The question was now, whether or not fortune, on her side, would vouchsafe us the reward of so much toil and struggle?

Communication with the stations.

I had again repeatedly questioned Marco; but his statements contradicted each other here and there, and so I encouraged myself to hope afresh that perhaps Emin was, after all, at Wadelai, and that it would be vouchsafed to me not only to reach the goal, but to effect the purpose of the German Relief Expedition.

If I should meet Emin in Wadelai, I would undertake from

thence to put myself in communication with Muanga, and by a united advance to overthrow Unjoro, and so force a free passage for our countryman across the Victoria Nyanza to the German East African coast, from whence assistance could be speedily obtained for him. If this were accomplished, we could afterwards, when I had been able to learn particulars on the spot, examine the Mahdi problem somewhat closer, to ascertain whether the attempt at least could not be undertaken to put into execution the plans, which the imagination of Europe had devised concerning the movements of the "White Pasha" in the summer of 1888. *Further intentions of Dr. Peters.*

Meanwhile I regarded the land and people of Usoga with a certain increase of interest. This country had been represented on the map until then as merely a white patch. Before we came there, no intelligence of any sort concerning it had been brought to Europe by whites; and yet it is well worth while to bring the knowledge of Usoga to the white world. For this same country is so fertile, and possesses such a high degree of cultivation, that it is an agreeable surprise for any one marching here from the east; and there is no question that the land promises to be of great importance in the future development of the dark continent. *Geographical particulars of Usoga.*

Akola forms a portion of the general territory of Usoga, in which it takes the leading position, through the power and intelligence of its sultan, Wachore. Usoga appears to extend 1½° northward from the lake. Its western boundary is formed by the Nile, which is here called Kiyira, or Nyiro. In the east, and again to the north-west, the Wissmann Hills form a frontier against the Walukuma and the Walundu. This whole little territory, seen from the top of a hill, resembles a billowy sea, the crests of whose waves are scattered by the wind. The tops of the hills are mostly crowned by rocks or stones. The journey over the rising ground can be made without any difficulty, generally lying through banana groves. The whole hill country is called in Usoga Namakokowa Wachore. The maximum difference of level between the mountain and the valley, which stretch out lengthways in an irregular *Scenery of Usoga.*

direction, may be about one hundred and fifty to three hundred feet.

Not until the western part of Usoga is approached do decided mountain chains appear, which stretch out from south-south-west to north-north-east. They cut off the valley of the Nile on the east. They have a breadth of some twelve miles, and exhibit heights of about 5,500 feet. Towards the north they lose themselves in immeasurable distance. The most southerly, and, as it appeared to me, the most important mountain in these chains which rises over the Nile, is called Ndira Wera (Wera means white. Whether Ndira again is connected with Kiyira or Nyiro, or whether it simply means "way," I was not able to discover). I named these border chains "The Reichart Ranges."

The hilly region.

I encamped under the Ndira Wera on February 17th, exactly on the spot where Bishop Hannington and his column were murdered five and a half years ago. The camping-ground is some distance to the north-eastward of Ukassa, and we found still a number of skulls and bones there. Here, on the following day, I visited the Nyanza for the first time, having had a view the day previous of a far-reaching creek belonging to it.

Relics of Bishop Hannington's party.

Some half-hour's journey from this camping-place there is a completely enclosed bay of about two square miles in extent, out of which three long narrow creeks extend landwards. This bay is connected by a river-like canal with the Nyanza, and, indeed, with the farther end of the Napoleon Gulf. Fishermen's huts, picturesquely scattered about in the banana fields, surround the shore. A long hilly ridge, visible on both sides during several days' march, separates this bay from the Napoleon Gulf on the west, and lends to it throughout the character of a large lake. I do not know if Stanley, on whose camping-ground we slept several times, ever saw this bay. I do not find it on the maps. Since it is a noticeable feature in the formation of this part of Usoga, I have given it a name, and I have called it "Arendt Bay," and the hilly ridge which closes it in to the west "Schroeder's Mountain."

The Napoleon Gulf.

Arendt Bay.

THE BANANA MEAT AND DRINK. 351

On February 18th we at last encamped on Schroeder's Mountain, and were only twelve minutes from Napoleon Gulf, which I beheld for the first time on that day.

This little enclosed country of Usoga, which, in its inland parts, may be compared to Thuringia, carries on chiefly the cultivation of bananas to a great extent. The banana is roasted, baked, boiled, eaten raw, and, above all, drunk; and the people have, moreover, various ways of preparing their drinks. The muenge, which resembles lemonade,

The banana as food and drink.

MOUNT SCHROEDER AND ARENDT BAY.

is prepared by pressing the juice out of the ripe fruit without fermentation.

Besides this there was a strong, bitter, intoxicating drink, which the natives simply call pombe, prepared with mtama; and still another medium beverage called mriffa, in which the admixture of mtama is wanting. The Wasoga drink or suck up this wine, or this beer, from early morning till late at night. As early as midday my friends, the Sultans, were, as a rule, in a state of considerable joviality. Besides these variously prepared bananas, many batatas are eaten, and also various kinds of grain and pulse.

The country is likewise rich in cattle, sheep, goats, and all sorts of poultry. Besides fowls, they eat a very delicate kind of fat quail, which were brought to us almost daily in little plaited baskets.

Everywhere we found the Wasoga an amiable, light-hearted people. Among them the beer-pot is never empty, and day and night the drum and flute are resounding. With regard to race, they belong altogether to the Waganda; a foundation of Bantu, with a strong addition of north-east immigration, to which I shall again refer. But they have softer features, and are undoubtedly among the best-looking races of East Central Africa. There is, in the expression of their eyes and the softness of the lines of their faces, something decidedly feminine; and it is accordingly the female portion of the population that attract most attention. Their dress, as among the Waganda, is usually of red bark-fibre stuff, which is confined to the waist by a girdle, and covers the whole body; but various cotton fabrics have already made their way among them, so that a good variety is noticed in their costume. For ornaments, they are fond of pearls and rings, of which latter they manufacture some very tasteful ones themselves in ironwork. Besides this, they are very skilful in twisted wood-work and mat-making. Indeed, they show in every department of such manufacture a remarkable degree of neatness and taste. The same advance from a primitive condition to a higher level of culture is shown in their style of arming themselves. Bows and spears seem to have been the original weapons of the people, with a shield of plaited wood, fantastically bedecked with skins. Nowadays, however, every one who wishes to be thought of any account endeavours to procure a rifle; and, indeed, among the men of higher rank, the original muzzle-loader is already thought an inferior weapon. In Usoga, as in Uganda, almost every make of weapon may be found represented, even to the very newest. As a rule, the difficulty is with the cartridges, and in these last days with powder and bullet. But I scarcely think that it will be possible ever again to root out the craving for these articles. These tribes will no more be turned back to an uncivilised kind of weapon than will the Arabs.

The houses are like great bee-hives, shaped like half a globe, or else built with ridges and gables. The interior is strewn with hay or straw, in a clean and comfortable manner. Wherever we came it was a matter of course for the inhabitants at once to vacate their houses, to make room for our people. *Wasoga dwellings.*

This country is divided politically into a number of little sultanates, of which the most important is Wachore, in Akola. Wachore means, strictly speaking, the people of Akola, or Achore, which is the same. It appears that every sultan of this country bears the name of Wachore, which, therefore, would seem to be not a proper name, but a title. All these sultans are subordinate to the mfalme, the King of Uganda, to whom they are obliged to send yearly a strictly-calculated tribute in ivory, cattle, slaves, and other articles. I believe Wachore would gladly have availed himself of the disturbances in Uganda at that time, to free himself from this obligation, if only he had had powder enough, and could have relied on all his own countrymen. The Waganda who accompanied me were, for two nights, in fear of an attack by him in Wachoreland; an apprehension which formed something of a contradiction to their former contemptuous treatment of the Wasoga. But, indeed, Wachore himself was unwilling, after all, to engage in a conflict with us, who had concluded a treaty of friendship with him. In short, the attack did not take place either time, and it is to be supposed Wachore has let the opportunity slip for ever. *The sultans and their power.*

My relations with Wachore were, from the first, of a most cordial nature. I reached the south of his capital on February 18th, and a banana plantation belonging to the Sultan was immediately allotted as a camping-ground for me and my people. The Sultan at once sent me, as a princely gift, two fine milch cows, with their calves, and *Friendly relations with Wachore.*

23

indicated his fields and banana groves as a foraging ground for my people. As a return present, I put together for him an Indian silk shawl, a handsome turban, a cask of powder, together with a breech-loader and a dozen cartridges, calibre twelve. I then made my two servants put on their smart, gold-embroidered liveries, and despatched the whole present to Wachore. He, meanwhile, had set out, with the ladies of his harem and a numerous suite, to pay us a ceremonial visit. My messengers met him on the way, and he had already adorned himself with the new turban when he entered our house, about three o'clock in the afternoon.

His Highness was in a somewhat "elevated" condition. Probably he had been drinking, to get his courage up. For, certainly, the most wonderful rumours had preceded us, which, if they did not precisely mark us out to be cannibals, yet represented us as something very much of the kind; and that the normal occupation of the Badutschi was that of murdering people, was a belief that I found to exist in quite intelligent Waganda men. According to what Marco told me, the English and Arabs spread reports of this kind on the Victoria Nyanza. What stamped us specially as such was the fight with the Mangati, and, above all, the driving off of the herds of the Massais. Wachore is a man of about forty years of age, with strikingly intelligent and attractive features. A deep sabre-cut on his face gives proof that he has not shrunk from the turmoil of the battle. He had brought with him large pitchers of various kinds of wine and beer, and whether we liked it or no, we were forced to pledge him more frequently than we would have wished. He talked and laughed incessantly, and we were soon good friends. His ladies, who glanced slyly out at us from under the fantastic shields, hung with asses' skins, which they held horizontally over their heads, inspected, in the meantime, with undisguised astonishment, the guests, whose like they had never seen, the tent, the motionless Somalis, standing by in their picturesque splendour. I caused a small mirror to be handed to each of them, for which they thanked me with many coquettish smiles, and, like true daughters of Eve, they immediately understood the use of them.

Wachore touched lightly upon his relations with the King of Uganda, with a certain diplomatic dexterity. He received us simply as friends of Muanga, and confined himself to explaining, on his part, that he was a friend of any one whom Muanga recognised as a friend. It struck me that though Marco treated him with an apparent friendliness and courtesy, there was yet a certain degree of self-sufficiency half hidden under ceremonial formalities.   *Wachore's visit.*

"My land is your land," said Wachore. "If you wish for anything, let me know, and you shall have it at once."

At half-past four o'clock he at length withdrew with his suite, and immediately afterwards large baskets of fowls, eggs, and quails, together with sheep and goats, were dragged up to us, as proof that the Sultan had been pleased by this visit to our encampment.

Scarcely had the sound of Wachore's drums and flutes died away in the north, when all at once the mixed music of many more drums and flutes, belonging to a new procession, approached my tent from the west. I asked Marco what this meant, and he answered,—

"This is the great chief of the Waganda (mkubroa). Do not be friendly with him; he is bad, and a liar, and he knows not the words of Jesus Christ."

With genuine astonishment, I presently saw coming towards me a personage, who, from his costume, might have been a fit denizen of an Oriental court, but was such an apparition as I certainly should not have expected to see in Central Africa.

A dark caftan, embroidered with silver, fell over wide sky-blue trousers, also adorned with silver embroidery. On his head he wore a diadem, made entirely of strings of beads of different colours, artistically interwoven, and rising in the form of a kind of crown. The wearer of this adornment was Kamanyiro Kanta, the cousin of the late King Mtesa, and uncle of Muanga, to whose party he belonged. At the overthrow of the Christians he had been driven across the Nile by the Arabs, and was now staying in Usoga, where he claimed to represent the interests of his country as ambassador   *Kamanyiro Kanta, Muanga's uncle.*

extraordinary of Muanga. Under this pretext he had got together a large amount of property, and among the rest a harem of extraordinarily pretty girls.

He came up to salute me with loud yells, which his musicians accompanied by a wild flourish on their instruments. I then took him by the hand, and led him with slow steps in front of my tent, where he took his seat upon a chair, which he had brought with him, while I seated myself opposite him in my own armchair. Herr von Tiedemann, who had been drawn from his tent by the noise, was not a little surprised to find this new procession with us.

Kamanyiro Kanta's feeling towards Marco seemed at first to be one of great irritation. As Marco informed me afterwards, he had asked him reproachfully why he had not brought up the great English expedition from Kawirondo. Kamanyiro's period of prosperity seemed to have been in the days of Mtesa, and especially during the months that Stanley spent at Uganda. Accordingly, he felt from the beginning a natural sympathy with the English; a sympathy which he certainly took care to hide from me, but from which he could never quite free himself. Marco, however, made him a very quiet report, in which he paraphrased the old Latin saying, "Ultra posse nemo obligatur" ("Since the Englishmen would not come, it had not been possible for him to bring them"). Then he passed on to a description of our expedition, pointed to the cattle that we had taken from the Massais, and further declared that it was I who had beaten the Mangati on the north-east of the Victoria Nyanza.

Career of Kamanyiro.

At every remark of this kind the old gentleman sprang from his chair, with loud yells, to clasp me in his arms, each embrace being accompanied with a loud flourish from his orchestra, which consisted of about seven performers.

When Marco had ended, Kamanyiro said to me, "I salute you, O German, as the friend of Muanga, and as my friend! We are all one. What we possess is yours, and what you possess is ours."

After this the whole procession, which was composed of

about seventy persons, went on its way, and presently had vanished, amid beating of drums and tootling of flutes, like a vivid mirage; and once again I sat alone in the sweet restfulness of the banana grove, on which the full moon shed its light.

On the following morning we paid our return visit to the Sultan Wachore.

For visits of this nature we donned a uniform which had been devised by Herr von Tiedemann—white trousers, trimmed with a broad stripe of gold down the side, stuck into high boots, coming up to the knee, and white jackets, with red lappets at the shoulders embroidered with gold, and cuffs to the sleeves to match. The helmet was also adorned with bands of gold, and I wore, in addition, a black and gold scarf. Appearances count for much in Europe, and for still more in Central Africa, and it would have shown very little wisdom not to have turned this fact to profit.

Return visit to Wachore.

Wachore received us in a dome-like hall, open on one side. He was reclining on an Indian divan, placed on the ground, and was dressed in a black caftan, embroidered with gold. He was smoking a pipe, and had, of course, a large bumper of banana wine at his side, from which he sucked up the intoxicating liquid through a reed.

"We are come to salute you," I said, when we had taken our seats before him on the chairs we brought with us, "and to tell you that we are your friends, and that we intend to remain your friends."

"Every one who is the friend of Muanga is my friend. I love white men, and am especially glad to be friends with the Germans, who understand war."

Compliments and ceremonies.

"Have you ever seen any white men?"

"Once before this, in Uganda."

"Now that we have been here among you, no doubt many more white men will come into your country."

"They will all be welcome," was the reply, "and especially the Germans."

The conversation continued in this style for more than an

hour, during which the banana wine circulated without intermission, and the pipes were refilled. Above Wachore's sofa a few guns were hanging. They were breech-loaders of various construction, and one in particular, a Martini rifle, Wachore ordered to be taken down and handed to us. It was both loaded and cocked, and suddenly went off in Herr von Tiedemann's hands. The bullet passed through the head of one of Wachore's attendants, so that his eyeball fell at our feet, and the man was dead in a moment; and a second was hit on the jaw, which was shattered, and he, too, afterwards expired. There was a moment's deep silence, and then I apologised to Wachore for Herr von Tiedemann.

A tragic accident.

"My friend weeps sorely," I said, "that the weapon went off in his hands."

Wachore suddenly burst out into a roar of laughter. "It does not signify in the least," he exclaimed; "the man was only a slave. Your friend did not do it; it was the gun that did it, so do not trouble yourselves about that."

The whole court joined in the laughter, that seemed, however, a little forced. The corpse was quickly removed, sand was strewn over the pools of blood, and the bowl of banana wine was immediately handed round again; just as when in Europe a guest has broken a valuable piece of china, and the well-bred hostess is anxious to pass over the unpleasant incident as quickly as possible. Such is the value set on human life in Africa.

Cheap estimate of human life.

This painful scene was just ended, when Kamanyiro Kanta appeared, with his attendants, and I arranged with them that I should march westward towards the Nile, by slow daily stages. As soon as the answer confirming the report of Emin Pasha's departure arrived from Uganda, I would be ready to march across the Nile with the Wagandas, who had fled to Usoga, and to make the attempt to bring back Muanga and the Christian party into that country.

We had scarcely returned to the camp before Wachore sent to Herr von Tiedemann a basketful of eggs, to show that he had no ill feeling against him on account of the occurrence at the morning's drinking party. On my side, I sent another gold-embroidered caftan in return to Wachore.

My people were still not quite easy as to the fate which lay before them. Thinking to inspire them with a greater feeling of security I gave orders that only one sentry should be on duty at night, instead of the four who generally kept guard; for I knew perfectly well that if we should be attacked in these regions it was quite immaterial how many men were on sentry duty. In any case we should, if attacked, be hopelessly lost.

My frame of mind during these days was somewhat agitated and uneasy, with respect to the approaching decision concerning the final object of the expedition. This decision was to be given earlier than I had anticipated.

According to the agreement, I set out on the following day, advancing slowly towards the west. We now always made short marches, with drums and fifes playing, and regularly pitched our tents in some banana grove. Our life was in every respect a pleasant one, for there were no immediate problems for the expedition to solve. Wachore alone was entirely responsible for the provisioning, and Wasoga provided guides.

On February 13th we happened to have a great number of Wagandas and Wasogas in our camp. Kamanyiro's band was playing, and the beer was flowing in streams, when suddenly some Waganda men came up to me, and handed me letters. These letters were addressed to the gentlemen of the English expedition, and I was on the point of returning them, when I suddenly perceived that on one of them H. M. Stanley was indicated as the sender. A joyful hope thrilled through me at this sight, that the news of Stanley's departure must be incorrect, for if he was now sending a letter to Usoga he could not possibly have left the Equatorial Province five months ago. Marco put an end to my uncertainty by tearing open the letter, and giving it to me to read; and under the peculiar circumstances in which I was placed, I felt myself perfectly justified in doing so.

And now the veil fell from the shrouded image, and I saw

it before me in all its nakedness. The letter was to the following effect:—

"Church Mission Station, Makolo.
"*September* 4*th*, 1889.

"Mr. H. M. Stanley and the expedition for the relief and rescue of Emin Pasha have arrived at Makolo Station, at the southern extremity of the Victoria Nyanza, accompanied by Emin Pasha, Signor Casati, forty Egyptians, and about four hundred Soudanese.

"The Equatorial Province is accordingly abandoned. Lado, Mugi Geri, and Dufilé have been for some months past in the hands of the Mahdi. After the evacuation of Wadelai and Nuguru Station most of the troops deserted in a body, and went to Makraka. A small body of troops were last heard of at Msua, but all the soldiers who were found in the province are rebels against the Egyptian Government, and cannot be trusted by a European. A letter containing similar information to this has been sent to Mr. Stokes. Mr. Stanley arrived here on August 28th, 1889. In a few days the expedition will start from here for the coast *via* Mpuapua.

Report from H. M. Stanley.

(Signed) "H. M. Stanley."

Such was the cold, dry purport of the letter. Not a greeting to his countrymen; not a word of counsel or of suggestion to Jackson and his colleagues! Although I had, for several days past, conjectured the kind of news contained in this letter, the effect on me was simply crushing. So, while I was yet in Muina, Emin Pasha had already been at the southern end of Lake Victoria. When I had landed in Kwaihu Bay he must have quitted his province long before. For this, then, we had endured all the dangers, anxieties, and toils; to receive this news there, at the very gates of the Equatorial Province! What could have been the design of Providence in permitting us to advance so far, only to make it clear to us at last that our labours had been all in vain?

Disappointment and discouragement.

AN OBJECT TO BE ACHIEVED. 361

"I will march on to Wadelai, in spite of it," was my first resolve. "Perhaps Emin Pasha will come some day or other to deliver us," was the mocking echo of my thought. But this impulse of defiance was soon succeeded by more reasonable considerations.

DR. PETERS READS STANLEY'S LETTER.

There was yet, I knew, a possibility of making the expedition, after all, conducive to the great aims out of which it had arisen. If Emin Pasha was gone, and the Equatorial Province evacuated, the solution lay in the great contrast between the Christian and the Arab system to the north of Lake Victoria in Uganda. Uganda must be made a rampart, to keep back the deluge of Mohammedanism from invading the north, and perhaps a starting-point for winning back all that had been lost there. The two English expeditions from the west and from the east had been fearful to interfere in the tangled disturbances of this country. If, then, the German Emin Pasha Expedition succeeded in contributing to the solution of the question in a Christian sense, we should have the right to say to ourselves, that the toils which had led us to Wachore's capital had not been in vain. The expedition would then have effected a tangible object, and we should be able, with a clear conscience, to meet those who had sent us out. At the same time, I might hope to have an opportunity of working for the furtherance of the special national interests of Germany in Uganda. I learnt afterwards that, even before my expedition started, Uganda had been ceded to England, but no information of the cession had been communicated to us. A great German expedition had been allowed to march into these countries, without its having been thought necessary to vouchsafe to it any information whatever on that important transaction.

On February 13th, 1890, I was naturally under the impression that the die that settled the fate of Uganda had not as yet been cast in Europe; that the prize of the contest was still there, and would fall to the lot of the boldest; and that in any case the monopolising of the country for the special interests of England could yet be prevented. This prospect could not fail to be a seductive one, and to nerve my resolution. Providence had rendered abortive all our plans regarding Unjoro and the north. To resist fate was beyond our power. On the other hand, it pointed us clearly and unmistakably to the south-west, where vast interests of civilisation were at stake. Up then, and away to Uganda!

Half an hour after the receipt of Stanley's letter,—which, by the way, I sent on to Kawirondo,—I gave orders to my column to hold itself in readiness for the march, to turn off towards Uganda early on the following day. I was well aware what risk I once more took upon myself by so doing; but I can honestly say, that although I saw that I could now make an honourable retreat upon the English expedition in Kawirondo, which I had reason to believe would at any rate not be hostile to us, I never for one moment entertained the thought of so doing.

In the evening I sat longer than usual in serious conversation with Herr von Tiedemann, in front of my tent. The twilight of the banana grove conjured up grotesque images before our eyes, and a gentle night wind rustled through the waving leaves. In the distance could be heard the drums, fifes, and songs of the Wasoga men; in the camp all was still.

Afterwards, when I lay down to rest, there came over my heart an infinite sense of forlornness and a profound self-pity. My thoughts wandered back to my country, which had allowed it to come to pass that a foreign power should dare to deprive us of almost every means of making our appearance effectively, here on the scene of action. I seemed to be a repudiated man, and my passion of distress was lightened by an outburst of convulsive sobbing. Without, the night wind swept through the rustling leaves of the banana groves; the lofty boughs of the tall fig-tree, beneath which my tent had been pitched, swayed in the wind, and whispered to each other strange weird stories. At last my spirit was soothed into a quiet composure, and bowed itself in submission to the eternal and inscrutable designs of Providence. *Conflicting emotions.*

The rising sun found us next day on our march towards the south-west. I wanted to cross the Nile at Jinga, above the Ripon Falls; and I again despatched letters to Muanga, with the request that he would send boats to Grant's Bay, that from there I might open communications with the Christian party across the lake.

Our further journey onward towards Usoga was accomplished in a very agreeable manner. The daily marches were short, out of consideration for Kamanyiro and his surroundings. There was abundance of food and drink, and in the afternoons and evenings we were entertained by the dances and songs of the girls of Kamanyiro's harem, to *Pleasant journey towards Usoga.*

which entertainments we were regularly invited after dinner; sometimes, also, an assembly of the people was called, in which Kamanyiro would convey our greetings to the Wasoga men, and assure them of the close friendship which united us to himself. As the afternoon drew on Kamanyiro invariably got drunk; but as he was always in a good humour, he contributed in no small degree to the hilarity of the expedition. Indeed, it was altogether an extraordinary contrast, when I thought of the times when we were marching over the high plateaus beneath the Kenia, or over the Angata na Nyuki. Kamanyiro's drummers, like all his other followers, were one-eyed. When I asked him how it happened that he had engaged none but one-eyed people, he made a gesture with his hand, to indicate the action of tearing out a man's eye, and, with a snap of his fingers towards the ground, cried, "Eh, it looks better!" This one-eyedness was, as it were, the livery of Kamanyiro's servants, and was not by any means the effect of accident; the old gentleman himself knew best how it had been brought about.

Kamanyiro's one-eyed men.

On February 16th, I at length received the letters from Uganda which confirmed the news of Emin Pasha's departure, and invited us to come to the aid of the Christian party. At the same time the French certainly told us that plague, famine, and black small-pox were raging in the country. This, however, did not have any effect on my decision.

On February 18th I encamped, as I have mentioned, on the spot where Bishop Hannington had paid with his life for the obstinacy with which he had persisted in his march from the east to Uganda, in spite of the warnings given him on the subject, in the most urgent manner, by the French and English. The Sultan Douba, who had executed the punishment of death on Hannington, had fled at the approach of our expedition, and kept entirely aloof from us. I should have dearly liked to avenge on him the murder of a white man; although, as a matter of fact, he had merely carried out a judicial sentence pronounced in the capital.

Bishop Hannington's murder.

The Waganda have an old prophecy, according to which an

expedition coming from the east is to "eat up" the land and make an end of the dynasty of the Wakintu. For that reason the approach from the east has always been strictly forbidden, and my expedition was the first which had entered the country from that direction. Muanga had, accordingly, forbidden Hannington to come to Uganda from Kawirondo, and had even sent him boats, to carry him to Usukuma, and thence to Uganda. Bishop Hannington's death, therefore, had no connection whatever with the persecution of the Christians, which happened later, but was occasioned by entirely different considerations, which had nothing at all to do with religion. *Cause of the crime.*

On February 19th the waters of the sacred Nile suddenly gleamed at my feet. I must confess that a thrill of proud triumph ran through me when I beheld the Nile. The little German Emin Pasha Expedition had achieved what none had ever accomplished before. Tana, Baringo, the Nile! With only some sixty men, we had penetrated through Gallas and Massais, to the eastern boundary of Uganda. Whatever Fate might yet have in store for us, in every case honour was saved. *Arrival at the Nile.*

I pitched my camp about fifty paces above the river bank. Hundreds of Christian Waganda, especially girls and women, came crowding round to greet us. They welcomed us as deliverers and liberators; but declared, in answer to my proposal that they should go with me to the opposite bank, that they were quite willing to do so, but would wait for "two days." The attachment and confidence of these people struck me as something quite touching and affecting. *Welcome from the Christian Waganda.*

When, on the following morning, I directed the passage of my expedition across to Uganda, the whole right bank of the Nile was covered with hundreds of these figures, clad in garments of brown fibre cloth. I had had my chair set up on a prominence, on the right bank of the river, so that from that position I might superintend the passage of the caravan.

Below me was displayed an extremely gay and animated scene; the fantastic Waganda boats, with their long projecting prows, adorned by branching antlers hung with skins and beads, crowded along on the water, to embark my people and the cattle. These boats are made of planks sewn together and held firm by a series of strong ribs. Above these ribs small benches are arranged for the rowers, on which, according to the size of the boat, from fourteen to thirty rowers take their places, and propel the vessel by means of a kind of paddle. On one of the benches aft stands the singer, who directs the whole, and whom the rowers accompany in chorus with their rhythmic songs. The helmsman sits in the bow. The whole presents a picturesque appearance. The rate of progress, when the men work lustily, is a very fair one—as much as five English miles an hour. The boat has a sort of keel, by means of which it cuts swiftly through the water; the end of this keel is prolonged beyond the fore part of the boat, and forms the great beak or prow before mentioned. The vessel, altogether, recalls the representations sometimes seen on Egyptian temples. But what a lavish waste of power is displayed by the whole arrangement of these vessels! From twenty-five to thirty men are required to transport six or seven passengers or eight or ten loads across the lake! No one can wonder that the result of work obtained is everywhere in Africa so insignificant, when power is wasted in this way.

Meanwhile the transport of my men and luggage and of the cattle was quickly effected. Load after load was deposited on the opposite shore, which I had already visited on the previous day. When all had been carried across, I passed over myself with the flag to the left shore, and then marched at once with my column in a southern direction to a plantation of Kamanyiro's, where I purposed to encamp for the day.

The crossing was accomplished a few hundred paces above Ripon Falls. The Nile is here about 6,500 feet in breadth. The Ripon Falls are precipitated on the left or Uganda side in a cataract, and on the other side in the form of rapids, towards the north.

The fall may be from twenty to forty feet in height. It is

PASSAGE OF THE NILE.

astonishing what a number of fish are carried down by these falls. The Waganda have a curious method of catching them. They drag them out of the water, at a place immediately under the falls, with a large hook, without using any bait. It is probable that the fish are so stunned by the fall down the cataract that they are easy to catch. I saw a man bring out nine or ten large fish in five minutes. The fish are excellent eating. There were both flat fish and some of the salmon kind, which made a very agreeable variety in our monotonous bill of fare. *Fishing by the falls.*

Towards twelve o'clock we had reached Kamanyiro's plantation, and established our first camp on the soil of Uganda. When the last of the boats which had carried Kamanyiro and his men across to us turned back towards Usoga, a kind of oppression stole over my heart. We were now manifestly face to face with dangers which exceeded all those that lay behind us. I neither knew Muanga and the temper of his faction, nor had I any information as to the position of the Arabs. How if the boats which I expected to meet me at Grant's Bay were not there? Must I not then assume that the Arab faction would try, under all circumstances, to prevent my joining Muanga? And how could I entertain any reasonable hope, if they resorted to force, to escape being destroyed, with my whole expedition? I knew for certain that we were in no condition to resist Karema, if he were to make a resolute attack upon us. We could certainly sell our lives as dear as possible, but there could be no thought of a victory, or even of escape, in case we were attacked by the Arabs. So that our position at this time was just that of men playing at hazard and risking everything against the bank. *First encampment in Uganda.* *A dangerous enterprise.*

When we entered Kamanyiro's plantation, with drums beating and colours flying, my people were jovial and of good cheer. But my own feelings were more serious than ever, and the immediate future rose in a threatening form before my mind.

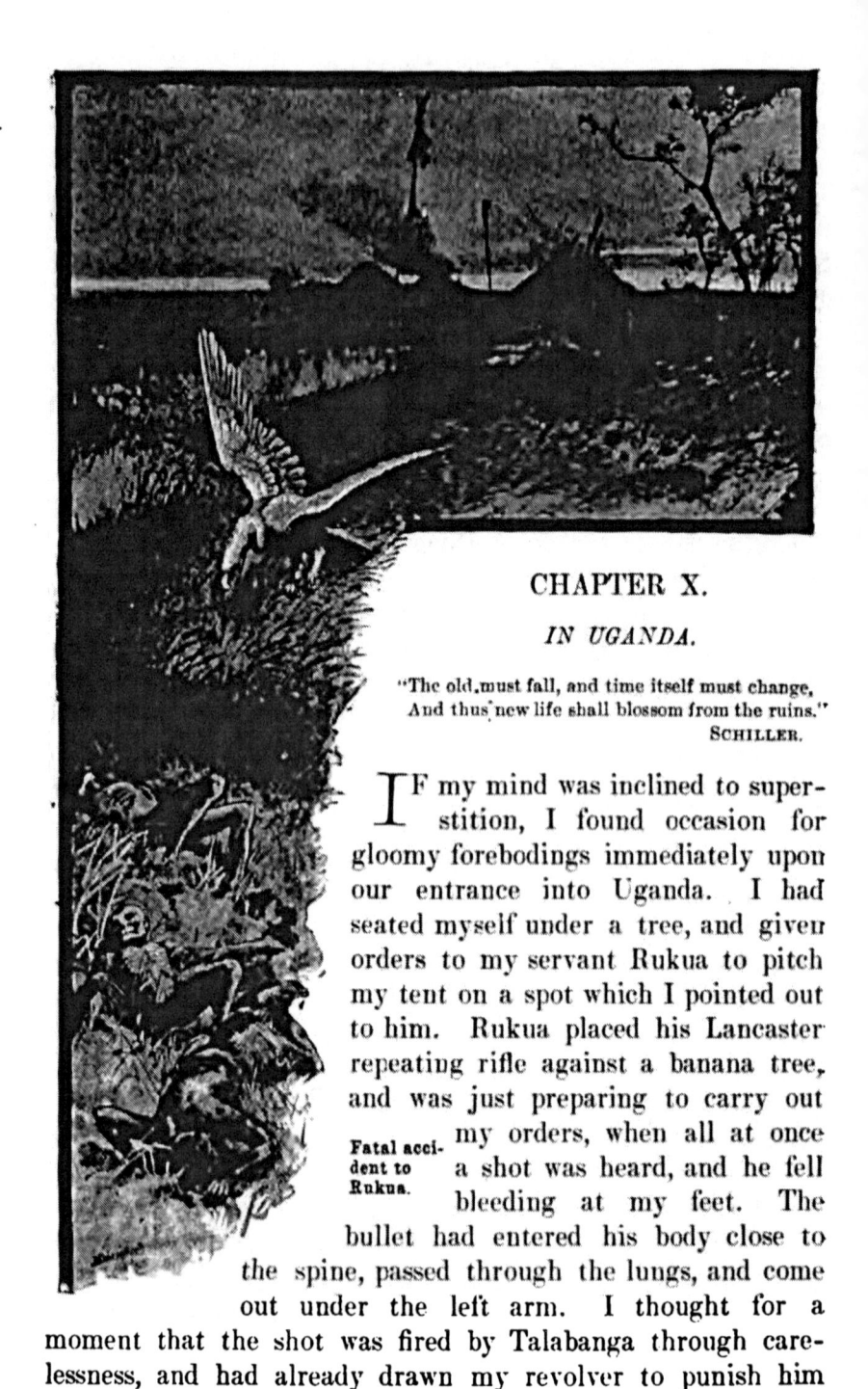

CHAPTER X.

IN UGANDA.

"The old must fall, and time itself must change,
And thus new life shall blossom from the ruins."
SCHILLER.

IF my mind was inclined to superstition, I found occasion for gloomy forebodings immediately upon our entrance into Uganda. I had seated myself under a tree, and given orders to my servant Rukua to pitch my tent on a spot which I pointed out to him. Rukua placed his Lancaster repeating rifle against a banana tree, and was just preparing to carry out my orders, when all at once a shot was heard, and he fell bleeding at my feet. The bullet had entered his body close to the spine, passed through the lungs, and come out under the left arm. I thought for a moment that the shot was fired by Talabanga through carelessness, and had already drawn my revolver to punish him

Fatal accident to Rukua.

for it, when I saw that Rukua had been shot down by his own weapon. He had again, in defiance of my repeated warnings, been carrying it not only loaded, but cocked; it had slipped down from the banana tree, and gone off as it fell.

There was no chance of the faithful fellow's surviving. We bandaged the wound at once, but every breath he drew came whistling through the shot holes, and black spirts of blood welled out on the ground. He at once began to wander, calling incessantly on my name, and that of his friend and countryman, Selek. I had him placed on my bed and carried into a hut close by; but he died within half-an-hour, and we had only the sad satisfaction of giving him an honourable funeral. I now forbade any further carrying of loaded guns throughout the whole expedition; for the mere marching with them was a serious danger to life and limb, quite apart from any hostile attack. *Rukua's death and burial. Precautionary order.*

In the afternoon Kamanyiro came to me as usual, and brought me the information that the boats which were to carry us to Muanga were waiting for us in Grant's Bay.

The next morning we accordingly started for that place. We marched first along the high road which leads from Usoga to Mengo, but soon after nine o'clock turned away from it to the left, and made a wide circuit round the bay so as to reach its south-western extremity. Here we arrived at noon, to find that no boats were there; but I received, instead, a letter from Mr. Gordon, inviting me to march overland to Mengo. *The boats not provided.*

"BULINGOGWE, *February* 18*th*, 1890.

"DEAR SIR,—Muanga, King of Uganda, thanks you for your letter of February 14th, 1890. He wishes us to tell you that the plague was ravaging the island where we all lived crowded together. We left that island, and intend to return to Mengo, to the mainland. We have no fear of the plague there, for there is not a human being living in the place. The king sends you a messenger, named Mika Sematimba, who *Letter from King Muanga.*

understands Kiswahili, and will be your guide to Mengo, where you will meet the king. Muanga invites you to come quickly, and if you will cross the lake to Usukuma, he will give you canoes.

"Yours faithfully,
"E. C. GORDON."

The correspondence with Muanga was carried on by means of boats on the Victoria Nyanza.

I now found myself in anything but an agreeable position. The Christians on the islands urged me to go overland to the capital, and they would then place themselves in communication with me from the opposite island. Between me and the capital lay a completely desolate region, and I had no accurate information concerning the attitude of the Arab party. I had, indeed, been informed that the Arabs had recently been driven back by the Christians before Mengo, but even after this occurrence the court had still remained on the islands, and the messengers told me expressly, that Karema also was still in the north of Uganda. How could I suppose that he would refrain from attempting to prevent my effecting a junction with the Christians?

Doubtful position.

I sent for Kamanyiro in the evening, and said to him,—

"You told me yesterday that I should find boats to-day here in Grant's Bay on Lake Victoria. Well, where are these boats?"

"The boats are not there."

"I know that myself. I am a German, and we Germans do not like people to tell us lies. If there were no boats here, why did you say yesterday that we should find some?"

Declaration of Kamanyiro Kanta.

"My people had reported it to me."

"Yes, indeed, your people had reported it to you. I do not believe your words, and I advise you in future to refrain from acting towards me in such a manner. I now inform you that we shall start to-morrow morning to march towards Mengo; but I shall no longer march after the manner of the Waganda men, as I did in Usoga, but in the German fashion; that is, we shall move quickly forward, from before sunrise in the morning till afternoon, to get to Mengo as quickly as possible. Have your men in readiness, therefore, and send everyone who is not able to march quickly, back across the Nile for the present, to Usoga. I especially advise you to send back your women there. If you are not able, yourself, to accompany me, you can also return to Usoga. These are my orders, and I now leave it to you whether you will obey them or not."

Definite instructions of Dr. Peters.

This tone was to some extent new to the old Uganda chief, who on the day before had had a whole village flogged, simply to give us an idea of his power. I may refer to the statements of Emin Pasha and of Stanley, to show with what arrogance these chiefs were formerly accustomed to behave towards white men. Kamanyiro had already tried once in Usoga to take that tone with me. One morning, when I gave the signal for starting and my tent was already taken down, he sent a servant with the message, that I might as well have the tent put up again, as we should not march that day. I thereupon sent for him, and asked him drily whether he was of opinion that I had lost my wits during the night, or whether that calamity had happened to himself;—after which, in three minutes' time, we found ourselves amicably marching along together.

Understanding with Kamanyiro.

Here on the Nile was the province of which Kamanyiro was Governor, and the very next day was to bring his antiquated claims into open conflict with the ideas which we had been accustomed to carry out in the expedition. On this day, before sunrise, we had already climbed the ridge that encloses Lake Victoria like the walls of a crater. Uganda in its southwestern portions is less fertile than Usoga. It may be said that in Usoga the greater part is cultivated, and in Uganda the greater part is steppe. The whole country parallel to Lake Victoria is framed by a hilly range forming a table-land; and a similar mountain formation extends along the Nile to the north, as far as the eye can range.

Through desert Uganda.

The formation of the mountains is very singular, such as I have never seen elsewhere; always table-shaped, with blunt flattened summits.

These hills stretch uninterruptedly as far as the north-east angle of the lake, to the mouth of the Katonga near Buddu. As I said before, the mountains generally slope abruptly down to the lake, in crater-like formation.

As the lake runs into the land in many bays, and a row of more or less beautiful islands lies facing the shore, the view *View from the heights.* from the heights is extraordinarily attractive and picturesque. If the eye is allowed to wander towards the right, over the plateau northwards, a broad plain is seen stretching out, only broken here and there by isolated hills. Where the land slopes away to the north lie the villages and plantations of Waganda, everywhere enclosed by ever-green banana groves, surrounded by fields of corn and batatas. The whole scene makes a curious but a very pleasing impression.

The billows of war had not yet rolled to this farthermost south-west corner of Uganda. It was not until the second day that we came to a devastated and burnt-out district. Here we *The astonished natives.* found people still left, who gazed in mute fear at the great black, white, and red flag, which in front of our expedition was carried for the first time through Uganda.

As I well knew that in the case of possible Arab enterprise I should have to rely principally on moral impressions, I had taken care that our reputation should precede us, and had been careful above all to bring with me from Usoga a band of war *March in military state.* drums, which should send the signal of war resounding before us over the far-spreading heights—three drums tuned in fifths, on which the roll was beaten, and the big drum coming in between, the whole producing a solemn and threatening effect.

In this way we went on the whole morning, in a westerly direction. We passed over one chain of hills after another, and in the valleys several watercourses were crossed, which

TRIUMPHAL ENTRY INTO UGANDA.

carry the waters of Uganda into the Victoria Nyanza. On February 22nd I encamped in Ischioragama, a large and well-preserved plantation belonging to the king, with a broad road running straight through it, alongside of which I established my encampment.

Kamanyiro Kanta did not make his appearance until an hour after our arrival, and even then he was very weary, and groaning from his exertions. I went a few steps forward to meet him and congratulate him, a little ironically, on his prowess in marching. I then took him by the hand and led him, as usual, to the chair in front of my tent. But now the old gentleman suddenly broke out into a flood of invectives and curses, of which I certainly did not understand all, as they were principally directed to the large crowd of Waganda men who stood round; but I gathered that they were chiefly levelled at the arrogance of white men, who imagined that they could now play the part of conquerors in Uganda. He wound up his address with the announcement to me, that the king had sent word I was now to remain for three days in Ischioragama. I answered Kamanyiro, very quietly, that in future, when he wanted to hold a conference with his assembled people, he must be kind enough to choose some other place for it than my tent; and, in addition to this, he was not to bawl so loud when he was close to me, as I could hear very well. As regarded his communication, I did not believe Muanga had made any such demand upon me. Moreover, even if this were the case, I should not be in a position to fulfil it, as it did not suit my manner of travelling.

"You say that this way of travelling is your custom in Uganda. Well, you Waganda may keep to it. So far as I am concerned, you can stay not only three days, but three years, here in Ischioragama. For my part, I am a German, and am accustomed not to copy the ways of strangers, but to follow my own."

Hereupon Kamanyiro poured forth a fresh torrent of imprecations. He had always said so—the white men would "eat up" Uganda yet,—but that all came from their allowing the words of Jesus there now, and letting the old religion perish.

Then I stood up, and said to Kamanyiro, "Now I desire to be alone. Go away to your own houses."

Then, as he did not obey this request, I summoned some Somalis to my aid, which had a completely terrifying effect on the Waganda men. Much as I was disposed to make some allowance for the self-willed obstinacy of an old Uganda chief, I did not think it conducive either to German or to our own interests to play the part which former travellers—Stanley above all—had been content to act. As I learned in Uganda, Stanley had been kept there a complete prisoner for seven months, and Kamanyiro always quoted him when he came to me with demands. Upon these grounds, I was very glad of the opportunity of making clear to the old gentleman, in the first place, that there was a difference between the year 1889 and the time when Stanley was in Uganda; secondly, that when a man came at the head of an armed expedition to the assistance of the King of Uganda, it was not the same thing as when Stanley entered the country alone, and only on a visit; and thirdly, that apart from all this, I was not inclined to play the traditional part accepted by white European travellers in this part of Africa.

Summary dismissal of Kamanyiro.

When I had dismissed Kamanyiro, I wrote the following letter to Mr. Gordon:—

"ISCHIORAGAMA, *February* 22nd, 1890.

"DEAR SIR,—Kamanyiro Kanta informed me to-day that the king had sent him word that I was to remain here three days. As this is in direct contradiction to your letter of yesterday, I cannot believe that it is true. But, however that may be, it does not in any way accord with my plans and the manner of my journey, and I shall consequently continue my march to Mengo. I shall encamp tomorrow at Katente, and the day after at Wakarimbue. Kindly ask the king whether it is really his wish that I should wait for

Letter to Mr. Gordon, the missionary.

three days in a plantation by the roadside. Let me have a brief answer. There is no food here for my expedition.

"Yours sincerely,
"CARL PETERS.

"To E. C. GORDON, ESQ."

I sent this letter at once to Kamanyiro Kanta, with the request that he would forward it across the lake to the king. Kamanyiro, who may very well have guessed the contents, after breakfast sent to me the supervisor of his harem—who was accustomed to preside at our afternoon entertain- ments—with the remark, that he noticed on the march my sheep did not get along very well. He feared that, if I continued to advance in the same manner, I should lose very many of my sheep. I could not restrain a smile at this, but I sent back the reassuring answer that from Massailand, where I had acquired them as spoils of war, to this place, the sheep had got used to much longer marches. Besides, it mattered little if some of them were lost; when this flock came to an end, I should very well know where to get another. {.sidenote: Kamanyiro Kanta's appre- hensions.}

Upon that, Kamanyiro sent word back: "Did I wish the letter to the king to be sent to-day or to-morrow?" I answered, "To-day," and, in fact, "immediately."

Meanwhile evening was drawing on, when suddenly I heard my old friend coming towards me in grand procession. He drove before him several oxen for slaughter, and brought fowls in baskets, and some bananas and honey. With loud yells, as was his custom, he sought to embrace me, which in a very cool, dry manner, I stopped him from doing. He then seated himself by my side, in front of my tent, trying to hide his confusion from his companions by continual chattering and laughing. He also tried repeatedly, after his old fashion, to drink with me, which I, however, courteously declined. I purposely refrained from speaking of my departure on the following morning, and was now curious to see whether Kamanyiro would stay behind or attach himself to me. {.sidenote: Renewed visit.}

Next morning, as we were about to start, we noticed that his women were already prepared for a journey; and when, towards mid-day, I had set up my camp in Katente, he came up to greet me, limp as a broken lily. On the way he had complained to Herr von Tiedemann, that he was an old man, and could not march as we young people did. I advised him accordingly to have a litter made for himself, and let his slaves carry him in it; but Kamanyiro declined this. He may well have feared that his slaves, who one and all hated him from the depths of their souls, would seize some opportunity of launching him down a precipice. However that may have been, from this time forward our relations to each other were established on a proper footing, and this remained a precedent in all my future dealings with the Waganda.

Kamanyiro joins the procession.

After we left Katente, we came into a perfectly desolate country. Not only were the villages burnt, and the groves of bananas destroyed, the whole landscape was simply burnt up, and lay there a black expanse. By the roadsides lay skeletons and corpses still in process of decomposition, poisoning the air. The sunshine, which had smiled over Usoga, had vanished; the heavens were for the most part covered with grey clouds, and the wind either in fitful gusts whirled the black heaps of ashes up in the air, or flung sudden cold showers on the expedition. The carrion vultures, who were gorging themselves with the flesh of the unburied corpses, seemed to be the only inhabitants of this land. Every trace of human beings had vanished. An oppressive desolation filled our hearts. For even if these impressions were not powerful enough to shake our resolution, they could not help to have a great influence on our spirits. Dull and almost spectrally echoed the roll of our drums from the hills, as we crossed the heights one after another. When we descended into the valleys, there would be a brook or a watercourse to pass over, whose broken bridge increased the aspect of desolation around us. And who was to warrant us that from behind any of the rocks on these hill ridges, over which we had to march, we should not be suddenly greeted by

A desolate region of horror.

A gloomy march.

A WELCOME REINFORCEMENT. 377

a volley from the Arab followers of Karema? Who could have deemed his own life secure from one five minutes to another, by day or by night?

So we went on, anxious and gloomy, and joyless was the time spent in the dreary encampment, which no longer yielded us any sustenance. Thus we travelled on, two days more, past Kigogorro and Numuyango, until, on February 25th, the road suddenly began to become lively once more. In the first instance, I received on this day the answer to my letter from Ischioragama, which informed me that the king had given no order whatever to stop me anywhere. On the contrary, he was desirous that I should come to him as soon as possible. *Answer to Dr. Peters's letter.*

The road, which for the last part of the way had wound round Murchison Bay in a north-westerly direction, turned suddenly to the southward. At this point some of Muanga's soldiers were stationed, who welcomed us with joyful shouts, presenting us with golden-yellow bananas, and pledging us in foaming drinks from mighty pitchers. *A scene of brightness and joy.*

We were approaching Kisallosallo, a plantation of the king's, some miles to the north of the capital, Rubaja-Mengo. From all sides Muanga's soldiers hurried up; their line of outposts had been pushed forward during the last two days as far as Kisallosallo. We now reached the place, and were so far in safety, since the united fighting power of Muanga and my own men would be sufficient to stand against the Arabs, Wanjoros, and the Mahdi's followers from the north.

We pitched our camp in Kisallosallo, and I immediately sent messengers to the king, to announce to him our arrival in the neighbourhood of his capital. I learned that I should meet Muanga in the morning at Mengo, and that the French mission intended to transfer its quarters thither from Bulingogwe on the following night. *Message to King Muanga.*
In the evening Muanga's drum-band met us, to honour us with a tattoo, and to accompany us solemnly on the following morning into the capital.

The early dawn found us, as usual, on the march. A broad

road led us over two more ridges of hills, now ever in a southerly direction; from all sides crowds of people came hurrying along, either to offer us joyful greetings or in respectful silence to watch us as we marched by. To the right

Approach to the capital. I noticed a line of buildings, which looked, from a distance, like pyramids, but were in reality cone-shaped. I learned afterwards that they were funeral monuments of Mtesas and the kings of the Wakintu dynasty.

Suddenly, a handsomely-dressed servant of Muanga's hurried up to me, murmured a few words, and vanished as swiftly as he had appeared. Marco informed me that he brought a message from Muanga, which expressed the anxiety of his master to see me at once. This was repeated three or four times.

A hill now rose up before me, on which I perceived some buildings. This, I was told, was Mengo. At the bottom of this hill we wheeled round towards the left hand, to turn into a banana grove, where a flourishing plantation had been set apart for us for our temporary abode. I quartered my soldiers in the huts, but had the tents set up for ourselves, according to my custom. I then made a hasty toilet and shaved myself, ready to present myself before the king.

Every five minutes messengers appeared from his majesty always repeating the same entreaty, that we would come as quickly as possible,—the king was dying of eagerness to behold us. This is Uganda courtesy, with which we were here made

Solemn procession. acquainted for the first time. We dressed ourselves and the soldiers, with a few selected porters, were marched up. With the flag borne in advance, we went slowly along the wide road up to Mengo, to pay our first greeting to Muanga, the Mfalme and Kabaka of Uganda.

The farther we advanced up the hill, the more dense became the throng. On the top of the hill was an enclosed space, like a meadow, into which we entered through a gate. To right and left were drawn up Muanga's soldiers, presenting arms lining the approaches to an impromptu hall of audience, built of reeds. The roll was beaten on European drums, and

RECEPTION BY MUANGA.

trumpets were blown, while we passed slowly through the line of soldiers, saluting as we went. At the entrance of the hall my Somalis were drawn up on guard, and we stepped forward into the closely-packed area, filled with the great men of Uganda, who sat or stood against the walls to the right and left. As soon as we had come inside the hall a man, still young in years, and dressed in complete European costume, rose from a seat at the far end of the room. His dark eyes were fixed on us with a kindly look; a dark beard surrounded his face, which had quite an European cast. His nose and mouth were regularly shaped; the latter certainly was rather large, but was remarkable for faultlessly white and beautiful teeth. His whole appearance had in it something which was, at the first glance, both agreeable and sympathetic. This was Muanga, King of Uganda, known for a long time past in the European press as the "bloodhound" Muanga. He wore a coat, trousers, and waistcoat of black and white check, which gave him the look of a well-to-do European gentleman in summer costume.

"Step this way," he said, in fluent Suahili (Karibu), advancing at the same time a few steps towards us and pressing our hands. "How are you? Take a seat!" pointing to two chairs which had been placed for us at his right hand.

At this moment I was addressed in French by a gentleman whom, at the first glance, I should not have taken to be an European. He was dressed in a long white garment, and had a small red cap on his head.

"Je suis le père Lourdel, et je vous ai envoyé des lettres."

This, then, was the Superior of the Catholic Mission in Uganda. He told me at once that he had only come over from Bulingogwe on the previous night, and that they had all, for the moment, established themselves, in a makeshift way for the time being, round Mengo. Immediately upon this, two more Europeans appeared in the doorway, and greeted us in the English language. These were Messrs. Gordon and Walker. During the formal ceremony of this reception, I witnessed the spectacle of my old friend Kamanyiro Kanta crawling on all fours to greet the king, according to the ancient Waganda custom; his majesty, however, received the homage with extraordinary coldness and indifference.

"I rejoice, Muanga, to behold the Kabaka of Uganda," were the words with which I opened our conversation. "I have *Address to* journeyed from the east up the Tana, past Mount *the king.* Kenia, and have had to fight with the Gallas, the Massais, and many others, and learned in Usoga that Emin Pasha, to whom I was marching, had gone away with Stanley, and that you were in need of help from Europeans. Therefore I have come across the Nile and marched hither through your territory."

"I have heard that you have beaten the Massais, and I know that the Germans understand war and are all soldiers. I welcome you. I am glad that Germans especially should come to visit my country. Now tell me of your combats with the Massais."

"The Massais are very savage," I said, "and are no friends to the white men. They dared to make attacks on my expe-*Dr. Peters's* dition, but we beat them back four times, killed a *explanation.* great number of them, burnt many of their villages, and drove off plenty of their herds."

Muanga laughed, well pleased at this description.

"The white men are not generally liked in the east of your land," I continued. "In Kawirondo, also, we were obliged to beat the Mangati."

"That too we have heard about here," answered Muanga. "Where have you your artillery?"

"I have left my artillery behind with the Gallas. Perhaps a second column of my expedition will march after me here, and if so I hope they will bring my artillery with them; if they do I will make you a present of it."

"I thank you much," he said. "I hope you will stay here with me, and wait for the second column. Anything that you *Muanga's* wish to have in my country shall be yours; only make *friendliness.* known your wishes, and send direct to me when there is anything you wish to have. I intend to have a large house built for you close to my own."

"I cannot stay long with you, because I must go onward to the German colony on the other side of the lake. If you choose to send any message by me to the coast, and I can be in any way of service to you, it shall likewise be done."

"I should like to send a message by you to the coast, but we will not speak of that to-day."

Everything that Muanga said gave us the impression of quiet, modest frankness, and when we parted from him at the close of our half-hour's interview we carried away with us the most favourable impression. We had imagined him to be a very different man. Mr. Gordon and Mr. Walker accompanied us to our tent, where, unfortunately, I could regale them with nothing better than tea and coffee. Directly afterwards Mons. Lourdel appeared, who stayed on after the Englishmen had gone away. He soon turned the conversation on the state of affairs in Uganda, and gave me details of the English proposals, *Père Lourdel's ideas.* which, he said, had afterwards come to nothing, since Mr. Jackson not only never came himself, but would not even send powder and ammunition." I asked him,—

"Does the king wish for any kind of European Protectorate at all?"

"Certainly not. Even during the time of his banishment from Uganda, we were only able, after much persuasion, to get him to enter upon any negotiation of the kind."

"Well, then, he should address himself to the European Powers, with the request that they would constitute his land neutral ground, exactly as has been done in the case of the Congo State. If we could get the Upper Nile neutralised, all the European Powers would be equally benefited thereby. Only Muanga would certainly then be obliged to make up his mind to adopt throughout his territory certain universally recognised principles of international law." *Dr. Peters's advice to the king.*

"Do you think that such a proposal on Muanga's part would find favour in Europe?"

"That I am unable to say. You know that I am sent out by a private German committee to the relief of Emin Pasha, to whom I thought of making a similar proposition. I have no kind of commission for Uganda from my committee; I have no official commission from Germany at all; but if Muanga is prepared to make proposals of the kind to the European Powers, I shall be very willing, for my part, to take charge of them and deliver them there. First of all, however, Muanga would have to accept the articles of the Congo Act for his own territory, and to furnish guarantees to the Powers that the slave trade and the exportation of slaves shall be suppressed in his own country."

Offer to carry proposals to Europe.

"The king will be very ready to do that, for he hates the Arabs, and, moreover, cannot witness with satisfaction the dragging away of his subjects. Before we brought him back from Usukuma to Uganda, we often held conversations with him on this subject. In the meantime we should have to reckon with the intrigues of the English in carrying out such plans."

"I cannot understand what interest England can have in proclaiming a Protectorate just here in Uganda."

"England wants the monopoly of trade."

"Such a thing is not possible on the face of it, since Uganda lies within the zone of land in which free trade is established by the Congo Act. A Protectorate without a monopoly of the kind would only be an expense to the English. If Muanga were to offer to us Germans the Protectorate of Uganda, and I were asked my opinion about it in Germany, I do not know whether I should not decidedly advise the rejection of the offer. England is in exactly the same position."

Conflicting interests.

Thus I came to an agreement with Mons. Lourdel as to the plan of our task on the very first morning.

In the afternoon, Herr von Tiedemann and myself were invited to dine at the English station. It was situated to the north of the capital, and was naturally of a very primitive description, as all the former buildings had been destroyed in the insurrection; but the sensation of being once more the guests of Europeans had in it, to our thinking, something extremely delightful.

After the dinner Muanga's minister, who bears the title Katikiro, made his appearance, to hold some conversation with

DESIGNS FOR THE FUTURE. 383

me on business. This personage was, like all the higher officials in Uganda, still quite a young man, with a very energetic and crafty cast of features, which did not make an altogether pleasant impression. He asked quite openly,— *Visit of the Katikiro.*

"What presents do you intend to make the king?"

"I will give him from one hundred to one hundred and twenty pounds of fine gunpowder, a Lancaster repeating rifle with fifty cartridges, a thousand percussion caps, and a number of small things besides, such as soaps, etc."

"And how long do you think of staying here? We are hoping for a visit of at least three to four months. Karema has posted himself in the north, and may at any moment attack the capital. So long as you are with us, this will scarcely happen, for he has already retreated northward on the advance of your expedition. Then, too, the fugitives from our Christian parties will be coming back to Uganda, from all directions, and our position will be materially improved thereby."

"I regret that I cannot stay here from three to four months under any circumstances. I have no commission of any kind to tarry here in Uganda; every day my expedition costs 50 marks (£2 10s.) in wages for my people. I am prepared"—(here I began to make a calculation)—"to remain here until March 16th; to-day is February 26th,—that makes three weeks." *Question of length of residence.*

"This is not the 26th, but the 25th of February," said the English missionaries.

"Excuse me," I said, opening my diary, "to-day is the 26th of February."

"Well, we make this the 25th of February," said both of them.

It turned out afterwards that by some oversight we had really got a day in advance in our calculations, and that the Englishmen were right. I have, nevertheless, always kept to our own reckoning in my previous account, because we were no longer able to verify on which day the disarrangement of dates had occurred.

"Be that as it may, we will fix March 16th, once for

all, as the day of my departure from Uganda. I have not enough ammunition to be able to propose to the king that I should attack and beat Karema and the Wanjoro in the north. If Karema, on the other hand, should advance towards the south, I should be prepared to support Muanga with my whole expedition, and, if he wished it, I would take the command of his people. If I am to do that, however, I must request that I shall be allowed to drill the soldiers, and, above all, the officers of his troops, every day from this time forward, so that they may become accustomed to our method of fighting."

Necessity for discipline.

After a long consultation, Katikiro declared himself satisfied with this agreement, which, to a certain extent, was concluded under the guarantee of the English mission, and which afterwards was accepted likewise by Muanga and the Roman Catholic party. By March 16th, I was confidently assured, the boats should be on the spot, to transport me over Lake Victoria to Usukuma.

On the following day there was another solemn reception held by Muanga, when I presented him with the gifts I had brought. Muanga was exceedingly pleased, for the hundred pounds of powder enabled him to provide five hundred of his soldiers once more with ammunition for a fight, a thing that under existing circumstances might be of the greatest importance to the maintenance of his throne.

Second audience of Muanga.

In the afternoon Herr von Tiedemann and I, dressed in uniform, paid a visit to the Catholic mission. Here we were introduced to Father Denoit by our acquaintance of the previous day, Father Lourdel. While Father Lourdel was an extremely energetic-looking man, with strong features, we beheld in Father Denoit, who may have been about thirty years of age, a figure that recalled St. John, with a mild, gentle face, with dark beard, the eyes of an enthusiast, and a very sensitively-formed mouth. Both of them belonged to the Algerian Mission, the so-called "White Brothers," and Father Lourdel had been already labouring for ten years in Uganda.

Visit to the French mission.

On my asking if he did not feel a longing to go back once again to his home in France, he replied,—" We have come here to die; we shall never return to our country."

He could have had no foreboding at that time how soon these words of his were to be fulfilled. He was accustomed to say also, " Si nous sommes en bonne santé nous ne voulons pas, et si nous sommes malades nous ne pouvons pas retourner" (" If we are well in health we will not, if we are ill we cannot return ").

I expressed to him my admiration of the courageous self-sacrifice shown by his Order. In the years during which that Order had laboured by the lake it had lost fifty per cent. of its brethren by sickness. I said to Father Lourdel,—

"People talk so much of us travellers, of Emin Pasha, Stanley, and others; what you are doing here is in reality much more heroic, and you do it exclusively for your great Ideal. Your names are scarcely mentioned by us in Europe; and the ambition which urges others on never enters into your calculations." *Various kinds of heroes.*

"We expect to receive our reward after death, if the Lord wills it so."

I have learned to know the work of this Catholic mission, everywhere round about the lake, in Uganda, on the Sesse Islands, and Usukuma, and I must express my sincere admiration for the achievements of these men. For the very reason that they have taken on themselves the vows of poverty, obedience, and chastity, because they may not possess any property of their own, nor ever look forward to returning permanently to their homes, they have a double interest in making their stations as comfortable as possible; and as they receive very little assistance from Europe, they are compelled to develop, to the utmost of their power, the natural advantages of the country. As the Protestant missionaries on Lake Victoria really work there only temporarily for salaries, and since they have before them the desire of returning, sooner or later, to England, and after that of finding some little provision awaiting them in London, they *Thoroughness of Catholic missions.*

are themselves less identified with the mission, they do not take root in the land in the same way, and consequently cannot be of so much use to the country. What I have seen of the English missions shows them to be behind the French ones in every particular. The Catholics have everywhere large and convenient houses, covered by far-projecting roofs, with pillared verandahs, which enable the inhabitants to protect themselves from the heat of the sun, and to take bodily exercise even in rainy weather. At these mission stations I found, everywhere I went, gardens, in which not only tropical vegetables, but all kinds of European vegetables were grown.

Practical means of success. While the English missionaries were obliged to live just as the natives do as to food, the Roman Catholics enjoyed European potatoes, bread and butter, cheese, which they made themselves, brandy manufactured from burnt bananas, colerabi, turnips, greens of all kinds, pineapples, oranges, and other fruits for dessert. While the English lived in badly-built houses, every Roman Catholic Father or Brother had his own cool whitewashed room, and they assembled for their meals in a pleasant refectory. As they cannot obtain any European labour in the country, and yet wish to establish themselves comfortably there, they are obliged, as indeed they are enjoined to do by the rules of their Order, to use all possible care in training their people to work. If they want to have tables, chairs, kitchen utensils, they must get them made by their pupils, and they have, therefore, a particular interest in teaching the people to make these articles properly. Hence again the system of *frères*, or brothers, serving for this purpose, is also especially practical, one or more of them are attached to each station. A settlement of industrious and skilled workmen is formed in this way by means of the Catholic mission, which consequently exerts a most beneficial influence upon its surroundings, and upon the whole land.

Mechanical ingenuity developed.

It is true that on February 27th there was not much to be seen of the Catholic station in Uganda. It had been destroyed by the Arab faction, and only the foundation walls were left standing. Mons. Lourdel, like all the rest, had been obliged to domicile himself in a makeshift fashion, and received me in a hall surrounded by a fence. Here we partook of tea, to which Monseigneur Lourdel contributed a tin of sardines in oil, a rare treat for us, and one which recalled memories of our distant home. {Mons. Lourdel's quarters.}

From the Catholic Mission we returned, under the convoy of Mons. Lourdel, to King Muanga. I was desirous, as soon as

A MISSIONARY AT THE PLOUGH.

possible, to convert the arrangements which I had drawn up the day before, in concert with Lourdel, into accomplished facts, and for that purpose I had asked for a private interview with the King of Uganda. We found Muanga, attended by only a few of his followers, sitting in a room of one of his houses, which sprang up like mushrooms in daily increasing numbers. Access is gained to the interior of the palace through a perfect labyrinth of courts, passages, and gateways, in which it is customary to station the soldiers of Uganda by day and night. Close by are buildings erected for {King Muanga's palace.}

the king's women and for his other court attendants. The whole place produced upon me an impression such as I always associated in imagination with the court of Attila in Hungary. All the buildings are of unplaned wood, but their spaciousness, and the great number of the rooms, give them an appearance of grandeur and suitability.

When we entered Muanga's presence, he, at my request, dismissed all his servants, and, without my asking him, he sent into the adjoining rooms to see if there were any persons there who might overhear our conversation. Père Lourdel then whispered my proposal in the ears of Muanga, whereupon Muanga took hold of Lourdel by the ear that he might in turn whisper his reply. The result of this somewhat singular interview was Muanga's declaration:—

Private interview with the king.

"If the Doctor will carry my message to Europe, I am willing to make a treaty with him, in which I resign, in favour of the Germans and the other Europeans, the right of the Mfalme that the people of Uganda may only travel, carry on trade, and build houses by his permission. I am also prepared to sell my ivory to none but the German Company, if they will supply me in exchange with powder and ammunition. I will be the servant of no European. They shall all have equal rights in my country, but I prefer to conclude friendship with the great Sultan of the Germans alone. If the Doctor will draw up a treaty to this effect, I will sign it, and I will see that all my chiefs put their names to it too."

Muanga's declaration.

This was exactly what I was aiming at. If I succeeded in binding the King of Uganda to such promises, I believed that I should do great service to the whole European cause.

Everyone who reads the accounts of travel in Uganda knows what restrictions on their freedom of movement are encountered by Europeans in this country. Felkin and Stanley, Emin Pasha and Juncker, have all experienced this. If the king accepted the principles of the Congo Act, the country would for the first time be really thrown open to European traffic. And that must be to the common advantage of all the nations who have any interests on the coast territory.

I immediately repaired to my tent with Mons. Lourdel, and proposed to him the following draft of the treaty, which, with a few alterations in the style, suggested by Lourdel, has been retained. The treaty was drawn up in French, in the language of Kiganda and in Kiswahili, and it was afterwards signed in all three languages. I have inserted it in the appendix in the French and Kiganda text; and I subjoin here a verbatim translation:— *Draft of a treaty prepared.*

"MENGO, *Feb.* 28*th*, 1890.

"Between King Muanga, Kabaka of Buganda, and Dr. Carl Peters, the following preliminary treaty has been agreed upon:—

"The King Muanga accepts the decrees of the Berlin Treaty (Congo Act) of February 1885, so far as they have reference to Buganda and its tributary countries. He throws open these countries to the subjects of His Majesty the German Emperor as to all other Europeans. He guarantees to the subjects of His Majesty the German Emperor, as to all other Europeans who may wish to avail themselves of it, entire freedom of trade, and the right of travel and settlement in Buganda and all tributary states.

"King Muanga enters into friendship with His Majesty the German Emperor, and receives for his subjects permission to trade, with the right of free passage and of settlement in all the territories of His Majesty the German Emperor. *Articles of the Uganda treaty.*

"Dr. Carl Peters undertakes to propose the ratification of this preliminary treaty to the German government.

"This treaty is drawn up in Kiganda, Kiswahili, and French. In case of any disputed interpretation, the French text alone shall be considered as binding."

On the following day, February 28th, we finished the three drafts of this treaty; and on March 1st I went again to Muanga with Mons. Lourdel, and was received by the king in his cabinet council. He had with him his two ministers, Cyprian, the minister of his household, called Kanta, the real minister of state, Katikiro, with a few other great men. I laid before them the principal heads of the treaty, explaining to them that since Uganda had become Christian, and the Christian party was here in the ascendant, it was necessary to frame the treaty in its general particulars according to European principles.

Interview with the ministers of state.

"The European powers," I continued, "in a treaty which was concluded in Berlin in 1885, have come to an agreement concerning certain general principles of law respecting Africa. I wish to see these accepted also by the Waganda, and I have accordingly drawn up the following treaty," which I then caused to be read aloud in the Kiganda language. "I now call upon you to sign it."

The king and Cyprian Kanta signed immediately, after Muanga had declared that he wished to enter into the same relation to the European powers as that in which the Sultan of Zanzibar stood towards them.

Signing of the treaty.

The Katikiro, the leader of the English party in Uganda, refused to affix his signature, saying that he wished first to talk over the affair with Messrs. Gordon and Walker.

The Katikiro's refusal.

This brought the whole matter to its second stage. The refusal of Katikiro had now made a conflict necessary, to bring the treaty to a full recognition by the government of Uganda.

I was the more determined to carry the matter through, when in Uganda the great importance of these countries from a political and commercial point of view became abundantly clear to me. Ivory comes pouring in, to Uganda, in the form of tribute, and as an article of trade to be exchanged for food and other things, from all the states to the north and west of Lake Victoria, as far as the Albert Nyanza, to be despatched from Uganda across Lake Victoria to Tabora and the coast. A good part of the trade of Uganda, which cannot indeed be calculated, but which anyone who understands African affairs may estimate from the fact that from sixty to eighty Arabs have settled in this country, has to do with the customs levied along the coast by the German trading company. The

Important trade of Ugnada.

same thing is shown by the quantities of European weapons, of ammunition, stuffs, manufactured ivory, and other articles to be found in Uganda. For all these articles have come, in the last place, from the coast and from Zanzibar, to be sold in exchange for ivory. The Arabs in Uganda cultivated the closest relations with their co-religionists in Tabora, and carried on, as factors, the exchange of goods between that place and Uganda, and indeed beyond Uganda to the north. As I was able to ascertain, gunpowder was carried to Unjoro by means of the Kimbulus in Busiba (Karague), and, as I was told in Uganda, even to the Mahdi himself. The whole traffic, therefore, of the Victoria Nyanza lies in the Tabora trade ; and all great commercial and political disturbances in Uganda must accordingly make themselves felt immediately in the traffic and barter on the coast, and also in the revenue drawn from the customs of Bagamoyo and Dar-es-Salam. The Uganda ivory filters through a thousand channels, apart from the direct exportation of the purchased goods across the lake to the south. It is the great medium of exchange for these regions, and passes perhaps through six, seven, or even more hands before it reaches Tabora or Irangi, where the Arabs have likewise settled ; and arriving at the coast, is absorbed into the commerce of the world. This internal trade is engaged in, among others, by the inhabitants of the island of Bukerebe, whose carvans of traders I have seen myself both in Busiba and also in Usukuma. They pay with fish and articles of iron, which they, on their side, exchange again in Usukuma. I think that in estimating the political and commercial affairs of East Africa too little stress is laid on this internal trade among the tribes. In it lies the chief investment of the slave trade. But there is another series of products, which have, as it seems, been exchanged for centuries between tribe and tribe. Thus Usukuma supplies hoes and iron goods to the tribes as far as Usoga. We sometimes met caravans coming from the southeast, as we were marching through the steppes. When I asked them, " Where to ? " they answered, " We are going to Usukuma." " What do you want there ? " " We want to buy hoes" (yembe). In this way it is that the barter trade of Uganda along the coast defies all direct calculation. It can probably be ascertained only in Uganda itself. But the facts which I have mentioned above leave no doubt of its importance as a whole.

As Uganda is entirely shut off from any approach from the east, the promotion of traffic in Uganda, which I had most urgently pressed upon Muanga, would in the first place be of the greatest advantage to traders from the German territory, but would in the end be of service to every nation that desired to enter *Arbitrary* into any undertaking in these countries,—among others *restrictions* especially to Mr. Stokes, whose agents I had met in *by the kings.* various places round the lake, and to the English missionaries, who after the ratification of this treaty were preserved from the fate which had often befallen them before, namely, from being forbidden by the king, for months at a time, to leave their houses, even to take a walk, which had happened to Messrs. Gordon and Walker; or from being suddenly banished from the kingdom, as Mr. Mackay had been; and from many similar restrictions of personal freedom.

I was therefore the more surprised when Mr. Gordon and Mr. Walker, who dined with me on the evening of March 10th, *Objections* told me that they must dispute Muanga's right of *of Gordon* entering into negotiations with a third power, since he *and Walker.* had already placed himself under British protection. On the other hand, this objection certainly gave me a welcome opportunity of formally and definitely bringing the affair to a conclusion.

I therefore wrote, putting a formal question to King Muanga. The English had told me, I said, that he was de-
Dr. Peters's pendent upon the British East Africa Company, and *letter to* had no longer the right to conclude treaties with any *the king.* other persons. Before I could proceed further in the affair, I must first know how this matter stood, as I had no intention of carrying an invalid treaty back to Europe. I must beg that not only Muanga, but also the great men of the country, would declare whether they were dependent (watuma—

slaves) on the English, or whether the king had still the same right as that enjoyed by Mtesa.

Meanwhile, on March 2nd, the treaty was signed in the house of Mons. Lourdel, and afterwards in my tent, by all the great men and governors of provinces of the Catholic party, who formed the majority in the country. On the morning of March 3rd Muanga assembled a state council, to which were invited all the great men of the land, and also the princesses of the house of Wakintu, as many of them, namely, as had escaped the murderous hands of Karema. I was the last man to arrive. The two Englishmen did not know what was the business on hand. Muanga first disposed of a number of less important matters of state, appointments of governors, and so on. Then I rose, and spoke to the following effect:— *Great assembly concerning the treaty.*

"I have come hither, at your request, to help you against the Arabs. I have become Muanga's friend and yours. We are all Christians; we all know the words of Jesus and love them; the white men and the Waganda are quite the same. It is necessary, therefore, that the Waganda should acknowledge the same things to be right towards us white men, which we in our countries acknowledge to be right towards them. When people from Uganda wish to come to Germany, they could travel, and live, and carry on their trade wherever they choose; and they can do the same if they go to France or to England. I demand that you Waganda should grant the same right to us Europeans; not to us Germans only, but to all Europeans, to whatever nation they may belong. Muanga has declared himself willing to give up the right claimed by Mtesa, of forbidding the white men to travel or trade in Uganda, or of banishing them out of the country whenever he likes. He has concluded a treaty with me to this effect. In this treaty he asks for the friendship of the great Emperor of the Germans. Now the Englishmen who are sitting here by me come to me and say, Muanga and the Waganda have no longer any right at all to make such treaties; they say that the Waganda have become the slaves of the English. Therefore *Full freedom of residence for white men.*

I ask the question of you Waganda—Have the Englishmen spoken what is the truth? Then I will tear up the treaty. Or have they spoken what is not the truth? Then declare it now openly."

These words called forth such a storm of indignation against the Englishmen from the whole assembly of the Waganda that I feared for a moment it would lead to acts of violence. Then Muanga sprang up from his throne and said, addressing himself particularly to Messrs. Gordon and Walker,—

Excitement in the assembly.

"You have heard what Dottore Patasi has said. Now tell me yourselves whether his words are true; whether you really did go to him and tell him what he has stated, or not."

A little taken aback, Mr. Gordon now explained that certainly the king had accepted the flag of the British East African Company, and that that was the same thing as accepting the British Protectorate. Such, at least, was their interpretation of it, and that was what they had told me.

Mr. Gordon's explanation.

To this Muanga made answer,—

"You all know that when we were on the island of Lake Victoria, we sent messengers both to Stanley and to Mr. Jackson, saying, 'Come and help us, and we will accept the English flag, and grant to the English a monopoly of trade in Uganda.' The Englishman alone was to be allowed to trade in Uganda. Bring me back upon Mtesa's throne, and it shall be as I have written. What happened then? Stanley, who came from Unjoro with Amdallemin, refused to listen to the entreaties of his Christian brothers, and made a wide circuit round Uganda. Mr. Jackson, who had been staying with many soldiers for a long time in Kawirondo, not only did not come himself to our assistance, but did not send a single cartridge or a handful of gunpowder to help us; and now the Englishmen say that because Mr. Jackson sent me his flag in a parcel I must consider myself to be under British protection. The only people who have come to our aid are the Doctor and the Germans (Badutschi). If I placed my land under any one's protection,

Muanga's plain speech.

it would be under that of the great Emperor of the Germans. But I will remain like Mtesa, I will belong to no one. They shall all be welcome in Uganda. If the Germans desire to come, let them come; if the French wish to come, let them come; if the English wish to come (and you can write this to Mr. Jackson), and wish to have the same right as the Germans, they shall be equally welcome. But if they wish to 'eat up' my land, I will make war upon them, for we Waganda will be free, and I will remain what Mtesa was."

Common rights for all Europeans.

This speech was received with what in Europe we should call "enthusiastic applause," in which the whole assembly joined, with the exception of a few leaders of the English party.

Every one sprang up and pressed forward to shake Muanga by the hand.

I then rose for the second time.

"I have heard your words, O King! and I see that you and your chiefs are agreed, and I know that you and all your chiefs will sign the treaty. Hear now what I intend to do to show you that I am really the friend of the Waganda. I hear, Muanga, that to the west of Lake Victoria there are still enemies, allies of Karema, who refuse to pay you the tribute which they owe. I am told that, in Busiba particularly, there is Kimbulu, who gets gunpowder from Unyanyembe for your enemies in Unjoro. If you want to make war in the north, you must first of all have the whole south in your power. I am ready to help you to do this. Give me some boats and a few men, and I will force the people of Busiba to acknowledge you, Muanga, as their lord, to pay you tribute, and banish Kimbulu out of the country. In this way I think to secure for you a safe communication with our German colony and with your friends the Christians on the coast."

Dr. Peters proposes to fight Kimbulu.

The king laughed aloud for joy when I had ended my speech, and the other Waganda, including Gabriel, the commander of the Waganda troops, came up to thank me for my offer. Then Muanga rose once more and repeated, "that all may know it,"—

"I am the son of Mtesa, and what Mtesa was in Uganda that will I also continue to be, and against every one who will not have it so I will make war."

The assembly dismissed. He then turned round suddenly and disappeared through a door at the back of the hall into his private apartments, thus putting an end to the sitting.

Upon this the stream of people, led by M. Lourdel, rushed to the house of the Katikiro, the leader of the English party.

To the Katikiro's house. I preferred to take no part in this assembly, by which Katikiro was to be forced to add his signature, and I withdrew to my tent. The crowd meanwhile demanded of Katikiro that he should either sign the treaty or resign.

In the afternoon Messrs. Gordon and Walker came to me and informed me that the deputation had very nearly come to blows, and that the temper of the people had been inflamed to such a degree that they feared the evening might witness a general butchery.

"Show us the treaty," they said; "we will read it, and then decide what we ought to do."

They then at once read the text, and it was Mr. Walker who said to Gordon, "I really think we should get our people to sign to the affair."

I answered,—

"You must know best what attitude you ought to take up. I attach no importance to the signature of the chiefs, because *Explanation to the missionaries.* the king's name legally binds Uganda with regard to other states. Moreover, in case of any collision between the two parties, which I should extremely deplore, and which I am resolved to endeavour to prevent, I offer you a refuge in my camp. For my own part, I shall give orders to fire on whichever party fires the first shot."

I then wrote at once the following letter for Mons. Lourdel:—

"MENGO RUBAGA, *Mars 4th*, 1890.

"BIEN CHER MONSIEUR,—J'apprends que les deux parties chrétiennes vont faire guerre entre elles-mêmes.

"Je crois que ceci sera la fin de la dynastie, par ce qu'il

enforcerait à l'Angleterre la nécessité d'une occupation, et je suis sûr que vous ferez tout ce qu'est dans votre puissance pour pacifier les cœurs de nos hommes et empêcher des actes de violence.

" J'expecte avec beaucoup d'interêt la réponse du roi sur ma proposition.

" Veuillez agreer, mon cher monsieur, les sentiments les plus respectueux de votre serviteur

" CARL PETERS."

(TRANSLATION.)

" MENGO RUBAGA, *March 4th,* 1890.

" DEAR SIR,—I am informed that the two Christian factions are on the point of commencing hostilities against each other.

" I think that this would be the end of the dynasty, because it would force upon England the necessity of an occupation. I am convinced that you will do all in your power to tranquillise the minds of your people and to prevent any outbreak of violence.

" I await with much interest the answer of the king to my proposal.

" I am, dear Sir,
" Respectfully and faithfully yours,
" CARL PETERS."

On the evening of this day, all the great men of the English party, with the Katikiro at their head, came and signed the treaty. On the other hand, I received a reassuring communication from M. Lourdel, to the effect that they, the missionaries, were there to do the works of peace, and not of war, and that it was a matter of course that they would make every effort in their power to secure peace ; which indeed was not in any way threatened, as no one meditated resorting to acts of violence.

The conclusion of my letter referred to a proposal which I had laid before the king on March 3rd, in which I urged him to place his admiral, the Djumba, at my disposal, in order to get together as many boats as possible among the Sesse Islands, for the projected expedition to the west of the lake. To give this affair more importance, I wished to send Herr von Tiedemann also to Sesse, where he would find safe quarters with Monseigneur Livinhac in the French mission station.

<small>Boats required for the expedition.</small>

At the same time I drew up a short report, to the German general consulate in Zanzibar, of the proceedings in Uganda, and the treaty which I had concluded, and despatched it direct to Usukuma, by a boat which the king had given me for the purpose. My own sentiments during this time are shown in a letter addressed to Dr. Arendt, written at the same time, and sent with the report across Lake Victoria :—

"RUBAGA IN UGANDA, *March 7th*, 1890.

"DEAR ARENDT,—You will, I daresay, have received the telegraphic communication that my expedition had penetrated to the boundaries of Emin Pasha's territory, when I received the information of his departure just in time to be able to turn to the south-west and march to Uganda. Strictly speaking, I had perfectly fulfilled my mission in Wachore's capital, for, as Emin Pasha could testify, there was no longer any difficulty in advancing from thence to Fauvera, where Emin once had a station. At this present time I am not very far away from Mwutan-Nzige, and could betake myself thither at any moment if Emin Pasha were still there, instead of the Mahdi and the rebels of the Equatorial Province. Emin Pasha, or Stanley, or Dr. Felkin, or indeed any one acquainted with the affairs of these localities would be able to confirm this statement for me. In any other country I could do without such a confirmation, since I myself know better than anyone else with what tension of nerve this result was attained. In Germany, I am anxious to have some such certificate to prove that I have accomplished my task like an honest man.

<small>Letter to Herr Arendt.</small>

"Without assuming to tell you anything new, I may also

make the following statement. Three times during my expedition the English have crossed my path ;. and each time, under very various circumstances, I have been fortunate enough to hold my own against them. *Opposition overcome.* The first time they wanted to close the way to Witu against me, and afterwards to prevent my advance from that place to the Tana. I have put an end to English influence in Oda-Boru-Ruva, and set up the German influence in its place. Then, according to Mr. de Winton's prophecy, I was to find an English expedition at Baringo. The English expeditions were obliged to turn back in the steppes of the Upper Tana, through which I made my way, and the German flag now waves over Baringo. Lastly, the English had already sent their flag to Uganda, and everything was ripe for the British protectorate. The English flag is now withdrawn from this place, and the king, Muanga, has recently solemnly withdrawn from English protection, or rather from his consent to it, and I am bringing back with me a treaty of commerce and peace.

"I have had occasion, in carrying out this expedition, to fight, one after another, the Wagalla, Wandorobbo, Wadsagga, Wakikuju, Massai, Wakamasia, Waelgejo, and Mangati tribes. None of these tribes have been able to check my advance, and they have all learnt to fear the German flag. *Advantages to the German flag.* I have attained this result with fifteen Askaris and about fifty bearers; and with articles of barter collected in Lamu from the refuse of the stock of the encampment, which had been described to us as probably sufficient for the march between Tana and Oda-Boru-Ruva. Such, my dear Arendt, is the German Emin Pasha Expedition, from the Bay of Kwaihu to the capital of Uganda :—Tana, and Baringo, and the Nile!

"The most important achievement of the expedition is undoubtedly the affair of Uganda. It was 1884 over again, but in a grander style. . . . I tell you these things, my dear Arendt, not from any feeling of boastfulness, but because I desire to make my standpoint clear in the sight of all men. For I cannot tell whether I shall return, having now undertaken the task of clearing the west of Lake Victoria of the Arabs, and if my cartridges hold out I intend afterwards marching on Unjanjembe, to observe for myself the position of Tippoo Tib.

"An effort has been made to hinder me from taking any share in my old work; and Fate has given me its revenge in truly grand fashion. If I fall, it shall not be in faint-hearted fashion, but proudly, and the German flag which I have carried thus far shall be spread over me for a pall. I have always been anxious, in my own way, to raise it to honour. That I have differed from the majority of my countrymen in my idea of the manner in which this was to be effected has been not the most unimportant reason of the hatred and vituperation which I have encountered in Germany. But I love the black, white, and red flag none the less passionately on that account, and for the rest a good deal of the blame is my own. . . .

"Uganda, a splendid country, is at present trodden down by war. . . .

"With kindest regards,
"Yours,
"CARL PETERS.

"POSTSCRIPT, *March 8th.*—A former servant of Emin Pasha's is just now sitting by my side. I have to-day succeeded in gaining from Muanga the prohibition of the export of slaves from his country.—C. P."

I sent to the Englishmen in Kawirondo a copy of the treaty in French, accompanied by the following letter:—

"Dr. Peters begs to enclose the above copy to the gentlemen of the B. E. A. A. Expedition, with the information that King Muanga yesterday, at a public meeting, at which the gentlemen of the English Mission attended, has declared himself free from any engagements which the B. E. A. A. may claim upon his letters addressed to Mr. Jackson, as the conditions, he thinks, have not been fulfilled which he made his terms under the protection of the abovesaid Company.

Explanatory letter to the English.

"Dr. Carl Peters leaves this entirely to be settled between the two parties, and thinks that his treaty does not injure the rights of any European nation."

PLEASANT QUARTERS IN UGANDA. 401

On March 6th I received the king's decision concerning my proposal of collecting boats at the Sesse Islands. Muanga declared himself willing to send his admiral thither, and to allow Herr von Tiedemann to travel in the same boat to the French Mission. I accordingly at once gave instructions to Herr von Tiedemann to hold himself in readiness to start on the following morning. The Djumba, however, did not appear at the time appointed, and Herr von Tiedemann had to defer his departure until the following day.

On the morning of March 8th he betook himself, with his personal attendants, to the shore of Lake Victoria, opposite to the island of Bulingogwe, and already on the day afterwards I received the information that he passed the night in Bulingogwe, and expected to arrive in Sesse in three days. *Departure of Herr von Tiedemann.*

I myself removed on March 8th, together with all my people, to a charming country house which the king had given me. It stood in a banana grove on the eastern slope of Rubaja hill. The house consisted of three large rooms, built of cane reeds after the Indian fashion. The kitchens and servants' offices were established in the adjoining houses. As is usual among the Waganda, the courtyard consisted of a number of squares, with partitions of twisted reeds. The houses for my column stood at the entrance of these courtyards, so that I had all my men around me, and yet was completely private and undisturbed. From the flagstaff by the principal gateway waved the great German flag. I may mention in passing that I had four sentries on duty day and night in Uganda, round our camp, according to my principle of considering a surprise, from whatever quarter it might come, as a downright disgrace to myself. *A pleasant camping-ground.*

On March 9th I had the great pleasure of making the acquaintance of Monseigneur Livinhac, who had come over from the Sesse Islands to visit the newly-established Catholic Mission. Monseigneur Livinhac, like so many of his brethren in these countries, is a strikingly handsome and dignified-looking man, with a magnificent long black *Monseigneur Livinhac.*

26

beard. A crucifix, set with brilliants, hangs down over his white cassock. I found him to be a very cultivated man, of great delicacy of feeling, and entirely free from prejudice; full of enthusiasm for the cause he served, and possessing a clear-sighted intelligence as to the great changes which are taking place, at the present time, in African affairs.

I had the pleasure of seeing him for the first time on March 8th. On Sunday, March 9th, we dined together at the Catholic Mission; the crown of the feast was a bottle of Algerian wine, brought by Monseigneur Livinhac,—a rare treat, which, together with the animated conversation, put us in a frame of mind that was almost European.

During the following days, I began to take in hand another great question of principle with respect to Uganda. If Muanga and his party wished to participate in the European and Christian system, it was absolutely necessary that he should take his stand, on principle, on the anti-slavery movement. Chiefly on account of the great beauty of the women of Beyma, Uganda had formerly been one of the greatest centres of the slave trade. Between March 9th and 16th Monseigneur Lourdel and I succeeded in obtaining from the king the following solemn declaration, which brought the whole matter to a conclusion:—

Uganda and the slave trade.

"Moi, Muanga, roi du Bouganda, j'affirme, en présence de Monsieur le docteur Carl Peters, et du R. P. Siméon Lourdel, que j'interdis la traite des esclaves dans le Bouganda, and les pays qui en dépendent; and que je ferai tout mon possible pour empêcher l'exportation des esclaves de tous les pays qui me sont soumis.

Muanga's desire concerning slavery.

"Muanga, Kabaka du Bouganda.
"Siméon Lourdel, de miss. d'Algers, Supérieur
de la Mission Catholique.
"Dr. Carl Peters.

"Mengo, le 16 Mars, 1890."

This decree was issued at the same time in the Kiganda

language, in which it was announced to the chief men of the country, at a solemn public assembly.

To bring out more clearly the Christian sentiments which underlay this decree, I induced the king, in a formal memorial addressed to the signatories of the Congo Act, to request the

MONSEIGNEUR LIVINHAC.

neutralisation of Uganda and the territory of the Upper Nile in the spirit of the Congo Act, and to pledge himself to make Christianity the one dominant religion in all his dominions. The king appointed me his plenipotentiary for the negotiations concerning this matter, in case I should consider, on my return to Europe, that there was any prospect of their leading to a practical result. The Christian religion was, moreover, formally proclaimed as the religion of the state, by the decree that all government appointments should be filled by Christians only, and that, accordingly, all heathens who refused to be converted to it must resign their appointments. This decree was carried out in Uganda to the fullest extent, and it was in this way that my old friend Kamanyiro Kanta lost his province. The queen-mother, Mtesa's widow, who had herself remained a heathen, was obliged, although I was on very good terms with her, to dismiss all her court officials who adhered to the old belief, and to surround herself with a retinue of Christians, a proceeding which was anything but agreeable to her. Mohammedanism, as such, was simply forbidden, under penalty of death. Heathenism was tolerated, but Christianity alone was in every respect to be the dominant religion.

I co-operated very zealously in all these matters, because I considered that these measures were suited in every respect to the existing condition of affairs in the north of Lake Victoria. Mohammedanism received its deathblow by the prohibition of the slave trade. It had to be forbidden in Uganda because it aimed openly at the extermination of Christianity; and if it were in any degree tolerated it could have easily gained the ascendency, supported as it was by the neighbourhood of the great Mohammedan powers in the north. Heathenism, from a political point of view, might be tolerated, if only its followers were prevented from holding any positions of influence in the country. To give them such positions would be dangerous, because in the old heathen religion a supernatural veneration was paid to the dynasty itself, and it was therefore to be assumed that although Muanga went with the Catholic party, there yet existed in that ruler a strong attachment to his former religion, which might easily become dangerous to the development of Christianity, unless the latter held in its hands the control of every department of the state. If heathenism were dealt with everywhere as we dealt with it in Uganda, it would hold something like the position which it occupied about the middle period of the Roman Emperors, and there is no doubt that it would very soon fall to pieces.

In order to deal a blow at Karema's party, I tried to induce the king to set a price of fifty frasilas of ivory upon his head, and to grant to all his followers, if they would abjure Mohammedanism, an amnesty and permission to return to Uganda. I did not, however, pursue this idea, owing to the representations of Mons. Lourdel, who said that in the utter absence of all truthfulness here no one would believe either that the price promised for the head of Karema would be paid, or that the amnesty would be observed, and that therefore an announcement of this nature would be unpractical. I certainly had not thought of that. *Mons. Lourdel's opinion.*

But in spite of all this, I had during these few weeks in Uganda the great satisfaction of being able to observe the rapid advance of the country in prosperity. In the north of Mengo, the daily market had been re-opened under lofty trees; and every day saw fresh crowds of Christian fugitives from every quarter streaming back to their home. Houses and villages sprang up on every hill, almost like blossoms after a spring rain. The fine broad roads, which had become overgrown with grass, were soon cleansed again, and presented the trim appearance which is peculiar to all these settlements. Digging and planting went on everywhere; and as, strangely enough, our entrance into the country had been accompanied by a return of the rain, every place seemed to burst out at once into verdure and bloom. The members of both confessions betook themselves at once to building places of worship. The symbol and the blessing of the cross were to be seen everywhere. *Prosperity of the country.*

This was to me the greatest satisfaction that I could possibly have received, for all the dangers and anxieties of the journey. Whenever I showed myself in public, which I always did with a certain display of ceremonial, men and women crowded round me rejoicing, to salute me, and thank me for the help I had brought them. I felt deeply moved during these hours and days, when I reflected what might be made of this country, so highly favoured by God, if it continued in the paths of industry under European influence, as it had shown itself happily disposed to do during these weeks of my stay.

As I was so entirely isolated, and generally lived alone, I had leisure enough, after my political labours, which never took up more than a few hours of each day, to study the country and the people, and to become acquainted with their manners and customs.

<small>Acquaintance with the country and people.</small>

I could not, of course, arrive at any definite conclusion in these respects; but for the very reason that I saw Uganda under such peculiar circumstances, my observations may be found not entirely devoid of interest.

If nations may be divided into two classes, those which are destined to rule and those which are compelled to obey, the Waganda belong unquestionably to the former class. Proud even to passionate vindictiveness, brave and courageous even to cruelty, they have within themselves that instinctive feeling of their superiority over others which is the natural and indispensable condition of sovereignty. It is not very long since the King of Uganda looked upon himself as the first monarch of the world, and looked down with an equal contempt upon white men and Arabs. Mtesa was unsophisticated enough to ask for the hand of a daughter of the Queen of England in marriage, and thought he was conferring a great deal of honour in so doing. The English missionaries prudently kept back in Usumbiro the document containing this proposal. But the individual Waganda also, however submissive he may be at home to the despotism of his Mfalme, understands perfectly well how to command when he is abroad. I had several opportunities of remarking this, both in Usoga and on my journey round Lake Victoria. There was with me as guide Stephano, a young servant of the Katikiro's, and I was delighted to see with what authority this man, who behaved like a slave towards me, ordered about hundreds of rowers from Wausu, and how he, standing alone, gave his commands to men of the western tribes. This gift of authority is, as it were, in the blood of the Waganda, and this superiority is

<small>Pride and ignorance of Mtesa.</small>

nowhere denied. "Oderint dum metuant" is most assuredly the only practical motto for Africa, and seems indeed to be the accepted principle of the continent in the treatment of other people.

In the development of their intelligence, the Waganda undoubtedly excel every other African nation. The missionaries have assured me of the fact, and I had occasion myself to remark with what quickness they caught up and assimilated ideas. In contrast to all other negro tribes, the Waganda feels the necessity of progress. Christianity has spread among this people with amazing rapidity, when once the superiority of the white race was understood; and in its train have come the arts of reading and writing. The missionaries of both confessions agree in their descriptions of the eagerness with which the Waganda presses forward to be taught, How utterly different from the morally and mentally degraded Uwangwana on the coast, or the stupid Usukuma and Mjammesi. In the Waganda there is fire, appreciativeness, and intelligence, and without question this tribe has a future before it.

Great abilities of the Waganda.

It is true that these advantages are accompanied by a number of faults. I never saw the simple impudence of which Emin Pasha complains. "Other times, other manners;" and it certainly makes a difference whether you come to Mtesa as a private individual, or to Muanga at the head of an efficient military expedition! On the whole, with Christianity there has come a greater respect for the white race which introduced it. The superiority of the white man, as I said before, has become clear to the Waganda, and they are eager to learn from us as much as possible. But their desire to hold a certain rank leads them to despise common unskilled labour, and, since they must live, they have recourse to begging or stealing. In a country where private property is entirely at the mercy of the ruler's caprice, the chief spur to honest solid acquisition is wanting, and the dangerous blessing afforded by the perennial banana, which, without demanding any cultivation to speak of, bestows everything necessary for the support of life, has naturally intensified

Respect called forth by resolution.

the general inclination to idleness. These fortunate people only need to build houses, for which the reeds of the country supply a convenient material, and to weave their clothing stuffs, mbugo, from the bark of a certain wild fig-tree; the rest of their time can then be wasted merrily in a *dolce far niente*. The unripe banana, when dried, yields the finest white flour I have ever seen. I prefer the ugali (or broth) made with banana flour even to that made with wheat flour. Or again, the green banana may be roasted, and yields a dish not unlike potatoes baked in their skins; while one variety of banana, when ripe, is boiled in the skin, and when it is afterwards peeled it makes a preserve which has exactly the taste of our stewed pears. For dessert a capital dish is afforded by the ripe banana, peeled, cut in half, and baked in a pan with butter and sugar; prepared in this way it is certainly quite equal to our European dish of apple cake or tart. There are other ways of cooking bananas, not to speak of the various effervescing drinks which are obtained from this fruit, from the light muënge (tamo tamo), which resembles champagne, to the heavy intoxicating varieties of pombe! Truly, the gods could not have bestowed a more valuable gift on the countries on the northern shore of Lake Victoria than its vast banana groves, which afford an easy and pleasant means of subsistence to millions of people. But, as is said to be the case in the South Sea Islands, this gift of the too easy provision of the necessaries of life is attended with dangers not always overcome, even by the restless energy of this race. The traveller in Uganda must look well after his goods and chattels, especially at night, and will do well to harden himself against the begging of high and low. Unless he does this, he will not carry much away with him from this country.

The form of salutation among the Waganda is lively and cheery. When two acquaintances meet, one of them says, as he grasps the other's hand, "*Otiano*." "*Eh*," replies the other, in a grunting tone; and now arises an interchange of complimentary grunts—"*eh*," "*eh*," "*eh*," "*eh*," "*eh*," "*eh*," varied with an occasional "*otiano*," the voice in diminuendo tones. The method of giving thanks is by falling flat on one's stomach, and holding the two hands palm to palm, waving them in a slanting direction through the air, uttering over and over again—"*Nianzig, nianzig, nianzig.*"

As might be expected from the lively, sanguine temperament of the people, a love of music is strongly developed among them.

Stanley translates Uganda as meaning "The Land of Drums." I have vainly sought to discover any justification for such a translation. On the contrary, Uganda means in Kiganda *the brother*, and Uganda should therefore be translated the "Brotherland," analogous to our German word "Fatherland." But if Stanley's interpretation be etymologically incorrect, it can certainly be justified practically, for Uganda is indisputably a land of drums in the fullest sense of the expression. Drumming goes on there day and night, from one end of the land to the other. The hilly country, with its surrounding heights and its echoing valleys, to a certain extent invites this proceeding. Indeed, from the heights of Mengo or Rubaga the country may be governed by means of signals given by beat of drum, certainly for a circuit of five miles around. This is fully taken advantage of at the royal court. Muanga has a whole houseful of the most various kinds of drums. By means of these the greatest variety of signals can be given, which are immediately understood by all the country round. Often when Gabriel, the head of the army, was with me, he would suddenly get up and say: "The gates are being closed," or "The king wants to see me," or "The Askaris are ordered to dance," or something of the sort. And when I asked him, "How do you know that?" he would answer, smiling, "*Nyoma*" ("Drum"). The drum used in war is especially effective, even to a European ear. Three drums, tuned in fifths, are beaten in a peculiar roll, which has a solemn, dignified, and at the same time menacing effect.

<small>The Waganda drum.</small>

Next to the drum the various kinds of flute are very plentiful in Uganda, both reed and wooden flutes of all kinds and sizes. An orchestra of flutes in Uganda is extremely comic.

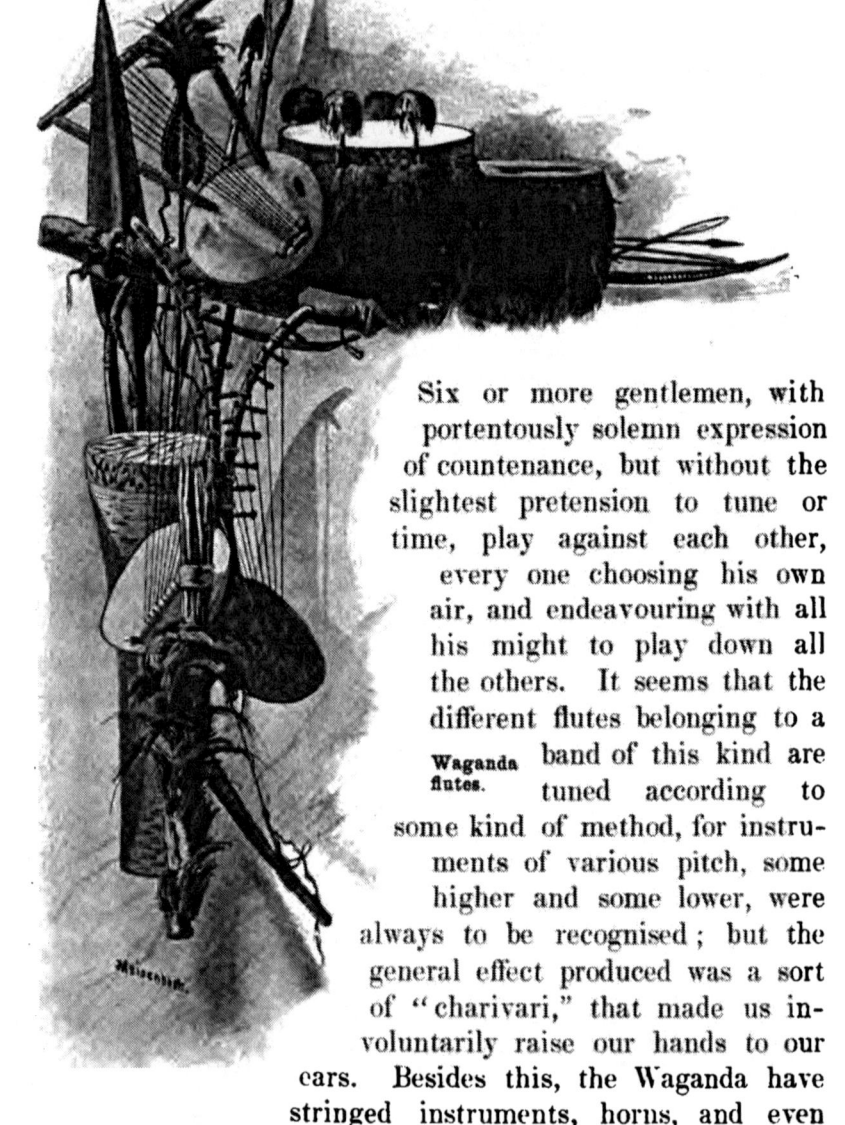

Six or more gentlemen, with portentously solemn expression of countenance, but without the slightest pretension to tune or time, play against each other, every one choosing his own air, and endeavouring with all his might to play down all the others. It seems that the different flutes belonging to a band of this kind are tuned according to some kind of method, for instruments of various pitch, some higher and some lower, were always to be recognised; but the general effect produced was a sort of "charivari," that made us involuntarily raise our hands to our ears. Besides this, the Waganda have stringed instruments, horns, and even little pianos of wood, of which I saw a very full-sounding specimen in King Muanga's collection of instruments. Together with these

MUSICAL INSTRUMENTS OF THE WAGANDA.

Waganda flutes.

instruments the singer makes his appearance. He recites to the accompaniment of a drum, beaten by himself. He appears to be performing love-songs, or songs in praise of the Msungu, or of some of the chiefs who are present. While singing the love-songs he smiles significantly, or accompanies his chant with a rhythmical dancing movement, without, however, moving from his place. The Waganda also sing in chorus, not unmelodiously; sometimes rather plaintively, sometimes with a wild and shrill sound. You never quite lose the feeling that they have picked up a fragment of a tune, like parrots, but that they do not know how to put the different parts together, so as to blend them into a real and complete melody. It is always a beginning, but never comes to any completion, as if they were trying to utter something they wanted to say, and could never find the right expression for it. However, my visit to Uganda was at too serious a time to allow me to form a proper opinion as to the joyousness and love of singing inherent in these people. There was dearth in the land, and war stood on the threshold. Such a time is not very favourable for singing and dancing merrily. But still the population streamed back into the land, day by day, in ever increasing-numbers. Everywhere building was going on, fields were being tilled, and on the whole I was able to gain, I think, a very fair idea of this side of the national character.

Musical proclivities of the Waganda.

The houses of the Waganda chiefs are very tastefully built; they are generally neatly made, entirely of reeds, in something resembling the Indian style of architecture.

My house at Rubaga, into which, as I have already mentioned, I moved in the second week of my stay, presented at the front and at the back two semi-circular halls, in which I established myself very comfortably. The centre was occupied by a large, partially-darkened room, which was approached from a third side by a door which could be locked. The trim little house was enclosed by a square of high fences made of matting, above which only the lofty trees of the banana grove appear, near which the house was situated. The courtyard was again divided, by similar fences of matting, into

Waganda architecture.

different parts, one of which contained the house used as our kitchen. Three doors on three sides led from the outer fence into the open country. Before one of these doors, at about ten or fifteen paces distant, lay the houses for the slaves, in which I quartered the Askaris and the bearers. I had installed my own servants and the kitchen in the separate parts of the courtyard, so that I had all my people at hand, and yet was entirely alone and undisturbed. It is certainly the pleasantest style of building that can be imagined for these countries. As the courtyards are paved with hard-trodden clay, the most scrupulous cleanliness can be maintained throughout.

The houses of the slaves and of the poor consist, like those of the Bantu, of huts shaped like haycocks, and entered by a door with locks or fastenings, and supported inside by a peculiar arrangement of pillars. The Waganda are extraordinarily skilful in house building. Give them three or four days, and whole villages appear where before there had been a desert. In Mengo not only reception halls of colossal dimensions arose, as it were, out of nothing, in the course of a single week, but also hundreds of houses for the guards, drummers, and slaves of the king.

Skilful builders.

Besides this aptitude for building, the Waganda, as Emin Pasha has observed, have a great turn for blacksmith's work. At Rubaga there is a smithy of this description, which I visited. The men were working there almost exclusively with European tools, and, in my opinion, with almost European skill. I had occasion myself to have several guns repaired here, and among other things it was necessary, at one time, to replace in one of the magazine guns a lost part of the machinery, by which the cartridges were rapidly thrown out after the weapon had been discharged. In every case the work was done in a neat, workmanlike manner. This particular trade is still held in honour in this place. The owner of the forge had lately been appointed one of the chiefs of the land. The Waganda import their iron either from Unjoro or from Usogora, on the west of the lake, or in the shape of iron wire from the coast. No minerals of any kind are obtained in Uganda itself.

The facts I have thus brought forward show that in all probability we have before us, in this lively and hearty people, a

HOUSEHOLD UTENSILS OF THE WAGANDA.

rising race, which has a future before it in the development of Central Africa. They pass their lives in their own mountain land, with its valleys and heights, like the Thuringians, loving song and merriment. But here are imprinted, more deeply than in the German race, the dark features of bloody revenge and brutal cruelty. In Uganda we are within the limits of the dark despotism of Central Africa. The stranger marvels at the number of human beings he encounters who have lost one eye, or both ears, or their noses, or lips; but the missionaries have stories to tell of much worse things. Everything in the whole of this country belongs to the ruler alone. He issues his command, and the people at once bring him their cattle, daughters, and wives. He commands, and hundreds of his subjects are dragged off to the place of execution, and there put to death with fearful tortures. The limbs of the victims are hacked off one by one, roasted before the very eyes of the unfortunate sufferers, who are then forced to eat their own flesh. The mutilated trunk is then slowly roasted, and everything is done to prolong the agony as much as possible. This is what Mohammedans and Christians have had to live among here, and only recently, with the introduction of Christianity, has the state of things taken a turn for the better. And yet this country is both in climate and scenery cheerful and beautiful, so that one wonders how, under these skies, such bestial cruelty can have established itself.

According to Father Lourdel, the thermometer in Uganda, even in the hottest season, which is in February, never rises above 28° C. (82° Fahr.) in the shade; while in the coldest period, July, it sinks to 13° C. (55° Fahr.) in the night. Strange to say, Uganda belongs, in its seasonable periods, to the southern hemisphere, while geographically it is in the northern. Moreover, there is not such a sharp division into a dry and a wet season as in other tropical countries, although the precipitation of rain is greater than usual between the months of March and May. It rains irregularly at all times of the year, owing to the influence of the lake, and the embraces of sky and earth are here of an extraordinarily fiery character. Nowhere have I met with such numerous storms of thunder and lightning, or of so violent a kind, as in Uganda. During a storm one can almost say that the space of time between the flashes is shorter than the time covered by the flash itself; it flickers continually like a gas flame in an autumn wind. It is accompanied by short rolls of thunder. Even when we had not thunder-storms just overhead, the horizon in one direction, generally to the north, was in flames every night in March. But the earth here shows herself grateful enough for the blessed rain of heaven. Everything blossoms and flourishes, and I am convinced, as are the missionaries, that the land here is able to bring forth, without exception, every product of the tropical and temperate zones. I will only mention the excellent Uganda coffee, which we drank regularly, and which grows wild here. Herr von Tiedemann bought fifty pounds of it for, I believe, four arm-lengths of stuff; I find no difference between this and Mocha coffee. Besides this I must mention tobacco, and sugar-cane, manioc, red sorghum, peas, beans, batatas, etc. At the Roman Catholic mission station every kind of European vegetable is grown. The country is also extremely healthy, no missionary having died here before Mons. Lourdel, and for lung diseases Uganda is probably as much to be recommended as Madeira.

Fertility and productiveness.

And now, whence come the inhabitants of this land? Whence have they their peculiar characteristics and their superiority in culture over the other Bantu races? for that they are of Bantu stock there is no question, as the construction of their language proves it; but among this original population a second element has been introduced, which came from the north. Emin and Felkin call these people from the north Wahuma (inhabitants of the north), and I found in Uganda the probably identical name Beyma in use. In Usukuma the Massais are called Wahuma, and this word is identical with Wasukuma itself, which signifies nothing else than North-folk. These Beyma came long ago from the far north, passed over the Nile, not far from Mruli, and conquered all the country to the north and west of the lake. They founded here a great kingdom among the Wakintu,

Origin of the Waganda.

from whose race springs the present dynasty of the Uganda kings. Their kingdom extended as far as Mwuta Nzige, and southwards to the north end of the Tanganyika; and the countries of Usoga, Uganda, Unjoro, Meru, Usagara, and Uhha, in the south, all belonged to it. In Uhha the Beyma race still exists, pure and unmixed. In the north they became absorbed into the aboriginal population, or were sharply distinguished from the general mixed race in the Beyma pastoral tribes.

These Beyma are still found in Uganda by hundreds of thousands. They keep entirely to themselves, though their women are everywhere sought for, on account of their remarkable beauty, and through them the Beyma blood is making its way everywhere. So far as I saw, the Beyma were of a slender type, with dewy, dreamy eyes, and features of almost a Caucasian cast; their colour is light brown, and their faces reminded me of the figures in an ancient Egyptian temple. Felkin states that they were also called Wawitu; an assertion that I was not able to verify. This name would seem to point to a connection with the countries east of the Samu. At present it is of the greatest importance to the history of Central and North Africa to know whence come the Beyma, and to what race they may belong. They speak Kiganda, but in an outlandish dialect. After a closer research, however, I succeeded in proving the existence of a number of words in their language, which are not Kiganda, and so may belong to the original language of the Beyma. I here give these words, hoping that more erudite men than myself will be able to draw conclusions from them :—

The Beyma people.

Comparison of languages.

English.	*Suahili.*	*Kiganda.*	*Special Beyma.*
day	siku	naku	birro
God	mhungu	katonda	Dubaga (or Rubaga, like the former capital of the Uganda)
devil	shetani	Rubale	batwesi (rather, as it seems, archangel)

English.	Suahili.	Kiganda.	Special Beyma.
star	tonda	ratonda	iguru
sheep	kondoo	diga	ntàma
rain	mwua	mkubá	njúrra
how are you?	haligani	otiano	mirembejo
honey	asali na njuki	nubiss	bugéme
peace	amani	kwegaisia	kwesengeléssa
hair	uĕlle	mwiri	söke
father	baba	sebo	tata.

Any one who wants to obtain an answer to this question must also examine the words which are common to the Kiganda and Beyma, but differ from the Suahili, for it is quite possible that words have crept into the Kiganda language from the Beyma. I must leave these enquiries to experts, since of the Kibantu languages I only know Suahili, and the tribes that differ from Suahili may simply be the Uganda dialects of Kibantu. I will here give a few such words, as specimens, which will perhaps repay examination:— *Suahili and Kiganda dialects.*

English.	Suahili.	Kiganda and Beyma.
ox	ngombe	nte, unte
bird	ndege	njungu
wife	manamke	mkasi
sultan	sultani	kabaka (Beyma, mukama)
child	mtoto	muana
night	usiku	kirro (comp. birro = day)
soul	roho	mtinsa
stick	fimbo	mkoni (Beyma, mugó)
fat	mafuta	msigo
milk	masiva	máte (Beyma, matá)
war	mwita	baruana (Beyma, turuani)

I content myself with these specimens, because the enquirer will doubtless find noted in Monseigneur Livinhac's grammar of the Kiganda language other non-Suahili tribes in Kiganda.

Felkin is of opinion that the Beyma are of ancient Abyssinian origin, and I should be inclined to believe that they belong to the Somali of the Wagalla race. They are unquestionably, like the latter, an entirely pastoral population, and a few words of their language sound to me like some well-known Somali or Wagalla words. Thus *birro*, day, is in Kisomal *beri*, in Kigalla *boru*, to-morrow morning. *Njúrra*, rain, is in Kisomal *górrah*. I leave this point undecided. I own that I await, with the keenest interest, the answer which will be given, by an Oriental scholar, to the question thus raised.

Meanwhile, I may be permitted to bring forward the reasons which have led me to suppose that there has existed intercourse, in very ancient times, between the lake district, especially Uganda, and the civilisation of ancient Egypt.

<small>Ancient relations with civilised countries.</small>

1. It is a well-known fact that the ancients were acquainted with the lakes of Central Africa. Aristotle, in his "Historia Animalium," viii., 2, mentions in a brief and sober way, that "the cranes migrate as far as the lakes beyond Egypt, where the Nile has its source. There dwell the pigmies; and this is no fable, but the simple truth. Both men and horses, so says report, are small size, and live in caves."

What seems to me remarkable in this passage is, that Aristotle mentions the fact that the Nile has its source in the lakes of the south country, not as anything new, but casually, as something already known to his readers. The additional remark "and this is no fable," etc., proves, moreover, that Aristotle had his information about the nation of dwarfs from a source he considered trustworthy, probably from travellers; and the story has been shown in our own day by Schweinfurth to be perfectly well founded. Schweinfurth also recognised the nation of the pigmies in the tribe of dwarfs of the Akka, to the south of Manbuttu.* Now, it is of course possible that such information may have arrived in Egypt at third or fourth hand. However that may be, the passage at least proves a certain intercourse. Eratosthenes also, about 200 B.C., speaks of the Nile as issuing from lakes.

<small>Ancient records and their teachings.</small>

Ptolemy seems to have had more accurate information, for on his map he indicates two Nile lakes (the Victoria and

---

* Accordingly, it was not Stanley who first discovered the dwarf tribes of Central Africa.

Albert Nyanza?), and marks down the Mountains of the Moon to the south of the lake. These Mountains of the Moon, accordingly, appear even before the Christian era, and are given in somewhat uncertain form by every subsequent geographer. Can it be doubted that these Mountains of the Moon point to a knowledge of Unjamwesi (*Un* land, *ia* form of the genitive, and *mwesi* moon, thus making Land of the Moon), to the south of the Victoria Nyanza, from which, as a matter of fact, issue the last streams flowing from the Nile?

Stanley thought, not long ago, that in the Ruwenzori he had discovered the fabulous Mountains of the Moon; but he gives no reasons of any kind for his belief. He reprints the accounts of the Mountains of the Moon given by the ancients, but adds nothing to show why these accounts should be applied to the Ruwenzori; while the ancient maps, that he himself prints, flatly contradict his hypothesis, as they one and all place the Mountains of the Moon to the south of Lake Victoria. There is no great difficulty in selecting some mountain or other, and saying, "Here are the Mountains of the Moon;" and one man has pointed to this mountain, and another to that. But the solution is evidently to be found much nearer at hand; and the fact of deriving the origin of the name from Unjamwesi, the name of the country at the present day, is supported above all by the places marked on the map by the Greeks and Arabs. It is probable that Uganda traders learnt that beyond the lake lay Unjamwesi, the Land of the Moon, and brought this information back with them to Egypt. The derivation of the name Unjamwesi itself is not quite clear; the mountains of Unjamwesi, seen from the east, are crescent-shaped, and give something like the impression of the rising moon. It may be that the name, Mountains of the Moon, may be traced to this circumstance; but that is not now to the point.

All that Stanley quotes from the reports of the ancients concerning these Mountains of the Moon belongs entirely to the realm of fable, and may just as well apply to any other mountain range as to the Ruwenzori. The mountain described in these accounts is called, not Ruwenzori, but Kumr, and there is

420   *NEW LIGHT ON DARK AFRICA.*

Ancient maps and charts. mention of caves and great buildings within it. It is well known that Thomson discovered large rock-cut buildings both in Elgami and, in fact, in Elgon. It cannot, of course, be proved that there is any reference to these buildings in Elgami in the legends told of the mysterious

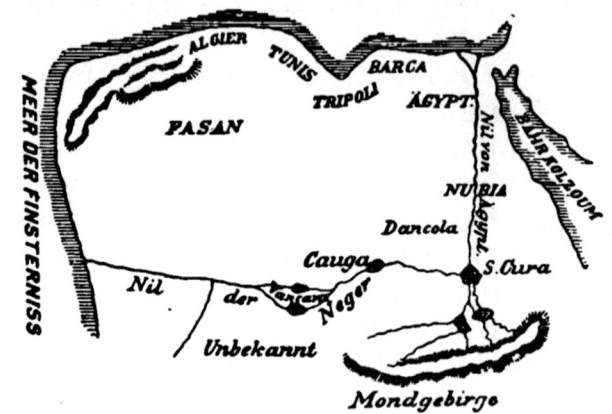

CENTRAL AFRICA, AFTER EDRISI, 1154.

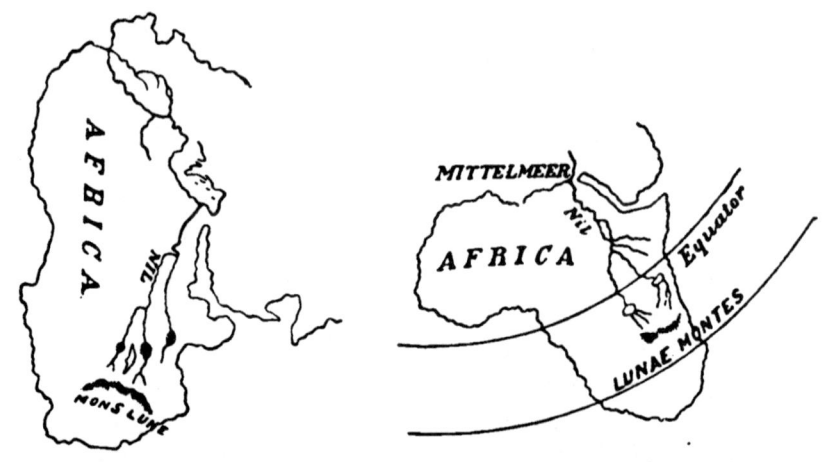

MAP OF SYLVANUS, 1511.   MAP OF JOHN RUYSCH, 1508.

mountain Kumr; but there is perhaps a clue better worth following up than that of the Ruwenzori,—which, by the way, was discovered, not by Stanley, but by Casati. We cannot really be induced to accept Ruwenzori as the Mountain of the Moon simply because Stanley happened to march past it. If it is granted, however, that we are justified in finding, in the reports of the ancients concerning the Mountain of the Moon, the proof that they were acquainted with Unjamwesi, we shall also be forced to conclude that their commercial intercourse extended as far as to the Victoria Nyanza, and that either travellers had penetrated from Egypt to the lakes, or from the lakes to Egypt. The latter is the more improbable, and therefore the historical expert will pronounce in favour of the former conjecture.

2nd. The name for the Nile is, in Uganda, Kyira, or Kyila, the "r" and "l" in the Kibantu language being the same sound. In Usoga also I found that the word for Nile was Nyiro or Nyilo. This is the ancient name for the river.

MAP OF SEBASTIAN CABOT (16TH CENTURY).

Accordingly, the Nile, at the present day, bears at its source the same name which it bore thousands

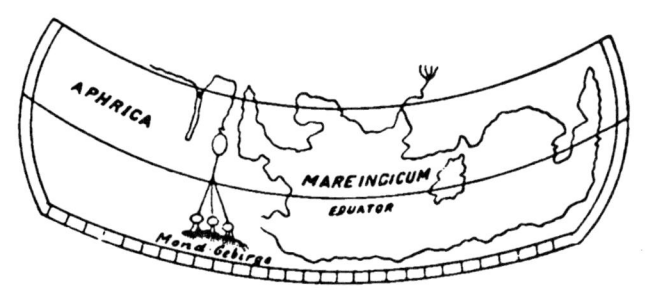

MAP OF THE MARGARITA PHILOSOPHICA, 1503.*

of years ago at its mouth. This may be explained, since it is highly improbable that it should have happened by chance, by

* In all the maps given above the Mountains of the Moon are marked at about the spot of the present Unjamwesi.

the assumption either that people from the north travelled the regions of its source, or *vice versâ*, and that there must have been a time when men were acquainted with its identity at both ends of the river. The force of this fact is in no way diminished by the circumstance that now immigrant tribes of later date, along the centre and upper course, have given new names to the river. It is quite possible that the old aboriginal inhabitants remained established only at the source and at the mouth of the river, which, accordingly, here retained the old name. This, again, can only be explained by the supposition that communications existed in ancient times between the territories at the mouth and those at the source of the river.

Theory concerning ancient relations.

3rd. There are at Mengo thirty-three royal tombs of the tribe of the Wakintu.* In the most ancient of these are said to be buried primeval records of the dynasty. I was not only informed of this by Muanga, but the missionaries confirmed his statement. I tried to obtain permission to have the records disinterred, but the superstition of the Waganda is still so deeply rooted that Muanga, though in very courteous words, refused my request. On the other hand, I received permission to visit some of these tombs. Dr. Felkin tells me that he has already seen the tombs, but he has not given any description of them. I mention, first of all, that the number of tombs being thirty-three does not prove beyond dispute that only thirty-three generations of the Wakintu have ruled over Uganda. From the statements of the Waganda it appears that the capital of this dynasty was originally situated more in the neighbourhood of the Albert Nyanza. The name Kitarra, *i.e.*, city of the Wakintu, that remains to the present day in the north-west of Uganda, seems to point to the conclusion that the race originally ruled in that place. We cannot determine with certainty the maximum, but only the minimum number of ruling generations from the number of the thirty-three tombs.

The royal tombs at Mengo.

---

* The title of the king, as has been before stated, is Kabaka, or Mfalme. Might Mfalme perhaps be a Bantu modification of the Egyptian title Pharaoh ? " L " and " r " have the same sound in Kibantu.

These tombs are arranged in the following manner: On approaching them from a distance the traveller thinks he sees pyramids before him, but in reality they are in the form of large cones, and are built of wood in Uganda fashion. On entering, the visitor finds himself in a dusky hall, supported by a row of columns. In the background of this hall is a painted curtain, before which are ranged the weapons and favourite movables of the deceased. On putting aside the curtain a dark area is entered, from which shafts and corridors have been excavated in the ground. In these passages textile stuffs, cowrie shells, and other articles of value, which in Uganda represent money, are heaped up. At the farthest extremity of these passages is deposited the coffin, with the embalmed corpse of the dead person. *Treasuries in the tombs.* It appears that the regular procedure for preserving the corpse is by drying it, and swathing it tightly in wrappings; but the Waganda also told me that they understood the art of preserving the body from decomposition by injections into the blood. In front of the curtain twelve girls watch day and night on behalf of the one last departed; at present, therefore, for Mtesa. From time to time all the great men of the land come to the dead man, with drums and fifes, to pay him a visit, as if he were alive.

What speculations may be founded on this? Manifestly, we have here to do with forms which are not met with, to my knowledge, among any other Bantu tribe. How is it that just the Waganda have this method of burying their dead? I know very well that customs of the kind exist also in Madagascar, and that the old Aztecs had a similar practice of sepulture; but these two regions of culture are too *Ancient sepulchres of Aztecs, etc.* far away to allow of the idea of any communication with them. It is much more probable to suppose here an influence from the north, from Egypt. Certainly this proof has nothing absolutely striking about it, but in connection with what I have already cited a certain probability for my conjectures will always be manifest.

I have already mentioned that Thomson found great rock-cut buildings in Elgon, which, according to his description, none but a civilised nation could have produced. The Elgon rears its height in the north-east of Uganda. By whom could such structures have been raised? Other relations may here be conjectured. Indians or Arabs might have pressed forward from the east coast over the Baringo, and have reared these buildings. The most probable conjecture is, perhaps, here again that which points to Egyptians. From an Arabian description of the Nile Stanley extracts the following narrative, which is interesting, though it sounds somewhat fabulous. (See "In Darkest Africa," vol. ii., p. 282.)

Elgon rock dwellings.

"Historians relate that Adam bequeathed the Nile unto Seth, his son, and it remained in the possession of these children of prophecy and of religion, and they came down to Egypt (or Cairo), and it was then called Lul; so they came and dwelt among the mountains. After them came a son, Kinaan, then his son Mahaled, and then his son Yaoud, and then his son Hamu, and his son Hermes—that is, Idrisi the prophet (Enoch). Idrisi began to reduce the land to law and order. The Nile used to come flowing down upon them, and they would escape from it to the high mountains and to elevated land until the river fell, then they would plant whatever country was left bare. Idrisi gathered the people of Egypt, and went with them to the first stream of the Nile, and there adjusted the levelling of the land and of the water by lowering the high land and raising the low land, and other things according to the science of astronomy and surveying. Idrisi was the first person who spoke and wrote books upon these sciences. He then went to the land of Abyssinia and Nubia, and gathered the people, and extended the distance of the flow of the Nile, or reduced it, according to the swiftness or sluggishness of the stream. He even calculated the volume of the water and the rate of the flow. He is the first man who regulated the flow of the Nile to Egypt. It is said that in the days of Am Kaam, one of the kings of Egypt, Idrisi was taken up to heaven, and he prophesied the coming of the flood; so he remained on the other

Arab account of Ancient Egypt.

side of the Equator, and there built a palace on the slopes of Mount Gumr. He built it of copper, and made eighty-five statues of copper, the waters of the Nile flowing out through the mouths of these statues, and then flowing into a great lake, and thence to Egypt."

"Idyar el Wali says: 'The length of the Nile is two months' journey in Moslem territory, and four months' journey in uninhabited country.' Its source is from Mount Gumr, beyond the Equator, and that it flows to the light, coming out of the river of darkness, and flows by the base of Mount Gumr." *Idyar el Wali's account.*

"King Am Kaam, mentioned above, is Hermes I. The devils carried him to this mountain, which is called Gumr, and there he saw how the Nile flows out of the Black Sea and enters into the Mountain of Gumr. King Am Kaam built, on the slopes of the mountain, a palace, having eighty-five statues, to which he collected all the water that flows from this mountain, conducting it in vaulted conduits until the water reaches the statues, and flows out of their mouths in measured quantities and calculated cubic contents."

If these descriptions have reference to any real facts, would one not naturally, at the sound of the name Gumr, be reminded of El Gumi, in which the Elgon towers aloft with its unexplained and mysterious cave dwellings? From Mount Elgon the Nsoia pours itself into Lake Victoria, and on in another direction, though at some distance from it, the Nile flows past the slopes of the mountain. Could the imaginative narrator have heard some confused rumours of magnificent Egyptian undertakings in El Gumi, of which the caverns discovered by Thomson are to the present day dumb but eloquent witnesses? In explanation I here give an extract of Thomson's description of them ("Through Massailand," pp. 510 and 512). *Gumr and El Gumi.*

"There lay before me a huge pit, thirty feet deep, one hundred feet long, and about twenty broad, cut perpendicularly out of a volcanic agglomerate of great compactness." In this cave Thomson found entire villages. "On inquiry as to who made this curious excavation, I was told that it was God's work. 'How,' said they, 'could we, with our puny implements' (exhibiting a toy-like axe, their only non-warlike instrument), 'cut out a hole like this? And this is nothing in comparison with others which you may see all round the mountain. See there, and there, and there! These are of such great size that they penetrate far into utter darkness, and even we have not seen the end of them. In some there are large villages, with entire herds of cattle. And yet you ask who made them! They are truly God's work!' ... There was absolutely no tradition regarding these caves among the people. 'Our fathers lived here, and *their* fathers did the same,' was the invariable reply to all my questions.... And yet the caves bore incontestable evidence on the face of them that they had neither a natural nor supernatural origin. They must have been excavated by the hand of man. That was a fact about which there could absolutely be no two opinions."

Thomson himself comes to the following conclusion: "Looking at everything, I can come to but one conclusion, and that is, that in a very remote era some very powerful race, considerably advanced in arts and civilisation, excavated these great caves in their search for precious stones, or possibly some precious metal.... Are we to suppose that the Egyptians really got so far south? If not, what other race could have cut these extraordinary recesses?"

And now let us hear what the people in Uganda still, at the present day, relate concerning the origin of the first Kintu. The first Kintu came from the north to Uganda, and was in every respect a supernatural being. He possessed the knowledge of all things, and brought civilisation and culture into the land. After having given many proofs of his supernatural greatness, Kintu married a daughter of heaven, and from this marriage sprang the dynasty that at the present day still sits on the throne of Uganda. (See Felkin, "Waganda, Tribe of Central Africa," "Proceedings of the Royal Geographical Society," pp. 764, 765.)

Thus we meet with mythical indications from Egypt concerning the undertakings of a remarkable man proceeding southwards, and in Uganda we find similar mythical recollections of the appearance of a hero from the north. Even at the present day we find in El Gumi magnificent monuments of old civilised work, and in Arabian narratives we meet with the name Gumri, which has a marvellous analogy in sound with El Gumi. Do not these facts combine to prove that there was a time when Egyptian enterprise actually extended as far as the source of the White Nile? The historic tradition which still lives in Uganda tells of the conquest of the entire territory by a white race that descended from the north, crossed the Nile at Mruli, and united the whole region around Lakes Victoria and Albert into one great kingdom. These are the herdsmen tribes of Beyma who, as I have stated, have remained to this day an unmixed race in Uganda, being either of old Abyssinian origin, or at all events representatives of nations from the north of Uganda. Does this tradition stand in any connection with the old fabulous myths which I have just mentioned, and according to which the son of an Egyptian king assembled the peoples of Abyssinia and the Soudan, to lead them to the source of the Nile? And to what a great historic revolution does not all this point! *Historic tradition of a white race.*

I must confine myself to throwing out all these ideas as problems for further investigations, and to suggest explanations for which, perhaps, no real premises may ever be found, as they come to us only through the misty dawn of prehistoric times. As memorials, there remain to us only the rock-cut dwellings of Elgon and the sepulchral monuments of the Wakintu; but who can assert that these stand in direct connection with each other? *Unproved theories.*

I sum up briefly, under the following heads, the result of my own observations and conclusions.

1. Ancient Egyptian relations and civilising influences spread, either directly or indirectly, as far as Uganda, and their fame at least reached even to Unjamwesi (the Land of the Moon).

2. In historic times an immigration took place into Uganda,

of a race stronger than the Bantu, and they founded a great kingdom, under the dynasty of the Wakintu, and from their intermixing here with the aborigines has arisen the Uganda nation of the present.

3. Perhaps it was this very immigration which brought about the cultured relations with Egypt to which the graves of the kings seem to point. One might conclude that these proceeded from nomad tribes of Southern Egypt or of Abyssinia, perhaps under the leadership of an Egyptian prince (Mfalme). Or it might be, that the trade relations of ancient Egypt, extending to Lake Victoria, and this authentic immigration from the north, were separate from each other, and only in Uganda became amalgamated into that system of which obscure traces can be still recognised.

4. The Wakintu are described, both in legend and tradition, as coming of a far superior race, which brought the first beginnings of culture to Uganda, and in consequence are venerated, to the present day, with divine honours. The members of this dynasty still retain, according to their own belief, the gift of prophecy, of which Mtesa frequently makes practical use. We may conclude that in them and their surroundings the reason may be found for the higher position occupied by the Waganda, compared with the other Bantu, and for their country possessing a proportionately greater history.

It was not possible for me to prove anything definite. It would be necessary either to seek for exact information in Egyptian hieroglyphic evidence, or, if the statement be true that records exist in the most ancient tombs of the kings, to disinter these records and decipher them. Were we to succeed in obtaining accurate knowledge, a new light would be shed both upon the history of the Egyptians and the development of affairs in Central Africa.

* * * * *

Amidst such occupations and conjectures the days in Uganda passed away rapidly enough. In the afternoons I was in the habit of taking longer or shorter walks with Mons. Lourdel; or the gentlemen of the English Mission would come to spend the evening with me. The afternoon hours I frequently spent with Muanga, with whom I continued uninterruptedly to maintain friendly relations. I also associated much and gladly with other great men of Waganda. With the Katikiro alone I could not get on a good footing. At the beginning he strove to win me over by clumsy flattery. Failing in this, he thought proper to adopt towards me the lofty demeanour of the Prime Minister of Uganda towards strangers. Every moment his servant Stephano brought me the message, "Katikiro amekwita" ("The Katikiro sends for you"). At first I would politely decline to go to him. At length the thing became rather too strong for me. "The Katikiro?" "Yes, you are to come to him immediately." "Ask the Katikiro whether he is gone mad. If he wishes to see me, he can come to me; if I wish to see him I will go to him; but I do not wish to see him." This put an end to his intrusiveness; but from that time forth our meetings at court were of a bitter-sweet character. *The Katikiro and his sentiments.*

In the English Mission in Uganda I had also found some books, amongst them Shakespeare, and Gibbon's "Decline and Fall," which I was accustomed to read. March 15th, the day fixed for my departure, came round; but nothing was to be seen of the boats. Dr. Felkin is right in saying that it is easier to get into Uganda than to get out of it. On reading the accounts of travellers through this country we find this statement fully verified. *Difficulties in Uganda.*

Consequently, on March 16th I betook myself to King Muanga, and said to him, "To-day the boats were to have been ready for me. Where are they?"

"I have received information," he replied, "that they are already assembled at Sesse, and are on their way to Uganda."

"As they have not yet arrived, I prefer to go by land, through South Uganda, to Bunjako, and to reach Sesse in that way. I intend to leave here on Monday."

"Wait another week," answered Muanga, "and if the boats have not arrived by that time you can depart; but I am certain that they will be here."

"Very well, then, I shall wait another week."

On arriving at home I received a letter from Herr von Tiedemann, confirming the statement made by Muanga regarding the assembling of the boats.

But the next week went by, and again nothing was to be heard of the boats. During this week I made friends with Muanga's mother, the favourite wife of Mtesa, whom I visited, and with whom I exchanged presents of various kinds. She is a woman who can be really called a lady, about forty years of age, of still youthful appearance, and extremely agreeable manners.

A lady in Uganda.

On March 21st I informed Muanga that I had finally decided to leave for Bunjako, opposite Sesse, and that I should break up my camp on Monday, March 24th. On the 22nd, just as I had finished dinner, and was smoking my pipe, the king sent to me with the request that I would step across to the court. I quickly donned my uniform and hurried off, in the hope of at length receiving tidings of the arrival of the boats. I found Mons. Lourdel and Messrs. Walker and Gordon already in waiting. On my arrival Mons. Lourdel informed me that a letter had arrived from Mr. Jackson, which I should request the king to let me see. Muanga sought at first, from what motive I do not know, to prevent my reading the letter. On my repeated request, however, he handed it to me, remarking, at the same time, I was not to allow myself to be disturbed by its contents, as he attached no sort of importance to it. I took Jackson's letter in my hand,—and who shall describe my astonishment on reading the following statement made by this gentleman? He had received information, he wrote, that Dr. Carl Peters and Herr von Tiedemann had reached Uganda, on their march towards Emin Pasha. He considered it his duty to inform Muanga that these two gentlemen were sojourning in these regions without the consent of their Government. With the sanction of the German and English Governments, he had undertaken the task of preventing their further progress, and, if necessary, of arresting them. Being absent himself, he now requested his friend Muanga to carry

Important interview with the king.

Mr. Jackson's letter.

out this arrest, as these two men had done mischief enough in Africa already. Moreover, he hoped soon himself to see Muanga, as he was coming with five hundred men.

The letter was dated in the first days of March, and was marked as being sent from Kawirondo. I have already stated that I had repeatedly offered Mr. Jackson friendly co-operation in these regions, that I had given him information concerning the road to Uganda, and had loyally made known to him my negotiations with the king. And this letter to the king of Uganda was Mr. Jackson's reply! He had been afraid to march into the place with five hundred men, and knew Muanga only as the murderer of Hannington and the persecutor of the Christians. He now requested this ruler of Uganda, dreaded by him, to arrest Herr von Tiedemann and myself!

Mr. Jackson must have known, by the whole tenor of my expedition, what such a request meant. Above all, he must have known that I would allow myself to be arrested alive by no man, and that, on the other hand, Muanga, if he felt inclined to accede to the wishes of the English, would certainly not have ordered simply our arrest, but would make things safe by the massacre of our whole expeditionary force. This did not deter him from sending such a proposal to Uganda. I must confess, that the first sentiment I experienced on reading this letter was one of contempt for the Englishmen in Kawirondo, who appeared to me to be just the people, indeed, to stop the German Emin Pasha Expedition, or even to arrest us! Mr. Jackson, with his pedantic way of carrying through his expedition, and his timid indecision, was the right man to make an impression on me! My second sensation was one of heartfelt pain, that an Englishman should venture, here in Uganda, to claim the authority of the German Government in taking measures against a German expedition. It was not until afterwards that I ascertained that Mr. Jackson was here speaking advisedly. On March 22nd, after reading this letter, I could quietly inform Muanga, from my firm belief, that this statement of Jackson's was contrary to fact.

Danger of massacre.

Painful sensations.

" It is well known in what relation Mr. Jackson stands to me."

"Certainly, certainly!" said Muanga, to whom this explanation appeared quite plausible.

After we had all taken leave of the king, I again returned to him with Mons. Lourdel.

Muanga once more took up Jackson's letter, spat upon it, and threw it behind him over his shoulder. Then he said to me,—

"Jackson is my enemy, and I am the enemy of Jackson. Now I am your friend. The Katikiro and the Englishmen have been here, and have urged me to invite Mr. Jackson again to Uganda. If you like, take my soldiers, go to meet them, and do with them what you think right."

Muanga's declaration.

"This does not appear to me to be either to your interest or to the advantage of us all," I replied. "It is in Europe that whatever is to take place here in Uganda must be decided, and it is better not to let myself be hindered in my departure towards the lake. Mr. Jackson is in the habit of marching very slowly, and who can tell when he may arrive here, or whether he will come at all? It is better that I should acquire for you the lands on the west side of the lake, and then make my way to the coast, to look after your affairs there."

Dr. Peters's reply.

"This appears to me the better way also," said Muanga. "I have received intelligence that the boats have already reached Ntebe. If you will, you can go thither and embark in them."

How right I was, in my supposition that Jackson would be long indeed before he came to Uganda, was proved in the following month. He did not arrive there until the latter half of April.

In those days violent disputes took place between Muanga and the Katikiro. Though Muanga was ready to permit Jackson's visit to Uganda, he persistently asserted that he considered himself freed from all obligations towards the English, and that he had not the slightest intention to renew such obligations with them.

Dispute between Muanga and the Katikiro.

I gave orders that everything should be made ready for my departure. On the afternoon of March 22nd I took a formal leave of Muanga.

"Tell the people of Europe," said he, "that in case the English should form an alliance with their friends, the Arabs, and attack me, I protest, through you, against every act of violence on their part. If the English try to set up their Protectorate in Uganda I shall make war against them. If I am beaten, I shall go forth with all my people to another country. This I empower you to make known in Europe, and do you come back to me soon, my friend. I know that you are my friend, and beg you to say this to your great Emperor. I shall always remain the friend of those Europeans who wish to live peaceably in Uganda, but especially the friend of the German people. This I swear by God and by Jesus Christ."

Muanga's message to Europe.

"Farewell, Muanga. I came willingly to Uganda when you called me, and have been glad to help you. You know for certain that I shall always remain your friend, and shall always be glad to help you."

Then Muanga replied, "Accept my thanks for what you have done for me and the Waganda, and tell the Europeans and tell your Emperor to send you to me again."

Contrary to his usual practice, Muanga accompanied me to the outer gate of his palace. Another pressure of the hand, and I hurried down the hill of Mengo towards my camp.

Civilities of the king.

Two hours later, a messenger from the king appeared before me, with the announcement that Karema was marching from the north, that he had burnt a number of villages, and that in a day or two he might arrive before Mengo. Under these circumstances Muango warned me not to proceed along the land route by Ntebe.

"Wait here a few days longer, until we receive accurate intelligence."

"How does Muanga know this?" I asked.

"The Katikiro is with him, and has brought the man with him who came with the news from the north."

"Then tell Muanga, no announcement made by the Katikiro shall prevent my carrying out our arrangements, and that I intend starting to-morrow morning."

Intrigues of the Katikiro.

I saw clearly at once, what proved a few days later to be the complete truth, that the Katikiro had made use of Karema's advance as a ruse to induce the king to call Mr. Jackson to his aid, and thus to serve the English cause. I was determined to put a spoke in his wheel in this matter.

The next morning I betook myself, with my whole column, which was kept in readiness for marching, in the first instance to the Roman Catholic Mission, to obtain further information. A heavy downpour of rain gave occasion for giving my men refuge in the barns of the station, and deferring their march. Mons. Lourdel informed me that the Catholic party, to which Muanga belongs, had meanwhile received reports of Karema's approach; and soon after I received, in addition, an imploring letter from Muanga.

Muanga's imploring letter. "Stay in Uganda, my friend. Karema and the Arabs and Wanjoro are coming. To-day or to-morrow we shall have war. Do not forsake me in this need, and I shall be eternally grateful to you."

My resolution was at once taken. I must not, under any circumstances, quit Uganda until this matter had been decided. On the morning of March 24th, believing a struggle to be imminent, and hearing that the boats had reached Kasi, opposite Bulingogwe, I first asked permission to send away the women and invalids of our expedition at once as far as Sesse, where they would be in safety under the protection of Herr von Tiedemann. This was at once granted, and the column set out, in consequence, at nine o'clock, for Lake Victoria. Retaining only *Collecting the forces.* twenty-five men at Uganda, I returned with these to my camp, and then sent to the king, requesting him immediately to call together a general council of war, consisting of the army and the great men of the Waganda. By one o'clock, all Mengo and Rubaja were full of Muanga's picturesquely adorned dancing soldiers. I then betook myself, with my Somalis, to the royal fortress, where the chief men of the land were already assembled. A fantastic and spirit-stirring impression was produced by the approach of the several troops of soldiers surrounding their king. Carrying their muskets sloped over the right shoulder, one column after another came dancing along, singing fierce songs, in which they swore destruction to Muanga's enemies, and fidelity to their king. The entire assembly rose on my entrance, and I addressed Muanga as follows:—

"Well, Muanga, Karema is advancing. This is good, for to-day we can bring this whole matter to an end."

An approving laugh rang through the spacious hall. Then I continued,—

"Well, this affair must be cleared up. If Karema is in the north of Uganda, burning your villages and driving away your subjects, let us go forth this very afternoon to beat him and drive him back to Unjoro. If this pleases you, I am prepared, with the few men that remain with me, to put myself at the head of your army, and will undertake the responsibility of overthrowing the enemy." *Defiance to Karema.*

"The tidings are still uncertain," replied Muanga. "What say you, Gabriel?"

Gabriel, the commander of the Waganda troops, and my very particular friend, prostrated himself before the king, and said, "O Mfalme! the white man, the Doctori, is right. Let us march northwards, and attack Karema." *Debate and difference of opinion.*

Thereupon the Katikiro's confidential man arose, and said, "We Protestants, when we returned with thee a few weeks since to Uganda, bound ourselves to fight Karema and the Arabs only in case they should attack your capital; but we are not bound to march to the north, and to attack Karema ourselves. Tell Dr. Patasi to wait here until Karema attacks us in Mengo. If he desires to go, however, let him await the arrival of Mr. Jackson with the English expedition, when we shall be strong enough to beat not only Karema, but the Wanjoro as well."

I rose and said, "We are strong enough as we are to beat both Karema and the Wanjoro, and if the Katikiro and his party do not wish to march with us, then let us go alone to attack Karema, or at least find out whether he is in Uganda at all. If you do not like this either, then send out scouts to bring in tidings from the north. If, as *Dr. Peters will attack Karema.*

the Katikiro asserts, Karema is really only one day's march north of Mengo, the scouts can bring us news by to-morrow afternoon. I will stay in Uganda till the tidings come. Should this prove not to be the case, I will then march to Lake Victoria to join my boats, and leave all the rest to you. This is my determination. Now say whether it is good or not."

Muanga replied, "Thou hast spoken rightly. If the Katikiro and his party will not join us in the fight, let us send out scouts, who shall bring us tidings by to-morrow afternoon. If they tell us that Karema is coming, fight with us against him ; but if they report that the news is a lie, go to the lake, where the boats shall remain waiting for thee in the meantime."

This proposal met with general acceptance, and I was told it was immediately to be put into execution. Accordingly, I returned to my camp. That evening Mr. Walker, of the English Mission, came to tell me that he did not believe any scouts had been sent out. He was already inclined to think that the whole matter was a fabrication.

Mr. Walker's visit.

I waited until the following afternoon, when Mons. Lourdel called, to inform me he had received confidential information that Karema was not in the country at all, and that the whole story had, according to my former supposition, been invented merely to frighten Muanga, and to force him once more to make the offer to Jackson that he would accept the British Protectorate in return for assistance. In the afternoon I received a letter from Gabriel, which I still have in my possession. He wrote thus: "My scouts have just come in, and they report that neither Mahdi, nor Karema, nor Wanjoro are in Uganda, and that the whole thing is a lie. Leave here to-morrow if you wish. If, on the contrary, you will stay here, we shall rejoice."

Gabriel's letter.

I now gave decisive orders for departure the next morning. That evening Gabriel spent at my supper table, where I regaled him with tea.

We talked much of Germany and Uganda, and he expressed a wish to visit me some day in Germany. But it would be still better if I should soon return to Uganda, to arrange all matters

DEPARTURE FOR BULINGOGWE. 437

in friendship between the Germans and the English. I may honestly say, that it was a matter of genuine sorrow for me to part from the distinguished and quiet-mannered young Waganda, the only real native gentleman whom I met with in this country.

It was still early next morning when, according to the old custom, we set off southward with beat of drum. The air had been cleared in the night by thunder-showers, that had lasted up to nearly six o'clock, and a brilliant sun illumined the smiling landscape. What a different picture I now saw before me from that of the desolated Uganda, on the day when I first entered it! Everywhere, once more, broad and well-kept roads and happy groups of people; everywhere the blessing of labour in field and village. A feeling of gratitude arose in my heart at the remembrance that it had been vouchsafed to me to assist in bringing about this peaceful state of things in the country, and I experienced a joyous hope for the future. The German Emin Pasha Expedition had been able to do good work after all; and who could tell what further results it might be instrumental in producing for the later development of Central Africa? *A start in the morning.*

Thus with light hearts we travelled ever in a southerly direction through the well-cultivated country. Soon the fields gave way to a park-like forest, traversed by a wide road. Now we enter the region of the hills which tower around the Victoria Lake on the north. Suddenly the water gleams at our feet on the left. The shimmering blue lake lies stretched before our astonished gaze. We descend the slope, and I ask,— *A land of plenty.*

"What country is it that we see before us over there?" *The land of Bulingogwe.*

"It is Bulingogwe," replied Marco.

The boats lay at Kasi, on the right side of the furthermost inlet of Murchison Bay. The Wasesse were speedily made aware of our arrival, and scarcely half-an-hour had elapsed before the quaint boats, with their far-projecting prows, were running across to take my entire column on board. In rapid course our boats go hissing through the calm mirror of waters to Bulingogwe. In ten minutes we reach the island, and I give orders to set up our camp upon the picturesque slope overlooking Murchison Bay and the broad lake towards the south. Behind us lies the dust of Uganda's intrigues; before us rises a new and great problem, which we have to solve. For the first time for weeks, the little marching flag of the German Emin Pasha Expedition, which had seen the Kenia and been carried before us in our Massai encounters, flutters in the breeze.

<small>Brilliant and cheerful expectations.</small>

The eye wanders with delight over the glorious bay, with its wood-crowned slopes, and the heart swells with exultant joy. Difficult tasks and serious obstacles may yet lie between us and our native country; but now, for the first time, the words of Schiller arise in our minds:—

<small>A grand prospect.</small>

> "For each vessel's stately prow
> Toward hearth and home is pointed now,
> And right homeward are we wending."

CHAPTER XI.

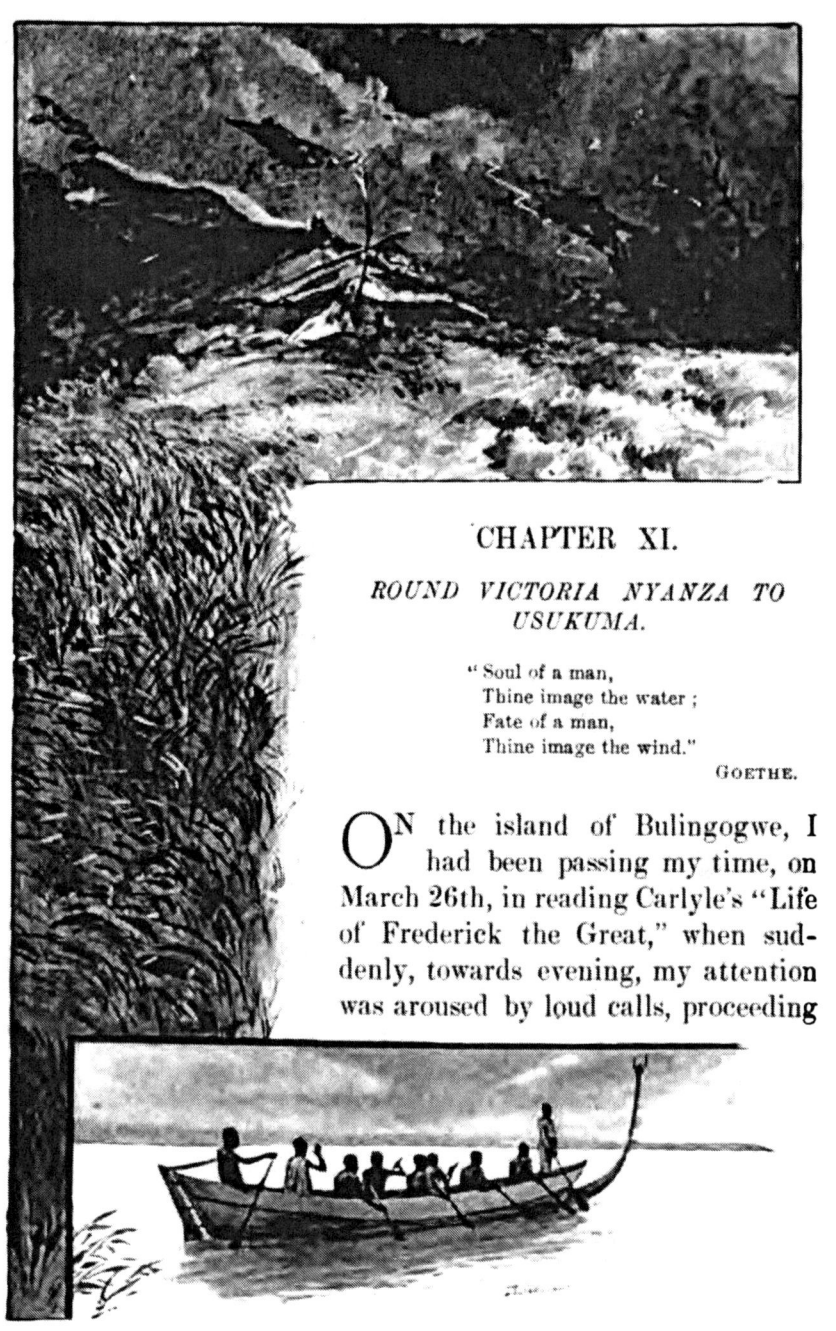

ROUND VICTORIA NYANZA TO USUKUMA.

*"Soul of a man,
 Thine image the water;
Fate of a man,
 Thine image the wind."*

GOETHE.

ON the island of Bulingogwe, I had been passing my time, on March 26th, in reading Carlyle's "Life of Frederick the Great," when suddenly, towards evening, my attention was aroused by loud calls, proceeding from the mountain ridge which intersects the island in a westerly direction. On going to the entrance of my tent, which was pitched upon the western slope of Murchison Bay, I perceived Mons. Lourdel descending the steep, with a few companions. I had presented one half of the donkeys I had taken from the Massais to the Roman Catholic, the other half to the English missionaries. Mons. Lourdel informed me, he had heard at Mengo that the Djumba had had us taken to Bulingogwe, but had then recalled the boats. It at once struck him that this was a trick of the Katikiro's, in whose power we were completely; so as soon as the boatmen received orders to return to Sesse with their vessels, accordingly he had ridden over on one of the donkeys I had given him, and was going to spend the night with me. I offered Mons. Lourdel my best thanks, and at once ordered a festive supper. During the meal Mons. Lourdel acquainted me with some interesting facts respecting Stanley's carrying off of Emin Pasha. I had already remarked, that in the first letter I received from the French in Usoga the news of the revolt of Emin's troops had been communicated in somewhat sceptical terms. "If credit may be given to certain rumours, Emin's troops are said to have mutinied." Now for the first time Mons. Lourdel distinctly told me, "Il n'a pas voulu; Stanley l'a pris comme un voleur;" ("He did not wish to go; Stanley captured him like a thief"); "and, as our people at Ankore have noticed, he treated Emin very badly."

Mons. Lourdel, the French missionary.

Particulars of Stanley and Emin.

As these communications made to me by Mons. Lourdel only represented what he had heard from others, I could not make up my mind to attach much importance to his words, as I could not imagine that Emin Pasha would allow himself to be removed by Stanley, against his will, from a province in which he was governor. Not until I reached Mpuapua did I discover that the tidings I had already received in Bulingogwe, and still further in Ukumbi, did not even convey the whole truth.

Incredulity of Dr. Peters.

By his coup of April 5th, 1889, Stanley not only obliged Emin Pasha to come away with him, but induced him, by holding out various promises, to submit to his dictation. He told Emin he would conduct him round Lake Victoria to

ARRIVAL OF MUANGA'S ADMIRAL.

Kawirondo, and then from Mombas furnish him with the means not only of recovering his former position in the Equatorial Province, but also of reconquering Uganda and Unjoro, though certainly it would be under the sovereignty of the British East African Company. These promises he did not keep, later on, at Usukuma, and thus he compelled Emin Pasha, against his will, to march with him to the coast. This behaviour of Stanley's is the more inexplicable as it was adverse to the interests of those by whom he was commissioned, the British East African Company. The plan, in his bold way suggested by Sir William Mackinnon, of acquiring for England the countries of the Upper Nile, must indeed be called grand. That it failed entirely is, in the first instance, the fault of Stanley and no less of Jackson, both of whom, on arriving at the place, were wanting in the necessary determination to put it into execution at the right moment. This matter formed the subject of conversation between Mons. Lourdel and myself during our supper, and Lourdel once more expressed his conviction that, in consequence of Jackson's indecision, England had certainly lost the opportunity of taking peaceable possession of Uganda.

Sir William Mackinnon's bold plan.

Our conversation was suddenly interrupted by the landing of people from boats just below my tent, and the arrival of a large procession. Muanga's Djumba (Admiral) appeared, bringing with him presents of honour for me; he was accompanied by Nugula, whom he introduced as the Kabaka (king's representative) in the Uganda expedition, of which I was to take the command for the clearing of the west shore of the lake. Nugula prostrated himself before me, and swore to obey me in all things. The flotilla, destined to carry the men employed in the collection of tribute money to Busiba, the projecting land of Karague, to the south of the Kagera, was assembled at Sesse, which I could reach from Bulingogwe in three days.

Arrival of Nugula.

"There you will find nearly a hundred boats. To-morrow morning the thirty-three boats especially destined for the transport of your column shall be in the bay, to take us first to Mfoh."

"And where shall I find the sick people I sent to Sesse a few days since?"

"These, too, will be here at Bulingogwe to-morrow. They lost their way the day before yesterday, and marched to Ntebe. When I learnt that you yourself had started for Sesse to-day I immediately sent boats to bring these back, and to-morrow they will be here again."

<small>Nugula's report.</small>

Here was a fresh proof of the way in which the Waganda keep their promises. I now dismissed Djumba and Nugula, once more giving them orders to have the boats in readiness at sunrise. Mons. Lourdel then retired to one of the huts by the shore, below my tent, where he passed anything but a comfortable night in a lounging chair, as these huts swarm with vermin. The following morning I was roused by a deluge of rain. It did not cease until 6.30, at which hour Mons. Lourdel appeared to breakfast. I take this opportunity to mention, that throughout the expedition I adhered to the principle of three meat meals a day. In the mornings, previous to the starting of our column, a cup of hot coffee, or cocoa, and milk was taken, at which meal cold meat and, as a rule, some porridge and honey were at our disposal. On the march I caused a halt to be made for a quarter of an hour between ten and eleven, when we partook of cold meat and mustard and cold porridge. On our arrival in camp a good soup was immediately prepared, and some meat was roasted, and this proceeding was repeated at six in the evening. Coffee, for which, having cattle with us, we were generally provided with milk, always formed the conclusion of each meal, and, as a finish, we smoked the tobacco of the country from a native pipe. The tobacco differs considerably in the various provinces, but sometimes, as among the Gallas, on the Tana, and in Kawirondo, for instance, it is an aromatic and fragrant luxury. At any rate, we vastly preferred it to some tobacco we found in Ukumbi, which had come from Europe. Occasionally an agreeable addition was made to our table by a good fish from the lake. Besides this, I had the good fortune to secure some large parcels of smoked grasshoppers, neatly packed in matting, which constituted an excellent

<small>Dietary on the march.</small>

<small>African tobacco.</small>

hors d'œuvre. Fried in fat, they taste very much like pork sausages(?); and having had the luck to avert a threatened salt famine by the purchase of ten pounds of Unjoro salt in Uganda, we could indulge in a little salt with them without any twinges of conscience. As at the lake we could always get bananas and other fruits, and often, too, refreshing buttermilk, our scale of provisioning during the next few weeks was an exceedingly satisfactory one for Africa, and, in consequence, we enjoyed good health.

Mons. Lourdel and I waited till half-past seven for the boats to come across; but the Sesse people, of whom the boats' crews entirely consisted, gave no signs of moving. As Djumba and Nugula had been taken back to the other side, we found ourselves in the very position which, on the previous day, Mons. Lourdel had feared would be mine. *Dilatoriness of the boatmen.* We went down to the shore, and signalled across to the Sesse people. No answer; not a sign that we had been understood, or that any one was willing to attend to our summons. I now proposed to Mons. Lourdel that he should go with me to the island, and try if we could not ferret out some small fishing boat, in which we could row across to the flotilla. In the bay, between the mainland and the island, a few of these boats were gliding about, with one or two men in each. In vain did Mons. Lourdel make signs to them to approach. At last, on his telling them that he commanded them in the name of the king, one of them came as far as the reeds on the margin of the island, but he refused to come close up to us. Then Mons. Lourdel lost patience. With one bound he was in the lake, and, before the fisherman had time to row off, he had seized the boat, and, with a vigorous blow of his fist, sent one *Lourdel's energetic measure.* of them overboard. He jumped into the boat, and, wet through as he was, he by himself pulled across towards the flotilla, calling out to me to remain where I was, and that he would bring the boats. So soon as the Sesse people perceived that we had got in possession of a boat, they immediately unmoored the whole flotilla, and began racing across to us, each striving to out-row the rest. They had evidently not intended, with *malice prepense,* to leave us in the hole, but being under no control, had given themselves up to a comfortable "dolce far niente." At the lake I was soon convinced that my way of conducting the expedition, by starting before sunrise, was utterly impracticable with these people. Every morning I had to begin the struggle afresh against the laziness of the boatmen.

<small>Difficulties with idle people.</small>

The Sesse Islands are the great naval station and the sailors' recruiting ground of the King of Uganda. Hundreds of boats are to be found here, which, at a moment's notice from the king, must be placed at his disposal. With this fleet the Waganda have conquered for themselves the supremacy over the whole of Lake Victoria. Any boats belonging to other tribes that make their appearance upon the lake, and do not at once submit to the Kabaka, are, without more ado, seized and destroyed. In this wise all the regions north and west of the lake have been laid under tribute by him.

About ten o'clock Mons. Lourdel, still wet through, returned to Bulingogwe. I immediately furnished him with a change of clothing, but I fear that morning laid the seeds of the fever to which, to my deep sorrow, he soon afterwards fell a victim. I had learnt to esteem very highly the calm and energetic man who so thoroughly championed the interests of his Church in Uganda. He was then thirty-nine years of age, had laboured in Uganda since 1879, and had taken his share in all the vicissitudes this country had undergone. He had, moreover, no desire ever to quit Uganda.

<small>Fatal consequences to Mons. Lourdel.</small>

I now took leave of him. My invalid column had actually been brought over from Kasi to the other side. My baggage and people were soon embarked on the boats, and I took my seat in the largest of them. In the front part of the boat is an open space, where the arm-chair was placed on which I sat. I protected myself against the spray that dashed over the bows with an antelope skin, which Mons. Lourdel presented to me in the moment of our parting.

"Au revoir, Mons. Lourdel; au revoir, either in Europe or in Uganda," I called out from the boat for the last time.

ON LAKE VICTORIA.

"Au revoir in Uganda, if it be God's will," he replied, waving his handkerchief vigorously in salute.

I returned his farewell salutation, and the boats went hissing through the blue waters towards the south. It was indeed a glorious sight, such as is seldom met with. The morning was cool after the downpour of the night, and the power of the sun was mitigated by the fleecy clouds that floated across it. To the right and left the sharp outlines of the coast of Uganda, studded with forests or plantations, stood forth along the wide-stretching Murchison Bay. Before us, in the far distance, was dimly visible a group of islands, of which as yet only the peaks of the mountains showed themselves above the horizon. And the fantastic boats careered onwards, like horses of the sea striving with each other in a race. A light southerly breeze refreshed the senses and nerves. To-day it was scarcely able to curl the surface of the water, nor did we as yet experience anything of the ocean-like motion of the waves which often, even without any great amount of wind, suddenly agitates the surface of Lake Victoria.

Parting with the good missionary.

View on the Lake Victoria.

Mobile as the expression of an intellectual face, is the aspect of the Victoria Nyanza. To-day it raises its blue eyes thoughtfully towards the lofty firmament, glowing with the sweet freshness of youth, awakening the heart to cheerful thoughts. Sparkling in the brilliant sunlight, it stretches before us into seemingly endless distance. On the horizon gleams a verdant isle, or perhaps the mountain summit of an island, like some beautiful Fata Morgana. Here we have before us the actual realization of the Islands of the Blest. White swans and ducks skim along the deep blue water. Eagles circle above it, intent on the capture of fish, which spring in shoals out of the waves, and here and there some large grey-bellied porpoise tumbles about, rollicking in the tepid flood. Thus in its holiday garb the Victoria Lake stretches before us, and only from time to time, like an apparition from dreamland, the shadow of a fantastic cloud glides across its mirror. By noon the eastern shore recedes more and more; we keep along the western side, passing sharply-defined groups of trees and pretty

Fish in Lake Victoria.

half-concealed villages. The boats of the flotilla are, by this time, widely scattered. My large vessel, propelled by twenty-six oarsmen, and bearing the large black, white, and red flag, shoots forward in advance, marshalling the rest on their way.

At three o'clock we reach a flat island, exactly facing Murchison Bay on the south. Here we make a halt, to give the men a short rest and collect the scattered flotilla. But I cannot stay here long. Already, in a quarter of an hour, I give the order to resume our voyage towards the island Mfoh, situated opposite Cape Ntebe, where we are to spend the night. We now turn to the west, leaving Uganda's characteristic coast behind us to the north. Forward we go at accelerated speed, and the foam hisses merrily on the bow of the boat. From time to time we take a wave on board, the spray rolling from my antelope skin. The lake, but this morning smooth as a mirror and almost languishing, seeming to draw the vault of heaven towards it, is now lightly stirred by the gentle evening breeze. Just as when a slight frown passes over a thoughtful brow, its surface now assumes a totally different aspect. Soon mysterious forms arise above the horizon, far in the south-west. At first the spectator cannot tell whether these are boats of strange shape, or what they are. Marco, who is seated behind me, tells me they are the western outlines of the Sesse Islands. The sun sinks lower and lower; the lake in the west is like a glowing mass of fire. My boat rushes swiftly through the waters. I look around me, and find that we are alone. Those distant specks upon the horizon are the nearest of the boats following me.

Our course is directed straight to the land that rises up, ever more sharply defined, before us. I am told, on enquiring, that these are the outlines of the Island of Mfoh. Uganda's coast winds along in a series of bays. Now it makes a sharp turn northwards, jutting forward into the lake, like an isthmus, towards the islands for which we are steering. "That is Ntebe," explains Marco.

The sun has sunk into the west; the evening glow in the sky has flamed up and died away, and now Lake Victoria lies bathed in the pale light of the full moon. The islands to the south-west are no longer visible. Straight in front of us, dark and rocky, rises steeply from the waters this volcanic island, covered with gnarled and often strangely-shaped trees. We involuntarily wonder how a landing-place is to be found here. On nearer approach I become aware of a canal penetrating into the land, which we now enter, and that we have to effect a landing on the Island of Mfoh. Whilst the coast on the east is very steep, to the south and west it is flat along the water's edge. Here the shore forms a wide bay, and now, at seven in the evening, our boat voyage for the day is to terminate. Soon the boat grates upon the flat sandy shore, and the Sesse people jump into the water, to pull it a long way further in. Then I am borne to the shore upon the shoulders of two sturdy fellows. We have reached Mfoh, after a passage of eight or nine hours, but we have still to wait for the other boats before we can pitch our tents and prepare supper. *The canal.*

Half-an-hour elapsed before the first boat came up, and at midnight, when I held a final muster, some of them were still missing. Fortunately the tents and accessories were in some of the foremost ones, so that by eight o'clock my tent was pitched close by the edge of the lake. I had to wait for my supper until nearly ten o'clock, but the moon shone bright, and the contours of the islands rose like phantoms out of the water. My people were lodged in houses in different parts of the island, and late into the night I was busy posting sentries, that the boats might be watched with sufficient care. In those days I still feared intrigues from Uganda. Should the flotilla disappear some night, we should probably all have been doomed to perish, imprisoned on one of the islands of Lake Victoria. It was late when I lay down to rest; but I was destined not to get much sleep that night. *Arrival at Mfoh.* *Necessity for vigilance.*

A storm came up that night, the like of which for grandeur I can hardly remember. Flash followed flash, and that I was in the very midst of the electric disturbance I knew by lightning and thunder being simultaneous. The rain came hissing down on the tent and into the lake. It was as if the floodgates of heaven had opened for another deluge, and the earth was about to be swallowed up by the raging elements. The storm howled and whistled. As my tent, with its iron-tipped poles, was the highest point in the landscape, my position was one of imminent danger. Yet I had no wish to rise. At last it seemed as if Providence intervened to rescue me. The storm and wind that stirred up the waves of Lake Victoria, and dashed them almost to the very door of my tent, caused the tent to rock to and fro, so that every moment I dreaded it would collapse. I may have lain thus for about half-an-hour, when my fears were suddenly realised. The ropes that held down the roof on one side gave way, and I lay buried beneath the weight of the tent. At the same instant the flagstaff in front of it was struck by lightning, and I felt the shock in every nerve. The next morning I discovered the flagstaff lying in pieces upon the ground, with its lance point bent and half melted away. For me there was but one thing to do. With nothing on but my shirt, I ran at a venture towards the huts, where I knew the Somalis were housed. I found them seated round a fire, and at once casting off my wet garment, I wrapped myself in a woollen blanket. Then Jama Ismael folded me in his arms, so that I was soon quite warm, and thus escaped the dangerous consequence of my involuntary shower-bath.

The dawn had come by this time, and I succeeded in finding my servant, and procuring a dry change of clothes out of my trunks. Having shaved and dressed, I refreshed myself with a hearty breakfast after the sufferings of the night. The storm was over, but the waves of the Victoria Nyanza rolled along hollow, with white crests, so that my Sesse people declared we could not proceed further that day. Meanwhile Stephano had arrived at Ntebe, sent by the Katikiro to convey letters to the English station at Usumbiro, and at the same time to carry out official measures for my expedition. He handed me a hypocritical letter from the Katikiro, which ran thus: "I send thee greeting, again greeting, and once again greeting, my friend! Wherefore didst thou depart, my friend? Wherefore didst thou leave us, thy friends, to yearn for thee in Uganda? What wilt thou reply when thy brothers on the coast ask thee, hast thou driven away the Arabs from Unjoro, and wherefore didst thou depart from Uganda before this was done? Greeting, again greeting, once again greeting!" *The Katikiro's letter.*

Two days later I replied to Katikiro from Sesse: "Greeting, again greeting, once again greeting! I have received your letter, and read it without pleasure. I was glad to leave Uganda because your quarrels with Muanga displeased me. You ask me what I shall say to my brothers if they ask me why I departed from Uganda? I shall tell my brothers that you are a liar, and that you and your friends are the ruin of Uganda. I will gladly return to Uganda, and indeed with soldiers and cannon, to help Muanga to gain the mastery over his bad subjects, at whose head you are. Greeting, again greeting, once again greeting!" *Dr. Peters's reply to the Katikiro.*

Although the lake was very rough all the morning, I gave the order at eleven o'clock to embark for the island of Vuvoh, where we intended to encamp that day. To-day the waves of Lake Victoria had the same motion as those of the Baltic; just then one could not recognise it, remembering the day before. Only by dint of great exertion could my men make headway against the south wind. The boat was dashed from side to side, so that every now and then I expected it would capsize. The waves broke over the bulwarks continuously, and we were soon all wet to the skin. *The lake under a new aspect.*

The Sesse people are accustomed to accompany the labour of rowing, almost uninterruptedly, with rhythmic songs. The leading singer stands upon one of the stern seats. He sings somewhat as follows, "Hei, hei, heia! Hei, hei, hei, hei, hei, heia!" Or different subjects form the burden of his ditty. He narrates, always in rhythm, long tales of robbers connected with the lake, and love stories, to which the chorus regularly sings a refrain. Or again, one of the *Songs of the Sesse people.*

Waganda stands up and sings the praises of Muanga and his friend the Msungu, called Kupanda. This song my people caught up, and made a practice of entertaining us with it every morning between the lake and the coast.

"Eh! Buana mkubua etu Kupanda scharo?"
Chorus: "Scharo?"
Solo: "Ia scharo!"
Chorus: "Scharo?"
Solo: "Ia scharo."
Chorus: "Scharo?"
Solo: "Eh! Buana mkubua etu Kupanda scharo!"
("Eh!" (drawn out) "Is not our leader the stormer of cities?"
Chorus: "Cities?"
Solo: "Yes, cities!" etc.
"Yes, our leader is the stormer of cities!")

To-day they endeavoured, by singing with half-hushed voices, to appease the storm; but in this they were not successful. It was not till towards four in the afternoon that my boat reached the island. This time I had taken the precaution of bringing with me my tent, its accessories, and my luggage, so that I was so far independent of the boats behind me, and could at once pitch my tent in a plantation of plantain trees, on the southern shore of the island. The sun of the previous day, and *Sunburnt and wind-burnt.* the wind of the present one, had burnt my face dark-red, and covered the skin with blisters. I became more prudent in future, and used completely to cover my face with linen during the hot hours in the middle of the day, so that, seated in the bow of the boat, I had the appearance of the "Veiled Picture of Sais." The voyage lost much of its charm in consequence, but by this measure I escaped the risk of sunstroke.

My little flotilla had been scattered by the storm, and even on the morning of March 29th the boats were not all together. *Starting afresh for Sesse.* Nevertheless, I resolved to pursue my passage to Sesse. It was necessary, in any case, to encamp there for a day, or for several days, to collect the whole fleet. I longed for the comfortable station and for the society of

Europeans. For that reason I left a few of the Waganda behind to look out for the missing boats, and started about ten o'clock, always steering parallel with the Island of Sesse, which lay before us. Once more Lake Victoria lay spread out smooth as a mirror, raising its dark blue eyes to heaven. The sun lit up with lovely splendour the richly-wooded shores of Sesse, along whose windings we darted like an arrow. In front of us, to the north-west, the mouth of the Katonga, where the land turns sharply to the south, was clearly and distinctly visible. Whilst the north of Lake Victoria consists of high table lands, the western coast is entirely flat. "What land is that?" I enquired. "Buddu," replied Marco. *Sailing by the mouth of the Katonga. Budduland.*

The experience of the previous day had taught me the wisdom of taking on board an ample stock of provisions. So I had well provided myself with meat and bananas, and this greatly contributed to make the voyage an enjoyable one. There was also much to be seen that awakened interest. The creeks of Sesse swarmed with aquatic birds of all kinds; and even if this had not been the case, it was an intense enjoyment in itself to feel in heart and mind the influence of all this gorgeous tropical splendour. The soul drank in, so to speak, the wondrous beauty of the landscape, and, full of idealised enjoyment, the mind gave itself up to poetic delight. Thus we continued our voyage westward, until four in the afternoon. At that time we reached the north-west corner of Sesse, and now the boats turned southward. Soon was distinctly visible the promontory where Sesse approaches nearest to the mainland of Buddu. Here I found, as I had been led to expect, the French missionary station. The rowers pulled in regular time, and the boat shot swiftly past the verdant shores. The figure of a white man, accompanied by a servant, came in sight amongst the bushes. "Buana mdogo!" ("The young master!" literally, "The little master!") cried my servants. It was indeed Herr von Tiedemann. His companion, as well as himself, had recognised us and our black, white, and red flag, and as a sign of rejoicing Herr *Beautiful landscape of Sesse. The French Mission. Meeting with Herr von Tiedemann.*

von Tiedemann fired off his gun. I returned his salute. Soon the boat grated upon the strand, and with a warm shake of the hand, Herr von Tiedemann and I greeted each other once more, after a separation of several weeks. He was much rejoiced to hear that the whole party was on its way hither.

The news of the disturbances in Uganda had penetrated as far as Sesse, and Monseigneur Livinhac had thought I should not get away from thence within any calculable time. All the more joyous were the feelings of my travelling companion, when he heard that, without any long stay at Sesse, we should push on southwards. We strode along the narrow pathway leading from the landing stage, and proceeded up the hill to where the French station stood. To the right, when the summit was reached, stood a long dwelling-house, in front of us the chapel, and all around the clean and well-kept houses of the parishioners, the whole surrounded by cultivated gardens, and framed in by a distant background of dark woods. Monseigneur Livinhac received me with the heartiest of greetings, and congratulated me upon my unexpectedly rapid departure from Uganda, which he declared to be unique in the history of travel in Uganda. I was taken to the refectory, and at once regaled with a glass of wine and with coffee. To my regret, I learnt that one of the fathers, named Schankmerl, was lying in a hopeless state with congestion of the liver. There was something truly sublime, to my thinking, in the calmness with which this state of things was accepted by the companions of the desperately sick man. "We are here to die," was their simple, modest reply. Here was no useless lamentation, no sentimental reflection ; nothing but manly resignation to the decrees of Providence. The well-prepared supper, served in European fashion in the refectory, which was illumined by wax lights, had, so it appeared to me, something of solemnity in it. The level of our conditions of life had been so greatly depressed, that to sup by artificial light seemed like unheard-of luxury.

When supper was over a scene was enacted, which sounds

CONVERSATION WITH MONSEIGNEUR LIVINHAC. 453

so romantic, that it might have formed a part of a drama. We conversed about the affairs of Uganda, Jackson's order for my arrest, and the events of the last few days, and naturally got to mention Mr. Mackay, the leader of the English party in this country. I spoke of the great influence

Mr. Mackay and his influence.

MONSEIGNEUR LIVINHAC BLESSING HIS PUPILS.

he appeared to exercise in Uganda; a view which Monseigneur Livinhac entirely confirmed. I had previously heard, that Mr. Mackay had expressed the hope he felt, of still being able to carry out his programme of making Africa an English possession, from Table Mountain to the Atlas, and also giving it as his opinion that the German companies working there had no real support from the German Government. When the right time came he would let loose the Arabs upon the Germans, and then we should see how soon the whole undertaking there would collapse. Thereupon I suggested the question, whether Germany would not be quite justified in issuing a decree of expulsion against such a man, as these plans really savoured of high treason.

"I should be quite ready to conduct Mr. Mackay to the coast. But," I continued, "when do you, Monseigneur, think of returning to Europe?"

"*Jamais!* I shall remain here until my death."

"That is a pity. I should be exceedingly rejoiced to have had you for my travelling companion thither."

At this moment a man entered the room and threw himself upon his knees at the feet of Monseigneur, whose hand he kissed. He said something to him in the Wasukuma language, which I did not understand. I thought I noticed Monseigneur turn somewhat pale, and I looked at him expectantly.

The bearer of an important communication.

"Mr. Mackay is dead," he said abruptly, "and I am recalled to Europe."

Naturally concluding that Monseigneur Livinhac might wish to be alone after receiving such important tidings, we at once took leave of him, and I remarked to Herr von Tiedemann that had the foregoing scene we had just witnessed been represented on the stage, the author of the piece would certainly have been accused of dealing in the improbable.

The next morning rose bright and clear, like its predecessor. The previous day I had sent Nugula to the smaller Sesse Islands to collect the large fleet with which I intended to make the attack upon Busiba.

I spent Sunday, March 30th, at the French missionary station, to collect my own expeditionary force there. I had had my tent pitched under a huge tree, and as Father Schaukmerl's condition was worse that day than before, we took our meals in the tent—Monseigneur, Herr von Tiedemann, and I. In the night a flotilla of Muanga's had

Sunday at the French station.

come up from Usukuma, laden with powder and ammunition for the king, and with stores for the Roman Catholic Mission. I asked the leader of this expedition to exchange some of his largest boats for smaller ones from my flotilla, which he agreed to do, after consultation with Monseigneur Livinhac. I sent for Stephano, and in Monseigneur's presence told him that from this time Uganda's intrigues must be at an end, and that I was well aware that he belonged to the English party.

"From henceforth I am again the head of this expedition, and no one else, and every one belonging to it must obey me. If you do this in every particular, faithfully and willingly, you shall receive presents from me at Usukuma; but if I once notice that you are working against me, either openly or secretly, you will be flogged and put in chains, and that is what you have to look to." *Serious advice to Stephano.*

If these words addressed to the official representative of the king were somewhat harsh, they produced their effect very completely. Throughout the entire remainder of the expedition I had no cause to be displeased with Stephano.

In the afternoon the last of the boats scattered on Friday made their appearance, and the same evening I learnt that the great flotilla had also assembled. I left orders at Sesse that Nugula was to follow me immediately with the fleet and meet me at Sango, north of the mouth of the Kagera, from whence we would go forward on the following day to Busiba. I then gave orders in my fleet to have everything in readiness for our leaving Sesse on the Monday morning, as provisions were scarce at Sesse, and I was, moreover, impatient to get nearer to the scene of action. So we started southwards already on Monday morning, March 31st. Before leaving we greeted Monseigneur Livinhac, and talked with him on the subject of our travelling together from Usukuma to the coast. *Arrival of the boats.*

Monseigneur intended to hurry after us so soon as he had received from Europe the order for his recall from Africa. This document, he expected, would be delivered to him that very day, as the boats had brought him the news that four French missionaries had left Usukuma to *Monseigneur Livinhac's intentions.*

strengthen the number of their brethren in Uganda. He told us we should probably meet them on Victoria Lake to-day or to-morrow.

The morning was gloriously fine. Upon the strand our people and the Waganda, who had come from the south, were bustling about. In half an hour the boats were unmoored and ready for departure. I entered the largest, which carried the German flag. Another good-bye and *au revoir* to Monseigneur, and away we went merrily upon the lake.

Our journey resumed.

So soon as we had got through the canal that separates Sesse from the mainland quite an oceanic swell made itself felt. The rocks swarmed with sea mews and other birds. The swelling billows dashed unceasingly against the cliffs. All our boats showed themselves equal to the occasion. If at one moment they lay in the hollow of the waves, the next they appeared upon the summit, and soon we lost the unpleasing apprehension of a possible capsizing. The men pulled steadily, singing rhythmic songs; and although their progress was retarded both by the south monsoon and the heavy, adverse swell, yet we got on rapidly enough, and towards the afternoon had lost sight of most of the other boats. Consequently I made my men row somewhat slower, that I might keep at any rate a part of my boats in sight. Between two and three in the afternoon we sighted a sail—doubtless the expected French missionaries. I gave orders to stop, and sent forward some of the boats.

Good boats and good rowers.

It was, indeed, the boat containing the French missionaries, who had no idea of our approach. My people caused them to lower their sail, and now I sped towards them in my large boat.

The French missionary boats.

"Bonjour, messieurs! Dr. Peters" ("Good morning, gentlemen! Dr. Peters"), I called out to them.

"Comment, Dr. Peters! Vous n'êtes pas mort? Nous avons lu la nouvelle de votre mort." ("Dr. Peters! Then you are not dead? We have read the news of your death.")

"Non, messieurs, je ne suis pas mort du tout. N'avez-vous

"How, Dr. Peters?—You are not Dead?"

A MEETING, AND IMPORTANT NEWS. 457

pas quelques bouteilles de cognac pour nous?" ("No, gentlemen, I am not dead at all. Have you not some bottles of cognac for us?")

"Malheureusement pas." ("Unfortunately not.")

We were now alongside, and I here learnt, according to the news from Europe, we had been reported as massacred either by the Massais or the Somalis.

"How do matters stand in Europe? Is there peace there or war?" I continued.

"No war."

"Has anything of importance in Europe taken place?" *Interchange of news.*

"Nothing that we know of."

"How are things looking in the East African colony?"

"The road to Bagamoyo is free, so far as the Arabs are concerned, but threatened by bands of robbers. Our last letter-carrier was attacked between Usongo and Massali, so that we are almost entirely without news from the coast." *Dangers of letter-carrying.*

"What is the state of Usukuma?"

"Food is to be had there, but the Arabs from Morgo threaten the Europeans."

"Have you any news of the Arabs in Karague, to whom we are now going?"

"No, we have always encamped on the islands, for fear of their attacks."

"We wish to spend to-night in Baale. Will you not go with us thither, that we may make one camp of it?"

"We much regret that we cannot do so, but we must reach Sesse to-day, as we are the bearers of important tidings for Monseigneur."

"Then it is true that Monseigneur returns to Europe?"

"Yes, we are now taking to him the order for his recall."

"Then I shall be able to travel with him. I shall expect him at Nyayesi."

This dialogue was carried on half in shouts, owing to the roughness of the lake.

My boat now moved off to give Herr von Tiedemann the opportunity of putting a few questions to the gentlemen. In ten minutes more we had concluded this conversation on Lake Victoria, which had taken place under such unusual circumstances.

Conclusion of the interview.

"Greeting to the gentlemen in Sesse and Uganda."

"Greeting to our brethren in Usukuma."

The sail was now hoisted, and we separated on our different ways towards north and south. The sun was just setting, and tinted the bays in the west with glowing red. Presently we rowed past places from which smoke ascended. I gave orders to land, but was informed that we were not far from Baale, and would find provisions there.

So we continued our voyage by moonlight. At eight o'clock our boats grated on the sand. Here, as everywhere along Lake Victoria, the coast extends flat and shelving very gradually into the water, and the boatmen are obliged to jump into the water and drag the boats a long distance. In fact, the entire lake, which occupies an area about equal to that of the kingdom of Bavaria, is rather flat-shored, and this accounts for the rapid formation of waves at every sudden squall. The whole is volcanic ground. The island groups in the south are, as a rule, nothing more than the edges of craters. It is said that similar crater ridges, forming hidden reefs, exist in some parts under the waters, rendering navigation dangerous. Keelless steamers of light draught are therefore advisable on Lake Victoria, but they should be decked and solidly constructed, to resist sudden squalls and dashing waters.

Flat shores of Lake Victoria.

On my arrival in Baale I had only eleven boats with me. The others, unable to breast the waves, had remained, as I heard later, to the north at Bujaju. A walk of five minutes from the shore, through woods and maize fields, brought us to the village of Baale, where I had the tents pitched, and quartered the people in the huts. As usual, I placed sentries near the boats. A few fowls were soon procured and put into the pot, so that by ten o'clock we were able to enjoy a hot meal. Our diet was still very good, as we had brought rice with us

Arrival in Baale.

DUMO AND ITS SURROUNDINGS. 459

from Uganda, and bananas were to be had everywhere. I had taught my Somali *chef*, Hussein, the culinary art. He understood how to prepare really good soup and to roast meat to my satisfaction. There is no fear of uncleanliness with the Somalis; they are patterns of cleanliness. I intended spending the next day at Baale, to wait for the coming up of the other boats; but as I was told, about noon, that they had been seen on the horizon making southwards, I gave orders to start, hoping to reach Dumo on that day, April 1st. This place is known from Stanley's descriptions of his travels, and, as he relates, he had thought of passing through it this time on his return from Lake Albert. Stanley might have fearlessly gone thither. Sweet peace reigned here, and, as the Christian party were always in possession of boats, he would most likely have been able to collect a flotilla with which to cross the lake to Usukuma.

<small>Hussein, the expert cook.</small>

<small>Start for Dumo.</small>

We arrived at Dumo by sunset. The place is situated on a little bay amidst fields, which we reach, as at Baale, by going through a marshy and wooded tract. Dumo is small. On April 1st it was deserted. This made a melancholy and somewhat discouraging impression upon me. But the evening, when we partook of our meal by moonlight in the open air, passed in lively conversation, and a deep sleep fortified us for the following day. In the morning the lake was rough, and the waves showed white crests, and my Sesse people had no inclination to put to sea; but I ordered them to do so, and though we got wet through, we reached Sango about three o'clock in the afternoon. The place is picturesquely situated on the summit of a hill, visible from afar, and lying to the north of the mouth of the Kagera. From thence an exquisite view is obtained across the mountains of Ankore or Busagalla. Here I had to collect my whole fleet, as the next day would bring us already to Busiba. Of the remainder of my own people I had seen nothing for three days, and was beginning to feel a little uneasy about the matter. Meanwhile we installed ourselves comfortably in our tents, in the midst of an upland furnished with banana trees. Food was here brought to

<small>Description of Dumo.</small>

<small>Waiting for the fleet.</small>

us in abundance, and we could thoroughly take our ease. To my great joy, the boats under Nugula's command arrived in the evening with a great shouting from the crews, and I learnt that all my people were on the way.

On the shore at the foot of the hill, upon which, slightly inland, stands Sango, a varied and lively activity was now manifested. In all ninety-three boats, manned by more than two thousand men, were here assembled. The line of camp-fires looked like the lights of a town. Food was being everywhere sought for, and joyous songs resounded, first from one camp-fire and then from another, and I looked forward to the events the coming day might bring with the greatest interest.

<small>Sango and the fleet.</small>

Early in the morning we were under weigh, in the hope, if possible, of reaching by noontide Tabaliro, one of the islands of Busiba, in front of the mainland, to the south of the mouth of the Kagera. We had a fine view of this river, which, in great breadth and fulness, throws itself here into the lake. At this spot a row of strange, conical rocks rises out of the water. They are mostly tenanted by birds only. The largest of these islands is the fertile and thickly-populated Tabaliro, which we reached at two o'clock. The inhabitants of this island were followers of Karema, and under the influence of Kimbulus.

<small>The River Kagera.</small>

Here my work was to begin. Immediately on my landing with twenty boats, in advance of my fleet, I called together the chiefs of the tribes to hold a council. These are quite a different race from the Waganda of the north. The men are clothed in short coats made of straw, and carry a short spear and lance, bow and arrow; the women wear long petticoats of straw, and look like walking brooms. The people have the unmistakable air of true savages. I was the more interested in them as here, for the first time, we had come within the domain of German interests. I let them know who we were and what was our business.

<small>A conference with the chiefs.</small>

"I come in the name of Muanga, the king of Uganda.

You are to recognise him as the Mfalme of Uganda, and pay him the tribute that you owe him. You must drive the Arabs

WASIBA OF THE ISLAND OF TABALIRO.

out of your country. If you do this you shall have peace; if you will not do it, I shall make war upon you."

It struck me that these people were less submissive than

I was accustomed to find the natives. I dismissed them, with the order to meet together in the morning, when we would hold a conference on these matters.

As several of my boats were visible on the horizon, I entered the village, where I intended, after turning out the inhabitants, to quarter myself. But I soon learnt that the people were preparing to make an attack upon us during the night.

An anxious night. preferred, therefore, to encamp, with my people, close to the shore in the vicinity of the boats, so we returned thither. The tents were then pitched, and soon, for the first time on German ground, the German flag waved merrily in the breeze over the glorious bay. On its shores boat after boat discharged its occupants, and in a short time the coast was covered with the long-beaked craft. To show the people of Busiba that we were not in the habit of being kept waiting by black men, I directed that all cattle in sight should be driven together and taken possession of, and threatened the people that if they did not submit by the evening I would fire the neighbouring villages.

"I have been informed that you are going to make war upon us to-night, and believe that you are foolish enough to do so; but you shall learn to know us. If you choose war with **Warning to the Wasiba.** us, not one of you will escape with his life. You see that your herds are already in my possession, and soon you shall see the flames rising from the roofs of your homes. Therefore decide. Will you recognise Muanga as your king, or die?"

"We will acknowledge Muanga and thee as our masters, and we will have nothing to do with the Arabs," was the answer; but all that evening I received contradictory reports from Nugula and other Waganda. At one time it was that the Wasiba were prepared to fall upon us; then again, when I was about to go at them, I was appeased by being entreated to wait **Reply of the natives.** until the morning. Accordingly, I had a good watch kept for the night, and waited for morning to come. In the early morning came Nugula, accompanied by the heads of the tribes, to tell me that all had been arranged between them. The Wasiba had submitted to Muanga, and would pay the tribute demanded by him, and indeed they would collect it that very morning. They said that Kimbuku and Mtatemboa, the leaders of the English party on the mainland opposite, had fled a few days previously on hearing of our approach. There was, therefore, now no question of a war, and he, Nugula, was prepared, if I so willed it, to carry on the further business alone. *Improved prospects.*

This communication was confirmed the following day, in another part of Busiba, by the arrival of a letter from Mons. Lourdel, dated March 31st. It ran as follows:—

"BIEN CHER MONSIEUR,—Le roi Muanga me charge de vous informer que Mtatemboa, l'un des chefs tributaires, chez qui vous devez passer, s'est sauvé avec une partie de son monde par crainte de votre passage. Le roi Muanga vous prie de passer par le milieu du pays de Mtatemboa, afin de frapper d'avantage de crainte les gens du pays. Je pense que vous n'aurez rien à craindre en passant par l'Uziba.

"Vous ferez bien de brûler la capitale de Mtatemboa et de le faire disparaître et mettre un des fils à sa place."

(TRANSLATION.)

"VERY DEAR SIR,—King Muanga desires me to inform you that Mtatemboa, one of the tributary chiefs, through whose territory you are about to travel, has fled with some of his people out of fear of your passage. King Muanga begs you to traverse the centre of Mtatemboa's country, to strike with all the greater fear the people of the land. I do not think you have anything to dread in passing through Uziba. *Père Lourdel's letter.*

"You will do well to set fire to Mtatemboa's capital, to cause him to disappear, and to set up one of his sons in his place."

The turn matters had taken was a most welcome one to us, as it relieved us of the necessity of fighting once more upon the west coast of Lake Victoria for what, after all, were foreign interests, against foes of whose strength we were not in a position to estimate. Had I received Mons. Lourdel's letter before leaving Sesse I should certainly have carried out Muanga's wish that I should burn the capital of the fugitive Mtemboa. As it was, the letter only reached me at Bukoba, when we had left that district far behind us; and as the report that the entire party of the Arabs in the country had everywhere taken to flight on hearing of our approach, proved correct, I thought it best, in view of my small supply of ammunition, and being ignorant of what might still be before me in the German colony, to desist from a pursuit into the unknown west. I therefore contented myself with carrying out to the letter the commission I had undertaken in Uganda, namely, to bring the Wasiba into subjection to Muanga and to collect the tribute for him. This I did on April 4th at Tabaliro, and afterwards at Bukoba, where I stayed one day for the purpose. I was still less inclined to make an adventurous raid upon the west that was unknown to me after receiving a letter at Tabaliro from Monseigneur Livinhac, describing the situation in the south of the lake, from which I was forced to conclude that there also the German Emin Pasha Expedition would have to fight its way. The letter ran as follows:—

Resolutions consequent on the news.

Collection of tribute.

Letter from Monseigneur Livinhac.

"BIEN CHER DOCTEUR,—Il est vrai que je suis rappelé en Europe par mes supérieurs. Je vais faire mon possible pour vous rejoindre au sud de Lac et profiter de l'offre gracieuse que vous m'avez faite de me prendre sous votre drapeau. Le courrier qui a apporté nos dernières lettres a été attaqué entre Usongo et Masali. Presque toutes nos lettres et nos journaux ont été perdus, ce qui fait que nous sommes toujours sans nouvelles. Le P. Schynse m'écrit de Zanzibar. La Caravane Stanley-Emin y arrivait heureusement à la fin de Novembre. La route est ouverte et le pavillon allemand flotte partout depuis Mpwapwa jusqu'à Zanzibar.

"Je vous prie de vous arrêter à Nyagezi, où vous trouverez une grande maison pour vous loger convenablement vous et vos hommes. De là au Bukumbi il n'y a que trois heures de marche. Les quelques Arabes qui se trouvent à Masawza (golfe de Speke) font ce qu'ils peuvent pour indisposer les populations contre les blancs. Votre arrivée les rendra plus polis, j'espère.

"Au plaisir de vous revoir bientôt et de voyager avec vous.

"En attendant ce plaisir je vous prie d'agréer l'expression des sentiments de profond respect et de haute considération avec lesquels je suis

"Votre affectionné,
"LÉON LIVINHAC,
"*Sup. des Miss. d'Alger.*"

(TRANSLATION.)

"VERY DEAR DOCTOR,—It is true that I am recalled to Europe by my superiors. I shall do my utmost to join you south of the lake, and to avail myself of your kind offer to take me under your flag. The messenger who brought us our last letters was attacked between Osongo and Masali. Almost all our letters and newspapers were lost, so that we are still without news. Father Schynse writes to me from Zanzibar. The Stanley-Emin caravan arrived there safely at the end of November. The road is open, and the German flag waves everywhere from Mpuapua to Zanzibar.

"I beg you will stop at Nyagezi, where you will find a large house to lodge you suitably, you and your men. It is only a three hours' march from thence to Bukumbi. The few Arabs who are at Masawza (Speke's Gulf) are doing all in their power to set the inhabitants against the whites. I hope your arrival will have the effect of making them more polite.

"Trusting soon to have the pleasure of seeing you again, and of travelling with you, I beg you will accept the expression of the sentiments of profound respect and consideration with which I am

"Yours affectionately,
"LÉON LIVINHAC,
"*Sup. of the Miss. of Algiers.*"

Taking into consideration that for the repeating guns we

had scarcely forty cartridges per man left, and that the ammunition for muzzle and breech-loaders had likewise dwindled considerably, it will be readily understood why, on receiving the above intelligence, I confined myself to simply fulfilling what I had undertaken to do.

Position of the expedition.

On April 4th, when all was in order, and Nugula declared that I might leave the rest to him, I quitted Tabaliro at eight in the evening, and travelled further south, with the intention of reducing the mainland of Busiba also to submission.

Departure from Tabaliro.

Night passages upon Lake Victoria are vastly preferable to those undertaken in the dazzling sun, when the reflection of its rays from the water mercilessly burns the skin, and the heat becomes unbearable if we strive, by covering ourselves up, to protect ourselves against them. At night it is cool; one can divest oneself of the troublesome sun helmet, and recline at ease in an armchair. The moon stands bright in the heavens, illuminating, with her gentle light, the land to the right and the mysterious surface of the lake. Far off in the east tower, like a strong wall, heavy thunder-clouds, in which the lightning quivers and flashes incessantly; but above our heads it is clear, and only, like the phantoms of a dream, a light cloud passes from time to time over the face of the moon. All nature lies in peaceful repose around us, and the soul is absorbed in contemplation of the great mystery of the Universe. Like panting horses in a race, our boats fly along, side by side, with the rapidity of arrows, past dark inlets and fantastically jutting points of land, clothed with primeval woods, and stretching precipitately down to the water's edge. My men are asleep, and no sound is audible save the loud breathing of the boatmen and the measured beat of the oars. Involuntarily our thoughts fly homewards to the dear ones in Germany; night bridges over the barriers of space. Thus we travel onwards through the night till towards the morning. From time to time we glide by small islands, rising out of the water on the left.

Pleasures of the passage.

I had intended travelling as far as Bukoba that night, but towards three o'clock the thunderclouds from the east spread above us, squalls of wind set in, and we considered ourselves fortunate that we were enabled, by the greatest exertions of the boatmen, to reach the Bay of Makonga just before the storm came rattling down upon us. The tents were rapidly pitched, and the baggage hurriedly deposited in them. Whilst the lightning flashed, the thunder rolled, and heavy rain came down, I made myself comfortable in one of the houses of the village, where my Somalis were quartered. For my column I had still at my disposal thirty-three boats, and the smaller ones, which were behind, had taken refuge where they

An approaching storm.

VOYAGE ALONG THE COAST OF BUSIBA.

could along the coast. In the morning, passing by Makonga, they proceeded earlier than ourselves direct to Bukoba, where the meeting-place had been appointed.

Before starting for that place I had to inflict a mild punishment on my servant Buana Mku. On the previous evening I had put aside from my supper half a fowl, which I now asked him to set before me that I might finish it.

<small>Buana Mku's misbehaviour.</small>

"The half fowl?" said Buana Mku. "Why, you ate that up yesterday evening," he continued, with a bold front, fancying that I had forgotten all about the affair.

My servants might have had half a fowl, and welcome, as there was no lack of provisions, but the audacity of lying thus to my face induced me once more to teach Buana Mku that it is best to stick to the truth in all the circumstances of life. Twenty-five lashes caused him to incline more and more to this opinion.

<small>Summary punishment.</small>

We then set off for Bukoba, which we reached after a passage of two or three hours. On the left, opposite the Bay of Bukoba, the little island of Bukerebe rises picturesquely from the water. To the south are grouped a few more small islands; they are all deserted. As the Waganda have taken possession of the whole lake, the inhabitants prefer to settle in the interior of the country, to avoid being continually molested by passing fleets from Uganda. Bukoba is the chief point of southern Busiba. From here I was told Karague could be reached in three stages. I gave orders to have the camp pitched upon a green meadow, about twenty-five feet above the level of the lake, commanding an exquisite view of the bay. High woods framed in the meadow at the back. The whole formed a landscape of remarkable beauty, and seemed, by its unique position, to invite the establishment of a station. Later on, in Mpuapua, I recommended the spot to Emin Pasha for this purpose. It is the more particularly suited for a station as provisions are to be had in abundance in the neighbourhood, and the harbour offers good anchorage for boats.

<small>Island of Bukerebe, etc.</small>

THE SULTAN'S SUBMISSION;—BUMBIDE. 469

Immediately on my arrival I sent Stephano, with some soldiers, to the Sultan of the country, to summon him to a conference. He had no desire to be on unfriendly terms with us, and at once sent considerable tribute offerings, both for the men and for ourselves. As a return gift, I sent him in the evening some gunpowder, pieces of stuff, and a few finger-rings, and again, on the following day, received from him three oxen for slaughtering, a flock of sheep and goats, as well as milk and honey in abundance. The Sultan, who, on the first day, had sent his sons to welcome me, himself appeared on the second day, a Sunday, to offer his submission. He promised most unequivocally to pay the tribute demanded by Muanga so soon as Nugula should arrive with his boats for the purpose of collecting it. Here, too, my task was now fulfilled, and I spent a most happy Sunday afternoon on April 6th.

The Sultan summoned.

Promises of submission.

It was Easter Sunday, and the spirit of Easter pervaded our hearts. The moon was full that evening, and we conversed together in front of my tent until late into the night.

We were awakened early next day by a downpour of rain, which lasted the whole morning, and prevented our starting till towards noon. At one o'clock the sun burst forth, and we set forth, hoping to reach the island of Bumbide (called by Stanley Bumbire) that evening. Here Stanley had experienced "the day of terror in Bumbire," as he calls it, on which the natives wanted to drag him out of his boat by the ears, and threatened him with death; a fate which he only escaped by rapid flight. From here he hastened back towards the south, to the island he calls "Refuge Island" (Banderema), lying opposite Soswa.

A quiet Easter Sunday.

Island of Bumbide.

I was most curious to make the acquaintance of the wild tribes that had inspired a Stanley with such fear.

Towards seven o'clock in the evening the high shores of Bumbide showed themselves straight in front of us. For an hour we rowed parallel with them, in a southerly direction. On landing at eight o'clock we went up a steep incline, upon which villages were scattered. Who shall describe my astonishment at discovering an inoffensive, timid people, who eagerly strove to anticipate all our wishes, immediately turned out of their dwellings for us, lent a hand in pitching our tents, and brought in as much food as was to be had in the island! It struck me these people must have changed considerably since Stanley's first visit, and this idea was in no way altered during my further stay on the island.

Friendliness of the natives.

The following morning was wet again, as usual, and I was unable to start until noon for the most southern of the three Bumbide islands, which I reached in the evening. Here the camp had to be crowded into a small space on the shore, which was unpleasant, as I had between nine hundred and a thousand men with me. The evenings were now very enjoyable for us, as we were provided with the materials for lighting, which I had devised in Uganda, namely, a large earthenware pot filled with grease, into which we stuck three or four wicks, which were set alight, and lit up the darkness with a flickering radiance. This was all the more convenient as the moon, upon whose light we had hitherto depended, was nightly on the wane.

On the morning of April 9th I climbed the steep ascent of Bumbide, to gain a view over the lake and the surrounding landscape. Far away to the south-east a speck was pointed out to me as being Soswa, the destination of our voyage for to-day. To the south extended a whole circle of islands, which partially veiled the south-west side of Lake Victoria from view, yet not sufficiently to prevent our being able to follow the line of the coast behind them. My people informed me this was the land of Usindja, extending along the south-west of the lake. I returned in joyful mood to the camp, for to-day would see the end of our southern course, and we were to turn to the east.

View of Lake Victoria.

We set off at about eight o'clock, and pursued our journey at first still in a southward direction. Then on reaching the island of Rubili, where some of the people hoped to be allowed to encamp, I gave the order to turn to the east, towards Soswa. It was a wonderfully fine afternoon. The air was clear, and we could see far into the

Course towards Soswa.

distance. The group of islands we left behind us on the south, whose circular wreath towards the north is formed by the Bumbide islands, looked picturesque and even strange, and led the mind to reflections as to their origin. On this afternoon I recognised more than ever that the region of Lake Victoria was one of powerful volcanic activity. Everywhere along the lake I could discover traces of the water having retreated, and at Ukumbi I learnt from Monseigneur Hirth that the water continued to rise during a period of seventeen years, and then fell again during an equal cycle of seventeen years. Whether this would lead to the conclusion that the bed of Lake Victoria is subject to periodical shocks, I am unable to say, but am inclined to conjecture that this is the case. In like manner, although in longer periods of time, the shores and beds of oceans rise and fall. If these regular alternations in the level of the waters really take place, they can hardly be explained in any other way. *Volcanic region of Lake Victoria.*

These were my reflections on April 9th, as we made for the island of Soswa, which became visible on the distant horizon. The sun went down, but Soswa was not yet reached. Our flotilla had long disappeared behind us; only Herr von Tiedemann's boat, my own, and a third one, kept an equal speed. It was nine o'clock when we came abreast of the foremost of the Soswa isles. It was covered with primeval forest, *The Soswa islands.*
and the wind, which had risen, dashed the waves with a weird sound against the wall of rock. We passed by several islands, bearing through a sort of canal, until at last, when it was already ten o'clock at night, we landed upon a rocky and inhospitable shore in the south of one of them. Pushing through low brushwood, we succeeded in reaching an open declivity, where we could pitch our tents. I established the men in some dilapidated huts, such as the Waganda have everywhere prepared for their night encampment on their voyages. *A primitive encampment.*
They were primitive straw huts, but offered protection from the inclemency of the weather. Many of my men, amongst them all the Somalis, had become seasick on the passage. Had it been necessary to fight just then we should have fared but badly.

That night another terrible thunderstorm, with wind and heavy rain, broke upon us, rendering the tent, with its projecting roof, highly dangerous, while the violent gusts threatened every moment to carry it away. We obtained but little sleep, but on the following morning the golden sun smiled once more upon the glorious lake, whose southern shores were now before our eyes, and cheerfulness reigned around, when at eight o'clock it was announced that some of the lagging boats of the previous evening had already passed Soswa in the early hours of the morning, on their way to Bandelundo, where it was our intention to encamp that day. At once I gave the order for the boats moored at Soswa to start, eleven of them having come in during the night.

Arrival of missing boats.

If our encampment in Soswa had been inhospitable and comfortless, we were richly compensated in Bandelundo. Here we were able to set up our encampment on level ground, beneath the shadow of a huge cotton tree. The sun shone bright. There was a sufficiency of provisions at hand, as we still had with us some of the sheep from the Massai flocks, and grain that we had brought from Sesse.

Encampment in Bandelundo.

Thus we passed a pleasant afternoon and evening at Bandelundo, cheered by the knowledge that the voyage, which gradually began to become very wearisome, would, please God, in two days be at an end.

All these small islands have a very singular appearance, as they are very rocky, and often form the quaintest shapes. They generally rise sharp and white out of the blue water, conjuring up fantastic ideas in the mind, especially in the moonlight. We continued to steer past groups or separate islands, which gave the mind cause for reflections of various kinds. But the charm of novelty had vanished from our passage. As a rule, I used to open my umbrella, and take up to read, out of our little library, some volume that had not been too often studied before. Just then I was once more reading Bulwer's "Last Days of Pompeii," and, in truth, surroundings more calculated to bring before the mind the events in sunny Pompeii could scarcely be imagined. That day we ran to the

A quiet journey.

island of Kuru, situated opposite to Kome, whose inhabitants alone have been successful in resisting the Waganda, and consequently live in bitter enmity with them. We saw cattle at Kome and the smoke of hut fires. I would gladly have sent across to get food from thence, as the corn for my men was beginning to run low, but I had no stuffs to offer in payment, and it went against my conscience to attack a tribe, whose bravery and independence, in the face of the dreaded Waganda, I could not but recognise and admire in secret. *Arrival at Kome.*

The shore of Kuru, by which we encamped, is very stony, and it was with difficulty that a place was found where Tiedemann and I could pitch our tents. We knew that on the following day we could reach Nyagesi, the French Mission station, and were consequently in a very excited state of mind as we sat after supper drinking our tea by the light of our primitive lamp. In Nyagesi, we were told, there was a fine dwelling-house, and we were even dazzled with the prospect of a room on the first floor. Besides, we had been told at Sesse, that European tobacco was to be had there, and that after months of abstinence we could once more indulge in a glass of cognac and water. All this excited the imagination to joyous anticipation, and it was eleven o'clock when, in high spirits, we retired to bed. *Encampment at Kuru.* *Comforts of civilisation.*

In the morning we continued our voyage, passing first along by the island of Kome, and then by the mainland, which in the south-west stood out every moment more sharply and distinctly. Once more the weather was glorious, and at twelve o'clock we passed the island of Djuma, where Stephano proposed to me again to set up our camp, which I, however, declined to do. We then turned south-eastwards, and now the shores to the left, leading in the direction of the creek of Ukumbi, became more and more distinctly visible. We could distinctly perceive that we were approaching the end of our voyage on the lake; but the whole afternoon passed away before we reached the entrance to the sound. At about half-past five we rowed by the marvellously shaped south-west corner of the entrance, and noticed to our left the peculiar, skittle-shaped granitic rocks and basalt *Djuma and Ukumbi.*

formations which lend to the coast of Usukuma such an original character. In the middle of the sound rises a steep little island, covered with primeval forest, which we left on our right. We approached nearer and nearer to the eastern side of the sound, where the settlements and fires of the Wasukuma could be seen. The oarsmen were extremely exhausted by the exertions of the last few days, but now they once more put forth all their strength, and with a cheerful singing of songs we approached the spot where, in the twilight, the outlines of the Roman Catholic Mission of Nyagesi were pointed out to me. I stood in the bows of the boat, expectantly awaiting the moment of arrival and the meeting with the brethren of the Mission. We approached the shore, passing by wonderful formations of rock. The boat ran in; I jumped out, and was accosted from the darkness with words of greeting certainly spoken in a strong Alsatian accent.

Catholic Mission of Nyagesi.

"Welcome to you, gentlemen! I am astonished to see you so soon. Your coming has already been announced to me by a letter from Monseigneur Livinhac. I am Monseigneur Hirth, and I presume that I am addressing Dr. Peters."

A welcome in German.

I called out joyfully, "Good evening! It is indeed a glad surprise to me to be greeted here in the German tongue. Herr von Tiedemann will be here directly; his boat is immediately behind mine."

My words were presently fulfilled; and so we strode onward together, through fields of maize and kitchen gardens, towards the large square yard surrounded by buildings, on the left of which the brightly lighted rooms of the priests' dwelling of the missionary station of Nyagesi gleamed a hospitable welcome upon us. We traversed a long corridor, and Monseigneur Hirth ushered Herr von Tiedemann and myself to the separate dormitories that had been prepared for us. After a hasty toilet, we repaired to Monseigneur Hirth's sitting-room, where Père Guyaut and the Brother of the station were introduced to us. I handed over the letters from Uganda, after reading which Monseigneur Hirth bade us welcome once again. We were then conducted to the refectory, where we found awaiting us what was, according

A sumptuous civilised meal.

to our ideas, a right royal meal. First came a vegetable soup, prepared in the French fashion; next came fish, potatoes, bread, kohl-rabi, beetroot and cabbage, roast mutton and fricassee of fowl; then, as a concluding course, cheese, butter, and fruit, with which we drank cool banana wine, the whole feast winding up with a small glass of clear banana spirit. Who could blame us if our mood was a very excited and merry one? Behind us lay the dangers and discomforts of the Victoria Nyanza, and we now were actually upon the soil of the German East African colony. Our return to the coast and to our homes, which hitherto appeared as a dream in the hazy distance, became from that day a fact upon which we could once more practically reckon, and our thoughts were duly directed to the future. True, I had still many cares before me. Considering the treatment I had experienced since the beginning of the expedition, I had to be prepared to encounter fresh difficulties of a similar kind, so soon as I should reach the territories adjoining the coast. But my nerves had been braced by what now lay behind us, and I had long accustomed myself, when new difficulties and dangers arose in our path, to apply to ourselves the old saying, "I think we also can bear this like men." *[Hopes and anticipations.]*

In holiday mood, I awoke the next day in a whitewashed bedroom. In Nyagesi, in the library of Père Schynse, I had come upon a number of German and French papers, though they certainly only came down as far as the previous August, amongst others the German Colonial newspaper and the *Mouvement Géographique*, of Brussels, in which we read the first account, though in a very distorted and incorrect form, of our landing at Kwaihu Bay. I rose, according to my custom, before six o'clock, and seated myself, in the quiet peace of that Sunday dawn, in the cloister of the station, giving myself up to peaceful reflection. *[News from Europe.]*

At six o'clock the Mission bell rang for service, and I too bent my spirit in humility before God, who had safely led us hither through all dangers and difficulties. We then met in the refectory for a sumptuous breakfast, after which I wrote reports to Germany, which were to be forwarded at once next morning to the coast by express messengers, namely, my two porters, Farialla, and Pemba Moto. I was the more anxious to send these despatches as quickly as might be, as further details had been made known to me in Nyagesi respecting our reported collapse, and I was ignorant whether our relatives in Germany had been already reassured as to our position, by later information. Therefore I wrote a report of some length to the German Emin Pasha Expedition committee, and to the German Colonial Company. As the first of these reports is characteristic of my state of mind on that day, I give it here, although extracts from it were published some time since in the German *Colonial Gazette* :—

Reports for home.

"I am told here, on my arrival in Usukuma, that it has been reported in Europe our expedition had failed, and that I myself was dead. The remark has been added, that this was just what had been predicted, for all the world knew that it would be impossible to pass through the Massai country with an expedition such as mine; that I had voluntarily rushed to my ruin, etc., etc. I beg the honourable committee kindly to allow me to make the following remarks, in all humility :—

Real condition of the Massai country.

"1. Firstly, being on the spot, I was probably in a better position than our critics in Europe, or on the coast, to judge of the possibility or impossibility of accomplishing my expedition with the means at my disposal. It was never my intention to endanger, like a madman, the lives of those entrusted to my care. If, nevertheless, I pushed forward with my small column, it was because I did not consider the obstacles in our path to be insurmountable, despite all the talk that was made about them; and the result fully vindicated the correctness of my view.

A small column preferable.

"2. The difference between my estimate and that of others regarding the difficulties to be encountered, simply lies in the fact that I have but little belief in Arabs or Africans taking the initiative, and therefore feel confident that a certain union

CAMP IN USUKUMA.

of prudence and quick resolve will carry one through. The dangers of Massailand did not frighten me. The travellers who tell us of them—Thomson and Dr. Fischer—never assumed a resolute attitude towards these somewhat impudent sons of the wilderness, and therefore could not be accepted as authorities concerning the difficulties of this march. In reality, these dangers are in nowise so formidable as people say and believe, and my march through this territory, though I had only about sixty or seventy men altogether, had nothing of the conjurer about it, though not without its difficulties, and though on certain days our situation was, to some extent, grave. I sincerely hope that if our example be followed, the so-called 'Massai dangers' will in a short time be heard of no more. At any rate, there can be no question of my having carelessly risked the lives entrusted to my keeping, seeing that I was enabled pretty correctly to estimate existing dangers; and, as the result has shown, I did not underrate them. *[sidenote: Arabs and Africans undependable.]* *[sidenote: Massai dangers exaggerated.]*

"3. It appears to me that, in general, a host of prejudices exist concerning African travel, which, in the interest of opening out this quarter of the world, ought to be set aside as quickly as possible. Foremost among these fallacies is the idea that it is necessary to start with a great quantity of articles for barter, and a large number of porters, to penetrate into Central Africa. As every porter consumes monthly, on an average, the value of a 'doti' and a half of stuff, it can soon be calculated in what space of time he will have eaten up the equivalent of his load. If it should be thought that the larger the number of men the greater the capability of resistance, I can only say that, in this respect, everything depends upon organisation, and that a small force is more easily organised than a large one. The Mgwagwana proper is cowardly, and by his bad example demoralises the better-disposed elements of the expedition. We have proofs of this in the Arab expeditions, thousands of men strong, who have been beaten by the Massais. The English expeditions in Eastern Africa that advanced at the same time as I did, though they counted their *[sidenote: Africa to be opened out.]* *[sidenote: Importance of expeditions.]*

hundreds, were not, I am convinced, nearly so well prepared for fighting, or so capable of resistance, as mine, in which I knew every man, and in which all were animated by one and the same spirit. The danger of being too well supplied with articles for barter is, that these are sometimes used to stave off fighting by paying tribute, which only lowers the feeling of respect for the white race, and increases the simple arrogance of the African. I shall be glad if a comparison between the Emin Pasha Expedition and those undertaken by others results in proving that I have never been guilty of this cardinal fault. The result has also shown, that our expedition has been respected, in all countries, in a manner becoming the dignity of the European race. Even in these countries our enemies prefer to take to flight at our approach, as, for example, in the west of the Nyanza the powerful Arab, Kimbulu, who has one hundred elephant-hunters, fled, with all his following, whom I had undertaken to drive out of the country. The tribes who wish to remain on friendly terms with us have always been well treated. Without exception, we never fought save when we were called upon to do so righteously, in our own defence.

Bribery to be avoided.

A resolute front to be maintained.

"4. In this way our expedition, although Emin had unfortunately been previously obliged to quit his country, which is ever to be regretted, has always been able to work in the spirit which led us hither. It was reserved to the German Emin Pasha Expedition to explore the whole Tana territory, and Usoga also. We were enabled to conduct Muanga and his party back to Uganda, and thus to erect in the north of the Nyanza Lake a Christian barrier against Islam; to attach Uganda, by virtue of the Congo settlement and the principle of the suppression of the slave trade, to the half-civilised states of Africa, such as Zanzibar, and to clear the western coast of the Victoria Nyanza from Arab influence. This was mainly the object kept in view in our movement for the countries of the Upper Nile, whereby we hoped to further the culture and development of Central Africa, of which we justly considered Emin Pasha as the pioneer. I believe

Use of the German Expedition.

Principles of Christianity and freedom.

that Europe generally will be inclined greatly to underrate the importance of this Emin Pasha Expedition. But perhaps the far-sighted will appreciate the moral influence which the advance of so many expeditions for the rescue of one remarkable white man must exercise over the whole of Central Africa. This fact has stamped us in these countries as a superior race, and this is a gain for all time. All honour to Stanley, to whom it was reserved to conduct Emin Pasha back to the world of the white race.* But we, too, have been allowed to help to establish the conviction that the abandonment of the position on the Upper Nile is only an episode, and that the word 'Tutarudi' ('We shall return') is still engraven on all hearts. If Europe wishes to extend this conviction over the entire north-eastern part of this portion of the globe, it would be desirable to send a strong expedition through the lands of the Somalis and Gallas, in order to impress these stubborn tribes too with a sense of our superiority, and at length to avenge the murder of Von der Decken. The exploration of the entire Juba territory would be the geographical outcome of this expedition, which is really demanded in our time. Such an expedition, although undertaken from quite other ethical and geographical points of departure, would naturally take up the views and, perhaps, too, the geographical aims of the Emin Pasha Expedition, and thus would be lifted the last fold of the veil of mystery that now hangs over Eastern Africa.

Stanley's achievements.

Intercourse to be maintained.

Idea of a new expedition.

"5. It appears to me, as I look back upon our own undertakings, that the great struggle for Eastern Africa, which was carried on there between Europeans and Arabs, has been decided in our favour. The Arab rule has been worsted along the whole line. This is due, in the first place, to the action of the German Government by means of Captain Wissmann; but Stanley, Count Teleki, and ourselves may have contributed to the result. Stanley, inasmuch as he defeated the tribes between the Congo and Mwutan Rzige, as well as the Wanyero and Wanera; Teleki,

* So I still thought on April 13th, 1890.

by overthrowing the Wakikuju and Wasuka; and we, by demonstrating the superiority of European arms to the Wagalla, Wadsagga, Wakikuju, and Massais, not to mention smaller tribes, supporting the Christian party in Uganda, and breaking Arab influence in the west of the lake, have worked for Christianity in Eastern and Central Africa. Lastly, all these undertakings represent one great general whole, and in this moral connection the German Emin Pasha Expedition must be included. If it were looked upon in this light, much of the former antagonism against this enterprise would vanish, and it would be allowed that, although apparently the enterprise has failed in its object, it has not laboured in vain in the service of the great moral ideas which are at this moment struggling for realisation in Africa.

Results already achieved.

"I have the honour to sign myself, with unalterable respect, the honourable committee's most devoted servant,

"CARL PETERS.

"P.S.—I hope to be in Zanzibar by the end of June, and to bring with us Monseigneur Livinhac, who has been appointed Superior of the Mission at Algiers."

After these reports had been finished, and I had written a few private letters, I took a charming evening walk, with Monseigneur Hirth, through the plantations of the Mission, which proved to me what can be accomplished in this country by honest persevering work. The most various kinds of European vegetables were growing here. A great stretch of land had been cleared and planted with bananas, which had been introduced from Uganda. Everywhere willing industry and the blessed fruits of work!

A prosperous region of industry.

We were still absorbed in these reflections, when suddenly a noise from the shore attracted our attention, and we were informed of the approach of the remainder of my boats, which had not come up on the previous evening. We hastened down to the shore, and, sure enough, there we could count more than twenty boats, all appearing at about the same spot from behind the islands we had passed the day before. As soon as they perceived the shore they fell into line, and went through some evolutions and manœuvres of various kinds. They then ran in, and I was quickly surrounded by my missing men, whom I had not seen since we were at Bumbide. I hastened to give out cloth stuffs among them the same evening, that they might provide themselves abundantly with food. They were lodged in the houses of the Mission station,

Arrival of the boats.

USUKUMA WOMAN PREPARING CORN.

and soon a cheerful bustling activity reigned amongst the men, who were now convinced—what they had hitherto often doubted—that they should succeed in getting back to their own country.

On April 14th I decided to remove, with some of my men, to Ukumbi, which lies some miles south of Nyagesi. Herr von Tiedemann also made up his mind to go there for a few days, and preferred to proceed by boat. As the Arabs at Margo had not yet acknowledged German supremacy, I considered it important at once to hoist the German flag in

Removal to Ukumbi.

Ukumbi, and, by treaty, to bring the country under German protection, the more so as the French Mission had directly requested me to do so.

On the morning of April 14th Père Guyaut had taken a photograph of our camp and our Askaris. In the afternoon I started, with Hussein Fara and a few other Somalis, and my private servants, and got to Ukumbi towards the evening. Heavy rain had again fallen, and everything looked fresh and green. It is true that the water, lying in the road, considerably impeded our progress, but a tropical landscape always gains by the watery element. The peculiar basaltic pillars, granitic formations, which I had already noticed from the boats, distinguished, as I now found, all this part of Usukuma. The road continues to lead past such formations, and here and there a glimpse is to be obtained of Lake Victoria on the right. On reaching a village half way between Nyagesi and Ukumbi I was met by a donkey, which Monseigneur Hirth, who had gone over that morning, had kindly sent for my use, so that the rest of my journey was accomplished in a very comfortable manner. Over a broad marsh we went slowly up hill, through villages intersected by broad roads between green hedges, surrounded by mtama and maize fields. Suddenly, on our left, upon the slope of one of the above-mentioned hills, the handsome Mission station of Ukumbi came in view.

The road through Usukuma.

The sun was setting as we approached, and the bells of the church were ringing for vespers. We entered, through an archway, into a square court surrounded by buildings. Monseigneur Hirth appeared on the verandah, and ran down the steps to welcome me.

Welcome by Monseigneur Hirth.

The bells rang out solemnly through the twilight, as Monseigneur conducted me to his study. Here the sight of a writing table, with a bookshelf above it, made me at once aware, that I was in a spot where the culture and mental industry of Europe were represented in the heart of Africa.

CHAPTER XII.

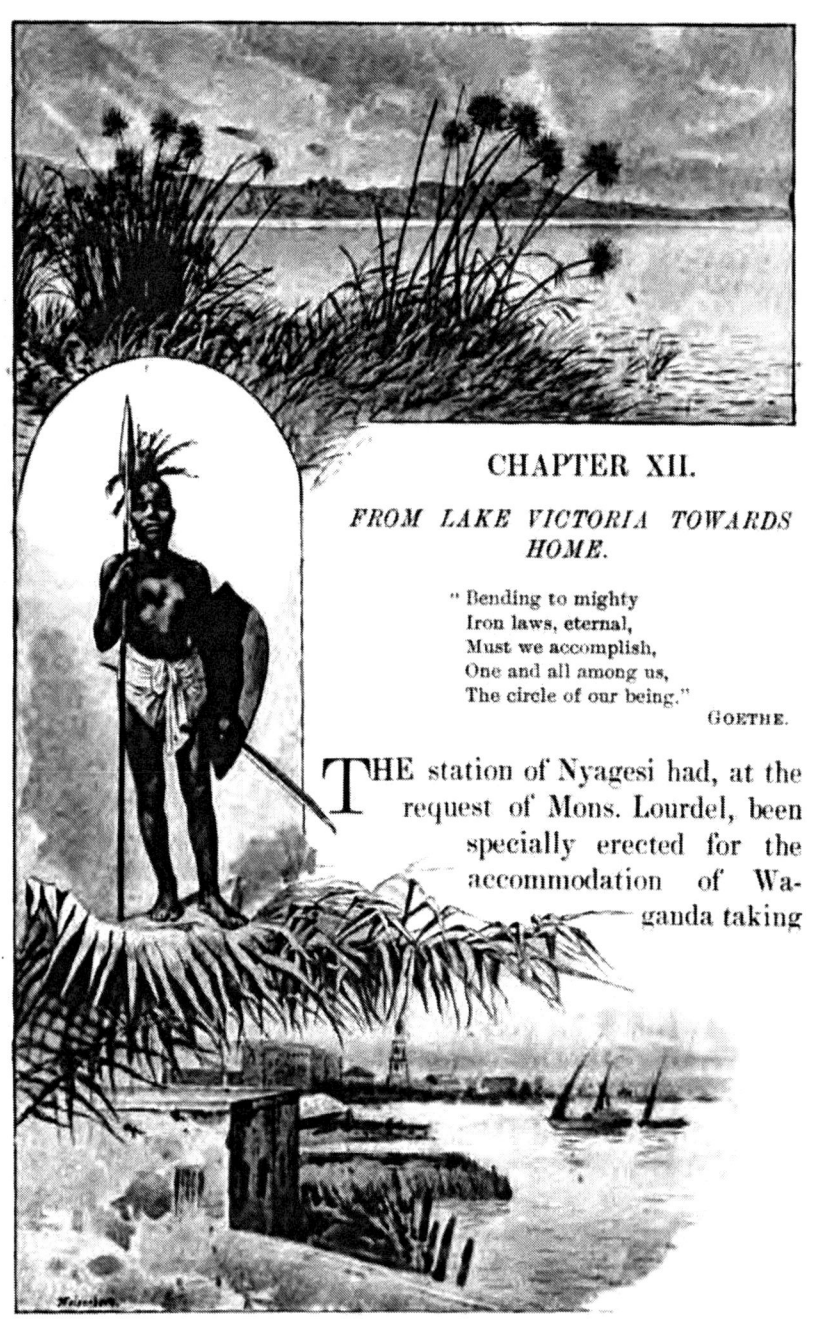

FROM LAKE VICTORIA TOWARDS HOME.

" Bending to mighty
Iron laws, eternal,
Must we accomplish,
One and all among us,
The circle of our being."
     GOETHE.

THE station of Nyagesi had, at the request of Mons. Lourdel, been specially erected for the accommodation of Waganda taking refuge in Usukuma. It was now managed from Ukumbi. As a rule, Père Guyaut went over on the Saturday to hold a service there on Sunday, returning to the station on Monday. During the weeks of our stay in these parts, Père Guyaut remained, with one of the Brethren, at Nyagesi, awaiting the arrival of Monseigneur Livinhac. Hitherto Monseigneur Hirth had been the superior of Nyagesi and Ukumbi, but he had just then been appointed head of the Catholic Missions round Lake Victoria in the room of Monseigneur Livinhac, who was recalled to Europe. Monseigneur Hirth is a tall, spare man, wearing a thin beard and gold spectacles. He bears the stamp of a German *savant*, and is deeply versed in the dogmas of his religion. He speaks and writes good German, though his pronunciation betrays a strong Alsatian accent. Our conversation was carried on alternately in German and French, and many an evening we discussed the differences in the doctrine of our several churches.

The Mission station and its occupants.

Soon after my arrival I was introduced by Monseigneur Hirth to Monseigneur Hautecœur, *Père Procureur* of the station, a very intelligent and interesting little man, who had spent long years in Unjanjembe, and was able to give me much important information concerning Arab doings there. Having a very strong sense of humour, Monseigneur Hautecœur contributed most essentially to our entertainment at table. He manages all the business matters of the station, and is skilful in all manner of industries, from turning and carpentering, to making cartridges and repairing guns. I used to enjoy walking over to his lodgings of an afternoon, and watching him at his work.

The Père Procureur Hautecœur.

Over and above these two, there was a serving Brother at Ukumbi, who, sad to say, soon after my arrival was attacked by dysentery, of which he died during my stay. This man had made himself very valuable to the station by laying out a garden, in which he had cultivated many European vegetables, and fruit from the coast, oranges amongst the rest. This garden was below the buildings, and was watered by a mountain stream, turned from its course for the purpose.

Labours of the serving Brother.

The whole settlement had, for the benefit of health, been

IN ASCKUMA.

built upon a height, upon the eastern side of the very interesting creek; but even this fact was not sufficient to protect it against fever miasmas. Unlike Uganda, the Usukuma country suffers from considerable drought, and, as I was informed, looks quite burnt up during eight months of the year. This drought is often very injurious to agriculture,

The dry season in Usukuma.

WASUKUMA.

and thus it comes that the inhabitants have mostly employed their energies in the rearing of cattle. I was told that during the dry season the beasts are driven into the forests, but I could not quite understand how the people contrived to feed such myriads of cattle the whole year through. When I saw Usukuma, which was during the rainy season, the whole country looked like a fresh, verdant meadow. In the fields maize and mtama were blooming and ripening, as well as sweet potatoes and flourishing bean fields, so that I was forcibly reminded of our marsh land in Lower Germany, when I looked across these plains bordered only by the distinguishing skittle-shaped rock mentioned above. The inhabitants of this country also exhibit the characteristics of the dwellers in marshy plains. They are heavy and sleepy, but, as it appears, reliable and steady. On the whole, we may regard Usukuma as a valuable possession as the Wasukuma, beyond a doubt, make the best bearers, and have in every way good capabilities for work. They have great predilection for establishing relations with the coast and the white race, and will unquestionably, in the future, count amongst our most useful subjects. I place them higher in value even than the Wanjamwesi, more particularly because the latter have for centuries been under Arab influences, to which the Wasukuma are decidedly averse. These people soon attached themselves to me, and from all sides came petitions and entreaties to give them a German flag; petitions was unable to grant, for the sole reason that I had no more flags in my possession.

General aspect of Usukuma.

Good qualities of the Wasukuma.

In solemn form I hoisted our flag at Ukumbi, on the morning of April 16th, thus taking possession, for Germany, of the south side of Lake Victoria. Through the intervention of Monseigneur Livinhac I had, in the first place, entered into a treaty with the Sultan of Ukumbi, in which he recognises German sovereignty, and begs for the flag. It was then with due solemnity hoisted in his capital, in a lofty position, and saluted by us with volleys from our firearms. It was visible, also, to all the boats coming from the north into the creek.

Hoisting the German flag.

The Arabs of Margo, as I learnt from Monseigneur Hirth, had fled into the forests on hearing of our approach, taking with them large quantities of ivory; and the opinion was general in the south of the lake that, after the hoisting of the German flag, they would altogether disappear from that region. Their wealth, in the shape of ivory, already at that time roused the people of the place to propose plundering expeditions against them; but I refused all offers of this kind, as

Flight of the Arabs.

was insufficiently acquainted with the country, and, in view of my small stock of ammunition, was obliged, moreover, to avoid every imprudent step. It was afterwards reported in Europe that the Wasukuma subsequently set to work, on their own account, to slaughter the Arabs, and probably took possession of their ivory.

MISSION HOUSE IN UKUMBI.

The day after the hoisting of our flag, Herr von Tiedemann returned to Nyagesi, as the accommodation at Ukumbi was rather limited; and now began a few exceptional weeks of wonderfully calm existence for the expedition, which had gone through so many adventures of every kind in getting here. In Ukumbi there was an establishment belonging to a Mr. Stokes, which comprised several Wangwana and a number of female slaves. Here my people found amusement by day and by night, and the beer-jug was never empty. The temper of the people

Mr. Stokes's establishment in Ukumbi.

was one of great self-complacence. I could scarcely refrain from smiling, when I saw them dressed up in all sorts of tinsel finery, strutting, with their heads high in the air, among the natives, at whom they scarcely deigned to glance; or when, lounging by the pombe-pot round the camp-fires, they related to the horrified listeners stories about the Massais and Waganda. They now, for the first time during the expedition, received regular poscho, the Catholic Mission having been enabled to sell me a sufficient quantity of stuff, accepting in payment a cheque on Zanzibar. They could pay for their own food; but, in the beginning, they still followed their old habit of simply seizing upon what they wanted, without taking the trouble of purchasing, and were intensely surprised when I responded to this action on their part by an energetic application of my hippopotamus-hide whip. Only by degrees did they become accustomed to respect, in the Wasukuma, German subjects and men, like themselves, under German protection.

Distribution of poscho.

Protection to the Wasukuma.

The course of each day in Ukumbi passed very quietly, in idyllic fashion for me. I occupied a comfortable little room, in which I made a practice of reading or writing during the morning. I rose at six to attend the roll-call of my men, who had to wait for me drawn up in rank and file in front of the verandah. We then partook of breakfast in the refectory, after which an hour was spent in each other's company in the cool verandah, smoking a pipe of European tobacco. Then I used to pay a visit to my Somalis, who occupied a tent to the left of the station. Afterwards I wrote reports or read until twelve o'clock, when the bell called us into the refectory to luncheon, which consisted of soup, roast meat, vegetables, bread, butter, and cheese; and a glass of cognac and water tended to promote cheerfulness. After luncheon, another pipe was smoked, to the accompaniment of a cup of coffee. Each one then retired to his own room. I read, or paid a visit to Monseigneur Hautecœur. Soon after four I called for Monseigneur Hirth or Monseigneur Hautecœur, to take a walk in the neighbourhood. We explored the country around,

The order of the day in Ukumbi.

Luxuries of civilised life.

or we would go to the lake to catch a fish, or into the village to buy honey. At six o'clock came vespers, and at half-past seven we once more met in the refectory for the chief meal of the day, which was followed by long conversations in the room, or, if the mosquitoes were not too dangerously inclined, in the verandah.

It will be allowed that such a mode of life in the interior of Africa is pleasant enough, and some surprise may be felt when I relate that no more than a week had passed before I became conscious of an almost irresistible longing to do something, no matter what—either to attack the Arabs of Margo, or to drive back the hostile inhabitants from the other side of the creek. This desire for action had been too highly strung up, to be rapidly brought down to the level of the quiet enjoyment of life. Then would come hours when the mind, almost exhausted, like an electric battery, was inclined to lose itself in dreamy reflections and poetic thought. Every effort of will subsided, and the soul became quite the "world-contemplating eye" of Schopenhauer. The great problems of existence stood forth in all their distinctness, and, as in earlier years, the mind struggled to solve them. *[Desire to be at work.]*

Sometimes I also took part in the Roman Catholic service. When at six o'clock the bell chimed for prayer, the longings of childhood crept into my heart. I betook myself to the chapel, which was illuminated by wax lights and redolent of incense. In this chapel was a harmonium, on which Monseigneur Hirth was accustomed to play with the touch of a master; and when, to the sound of this instrument, the children sang their Latin hymns with harmonious voices, the soul was touched with a sweet melancholy. On listening for the first time to this music a profound feeling of sadness and pity for myself came upon me. All the passionate struggles and combats of the last few months passed in review before my mind, and I was fain to cover my face with my hands, to repress a convulsive sobbing. *[Service in the chapel.]*

At such moments, differences of doctrine in the several creeds vanish from the mind. "Feeling is everything, name is but sound and smoke;" and music, which, according to Schopenhauer, is the direct reflection of human aspirations, awakens sentiment, even in a higher degree, amidst the threatening surroundings of African life, than it does in the concert stalls of Europe.

Thus the days went by in a dreamy uniform fashion. Of Monseigneur Livinhac we heard no tidings. The rainy season was now upon us in all its force; torrents of rain poured daily from the clouds, mostly accompanied by thunder and lightning. From Usukumba, as well as from Usumbiro, came tidings of heavy floods, which, it was said, rendered the roads to the coast impassable for the time. My men fell ill one after another, and on April 24th Herr von Tiedemann himself was attacked by violent fever. On the 25th I lost my efficient little Musa from Dar-es-Salam, who, after Nogola's death, had been sole leader of the porters. He had gone with two companions from Dar-es-Salam, to bathe in an inlet of the Nyanza. Hassani, who, by the way, was Musa's brother, and one of his two companions, standing on the shore, suddenly noticed a crocodile approaching the bathers. Instantly they both endeavoured to gain the shore by swimming, which Maniumku, the second of Musa's companions, succeeded in doing, but before Musa could reach the land the crocodile had overtaken him, and seized the unfortunate man by the back of the neck; and, before he could utter a cry, both disappeared together beneath the surface of the water.

Waiting for Monseigneur Livinhac.

Musa devoured by a crocodile.

We were just sitting at dessert after our dinner, when Hassani and Maniumku entered, howling lamentably, with the tidings, "Musa has been devoured by a crocodile!" I sprang from my seat, put on my helmet, and shouldered my gun, hoping at least to be in time to execute vengeance upon the crocodile; but the creature had swum with its prey to one of the small islands in the creek, and was no more to be seen. I learnt from the Fathers that the crocodiles of Lake Victoria are particularly dangerous. They overturn small fishing boats to seize the crews, and sometimes even attack people standing on the shore. I was told that many of the

Ferocity of Lake Victoria crocodiles.

Wasukuma lose their lives in this way. I regretted poor Musa much, and forbade my men to bathe any more; but such a prohibition was now scarcely necessary.

As the news from Nyagesi appeared somewhat grave, I betook myself thither on April 27th, to call on Herr von Tiedemann. He was afraid, on the afternoon of that day, that he was suffering from inflammation of the liver; a supposition which fortunately proved to be erroneous.

THE CHIEF PORTER MUSA KILLED BY A CROCODILE.

I remained at Nyagesi on the 28th and 29th, where we one afternoon went out for a general lion hunt, in which Herr von Tiedemann was also able to take part. Every afternoon a lion had carried away a sheep from the flock belonging to the Mission. We took up our position upon a height in the vicinity of the flock, to lie in wait for him; but the impudent fellow must have scented us, for that afternoon he carried off a sheep from another flock that was grazing just behind us. We heard him roaring quite close to

An attempt at lion hunting.

us, when my servant Mabruk disturbed him, but we could not get within range of him.

I returned to Ukumbi on April 30th, with my mind relieved concerning Herr von Tiedemann's health. We sat up late into the night, as I had taken a fancy to watch for the Walpurgis hour.* Unable to sleep any longer in a room, on that night I once again set up my tent in the yard of the Mission station, and retired to it at midnight.

The "Walpurgis night" watch.

But this long watch was destined to have its consequences. On May 1st, after breakfast, I was suddenly seized with a slight shivering fit, and at once felt a longing to go to bed. An hour afterwards I was lying in a high fever, and it proved to be the real marsh fever, or malaria, by which I was attacked. The peculiarity of this illness is, that it acts, in the first place, on the nervous system, and paralyses the will. The patient suffers greatly from depression and from all kinds of distressing hallucinations. He is either shivering with cold, or lies groaning, half dead, with burning heat. In this state he gets to think he will not live through the day. I was quite convinced I should die, and I can say that there was something exceedingly consoling to me in the thought that after all my anxieties and struggles I should lie at rest at last on the shores of Lake Victoria.

Dr. Peters attacked by fever.

But Providence had decreed it otherwise. Strong doses of tartar emetic relieved the system, and then Père Hautecœur, who had taken my case in hand, prescribed regular doses of quinine, which at last subdued the fever, after I had had three days of delirium. But what havoc this attack had made of my bodily frame! Only three days before I was brisk and strong as in Europe; now I had become emaciated and weak to such a degree that I could hardly stand up to crawl the twenty paces that divided the Mission house from my tent. I mention this to show what the malarious fever is on Lake Victoria.

The Doctor's recovery.

---

* The night between April 30th and May 1st (in some calendars the vigil of St. Walpurgis or Walburga) had already in pagan times been a great festival. See the " Walpurgis-Nacht " in Goethe's Faust.—Tr.

Whilst I was prostrated with fever, the Brother of the Mission had died, and had been buried. On May 4th my attack of fever had been overcome, and on the 5th I could once more seat myself in my arm-chair. Meanwhile the report concerning Herr von Tiedemann was a disquieting one. He, too, was pursued by hallucinations. One night he had alarmed the whole Mission station by firing shots from his revolver at some imaginary foes. Such were the tidings Père Guyaut brought to Ukumbi on May 6th. *Herr von Tiedemann's illness.*

Only one course was left for me to take. I must give up waiting any longer for Monseigneur Livinhac, of whom we had not yet heard anything. If we remained in this region of fever, the attacks would infallibly recur, and in the end prove fatal to us. Away, therefore, from Ukumbi, however weak we might feel ourselves,—away to other regions! Change of climate alone could cure us. *Resolution to make a start.*

On May 6th I wrote to Herr von Tiedemann that on the 8th we should leave for the coast. On the 7th he arrived at Ukumbi, where I had meanwhile made every preparation for our departure.

I had engaged twelve new porters, and had bought from the Mission sufficient cloth stuffs to supply the column with maintenance until we should reach the coast. Besides that, I had laid in some provisions for our personal use, from stores which Dr. Hans Meier had sent to the Lake through Mr. Stokes's instrumentality. I took with me eleven bottles of cognac and a few boxes of biscuits. I had also procured two loads of rice. *Stores for the march.*

By the evening of May 7th, we were so far recovered as to be able to take our places at the general supper-table in the Mission. I shook off the effects of the fever with extraordinary rapidity, and on the morning of May 8th was already quite on my legs again. Heavy showers of rain made us defer our departure until eleven o'clock. We were still sitting in the verandah in front of my room, engaged in earnest conversation with Monseigneur Hirth, when the sky cleared. Then I gave the order to sound the trumpet for the start. A loud burst of cheering from all our men proved to me how they, too, had been longing for the hour of departure. The drum was beaten. Accompanied by Monseigneur Hirth and Monseigneur Hautecœur, I placed myself at the head of the column. We left the courtyard of the Mission station, turned to the right, and then our way led over the brow of the heights that shut in the Mission at the back, in a southerly direction, parallel with the creek of the Victoria Lake.

The start from Ukumbi.

The march on that day was somewhat toilsome, but we kept up our courage by the consciousness of being on the road. We had repeatedly to cross swampy lakes and pools, so that it was nearly six o'clock before we reached Ndinga, our camping-place for that day. A great popular festival was in progress at Ndinga. Dancing and singing groups passed continually across the open space by the village, on which I had given orders to pitch the tents, until I had to forbid their noise.

March to Ndinga.

It was a delicious feeling, after the rest of the previous weeks, to feel oneself once more making way; and in joyous mood we sat down that evening together in my tent, the first occasion on which we had done so for a long time. Unhappily our enjoyment was disturbed after supper, for Herr von Tiedemann had a fresh attack of fever, which compelled him immediately to retire to bed. The next morning early we pursued our journey, past well-kept, clean villages, and through a fertile and highly-cultivated country. The contrast between travelling through this sphere of German interests and through the desert steppes in the north made itself felt in a striking manner. I was in the habit of saying that we danced on our way, from the lake to the coast, like ballet girls. Our commissariat was accurately regulated; we had guides to lead us every day who knew the capabilities of the country with regard to the water supply, and I had really no further trouble, excepting that of actual marching. Moreover, at Ukumbi, three Wangwana, who were in the service of Mr. Stokes, attached themselves to our party, under the direction of Salim and Pangani. These men knew the country and the

A pleasant day's march.

Intelligent Wangwana guides.

people well, and I was able, from that time, to make use of them in regulating my relations with the natives. Besides this, on the second day of our march one hundred Wasukuma joined my expedition, in order to travel to the coast under its protection. These people had herds of cattle with them, which they intended to sell at Bagamoyo.

The Wasukuma are a people fond of travel, and in consequence of the great wealth of the land in cattle, which enables them to procure from the coast the coveted cotton goods, the traffic between this country and the places on the coast will, the next few years, be increased beyond all calculation, the more so if, by the establishment of a steamer on Lake Victoria, the activity of the trade between the northern and southern shores is promoted, which will enable the Waganda also to open up trade directly with the coast.

Probable future importance of the Wasukuma.

After heavy rains, the country of Usukuma has very much the appearance of the marshy plains of Lower Germany and Holland. It is as flat as a trencher, completely verdant, and only remarkable for the conical rocks already described. Among these, the eye rests upon mighty herds of cattle, to be counted by many thousands of head, reminding us of the wealth of the Massais in this particular. From these numerous cattle we derived a great advantage, as we could command large supplies of milk, which, especially in the form of curds and whey, furnished a refreshing article of food. I was now accustomed, throughout the whole march, to carry a great gourd containing buttermilk, a beverage equally nourishing and refreshing, which soon restored my bodily strength, that had been greatly diminished by the fever.

A land of plenty.

During the first days of our march, our one inconvenience arose from the marshy state of the ground. Fate appeared unwilling to spare our expedition any of the difficulties of African travel. In the north we had been obliged to struggle on amid dry primeval forests and bush steppes; now we became acquainted with the far greater disagreeables of stamping along for hours through water or mud, risking at every step the loss of our boots, as we often sank up to our knees in the

Difficult marching.

morass, while every day brought with it the danger of a rene[w]
attack of marsh fever; for these swamps are the most pro[l]
hotbeds of malaria.

On May 9th we encamped in the precincts of a very r[]
village called Kabila, which is surrounded by good cultivati[]
and especially noted for its enormous herds of cattle.

Encampment at Kabila. heavy downpour overtook us in the afternoon, fill[]
us with gloomy forebodings with regard to the ma[]
for the following day.

On that day, after crossing a stream, we were to reach
country of Nera proper, where we should come upon Stanl[e]
route. We left Kabila early, and soon found ourselves i[]
horrible quagmire, through which we could manage to cr[a]
with dragging footsteps, in the slowest of time. We contri[]
to reach the ford of a tributary that emptied itself into L[]

Stopped by a river. Victoria, but every attempt to cross it was fruitl[]
The current was violent, and the water rose higher t[]
the men's heads. What was to be done? The guides propo[]
that we should return to Kabila. This I declined to do. A[]
had heard that this river was formed by the junction of [t]

The two branches. streams higher up, I decided to try whether it wo[]
not be possible to cross these separately, one after [the]
other. So we went pounding slowly along towards the east, a[]
succeeded in finding, in the stream that flowed from the nor[]
east, a broad part, where the water only came up to the me[]
chests, and where we at last managed to cross. Forward n[]
for the southern branch! But every effort to find a fordi[]
place here was unavailing; and as the sun had already passed [the]
zenith, I had to make up my mind, willingly or unwillingly,

Encampment by the river. look out for a spot in the swampy plain where it wo[]
be possible to pitch our camp. Such a spot was fou[]
below one of the stony hills characteristic of Usukum[]
just to the north of the place in the river near which we t[]
were, and thither I led our whole caravan. "The water h[]
will have run off by to-morrow morning," said one of [our]
Ukumbi guides, "unless it comes on to rain again."

An alteration had been made in the manner of living in [c]

expedition, inasmuch as I had brought with me a packet of wax lights from Ukumbi, and we could accordingly make ourselves comfortable in the evening in our tents. One candle had certainly to last us for four evenings; but, at any rate, it gave us two hours' light every evening ; and as Herr von Tiedemann generally lay down of an evening, I could devote myself to reading during the hours after supper, whilst enjoying my pipe. This fact, more than anything else, took from our mode of living the makeshift or journeyman workman-like appearance that had characterised our march into the country.

The next morning we returned to the river, and behold ! the guide had been right ; the waters had so far subsided that we were able to overcome this troublesome obstacle, and though we had an hour's wading through the mud for it, we reached the land of Nera, and, in fact, came to a wealthy village in the same. *Fording the stream.*

Before leaving Ukumbi, I had ordered two donkeys to be in waiting here, intending thus to secure an agreeable variety in our method of progress for Herr von Tiedemann and myself. These donkeys were driven up in the afternoon, and although they had not been broken in, and required careful watching, especially at the beginning, as they had a tendency to run away at any moment into the thorny brushwood, they nevertheless proved exceedingly useful to us on the march as far as Mpuapua. The following was now my method of travelling. In the morning at 5.30 the first signal to rise was given, after I had washed and dressed myself. The men had at once to go to their loads, and especially to the tents, which were struck in a moment. Two minutes later the second trumpet sounded, whilst we, generally standing about the kitchen, consumed some hot coffee, porridge, and, since our departure from Ukumbi, a few biscuits, so long as they lasted. Some two minutes more and the third signal was given, the drums beat, and we started on our journey, I marching in front with the guides and our flag, whilst my column quickly fell into order behind me. I usually marched on for two hours, then, at about eight o'clock, the donkey was *The two useful donkeys. A morning's march.*

32

brought, and I rode on it for about another hour. From
to eleven I marched again on foot, and then made a halt
quarter of an hour for breakfast. This meal consisted regul
of cold meat, with usually the addition of porridge. Thereu
we went on again till noon, or past noon, according to
distance of our place of encampment. If it was necessary
march until the afternoon, I made a halt between twelve
one o'clock, and, as a rule, I had cocoa or tea made for I
von Tiedemann and myself; but, on these occasions, I allo
no previous halt. The last stage of the journey I generally r
on the donkey.

In this way we covered from nine to eighteen miles a
The average on our return journey was daily about tw
miles. Here it was, in Nera, that Salim and his compani
joined us, and under their guidance we, on the following mo
ing, pursued our way southwards, further into the land. H

The Nera country. in Nera Stanley had been compelled to fight,
months previously. I consider that Stanley, in
accounts of his travels, draws far too threatening a picture
his position in Nera. The people of this country have alw
had a tendency to be insolent in their behaviour to all carava
but when, like Stanley, a man has the command of a thous
men and a Maxim gun, this insolence is no more than that
a fly annoying an elephant. In all these countries there p
vails what I may call the *vice* of demanding tribute fr

Payment of tribute a mistake. travellers, an evil custom, which is all the more to
condemned as the native chiefs do nothing whatev
either in the way of maintaining the roads or
rendering them safe. Nevertheless, all travellers, Mr. Stan
at their head, have consented to pay this tribute. I alwa
refused on principle to do so, and more decidedly than ever
our return journey, because we were now marching in Germ
territory, and it would have been reversing the natural order
things for the masters of the country to pay tribute to th
subjects. This proceeding of mine one day led to a slig
skirmish with the most southern inhabitants of the land,
Wasekke. These people employ the tactics, if I may so c

DIFFICULTIES WITH THE WASEKKE. 499

them, of shrieking and howling at caravans, in order to intimidate them. As I learned from my servant Selek, a native of the country, it is by no means the fashion with them to kill people, but they only do this as a pretence, and generally cause the bearers to drop their loads, *Tactics of the Wasekke.*

ANIMAL LIFE IN THE DESERT.

which then become the welcome prey of the natives. When they endeavoured thus to intimidate our expedition, they certainly tried it on with the wrong people. We fired in among them, and four of them had to pay for their folly with their lives. I laid three of them low, and Herr von Tiedemann one. In two minutes the whole body of them had disappeared. I suppose that to Stanley's fancy the dangers of such a position were more vivid than to my brain of Lower Saxony, but this kind of description of travels has the disadvantage of awakening in those who come after a timid frame of mind, which causes them to give way to the unjustifiable and impudent demands of the natives more than is advisable in the interests of the opening out of these countries. *The African character.*

Truth to say, from a warlike point of view, the Africans ar
greatly to be feared, least of all the Bantu tribes in the ter
of the German Protectorate and the rascally Wangwana o
coast. The only people who may inspire any fear in
respect are the Massais of the tablelands.

From May 12th onward I found myself upon the
which Stanley and Emin Pasha had taken. On the 13t
crossed the Wami, one of the tributaries of Lake Victori

Crossing the Wami. Muamara, and on the 14th we reached the co
of Sekke, where we had to fight a little in the m:
above described on the next morning. In entering Sekk
had reached the last border country of Usukuma, and we en
Unjamwesi territory after a four hours' march through a
region wonderfully rich in game animals, amongst whi
was especially struck by the numbers of giraffes and ze
The Wasekke pursued us for a short distance into the prin

Prudence of the Wasekke. forest, but had carefully kept beyond the range o
guns. At length they gave up the vain pursuit,
as in former days, we continued our way alone
unaccosted through the wilds. At one o'clock we reache
first Unjamwesi kraal, Sijanga, where we were receive
the inhabitants with great heartiness.

In this country Mr. Stokes, formerly a member of
English Mission at Usumbiko, carries on his business. He

Mr. Stokes's business activity. his principal settlement at Usongo, from which
he chiefly trades to the Victoria Nyanza. I
already mentioned that I met his agents in Ug
and in the west of the lake, where they were purchasing i
Stokes, like a shrewd Irishman, has hit upon just the
thing in pushing the buying-up trade in the interior, whic
indeed, the one branch in which money is still to be n
There is no room left for large profits in the purchasing
on the coast, where the European has to compete with
Indians, and where the prices depend entirely upon the ma
of Europe. For this reason, from the very beginning, I a
cated the view that the German East African Company sh
establish the centre of its commercial undertakings in

interior, where ivory has still no fixed rate of sale, so that practically its price on the coast is regulated only by the expenses of transport. This course the Company has in these last days adopted, and it is to be expected that it will not only be a gainer, but that it will also contribute in a much greater degree to the opening up and civilising the interior of Africa, than if it had confined itself to erecting factories at different places on the coast. The British East African Company, too, naturally started with this idea from the beginning. The first thing that William Mackinnon did was to erect English stations along the course of the Tana upward, at Miansini on the Naiwascha Lake, and at Kwasundu on the Victoria Nyanza. Through Mr. Stokes's establishment, which is situated about four or five days' journey from Tabora, Usongo has become, in reality, the second commercial and political centre of Unjamwesi, and, as such, stands in a certain contrast to Tabora. *Ideas of trade in Africa.*

The result of all this has been that the traffic from Lake Victoria to the coast has become accustomed to make the circuit over Usongo on the so-called Ndjia Stokisi. As Stokes had to keep up caravan communications from Usongo to Lake Victoria, and, on the other hand, sent his wares from Usongo to the coast, other caravans also followed this same route, so, amongst others, Stanley and his expedition. A glance at the map, however, will show that this route is a very circuitous one. Many a morning I experienced a certain feeling of annoyance at the thought that we were moving in a south-south-westerly direction, instead of proceeding towards the south-east, where lay the goal of our march. Monseigneur Livinhac had, already in Uganda, suggested to me the idea whether, in the interests of the trade between the coast and Lake Victoria, I should not strive to open up a direct way from Ukumbi, or even from Speke's Gulf to Bagamoyo. I decided to act upon this suggestion, at least in part, and already in Sijanga made up my mind not to take the circuitous route through Unjamwesi, but to make my way straight towards Ugogo, and thus to cross the Wembaere *The routes of caravan trade.* *Opening up a direct trade route.*

steppe in a diagonal line. Salim tried, indeed, to dissuade me from this intention by calling my attention to the dangers to be encountered at the hands of the Massais, which had been the cause of Stanley's taking the circuitous route through Unjamwesi. I replied: "We know the Massais, and are not afraid of them. Let those who fear the Massais march to Ugogo through Unjamwesi. I shall avail myself of the nearest road thither, and must, therefore, procure guides through the Wembaere steppe."

Unfortunately I was unable immediately to carry out this intention. At Sijanga I had pitched my tent in the middle of the village. In the afternoon, on stepping forth from my tent into the open air, I was startled by a slight attack of giddiness. I went back immediately, sat down in my chair, and took a strong dose of quinine. In spite of this, my Ukumbi fever returned in the night, just one fortnight after the first attack. In consequence, I was under the necessity of making only short marches during the next few days, pitching our camp only about five miles further south each day. On the 16th we encamped at Lindilindi, on the 17th at Sai, and it was not till May 18th that, when my fever had altogether subsided, I was able to push forward in a long day's march, in an easterly direction, to Busiba.

Return of the Ukumbi fever.

Busiba is the furthest Bantu settlement in the Massai wilderness. Here reigns that Sultan Keletesa whom I had seen in Bagamoyo a year previously. The Wasiba people have constantly to defend themselves against the rapacious Massai tribes. A warlike spirit has, in consequence, been developed among them.

The settlement of Busiba.

I was conducted to Sultan Keletesa by a guide who had just returned from the coast. He was the very ideal of an Usukuma dandy. The young gentleman sported European trousers and a European shirt; his head, that he waved in an impressive way, was protected by a European tropical helmet from the rays of the sun, so dangerous to finely-organised brains. But this was not enough for our friend. As he had seen it done in Bagamoyo, he used, when the sun mounted higher, towards

A dandy of Usukuma.

eight o'clock, to put up an umbrella; and for the protection of his delicate hands he would draw on a pair of woollen gloves, No. 13. He looked down with an eye of pity upon our dilapidated condition, and received with dignified gravity the well-deserved homage offered by his compatriots, especially by those of the female sex.

Keletesa had no sooner heard of my arrival, than he hoisted in his capital the German flag he had brought from Bagamoyo, and presently he appeared in person to bid us a hearty welcome. He also showed me a letter from Bagamoyo, signed by Captain Richelmann,—the first German document I had set eyes on for a whole year.

Keletesa's cordial behaviour.

I pitched my tent under the shade of a widespreading tree, and my people quartered themselves in the houses of the Wasiba, which were hospitably placed at our disposal. Mirth and dancing were the order of the day in the kraals, and Keletesa held two long conferences with me. I questioned him as follows:—

AN USUKUMA DANDY.

"When you go from here to Bagamoyo which road do you generally take?"

"I go through the Wembaere steppe in seven days to Usure, and then from Usure to Muhalala and Ugogo, likewise in seven days."

Particulars for the journey.

"Is water to be found for a caravan in the Wembaere steppe?"

"Plenty of water is to be found there now. When the river beds are dry you have only to dig in the sand, and you will find water below."

"Will you give me guides to take me through the steppe?"

"I cannot provide you with guides, as they could not return alone. The road leads all the way close along the Massai country, and you must keep a good watch that they do not attack your expedition. If you want guides, some may accompany you as far as Mpuapua, and wait there till your expedition returns here; but you cannot miss the way if you always follow the traces left by me and my people. Each day you will also find a camping-place I have used, where your people may sleep. There is only one way through the Wembaere steppe."

"Then I shall find water each day?"

"Every day much water," he replied; "but you ought to stay here a few days, and provide yourself with food, for you will find nothing to eat in the desert."

"Ah, I need not stay here some days for that purpose," I answered. "My people have sufficient poscho to last them as far as Mpuapua."

I then summoned Musehe, the head man of the porters, and Hussein, and ordered them to tell the people that each man must buy food for himself for seven days, as we were going to cross the Wembaere steppe.

We started early on the following morning. At first our way led us past a few settlements. To the left the white steppe lay stretched out in immeasurable distance before us in the clear sunlight. When we had left the last settlement of the Wasiba behind us, we entered a remarkably barren country, a grey and dingy region of thickets, with dried-up trees everywhere. At each step we took a sandy dust cloud whirled up, enveloping the whole column. Thus we toiled along in a south-easterly direction until past noon. Suddenly a river came in view. "That is the river Sanguke," said Salim; "it flows to the Manonga, by which we shall sleep to-morrow."

A region of thicket and scrub.

The river Sanguke.

As we had not had a rest the whole morning, I decided to

make a short halt here, and then to go on in the afternoon to Keletesa's first camping-place.

A march of this kind through barren steppes has a depressing effect on the mind; and it was in a somewhat mournful mood that I threw myself down on the river's bank, to await the arrival of my colu

Herr von Tiedemann had remained a long way behind. When he came up he informed me, very sorrowfully, that he was once more suffering from dysentery, and that it would be impossible for him to march further that day. So I set myself to the task of seeking for a camping-ground in the neighbourhood. This was difficult enough, as the ground near the water was slimy, and manifestly a fever trap, whilst stiff and thorny brushwood cut us off from the steppe. *Herr von Tiedemann's illness.*

At last, about twenty yards northward from the watercourse, I found a spot that was somewhat more open, and had it cleared by the axe. The Sanguke and the Manonga already belong to the water feeders of the Wembaere. Day by day we now encamped near some tributary of this river, and crossed the river itself a few days later. I was unable to discover whither it flowed. Salim declared that it belonged, after all, to the Kufidschi system; a theory which, however, I consider entirely unwarranted. It appears to find its way north-eastward into the Wembaere steppe, and perhaps forms the upper course of one of the tributaries of Lake Victoria, flowing into Speke's Bay. *Crossing the Wembaere.*

In this steppe we passed a sufficiently melancholy afternoon. By making use of his bedstead, I had a sort of litter constructed for Herr von Tiedemann, on which he could be carried on our marches by a few Wasukuma porters. For any one suffering from dysentery, marching should by all means be avoided.

Thus we pursued our journey next day in a south-easterly direction. The aspect of the country underwent, in so far, a favourable change, that the foliage had a somewhat fresher appearance, and tracks of game animals were visible here and there. Many ostriches, in particular, showed themselves in the desert, but none came within range *A region of game animals.*

of our guns. The porters who were carrying Herr von Tiedemann remained far behind, so that I began to feel anxious on his account, and sent back men to look after him. However about an hour after my arrival at the camp at Manonga, which I reached at two o'clock, Herr von Tiedemann came in. He **Travelling in a litter.** complained that the stretcher, which exposed him to the burning sun and to the risk of being thrown down at any moment, had rendered the march altogether intolerable to him. Presumably it was to the heat of the sun that we had to ascribe an alarming attack of palpitation of the heart by which Herr von Tiedemann was seized that afternoon, which filled me with dismal apprehension. But on the following morning he felt much better, and was once more able to march.

On our horizon a sharply-defined mountain land now showed itself, which Salim, in reply to my inquiry, designated as Iramba. **The true Wembaere steppe.** Towards the left the eye wandered over a barren tract of desert land, studded here and there with bush—the real Wembaere steppe, which leads into the land of the Massais. At intervals rose a small group of high trees, under whose shade a fresher flora was able to develop itself. Here great herds of giraffes and zebras were grazing, but I was never able to knock over one of them. Our march now always lasted until after midday, as we were compelled, on account of the necessity for water, to keep scrupulously to Keletesa's camping **March through the wilderness.** places. My people generally found there the small straw huts of the Wasiba, in which they established themselves, and we could always rely upon finding water in the vicinity. On the whole, this renewed march through the wilderness had great attractions for me after the long stay in a civilised country on the shores of Lake Victoria. The recollection of my forward march along the upper course of the Tana arose in my mind, and my heart could once more hold quiet communion with itself.

Perhaps an expedition of this kind through Africa offers more opportunities than are found elsewhere for thought and quiet reflection. A man is alone almost the whole day, the di-

and turmoil of the world are far off, and only the great impressions of pure and unsophisticated nature work upon the fancy. Sedately, and free from the feverish strife of Europe, existence flows onwards, and the mind is necessarily raised to the contemplation of the great and the eternal. *Thoughts in the solitude of nature.*
Thus life here gains in mental depth and purity of aspiration, and in the midst of European civilisation the fact of being able to look back upon these weeks lends to this memory something of the longing desire for the purity and innocence of Paradise. In the throes of the grasping strife and struggles of civilisation the mind longs for the grand impressions and feelings of the wilderness, where the Creator Himself appears to come nearer to us in His works, and eternity seems to speak to us in its own mighty language.

May 23rd saw the end of our march through the steppe. This day was one of the most disagreeable I experienced throughout our entire expedition. In the morning we proceeded in a southerly direction, always keeping in view the abrupt blue slope of the Iramba plateau, illumined by the clear morning sunlight. Suddenly a surface of a bright green colour appeared before us, which I was inclined to take for a beautiful meadow. But on this occasion I fared like the grenadiers of Frederick the Great at the Battle of Prague. I was soon convinced that the supposed meadow was nothing but an infernal swamp. At first I tried to march round it, but in half an hour's time I found that it stretched out before us in apparently endless width, and that we must of necessity wade through it. So now for it. From half-past nine in the morning until past midday we waded, always up to the hips, sometimes to the waist, in water, through rushy ground and clinging slime. From time to time I was obliged to call some of my men, as my boots were actually sticking in the slime. With enormous exertion we at last reached an elevated place in the middle of the swamp, where we were able to rest for a short period. Then the business began again, until at last the cause of this marsh became apparent; it arose from the swelling of the Wembaere river, *A difficult and dismal swamp.* *A haven of rest.*

which had overflowed its banks, and which, as a finish, we had to cross in water up to our chests. We all recollected the fate of Musa, and this remembrance, together with the thought that some hungry crocodile might seize the fine opportunity of securing a substantial breakfast, naturally did not contribute to make the wading more agreeable. Exhausted and wet through, we at length climbed out of the swamp on to higher land, where we quickly changed our clothing, so as to avoid catching a deadly fever in addition to all the rest. We now saw before us grazing herds, with their herdsmen, but these latter scampered off at the top of their speed when I attempted to open a conversation with them.

In a state of extreme exhaustion, our column halted at half-past one o'clock, under the shadow of some trees, to get a hasty meal; but we had to march until past three before we reached Keletesa's encampment. I decided to rest here for a day, to collect a fresh stock of provisions for the column for the march across the steppe between Iramba and Ugogo that lay before us. That very afternoon I sent to Sultan Kilioma, requesting him to be kind enough to come to me, to enter into negotiations respecting our relations to each other. I asked him not to forget the tribute due to me; I should require a few donkeys and some sheep. It appeared that the people of Iramba are of the same race as the Wagogo, a mixture of Bantu and Massai blood. They were said to be formidable people, who attack passing caravans, to force them to pay a tribute. Salim told me, however, that the people of northern Iramba were on friendly terms with the Wasiba under Keletesa.

Provisioning the column.

The people of Iramba.

On the afternoon of the 24th the Sultan appeared with a large retinue, amongst whom my attention was especially attracted by a number of young girls, whose whole attire consisted of short skirts made of beads, that were very becoming. I laid before the Sultan the reasons that had induced me to send for him.

"I know very well that you dwell here, close to the Massais, who come to burn your villages, murder your people, and carry off your cattle. Now, I am the enemy of the Massais, against whom we have repeatedly fought, and all enemies of the Massais are my friends. The nearest way from the Nyanza to the coast leads through your territory, and I conclude that in the future many Germans will pass through it. For this reason I will give you our flag, which will perhaps frighten away these Massais. But, above all, my brothers, when they travel through your country, will know at once you are our friend. You will bring them food, and they will then give you presents, and if they want to have guides you will furnish them with guides to Busiba. Are you ready to enter into such friendship with me?" *Address to Sultan Kilioma.*

"I am very willing to do so. The Massais came here only half a year ago and drove away my herds of oxen, and I know that they will come again as soon as they see that my herds have grown large once more. Therefore I shall be glad if the Germans pass frequently through my territory, and I pray you give me your flag, and then I will be the servant of the Germans." *Sultan Kilioma's reply.*

"Very good. Here is our flag for you, which my soldiers shall hoist for you to-day, and here I give you your letter. But understand well, that I also now demand of you that you shall give your support to every expedition under the German flag. So soon as you have had the German flag given you you are of necessity bound to give them whatever they require of you, otherwise we shall make war upon you and destroy you all. But if you are faithful and true to us, my brothers, who will perhaps come, will, on their part, always be willing to make you presents."

After an hour's interview the Sultan left me, and I sent a few Somalis with him, who hoisted the black, white, and red flag on a lofty position. This country is of importance for caravan traffic, chiefly on account of its lying between two steppes, and thus from its position it necessarily becomes a point of support for the journey. *Hoisting the flag.*

On May 25th we pursued our march southwards, still keeping the Iramba mountains on our left. I noticed that in the distance the mountain chain was levelled down, and I decided to cross its most southern spur. Behind it we came upon the productive settlement of Usure, where we were able to provide ourselves with food for the desert march to Uweri-weri. The plateau of Iramba is covered with handsome forests, in the midst of which the people have formed their plantations. In north Iramba we had been told that we should have to fight with the people in the south; therefore on that day I accomplished the march with all the vigilance I had formerly used in the Massai country. But the Wairamba had evidently no desire to measure themselves with us. In the forest, through which our road lay, we met with several wood-cutters, who willingly gave us information, when we asked them, regarding our route. A hostile disposition was nowhere noticeable, and soon we left all trace of this settlement behind us, and were once more surrounded by the vast and barren bush steppe. Here we lost the track of Keletesa's caravan, and had to seek our way for ourselves. About noon, however, we found water, and Salim's Wangwana succeeded in finding Keletesa's track again, so that we managed to reach his encampment, in a sort of moor-like water hollow, towards four o'clock.

The night before I had had the ill-fortune to be found out in my bed by a centipede, which stung me in the finger, so that for the next few days my arm was painfully inflamed and almost paralysed. The following night, when we had gone to bed at nine o'clock, I had a second unpleasant surprise. My servant had placed my washing basin, which consisted of a waterproof bag hanging in a three-footed stand, close to my bed, ready for the morning's use. During the night, as usual, the wind rose slightly, and by moving the tent backwards and forwards it caused the basin to overturn, and to pour its whole contents over my blanket and myself. I called my servant, but could not make up my mind to get up, and so remained lying in my wet blankets. The consequence was, that all the next day I experienced the uncomfortable sensations of coming fever.

ON THE IRAMBA PLATEAU. 511

During this day we continued the course of the expedition towards the southern incline of the Iramba plateau. The ground became more and more undulating, and, in consequence of the moisture, was productive of a richer vegetation. Mighty ferns, like those we had seen along the Tana, towered under the shadow of primeval forest trees, and a growth of fresh grass appeared in the beds of rivers now dried up. From ten o'clock we were continually on the ascent, until, between eleven and twelve, a very steep and difficult mountain barrier had to be scaled. I reached the summit and halted, to await the arrival of my column, that had fallen behind. We partook of some breakfast, and pursued our way along the plateau till towards three in the afternoon. Then the forest opened, and suddenly we saw a field of maize just in front of us. Half an hour's march brought us through the corn fields, and then, upon a hill straight before us, rose a fortified place, with ramparts of clay, strongly reminding me of Kabaras and Kwa Tindi.

The Iramba plateau.

In these countries it is customary for an approaching caravan to announce its friendly intentions by beat of drum. This I was not aware of, and so it came to pass that the inhabitants began swarming about like bees, especially when they saw the German flag. They were afraid we were going to attack and plunder the place. By means of Salim I soon established friendly relations with them, and learnt that we were now in Makongo, in the vicinity of Usure. I had the tents pitched under a huge tree on the left side of the ramparts, and, at the request of the elders, I forbade my people to encamp within the walls of the town. It might otherwise soon come to a quarrel, the chiefs thought.

A panic among the natives.

My efforts to enter into friendly relations with the Sultan of the place himself were certainly unavailing. His relatives came presently, begging me to excuse him, saying that he could not possibly appear, being just then so exceedingly drunk. They were prepared to accept my suggestion to pour water upon him, so that perhaps he might be able to appear in the evening. On my sending in the evening to request that the Sultan might now be brought to me, I

A self-indulgent Sultan.

was informed that the application of water had had no effect, and that he was still drunk, but that he would come to me at five o'clock the next morning. At that hour, however, the state of intoxication continued as strongly as ever. They tried to bring him to me, but he staggered and tumbled down at the gate. As a proof of their friendly intentions, his brother presented me with two oxen for slaughtering, with which I had to console myself for the unsuccessful attempt at concluding friendship.

On leaving Makongo we proceeded in a south-easterly direction, leaving the southern incline of the Iramba plateau behind, to the north of us. We had soon left the plantations, and were once more out in the bush forest.

That morning I had the misfortune that my donkey ran away with me, without any apparent reason, into the midst of the thorny thicket, where my left hand was mercilessly lacerated. From that time I adopted the plan Herr von Tiedemann had always followed, namely, that of having my untrained donkey soberly led by a Somali; which method, although it did not present a very imposing appearance, was at least a comfortable and practical proceeding.

<small>A mischance through my donkey.</small>

At eleven o'clock the forest once more opened before us, and we saw more plantations, which were, indeed, the fields of the sultanate of Usure. But I passed by the first villages without halting, as I wished to press on to the capital, where a Sultana wields the sceptre. We did not reach this place—which is also surrounded with strong walls—until after one o'clock. To our sorrow we were told, immediately on our arrival, that the Sultana very much regretted that she could not receive us, but that she and all her court were very drunk. It was just harvest time, when, as I might easily see, the corn-cultivating tribes of Africa are more or less drunk every day. The movement that hopes, by preventing the importation of spirits, to put an end to the consumption of alcohol in Africa, is in error; for this reason, that the natives have for thousands of years prepared their own beverages, and make themselves drunk so long as a grain of yellow corn is to be had anywhere. The different sorts of native pombe

<small>The unladylike Sultana.</small>

<small>Native and foreign alcohol.</small>

are certainly lighter than European brandy, and as the natives have always been accustomed to put away large quantities, there can be no doubt that brandy is far more injurious to them than their native alcohol.

I was compelled here in Usure also, on this day, to dispense with the personal acquaintance of the Sultana, formerly a friend of Dr. Fischer. Her prime minister, however, who was dressed altogether in red, visited me several times, enquired respecting our wishes, and very readily supplied us with all sorts of food.

The fever of which I had felt the premonitory symptoms the day before, now broke out. The attack was indeed a slight one, and passed off on the following day; but it was tiresome, nevertheless, as it had reduced the bodily strength I was only just regaining. *Return of fever.*

In Usure also I determined to enter upon a treaty, by which the Sultana acknowledged our supremacy, and to hoist our flag. This was done on May 29th, 1890. On a height, visible from afar, the black, white, and red flag was displayed, and greeted by three volleys from three Somalis.

The importance of Usure, for the development of the caravan road opened up by me, is similar to that of north Iramba. Caravans coming from either side can here recover from the fatigues of the march across the steppe, and take in a fresh stock of provisions. *Importance of Usure.*

When we were just about to make a start, I was informed that Mandutto had disappeared. I learnt that the reason for this step was that, a few days previously, he had wounded his wife—a young and very handsome Galla-woman—in the hip with a knife. In consequence of this she was unable to march any further with us, and Mandutto would not leave her behind. Negroes are all very faithful to their wives and sweethearts, a fact I was able to verify during my entire journey. So far as regarded Mandutto, I was sorry he had not spoken to me about it, for I would willingly have paid him his well-earned wages, and I now had porters in abundance at my command. It was a great sacrifice on the part of *Sudden departure of Mandutto.*

the intelligent fellow, who forfeited his whole pay in order to remain with his sick wife.

On May 31st we left Usure, and once more made our way into the bush. The Sultana had presented me with three oxen, which I had taken with us, intending to have one killed every second day. Besides these, I also provided myself with eighteen fowls, which were carried in baskets for us, as well as several sheep, that were driven. I may mention, by the way, that the food for these fowls gave out in the desert. In order, at any rate, to preserve some of them for our use, I thereupon adopted the somewhat original method of having two fowls killed, cooked, and chopped up every day as food for the rest; by which measure our stock indeed rapidly dwindled, but nevertheless lasted us for the march through the steppe. Sometimes, too, the fowls were fed with scraps of mutton cutlets.

Departure from Usure.

Our cannibal fowls.

On the day we started, I had to break our march near a pool of water we found in the forest, as Herr von Tiedemann once more fell seriously ill. He was again attacked by dysentery, which, especially on the first day, assumed a truly alarming character, so that I feared the worst. He had faithfully gone through all the fatigues and dangers of the expedition with me; I could not bear the thought that I might lose him on the last stage of it.

Herr von Tiedemann's illness.

To give him a little rest, I remained encamped in the forest on June 1st. In these last days I had entirely recovered from my last attack of fever, by sleeping, literally, day and night. On that June 1st I slept nineteen hours out of the twenty-four, the remaining five being seriously devoted to the taking of nourishment.

A day's rest.

On June 2nd I started, a man completely refreshed, but Herr von Tiedemann was so weak that he could hardly keep up with the expedition. In consequence, I ordered Salim and the Wangwana, in the evening, to make him a comfortable hammock, and persuaded him to make use of it from that time forth, taking care to appoint four sturdy Wasukuma to act as his bearers. Thanks to his strong constitution, which time

Hammock travelling.

after time shook off the attacks of illness, his health gradually improved under these circumstances, so that he was fairly convalescent on arriving at Mpuapua, where Emin Pasha prescribed more effectual remedies for him.

Thus we journeyed onward through the arid steppe, ever in a southerly direction. We had always to march until past noon before we came to water, but still we found some every day, although we were compelled every now and then to dig for it. Three or four wells along this route would be quite sufficient to make it practicable all the year round, and this would mean a shortening of the way, to the saving of nine days in the journey between the coast and Lake Victoria. The road is even and good, although occasionally rendered somewhat difficult on account of brushwood, and beasts of burden can also find ample fodder. Therefore I think this route has a future before it.

A practicable and short route.

On June 6th, after a long day's march, we at length reached the district of Uweri-weri, which Dr. Fischer, so late as in 1886, had found still in a flourishing condition, but which was now entirely devastated by the Massais. Instead of prosperous settlements, we found a wilderness, and what had once been corn-fields was already choked with brushwood. Only a few miserable ruins remained of the villages, and no human being inhabited the desolate land. The same indignation that had possessed me on the Angata na Nyuki now again stirred within me, against these barbarians of the tablelands, and I sincerely regretted that our old friends did not here make another attempt to try their strength with us. I established our camp just below a hilly ridge, from whence, however, we had an open view of the desert Massai steppe. The day was grey and dreary; an unpleasant wind swept across the steppe, and I sat, in much depression of mind, in the midst of the desolation around us. Water was only to be found in dirty pools. I ordered the tents to be pitched, and was greatly rejoiced at the arrival, an hour later, of Herr von Tiedemann, who was carried along in his hammock; he had borne the fatigues of the day better than I had expected.

The district of Uweri-weri.

For the first time for several days we took our supper together. On leaving my tent, when the meal was over, to give some orders, I perceived that the western sky was illumined by a most peculiar red, which, at so late an hour, hardly appeared to me to be caused by the sun. I called to Herr von Tiedemann to come out. He now told me that during the afternoon he had several times fancied he heard the booming of cannon, which appeared to proceed from the west. This excited our imagination to all kinds of conjectures. Could the struggle between our countrymen and the Arabs have extended so far to the west? Could measures have been taken to occupy Tabora, in order there also to make a clean sweep of the Arab rabble; a step which we already considered necessary when at Lake Victoria? But Hussein, whom I questioned respecting the redness of the sky, destroyed the illusion by soberly declaring that the light came from the sun, which, although it seemed very extraordinary after seven o'clock in the evening, was not impossible.

A strange natural phenomenon.

On the following morning we left Uweri-weri, and proceeded southwards, continually through bushland, arriving between ten and eleven o'clock at Kabaragas, which is inhabited by the tribes of the Wakimbu. The place lies in a hollow, and the people, full of eager curiosity, ran out from behind the red clay walls as we descended the slope. Friendship was quickly established between us; the camp was pitched to the west of the village, and food of every kind provided. For the first time for a week we were again among strangers. The people at once reported to me: "A week ago three messengers of the Badutschi, from Mpuapua, passed along the Usonga road; they are said to be carrying letters for the white man who is coming from Uganda." These tidings were afterwards confirmed to me at Mpuapua. The gentlemen of the Mission had wished to send me a friendly welcome, and also news from Europe. Unfortunately these tidings failed to reach me, because—what no one in Mpuapua could have foreseen—I had marched through the Wembaere desert, and not by way of Unjamwesi. These letters only came into my hands in

In Kabaragas; exciting news.

Germany, several months later. This was the more to be regretted, as they would have spared me much of the anxiety I experienced, even in Ugogo, respecting our possible reception on the coast.

On June 8th we at length entered the country of Ugogo. Towards one o'clock we arrived at the town and district of Muhalala in 5° 47' S. lat., situated three thousand four hundred and fifty feet above the level of the sea. To those coming hither from the north this country lies extended in a charming prospect in the hollow. Before us, to the south, rise the mountains of Bunduko, and on the left are other dark ridges. These are the Bachi Mountains. To judge by the maps, one would imagine the whole of Ugogo land to be a flat savannah plateau. Doubtless this arises from the fact, that every traveller considers Ugogo to be so well known, that it is unnecessary to give any details about it. The consequence is that the map of this country is particularly inexact. *District of Ugogo. Physical aspect of Ugogo.*

That day I pitched my camp in an enclosed space on the northern slope, just above the villages. We had a splendid view over the whole surrounding country. I had scarcely established myself comfortably in my tent, when Salim arrived with the announcement that two Germans had encamped down below at Muhalala, who were on their way from Tabora to Mpuapua. I immediately sent off a letter to these reported white men, by some of my Somalis. My messengers returned in about an hour's time, and said: "There is only one traveller down below, instead of two. This one does not belong to any expedition, but is alone; nor is he a European, but an Arab, and he is not going to Mpuapua, but to Irangi." Here was another proof of the amount of reliance that, generally speaking, may be placed on the communications of black men. *An exaggerated report.*

In point of fact, the man in question was the Arab Mohammed Bin Omari, one of the great Tabora Arabs; he possessed places of business in Irangi, and was now following his caravan thither, for the purpose of sending the ivory stored up there to the coast. *The Arab trader, Bin Omari.*

From all I have heard about Irangi in these latter da[y]
I cannot but think that this country has perhaps a future bef[ore]
it. Like Iramba, it appears to be a damp oasis in the wat[er]
lacking desert, and I was informed that its inhabitants w[ere]
"good," from which it may be concluded that there are [no]
Massais dwelling in it. The inhabitants are probably of [the]
same race that we met with in Iramba, who are closely rela[ted]
to the Wagogo.

Mohammed Bin Omari arrived at my tent after breakfa[st]
to pay his respects to me, and to bring me tribute.

Interview with Mohammed Bin Omari. "Come nearer," I said, on his appearing with so[me] of his followers at the entrance of my tent. "Y[ou] come from Tabora?"

"I come from Tabora," he replied, "and am going [to] Irangi."

"Well, how are things looking in Tabora? Do you Ara[bs] there wish to have war upon the Germans, or do you prefer [to] have peace?"

"We Arabs of Tabora wish to have peace, and have alrea[dy] sent this message to the coast."

"Well, that is right. I think, too, that it is the very b[est] thing for your own interest, for you must have understood t[hat] you are not able to fight against the Germans. You will h[ave] heard that my brothers have defeated Bushiri. We, on [our] part, have defeated the tribes in the north, the Gallas a[nd] Massais, and have come down from Uganda."

"What tidings do you bring from Uganda?"

"In Uganda the Arabs have been beaten just the same [as] in the east. They have all been killed, or have been obliged [to] flee to Unjoro. The Christians rule in Uganda, and [if]

Achievements of the Badutschi. the Arabs wish to carry on trade there again, they w[ill] have to submit to the Christians there too. The w[ar] is at an end; you are beaten at all points, and it is to be ho[ped] you will not be unwise enough again to begin fighting agai[nst] the Badutschi."

"The war is at an end," repeated Mohammed Bin Oma[ri] "and we, all of us, wish for peace. Pray make our peace wi[th]

Uganda. The news about you has already reached us in Tabora, and we know that you can also procure peace for us at Lake Victoria."

"I must first learn what are the commands of the great Sultan of the Badutschi. If he wishes it, then I shall be quite ready to make your peace with Uganda."

"Will you not, then, give me a letter to show that I am the friend of the Germans, and wish to have peace with them?"

"Such a letter I will willingly give you, but know that it depends entirely upon your own behaviour whether you will permanently remain the friend of the Germans or not. Our eyes are sharp, and we soon find out if any one is acting honestly by us, or wishes to play us false." *Conditions of friendship.*

Mohammed Bin Omari now presented me with a few sheep, some rice, honey, and milk. Then he inquired,—

"Is there anything else that you require me to do? If so, let me know; I will give you all you demand. You perhaps wish for stuffs or beads?"

"No, thank you. I want neither cloth nor beads, but give me accurate information concerning the condition of Ugogo. How many days' journey have we to Mpuapua?"

"You will want nine or ten days to get to Mpuapua, if you march well."

"Shall we have war on the road?"

"No war as far as Nsagara, if you pay tribute to Makenge."

"I am a German, and pay no tribute. I paid no tribute to the Massais, and I expect of Makenge that he will not come to us with any demand for tribute. Then, farewell!"

When we descended the slope the next morning, and marched past Muhalala, we found Mohammed Bin Omari standing by the wayside, with some of his followers, to greet us once more, and to make me further presents of rice, sugar, milk, and sheep. It must be said of the Arabs that they are most polite and respectful in their manners, and their behaviour shows more refinement than is found in the majority of the white race. *Mohammed Bin Omari's homage.*

I now continued to advance towards the east. At ten o'clock

there suddenly opened upon my astonished gaze a far-stretching region, lying considerably below us, bordered in the distant east by blue mountains. This was the land of Ugogo proper, and the rocky incline before which we stood was no other than the southern spur of the skirting range of Mau, which we had climbed months previously at Elgejo. The eye rested delightedly upon the flat country lying in the valley, that spread out before us like a sea covered with ice and snow.

The difficulty now was to find a place where we might descend. But the Wagogo, who stood around, pointed out the way, and with some trouble the column, as well as the beasts of burden, were successfully transported to the foot of the mountain in the course of an hour. This mountain ridge is called in Ugogo Kilima Tindi. The mountain ridges shining with bluish tints on the distant horizon, belonged to the Marenga Mkali, or to the western boundary of Mpuapua. Salim, who was well acquainted with the country, pointed out all this to me. My troop of Wanjamwesi and Manyema broke into loud shouts of rejoicing on seeing before them the Ugogo they knew so well.

The Kilima Tindi ridge.

We now proceeded eastwards until past midday. The sun shone hotly down upon us. Stanley calls Ugogo a garden, and regrets that he is unable to have a hand in cultivating it as such. He would probably experience a great disappointment if he attempted to do so. This supposed garden, more than any other country in Eastern Africa, is simply a dry savannah, in which the watercourses themselves contain water only in the rainy season, and where even those expeditions which, like our own, traverse the country immediately after the rainy season have continually to combat against the drought.

Deceptive appearances.

The river Bubo, flowing from the north to Ugogo, and forming part of the Rufidschi water system, was already, by the middle of June, entirely dried up, and we had to dig for water in its bed. Out of such a country no garden could be made; cattle-breeding alone is possible, and the cultivation of maize and corn only in a very limited area, in particular positions. Of all the countries through which we travelled

A dry arid region.

Ugogo is the ugliest, and, I may add, the most repulsive; and the disposition of the people is in keeping with the character of the country. The Wagogo are originally of Bantu race, but

VIEW OF THE PLAIN OF UGOGO, NEAR MTIVE.

apparently have a considerable admixture of Massai blood. Like the Massais, they are arrogant and addicted to thieving. They look upon strangers simply as enemies; and as for thousands of years traffic has taken its course through their land, they have established for themselves a predaceous custom of exacting tribute, under which all the trade caravans have to suffer grievously.

In his work "In Darkest Africa," vol. ii., p. 406, Stanley

thus complains, in a somewhat sentimental strain:—"There is no country in Africa that has excited greater interest in me than this. It is a ferment of trouble and distraction, and a vermin of petty annoyances beset the traveller from day to day while in it. No natives know so well how to aggrieve and be unpleasant to travellers. One would think there was a school somewhere in Ugogo to teach low cunning and vicious malice to the chiefs, who are masters in foxy-craft. Nineteen years ago I looked upon this land and people with desiring eyes. I saw in it a field worth some effort to reclaim. In six months I felt sure Ugogo could be made lovely and orderly, a blessing to the inhabitants and to strangers, without any very great expense or trouble; it would become a pleasant highway of human intercourse with far-away peoples, productive of wealth to the natives, and comfort to caravans. I learned, on arrival in Ugogo, that I was for ever debarred from the hope. It is to be the destiny of the Germans to carry out this work, and I envy them. It is the worst news of all that I shall never be able to drain this cesspool of iniquitous passion, and extinguish the insolence of Wagogo chiefs, and make the land clean, healthy, and even beautiful of view. While my best wishes will accompany German efforts, my mind is clouded with a doubt that it ever will be that fair land of rest and welcome I had dreamed of making it."

What a pity for Ugogo that Stanley cannot carry out his plans respecting this country! It would indeed be an enormous advantage for the whole of Eastern Africa if the caravans, instead of passing through an entirely dried-up savannah at the back of Usagara, could make their way through a verdant and flourishing garden. Certainly Mr. Stanley had a capital opportunity offered him "to extinguish the insolence of Wagogo chiefs" when he last traversed this country, and it is only to be regretted that he took no advantage of it.

Lost opportunities.

On June 9th we found ourselves in the western part of Makenge's country, and on this day I set up the camp at Mtive, once again in an encampment that had been occupied by Mr. Stokes. When Stanley passed through Makenge's country nine months previously the latter had sent to him with the request that he should pay tribute immediately. Stanley, at the head of one thousand men, and possessing a Maxim gun, could have utilised this excellent occasion "to extinguish the insolence of Wagogo chiefs," for a demand of this kind for tribute, in the face of so strong an expedition commanded by nine white men, may well be called insolence.

The disagreeable question of tribute.

Instead of setting to work "to drain this cesspool of iniquitous passion," however, Stanley sent Makenge the accustomed tribute paid by caravans. But with this Makenge was not satisfied. He returned the simple tribute, and now demanded of Stanley that he should give him up his men for feudal labour. He desired Stanley to have a fortified camp built for him.

Makenge and Stanley.

Here was the second opportunity for Mr. Stanley "to extinguish the insolence of Wagogo chiefs." He was certainly sufficiently angry at this demand of Makenge's, but instead of refusing it, and waiting for the consequences, he considered it the wiser course to give way, and sent Makenge four times the usual tribute, with which the latter was graciously pleased to declare himself satisfied.

This small episode, which took place during Stanley's sojourn in Ugogo, is not related by him, and I only mention it to make the following circumstances more intelligible.

It is as clear as possible that if an expedition of the strength of Stanley's in Ugogo consented to pay tribute, one could scarcely expect either great respect or corresponding humility towards the white race from the people of the land. Accordingly, what happened to us in this country is not in any way to be wondered at.

Tribute-payers not respected.

We were still sitting at breakfast, when some rascally Wagogo began to crowd round our tent, and one of them placed himself rudely in front of the entrance. On my requesting him to be off, he grinned impudently, but remained where he was. Hereupon Herr von Tiedemann, who sat nearest to the door, sprang from his seat, seized the fellow, and flung him on one side. I too jumped up, and called out to Hussein to la hold of him, and to teach him a lesson with the hipp potamus-hide whip. This was done amidst howls lamentation, whilst the Wangwana informed us that th offender was the son of the Sultan of the country. Whilst th was going on there arose, to the north of the camp, the war-c of the Wagogo, which we knew so well. These people ha driven away my men from the water because I had paid tribute, and now came rushing towards the camp. I in mediately betook myself to the north side of it, and saw ho the Wagogo warriors, armed for the most part each with tw lances, came dancing along, challenging us to fight.

A lesson to the Wagogo.

As they began to shoot their arrows at us, I fired among them, knocking one over, and hitting another in the arn They now took to headlong flight, and immediately som of the chiefs came to me to open peace negotiation The debate upon these continued all the afternoon, an in the evening it was at last decided to send messengers Makenge, to whose capital we were to march on the followi day, and to leave the settling of the matter to him.

A decided check to insolence.

I stationed twelve sentries to guard the camp during t night, and the following morning set out, with beat drum, on our march eastward, passing great crow of the Wagogo as we went. Our way led through almost dried-up river, into the country of Unjanguira. eleven o'clock we came to a well-cultivated territory, whi strongly reminded me of the country bordering Lake Mör near Alexandria. I remarked that large bodies of men we running about behind the maize fields, and was further di agreeably impressed by the hyena-like howl of the Wagogo, which I plainly recognised a war-cry.

March towards the east.

When we had pursued our way through the maize fiel lying east of the villages, I suddenly became aware of sever hundred Wagogo warriors, who were kneeling by the left side the road, with bows bent and lances ready for battle, and o of the chiefs came running towards us, shouting in impude tones the demand for tribute ("Mahongo! Mahongo!"

THE WAGOGO ATTACKED AND DEFEATED.

My contempt for these rascals had been increased by the occurrences of the previous day. I handed my gun to my servant, and, taking my long knotted stick in my hand, made straight for the Wagogo, calling out to them:— *Renewed demand of tribute.*

"Take yourselves off from here, and mind what you are about!"

They all rose, and moved slowly away. I then marched to an encampment in the south of Makenge's capital, and immediately sent a message to the Sultan, requesting him to put himself in communication with me, as I desired to know whether he wished for war or peace.

The messengers returned with their commission unexecuted. They had been warned by a caravan of Wanjamwesi, encamped in the vicinity, not to enter Makenge's capital, where, they declared, thousands of warriors were collected to attack us. To be prepared for this emergency, as I was almost without ammunition for my muzzle-loaders, I sent in all haste for the only load of wire I had brought with me on the expedition, had it filed into pieces, and distributed these among my men. We then seated ourselves for breakfast, during which messengers, sent from the Wanjamwesi caravan, appeared to offer us their friendship. *Makeshift ammunition.*

Whilst I was speaking to them messengers suddenly arrived from Makenge.

"Our Sultan sends you word that he wishes for peace with you. He wishes to be the friend of the Germans, and you are to pay no tribute in his country."

"Tell your Sultan," I replied, "if he desires to be the friend of the Germans, and our friend, he must exchange presents with me. Let him send me corn and honey, and I will give him powder and cloth stuffs." *Makenge's messenger rebuked.*

We were still in conversation, when the clatter of guns, proceeding from the west of our camp, again near the water, suddenly resounded. In wild haste my men came rushing to the camp from that direction. Seizing my double-barrelled gun, I stepped forth from my tent, and cried,—

"Where are the Wagogo?"

"There, and there, and there! From every side they come!"

And so it was. From every direction I could see the Wagogo in crowds dancing forward.

This sight so roused my anger that I cried out to my men:

"Dererah, Somal!" ("Fight, Somalis!") "To your guns, sons of the Unjamwesi, sons of Usukuma, and sons of Manyema! Forward! Down with the Wagogo!"

<small>War with the Wagogo.</small>

The plan of action was soon settled. A few of the Somalis had to protect the east and north side of the camp. To the west and south, from whence the chief attack proceeded, I hastened forward with about twenty men to oppose the enemy. Herr von Tiedemann was at first at my side, but I ordered him back to the eastern side.

The Wagogo, between two and three thousand strong, according to Von Tiedemann's computation, and many of them armed with muzzle-loaders, began the attack. An unfortunate circumstance for me was that my men could only shoot at short distances with those wretched pieces of wire, which somewhat lessened the superiority of our firearms. My double-barrelled gun, however, and the repeating guns of the Somalis, maintained their usual efficiency. In accordance with my old Massai tactics, I gave orders to fire several volleys, so as to begin by knocking down some of their warriors. With loud cheers we then advanced, but in such a way as to carefully watch the movements of our adversaries, and when they halted we halted too, and fired upon them again.

<small>A fight under difficulties.</small>

The sun shone fiercely, but in half an hour the Wagogo had been repulsed from the camp towards the south and west; and now I sent a message to Herr von Tiedemann, requesting him to remain in camp and guard it, as I intended to advance against the villages situated about half a mile to the southward, and there to attack the Wagogo in my turn. I was in the act of carrying out this intention, and was pushing forward against the villages, when I was suddenly met by messengers from Makenge.

STRAINED RELATIONS WITH THE WAGOGO. 525

"The Sultan wishes for peace with you, and will pay you tribute in ivory and oxen."

I replied, "The Sultan shall have peace. It shall be the eternal peace. I will show the Wagogo what the Germans are." *The Sultan sues for peace.*

So I advanced against the first village, where the Wagogo at first tried to defend themselves; but after several of them had been shot down, they rushed in wild flight out at the south gate, and the village was in our hands.

"Plunder the village, set fire to the houses, and smash everything to pieces that will not burn!"

But unfortunately it soon became apparent that the Wagogo villages themselves do not burn easily, being composed of wooden buildings covered with clay, with a circular enclosure around them. I ordered large quantities of wood to be placed in the houses, which were systematically set on fire. The axes that I sent for to the camp did their work also in knocking down the walls, so the first village was soon in ruins. Whilst this work was proceeding I placed three Somalis as a guard on the south side, and frightened away the Wagogo with my shots. *Burning of Wagogo villages.*

Meanwhile, I sent off a message to the neighbouring Wanjamwesi caravan, with which we had already concluded terms of friendship: "Come and help us. If we capture the herds of the Wagogo you shall have a share of the booty."

This was between two and three in the afternoon. The Wanjamwesi, however, did not probably feel very confident about the matter, for they did not appear upon the scene of the encounter until five o'clock. Now Hussein called out to me: "Master, come! the Wagogo are attacking the camp!" *A renewed alarm.*

I answered, "I will show you how to drive the Wagogo away from the camp."

We crept through the maize fields, and suddenly began to fire upon the hordes, who were rushing on from the east in flank and in rear. They fled wildly, scattering in every direction. My contempt for the Wagogo was so great, that during this fight I said repeatedly to my men, "I *Cowardice of the Wagogo.*

to our camp. But they were unable to regain possession of a single head of their cattle. On the following morning, they reported their loss on that afternoon as "over fifty."

When we approached the camp, Herr von Tiedemann and the men there came out joyfully to meet us.

"Well, Herr von Tiedemann, I think those will last us as far as Mpuapua," I said, pointing to the cattle.

We shook hands and walked towards the camp. My men performed warlike and triumphal dances round the animals. On entering my tent, I again quenched my thirst, this time with cognac and water; I then distributed the remaining powder and bits of wire, and posted sentries round the camp. I experienced a peculiar heaviness in the head, from running so much in the hot sun. As became manifest on that very night, I had contracted an affection of the brain, which made itself felt during the next few days in deafness, as well as in feverish temperature and a general feeling of discomfort.

Symptoms of sun-stroke.

Before turning back from the villages of the Wagogo, I had shouted to them,—

"You now know Kupanda Sharo and the Germans a little better than you did this morning; but you shall learn to know them in quite another fashion. I shall now remain amongst you in your country, so long as a man of you is alive, so long as one of your villages still stands, and a single animal of your herds is to be seized!"

Threatening the Wagogo.

A great slaughtering of cattle was now going on in the camp, and a joyous spirit pervaded the men seated round the camp-fires, before which reclined also the Wanjamwesi, who had been invited to stay till evening.

At nine o'clock Makenge sent his sons to me. They brought some ivory, representing a net value of about one thousand marks, as a first tribute, and requested to know what were my conditions of peace.

Makenge's submission.

"Tell your Sultan that I want no peace with him. The Wagogo are liars, and must be destroyed from off the face of the earth. But if the Sultan wishes to become the slave of the

Germans, then he and his people may live. As a proof of your submission, let him send me to-morrow morning a tribute of oxen, sheep, and goats, let him send me milk and honey, and then we will negotiate further."

That night I fell into a heavy sleep, from which I was awakened before sunrise by the lowing of cattle. Makenge had sent me thirty-eight oxen, as well as a number of sheep. In the course of the day, milk and honey and other articles arrived in addition. I now consented to enter into a treaty with him, by virtue of which he was placed under German authority. I promised to send him the flag, as soon as I should reach Mpuapua.

Makenge sends tribute.

The great Wanjamwesi caravan, which was encamped in the neighbourhood, sent me a deputation on that day to say, "Be our leader; we will be your people." This caravan numbered over twelve hundred men, and possessed, amongst other advantages, a great many drummers.

The Wanjamwesi caravan.

Having settled everything by June 11th, we started again on our eastward march on the 12th, the black, white, and red flag waving gaily in the morning breeze, the drums beating lustily, and the Wagogo herds in the van. Not a Wagogo was to be seen in the whole country side.

We encamped this day on the banks of the Bubo river, which flows from north to south, but which was at that time dried up, as I have already mentioned. I could scarcely move at all, and on this day had a kind of litter constructed for myself also, in which it was my intention to be carried on the morrow. After a march of some seventeen miles, we reached Ungombe on June 13th. The water standing here in small ponds had been rendered so dirty by the drinking of herds of cattle at them, that we could not make use of it even for soup.

By the Bubo river.

On this day Makenge's son, who was governor here, voluntarily sent me twenty oxen as tribute. Here we found encamped a large Arab caravan, which was still negotiating with the Wagogo respecting tribute. It was the caravan belonging to Mohammed Bin Omari, whom

Mohammed Bin Omari's caravan.

I had met at Muhalala. Scarcely had they heard of our arrival, when a deputation came to request that I would become their leader; they would be my people, if I would conduct them safely out of Ugogo. I accepted this proposal, and thus became the commander of more than two thousand men.

In the night I broke out into a healthy perspiration, which brought me relief from my attack of something like a sunstroke, but on June 14th my deafness still continued. On that day I did not give the order to start till the afternoon, a proceeding always to be recommended when one cannot hope to reach water in a single march: the people have time to cook their food in the last encampment, the animals can be watered for the day, and on the second day water will be reached.

On June 14th we turned slightly from our easterly course, and proceeded east-north-east, to avoid the so-called Lindi mountain chain. Having marched for some hours through forest and bush, we reached an open space, grassy but dry, at five o'clock. Here we encamped. It was a dull evening. The wind whistled loudly, and we sat in my tent feeling remarkably chilly. I retired to rest in a depressed state of mind, thinking of my deafness. All kinds of anxious thoughts passed through my brain. What if I were to become blind as well as deaf? How sad would be the future before me! I fell asleep at a late hour, and, awaking about two o'clock, called to my servant to bring me something to drink. I had brought sufficient water with me for Herr von Tiedemann and myself. Who shall describe my feelings of joy on my distinctly hearing Buana Mku's answer, and recognising that my deafness had entirely left me, for I could hear as well as ever!

Circuit round the Lindi mountains.

A great relief from anxiety.

I started, in consequence, early the next morning, in the brightest spirits; leaving the Lindi chain far behind us, we reached Matako. It was said to be a twelve hours' march from here to Msanga, the nearest place where water was to be had. I therefore determined to alter our ordinary method of proceeding, and gave orders for marching at midnight, that I might reach Msanga at noon on the following day. We certainly overslept ourselves and missed the midnight hour, so that we could not leave Matako before three a.m.; but as the distance proved to comprise a march of only ten hours instead of twelve, we reached our destination soon after midday. *An early start for Msanga.*

These night marches possessed one advantage, in that I could comfortably be carried over the ground in a litter, a proceeding for which in the daytime I had never patience, even when I felt unwell. When morning dawned, I generally called a halt in some camping-ground, and set fire to the straw huts, at which we warmed ourselves, and in the glow of which we partook of our breakfast. Then came the best part of our march. During a few hours thereupon the donkeys were requisitioned, and, as the country bordering the west of Ugogo became gradually more fertile and attractive, that march to Msanga was one of the pleasantest during the whole of our return journey.

At Msanga we found a great Wanjamwesi caravan, that had come from Mpuapua. The chiefs immediately came to salute me. They carried the German flag, and gave us some news from the coast, though their tidings were somewhat confused. *A caravan under the German flag.*

"We had heard that you had defeated the Massais, and now the Germans are waiting for you at Mpuapua. There, too, is Min Pasha, who has brought loads for you, and with whom you are to return to the Nyanza." *Tidings of Emin Pasha.*

"Do you mean to tell me that Emin Pasha is at Mpuapua?"

"Yes, in Mpuapua is Min Pasha, and they have cattle as the sand. There is a large house of stone."

These tidings were so altogether surprising, that they furnished subject for conjecture and conversation during the whole day, and yet, in my inmost heart, I was little disposed to credit them. I expected to find, as usual, that it would turn out to be some mistake. But this time I was to find myself in the wrong.

June 17th brought us but a short march. We now entered

the country of Mahamba, and reached a place called, after the Sultan, Yagallo. Kwam Yagallo is situated on the south-western slope of the Pameda hills, that separate Ugogo proper from Marenga Mkali, and which we had to march round on the southern side. Here we found a number of caravans, which had come from the east under the German flag. The camp was pitched near a watercourse, whose contents, though somewhat brackish, were drinkable. Marenga Mkali means "salt water," and takes its name from the mineral nature of the waters in this district.

Arrival at Kwam Yagallo.

Hardly had the tents been pitched, when my people suddenly reported, "Massais! Massais!" Sure enough, on the other side of the camp, were the Massais, driving their herds to the river to water them. Here they were again at last, our good old friends; certainly a little more slovenly in appearance than the proud sons of Leikipia. The Massais here, in northern Ugogo, also till the soil, and have certainly a little degenerated through the admixture of Bantu blood; but in outward appearance, and especially in the way in which they were armed, they bore a strong resemblance to their brothers of the north.

Appearance of Massais.

"Come over to this side of the river," I shouted to them. "Bring me presents, and you shall receive presents from me."

"Who are you?" they replied.

"I am Kupanda Sharo, and we have defeated the Massais of Leikipia."

"Kupanda Sharo's" acquaintance declined.

"No; stay you upon that side, and we will remain upon this side. We are afraid to come over."

This open declaration was received by my people with a roar of laughter; but, inviting as the fine herds of Massai cattle were to the Somalis and to ourselves, I considered it more prudent to refrain from attacking the Massais on the other side. By two o'clock they had marched away again into the steppe with their herds.

That night we were really on the march soon after midnight. We were going into the Marenga Mkali country, and had left a long stretch behind us before daybreak. After we had breakfasted we once more pushed on, and we entered the mountain district that separates Ugogo from Usagora, our road winding through attractive scenery, over easy mountain passes. We were repeatedly met by caravans of Wanjamwesi, who greeted us with a respectful "Jambo" or "Morning." At times the view opened into the Massai steppe on the left. Once, an eminence was pointed out to me by Salim, on the north-eastern horizon, as Kilima Ndscharo, but I cannot undertake to say if he was right. *The Marenga Mkali country.*

All that morning we marched through glorious mountain scenery. The air was cool, for a breeze in the valleys continually refreshed us. We came upon great herds of giraffes and zebras. Thus we continued our march until mid-day. Here the road wound down a far-stretching mountain slope to the left. We turn off towards the north, and see before us a narrow mountain pass; the sides of the hills are clothed with fields of maize and mtama. We are at Kampi, the Marenga Mkali lies behind us, and we have only one short day's march to get to the German station in Mpuapua. Here, too, we found more caravans encamped. The traffic all along this route is very considerable. I know no German high-road on which there is such a regular and uninterrupted personal and vehicular traffic, back and forwards, as upon this caravan route from Ugogo to the coast. The number of people who annually pass this way must be reckoned by hundreds of thousands. *Arrival at Kampi.*

On arriving at Kampi my first proceeding was to write a letter and send it by some messengers to "The gentlemen at the station in Mpuapua," telling them that I should arrive there at half-past ten on the following morning.

The water was more than two miles distant from our camp, so on that day we had to wait until evening before we could get a meal. After supper, so strong a wind blew from the east, through the valley where we were encamped, that the tent soon began to bend to one side, and was twice blown down. As there was not the least prospect of the wind lulling during the night, I had to make up my mind to have my camp bed placed in the open air, sheltered only by a few *A disagreeably windy night.*

the country of Mahamba, and reached a place called, after the Sultan, Yagallo. Kwam Yagallo is situated on the south-western slope of the Pameda hills, that separate Ugogo proper from Marenga Mkali, and which we had to march round on the southern side. Here we found a number of caravans, which had come from the east under the German flag. The camp was pitched near a watercourse, whose contents, though somewhat brackish, were drinkable. Marenga Mkali means "salt water," and takes its name from the mineral nature of the waters in this district.

Arrival at Kwam Yagallo.

Hardly had the tents been pitched, when my people suddenly reported, "Massais! Massais!"

Appearance of Massais.

Sure enough, on the other side of the camp, were the Massais, driving their herds to the river to water them. Here they were again at last, our good old friends; certainly a little more slovenly in appearance than the proud sons of Leikipia. The Massais here, in northern Ugogo, also till the soil, and have certainly a little degenerated through the admixture of Bantu blood; but in outward appearance, and especially in the way in which they were armed, they bore a strong resemblance to their brothers of the north.

"Come over to this side of the river," I shouted to them. "Bring me presents, and you shall receive presents from me."

"Who are you?" they replied.

"I am Kupanda Sharo, and we have defeated the Massais of Leikipia."

"Kupanda Sharo's" acquaintance declined.

"No; stay you upon that side, and we will remain upon this side. We are afraid to come over."

This open declaration was received by my people with a roar of laughter; but, inviting as the fine herds of Massai cattle were to the Somalis and to ourselves, I considered it more prudent to refrain from attacking the Massais on the other side. By two o'clock they had marched away again into the steppe with their herds.

That night we were really on the march soon after midnight. We were going into the Marenga Mkali country, and had left a long stretch behind us before daybreak. After we had breakfasted we once more pushed on, and we entered the mountain district that separates Ugogo from Usagora, our road winding through attractive scenery, over easy mountain passes. We were repeatedly met by caravans of Wanjamwesi, who greeted us with a respectful "Jambo" or "Morning." At times the view opened into the Massai steppe on the left. Once, an eminence was pointed out to me by Salim, on the north-eastern horizon, as Kilima Ndscharo, but I cannot undertake to say if he was right. *The Marenga Mkali country.*

All that morning we marched through glorious mountain scenery. The air was cool, for a breeze in the valleys continually refreshed us. We came upon great herds of giraffes and zebras. Thus we continued our march until mid-day. Here the road wound down a far-stretching mountain slope to the left. We turn off towards the north, and see before us a narrow mountain pass; the sides of the hills are clothed with fields of maize and mtama. We are at Kampi, the Marenga Mkali lies behind us, and we have only one short day's march to get to the German station in Mpuapua. Here, too, we found more caravans encamped. The traffic all along this route is very considerable. I know no German high-road on which there is such a regular and uninterrupted personal and vehicular traffic, back and forwards, as upon this caravan route from Ugogo to the coast. The number of people who annually pass this way must be reckoned by hundreds of thousands. *Arrival at Kampi.*

On arriving at Kampi my first proceeding was to write a letter and send it by some messengers to "The gentlemen at the station in Mpuapua," telling them that I should arrive there at half-past ten on the following morning.

The water was more than two miles distant from our camp, so on that day we had to wait until evening before we could get a meal. After supper, so strong a wind blew from the east, through the valley where we were encamped, that the tent soon began to bend to one side, and was twice blown down. As there was not the least prospect of the wind lulling during the night, I had to make up my mind to have my camp bed placed in the open air, sheltered only by a few *A disagreeably windy night.*

bushes, and there to compose myself to sleep; but I slept none the less soundly after all, for the fatigues of the previous night and of the day had thoroughly exhausted me.

And now the day was breaking for our last march before meeting with German countrymen. Full of excited expectation we started, first to climb the mountain pass before us, from whence, we were told, the valley of Mpuapua was to be seen. I hastened onwards with a few men of the column. The descent was an easy one. The bush gradually developed into a forest, and we continued to proceed further towards the east. All at once, soldiers in the uniform of the German protecting troop met us, and saluted us. Consequently we must now be close to the station. There—one more turn of the road, and on the heights of Mpuapua we descried the black, white, and red flag.

Final day's march to Mpuapua.

Our hearts beat higher at this sight, and, in a state of joyful excitement, we pursued the path, which wound round the north side of the station. Meanwhile we must have been seen from thence, for, behold, some gentlemen issued from the gateway.

Friends at the German station.

Soon, one of them, who was mounted on a donkey, galloped quickly towards me. He jumped down, and, taking off his hat, greeted me warmly. This was Herr Janke. Behind him came two gentlemen on foot. These were the officer in charge of the station, Lieutenant von Bülow, and Lieutenant Langheld. "Emin Pasha is here, also." A gentleman under the middle height, wearing a simple blue uniform and helmet, now came forward. A black beard framed in a face whose deep wrinkles told of long-continued mental strain. This was Emin Pasha!

"May I introduce Dr. Peters to your Excellency?" said Herr von Bülow.

"I am very glad to see you," replied Emin Pasha, taking my hand and stroking it. "I do not know how I am to thank you for all you have done for me."

Meeting with Emin Pasha.

I was so much agitated at meeting my countrymen and at encountering Emin Pasha, which was after all a surprise for

The Meeting with Emin Pasha.

me, that I was scarcely able to speak; therefore I contented myself simply with pressing Emin Pasha's hand.

"What an expedition you have behind you," continued the Pasha. "None of us believed it possible that you could make your way through. But now, come into my tent."

"Where is Herr von Tiedemann?" asked Herr von Bülow, who was an old comrade of Tiedemann's in the cadet corps.

"Herr von Tiedemann is following with the caravan," I replied.

"Then I will ride on a little way to meet him," said Herr von Bülow; and he took his leave.

Meanwhile, Emin Pasha, still holding me by the hand, led me to his tent. Emin Pasha's camp was pitched under gigantic trees, upon the north side of Mpuapua. Above the tent little flags fluttered gaily in the breeze, and they bore, to my astonishment, the same initials as our own flags, P. E. P. E. (Peters's Emin Pasha Expedition). Emin Pasha smilingly explained. "You see we, too, bear the device of your expedition." He had taken over the tents which I had left behind at Zanzibar. In front of Emin's tent waved the large black, white, and red flag, flanked on either side by a gun. His Soudanese soldiers were drawn up, and saluted us by presenting arms.

Encampment of Emin.

"Now, what can I give you in the way of refreshment? Will you take claret, or port, or a glass of beer, or——Dr. Stuhlmann," he called out to a delicate-looking gentleman now approaching us, "here we have Dr. Peters."

I greeted Dr. Stuhlmann, whom I had known in Zanzibar, and who was just getting about again after a severe attack of fever.

"Now, Doctor, you will let us have a bottle of *sekt*, will you not?" said Emin to Dr. Stuhlmann.

Meeting with Dr. Stuhlmann.

Emin Pasha had arranged his tent very tastefully, having pushed his bed into the background, and placed a table and chairs in the front. The table was covered with writing materials; books, too, were at hand. Above the table hung carefully-prepared birds' skins. The whole almost conveyed the impression of some German professor's study.

"And now, Dr. Peters," Emin Pasha went on, "something that will greatly interest you. Prince Bismarck is no longer Imperial Chancellor."

"What! Prince Bismarck no longer Imperial Chancellor! Is he dead?"

Startling news from Europe.

"No, he is not dead. He has resigned."

"And who is his successor?"

"General von Caprivi," he replied. "I may inform you," he continued, "that His Majesty the Emperor appears to take the greatest interest in our colonial affairs. In consequence of this interest, he has commissioned me to lead an expedition in the Lake Country, in order to restore German influence there. But I should wish thoroughly to talk over with you the manner of executing this commission, as you are, at this moment, among all of us the person best acquainted with the state of things in the Lake Country. But we will speak more about that to-morrow; and now, ask me what you wish to know further."

"What has become of Count Herbert Bismarck?"

"He retired at the same time as his father, and Freiherr von Marschall has succeeded him as Secretary of State for Foreign Affairs. Altogether, you will find the position of affairs in Europe, as well as the feeling about your expedition, much altered. We all work with renewed zeal, full of confidence for the future of our undertaking," said Emin Pasha.

Improved prospects for African colonisation.

I now related to Emin Pasha my arrangements with Uganda. He interrupted me several times by throwing in the word, "Charming, charming!" turning with a pleasant smile to Dr. Stuhlmann.

Emin Pasha's approbation.

Meanwhile Herr von Tiedemann came up, and was likewise welcomed by Emin Pasha in the heartiest manner. I imparted to Herr von Tiedemann the intelligence I had just received, that Prince Bismarck was no longer Chancellor of the Empire.

"I know it," replied Herr von Tiedemann shortly. "I've full information."

His friend Bülow had already told him the startling news.

For about three-quarters of an hour we thus sat in lively conversation in Emin's tent. I gave orders that my expedition should establish its camp close to his; and thus, through all the hollow between the hill of Mpuapua and the mountain slope in the north, waved the German flags and streamers.

"Gentlemen, it is time for dinner," said Herr von Bülow. "May I beg you to step across to the station? I have also invited both the gentlemen from the French Mission, Père Schynse, a German, and a French Father, so we shall have a large party to-day. I will now make you and these gentlemen acquainted with each other."

He rose, and Emin Pasha remained behind for a short time to make his toilette. By this time the two gentlemen from the French Mission had come up, to whom we were likewise introduced. As soon as the Pasha was ready, we proceeded up a path into the station of Mpuapua. It is very solidly built of rock stones, and has a tower more than two yards in thickness. Herr von Bülow was likewise having a well dug within the station, and the work was being carried on sturdily. *The station of Mpuapua.*

This settlement is, in truth, an achievement worthy of all respect. It may be confidently asserted, that Mpuapua is entirely impregnable, if properly defended, with regard to any attack where the assailants are not provided with artillery. I also believe that the neighbourhood is healthy. It is certainly very windy in Mpuapua, and accordingly colds must be guarded against; but, with proper precautions, people will certainly enjoy better health there than in the damp and heavy air on the coast. We looked at the various buildings, and soon entered a solidly-built dining-room, where a banquet awaited us that might be considered, according to African ideas, worthy of Lucullus, inasmuch as it included European vegetables of various sorts. In addition, there were good strengthening dishes of meat, from captured herds of oxen, and *A strong position.*

540   NEW LIGHT ON DARK AFRICA.

European delicacies in the way of preserves. The gentlemen [of] the station had also been kind enough to save up [all] they possessed in the way of drinks for the last f[ew] weeks, against our arrival, so that in this departme[nt] we had such a choice as could hardly have been exceeded, [on] similar occasions, in Europe itself.

A sumptuous banquet.

When we had satisfied the first cravings of hunger, Em[in] Pasha stood up, rang his glass, and welcomed us in wor[ds] full of heartiness, alluding to the rumours that had been ri[fe] concerning our destruction, and repeating that he had not co[n]sidered it possible to reach his province from the east.

I returned thanks to Emin Pasha, expatiating on his wo[rk] on the Upper Nile, and declaring that we had gladly endur[ed] every toil and danger, in the hope that we might be of use [to] our great "African" fellow-countryman. Herr von Tiedema[nn] proposed the health of the chief of the station, Herr von Bülo[w] and so the meal went on; for the first time for a year, we we[re] feasting among our compatriots, and naturally in a very exalt[ed] and excited frame of mind. For a long time we sat th[ere] together, and the sun was already sinking when I ro[se] to take a walk with Emin Pasha through the camp, [to] see if all my people had been well lodged. This proved to [be] the case. They were all feasting, in the highest spirits [at] having reached the strong fortress of the Badutschi. Now, th[ey] considered, all trouble and care was over and past, and t[he] German Emin Pasha Expedition was virtually ended.

A jovial encampment.

The evening found us all assembled again at the comm[on] table; the conversation of the dinner was resumed, and notab[ly] I had more opportunity than in the morning to make the a[c]quaintance of Father Schynse, with whom I continued sitti[ng] for a long time after the other gentlemen had betaken the[m]selves to their rooms for the night.

Next morning, before six o'clock, I had already repaired [to] the camp of Emin Pasha, to hold a practical coun[cil] with him. In company with Lieutenant Langheld [I] breakfasted in the open air, and then I retired with Em[in] Pasha into his tent, for a closer consultation. I began by layi[ng]

Consultation with Emin Pasha.

DESIGNS AND PROCEEDINGS OF EMIN PASHA. 541

before him all my treaties from Uganda and Lake Victoria, of which he afterwards caused copies to be taken. I called his attention to the probability of an attempt by the English party in Uganda, assisted by Jackson, to force Muanga to overturn these arrangements, and to make others in the British interests. To safeguard the German interests in Uganda, pending the decision of His Majesty the Emperor, Emin Pasha determined at once to send messengers thither, to announce to the king that at the command of His Majesty the German Emperor he would come to Lake Victoria, and to exhort Muanga to make no new arrangements of any kind differing from the treaties I brought with me, until the decision of the Emperor should be known. The messenger who carried this letter started for Ukumbi on the very next day.

When this had been done, we talked together of the state of things in the Equatorial Province. Emin Pasha drew my attention to the fact that he was now in the service of the German Empire, but that if through any circumstances he should get back into his old territory, he was prepared to undertake for that territory the same responsibilities which Muanga had taken upon himself for Uganda, and to work in the sense of these arrangements on the Upper Nile. Before he decided anything in this direction, he said, he must naturally be made aware of the position taken up by the Imperial Government, and he hoped, if possible, to see me again in Africa. *Emin in the German service.*

On this subject also a document was set up and completed.

As a third point, we discussed the object that lay before Emin Pasha's expedition. Emin asked me to give him accurate particulars concerning the countries in the west, and asked my advice respecting what he might have, in the first instance, to do to fulfil the commission entrusted to him by His Majesty. I could only counsel him, to the best of my knowledge and convictions, that before doing anything else he should at once occupy Tabora, or some other suitable place in its vicinity. *The occupation of Tabora advised.*

"Then that is also your view," said Emin Pasha. "That

coincides entirely with my own opinion, and with what Fat[her] Schynse has told me."

I replied: "I am even in a position to make you an o[ffer] in the name of Monseigneur Hirth, that in case you [are] prepared to occupy Tabora, the Catholic Mission will willin[gly] place their station, Kipullpulla, there at your disposal, [for] your objects. On the question of the practical advantages [of] occupying Tabora, in the first instance, there is no neces[sity] for much debate. Tabora is the central point of all the A[rab] influence for the entire Lake territory. Whoever is master [of]

Importance of the position. Tabora has in his hands the key to the three la[kes,] and therefore the occupation of Tabora is the f[irst] thing that has to be done on the part of the Germa[ns.] If you should decide first to establish a station by one [of] the lakes, you would, after all, only bring about local resu[lts.] With Tabora you produce an effect upon all the three la[kes] together."

"I am very glad," said Emin Pasha, "that we are entirely of the same opinion upon this point, and I am de[ter]mined also to act in this sense. As it appears you have, a[fter] all, had a very severe fight in Ugogo, I shall request Herr [von] Bülow to attach himself, with a part of his force, to [my] expedition into the interior. You would oblige me if [you] would now give me some particulars on the condition of Ug[ogo] specially."

"I shall take the liberty of working out for you a v[ery] accurate record of routes, in which the peculiar question [of] water supply in that country shall be specially treated."

"And what places on Lake Victoria," continued Em[in,] "would you recommend to me for the establishment o[f a] station?"

"I would recommend your Excellency with this view [to] inspect Bukoba, in the south of the Kagera. The southe[rn]

Advantages of Bukoba. margin of the lake is flat and unhealthy; the weste[rn] border is fertile, and as I think more healthy, as [it] lies higher. Bukoba appears to me to offer all the conditi[ons] necessary for the establishment of a station."

Emin Pasha noted down all these details very carefully; and it was past ten o'clock by the time we went up together into the station, where we at once proceeded, with the help of the other gentlemen, to reduce the important discussion of the morning to writing. Thereupon I wrote letters to Monseigneur Hirth and Mons. Lourdel in Uganda; and thus we had a very satisfactory day's work behind us when, towards one o'clock, we sat down to luncheon. During this meal there came an English missionary, from the neighbouring English Mission station of Kisokwe, an amiable, unassuming gentleman, who enquired with great interest concerning our adventures in the north. He remained sitting beside me the whole afternoon, after the other gentlemen had retired for a short midday sleep. This was the second day. *An English missionary.*

After four o'clock I betook myself to Emin Pasha, who now gave me a number of particulars concerning his expedition and Stanley's proceedings on the Upper Nile. To my great astonishment, I here received the full confirmation of what I had already heard, here and there, in the shape of rumours, by Lake Victoria, namely, that Stanley had carried off Emin Pasha actually by force from the Equatorial Province. *Emin carried off by Stanley.*

Emin Pasha told me: "When Stanley came, for the first time, to Lake Albert, he would have been lost if Casati and I had not gone to him. Stanley did not come to us, we went to him. He did not reach the Equatorial Province any more than you did. When he first arrived at Kiwalli, and found no tidings of us, he did not venture to make an advance along Lake Albert to Wadelai, but went back for four months, to bring up a boat. Then the expedition came back, and we sought them out, brought them provisions and clothing, and in this way the expedition was saved from destruction." *Criticism of Stanley's proceedings.*

Exactly in the same manner did Signor Casati express himself to me, a few months later.

"Then Stanley began to press me to give up my post. He told me the Khedive had sent him hither, for the definite purpose of delivering to me the order commanding me to evacuate the Equatorial Province. Stanley gave me to understand that he was empowered, in case of need, to carry me away from the Province by force. At that time my position on the Upper Nile was still of such a nature, that if I had had ammunition and stuff goods left, I could have maintained myself permanently there. Not until afterwards and prompted, if not directly by the intrigues, at any rate the appearance of the English, my people put themselves opposition to me, and in fact solely on the ground that they would not go away out of their Province. I am convinced that if I returned there now, with an equipment, they would rejoicingly bid me welcome. But if Stanley had a commission from the Khedive to lead me away from there, he has certainly not been loyal to the Khedive; for a few days later he came with an offer from the King of the Belgians, that I should hoist the flag of the Congo State in the Equator Province, and that King Leopold offered me a contribution of £1,000 per month for the expenses of the government. After a short time he advised me not to accept such an offer, for that the Congo State, from which he just then came, was in a condition of great confusion and distraction. Besides, he said it was well known to Emin how King Leopold had formerly treated him (Stanley). Therefore Stanley could not counsel him to close with this offer, but he would make him a third proposal. A British East African Company was about to push forward towards the Upper Nile, from Mombas. Stanley accordingly proposed that Emin should enter the service of the company. Emin was to march with all his troops round Lake Victoria, under the command of Stanley, to Kawirondo. There they would find out a suitable island on Lake Victoria on which Emin Pasha could fortify himself. Then Stanley would hasten back to Mombas, to bring up reinforcements for him. Every officer of Emin Pasha and his men would, on entering the service of the British East African Company, receive the same salary they had had from the Egyptian government. Emin Pasha might himself negotiate with the company in London, respecting his own salary.

Emin's position on the Upper Nile.

Offer of the King of the Belgians.

The British East African Company.

After my return to Europe, I naturally read with lively interest Stanley's account of these propositions, which are also to be found in his book "In Darkest Africa," but in another connection, and, above all, with other surroundings. Especially does Stanley assert that he made this last proposal to Emin Pasha, not in the name of the British East African Company, but only as a proposal emanating from himself.

In contrast to this, Emin Pasha repeatedly asserted, in Mpuapua, in the most positive manner, that Stanley, to provide for the case that Emin might be inclined to accept this proposal, had brought with him from London an agreement signed by the founders of the British East African Company, officially drawn up and with seals attached, at the foot of which agreement Emin had only to sign his name to conclude the affair. This narrative of Emin's is to be implicitly credited, inasmuch as he had no reason at all for stating what was incorrect, whereas it will be understood that the British East African Company had reasons subsequently, when Emin had entered the German service, to disconnect itself from the fact that a proposal had been made to him. *Discrepancy between Stanley's and Emin Pasha's accounts.*

"However," continued Emin, "even this last proposal, the acceptance of which Stanley forced upon me, half by threats, he did not carry out. When we had arrived in the south of Lake Victoria, he suddenly found that he did not care to lead me round the lake and to take me to Kawirondo, from whence, as had been expressly agreed, I was to reconquer my territory of Unjoro and Uganda with the reinforcements Stanley was to bring up; on the contrary, he suddenly declared that I must go with him to the coast, to complete the affair. He said that without the express command of the Queen of England he could not mix himself up with the troubles in Uganda. In this manner I have been compelled to march with him to the coast, whereas originally the question was only that of a transfer of my capital from Lake Albert to Lake Victoria." *Emin compelled to follow Stanley.*

"To interfere in Uganda"—this was Emin's opinion, which he repeatedly expressed—"Stanley did not venture; as indeed in general in the conduct of his expedition, for the details of which I have the greatest admiration, he often made wide circuits, to keep out of the way of the tribes he considered as warlike. This accounts for the wonderful bends and corners to be found in the route of his expedition."

Emin frequently made the remark: "If at any time Stanley suffered from a slight illness, as, for instance, from catarrh, we used to be kept waiting for weeks in one spot. On the other hand, no particular notice was taken of the state of health, good or bad, of the other members of the expedition. But what distinguishes this man is the extraordinary presence of mind and the merciless resolution with which he carried out what he had made up his mind to do. If any unexpected incident occurred, very little time elapsed before Stanley had resolved upon his measures, which were then put in execution, let the cost be what it might."

Emin's estimate of Stanley.

I must here declare that, for several reasons, I cannot consider this eulogistic opinion concerning Stanley as the leader of an expedition, which Emin Pasha expresses, especially with regard to his last undertaking, as warranted. Respecting the presence of mind displayed by Stanley in certain dangerous situations I can give no sort of opinion; but his arrangement of the expedition as a whole, and his decisions at important turning-points of the enterprise, appear to me in a high degree incomprehensible, I may even say confused. It is incomprehensible to me why Stanley, to get to Emin, did not, in 1887, take the more convenient route from the eastern coast. What he says in favour of the western route does not in any way apply. I was afterwards told that in this particular a wish had been expressed by the Congo State, in whose service Stanley still was in the year 1887. That would render his general plan intelligible. But then his connection with Tippoo Tib becomes incomprehensible to me. Stanley seeks to explain this connection on the ground that Tippoo Tib was too dangerous, and therefore he could not leave him behind as an enemy. But then Tippoo Tib was in Zanzibar in 1887, and was brought to the Upper Congo by Stanley himself. Stanley

Dr. Peters's opinion.

Relations with Tippoo Tib.

knew Tippoo Tib as a faithless man. A man of that description is not generally left to guard one's house, nor is it usual to give any post of confidence to him.

But most incomprehensible of all appears to me the going back to bring up the iron boat after the first arrival at Lake Albert, which cost him four months, when he might have been with Emin Pasha in fifteen days. Precisely from the point of view of an African expedition, I cannot at all understand why Stanley did not at least put himself into communication by letter with Emin Pasha before he went back, and when he did go back, why he did not at once try to put himself in touch with his rear-guard. There appears in these movements of Stanley's, supposing him to be unable to give a better reason for them than that cited in his book of travels, a degree of indecision which I am at a loss to reconcile with the general picture I have formed for myself of this man; partly, too, from personal acquaintance. Through these movements the period of the expedition was lengthened out to three years, which certainly increased the cost of the undertaking in a disproportionate degree. The same rule holds good with African travels as with every other thing, that they are most complete when the greatest possible results are achieved with the smallest possible means.

Indecision in Stanley's proceedings.

It is in this case as in solving mathematical problems—the simplest and readiest way is certainly also the best one. Looked at from this point of view, Stanley's undertaking appears to me like working an equation with totally unnecessary circuitous ways and formulas. And what was achieved in the end by this great expenditure in money and men? The Equatorial Province is deserted; neither Uganda nor Wadelai has been brought under the British Protectorate; and, on the other hand, Emin Pasha, who was formerly a sincere friend of England, has been turned into an equally sincere opponent—at least, of Stanley personally. That is the final outcome of an undertaking which was announced as calculated to serve the interests of civilisation and of Christianity in Central Africa, and, as certainly appears from

Want of result of the expedition.

Stanley's third proposal, at least aimed at getting the territories on the Upper Nile included in the sphere of British influence. Neither the ostensible nor the real object has been attained. Even the Mahdi himself could not have been more injurious to the civilising of the Upper Nile than Stanley has been in reality. But as regards the establishment of the English in these countries, Stanley, by refusing the assistance of Muanga, and by avoiding co-operation with Jackson's expedition, has contributed to convert the sentiment in Uganda into positive enmity to England. This matter Stanley may settle with those who commissioned him. These facts must, however, be kept in view, if a just estimate is to be formed of the value of his last expedition.

Effect on civilisation.

It was not till I reached Mpuapua that I learned how it was Stanley's undertaking that frustrated our own plans with regard to the Equatorial Province. Emin Pasha has corroborated me in the assertion that even with the small powers we possessed we might have materially assisted him; inasmuch as we should, as I have already stated, have established for him communications with Uganda, and consequently with the German East African colony. If Stanley had stuck fast in the swamps of the Aruwimi, Emin Pasha would at this day, according to all human calculation, be still in Wadelai in a perfectly secure position. The whole territory in the north of Lake Victoria would be a firm bulwark, under Christian influence, which in time could have been extended step by step down the Nile against the Mahdi influence, whereas now the Arab influence extends to the northern boundary of Uganda; and Uganda itself is torn by the confusion of the strife of parties, and its development is hindered to an immeasurable extent. Therefore it must be stated that Stanley's enterprise has been absolutely hurtful in its effects for the general interests of humanity, and for the special interests of England.

Effect in frustrating Dr. Peters's expedition.

It can be understood that observations such as these, which we naturally made during our meeting in Mpuapua, were always attended by painful feelings in Emin Pasha and in myself; but we united in the resolution, even if much had been lost, to hold fast to the idea of winning back in common what had been lost, in one way or another. We entertained the hope of gaining for this object the sympathies not only of the continental Powers, but, in the end, those of the English Government likewise. In Mpuapua we were not yet aware of the contents of the new arrangements between Germany and England, which have materially delayed all these things in the north of Lake Victoria. Hopes for the future.

Meanwhile, I had an opportunity, in the days we passed together, of studying the purely human qualities of Emin Pasha somewhat more closely, to note his truly German thoroughness in the scientific labours he prosecuted incessantly, and also the natural goodness of heart that speaks out of his whole being. Often when we were talking of the most important things, his bird shooter, who was always at work, brought him a bird he had killed; which Emin would take in his hands with a kind of haste to examine accurately, register it, and lay it aside for skinning. All his works, including his journals of travel, showed the greatest closeness of observation and accuracy of insertion. In this particular there is certainly a decided difference between Emin Pasha and Stanley. While, wherever the maps rested on Stanley's declarations alone, I used, after a few trials, as, for instance, at Uweriweri, simply to put them aside, I should accept as authentic, without trial, every particular to which Emin Pasha has put his name. His provident, almost fatherly kindness of heart towards us showed itself in a series of instances that were really touching. Though we were hastening to the coast, and he, on the other hand, was going for an indefinite time into the interior, he would not rest until we had accepted from him a number of presents, for the greater comfort of our situation. Clothes, linen, perfumes, drinks, all these things were literally pressed upon us, and always in a very delicate manner, and with friendly smiles. Though his saddle-horse had fallen, he was almost angry when for a long time I protested against receiving one of his handsome Muskat donkeys as a present. At the very last moment, when I took Character of Emin Pasha. His amiable qualities.

leave of him, and was looking around for a stick for my donkey, he forced his own riding-whip upon me, and to my remonstrance, "But, your Excellency, then you will have none!" he replied, "Oh, I shall manage, I shall find something."

For everything that, on the other hand, we were able to do for him, his gratitude was simply heart-moving. I left with him some scientific instruments, and also a few books, among others a few volumes of Arthur Schopenhauer, which seemed especially to please him.

Gratitude for small services.

In the few days of our intercourse I was not in a position to form an opinion concerning Emin Pasha as a politician or an organiser; in that respect his deeds must speak for themselves. But to the man Emin Pasha both Herr von Tiedemann and myself became sincerely attached, and we shall always think upon him with grateful recollection. On those days of Mpuapua rests a halo of pleasant heartiness, which always arouses a wish once more in life to experience such hours and days.

On the afternoon of June 21st we had our photographs taken by Herr Janke, in front of Emin's tent, in a group, and then Emin Pasha and myself separately. Our breaking up was fixed for the following day. We were going to the east and to the coast, and Emin Pasha wanted to commence his march upon Ugogo. Once more we passed a pleasant evening together. Next morning at six o'clock we were all in our camps, making ready for the march.

Photographic portraits.

At half-past six the two expeditions started simultaneously, with waving flags and drums beating, in opposite directions. On the previous day I had been able to supply Emin Pasha with twenty-seven porters from among my Wasukuma, a circumstance of which he was glad, as a number of his porters had run away on the coast. We, on the other hand, departed from Mpuapua well provided with all kinds of eatables, especially with bread and vegetables. The gentlemen remained together half an hour longer; then came the time for saying good-bye. Herr von Tiedemann had received from Herr von Bülow a riding ox as a present, and I mounted Emin Pasha's white donkey. "Greetings to Germany, and greetings to Lake Victoria, and may we soon meet again!"—and then there was a shaking of hands, and without many more words I rode off after my column, that had gone on in advance, towards the east. At a turn of the way I looked round again, and once more my eyes rested on the short, peculiar figure of Emin Pasha. Hats are waved; and behind me, like a fair dream, Mpuapua and my experiences there sink back together into memories of the past. *Parting from Emin Pasha.*

Over the further march to the coast I may pass lightly, for the route from Mpuapua to Bagamoyo is well known. I followed the southern road through Usagara. I confess that I wanted to make the last part of my journey as easy to myself as I could. There were no more perils to be encountered, and I was anxious not to arrive in an exhausted state at the coast, where the danger of attacks of fever is especially strong. The northern way over Mamboyo is steeper, but a few days shorter; the southern way is the easier and pleasanter one. Every marching day was now, to a certain extent, a holiday for us. Eating and drinking we had in plenty; and already in Tubugue, our first camping-place, I received letters from the coast, informing me that seven more loads of European dainties, notably sausages, preserves, and champagne, had been sent up the country for us by our friends in Zanzibar, and that we might expect every day to receive them. Though they, in fact, only reached us seven days before our arrival at the coast, the very expectation of them was an enjoyment. So material does man become, when for many months he has been restricted to the barest necessaries of life. *The northern and southern routes.*

From our second camping-place, Mlale, I sent forward to Zanzibar my last report for Europe, and a telegram, in which I especially related the fight at Ugogo, and my meeting with Emin Pasha.

At midday on June 25th, from the lofty plateau in the north of the Mkondogna river, my eyes rested for the first time again with delight on glorious Usagara, and my heart was so stirred that tears came into my eyes, when I *Arrival at Usagara.*

thought that we had been privileged, six years ago, to gain this land for Germany. My thoughts wandered back to the hours I had passed in the Mkondogna valley with my friend Jühlke, and of the world of adventures and emotions that lay for me between the December days of 1884 and the July of 1890.

In slow and easy marches we now moved on, down the charming Mkondogna valley, which again reminded me vividly of the Rhine or the Neckar, as it had done six years ago.

On the 26th I marched past Mninin-Sagara. At all corners the German flag was now waving, the people came out of the gates, and persisted that they remembered me from my last stay here, which, however, I did not believe. We encamped in the same spots where my first expedition had pitched its tents.

The Arabs of Mkondogna. On June 27th, when I entered Mkondogna, the Arabs resident there prepared a solemn reception for us. They came in a body to meet us, conducted us to the Barasa, brought us fruit and milk, and when we had taken leave of the first Arab, we had to go to a second, a certain Buana Sani, to partake of a breakfast which the Catholic missionaries in Loanga had sent down for us. Father Horné, to whom I had, from Kedar, sent tidings of our approach, sent some pupils of the Mission before us to Mkondogna, who presented us with a large bouquet, and brought us a hearty letter of welcome, with an invitation. We were on no account to pass by Loanga without partaking of the hospitality of the Mission.

On the afternoon of June 27th we therefore rode with a few men to Loanga, where we found a warm welcome, and **Stay at Loanga.** a quantity of news from Europe. I have forgotten to remark that in Tubugne we had received our European mail communications from the German Emin Pasha committee, and letters from our dear ones at home, the reading and re-reading of which gave these last days of the expedition a peculiar charm.

June 28th, a Saturday, we spent agreeably in the pleasant station of Loanga, which is built neatly and tastefully by the Loanga brook on the slope of a mountain, from whence the prospect opens on the mountains of Ukami. We spent hours

TRAVELLER'S RELAXATIONS AND ENJOYMENTS. 553

there in the shady verandah, telling the narrative of our

USAGARA LANDSCAPE.

expedition, or hearing about Europe, sitting over a glass of claret and water, looking out upon the ravishingly beautiful landscape. Father Horné is a German, a Hessian, if I do not mistake, and a solid and amiable man. On the 29th we stayed to dinner at the Mission. I had just sent the order for starting the expedition to Farhani, towards Koberenga, when Herr von Tiedemann was seized with an attack of fever; so I advised him to remain in Loanga till it had passed over. I would wait for him in Mrogro, another mission of the Catholics. I was obliged to march away, because the expedition was already on the road. So I had now to make four days' marches alone through the Mkata plain as far as Mrogro. When I was encamped in Wiansi, a day's march short of Mrogro, I heard that a German expedition was lying in the neighbourhood. I sent Hussein with the announcement that I was here in Wiansi; and, in the evening, when I was already in bed, Herr de la Frémoise, the chief of the expedition, which was bound to Mpuapua, came galloping up on horseback. He brought with him a bottle of champagne and another of absinthe, and we remained together in animated conversation until late in the night. Next morning we breakfasted together in the open air, and then I marched onward to Mrogro, crossing the Lugerengere. From this side the mountain plateau of Ukami appears rising massively, and on its slope lies Mrogro, the most beautiful of all the stations I met with. This morning I received the seven loads of European dainties, close to Mrogro, and, somewhat weakened in body, I resolved to make a break of seven days in my journey, here in beautiful Mrogro, so that I might get to the coast in full health and strength, and, likewise, that we might enjoy the good things in the packages, especially the sausage and preserves, in all tranquillity of spirit. The value we put upon these things was a very different one from our estimation of them in Europe. We quite forgot that when once we got back to Zanzibar or to Europe, we should probably be able to buy sausage and beans, carrots and cabbage, every day.

In Mrogro, also, I found the heartiest welcome from Father Karst and Brother Basilid, two Lorrainers, who speak German quite fluently; and in the plantations of this station, which have quite a European appearance, I passed a quiet and reflective week.

On July 5th Herr von Tiedemann arrived, safe and sound. We had a really capital kitchen, to which Brother Basilid himself attends; the coast was close before our eyes, and we also found some new reading in the station, among other things some European periodicals. I felt especial interest in the coffee plantations of this place, which Brother Basilid has laid, utilising in the work a rushing mountain stream. They not only supplied the station itself, but also all the remaining Catholic mission houses, with coffee, and Basilid thinks they will very soon have a surplus for trading.

Brother Basilid's plantations.

I should recommend anyone who proposes to establish plantations in Eastern Africa, to betake himself to Mrogro for awhile, to learn there. Mrogro is in reality a pattern for the German East African territory.

On July 10th I at length started again, to accomplish the remainder of the journey in long marches. I took with me Herr Neuhaus, an hospital attendant from the Protecting Corps, who had been left behind, sick of a fever, by Emin Pasha, and whom I caused to be carried along with us to the coast. We journeyed towards Bagamoyo by the well-known route. We were in excellent health, and the expectation that in a few days we should have left behind us all the toils and dangers of this expedition, out of which, for months together, we had had no hope to emerge alive, made every heart beat high.

March to Bagamoyo.

On July 15th I encamped in Pigiro, about two miles from the ferry across the Rufu. I heard that a German official was stationed here, and at once sent my servant Selek and the Somali Mohammed Ismael to him, to announce our arrival. They came back and reported that the white man was suffering from fever to-day, but sent his greetings and some fowls.

Next morning early, we went on towards Mtone. The way led through fresh grass, which was still damp from last night's rain. After we had marched for an hour I saw the Rufu I knew so well glimmering on the right. On the opposite bank I noticed a very large shed and a European tent. I had a gun fired, and immediately some boatmen appeared, and passed the ferry boat across to us by a chain; and directly afterwards a white man came out in front of the tent. I got into the boat with a few of my people, and when we were in the middle of the river, the white man cried out, from the opposite side,—

The ferry at Rufu.

"Are you Herr Dr. Peters?"

I answered, "Yes, certainly; and who may you be?"

"I am Bohndorf."

"I am exceedingly glad that you should be the first man I meet here."

Herr Bohndorf welcomed me heartily. I had made his acquaintance a year and a half previously in Egypt, and afterwards I had seen him again in Bagamoyo. He led me into his tent and opened a bottle of champagne, which had been sent there, he told me, for our arrival. Herr von Tiedemann, who came in afterwards, found us already engaged in animated conversation upon our expedition and the occurrences on the coast. Unfortunately my travelling companion was once more attacked by fever, so that he preferred to rest for a few hours at Herr Bohndorf's, and I had to traverse alone the short distance that still remained between us and Bagamoyo. Herr Bohndorf told me the gentlemen had intended to meet us at Mtoni, and I should probably find them on the way there. So with a heart beating high with expectation, I marched along the rest of the way, first through brushwood and then through the plantations of cocoa palms which already belong to Bagamoyo. Suddenly the place stood revealed before us. To the right, along the cocoa palm grove, we marched, with drums beating. When we came in sight of the German station I ordered my soldiers to fire three volleys. Then the gates opened, and all the gentlemen came out to us; in front was Herr von Paerbrand, acting as deputy for the chief of the station, who was absent at the time on an expedition. I could hardly speak from joyful emotion, when I

Herr Bohndorf's welcome.

The German station at Bagamoyo.

greeted these gentlemen. My soldiers were quartered in outhouses, and I was taken into the salon of the station. On the way, Herr Paerbrand informed me of particulars of the arrangement with England by which the gains achieved by our expedition north of the first degree of south latitude had been transferred to England, in return for which Germany received Heligoland ; that the Protectorate of Zanzibar had further been given to England, in exchange for which the German East African coast had been definitely ceded to Germany. *Important news from Europe.*

I will pass in silence over the emotions these tidings excited in me. I remained two hours in the salon to regain my composure, and begged the gentlemen to say nothing more on the whole subject. Here, in the room, I found a great number of telegrams from Europe, congratulating me on my return, and among these there were letters from my relations and friends. *Despatches from home.*

Telegrams of this kind I received from the German Emin Pasha committee, from the German Colonial Company, from Karl von der Heydt, from Wissmann, from various divisions of the Colonial Company, from the German East African Company, and also from Fritz Krupp and other dear friends and acquaintances.

When I had in some degree recovered from the perturbation of mind into which I had been thrown by the tidings received, and by reading these proofs of sympathy, Herr von Paerbrand came in again to carry me off to a banquet to which were invited all the German gentlemen in Bagamoyo, among them the Austrian Consul from Bombay, a very amiable and sympathetic gentleman, who was on a visit in Bagamoyo; besides my friends from the Mission, Father Etienne and Brother Oskar, and all the officers and officials of the Protecting Corps and of the German East African Company. Among others appeared Herr von Sievers, the chief of the Maritime Division of the Imperial Commissariat, who had come over with Herr Domarsky from Zanzibar, in the most civil manner, to put the *München* at my disposal for my passage to Zanzibar. *A genial dinner.*

It was a most cordial gathering at that dinner, the wine was not spared, and the general feeling was one of festivity.

In the afternoon came Herr von Tiedemann, who, to my great satisfaction, was entirely cured, and was able to join us at supper. As he was an old friend of Herr von Paerbrand, he resolved to stay a few days in Bagamoyo. We settled that we would go together to Europe by the French mail line, and at nine o'clock the next morning I took a hearty leave of all the gentlemen to cross to Zanzibar on the *München*, of which Herr von Sievers himself took command on that day. I took the whole of my little caravan, which had now shrunk to thirty-six men, across with me, and also the Austrian Consul and Herr Domarsky. The Countess Blücher, the President of the Women's Union, was also on board, so that we had an agreeable passage over to Zanzibar.—It was an ennobling sight for me when the continent of Africa, on which I had been employed exactly one year, one month, and one day in the carrying out of the expedition, began to sink below the western horizon. It seemed almost as if a great gulf were lying between me and my former life in Europe. The year 1889-90 had been so rich in emotions and impressions of every kind, that it appeared to contain a space of many years, even of a lifetime. I seemed to be quite a different man from the one who had gone off in June 1889 from Bagamoyo to the south, to begin the Emin Pasha Expedition. The continent of Africa disappeared in a hazy twilight, and soon the island of Zanzibar arose before us. Then I recognised all the old places which I had so often visited in the year 1887. Presently the masts of the ships became visible to us, then the houses and the flags of the consulates. We passed close by the German men-of-war the *Carola* and the *Schwalbe*, the gentlemen on board giving us a friendly salute. The anchor was dropped, we stepped into the boats, and soon we stood on dry land, on the well-known spot next to Oswald's house. I immediately betook myself to the German Imperial Commissariat, where the officer in charge at that time, Captain Richelmann, welcomed me in the most friendly manner, and invited me to join him at his dinner-table.

Chance ordained that, living with Captain Richelmann and Herr von Sievers, I found myself in the same house that I had occupied before the expedition started. But in this domicile, too, I could hardly recognise myself for the same man, so deeply and emphatically had the impressions of the year worked upon my inner life.

The old quarters in Zanzibar.

In Zanzibar I passed some happy days in the German colony. As I received intelligence from Berlin which rendered my speedy appearance there desirable, and as Lieutenant-Captain von der Gröben, whose acquaintance I had made on board the *Schwalbe*, informed me that the new English steamers, which ran as far as Naples, were very comfortably fitted up, I asked Consul-General Michahelles to put himself in communication with the British Consul-General to procure for me a guarantee for an unintercepted voyage home on one of the steamers of the English line. But here, also, public sentiment seemed to have undergone a change; the Englishmen met us in the most obliging way, and so, on the Tuesday, on board the British steamer *Madura*, in the company of Lieutenant-Captain von der Gröben, I commenced my voyage home to Europe. Herr von Tiedemann preferred, after all, making use of the French mail. On August 9th I was in Naples; on the 15th I was greeted in Milan, by Herr Oskar Borchert, in the name of the Emin Pasha committee; on the 18th, at Wildbad, I was again on German territory; and on August 25th, in Jüterbock, at the Anhalt station, I was heartily welcomed home, after an absence of exactly a year and a half, to the very day.

To Italy and Germany.

On the evening before my departure from Zanzibar, as I was standing, after taking my walk, at the gate of the German club, I had the pleasure of once more seeing Admiral Fremantle. He was going past, towards the sea, with one of the British captains, when he caught sight of me. He went a few steps further, then turned round, came towards me, and said,—

A few words with Admiral Fremantle.

"How do you do, Dr. Peters? I must congratulate you on the successful accomplishment of your expedition."

"Many thanks."

"You have a great work behind you. It required much energy and courage."

"Many thanks; yes."

"You have found many difficulties?"

"Especially on the coast."

"Yes, I know."

APPENDIX.

SUPPLEMENT I.

THE GERMAN EMIN PASHA COMMITTEE.

ACKERMANN, Privy Court Councillor, Member of the Reichstag, and of the Saxon Assembly of Estates, Dresden.
ARENDT, Dr., Member of the Executive Committee, Berlin (Secretary).
ARNIM, MUSKAU, Count, Member of the Reichstag, Muskau.
BALAN, Von, Land Councillor, Member of the Executive Committee, Schlawe.
BECKER, FRITZ, Dr., Worms.
BEHR-BANDELIN, Count, Chamberlain of H.M. the Emperor, Bandelin.
BELOU, Von, Landed Proprietor, Major on retired list, Member of the Executive Committee, Saleske.
BENNIGSEN, Von, Upper President, Member of the Reichstag, Hanover.
BOKEMEYER, Dr., General Secretary, Berlin.
BUECK, H., General Secretary, Berlin.
BUSSE, M., Dr., Mining Councillor, Dortmund.
CAMPE, Von H., Dr., Hanover.
CHRISTOPHERSEN, Member of the Executive Committee, Schleswig.
CLAUSZ, Manufacturer, Member of the Reichstag, and of the Saxon Assembly of Estates, Chemnitz.
CORNELIUS, F., Member of the Council of the German Colonial Company for South-west Africa, Berlin.

CRANACH, Von, Government President, Hanover.
CREDÉ, Dr., Court Councillor, Dresden.
CREDNER, Professor, Leipzig.
CUNY, Von, Privy Councillor of Justice, Member of the Reichstag, Member of the Executive Committee, Berlin.
DOUGLAS, Count von, Member of the Executive Committee, Aschersleben.
DRIGALSKI, Von, Lieutenant-General, retired, Berlin.
DZIEMDOWSKY, Von, Member of the Executive Committee, Schloss Meseritz.
FABRI, F., Dr. (theological), Godesberg.
FABRI, T., Dr., Hamburg.
FRIEDBERG, Dr., Professor, Member of the Executive Committee, Halle.
FRIEDERICHSEN, L., Hamburg.
GERLICH, Dr., Land Councillor, Member of the Executive Committee, Schwetz.
GRAIS, HUE DE, Count, Privy Government Councillor, Member of the Executive Committee, Berlin.
GRIMM, Dr., Ministerial President, retired, Karlsruhe.
GROSSE, RUDOLF, Dr., Strassburg in Elsass.
GROSZ, Advocate, Pforzheim.
GUILLEAUME, Cologne.
GÜNTHER, F., Commercial Councillor, Dresden.
HACKE, Count von, Rear-Admiral, retired, Berlin.
HANIEL, Dr., Land Councillor, Member of the Executive Committee, Mörs.
HANSEN, Land Councillor, Member of the Executive Committee, Tondern.
HERMANN, Prince of Hohenlohe-Langenburg, Langenburg.
HERWIG, Vice-President, Member of the Executive Committee, Berlin.
HESZLER, Government Architect, Erfurt.
HEYDT, CARL VON DER, Banker, Elberfeld, Treasurer.
HOBRECHT, Actual Privy Councillor, Minister of State, retired Member of the Reichstag, Berlin.
HOFMANN, Von, Minister of State, Berlin, First Deputy President.

IRMER, Dr., Keeper of the Royal Archives, Hanover.
JAEKEL, Land Director, Member of the Executive Committee, Dantsic.
KAAPCKE, Landed Proprietor, Member of the Executive Committee, East Prussia.
KARDORFF, Von, Member of the Reichstag, Wabnitz.
KENNEMANN, Landed Proprietor, Member of the Executive Committee, Klenka (Province of Posen).
KRESZMANN, Major, retired, Karlsruhe.
KRUPP, F. A., Privy Councillor of Commerce, Essen.
LANGEN, EUGENE, Privy Councillor of Commerce, Cologne.
LANGERMANN-ERLENKAMP, Baron von, Member of the Executive Committee, Lublin (Province of Posen).
LINDEMANN, M., Dr., Bremen.
LIVONIUS, Vice-Admiral, retired, Berlin.
LUCAS, Assessor, retired, Director of the German East African Company, Berlin.
LUCIUS, Privy Councillor of Commerce, Member of the Executive Committee, Erfurt.
LÜCKHOFF, Manufacturer, Member of the Executive Committee, Silesia.
MAERCKER, Lieutenant, Strassburg in Elsass.
MEHNERT, Dr., President of the Agricultural Credit Union in the Kingdom of Saxony, Member of the Reichstag, and the Assembly of Estates, Dresden.
MEISTER, Landed Proprietor, Member of the Executive Committee, Sängeran by Thorn.
MINNIGERODE, Freiherr von, Member of the Executive Committee, Rositten.
MIRBACH-SORQUITTEN, Count von, Member of the Reichstag, Sorquitten.
MÜHL, District Judge, Member of the Executive Committee, Segeberg.
NEDDEN, ZUR, Land Councillor, Member of the Executive Committee, Marienberg.
NEUBARTH, Landed Proprietor, Member of the Executive Committee, Wünschendorf.

NEUBAUER, F. A., Privy Councillor of Commerce, Magdeburg.
NIETHAMMER, Councillor of Commerce, Member of the Reichstag, and of the Saxon Assembly of Estates, Krebsstein.
OPPENHEIM, HUGO, Banker, Berlin.
O'SWALD, W., & Co., Hamburg.
PALÉSIEUX, Von, Major and Adjutant of H.R.H. the Grand Duke of Saxe-Weimar.
PETERS, CARL, Dr., Berlin, President.
PILGRIM, Von, Government President, Member of the Executive Committee, Minden.
POPELIUS, Member of the Executive Committee, Sulzbach.
RITTER, Dr., General Director, Waldenburg in Silesia.
ROEDER, E. von, Chief Master of Ceremonies, Berlin.
ROHLFS, GERHARD, Consul-General, Weimar.
RUMPFF, Manufacturer, Member of the Executive Committee, Schloss Aprath (Rhine Province).
SACHSE, Director in Imperial Post Office, Berlin.
SCHAEFFER, G., Member of the Executive Committee, Görlitz.
SCHMIDT, Member of the Executive Committee, Sangerhausen.
SCHREIBER, Member of the Executive Committee, Wolkramshausen.
SCHROEDER, Dr., Landed Proprietor, Poggelow, Second Deputy President.
SCHULTZ-LUPITZ, Member of the Executive Committee, Member of the Reichstag in Lupitz (Province of Saxony).
SCHWARTZKOPF, Von, Member of the Executive Committee, Neustadt in Hanover.
SCHWEINFURTH, Dr., Professor, Berlin.
SIMON, Privy Councillor of Government, retired, Berlin.
SOLMS-BRAUNFELS, HERMANN, Prince of.
STEINRÜCK, Von, Land Councillor, Member of the Executive Committee, Member of the Reichstag, Seclow.
STENGEL, Member of the Executive Committee, Stassfurt.
STEUN, Von, Major, retired, Berlin.
TEICHMANN-LOGISCHEN, Von, Lieutenant-General, Berlin.
TIEDEMANN, E. von, Member of the Executive Committee, Bomst.

APPENDIX. 565

TIEDEMANN, Von, Government President, Bromberg.
TRAMM, Member of the Executive Committee, Hanover.
TRUPPEL, G., Rudolstadt.
TUCHER, Freiherr von, Government Councillor, Nürnberg.
UECHTRITZ-STEINKIRCH, Von, Councillor of the Kummergericht, Member of the Executive Committee, Berlin.
ULRICH, J., Member of the Reichstag, Pfrengstadt.
WAGNER, J., Teacher at High School, Berlin.
WESSEL, Land Councillor, Member of the Executive Committee, Stuhm.
WETTICH, Town Representative, Member of the Executive Committee, Havelberg.
WIBEL, Dr., Wiesbaden.
WIED, W., Prince of, Neuwied.
WISSMANN, First Lieutenant, retired, Berlin.
WITTENBRINCK, High School Teacher, Burgsteinfurt.

SUPPLEMENT II.

RELATIONS WITH ADMIRAL FREMANTLE AND THE BRITISH BLOCKADE.

"To the Executive Committee of the German Emin Pasha Committee.

" I HAVE the honour very respectfully to report the following concerning my conference with Rear-Admiral Fremantle, which has just taken place.

" It lasted about three-quarters of an hour, and was in a high degree interesting.

" Admiral Fremantle was engaged on the quarter-deck. He immediately received me, and conducted me to his saloon.

" I introduced the subject of the prohibition that forbade me to visit any of the English places, and my *Neœra* to run in at any of them. To this Admiral Fremantle replied, in the first place, with some lengthy observations. My past doings in Eastern Africa, he said, must naturally awaken the suspicions of the English. I had come here, into their territory, and had everywhere hoisted the German flag. He had been suspicious of me before I came here. My behaviour here had greatly strengthened his suspicions. No one knew what my real intentions were. I had visited neither him nor the English Consul-General; here and there I had looked about me on the coast. Rightly or wrongly, he felt fully convinced that I had again political objects in the background. And these aims he would oppose. He was an Englishman, and no one could blame him for doing so. If, indeed, I were protected by my own Government, he could put no obstacle in my way. I ought to report to Berlin. So long as my Government did nothing for me, nobody could blame him if he tried to frustrate my endeavours.

He would readily admit that the blockade was a welcome implement to him, for this end. And he intended to use it. If this was 'unpleasant' for me, I must at least allow that he met me openly. I replied, his good will was not the point in question, 'but,' I said, 'I only want my right. You must yourself know how far you can justify such measures against me. It is plain that ultimately they will have to be adjudicated upon in another place.' I would have visited him before, but it had several times happened that he was absent when I was in Zanzibar. So far as my objects were concerned, they were expressed in the aim of my expedition. I wished to carry help to Emin Pasha. As regarded the attitude of the German Government, I was not entitled to express an opinion why it took up this or that position; at any rate, both our Emperor and the Imperial Chancellor had assured us of their sympathy, and I also believed that we possessed the sympathy of our nation.

"Admiral Fremantle said, that so far as regarded his right, there existed a state of war. That I was, or at least appeared to be, dangerous to the peace of Africa. That when, a short time ago, Sir John Kirk had been here, *entirely* on private affairs, the Germans had shown themselves to be disquieted, and that Sir John had been obliged, after three days, to take his departure. Now, he had personally a very high esteem for Sir John Kirk. Therefore I should receive more justice than Sir John Kirk. I was, for the English, exactly what Sir John Kirk was for the Germans. If Deinhard declared that he did not want to have Sir John Kirk in Saadani, he could do nothing against it; and the English did not want to have me in any of their places. Besides, there were such things as telegraphs. I had better complain of him; an order to him from London would alter the situation for him.

"I replied that I did not think he was justified in the measures he was taking, for a state of war did not actually prevail; and for the blockade there were definite normal bounds, which I did not intend to overstep. I should leave it to the public opinion of Europe to form a judgment on the attitude he was maintaining. Beyond this, I was especially anxious to know accurately, to what extent I had to calculate upon his opposition. 'What are the places you blockade?' Admiral Fremantle replied, 'The places from Lamu to Umba.' I said, 'Then outside these I have not to anticipate your enmity?' He answered, after a short hesitation, 'Outside these places I shall not interfere with you.' I said, 'Very well; I now know what I have to expect, and you may be sure that it is not my intention to interfere with the sphere of British blockade.'

"I then brought forward the subject of my wish with respect to the delivering up of the hunting weapons; the German authorities had, as I reported to the Committee yesterday, declined to mediate for me in this matter. Admiral Fremantle explained to me, in the first instance, that for his part he had never had any other idea than that there was a 'misunderstanding' in this matter. He had also said to his superiors, that I might have sent the weapons by Wissmann's steamer, so that I had given no cause of complaint. He would send my hunting weapons to me, on board the *Neæra*, and only requested me to give him a receipt for them.

"During our interview, an impression had evidently come upon the old gentleman, that this attitude towards a single man was not, after all, a very brilliant one, and it was manifestly agreeable to him to do me this favour.

"In conclusion, I asked him whether I might, if necessary, send the *Neæra* to Lamu. He replied, 'Well, if no arms are on board, and' (with a smile) 'if you yourself don't go.'

"I have to apologise if this short extract from our conversation should be found incorrect, here and there, with respect to style. I have been anxious to give the decisive declarations as literally as possible.

"I believe this report may be of use, in case of necessity, in characterising the condition of things here, and beg to refer this, with all respect, to the judgment of the honourable Committee.

"With much respect,
(Signed) "CARL PETERS."

"To Captain Cardale,
"Commander of H.B.M.S. *Agamemnon*, Zanzibar.

"Sir,—When I had the honour to call upon you this morning, you kindly informed me that you had orders not to allow my person to land at any place within the sphere of British blockade; neither should my steamer be entitled to call at any port or place blockaded by the British fleet.

"As it is absolutely necessary that I should have a personal interview with the Commander-in-Chief, Rear-Admiral Fremantle, and as I have hardly time to wait till next Thursday, I kindly beg of you either to give me passage on board one of H.B.M. ships that is going to Mombassa within the next days, or to give a pass for my steamer *Neæra*, on board of which I then will go to Mombassa. As this demand is in entire conformity with the conditions of the blockade, I trust that you will kindly agree to it.

"Your immediate answer will greatly oblige

"Yours very respectfully,
(Signed) "Carl Peters.
"*On board S.S. 'Neæra.'*"

"To Dr. Carl Peters,
" British S.S. *Neæra*.

"H.M.S. 'Agamemnon,' Zanzibar, *May 27th*, 1889.

"Sir,—I regret to inform you that it is not in my power either to give you a pass to Mombassa, or to grant you a passage in H.M. ship proceeding to that port.

"The Rear-Admiral Commander-in-Chief will arrive at Zanzibar at daylight on Thursday next, when you will have no difficulty in seeing him.

"I am, Sir, your obedient Servant,
"C. S. Cardale,
"*Captain and Senior Officer.*"

"Bagamoyo, *June 9th,* 1889.

"Your Excellency,—I have the honour kindly to inform Your Excellency that I shall most likely have to send the *Neœra* to Lamu.

"According to the promise kindly given by Your Excellency to me, that you will raise no objections to my doing so, in case there are neither arms, nor war ammunitions, nor my own person on board, I kindly beg from Your Excellency to instruct the commander of H.M.S. at Lamu of my intention.

"I probably shall send to Lamu either Herr Borchert or Herr Friedenthal, or both, and this will be about from the 25th to the 30th of June.

"With the expression of my sincere respect,
"I remain
"Your Excellency's most obedient Servant,
(Signed) "Carl Peters."

"'Boadicea,' at Zanzibar, *June 11th,* 1889.

"Sir,—I have the honour to acknowledge the receipt of your letter of the 9th inst., informing me of your intention to send the *Neœra* to Lamu, but that in accordance with what I mentioned in our recent interview you would not go yourself, and no arms or ammunition would be on board the ship.

"Under the above circumstances I shall not object to the *Neœra* going to Lamu, and I will give instructions to our blockading ship accordingly; but her proceedings there will be watched, and I shall direct that she is ordered to quit the port if anything whatever is being done or suspected which would at all be liable to create disturbance or injure the British Imperial East African Company.

"It would tend to remove suspicion if you were to make a candid statement of the object for which the *Neœra* is required to go to Lamu.

"I have the honour to be, Sir, your obedient Servant,
(Signed) "Fremantle,
"*Rear-Admiral Commander-in-Chief.*

APPENDIX.

"To Oskar Borchert, Esq.,
"Member of the German Emin Pasha Expedition, Lamu.

"Lamu, *June* 21*st*, 1889.

"Sir,—I have the honour to inform you that I have received orders from Arbuthnot, commander of H.M.S. *Mariner*, to prevent the S.S. *Necera* from landing the cargo consigned to the German Emin Pasha Expedition in Lamu.

"I further have to state that I have examined every package, and hereby certify that I have found neither arms nor ammunition nor powder amongst them.

"I have the honour to be, Sir,
(Signed) "D. R. Roberts,
"*Seaman, H.M.S. 'Mariner.'*"

"H.M.S. 'Mariner,' at Lamu,

"22*nd June*, 1889.

"Sir,—Acting under orders from the Naval Commander-in-Chief in these waters, and in consideration of the existing blockade of this part of the coast of Africa, I have to inform you that [the stores at present on board your ship for Dr. Carl Peters cannot be landed at this place, or at any other part within or adjacent to that part of the coast which is at present under blockade. Those stores, now in a lighter alongside your ship, must be taken on board again, and you are to quit the port as soon as this is accomplished. I shall send an officer and an armed party on board to support you in carrying out this order. The officer will accompany you to Zanzibar, in order to see that the stores are not landed in any other port on this part of the coast. His passage to that place will be taken and paid for.

(Signed) "Charles R. Arbuthnot,
"*Commander.*"

"WITU, 29th June, 1889.

"YOUR EXCELLENCY,—It is with the greatest surprise that I learn Your Excellency has given orders to seize the *Neæra* at Lamu, and prohibit her to discharge her cargo at this place. Your Excellency, I am sure, will understand my surprise, as you will remember our arrangement made at Zanzibar on May 31st. Your Excellency declared my calling at any place under British blockade objectionable, but promised not to interfere with me outside the line of this blockade. When I asked Your Excellency what you meant by ports and places under British blockade, you answered clearly and distinctly that this meant the coast between Lamu and the mouth of the Umba River. The official declaration limits the blockade between 2° 10′ and 10° 27′ southern latitude. Therefore, complying with your demand, I took the trouble to land the goods of the German Emin Pasha Expedition at Kwaihu Bay, about 2° 5′ southern latitude, therefore 'outside the line of blockade.' You further promised me not to interfere with the *Neæra*, should she call at Lamu, if neither men nor arms and war ammunition were on board. Now the *Neæra*, trusting to your promise, called at Lamu without me and war ammunitions of any kind. In spite of the promise given by Your Excellency to me at Zanzibar on May 31st, you have given orders to seize her by force, in contradiction to international law, and in conflict with the terms laid down in the declaration of blockade.

"I shall leave it to the public opinion to judge about this conduct, and I have taken steps to have this letter published in Europe.

"But I may take the liberty to inform Your Excellency that I had transferred the *Neæra* to Herr Oskar Borchert already on the 15th day of this month at Kwaihu Bay, and that I consigned the merchandise on her to Herr Toeppen on the 19th day of this month at Shimbye. For these goods, representing merchandise to be used on the Pangani route, were not of essential value to me while marching north of the Tana river, and therefore I sent

APPENDIX. 573

them to Lamu instead of landing them at Kwaihu. I expect that Herr Oskar Borchert as well as Herr Toeppen will claim damages from Your Excellency by legal proceedings for the losses they incurred through your orders, which you will have to answer for.

"I have the honour to be,
"Your Excellency's most obedient Servant,
(Signed) "CARL PETERS.

"To his Excellency the Rear-Admiral and Commander-in-Chief, FREMANTLE, on board H.M.S. *Boadicea*."

SUPPLEMENT III.

THE "NEŒRA" LAWSUIT.

THE English steamer *Neœra* was chartered in April 1889, through the instrumentality of the Indian merchant Sewa Hadji, by Dr. Carl Peters for a period of six months, at the stipulated price of 6,500 rupees per month, for the German Emin Pasha Expedition. After the landing, which took place in Kwaihu Bay on June 15th (outside the blockaded region on the coast), the articles required by the expedition, especially arms, munitions, wares, etc., were landed. There remained on board about one hundred cases of various articles which were not immediately required for the expedition. According to the arrangements made by Dr. Peters, these goods were to be sold in Lamu or Zanzibar, and in their stead articles of barter were to be provided, which were to be sent after the expedition. To this end, Dr. Peters consigned the goods left on board to the representative of the German Witu Company, Herr Curt Toeppen, in Lamu; while the charter was transferred on June 15th to Herr O. Borchert, member of the German Emin Pasha Expedition. Herr Borchert arrived with the ship at Lamu on June 18th. There eighty-seven cases were put on board a dhow, after they had been opened and not objected to by the English naval officer who carried out the blockade service in Lamu. This officer, in a letter to Herr Borchert, dated June 21st,* especially acknowledged that he had found in the cases neither arms, nor powder, nor ammunition of any kind. Nevertheless he informed Herr Borchert, in the same letter, that he had received orders from Mr. Arbuthnot, the commander of the English ship of war *Mariner*, to prevent the landing of the goods in Lamu. A letter from Mr. Charles R. Arbuthnot,

---

* See Supplement II., p. 571.

dated June 22nd,* confirmed this order, with the addition that the goods already transhipped to the dhow were to be put back on board the *Neœra*, and that the latter was to quit the harbour of Lamu immediately. The captain of the *Neœra* was compelled to obey this order, and to proceed to Zanzibar, accompanied by an English officer.

In Zanzibar the cargo of the ship was again inspected. A case was now found which contained, among other paraphernalia, a few leather belts and bags, besides a number of knives, or hunting knives, and a small quantity of sounding lead. Hereupon proceedings were taken in the English Prize Court in Zanzibar. There appeared as plaintiffs, demanding the release of the ship: (1) The proprietors of the *Neœra* (the English firm Messrs. Shepherd & Co.); (2) Sewa Hadji and O. Borchert as charterers; (3) Herr Toeppen as consignee of the goods. The judge had to decide whether the ship had been rightfully seized for breaking the blockade, and the decision turned upon the question whether the articles above described (leather belts, bags, etc.) were to be looked upon as materials of war. On this question English as well as German witnesses and experts were heard. The Englishmen (especially Captain Cardale of the man-of-war *Agamemnon*, and General Matthews, commander of the troops of the Sultan of Zanzibar) answered the question in the affirmative, while on the German side (especially by Imperial Commissary Wissmann) the opinion was maintained that we had here to do with articles the importation of which was in no way forbidden by the decrees and orders for the blockade. The judge took the latter view. The decision was given, to that effect, on August 5th, 1889. Though it was favourable as to the main issue, inasmuch as an order was made for the release of the ship, the judge not only refused the claim for damages set up by the plaintiffs, but also condemned the owners of the ship in the costs of the suit. At the conclusion of his plaint, Herr Borchert had not only asked for the release of the ship and her cargo, but had

---

* See Supplement II., p. 571.

sought to make the authors of the seizure of the vessel responsible for all damages he had suffered by that proceeding.

The question accordingly arose, whether, in view of this last decree, an appeal should be lodged against the decision of the Prize Court, that had been favourable on the chief point. This question was urged upon the German Emin Pasha committee also by the Foreign Office of the German Empire.

The executive committee of the above-mentioned association had applied to the Foreign Office with a complaint concerning the hostile measures of the English authorities (preventing the Somalis from landing in Lamu, confiscation of the weapons in Zanzibar, prohibition to Dr. Carl Peters and to the *Neæra* to land within the English line of blockade, seizure of the *Neæra*), and put forward claims for damages. The Foreign Office, after receiving the report of the Consul-General in Zanzibar, did not, indeed, acknowledge the complaint in all its bearings, but allowed it to be well founded in respect to certain points. With regard to the affair of the *Neæra*, it was proposed to the executive committee that the judgment of the Prize Court should be appealed against to the Privy Council in London, as the English Government could only be moved to give an indemnity in case of the "unconditional acquittal" of the ship. Thereupon enquiries were instituted on the part of the committee in London, in the proper quarter, with respect to the cost and the probable issue of an appeal. The answer was that the proceedings in London would involve an expense which would go beyond the means of the committee, and that the issue appeared doubtful; possibly, the appeal might lead to a reversal of the favourable verdict obtained on the chief point—the release of the ship. The German Emin Pasha Committee accordingly resolved to refrain from lodging the appeal. This resolve was communicated to the Foreign Office, with the reasons that had led to it. At the same time the claim for damages on account of the seizure of the *Neæra*, which the Prize Court had pronounced unjustified, and also for the other measures adopted on the side of the English against the expedition, was maintained. Respecting one portion of these claims the Foreign Office had entered into negotiations with the English Government. The provisional German-English agreement of June 17th, 1890, among various yet unsettled points in dispute, which were reserved for further friendly consideration, after it had been declared that there were in principle no serious differences of opinion upon them, had included the "claim respecting the detention of the steamer *Neæra*." The definitive agreement of July 1st brought no decision on this point. To the questions, whether there was still a future prospect that the claims raised for compensation for the illegal treatment of the German Emin Pasha Expedition by the English navy would receive any kind of acknowledgment and satisfaction, or whether all prospect of receiving such compensation must be abandoned, the German Emin Pasha Committee finally received from the Colonial department of the Foreign Office the answer that compensation for the seizure of the *Neæra* by the English Government was not to be expected. Apart from the occurrences that had accompanied the commencement of the expedition, the foundation on which such claims could have been enforced in a diplomatic manner had been taken away from the Imperial Government, by the fact that the committee had not adopted the available means for appealing against the judgment of the Prize Court.

In the report of the English negotiator Anderson on the decision of July 1st, a report which was laid, together with the decision, before the English Parliament, the following passage occurs:—

"Certain points of difference were specially reserved for negotiation between Dr. Krauel and myself.

"The first of these related to claims of German subjects connected with the capture of the *Neæra* in Lamu harbour by the British blockading squadron, and her condemnation (?) by the Zanzibar Prize Court, and to further claims on account of the alleged refusal of the British blockading squadron to permit the landing at Lamu of some Somali porters engaged for the expedition of Dr. Peters into the interior.

"*I have been able to give satisfactory explanations on both points, and the claims have been withdrawn.*"

SUPPLEMENT IV.

THE FATE OF THE SECOND COLUMN.

IN my narrative of the occurrences of Oda-Boru-Rûva, I described in what a painful position I was placed by the non-arrival of all intelligence respecting the second column. At the time I could not at all explain this to myself. It was only afterwards, in Zanzibar and in Europe, that I learned that Lieutenant-Captain Rust had pushed forward beyond Massa to unite with me, that he had landed a number of articles in the steppe forest, under the care of a Somali, and had then gone back to bring up the rest. Lieutenant-Captain Rust had afterwards lost the greater part of his loads in Kena Kombe by an explosion of the powder chests, had afterwards fallen seriously ill, and had returned to Europe. Some messengers whom he despatched to me appear to have been killed. As Lieutenant-Captain Rust has already made public his adventures in a book of his own, "The German Emin Pasha Expedition," which was published by F. Luckhard of Berlin, I may here content myself with referring the curious to his detailed account.

I shall, accordingly, only subjoin here a short account by Oskar Borchert, which will suffice for the continuity of this narrative. Herr Borchert intends also to describe and publish his experiences in detail, and his descriptions may be looked forward to with interest. From the following report, it is manifest that he set about his task with determination and energy, and that it was not his fault that he did not reach my column. The attempt of Oskar Borchert to overtake us, his march for this object, with a disproportionately small equipment, up the Tana, is in itself an achievement which, indeed, only stands in indirect connection with our expedition, but nevertheless gives Herr Borchert a claim to my acknowledgments, and the approval of the parties interested in Germany. For services must not always be estimated only according to the material results. He who does honour to the German name by the fulfilment of duty, and by courage, serves his nation too, though the effects of such conduct cannot be estimated in figures. This is what Herr Oskar Borchert has done by his march beyond Oda-Boru-Ruva. And now I think it best to let him speak for himself.

CARL PETERS.

"TO THE LEADER OF THE GERMAN EMIN PASHA EXPEDITION, HERR DR. CARL PETERS.

"Herewith I transmit to you, Sir, a brief report of my proceedings in connection with the German Emin Pasha Expedition. I begin my narrative from the period of our parting in Mbaya, on June 16th, 1889.

"After we had, on the day before, run into the Kwaihu Bay with the steamer *Neæra*, and from thence had happily accomplished the landing of the expedition, I received from you the command of the steamer, with directions to take the articles of barter from Kwaihu Bay to Lamu, to unload them there, to act *re* steamer *Neæra*, and then to betake myself, with the articles of barter that could be transported on the camels that were in Lamu, into the Sultanate of Witu, and there to rejoin your column that you had led thither in the meantime.

"After an exceedingly troublesome passage of three days, against the tide and monsoon, we came in sight of Lamu. But the *Neæra* had sustained great damage from storm and waves; and the storm, foretold by the captain, came on before we were able to run into the sheltering harbour. Parts of the engine were broken; the ship, without a rudder, at the mercy of the stormy sea, got off its course into the raging breakers, the waves tore away the companion ladder leading to the after deck, there was a foot of water in the saloon, and the captain prepared me for the worst. After many fruitless efforts, we at length succeeded, in this dangerous position, in throwing out the sheet anchor, a difficult thing to do in the situation in which we were.

After temporarily repairing the ship, I was able, with the help of a pilot, who had meanwhile come aboard at my signal, to run into the harbour of Lamu.

"The occurrences here,—that is to say, the uncalled-for confiscation of our articles of barter and the unjust seizure of the *Neæra* on the part of the English Admiral, Fremantle,—I have already had the honour of reporting to you in detail, in the camp at Hindi. In Hindi I received the order to betake myself to Zanzibar, and there, by resorting to law proceedings, to procure the restoration of the *Neæra*. It was only by chance that I succeeded in reaching Zanzibar from Lamu in a steamer of the Sultan line. I now entered an action against the English naval authorities, the captors of our steamer, and addressed a memorial to His Highness the Imperial Chancellor, Prince Bismarck, informed the executive branch of the German Emin Pasha committee of my proceedings by means of a telegram, and with the help of an Indian advocate carried through the so-called *Neæra* lawsuit, which in its details was interesting. I won it. The *Neæra* with her whole cargo was given up to me; but by the seizure our expedition had incurred an expense of 54,000 rupees, and in a report transmitted to Berlin I put it to the executive branch of the German Emin Pasha Expedition to decide whether they would appeal against the decision, and institute a separate lawsuit for damages. I transferred the charter of the liberated *Neæra* to Captain Wissmann, with the stipulation that he must send me to Lamu in one of his steamers. On September 4th I was at length able to start in the *Harmony* for Lamu.

"There I received the news that you, Sir, had already in July started from Witu for Ngoa on the Tana; according to the instructions left behind for me, I was to follow you to Kitui on the Kenia. I was obliged in Kenia to bring an expedition of my own together for myself, so far as I could manage it; and I left there on September 12th. Arrived at Witu, I established friendly relations with the Sultan Tumo Bakari, and from thence led the expedition to Ngoa, to wait there for the remainder of my articles of barter, which I wished to have brought by the maritime route by dhow, through Herr Schlunke, whom I had engaged as far as the mouth of the Tana, to be transported from thence up the Tana as far as Ngoa. After I had waited for some time in vain for Herr Schlunke in Ngoa, there arrived one day from him the bad tidings that the dhow had got on to a sandbank at the Osi mouth and had capsized, whereby many things had been lost, and asking me to come to assist with my people in saving the rest. Just as I was about to start, I received news which had very extensively disagreeable consequences for me, and overthrew all my plans. Lieutenant-Captain Rust sent me information from Kena Kombe, a place situate on the Tana, about six days' march above Ngoa, to which place he had meanwhile brought the articles of barter intended for you, that he had lost the greater part of the things, such as guns, ammunition, etc., by a fire, and asking me to help and endeavour to make up the loss of the articles. As I heard at the same time from Lieutenant-Captain Rust that you were going to wait on the Upper Tana for the arrival of the articles of barter, I wrote to Lieutenant-Captain Rust that I would try to parry the blow, and that he should go to you as quickly as possible with the portion of the things that had escaped. With a heavy heart I had now to retrace my steps for the second time.

"I proceeded with my column through the Belodsomi canal over Kau to Kipini, where with the help of Herr Schlunke I raised the wrecked dhow; then went on through German Witu land over Mpekotoni to Lamu, made up, by new purchases, for the things that had been burnt, and marched over Mkonumbi to Witu. Here I found news from Berlin, telling how in Germany it was believed the whole expedition had been ruined, and that you yourself had been murdered; and I also received a letter from the Imperial Commissariat in Zanzibar, wherein was announced the return of Emin with Stanley. These were truly tidings which disturbed me most profoundly. The foremost thing to do was to make certain as to the fate of the first column.

"On the same day, by a forced ride, I reached Ngoa on the Tana, just as a messenger, Amiri, arrived from Oda-Boru-Ruva, with letters from you, from which I could see that at the time when you were being mourned in Germany as a murdered man you were safe and sound with your column in Oda-Boru-Ruva. I therefore at once sent a despatch to Germany, to quiet the public mind there, in which despatch I stated that it was not the German expedition but an English one that had been destroyed by the Somalis; that you with your column, as well as Lieutenant von Tiedemann, were in good health, on the Upper Tana.

"The news of the return of Stanley and Emin Pasha to the coast was officially announced to me by the Imperial Commissariat; I could no longer doubt it, and was obliged to try and reach you, however small the prospect appeared of my doing so. For some time after I had sent off the despatches to Germany, new rumours were always springing up on the Tana, describing the expedition as having perished, which I certainly did not believe, but which startled me by their continual recurrence. The rumour said that your column had been completely destroyed in a fight with the Borani Gallas, and I was enabled to ascertain that nearly all the Gallas who were fit for war, and who lived scattered along the Lower Tana, had gone to Oda-Boru-Ruva. My duty bade me go forward to ascertain the truth.

"A few days after my departure two of Rust's Somalis overtook me, bringing a mournful message. Rust, whom I supposed to have joined your column long before, was lying sick, they said, in Mnina, in my immediate neighbourhood, and they asked me to come quickly to his rescue, or else he would die, for he had not been able to reach Oda-Boru-Ruva, but had been obliged to turn back, because of his illness. A few forced marches brought me to Rust, and I had the great satisfaction of keeping him alive by my appearance. The situation in which I found him was the most helpless and saddest that can be imagined. I brought Rust by the water route to Kulessa, my last camping-place, and the next morning I had him rowed by a few trustworthy Wapokomo to Ngoa, where he could receive hospitality and every care at the hands of the benevolent, dated June 22nd,* confirmed this order, with the addition that the goods already transhipped to the dhow were to be put back on board the *Neæra*, and that the latter was to quit the harbour of Lamu immediately. The captain of the *Neæra* was compelled to obey this order, and to proceed to Zanzibar, accompanied by an English officer.

In Zanzibar the cargo of the ship was again inspected. A case was now found which contained, among other paraphernalia, a few leather belts and bags, besides a number of knives, or hunting knives, and a small quantity of sounding lead. Hereupon proceedings were taken in the English Prize Court in Zanzibar. There appeared as plaintiffs, demanding the release of the ship: (1) The proprietors of the *Neæra* (the English firm Messrs. Shepherd & Co.); (2) Sewa Hadji and O. Borchert as charterers; (3) Herr Toeppen as consignee of the goods. The judge had to decide whether the ship had been rightfully seized for breaking the blockade, and the decision turned upon the question whether the articles above described (leather belts, bags, etc.) were to be looked upon as materials of war. On this question English as well as German witnesses and experts were heard. The Englishmen (especially Captain Cardale of the man-of-war *Agamemnon*, and General Matthews, commander of the troops of the Sultan of Zanzibar) answered the question in the affirmative, while on the German side (especially by Imperial Commissary Wissmann) the opinion was maintained that we had here to do with articles the importation of which was in no way forbidden by the decrees and orders for the blockade. The judge took the latter view. The decision was given, to that effect, on August 5th, 1889. Though it was favourable as to the main issue, inasmuch as an order was made for the release of the ship, the judge not only refused the claim for damages set up by the plaintiffs, but also condemned the owners of the ship in the costs of the suit. At the conclusion of his plaint, Herr Borchert had not only asked for the release of the ship and her cargo, but had

* See Supplement II., p. 571.

to me the details of your fight with the Gallas, in which Sultan Hugo lost his life. I now also ascertained definitely that you had marched away with the column as long as six or eight weeks before, and that there was no chance of my overtaking you. Still, I would not yet turn back; I was anxious to get as far as the mountain chains that could be descried from the Von der Heydt House. After six days of strenuous marching, I reached the mountain region through which the Tana forces its way. For a day and a half I traversed that district. The furthest place I reached was called Garebantai.

"My march back led me again to Oda-Boru-Ruva. In the meantime a number of Gallas had banded themselves together here, and during a two days' rest I took they twice tried to surprise me, but each time they were driven off by volleys of musketry. When I began my retreat, my situation was an unfavourable one. Already on my arrival at Oda-Boru-Ruva I had no articles of barter left, my ammunition was decreasing at a serious rate, and some of my people, footsore and enfeebled, entirely gave in.

"I now chose for my march the region on the right bank of the Tana, to get acquainted with this part likewise. Though I had to contend with difficulties of various kinds, and myself fell ill at last through want of water and proper provisions, I had many interesting experiences during this part of my journey. At length I reached the abode of the hospitable missionaries on the Tana, and here I still had the opportunity to observe the arrangement and management of the Mission; then I went on to Lamu, from whence I at once despatched to Germany the news that you had left the Tana station with your column in good health, and were probably across the Baringo. In the beginning of March I reached Zanzibar once more; there I saw Emin Pasha, and was able to deliver to him some of the things our expedition had brought from Germany.

"I have the honour to sign myself
"Your most obedient
"OSKAR BORCHERT."

SUPPLEMENT V.

THE UGANDA TREATY.

ENTRE le roi Mwanga Kabaka du Bouganda, et le Dr. Carl Peters est agrée le suivant traité préliminaire.

Le roi Mwanga accepte les stipulations du traité de Berlin (acte de Congo), février 1885, pour ce qui a rapport au Bouganda et à ses pays tributaires. Il ouvre ces pays à tous les sujets de Sa Majesté l'Empereur d'Allemagne, comme à tous les autres Européens. Il garantit aux sujets de Sa Majesté l'Empereur d'Allemagne, comme aux autres Européens qui voudront en profiter, entière liberté de commerce, liberté de passage, liberté de résidence dans le Bouganda et tous les pays tributaires.

Le roi Mwanga entre en amitié avec Sa Majesté l'Empereur d'Allemagne, et reçoit la liberté de commerce, liberté de passage, et liberté de résidence pour ses sujets, dans tous les territoires de Sa Majesté l'Empereur d'Allemagne.

Dr. Carl Peters se charge de proposer la ratification de ce traité préliminaire au gouvernement allemand.

Ce traité est fait en langue kiganda, kiswahili et français. En cas de différente interprétation le texte français seul fera foi.

27 *février*, 1890.

Signed
- MWANGA, Kabaka wa Buganda; and all the great men of the land.
- DR. CARL PETERS.
- TÉMOIN.
- SIMÉON LOURDEL, Supérieur de la Mission Catholique de Bouganda.

LUGANDA.

Kilagano ekyo ekisose, Mwanga kabaka wa Buganda kye alayana na Dr. Carl Peters.

Kabaka Mwanga, ebigambo eby o Buganda ne bye nsi

APPENDIX.

eziingila mu Buganpa ebyatabibwa mu Kilagano kya Berlin (acte du Congo, février 1885) abikkiriza. Ate abantu bonna aba kabaka wa Budatshi, abawa nga bwe yawa abazongu bonna obwinza bwo kuja mu nsi ye. Ate abantu bonna aba kabaka wa Budatshi abalaganya nga bwe abaganya abazongu bonna abalyagala, obwinza bwonna o bwo buguzi, o bwo kutambula, ne bwo kuzimba mu nsi ya Buganda ne nsi zonna eziingila mu.

Ate kabaka Mwanga aingidde mu ayagalo mkwano gwa kabaka o Mukuru wa budatshi, ate abantu be bonna ne bawebwa o bwinza o bwo buguzi, ne bwinza bwo kutambula no bwinza bwo kuzimba mu nsi zomu za kabaka o Mukuru wa budatshi.

Dr. Carl Peters alitwala ekilayano ekyo ekisose, eri Governement datshi, kitukkirizibwe.

Kilagano-ekyo ba kiwandise mu luswaili ne luganda ne lufransa naye oba walio empaka mu bigambo olufransa lme lulisara o msango.

27 *februari*, 1890.

> MWANGA, Kabaka wa Buganda.
> DR. CARL PETERS.
> SIMÉON LOURDEL.

THE END.

INDEX.

A.

Aberdare Range, the, 210.
Accident, a tragic, 258.
Achmed Somali, death of, 285.
Aden, proceedings at, 22.
Adventurous boat voyage, 161.
African tobacco, 442; character, 499; ideas of trade, 500; colonisation, improved prospects for, 588.
Agreement, the London, 133.
Ali Somal, arrival of, 304.
Ambassadress, a Massai, dialogue with, 250.
Amdalla, porter, 210.
Ammunition, serious expenditure in, 240; makeshift, 524.
Ancient records, their teaching, 418; maps and charts, 420, 421.
Angata-na-Nyuki, march to the, 290.
Announcement, a startling, 263.
Ants and mosquitoes, 85.
Anxious night, an, 242.
Appendix, 561.
Arab treachery, a piece of, 109; account of Ancient Egypt, 424; trader, Mohammed Bin Omari, 517.
Arabs, conversation with, 282; visit from, 284, in Uganda, 391; and Africans, undependable, 477; flight of, 486; of Mkondogna, 552.
Arendt, Herr, explanatory to the English, 400.
Arendt Bay, 350.
Articles of barter, 49; of the Uganda treaty, 389.
Augusta Victoria Fall, 201.
Aztecs, ancient sepulchres of, 423.

B.

Baale, arrival in, 458.
Badutschi, the, achievements of, 518.
Bagamoyo, passage to, 30; departure from, 83; march to, 555.
Bamberger, his philosophy, 206.
Banana, the, as food and drink, 351; capacities of the tree, 408.
Banquet, a sumptuous, 540.
Barakka, formidable accident of, 179.
Baringo Lake, its surroundings, 267; shores of, 272.
Basilid, Br., his plantations, 555.
Belgians, King of, his offer, 544.
Beyma people, the, 416.
Bin Omari, 517; interview with, 518; homage of, 519; his caravan, 531.
Bismarck, Count Herbert von, communication from, 16.
Bismarck, Prince, encouragement from, 12; change of front, 14.
Bley, Herr, departure of, 31.
Boadicea, the, 49.
Boatmen, dilatoriness of, 443.
Bonfire, a grand, 189.
Borchert and the *Neœra*, 55.
Brag, a game of, 229.

INDEX.

Bridge, failure of, across the Tana, 200.
British blockade, relations with, 566.
British East African Company, the, 544.
Buana Mku, parting with, 284; misbehaviour of, 468.
Buana Shama promises a guide, 79.
Bubo river, the, 531.
Budduland, 451.
Bukerebe, island of, 468.
Bukoba, advantages of, 542.
Bulingogwe, 437.
Bumbide, island of, 469.
Busiba, settlement of, 502.

C.

Camel, the voracious, 287; death of the last, 28.
Camp, poetry of life, 79; fortifying the, 258; Stanley's, 344.
Camping, among friends, 269; ground, a confused, 278, a pleasant, 401.
Canal, Siyu, 42.
Candle manufacture, 284.
Cannibal fowls, 514.
Caravan, the Wanjamwesi, 531; Mohammed Bin Omari's, 531; under the German flag, 533.
Centipede, a, 510.
"Chief," confidence in the, 261.
Christianity, prospects of supremacy, 404.
Christmas Eve, a disturbed, 245.
Civilisation, effect of Stanley's expedition upon, 548.
Civilised life, delights and luxuries of, 452, 488.
Coldness of nights, 218.
Combat, a, 289.
Commissariat, importance of the, 277.
Cooking under difficulties, 296.
Crocodiles, ferocity of, 490.
Culinary science and sport, 206.

D.

Dar-es-Salam, 33.
Deluge, a, 510.
Demand, a categoric, 186.
Deserter, arrival of a, 286.
Desertion, tendency to, 340.
Desolate region of horror, a, 376.
Dhow navigation, dangers of, 41.
Dialects, Suaheli and Kiganda, 417.
Dika, fording the, 208.
Discipline, strict, 94; necessity for, 384.
Discrepancy between Stanley's and Emin Pasha's accounts, 545.
Djuma, 473.
Döngo Gelesha Range, the, 252.
Donkeys, two useful, 497; mischance through, 512.
Dream, a curious, 293.
Dsagga, land of, 182.
Dumo, description of, 459.

E.

East African disturbances, progress of, 10.
Eclipse of the sun, 243; effect on Massais, 244.
Elbejet, chief kraal of, 230; reception at, 231; attacks on, 236, 239.
Elgejo, land of, 279; people of, 285; great plateau, 288.
Elgon rock dwellings, 424.
Elmorán, the, among the Massais, 226; villages, 227; attack by the, 237; kraal fired, 241.
Emin Pasha, services of, 4; conflicting rumours concerning, 14; accounts of, 305, 306; proposal to, 316; conjectures about, 339; question of his whereabouts, 844; tidings of, 533; Dr. Peters's meeting with, 536; approbation of,

338; consultation with, 540; in the German service, 541; carried off by Stanley, 543; his position on the Upper Nile, 544; discrepancy between his accounts and Stanley's, 545; compelled to follow Stanley, 545; estimate of Stanley, 546; character and amiable qualities, 549; photographic portraits of, 550; Dr. Peters's parting from, 551.

Emin Pasha German Expedition projected, 3; managing committee appointed, 5, 7; resolution for postponement, 12.

Encampment at Ischioragama, 373; a primitive, 471; in Bandelundo, 472; at Kuru, 473; at Kabila, 496; Emin's, 537; a jovial, 540.

Engatana, departure for, 76; camp at, 97.

England, question of co-operation with, 11.

Enterprise, a dangerous, 367.

Envoys, account of themselves, 343.

Europe, startling news from, 538.

Expedition, Dr. Peters's, frustrated by Stanley's undertaking, 548; another German, 554.

—— Emin Pasha, resources of, 31; division of, 56; strength of, 70; a previous, 276.

—— English, rumours of, 95; traces of, 120; letters for, 359.

—— expected British East African, 316.

—— German, 3, 5, 7; preparations for, 17; difficulties to be encountered, 18; plan of, 221; use of, 478.

—— idea of a new, 479.

—— Mr. Pigott and his, 132; traces of, 165.

—— Mr. Smith's, 96, 132; reported defeat of, 117.

—— Thomson's, 222.

—— Mr. de Winton's, 275.

Extract of report to Emin Pasha committee, 29.

F.

Fabian tactics possible, 244.
Famine, prospect of, 169.
Feast, a, for the black men, 241.
Fever, return of, 513.
Fighting, the best tactics in, 309.
Fire, an accidental, 266; fire signal, 120.
Flag, the German, advantages to, 399; caravan under, 533; hoisting, 113, 136, 258, 486; at Njemps, 273.
Flagstaff struck by lightning, 448.
Foreign Office, endeavours to interest, 28.
Forest scene, grand, 201.
Fremantle, Admiral, conference with, 32; proceedings of, 41; congratulations from, 559; relations with, 566.
French Mission, the, 384, 451.
—— missionary boats, 456.
—— station, arrangements of the, 452; Sunday at, 454.
Fugitives on the Tana, 155.
Fumo Bukari's declaration of friendship, 68.
Funga Sombo, swamp and forest of, 65.

G.

Galamba, 154.
Galla, arrival at settlement, 122.
—— guides, the, 162.
—— regions, 116.
Gallas, the, as police, 85; with the, in Oda-Boru-Ruva, 124; description of, 126, 127; sojourn among, 137; unsatisfactory relations with, 139; decisive measures against, 141; policy to be adopted towards, 149; delays of, 153.

Gall-Galla, cunning of, 144.
Game animals, a region of, 505.
German Government, embarrassing position with regard to, 15.
German station, the friends at, 536.
Germany, lively interest in, of expedition, 10.
Gnare Gobit, crossing the, 228.
Gordon, Mr., missionary, and Walker, 379; objections of, 392; explanation to King Muanga, 394.
Grain, scarcity of, 117; stores seized, 142; necessity of providing, 153.
Gratitude of Emin Pasha for small services, 550.
Gretchen-Thal, the, camping in, 220.
Guaso na Nyuki, crossing the, 268.
—— Narok, march by the, 259.
—— Nyiro, region of, 217; river, 219.
—— Tien river, 264; course of, 265.
Guide, an inefficient, 81; the incorrigible, 289.
Guides, arrangement for, 283; three Elgejo, 288.
Gumr and El Gumi, 425.

H.

Halt, a compulsory, 257.
Hameje, glorious, and its islands, 158.
Hamiri, failure of, 97; imaginative eloquence of, 103; arrival with the miaus, 113; his quarrel with Pembomoto, 118.
Hammock travelling, 514.
Hannington, Bishop, relics of his party, 350; his murder, 364.
Hautecœur, the Père Procureur, 484.
Heddenström, missionary, 98.
Heroes, various kinds of, 385.

Hindi, the rendezvous at, 51; start from, 59.
Hippopotamus shooting, 203.
Hirth, Monseigneur, welcome by, 482.
Hofmann Falls, the, 159.
Hostage, Sultan as a, 115.
Hostility, tokens of, 176.
Human life, cheap estimate of, 358.
Hussein, his idea of justice, 119.
Hussein, the expert cook, 459.
Hussein Fara's comparisons, 181.
Hussein Sheriff, conversation with, 73.

I.

Idyar el Wali's account of the Nile, 425.
Industry, a prosperous region of, 480.
Ingenuity, mechanical, developed, 386.
Insolence, a decided check to, 523.
Instructing the Somalis, 76.
Insurrectionary districts to be avoided, 19.
Intertropical starlight, 137.
Intervention, importance of, 273.
Iramba, people of, 508; plateau, 511.
Ischioragama, encampment at, 373.

J.

Jack, Mr., proceedings of, 318.
Jibije, 164.
"Junker" Range, march through the, 334.
Justice, to be shown and enforced, 193.

K.

Kabaragas, exciting news in, 516.
Kabaras, fortunate route to, 295.
Kabila, encampment at, 496.

INDEX. 591

Kamanyiro Kanta, 355; career of, 356; his one-eyed men, 364; declaration of understanding with, 370, 371; diplomacy of, 373; summary dismissal of, 374; his apprehensions, 375; joins procession, 376.
Kamasia Plateau, climbing to the, 278.
Kampi, arrival at, 535.
Karema chosen king, 314; defiance to, 435.
Karl Alexander Fall, 205.
Katikiro, visit of the, 383; refusal of, to sign the Uganda treaty, 390; rush to house of, 396; sentiments of, 429; intrigues, 433.
Katonga, sailing by mouth of the, 451.
Kawirondo, report on, 283; people of, 297.
Keletesa, cordial behaviour of, 503.
Kenia Mountain, the, 210; Peak, 219.
Kidori on the Tana, 116.
Kikuyu, stay at, 213; mode of killing cattle, 252.
Kilima Tindi Ridge, 520.
Kiloluma river, erroneous theory of, 181.
Kina Kombe, arrival at, 111.
Kirobani, the guide. 286, 287.
Kiswahili and Kisogo languages, 322.
Kiwewa, the rule of, 313.
Kome, arrival at, 473.
Konse, solemn entry into, 212.
Kraal, burning of a, 239.
Kraals, fortified, 230.
Krapf country, 203; Hill, 207.
Krapf's conjectures concerning the Tana, 162.
Krupp Mountain, 185.
"Kupanda Sharo" feeling, 188; acquaintance declined, 534.
Kwaihu Peak and Island, 38; Bay, arrival at, 39.

Kwam Yagallo, arrival at, 534.
Kwa Sakwa, 303.
—— Sundu, advance to, 311.
—— Telessa, march to, 335; description of, 336.
—— Tindi, particulars concerning, 333.
—— Tunga, march to, 335.

L.

Lake Victoria, fish in, 445; after a storm, 448; under a new aspect, 449; flat shores of, 458; view of, 470; volcanic region of, 471.
Landmark, a useful, 292.
Languages, comparison of, 416.
Leikipia, elevated plateau, 163, 219.
Letter-carrying, dangers of, 457.
Letters.—To a possible European, 297; of Père Lourdel, 319; of Dr. Peters, 340; of Père Denoit, 345; to Monseigneur Léon Livinhac, 346; for the English expedition, 359; from King Muanga, 369; of Dr. Peters to Mr. Gordon, 374; answer, 377; to King Muanga, 392; to M. Lourdel, 396; to Herr Arendt, 398; Mr. Jackson's, 431; Muanga's imploring, 434; Gabriel's, 436; the Katikiro's, and Dr. Peters's reply, 449; Père Lourdel's, 463; Monseigneur Livinhac's, 464; from Dr. Peters to executive committee of German Emin Pasha committee, 566; to Captain Cardale, etc., 573.
Lindi Mountains, circuit round, 532.
Lion hunting, an attempt at, 491.
Livinhac, Monseigneur, 401; opinions of, 405; mentioned, 452; intentions of, 455; waiting for, 490.
Loanga, stay at, 552.

INDEX.

Lourdel, Father, 379 ; his ideas, 381 ; his quarters, 387 ; about Stanley and Emin, 440 ; energetic measures of, 443 ; fatal consequences of wet to, 444 ; parting with Peters, 445.

M.

Mackay, Mr., despatch, 313 ; opinion of, 315 ; his influence, 453.
Mackinnon, Sir William's, bold plan, 441.
Magic ceremonial, 216.
Maize fields, tribute from, 110.
Makenge and Stanley, 522 ; his messenger rebuked, 525 ; submission of, 530 ; sends tribute, 531.
Malalulu, German flag hoisted at, 113.
Mandutto, water found by, 262 ; departure of, 513.
Mansamarabu, camp at, 63.
Maps and ancient charts, 420, 421.
Marawa, passage of the, 211.
March, a weary, 119 ; triumphal, to Oda - Boru - Ruva, 123 ; through mountain regions, 191 ; of December 24th, 244 ; by the Guaso Narok, 259 ; through the Junker Range, 334 ; to Kwa Telessa, 335 ; towards the west, 340 ; dietary on, 442 ; a gloomy, 376 ; a morning's, 497 ; through the wilderness, 506 ; towards the east, 523 ; to Bagamoyo, 555.
Marching, routine of, 121.
Marco, 342, 347.
Marenga Mkali country, 535.
Marfano, the boats at, 88.
Marka, 25.
Marongo submits to his fate, 187 ; securely guarded, 192 ; a gentleman at large, 212.

Marthe, the, arms shipped on board, 21.
Massa, arrival at, 114.
Massacre, danger of, 432.
Massai herds, 229 ; hostile appearance of, 253 ; real condition of country, 476.
Massailands, guide to the, 217.
Massais, the, management of, 222 ; character of, 224 ; equipment and marriage, 227 ; systematic speech to the, 233 ; preparations to fight them, 235 ; routed, 241 ; re-appearance of, 248 ; peace proposal from, 249 ; excluded from camp, 251 ; fear of, 300.
Mbaja, 44.
Mbe people, communication with the, 191.
Mboni, native of, 117.
Mbuji, crossing the Tana at, 108.
Mengo, royal tombs at, 422.
Mfoh, arrival at, 427.
Mgine, landing at, 50.
Miau, the captured, 94.
Miaus, and grain, failure of contract for, 88 ; a supply of, 110.
Mission, Catholic, thoroughness of, 385.
—— station, Nyagesi, 474, 484.
Missionaries, Mr. Stanley's opinion of, 317.
Missionary, an English, 543.
Mitole, dangers at, 99 ; complaints of elders, 102.
Mkondogna, Arabs of, 552.
Monsoon, the, 89.
Mountain ranges, discovery of, 146 ; region a, 218.
Mountains of the Moon, 419 ; the Emperor William II., 161.
Mpuapua, 536 ; station of, 539.
Mrogro, short holiday at, 554.
Msanga, an early start for, 533.
Muanga, son of Mtesa, 313 ; at the

Sesse Islands, 314; position of, 315; victory of, 318; his message to Europe, and civility, 433; proposal to write to, 344; and the English, 347; his uncle, 355; letter from, 369; message to, 377; audiences of, 379, 384; friendliness of, 380; palace of, 387; private interview with, 388; desire concerning slavery, 402; dispute with the Katikiro, 432; plain speech of, 394.
Muina, difficult march to, 104; departure by the boats from, 106.
Musa devoured by a crocodile, 490.

N.

Napoleon Gulf, the, 350.
Nature, grand solitude of, 291.
Nderani, fortified camp at, 109.
Ndinga, 494.
Neœra, the, chartered at heavy cost, 28; arrival at Zanzibar, 29; running out from Dar-es-Salam, 34; brought to book, 51; lawsuit, 55, 574.
Negroes, severity necessary with, 192.
Nera country, 498.
Ngao, seeking for, 82; German missionary station, 83; march from, 87.
Nile, the, questions concerning, 336; Emin's position on Upper, 344; arrival at, 365; passage across, 366.
Njemps, start for, 263; arrival at, 268.
Nocturnal festival, 115.
Nogola, misbehaviour and punishment of, 171.
Nomadic herdsmen, social status of, 224; propensities and deportment of, 225.
Nugula, arrival of—report, 441, 442.

O.

Oda-Boru-Ruva, triumphal march to, 123; with the Gallas in, 124; communication with, 273.
Omar Idlé's exploit, 195.
One-eyed men, Kamanyiro's, 364.
Optical delusion, a strange, 200.

P.

Papyrus swamps, 259.
Parisa's neglect, 169.
Path, a difficult, 264.
Peace, proposals of, from Massais, 249.
Pemba Motu, 279.
Pembomoto's quarrel with Hamiri, 118.
Peters, Dr., appointed commander in the Emin Pasha Expedition, 8; his opinion of route, 13; expedition to start under, 17; illness of, 89; proposed route of, 148; speech to the Wandorobbo, 167; account of himself, 283; proposal of, 338; experimental letter of, 340; proposal to visit Unjoro, 343; further intentions of, 349; definite instructions of, 371; reply to Kamanyiro, 373; advice to Muanga, 381; letter to Muanga, 393; proposes to fight Kimbulu, 395; reply to Muanga's declaration, 432; will attack Karema, 435; incredulity of, 440; attacked by fever, 492; parting of, from Emin Pasha, 551; return to Europe, 559.
Plenty, a region of, 342.
Philological studies, 96.
Poisoned arrows, attack with, 172.
Political missionary interference, 317.
Porters, disregard of application to hire, 27; unruliness of, 61; rewards

and punishments of, 62; importance of, 86; exciting news concerning, 105; poor Amdalla, 210; cheating, 216; desertion of, 260; from the English expedition, 303.
Poscho, distribution of, 488.
Potentate, a jovial, 354.
Purchasing supplies, 271.

Q.

Quarrel of Pembomoto and Hamiri, 118.
Question of ways and means, 270; of reprisals, 279.

R.

Rainy season, the, 58; and sickness, 89; stormy indications of, 179.
Ratification by spitting, 174.
Rebellion raised by Muanga, 314.
"Red letter day," a, 202.
Reichardt's opinion, 221.
Reports, missing, 146.
Resolution for unity of command, 15.
Rhinoceros hunting, 204.
Ripon Falls, 366, 367.
Routes, Thomson's, unadvisable, in dry season, 260; northern and southern, 551.
Rukua, first servant to Dr. Peters, 80; as interpreter, 232; fatal accident to, 368; death and burial, 369.
Rumours, disquieting, 340.
Rust, Lieut.-Capt., 20; instructions for, 148; measures to be taken by, 149.
Rust's column, waiting for, 146.

S.

Sakwa, Sultan, possessions of, 302; politeness of, 308; treaty with, 310.

Sango and the fleet, 460.
Sanguke river, the, 505.
Schopenhauer's philosophy, 250.
Schweinfurth, Professor, first ideas of expedition, 2.
"Schweinfurth Fall," 207.
Sesse Islands, the outline of, 446; starting afresh for, 450; beautiful landscape of, 451.
Settlement, new, the Von der Heydt House, 138.
Severity necessary with negroes, 192.
"Shauri" with porters, 85.
Shimbye, landing in, 43; passage to, 44; doings at, 47.
Short allowance, 94.
Siyu, recruiting at, 39.
Siyu Canal, a new plan, 42.
Somali Achmed, death of, 285.
Somalis, the character of, 58; friendly demonstrations of, 72; untrustworthy messengers, 94; the hostile, 143; excited, prospects of plunder, 175; and "strayed" cattle, 177; the discouraged, 254.
Soswa, course towards, 470; islands, 471.
Spitting, ratification by, 174.
Sport and culinary science, 206.
Stanley, H. M., departure of, for Africa, 2; camp of, 344; his refusal to march to Uganda, 345; report from, 360; and the Mountains of the Moon, 419; achievements of, 479; and Makenge, 522; carries off Emin, criticism of proceedings, 543; discrepancy between his accounts and Emin Pasha's, 545; Emin's estimate of, and opinion of Dr. Peters, 546; indecision, 547.
Stephano, serious advice to, 455.
Steppe, the, animal life and climate of, 101; marching through, 120;

its plants and animals, etc., 209; difficult march across, 257.
Stokes, Mr., enterprise of, 315; his establishment in Ukumbi, 487; business activity of, 500.
Stuhlmann, Dr., meeting with, 537.
Suaheli the, of the Tana, 126.
Subakini, English station at, 112.
Suffering, remembrances of, 99.
Sultana, the unladylike, 512.
Sultanas of Wachore, 354.
Sultans:—Hugo, of Gallas, 125, negotiations with, 129, his concessions, 131, great consultation with, 133, remonstrance of, 139; Sadeh, 144; Gollo, 144; Sakwa, of Kawirondo, messages from, 301, proposal of, 307; of Kwa Sundu, visit from, 312; Telessa, visit of, 336, second interview with, 338, his messengers, 339; Wachore, power of, 353; Kilioma, address to, 509; a self-indulgent, 511; Wagogo sues for peace, 526.
Sunstroke, symptoms of, 530.
Supper, a comfortable, 256.
Swamp, a difficult and dangerous, 506, 507.

T.

Tabaliro, departure from, 466.
Tabora, occupation of, advised, 541.
Talabanga, 342.
Tana, proposed route by, to Equatorial Province, 13; arrival at, 83; on the banks of, 93; scenery of the, 100; exhilarating climate of, 101; crossing at Mbuji, 108; lowest middle course of, 114, 129; fire signal at, 120; landscape near Oda-Boru-Ruva, 129; how to get to it, 142; settlement on, 157; mountain chains of, 161; question of fords, 178; great cataract of, 181; abortive attempts to cross, 193; sinking, 196; how to build a bridge across, 197; rising, 198; difficult again, 205; tributaries of the, 207; difficulty of, overcome, 209.
Teleki Rock, the, 252.
Tell, death of, 205.
Tempests, tropical, 414.
Thomson, effect of his treatment of Massais, 222; "Among the Massai," 299.
Thoughts in the solitude of nature, 507.
Thunderstorms, 291, 448.
Tiedemann, Herr von, 21; illness of, 137, 257, 271, 493, 505, 514, 552; position of, 176; in peril, 238; joyful meeting with, 256; grave condition of, 261; departure of, to Lake Victoria, 401; meeting of Peters with, 451; ill again, 554; return to Europe, 559.
Tiedemann Hill, 160.
Tippoo Tib, Stanley's relation with, 546.
Tombs at Mengo, 422, 423.
Traces of travellers, 209.
Trade, egotistical ideas of, 184; with Wakikuyu, 215; important, 390, 391; routes of caravan, opening a direct, 501.
Treaty between Dr. Peters and Sultan Sadeh, 135, 145; of peace, 251; signing the Uganda, 390; assembly concerning, 393; articles of the Uganda, 389; the Uganda, 585.
Tribute, payment of, a mistake, 498; disagreeable question of, 522; renewed demand of, 524; Makenge's, 531.
Tropical storm, a, 221.

U.

Uganda, chances of an attempt on, 316; up to, 362; journey towards, 363; first encampment in, 367; through desert, 371; treaty, 389, 585; important trade of, 390; and slave trade, 402; cruelty of the people, climatic advantages of, 414; difficulties in, 429; a lady in, 430.
Ugogo, district of, 517.
Unjoro, 343.
Ukamba Kitui, steppe of, 207.
Ukumbi, 473; removal to, 481; road through, 484; Mr. Stokes's establishment in, 487; order of day in, 488; start from, 494.
Ukumbi fever, 502.
Usagara, arrival at, 551.
Usoga, pleasant life in, 348; scenery of, 349.
Usukuma, important trade with, 391; dry season in, 485; general aspect of, 486; a dandy of, 502.
Usure, settlement of, 510; importance of, 513; departure from, 514.
Uweri-weri, 515.

V.

Victoria, Lake, fish in, 445; under a new aspect, 449; flat shores of, 458; view of, 470; volcanic region of, 471.
Visit to Wachore, 357.
Visitor, a mysterious, 341.
Volcanic region, 265; formation, 334.
Voltaire, our Kikuyu, 251.
Von der Heydt House, 138; Islands, 157.

W.

Wachore, friendly relations with, 353; visit of, 355.
Wadelai, 1, 3.
Wadsagga tribe, the, 182; haughtiness of, 183; insolence of, 185; retribution on, 189.
Waelgejo, quarrel with the, 288.
Waganda, the, report on, 308; Christian welcome from, 365; boats of, 366; great abilities of, 407; drum, 409; musical proclivities and architecture of, 411; origin of, 415.
Wagandaland, life easy in, 408.
Wagogo, a lesson to the, 523; war with, 525; burning of villages, 527; cattle seized, 528, 529; threatening, 530.
Wairamba, peaceable conduct of the, 510.
Waiting, weeks of dreary, 90.
Wakamasia, the, and Pemba Motu, 279; the friendly, 280; demand tribute, 281.
Wakamba, warriors, 167; securing them, 182; advice of, 194.
Wakawirondo, 298, 299.
Wakikuyu men in the camp, 210; characters of the, 214; hut of, 215; trade with, 215.
Wakuafi, the, or dealers, treaty with, 272, 274.
Walker, Mr., visit of, 436.
"Walpurgis Night" watch, 492.
Wami, crossing the, 500.
Wandorobbo tribe, the, 165; embassy to the, 167; insolence of ambassadors, 168; negotiations a bad bargain, 170; insolence, 171; threatened attack by, 173; delays and evasions, 174; talk with the, 263.
Wanga, visit to, 48.
Wangwana guides, 494.

INDEX. 597

Wanjamwesi, arrival of the, 528, 529; caravan, 531.
Wanjoro, white men in, 337, 338.
Want, terrible suffering from, 122.
Wapokomo, camping-place, 82; parting from the, 100, 126; characteristics of the, 112; cheerful dance of, 114.
Warriors, defiance of Galla, 141; Wakamba, 167; first meeting with Massais, 229, 253.
Wasekke, tactics of the, 499; prudence of, 500.
Wasiba, the, warning to, and reply, 462.
Wasoga, the, report on, 308; men, the, conversation with, 321; appearance, costume, and weapons of, 352; dwellings, 353.
Wasukuma, good qualities of the, 486; protection to the, 488; probable future importance of, 495.
Water, scarcity of, 36.
Water supply, important question of, 220; anxiety concerning, 248; seeking for, 261.
Weapons, confiscation of, 28.
Wembaere, crossing the, 505; Steppe, 506.
White race, historic tradition of a, 427.

Widow of Mtesa, her heathen officials dismissed, 404; ignorance of, 406.
Wild cattle, enormous herds of, 294.
Wissmann, Lieutenant von, co-operation with, proposed, 6; arrangements with Peters, 8.
Witu, safe arrival in sultanate of, 45; on the march to, 65; importance of, 66; statistics of the sultanate, 67; stay at, 70; supplies from, 93; no hope from, 98.
Women, Wandorobbo, 166; footsteps of, 166.
Women and children, decision concerning, 155.
Würz, missionary, 86.

Y.

Year, beginning a new, 262.
Yembamba, narrative of, 156.

Z.

Zanzibar, 2; Sultan of, 23, 27; difficulties and troubles at, 23, 26; caravans, curious behaviour of, 284; crossing to, 558; old quarters in, 559.
Zoology, lion and hippopotamus, 180; lions in the bush, 203.